TEXAS LAWMEN

1900 ★ 1940

More of the Good & the Bad

CLIFFORD R. CALDWELL
& RON DeLORD

Charleston — London

THE
History
PRESS

Published by The History Press
Charleston, SC 29403
www.historypress.net

Copyright © 2012 by Clifford R. Caldwell and Ronald G. DeLord
All rights reserved

First published 2012

Front cover courtesy of Clifford R. Caldwell, with the firearm and accoutrements provided
by Drexel Doran of Kerrville, Texas.

Back cover courtesy of Lon and Beth Rice, Morrison, Illinois. The names of the individuals
pictured are (from left to right): Alfrio Munoz, mounted customs inspector, Roma, Texas;
Domingo Garza, mounted customs inspector, Rio Grande City, Texas; James Stewart,
deputy captain of customs; William Hansen, deputy U.S. marshal; F.D. McMahan, Texas
Ranger, Alice, Texas; Tupper Harris, Texas Ranger, Alice, Texas; and Rufino Clarke,
mounted customs inspector, Rio Grande City, Texas.

Manufactured in the United States

ISBN 978.1.60949.452.0

Library of Congress CIP data applied for.

Straight is the line of duty;
Curved is the line of beauty;
Follow the straight line, thou shalt see,
The curved line will follow thee.

—*William MacCall*

Contents

Preface

Texas Lawmen, 1900 to 1940 is a continuation of the chronicle of brave peace officers, and some not so brave, who laid down their lives in the service of the State of Texas. The first volume covers the period from 1835 to 1899. This book carries forward from where volume one left off, beginning in 1900 and continuing through to the last known Texas lawman to have died in 1940.

At the time of Texas independence in 1835, the population of the state was roughly 25,000. By 1900, it had grown to over 3.0 million. By 1940, when the number of Texas residents hit a whopping 6.4 million, many thought the state would burst at the seams. The new century brought with it new challenges. More people equated to more lawlessness.

In 1910, the Mexican Revolution began with Francisco Madero's pro-democracy *antirreeleccionista* volunteers confronting Porfirio Díaz's federal troops. As the revolution spread, Pancho Villa joined with Madero's forces and aided in winning the first Battle of Ciudad Juárez in 1911. Soon, the violence was spilling over the border. Mexican raids into Texas in 1915 and 1916 caused an estimated twenty-one American deaths. Texas lawmen quickly rose to meet the new challenge. As many as three hundred Mexicans or Tejanos may have been killed in South Texas by the actions of rangers, vigilantes and citizens. Some sources place the death toll as high as three thousand.

By 1918, the National Prohibition Act had been passed. With this new and largely unpopular law came widespread illegal whiskey trade, as well as a more sophisticated form of violence. County and municipal lawmen—augmented by Texas Rangers, United States marshals, Border Patrol agents, customs inspectors and federal Prohibition agents—battled bootleggers and profiteers throughout the state.

The start of the Great Depression is usually connected to the stock market crash of Black Tuesday on 29 October 1929, when the Dow Jones Industrial Average fell almost 23 percent and the market lost between $8 and $9 billion in value. That day's havoc was just one in a series of losses during a time of extreme market volatility that devastated those who had bought stocks "on margin," meaning with borrowed money. By 1933, the unemployment rate had soared to 25 percent. Riding on the heels of what seemed at the time to be economic doom came an almost apocalyptic event that hit Texas and Oklahoma like something from the Book of Revelations: Black Sunday, 14 April 1935. It has been estimated that 100 million acres of farmland suffered the loss of all or most of its topsoil to the ferocious and unrelenting winds. By Black Sunday, there had already been weeks of dust storms. The cloud that appeared on the horizon that day was the worst by far. Sixty-mile-per-hour winds blew dust as coal black skies sent Texans scurrying for shelter, clutching their Bibles and praying for deliverance. Farms failed across the state. Livestock wandered aimlessly, searching for shelter and water. Faced with record unemployment, and little prospect of finding jobs, many Texans simply gave up and took to lives of crime.

Throughout the early 1900s, Texas lawmen were challenged with a period of drought, border war, Prohibition and a climate of economic collapse. Lawlessness in Texas did not end with the close of the cowboy era, nor did it slow with the advent of new technologies and more sophisticated criminals. Rather, the turn of the last century brought with it a gradual transformation in the type of crime—and criminal—with which Texas peace officers had to contend. The cap-and-ball revolvers of the mid-1800s were replaced by metallic cartridge firearms and smokeless gunpowder by the end of the century. The first decade of the 1900s saw the advent of the semiautomatic rifle and pistol, placing better and more powerful firearms in the hands of lawmen and criminals alike. Travel on horseback gave way to the automobile era and the age of flight. Texas lawmen were mounted on motorcycles and automobiles and used telephones to communicate with neighboring communities about criminals and fugitives. In spite of all the progress this era brought, the challenge of the Texas lawman, and the associated mortal danger he faced, remained largely unchanged. Heartless attacks from ambush by assailants, brutal beatings at the hands of prison inmates, feuds and whiskey-fueled disagreements—all dot the chronicles of the Texas lawmen of this era.

This book includes brief biographies of all the lawmen we have been able to identify who died between 1900 and the last day of 1940. The chronicle includes City Marshal James Robert Cotner of Nevada City, who, having passed his seventy-eighth birthday at the time of his death, holds the distinction of being the oldest Texas lawman to be killed in the line of duty. It also contains an entry for Malcolm Davis, who on 6 January 1933 was shot and killed by the notorious Clyde Barrow. The list of tales ends with Whitesboro chief of police William Thomas "Will" Miller, who died of injuries he received when a vehicle struck him on Christmas Day 1940. He died two days later on 27 December, thus marking the last death of a Texas lawman in the line of duty during the period from 1900 to 1940.

The lawmen are listed by the agency for which they served, in chronological order, beginning with the earliest date of death and working down to the most recent. If you are uncertain of the agency for which the lawman you are searching for worked, we suggest you begin your quest with the index at the end of the book. Early historical records are often less accurate than we would desire them to be. Please keep this in mind, because you may encounter alternate spellings for some surnames and given names. Wherever possible, multiple sources have been used to verify the information contained herein. For a more in-depth study of a particular lawman, we suggest you refer to the bibliography at the end of the book for more thorough reference material.

Throughout the text of this book, you will confront situations where more than one lawman was killed in the same incident. In those situations, the reader should look to the full description of the event in an account that generally follows, but may precede, the entry for the respective lawman.

This book is intended to be a comprehensive reference of the Texas lawmen who died between 1900 and 1940. Due to the volume of entries it contains, and in many cases the scarcity of information available, the authors did not intend to offer complete biographies of every man or an exhaustive summary of the circumstances of each death.

This book is the product of decades of research. Great care has been taken to include all of the lawmen we have been able to locate. But new cases are discovered each year. This volume includes lawmen we know were killed in the line of duty and who are included on the National Law Enforcement Officers Memorial, Texas Peace Officers' Memorial, Lost

Lawman's Memorial of the Sheriffs' Association of Texas or the Officer Down Memorial Page.

For purposes of historical interest, as well as completeness, this book also includes the names of many lawmen whose deaths occurred under circumstances that did not meet the rigorous criteria that have been established by the various memorial organizations for classification as "line of duty" death. In some cases, an officer's death may have been the result of a personal feud or an accident. It may have occurred after the officer had left his respective agency, or it may have taken place under circumstances where sufficient information could not be found to meet the criteria for inclusion on the list of those killed in the "line of duty."

The officers whose names have been listed on a memorial will have reference numbers listed next to their names in the "Memorials" appendix at the back of the book. The reference, or location number, will aid you in finding that name on one of the memorials, either in Austin, Texas, or Washington, D.C.

Acknowledgements

A s was the case with the earlier volume covering the period from 1835 to 1899, the roster of names and summary of events took years to assemble. It is the product of thousands of hours of work by numerous volunteers, logging an incalculable number of hours digging through archives all across the state of Texas. A mountain of files and correspondence was assembled containing what few documents researchers could find about the lives of these lawmen. Some of the files are extensive, while others may contain just a few scraps of paper or a newspaper article.

The people who were involved in the research necessary to produce this book derive their satisfaction from knowing that the passing of some of these obscure lawmen will not go unrecognized. Special recognition is due to retired Dallas County sheriff's assistant chief deputy Terry Baker; Bexar County sheriff's lieutenant Kyle Coleman; retired Fort Worth police sergeant Kevin Foster; retired Harris County sheriff's deputy Doug Hudson; Donaly E. Brice, senior research assistant at the Texas State Library and Archives Commission; and all the volunteers who have worked so hard to research the history of these lawmen.

A heartfelt thank you goes out to the founders and members of the Officer Down Memorial Page, Inc., including Chris Cosgriff, Mike Schutz and Steve Weiss, who have taken the time to honor our fallen lawmen on their website. Craig Floyd, Caroline Heyliger and Berneta Spence at the National Law Enforcement Officers Memorial Fund have devoted their lives to researching the deaths of all U.S. officers. Thanks to Sherlynn Kelly at the Lost Lawmen Memorial of the Sheriffs' Association of Texas for memorializing the sacrifices of sheriffs, deputies and jailers. Kathryn Nickell and Jim Willett at the Texas Prison Museum are dedicated to honoring the state's correctional officers and have assisted the authors greatly with their research. Special thanks to the staff at the Texas Commission on Law Enforcement Officer Standards and Education (TCLEOSE) for their work in maintaining the Texas Peace Officers' Memorial at the State Capitol in Austin. And thanks to the volunteers who assist with the Peace Officers' Memorial Foundation, Inc. (POMF), a charitable corporation of the Combined Law Enforcement Associations of Texas (CLEAT).

Numerous authors contributed by way of the research they have done in preparation for the many wonderful books contained in the bibliography section at the back of this book. You will find landmark work by authors such as Bob Alexander, Stephen Moore, Darren L. Ivey, Mike Cox, Robert DeArment, Leon Metz, Chuck Parsons, Robert W. Stephens, Robert Utley and Walter Prescott Webb.

Finally, we wish to recognize and acknowledge the hundreds of family members, researchers and librarians, law enforcement agencies and historians who have aided us in collecting the date necessary to produce this book. Without their help, this book could never have been completed.

1
County and
Municipal Agencies

ABILENE POLICE DEPARTMENT

Burch, Robert E. "Bob"
Born 17 December 1857—Died 27 July 1929

At about 4:45 p.m. on Saturday, 27 July 1929, Chief of Police Robert Burch was in pursuit of a Chrysler roadster automobile driven by a man who was suspected of stealing a purse belonging to Miss Andrews. The handbag, which contained about forty-five dollars in cash and the woman's watch, was taken while Andrews was at the Merkel Café. During the high-speed chase, which occurred on the Merkel–Trent road, Burch's blue Buick coupe automobile accidentally skidded off the road, overturned and was demolished. Burch was trapped beneath the wreckage until passersby extracted him. He was taken to the hospital but unfortunately died en route.

Burch was survived by his wife, Elizabeth Cunningham, and one son. He is buried at the Abilene Municipal Cemetery. Burch served as sheriff of Hale County from 1894 to 1906. He had been elected chief of police on 2 April 1929.

Jones, James Edgar
Born 5 February 1900—Died 14 December 1930

Officer James Jones was killed in a motorcycle accident while trying to stop a traffic violator. The incident took place on College Drive near Pine Street.

A vehicle turned left in front of Jones, causing him to hurriedly apply his brakes. Jones skidded thirty feet before striking the oncoming vehicle head-on. He was transported to a local hospital, where he died from the severe head injuries he received in the crash.

Jones was survived by his wife. He is buried at Merkel in Taylor County.

Beam, William Samuel "Sam"
Born 19 November 1869—Died 18 July 1940

Shortly before midnight on Thursday, 18 July 1940, Officers "Sam" Beam and Dee Bland were sent to the 1000 block of China Street to pick up a drunk who had kicked in the windows of a house. When the officers arrived and aroused the drunken man, he began fighting and fled the scene. Bland chased the suspect into a barn and left two men to guard the building while he returned to his patrol car to get a flashlight. When he returned, Bland found Beam slumped over in the seat, facedown, with the radio microphone in his hand. Beam had apparently reported the fleeing suspect and died shortly thereafter. Beam was seventy-one years old. The suspect, who was reported to have been an ex-convict, was arrested.

Beam was survived by his wife and six children. He had been on the police force about twenty years. Beam is buried at the Cedar Hill Cemetery in Abilene.

AMARILLO POLICE DEPARTMENT

Burnam, Presley George "Pres"
Born 2 June 1872–Died 5 January 1934

Captain Pres Burnam was shot and killed when he responded to a call involving an intoxicated man with a gun. The incident took place at the Western Motel in Amarillo.

The gun-toting fellow, Frank "Shorty" Crutchfield of White Deer, was creating a drunken disturbance in his room. The occupant of a nearby room called the front desk and complained about the noise. The desk clerk went to the room and asked Crutchfield to be quiet, but unfortunately he did not comply. Angered by the clerk's admonition, Crutchfield ran out into the hall carrying a gun, demanding to know who was complaining.

Crutchfield and the fellow who had lodged the grouse soon began fighting in the hall. During the struggle, Crutchfield's weapon discharged. Although no one was injured, the surprise shot ended the fight. Still in a state of agitation, Crutchfield ran downstairs and into the lobby of the hotel, where he assaulted another guest, holding his gun on that person and ordering him outside. As the armed troublemaker and his hostage made their way outdoors, Burnam and his driver, patrolman George Hayden, arrived at the scene.

Seeing Burnam, Crutchfield fled around the corner of the hotel. Burnam chased him, while Hayden remained behind to interview the complainant. Gunshots were soon heard emanating from the corner of the hotel where Burnam had gone. When Hayden ran to investigate, he discovered Burnam lying on the ground suffering from four gunshot wounds that had been fired at close range.

Burnam was helped into the hotel, where he soon died. He had been shot four times with a .32-caliber Colt revolver. Burnam's weapon was still in its holster.

Crutchfield, who had been declared insane in 1928, was later apprehended at a nearby tourist camp. The murder weapon was recovered. He was tried, convicted and sentenced to life in prison.

Burnam was survived by his daughter. He is buried at Dimmit in Castro County.

Grounds, Chester Lewis
Born 18 March 1909—Died 14 February 1934

Officer Chester Grounds was shot and killed when he responded to a family disagreement at 1413 East Fourth Street.

At about 1:30 a.m. on Wednesday, 14 February 1934, Sergeant A.L. Anderson radioed a report that a woman was being beaten on the head at a residence on Cleveland Street. When Grounds and Officer Audrey Giles arrived at the residence, they found eighteen-year-old Hazel Hammonds, wife of Clarence Hammonds, standing in the street looking frail and frightened. Grounds was unable to locate Hammonds at his residence, so the officers went around the corner to Roberts Street, to Hammonds's mother Clara Jane Hanawall's house, in an effort to locate him. When Hammonds was not found there, Grounds and Giles returned to the Hammonds home on Cleveland Street to continue the search.

Hammonds had concealed himself in the darkness by a fence in the backyard. When Grounds entered the yard, Hammonds fired at him three times, hitting Grounds in the chest. Hammonds ran from the scene. Grounds was rushed to the hospital, where he was pronounced dead.

A thorough search of the area began immediately. Hammonds, who had been drinking heavily prior to the incident, was eventually located by officers Curtis Gray and Sales Coffey at a filling station, where he was refueling his automobile. When Gray and Coffey approached Hammonds, he pulled a gun and pointed it at them. The officers immediately fired their weapons, killing him. Hammonds was hit in the right side by five pistol bullets and received a shotgun blast to the shoulder. He died instantly while clutching the .38-caliber revolver that he had just used to murder Grounds.

Grounds was survived by his wife and daughter. He is buried at the Happy Cemetery in Swisher County.

ANDERSON COUNTY CONSTABLE'S OFFICE

Pierce, Dave
Born 15 June 1878—Died 30 January 1908

Precinct 4 constable Dave Pierce, along with a man named D.W. Hart, went to the residence of Sam Tubbs (alias Sam Tubb) to settle a debt. Hart had sold Tubbs a gasoline engine and some assorted sawmill equipment, which Tubbs had failed to pay for. Pierce had civil papers to serve on Tubbs, along with a writ for the attachment of the equipment.

Although Tubbs was not at home when Pierce and Hart arrived, Tubbs's son allowed the men to enter the residence. When Sam Tubbs returned, he was carrying a shotgun. An argument ensued during which Tubbs shot and killed Pierce. Pierce died within minutes of being shot.

In June 1908, Tubbs was sentenced to life in prison for the murder of Pierce.

Pierce is buried at the Olive Branch Cemetery in the community of Brushy Creek. He was survived by his wife, Mary Della Cely.

Cox, Floyd Carl
Born 1 July 1903—Died 14 February 1930

Precinct 1 deputy constable Floyd Cox was shot and killed by a sixteen-year-old boy named Wendell Sanders. The incident took place after

Cox had arrested both Wendell Sanders and his older brother, Jim, the preceding day.

Wendell Sanders had been arrested on a minor theft charge. While taking Sanders into custody, Cox had difficulty with the youth and hit him over the head with the butt of his revolver to quiet him down. The young man was quite aggravated about the treatment and carried the full force of his anger into the following day.

Cox was eating lunch at a local restaurant when Wendell Sanders approached the café. Sanders was carrying a double-barreled shotgun. Seeing the armed youth, Cox went outside to confront him. Without speaking, Sanders discharged both barrels at Cox, hitting him in the head with the full force of the blast. In an astounding act of cold rage, Sanders reloaded and shot again. Once again, he discharged both barrels of the scattergun, finishing off the already fatally wounded Cox, who was lying in the street bleeding to death.

Sanders was captured at his home the following day. He was tried and convicted of the murder of Cox. On 18 April 1930, Wendell Sanders was sentenced to serve fifty years in prison.

Cox was survived by his wife, Cumie, and one child. He is buried in Ashdown, Arkansas.

Long, James Glover
Born 20 August 1885—Died 12 September 1935

Precinct 2 constable James Long was killed in an automobile accident. His vehicle collided head-on with a grocery truck on Highway 19 near Elkhart. Long suffered fatal injuries in the crash.

Long was survived by his wife and four children. He is buried at the Garden of Memories Cemetery in Elkhart.

ANDERSON COUNTY SHERIFF'S OFFICE

Ledwith, Charles
Born circa 1879—Died 15 October 1913

At about noon on Wednesday, 15 October 1913, John T. Groves was in Opperman's Saloon at Palestine. For no apparent reason, Groves pulled a knife and severely slashed and cut a man named McCullough. Afterward, Groves left the saloon.

Policeman W.M. Micheaux notified Deputy Sheriff Charles Ledwith of the assault. Ledwith went to Groves's residence to arrest him. As Ledwith reached the front porch of Groves's home, he was shot and killed. According to the medical report filed after the incident, Ledwith had been shot in the back.

Groves was arrested and charged with the murder of Ledwith, as well as the assault to murder McCullough. On 10 January 1914, Groves was found not guilty of the murder of Ledwith. Two weeks later, the assault to murder charge was also dismissed.

Ledwith was survived by his parents and one sibling. He is buried at the Jasper City Cemetery in Jasper County.

ANGELINA COUNTY CONSTABLE'S OFFICE

Martin, Arthur B.
Born circa 1881—Died 25 December 1912

On Christmas Day 1912, Constable Arthur Martin of the Pollock Precinct was shot and killed by a man named B. Ladd.

The trouble started when Ladd disarmed Martin during a struggle. It is claimed that Martin attacked Ladd with a knife and inflicted several knife wounds. Ladd shot Martin with the service revolver he had taken from him.

Ladd was arrested. An examining trial was set for 28 December 1912. The disposition of any charge against Ladd for the murder of Martin is unknown.

Martin was survived by his wife, Timmie, and two children. He is buried at the Pollock Cemetery. No marker has been located.

Ladd died on 8 September 1916 and is buried at the same cemetery.

Smith, Benjamin Franklin "Ben"
Born 10 August 1884—Died 15 September 1924
Date of Incident: 14 September 1924

Deputy Sheriff Ben Smith was shot and killed by fellow deputy sheriff Grover C. Dunn. Dunn also carried a commission as a special Texas Ranger, without pay, beginning on 15 November 1923.

Smith was the defeated candidate in an election for Angelina County sheriff. According to reports, Dunn was a supporter of the opponent, A.B. Young. Dunn claimed that he had tried to avoid Smith for several days. On 14 September, Dunn was having dinner at a local café when he noticed that Smith had parked his vehicle behind Dunn's. Dunn exited the café with Homer Garrison. Garrison, who would later become the director of the Texas Department of Public Safety, sat down on a bench alongside Dunn. Smith entered the café, looked around and then exited and stood in front of the bench where Garrison and Dunn were seated. Without saying a word, Smith walked back to his car. When he returned, he appeared to be reaching for his pistol. Dunn threw down his flashlight, drew his pistol and fired. Smith was shot a total of three times. All three bullets found their mark. Smith survived through the night but died the following day.

Dunn claimed that he had fired in self-defense. Smith did have a pistol, but it was still in his pocket. Dunn was charged with the murder of Smith and brought to trial in 1926. He was acquitted.

Dunn's special ranger commission was cancelled, but he remained a deputy sheriff.

Prior to his trial for the murder of Smith, Dunn had shot and killed a Mexican during a raid on a railway boarding car in 1925. He was charged with assault to murder but was acquitted. On 23 July 1928, Dunn, while acting as a deputy sheriff, shot and killed a man named Jim Rushing during an arrest attempt at a dance. He posted a $2,500 bond and was released.

The disposition of the charge in the Rushing murder is unknown. On 14 March 1933, Dunn was again appointed a special ranger for Atlas Pipe Line Company in Longview. He was a deputy sheriff for Gregg County at the time of that appointment.

Smith is buried at the Bennett Cemetery in Trinity County.

ARCHER COUNTY SHERIFF'S OFFICE

Ikard, Elijah Harrison
Born 8 March 1892—Died 22 September 1925

Sheriff Elijah Ikard was shot and killed during a gun battle that involved several lawmen and a group of three thieves.

At about 10:30 p.m. on Tuesday, 22 September 1925, Ikard was on a stakeout with other officers in a mesquite pasture near Megargel. The lawmen were watching a cache of stolen property that had been hidden by thieves in the field. The loot consisted of about $1,500 worth of groceries and tobacco products that had been taken from a local store. Along on the stakeout with Ikard was Deputy R. "Cowboy" Munsford. Other lawmen were also involved and had dropped Ikard and Munsford off in the pasture to watch and wait.

Not long after Ikard and Munsford arrived, an automobile approached nearby. Three men got out of the car. Ikard stepped forward and said, "We're officers, boys. Throw up your hands." In an instant, the shooting began. During the mêlée, a .45-caliber bullet struck Ikard's belt buckle and ricocheted into his body, inflicting a fatal wound and killing him almost instantly. Ikard managed to get off one shot at his assailants before he dropped. Munsford kept firing with a shotgun and pistol until he ran out of ammunition. When the smoke cleared, Ikard and two of the three attackers, Charles Crabtree and Frank Looney, lay dead. The third man, Bob Barnett, surrendered sometime later.

Barnett was eventually charged and convicted. He was sentenced to serve life in prison.

Ikard was elected sheriff on 4 November 1924. He was survived by his wife, Maude Parnell, and ten children. Ikard is buried at the Archer City Cemetery. Ikard's wife was appointed sheriff and served the remainder of his two-year term.

ARLINGTON POLICE DEPARTMENT

Johnson, James Evan
Born 16 August 1908—Died 23 November 1930

Officer James Johnson was shot and killed while he was attempting to arrest a man for disturbing the peace.

Johnson went to the front door of Sam Louder's home and identified himself as a police officer but received no response. When Johnson went to the side door of the residence, Louder opened fire. Johnson was hit in the neck.

Louder turned himself in to authorities. He was charged, convicted and sentenced to death for the murder of Johnson. There is no record of that death sentence having been carried out.

Johnson is buried at the Parkdale Cemetery in Tarrant County. His death certificate indicated that he was divorced. Johnson's given name is occasionally listed as "Evans."

ATASCOSA COUNTY SHERIFF'S OFFICE

Matlock, Abner
Born circa 1871—Died 12 August 1911

Deputy Abner Matlock was shot and killed when he attempted to arrest a man for firearm possession.

Matlock was advised by a citizen that a man was in possession of a pistol. Matlock knew the man, Lorja Trevino. He had removed him from a dance several weeks earlier for causing a disturbance.

At approximately 5:30 p.m., Matlock approached Trevino and demanded that he turn over the pistol. Trevino drew the gun from his pocket and pointed it at Matlock. Matlock drew his own gun and fired at Trevino. Trevino was wounded in the side but was able to fire his weapon, hitting Matlock in the hand with one bullet. The impact caused Matlock to drop his gun. Trevino then grabbed Matlock's pistol and shot him four times with it.

Matlock died from his wounds two hours later. Trevino fled the scene and was pursued by a posse. During the chase, Trevino fired two shots at the possemen, who returned fire and killed him.

Matlock had served with the agency for approximately three years. He is buried at the Mission Burial Park in San Antonio.

AUSTIN COUNTY CONSTABLE'S OFFICE

White, Raymond G.
Born circa 1867—Died 22 January 1902

At around 6:00 p.m. on Wednesday, 22 January 1902, a shooting affray occurred at the passenger depot at Bellville. The incident resulted in the death of four persons and the injury to three more.

Two years earlier, Walter Pennington had killed J.C. Odom. The case was set for trial in the district court on 22 January 1902. The deceased, Odom, had a brother named Milam Odom and a half brother named Raymond White. White was constable in the Wallis precinct. The parties converged at the depot. A large crowd was there waiting for the train. Reports of the day indicate that most believe the shooting was instigated by the Odom faction. Pennington was the first man shot. The bullet entered his stomach and traveled upward, passing entirely through his body.

The wounded Pennington managed to draw his revolver and use it with deadly effect. Next to fall was White, who dropped over dead with his revolver ready to fire. Near him, Milam Odom fell mortally wounded. A bystander named Henry Dittert was also killed. Pennington fired a total of six times, using all six cartridges in his revolver. Among the wounded were Elihu Pennington, who received a scalp wound; Antone Dittert, who suffered a flesh wound in the side; and John Havkath, who was shot in the foot.

Elihu Pennington, the father of Walter Pennington, was charged with murder. The shooting took place in the midst of the crowd. The gunfire was unexpected and rapid.

None of the wounded men—including Henry Dittert, who was killed—were parties to the shooting episode.

White was survived by his wife, Lucy Lenora Clark. His place of burial has not been located.

AUSTIN POLICE DEPARTMENT

Gaines, John H.S.
Born 4 August 1863—Died 19 November 1913

Officer John Gaines, who was a black policeman, was shot and killed by a man named George Booth, who was a deputy constable. The incident was the result of a shooting affray that occurred at Sixth and Neches Streets shortly after 8:40 a.m. on Wednesday, 19 November 1913. Booth is said to have fired two shots at Gaines. In return, Gaines fired five times at Booth. Each managed to find the mark with at least one shot.

At the time of the incident, Gaines was waiting for backup assistance from white officers. In those days, white men could only be arrested by white officers. Gaines was in the process of trying to arrest a white man for drunkenness. Booth had been causing a disturbance. He shot Gaines while Gaines was on the telephone calling the police station for help. After he was shot, Gaines, according to his own story, raised himself to a sitting position and emptied his pistol at Booth. Booth claimed that Gaines fired first. No one could give a convincing reason for the shooting. Gaines died at the City Hospital at 12:40 p.m. Before expiring, he made a statement to Police Chief Morris.

There were very few black officers in Texas until after the 1930s, and most of them did not wear uniforms. For the most part, they were forbidden from arresting whites.

Booth was charged with the murder of Gaines. After a speedy trial that began on 16 January 1914 and concluded with a forty-two-hour jury deliberation three days later, the jurors were discharged when they were unable to reach a verdict. The vote stood nine to three in favor of acquittal.

Gaines was the first black policeman in Austin. He was survived by his wife, Sarah. Gaines is buried at the Evergreen Cemetery in Austin.

Allen, Tom
Born circa 1876—Died 24 October 1915

Officer Tom Allen was shot and killed by a newspaper reporter named G.W. Bouldin during a dispute regarding some articles that the reporter had written.

The pundit had written several compositions claiming that Allen, who was a black officer, had mistreated black women during arrests. One article written on 23 October 1915 had made specific complaints against Allen for not being more "genteel in his search for Negro women suspected of crime."

Allen was on duty when, at approximately 9:30 p.m. on the night of 24 October 1915, according to some accounts, he ran into Bouldin at the wagon yard located just off Sixth Street near the east 400 block to Red River. Still angry about the articles and the things that were being said about him, an argument ensued between Allen and Bouldin. Bouldin broke off from the discussion and went into the Jennings & Jennings Drugstore, located at 421 East Sixth Street. According to reports, Allen followed Bouldin into the drugstore and asked him to step outside. Once again, harsh words were exchanged that soon escalated into fisticuffs. Bystanders broke up the pair, and Bouldin retreated into the drugstore. Allen soon followed him. As Allen stepped through the door, Bouldin, who was sitting behind a box, started shooting at him with a .32-caliber revolver. The first shot passed through Allen's broad-brimmed black fur hat and traveled out through the glass door at the front of the store. Three additional bullets found their mark, hitting Allen in the neck and both shoulders.

After Bouldin had let loose with the first volley, the wounded Allen managed to pull his pistol and return fire, harmlessly hitting a glass display case with three shots. One report claimed that Bouldin was wounded in the exchange; however, witnesses say he was not.

According to newspaper reports, Allen was killed only thirty feet from the spot where Officer John Gaines had died two years earlier, in 1913.

Bouldin went to trial for the murder of Allen on 14 November 1915. On the morning of Saturday, 18 December 1915, the jury returned a verdict finding Bouldin not guilty of murder or of the secondary charge of manslaughter.

Allen was part of Austin's Mounted Patrol and the second black lawman on the police force. He is buried at Round Rock Cemetery in Williamson County.

Sawyer, Fred P.
Born 27 March 1894—Died 3 December 1916
Date of Incident: 2 December 1916

At about 10:00 p.m. on Saturday, 2 December 1916, Special Officer R.L. "Dick" Morris, son of City Marshal Will Morris, went to a pool hall at East Sixth Street and Congress Avenue. His brother-in-law, Fred Sawyer, was reported to have been at the pool hall. Morris threatened to arrest two brothers, B. Bedell and C. Bedell, for using abusive language and disturbing the peace. The brothers went upstairs to the poolroom. Morris followed to make the arrest. A fight broke out between Morris and the Bedell brothers, during which the pair used billiard balls and pool cues as weapons. Sawyer went to assist with the arrest. Morris drew his pistol, but one of the Bedell brothers grabbed the gun away from him. Sawyer was accidentally shot during the struggle and was hit once in the foot and once in the thigh. B. Bedell was shot in the hand. Morris apparently used a large knife during the affray. It is unclear if the weapon was his or if it was taken from one from the Bedell brothers. In any case, C. Bedell was cut twice across the back near his kidneys.

Sawyer and C. Bedell were taken to the hospital. B. Bedell was taken to the police station, where he was charged with being intoxicated.

Sawyer died from loss of blood at the Seton infirmary at 3:00 a.m. on Sunday, 3 December 1916. He is buried in the Oakwood Cemetery in Austin. Sawyer was survived by his parents and six brothers and siblings.

It is not known if any charges were filed against C. Bedell or whether either brother was charged with the murder of Sawyer.

Littlepage, James Noel
Born 21 July 1863—Died 9 October 1928

Chief James Littlepage was shot and killed while trying to stop a man who was on a shooting spree in South Austin.

Littlepage and several officers set out from city hall on a report that a deranged man named Armand (Arman) Alexander, who was wielding a shotgun, had killed two women near the 300 block of Elizabeth Street. Later reports claimed that Alexander had shot his wife and another man. According to his wife, Alexander started acting strangely over what she described as a "family matter." On the evening of Sunday, 8 October, Alexander had kicked his wife and three kids out of the house and forced them to spend two nights sleeping out in the open. On the morning of the ninth, Alexander drove up the road in a touring car of questionable ownership and made his family get in the vehicle with him. It is unknown where the car came from. While driving into Austin, Alexander threatened to kill his wife and to give his children away and then kill himself.

Near Post Road, between the gate of La Prella place and Lone Oak filling station, Ms. Alexander jumped or was pushed from the moving car. The car containing Alexander and his three children then went on to the home and store of Mr. D. Pyburn on Elizabeth Street. Pyburn said that when Alexander drove up in front of the store, he heard him call for Mrs. Pyburn and their daughter, Ethel, to come outside. When they did so, Alexander stepped from the car with a pump shotgun in hand and shot Mrs. Pyburn in the top of the head. Next, Alexander hit Ethel Pyburn with his next shot, almost separating her head from her shoulders. Both women died near the small store and within view of husband and father. Five additional shots were fired at this residence, but neither Mr. Pyburn nor his nineteen-year-old son was hit.

Alexander returned to the car, which contained his now screaming children, and discovered the vehicle had a flat tire. He left the kids behind and began walking with the shotgun and a .22 rifle. He left almost a dozen shotgun shells in the car.

Alexander walked east on Elizabeth Street past the Brackenridge school and turned south along the banks of a creek. Mrs. J.C. Edwards, a teacher at Brackenridge, watched Alexander walk by the school with the guns in his hands. When she asked what he was shooting at, his response was: "Getting rid of a bunch."

Littlepage and other officers responded to the incoming call of a shooting incident. Littlepage came upon Alexander while he was driving in the 2400 block of Wilson Street, left his vehicle and began to chase Alexander on foot. Littlepage overtook Alexander and attempted to talk him into surrendering. A man named R.E. Chapman lived on Wilson Street and witnessed the incident. According to Chapman, Alexander fired several times at Littlepage with his .22-caliber rifle, hitting him in the hat and cheek. While continuing to run, Alexander pointed the shotgun behind him at Littlepage and fired, hitting Littlepage in the abdomen. Littlepage went down. Alexander fired at least two more times before taking Littlepage's .38-caliber pistol and running off down Wilson Street. Chapman; his brother, Officer Jack Newman; and at least one other officer put Littlepage into the backseat of his own car, and Newman drove him to the Emergency Hospital. Littlepage died on the operating table at the emergency hospital at 11:30 a.m. on Tuesday.

Alexander next ran to a house on Newton Street, where he shot and killed a carpenter named Joe Blunt, who was outside working on the home. Eventually, Alexander barricaded himself inside the Arnold home on South First Street. Officers gathered at the house. Sergeant William "Bull" Stuart, Harvey Maddox, Rex Fowler, Detective Chief A.L. Bugg, Jim Parker and Texas Ranger Frank Hamer had all surrounded the house and were firing rounds into the building anytime they had a target. After a few moments of quiet, a single shot was heard inside the residence. Hamer went in one door, and Stuart went in the other door to investigate. The body of Alexander was found in the bathroom with a self-inflicted shotgun wound to his throat.

Littlepage was survived by his wife, Etta, and three children. He is buried at the Oakwood Cemetery Annex in Austin.

Stuart, William Murray "Bull"
Born 12 January 1904—Died 16 October 1933
Date of Incident: 14 October 1933

Sergeant William "Bull" Stuart was killed in a motorcycle accident.

On Saturday, 14 October 1933, Stuart was northbound on Congress, traveling behind a truck that was marked as a United States government vehicle. Stuart pulled to the left of the truck and was apparently attempting to waive the vehicle over when he came into contact with another automobile driven by Gilford Hanna that was traveling southbound. The two collided. Witnesses reported that Stuart was thrown under the back wheels of the truck he was attempting to stop. The Hanna vehicle stopped as soon as the collision occurred. The truck also stopped for a few minutes but then left the area.

Injuries to Stuart were listed as fractured pelvis, fractured vertebra in his lower back, ruptured bladder and a fractured left foot. Further investigation revealed that Stuart's injuries resulted in a collision with the car, not the truck, and from the impact when he hit the roadway. Stuart died at about 2:00 p.m. on 16 October 1933.

Hanna was charged with negligent homicide by automobile.

Stuart was survived by his wife, Vivian Ferne Eanes, and two children. He was first buried at the Oakwood Cemetery in Austin, and then in 2000, he was moved to the Austin Memorial Park Cemetery to be buried next to his wife.

Cummings, James Redford
Born 13 June 1902—Died 3 December 1933

Officer James Cummings was responding to a "shots fired" call on his motorcycle when he struck another vehicle. The incident took place at Fourteenth Street and Red River Road.

At about 12:10 a.m. on Sunday, 3 December 1933, Cummings and Officer H.H. Kullenberg were riding their city-issued motorcycles in the downtown area of Austin when they received an emergency call involving a shooting in the 1700 block of East Sixth Street, where two people had been shot. The officers were traveling south on Red River toward the intersection of Fourteenth Street when a vehicle approached them coming up the hill east on Fourteenth Street. According to Kullenberg, since the car was going uphill, they did not see the vehicle's headlights. When the oncoming Chevrolet car entered the intersection, Kullenberg was able to swerve past the vehicle. Cummings was not. He collided broadside with the automobile, hitting the door, fender and hood on the left side of the vehicle and breaking out the driver's side window in the process. The car stopped some 150 feet past the intersection. Kullenberg turned around and went back to Cummings, who was partially pinned by his wrecked motorcycle.

After removing the wrecked motorcycle from Cummings, Kullenberg, along with A.J. Quentin and Frank Richardson, the occupants of the Chevrolet, carried Cummings to Brackenridge Hospital just a block away.

Cummings never said a word. He died at some point while he was being carried to the hospital. His cause of death was listed as a crushed skull and a lacerated artery in his leg.

Cummings was survived by his wife, Marguerite A. St. John, and one son. He is buried at the Oakwood Cemetery in Austin.

Morrison, Elkins Pond
Born 24 September 1906—Died 3 February 1936
Date of Incident: 2 February 1936

Officer Elkins Morrison was struck by a vehicle while attempting to cross Congress Avenue. The incident took place during foggy conditions.

At about 11:00 p.m. on Sunday, 2 February 1936, Elkins was hit by a car driven by Edgar Wilson. Wilson reported that he was only driving about twenty miles per hour and had not seen Morrison due to the rain and foggy conditions at the time, made more severe by the fact that his windshield wipers were not functioning. Morrison was taken to Brackenridge Hospital, where he died at approximately 4:00 a.m. on 3 February.

Morrison was survived by his wife and three children. He is buried at the Oakwood Cemetery in Austin.

BALLINGER POLICE DEPARTMENT

McMillan, Willard LaRue "Bob"
Born 5 January 1888—Died 27 October 1927
Date of Incident: 25 October 1927

On Monday, 24 October 1927, Mr. L.P. Payne went to work at the café as usual. According to Mrs. Payne, shortly after midnight she heard someone at the back porch of their home and asked who was there. From the darkness, the person replied that it was "Willard."

The mysterious voice identifying itself as "Willard" was City Marshal Willard L. McMillan. Mrs. Payne indicated that she had told Marshal McMillan not to come to her house anymore. He had apparently come calling previously, on two separate occasions. She also indicated that she warned him that she would kill him if he came back while her husband was absent.

After a conversation with McMillan, Mrs. Payne picked up a revolver and fired one shot through the screen door. Next, she swung open the screen door and fired a second shot.

Immediately after firing the two shots at McMillan, she called her husband. He returned home with a companion. Runnels County sheriff Matt Williams and Mitchell Moore, who was McMillan's brother-in-law, arrived at the Payne home. Seeing the wounded McMillan, Moore called for an ambulance.

McMillan made a statement claiming that Mrs. Payne had called him and asked him to come to her house that night. Mrs. Payne adamantly denied extending the solicitation.

McMillan died on 27 October 1927. A grand jury was convened to investigate his shooting death. The results of that inquiry are not known.

McMillan was survived by his wife, Beulah Lorena Bradshaw, and five children. He is buried at the Evergreen Cemetery in Ballinger.

BANDERA COUNTY SHERIFF'S OFFICE

Hicks, Elvious
Born 29 December 1879–Died 20 March 1932

Sheriff Elvious Hicks was shot and killed by a man named Ben Clark. The incident took place shortly after midnight during an ambush at a dance at Mansfield Park.

Hicks, who was indoors at the time, was told that someone wanted to speak with him outside, at the barn near the dance hall. Suspicious of the request, he went out with his gun drawn and a flashlight in hand. A man named Ben Clark was seated in his automobile nearby and opened fire at Hicks, hitting him with a blast of buckshot from a .12-gauge shotgun as he drove past the gathering. Clark also fired at deputy Billy Burns, who was coming to the aid of Hicks. Burns returned fire, hitting Clark twice. Clark got out of the car and was trying to reload when Burns shot him a third and final time.

Both Hicks and Clark were dead at the scene. Hicks's body had six buckshot pellets in the chest. His left arm had nearly been severed by the blast from Clark's shotgun. Hicks had no chance to defend himself.

It was later revealed that Clark had murdered Hicks in revenge for an earlier incident involving Hicks. It seems that Hicks had confiscated Clark's whiskey still several months before, on 7 January.

Hicks had been with the agency for five years. He was survived by his wife, Pearl Harris, and two children. Hicks is buried at the Bandera Cemetery.

BASTROP COUNTY CONSTABLE'S OFFICE

Jenkins, Daniel "Dan"
Born October 1858—Died 23 November 1900

Constable Dan Jenkins was shot and killed by a man named Stephen E.V. Wilson.

Jenkins heard gunshots fired in or near Eagleton's Saloon, located on Main Street in Smithville. As he stepped inside to investigate, someone opened fire on him. Jenkins was hit in the left chest near the nipple and in the lower left groin. He sat down in a chair and asked for a doctor. Unfortunately, he died within minutes, before help could arrive.

Wilson was charged with murder and placed under a $7,000 bond. He was indicted by a grand jury on 17 December 1900. On 3 January 1901, the case was called to trial, but the district attorney requested a continuance. The case was next set for trial on 27 June 1901. On 18 June 1901, the district attorney once again requested a continuance. It was apparently not granted, because on 10 July 1901 his file indicates that two witnesses failed to appear and testify as state witnesses. On 30 December 1901, the district attorney was granted another continuance. This time, the case was set for trial on 25 June 1902. Although the file folder for this case has gone missing, it appears as though the district attorney was unable to convince the witnesses to testify, thus the state dismissed all charges against Wilson sometime in December 1902 or January 1903.

Jenkins had been elected constable of Precinct 2 in Smithville on 6 November 1900. His place of burial is unknown. Jenkins was survived by his wife, Mattie Reid Jenkins, and four children. The Jenkins family were early settlers of Bastrop County. William E. Jenkins served as sheriff from 1876 to 1886.

McDavid, Dock "Doc" F.
Born 4 or 8 April 1877—Died 8 August 1908

Most records list McDavid's given name as Doc and his date of birth as 4 April. However, some family genealogists indicate that the correct spelling is Dock and give his birth date as 8 April. It is unclear which is correct.

Constable J.V. "Verge" Dunbar deputized Doc McDavid to assist him in arresting Joe McNeil. McNeil was wanted on a charge of using abusive language. He was well known in the community and feared by many people.

Dunbar and his deputy went to McNeil's home, which was located about five miles from Paige. There they arrested him without incident. On the trip back to town, McNeil was seated between the two lawmen in a buggy. While en route to Paige, Dunbar reported that McNeil made a sudden move to escape. He managed to get halfway out of the buggy when McDavid snared him. Dunbar was trying to manage the team of horses when he saw the prisoner attempting to grab McDavid's pistol. Dunbar, with his free hand, pulled his pistol and fired at McNeil. In his haste to shoot, he accidentally hit McDavid. The bullet struck him in the side and passed through his heart. McDavid reportedly cried out, "You've killed me for the man!" McDavid staggered and fell against the wagon wheels, relinquishing his hold on McNeil. He expired in a few minutes. As the prisoner was fleeing, Dunbar leaped from the buggy and shot him twice in the head.

McNeil died instantly. Dunbar was arrested and placed in the county jail. He waived an examining trial and was released on a $2,500 bond for the death of McNeil and $1,000 for the death of McDavid. On 8 January 1910, a jury acquitted Dunbar in the McNeil incident. The district attorney dismissed the case against Dunbar for the death of McDavid.

Doc McDavid was survived by his wife, Mollie, and four small children. He is buried at the Ridgeway Cemetery in Paige.

BASTROP COUNTY SHERIFF'S OFFICE

Gray, Robert William "Bob"
Born 27 October 1875—Died 16 April 1918

Shortly after midnight on Tuesday, 16 April 1918, Bastrop County sheriff Eli Hardin Perkins, Deputy Bob Gray and another deputy went to a nearby farm to arrest an escaped convict. When they arrived at the residence, the three lawmen split up in order to encircle the house. Gray encountered a man sitting in front of the dwelling. As he placed his hands on the man and told him not to run, the fellow suddenly pulled a gun and shot Gray in the leg and lung. The man then exchanged shots with the other lawmen and was killed during the affray. The sheriff was not injured, but the other deputy suffered a minor bullet wound.

Gray was taken to a nearby home where he died of his wounds several hours later.

Gray had been with the agency for four years. He was survived by his wife, Mary Anne Smith, and eight children. Gray is buried at the High Grove Cemetery in Red Rock.

BAYLOR COUNTY SHERIFF'S OFFICE

Board, Abner Leonard
Born 18 May 1848—Died 21 October 1913

Abner Board was assassinated by the brother of a man who was killed during an arrest several years earlier in 1901 while he was serving as sheriff.

By means of background, on 18 August 1901, Arnold Bruce and another man were camped on Wagner Creek in Throckmorton County, just over the county line from Baylor County. Bruce was acting irrationally, and several people went to Seymour in Baylor County to report his behavior to the sheriff. Sheriff Board and Deputy S. Suttlemeyer responded to the complaint. Bruce and the other man were standing while their horses drank from the creek. The lawmen ordered them to surrender and consider themselves under arrest. Bruce ran to a wagon and reached for a gun. As he began to raise the weapon, Suttlemeyer shot and killed him.

On Tuesday, 21 October 1913, P.J. Bruce of Ranger, the brother of Arnold Bruce, arrived in Seymour on the morning train. Bruce went to the second floor of the First National Bank, where former sheriff Board worked selling real estate. P.J. Bruce shot him six times, killing him instantly. Bruce ran down the steps and opened fire on Baylor County sheriff W.L. Ellis. In the ensuing shootout, Bruce was shot two times and was killed. Sheriff Ellis was seriously wounded.

Bruce had apparently planned the episode in advance because he had a letter on his person, addressed to his wife and children, asking that the people of Seymour ship his body back to Ranger for burial.

Although Sheriff Ellis survived this shooting incident, he was not so lucky several years later when, on 6 August 1916, he was shot and killed by a prisoner.

Board was survived by his wife, Annie Eunice Kenan, and three of the couple's five children. He is buried at the Seymour Cemetery in an unmarked grave. Board served as sheriff from 1884 to 1888 and again from 1900 to 1902.

Ellis, William Louis
Born 25 January 1861—Died 6 August 1916

On 21 October 1913, P.J. Bruce shot former sheriff A.L. Board six times, killing him instantly. Bruce ran down the steps and opened fire on Baylor County sheriff W.L. Ellis. In the ensuing shootout, Bruce was shot twice and killed. Sheriff Ellis was seriously wounded. Bruce killed the former sheriff out of revenge for the killing of his brother, which had occurred on 18 August 1901.

At about noon on Sunday, 6 August 1916, a prisoner named Brown shot Sheriff Ellis. He died at 2:30 p.m. the same day. Ellis had arrested Brown in connection with a theft from a local store and was bringing him to town. At a point about two miles south of Seymour, Brown struck Ellis with his handcuffs, stunning him. Brown then took the sheriff's pistol and shot him. He fled the scene.

A posse was assembled and caught up with Brown four miles west of Seymour. Brown was shot and killed during the encounter. He was still wearing the handcuffs and carrying Ellis's pistol.

Ellis is buried at the Seymour Cemetery in Baylor County. He was survived by his second wife, Sarah Ellen Scott, and two children. Ellis's first wife, Barnetta Thrasier Ashton, died in 1885. Ellis was elected sheriff of Baylor County on 5 November 1912 and reelected on 3 November 1914. He served until his death.

BEAUMONT POLICE DEPARTMENT

Stansbury, Walter W.
Born 17 October 1869—Died 23 July 1903

Mooney Allen had shot his wife the previous year and was known by the police as a desperate character.

At about 11:00 a.m. on Thursday, 23 July 1903, neighbors called the police about a family disturbance at Allen's house. When an officer arrived, Allen shot at him with a Winchester rifle. The officer quickly retreated to safety.

Officer Stansbury lived near where the incident was taking place and responded to the shooting. As he approached the house, Allen shot him once in the chest, mortally wounding him. Stansbury was taken to the hospital, where he died at 4:50 p.m.

Allen fled the scene but was later located by the sheriff and a deputy, who were on horseback at the time. Allen refused to surrender, so the sheriff told him that Officer Stansbury was not seriously wounded and that he could make bail if he returned to town peacefully. Allen agreed. The sheriff and the deputy rode in front of Allen on the way back to town. Allen was still armed. He stopped along the way at a saloon and had four shots of whiskey.

As the group entered the downtown area, they saw that a crowd had assembled. At that point, the sheriff tried to position himself behind Allen to prevent him from breaking and running. Allen is said to have pointed his gun at the sheriff. Gunfire erupted. During the mêlée, the sheriff shot Allen in the right arm, rendering him unable to operate his rifle. According to reports, during the shooting exchange the sheriff fired five times and Allen fired four times—all at close range.

Allen fled down a city street with the crowd of angry citizens hot on his heels, firing at him as they ran. Eventually, a bullet from the mob hit Allen, and he fell to the ground mortally wounded. Several members of the now highly excited horde fired numerous times into Allen's lifeless body before finally regaining composure and returning to civilized conduct.

Stansbury was survived by his wife and son. He is buried at the Magnolia Cemetery in Beaumont. The police force raised the funds to place a marker on his grave.

Merritt, Byron
Born November 1876—Died 17 December 1905

At about 9:00 a.m. on Sunday, 17 December 1905, nineteen-year-old Walter Powell (also referred to as Henry) was observed walking along the streetcar tracks near the terminus of the Sabine Pass line at Beaumont with a pistol in each hand. Motorman Byron Merritt, who was also commissioned as a Beaumont police officer, brought his streetcar to a stop just in front of Powell. Merritt stepped to the right side of the vestibule and ordered Powell to consider himself under arrest. Powell spoke to Merritt and asked him if he had a gun. Merritt answered that he did not. Powell immediately raised one of his revolvers and fired at Merritt. The shot was at close range and hit Merritt in the chest. Merritt ran about twenty steps, fell facedown alongside the track and died.

Powell proceeded to a nearby house and told the resident to take his wife and child and flee because he intended to kill the officers who would soon be coming after him. He also indicated that he wished to die along with them.

Deputy Constable Elijah Pevito, Deputy Sheriff Reed Tevis, Beaumont policemen John Sheffield and Nott Smith arrived at the residence and at once began to surround the house. Pevito approached the dwelling from the front, while the other officers took up positions on each side and to the rear of the building. Without warning, a shot rang out, and Pevito was seen staggering backward near the fence. He finally fell to the ground, shot through the heart. Pevito died almost instantly.

Tevis remained at the rear of the building. Powell was ordered to come out, which he did but with a revolver in each hand. Tevis ordered him to drop the guns. Powell made a move to shoot. Tevis raised his Winchester and fired one shot, striking Powell in the temple and penetrating his head. He was killed instantly. As Powell fell mortally wounded, one of his revolvers discharged. Fortunately, the shot went wild and did not strike anyone.

Merritt, who was twenty-nine years old at the time, had applied for a position on the Beaumont police force at the beginning of December and had asked for a fifteen-day layoff from the streetcar company to see if he liked police work. He was assigned the night beat at Pearl and Crockett Streets for seven to ten days. Merritt had already decided that police work did not suit him and, a few days prior to his death, had made plans to return to the streetcar company.

All the local newspaper accounts indicated that Merritt was still a commissioned Beaumont police officer at the time of his death and that he was attempting to arrest Powell when he was killed.

Merritt was survived by his wife, Gertrude, and two small children. He is buried at the Magnolia Cemetery in Beaumont. Due to an error on the 1900 census, Byron Merritt's given name has been recorded as Bryon on several memorials.

Related Case: Jefferson County Constable's Office, Elijah Peveto

Sterling, Alexander Rufus
Born 25 July 1884—Died 7 August 1920

Alexander Sterling had been a Beaumont policeman for fifteen years. In 1919, he pleaded guilty in federal court to violating the Reed Amendment (liquor laws) and was sentenced to forty-five days in jail. He was also fined $250. Sterling was suspended from the police force but was reinstated in the mid-1920s by the new chief and assigned to assist federal officers with Prohibition enforcement.

There are many conflicting stories concerning the cause of the incident that resulted in Sterling's death. According to reports, he had entered a hotel on Crockett Street and was met by the manager, John Macey. Sterling allegedly started shooting at Macey, who in turn grabbed a pistol from behind the bar and returned fire. Sterling was hit. He died at the scene with an empty pistol in his hand. Macey was wounded, and an innocent bystander, a Mexican cook, who was seated on a stool at the rear of the building, was also fatally wounded.

Macey was charged with the killing of Sterling. He alleged that Sterling was extorting money from him in exchange for his silence regarding Macey's liquor law violations. The outcome of that charge is unknown.

Sterling is buried at the Magnolia Cemetery in Beaumont in an unmarked grave. He was not married.

Brammer, Clarence Adam
Born 29 July 1885—Died 19 September 1923
Date of Incident: 12 September 1923

Officer Clarence Brammer died when a fellow officer accidentally shot him in the legs.

The other officer dropped his revolver on the ground. The impact caused the weapon to discharge accidentally. The bullet went through both of Brammer's legs. He was transported to a local hospital, where he died of lead poisoning one week later.

Brammer is buried at the Aurora Cemetery in Wise County. He was married.

Davis, James A.
Born 18 June 1872—Died 6 December 1925
Date of Incident: 5 December 1925

Officer James Davis was killed when he attempted to stop a team of runaway horses pulling a wagon.

Davis noticed the fleeing animals entering a busy street and tried to stop them to save nearby citizens from injury. Part of the wagon struck Davis, causing severe head and internal injuries. He was transported to a local hospital, where he died the following day.

Davis is buried at the Magnolia Cemetery in Beaumont. He was married.

BELL COUNTY CONSTABLE'S OFFICE

Mitchell, James W.
Born 9 November 1880—Died 22 July 1910

Precinct 1 constable James Mitchell was shot and killed at Belton by a man named Henry Gentry.

Gentry was suspected of being a peeper, and Mitchell had been tracking him. Gentry had tried to enter the bedroom window of a widow named Lamb. This was Gentry's third attempt to break into the house in the proceeding five-week period. On this occasion, the woman's daughter took a shot at him with a shotgun but missed. The daughter then fled to a neighbor's house. The neighbor called the constable and asked that he come with the bloodhounds and locate the "peeping Tom."

Mitchell was returning to his home with the dogs after conducting an unsuccessful search for Gentry when he was called to return. A brown derby hat and a pair of shoes had been found at the site. Mitchell's bloodhounds were unable to pick up the scent. Mitchell and neighbors were gathered together, having a conversation, when a lady in the group spotted a hatless man walking nearby. Mitchell saw the man round a corner, so he spurred his horse and gave chase. As he approached Gentry, who was hiding behind a tree, Gentry suddenly emerged and shot Mitchell in the back with a shotgun. Mitchell fell from his horse and died within a few minutes. Before he died, however, Mitchell was able to identify Gentry as the assailant to other officers.

A massive manhunt was undertaken. A posse of between two hundred and five hundred men surrounded the field and systematically conducted a thorough search for the killer. Suddenly, a shot was heard, and someone yelled, "We've got him!" Gentry had been located in a cornfield at about 4:00 a.m. The posse fired their guns in the air in celebration of their success.

Using a rope, the revelers hauled Gentry's body from the field. They photographed him and then loaded his corpse into a wagon and brought him back to town. A rope was thrown around his neck, and his naked, lifeless body was towed through the town's main streets by a mob of enraged citizens. Not yet satisfied that they had exacted a sufficient measure of revenge for his deeds, the swarm of outraged townsfolk burned Gentry's corpse at the stake—just for good measure. The incident made the news nationally.

Mitchell is buried at the North Belton Cemetery. He was survived by his wife and three children.

BELL COUNTY SHERIFF'S OFFICE

Grubbs, Isaac B.
Born September 1869—Died 6 August 1903

Deputy Isaac Grubbs was shot and killed by a woman named Catherine White.

Grubbs was attempting to serve Ms. White with an eviction notice at the time the incident took place. As Grubbs and another deputy approached the house, they were confronted by White, who stated that she would not be moved. Ms. White further reinforced her unwillingness by indicating that she would kill the officers if they proceeded. The resolute Ms. White, true to her word, fired several shots at the lawmen. Grubbs was fatally wounded.

White was acquitted of the murder of Grubbs in 1905, after her second jury could not make a decision.

Grubbs was survived by his wife, Eula White. Newspaper reports of the day indicated that his parents were well-to-do people and longtime residents of the area. Grubbs's is buried at Hillcrest Cemetery in Temple.

Bonds, Albert W.
Born 5 October 1881—Died 11 May 1927

Albert Bonds was elected sheriff on 2 November 1920 and was reelected on 7 November 1922. He was defeated for reelection on 4 November 1924 by John R. Bigham. Bigham had been endorsed by Temple chief of police Wiley Fisher. Bonds filed a criminal libel complaint against Chief Fisher.

Their hostility finally boiled over into violence. Bonds shot and killed Fisher shortly before noon on Friday, 20 August 1926, while Fisher was standing with his wife and the three small children of a man who had been killed in an automobile accident several days earlier. Bonds drove slowly past Fisher in his car and fired three shots in all. Witnesses to the incident claimed that as Fisher saw Bonds approach, he shouted a warning to his wife, saying, "Look out!" as he shoved her out of the way. Other witnesses claim that no words were spoken by either Fisher or Bonds.

Fisher died en route to the hospital. Bonds fled and abandoned his automobile about fifteen miles south of Belton. A $1,000 reward was offered for his capture.

Bonds eventually crossed the Rio Grande into Mexico on 19 September 1926 at a point known as Cow Creek, which is located about twenty-five miles south of Del Rio. By 30 September, Bonds was reported to have sought refuge deep in the interior of Mexico. He was eventually brought back to Belton and released on a $10,000 bond.

On Thursday, 2 December 1926, Bonds was shot and severely wounded while seated in his automobile in the public square. Monroe Fisher, the chief's son, was arrested and released on $2,500 bond. Bonds recovered, and his trial for the murder of Chief Fisher was set for 20 June 1927; however, no trial would ever take place. At about 11:40 a.m. on Wednesday, 11 May 1927, Bonds was walking by the Belton National Bank when an unknown person shot him five times with a rifle. He died an hour later at the Belton Sanitarium.

Bonds was survived by his wife. He is buried at the North Belton cemetery.

Related Case: Temple Police Department, Wiley V. Fisher

Zivley, George Dinkins
Born 14 May 1880—Died 26 October 1934

Sheriff George Zivley was killed in an automobile accident near Lorena at about 10:00 p.m. on Friday, 26 October 1934.

Zivley was driving from Temple to Waco at the time and was accompanied by a woman named Lillian Humphries. The Ford V8 coupe automobile in which the couple was driving was demolished when the vehicle crashed into the back end of a truck about one mile south of Lorena. Miss Humphries was also killed in the collision. The man driving the truck, Arthur Greer of McAllister, Oklahoma, was not injured.

Zivley was elected sheriff on 8 November 1932 and served until his death. After Zivley's death, Deputy Sheriff Meade S. Miller was appointed to fill his remaining term, which ended on 1 January 1935.

Zivley was survived by two children. He is buried at the Hillcrest Cemetery in Bell County. Zivley's wife, Leta Alina Witcher, preceded him in death. She passed on 30 May 1934, after a bout with leukemia.

BEXAR COUNTY CONSTABLE'S OFFICE

Berliner, Bernard "Barney"
Born 20 April 1908—Died 29 September 1931

Deputy Constable Bernard Berliner was killed in an airplane crash near south San Antonio.

Berliner and a man named Harry Schrader had taken off earlier in the day from Grozvenor Field, south of the city, for a pleasure flight. They had been airborne for only about ten minutes when the crash occurred. The aircraft, an American Eagle model, came to rest in a field near Somerset and Pleasanton Roads. Witnesses say the airplane fell into a spin and dropped from an altitude of about two hundred feet. Both men sustained serious injuries, with Berliner's being the most severe. They were taken to the Kelly Field hospital, where Berliner was declared dead on arrival.

Berliner is buried at the Agudas Achim Cemetery in San Antonio. He was not married.

BEXAR COUNTY SHERIFF'S OFFICE

Baird, Orie A., Sr.
Born 12 October 1870—Died 20 July 1912

Deputy Orie Baird was fatally wounded in the abdomen, and Deputy Constable Felicano Flores Sr. was shot in the groin when the two men were involved in a heated political discussion at a local saloon in San Antonio. Baird's wound was so serious that he died within an hour of being transported to the hospital. A bystander named Manuel Ochua had just arrived from Mexico after escaping two revolutions there. He was wounded in the arm during the same shooting incident.

Baird was survived by his wife, Paula Ida Boek, and seven children. He is buried at the Mission Burial Park in San Antonio. Some sources cite his given name as Ora.

Two years earlier, on 7 June 1910, Deputy Constable Flores was stabbed by a man named Garland Walker during an arrest attempt for domestic violence. Flores was able to pull his pistol and defend himself, firing a fatal shot that felled Walker.

Holloway, John Thomas "Bud"
Born 26 July 1877—Died 23 July 1924

Deputy Bud Holloway was shot and killed in an incident that took place while he was transporting a prisoner between Eagle Pass and San Antonio.

The prisoner, Eugeno Blanquini, was somehow able to overpower Holloway. Blanquini used Holloway's weapon to kill him. After killing Holloway, Blanquini escaped to Mexico.

Holloway was survived by his wife and two children. He is buried at the Mission Burial Park in San Antonio.

Mangold, George L.
Born 10 June 1891—Died 18 September 1932

Deputy George Mangold was shot and killed when he and other deputies responded to a reported burglary at a local business.

As the deputies began searching the store, one of the three burglars, all of whom were still inside the building, opened fire from ambush. Mangold was struck in the chest with a shotgun blast. The three men, Edgar McDonald, Eugene Banspach and Joe Demack, fled the store but were all later apprehended. No information has been found regarding the outcome of any charges against the threesome.

Mangold had been with the agency for only nine months. He was survived by his wife and two daughters. Mangold is buried at the San Fernando Cemetery in San Antonio. Some family genealogists cite his middle name as Joseph.

Musgrave, Joe Clyde
Born 13 April 1897—Died 3 November 1934

Former deputy sheriff Joe Musgrave was shot six times and fatally wounded near a saloon on Concho Street in San Antonio. His killer, city investigator Bryan Mauerman, was taken into custody immediately.

Mauerman claimed that he shot Musgrave out of self-defense and that Musgrave had slapped, kicked and otherwise abused him before he fired the fatal gunshots.

Musgrave was survived by his wife, Libbae Cooper, and one child. He is buried at the Roselawn Cemetery in San Antonio.

Ackermann, Frank B.
Born 7 May 1883—Died 20 September 1937
Date of Incident: 17 September 1937

Deputy Frank Ackermann was shot and killed when he responded to a call involving a man with a gun at a hotel on Medina Street.

When Ackermann and his partner entered the establishment, they encountered the gun-toting Ray Pryor in the lobby. Seeing the officers, Pryor ran upstairs. Ackermann gave chase. Once upstairs, shots were exchanged between Ackermann and Pryor. Both men were wounded. Pryor, a Donna café owner, was arrested and charged with murder.

Ackermann died of his injury three days later. Although Ackermann had only been with the Bexar County Sheriff's Office for nine months, he had five years' previous experience as a lawman. Ackermann was survived by his wife and three stepsons. He is buried at the Bueche Cemetery in San Antonio.

de la Garza, Jesus
Born 5 September 1905—Died 13 December 1937

On Monday, 13 December 1937, Special Deputy Sheriff Jesus de la Garza was inside the 2-X bar and café at Houston and Laredo Streets in San Antonio. Santiago Cervantes operated the lunch room concession at the café and was dancing with a woman named Hope Rocha when they passed Garza, who was seated on a bar stool. Rocha was a tall woman and Cervantes a short man. Apparently, Garza thought that the pair looked humorous while dancing and began to laugh out loud. When the couple danced past Garza for the second time, Ms. Rocha asked him why he was laughing. He told her to shut up, and then he laughed and cursed her in Spanish. Enraged by the insult, Cervantes confronted Garza, who by this time was intoxicated. Garza pulled his .32-20-caliber revolver and fired four times, striking Cervantes once in the back. The wounded Cervantes pulled his .38-caliber pistol, inserted one cartridge into the cylinder and fired. Cervantes' bullet struck Garza in the heart, killing him almost instantly. By the time police arrived, there were only four people left inside the once crowded bar.

Garza was divorced. He is buried at the San Fernando Cemetery #2 in San Antonio.

BIG SPRING POLICE DEPARTMENT

Burk, James P. "Jim"
Born circa 1871—Died 25 April 1907

City Marshal T.B. Sullivan had received information regarding a sporting house that was operating in the city. At about 12:15 a.m., Sullivan decided to raid the business and arrest the occupants. As he headed to the establishment, James P. "Jim" Burk volunteered to go with him. Once there, Burk took the marshal's pistol and walked around the building. Suddenly, gunfire erupted from inside the brothel as one or more of the occupants opened fire. Burk was shot through the heart and died in about four minutes. Sullivan rushed to Burk's aid and caught him as he was about to collapse from his wounds.

Sullivan and sheriff's deputies arrested three men inside the house who were suspected of doing the shooting: Ed Hargrave, Will Manning and Albert Smith. Hargrave was tried and convicted of murder in the second degree and sentenced to serve twenty-five years in prison.

Very little information is known about Jim Burk. He was reported to have been thirty-six years old and not married. His body was sent to Denison, in Grayson County, for burial. The exact location is unknown.

Andrews, Cullen Battle "C.B."
Born 21 March 1866—Died 23 March 1920

At about 2:00 a.m. on Tuesday, 23 March 1920, night watchman C.B. Andrews was shot and killed by a man named W.A. Huddleston.

Andrews was hit by two bullets that had been fired by his assailant. The wounds proved fatal. The circumstances surrounding the shooting death of Andrews are unclear. Huddleston was arrested. The disposition of any charges against him is unknown.

Andrews was preceded in death by his wife, Iona Parthenia "Annie" Frost. He was survived by his nine children. Andrews is buried at the Mount Oliver Cemetery in Big Spring. Some family genealogists report his given name as Curlin.

Howie, Henry Franklin
Born 8 June 1878—Died 10 August 1931

Officer Henry Howie was shot and killed while responding to a disturbance that involved two men.

Howie had received a call from J.D. York, who claimed that his life had been threatened by two men at a nearby tourist camp. Howie apprehended one of the men and was sitting in his patrol car discussing the incident with him when the second man, Julius (Louis) Whisenhunt, suddenly appeared on a nearby hillside and opened fire, shooting downward into the automobile. The bullet fired by Whisenhunt struck Howie in the right shoulder and ranged downward. The wound proved fatal. Howie died on his way to the hospital.

York was arrested under suspicion of being an accomplice. There is no information available regarding any charges against him. Whisenhunt fled to the badlands area near Scenic Mountain. Constable Miller Nichols and Deputy Andrew Merrick arrested him about an hour and a half after the incident. Whisenhunt was tried and convicted of the murder of Howie. He was sentenced to serve four years in prison. That sentence was later suspended.

Howie was survived by his wife, Mary Ann Cox, and five children. He is buried at the College Mound Cemetery in Kaufman County. The Junior Chamber of Commerce of Big Spring established a fund for Howie's widow and presented her with the money it had collected through generous donations on 3 September 1931.

O'Leary, William Joseph
Born 2 January 1896—Died 28 November 1939

Assistant Chief William O'Leary was shot and killed while he was struggling with a man named Rafael Camacho in front of a grocery store in Big Spring. Camacho had apparently been burglarizing the establishment when

O'Leary caught him by surprise. There were no witnesses to the shooting, but somehow Camacho was immediately identified as a suspect.

On 4 December 1939, Camacho committed suicide by hanging himself in his cell at the Parker County Jail at Weatherford. He left a note stating that he was the one who had killed O'Leary. The note identified the location of the murder weapon, which was recovered in a lake near Sweetwater and later linked through ballistics to the bullets recovered from O'Leary's body.

O'Leary had been with the agency for only five months. He was survived by his wife, Agnes Gertrude Clifford, and three children. O'Leary is buried at the Maverick County Cemetery (also called Eagle Pass Cemetery) in Eagle Pass.

Cass, Elijah James "Eli"
Born 27 July 1900—Died 6 November 1940

Patrolman Eli Cass suffered a fatal heart attack following a foot pursuit through the Texas & Pacific Railroad yard at Big Spring.

Cass had responded to a report of a shoplifting and arrived just as the suspects fled. He chased the men into the yards and managed to catch one of them. As he was walking the man to his patrol car, he collapsed and died.

Cass had been with the agency for eighteen months. He was survived by his wife and four children. Cass's wife, Genevieve Gibson, died the following day, on 7 November 1940. Cass is buried at the Mount Olive Cemetery in Big Spring.

BLOSSOM CITY MARSHAL'S OFFICE

Hill, Benjamin Joseph
Born July 1872—Died 19 October 1902
Date of Incident: 18 October 1902

City Marshal Benjamin Hill died from gunshot wounds he received when he attempted to detain a man for firing a gun at an outdoor church festival. During the arrest, the man, John Harris, shot Hill three times. It remains unclear why Hill thought it was a good idea to fire his weapon at a church bazaar.

Harris was convicted of Hill's murder on 27 October. He was subsequently executed by hanging between noon and 1:00 p.m. on 19 December 1902 at the town of Paris in Lamar County.

Hill was survived by his wife, Sarah Ida Holcombe, and three children. He is buried at the Knights of Pythias Cemetery in Lamar County.

BORGER, CITY OF

Dodd, Harry Benjamin
Born 22 November 1893—Died 19 December 1927

Night watchman Harry Dodd was shot and killed by a man named Louis Crimm. Crimm was wounded during the exchange of gunfire. According to reports, this fatal incident grew out of some sort of personal disagreement between the two men.

Dodd is buried at La Junta, Colorado. He was not married and was survived by his parents.

BORGER POLICE DEPARTMENT

Rigney, Irl Wilkerson
Born 11 February 1896—Died 30 November 1926

Captain Irl Rigney was shot and killed while attempting to arrest a murder suspect.

At about 7:00 p.m. on Tuesday, 30 November 1926, Rigney was making his nightly rounds when he recognized a man named M.F. "Toughey" McWilliams, who was allegedly wanted in Mexia. As Rigney attempted to arrest McWilliams, he was shot in the back three times at close range. As Rigney fell wounded, he drew his pistol, fired and hit McWilliams in the hip and chest.

Seriously injured, Rigney tried to make a statement, but he died before he could do so. McWilliams died from the wounds he received in the incident on 2 December.

At the conclusion of an investigation by police, officers reported that no weapon was found on McWilliams. Therefore, considering that Rigney had been shot in the back, it was suspected that one or more other persons might have been involved in the incident. Before he died, McWilliams denied shooting Rigney. It is not known if anyone was ever arrested for or convicted of Rigney's murder.

Rigney had been with the agency for twenty years. He had also been a deputy sheriff in Bristow, Oklahoma. Rigney was survived by his wife, Nellie M. Brown, and three children. He is buried in Shroud, Oklahoma.

Buchanan, Richard Coke
Born 28 December 1874—Died 19 March 1927

Patrolman Coke Buchanan was shot and killed while coming to the aid of a fellow officer who was being beaten by several men.

Another patrolman named Beal had stopped an automobile that was occupied by members of the noted Cotton Top Walker Gang. Five passengers exited the vehicle and began to beat Beal. Buchanan observed the incident from across the street and ran to the aid of his fellow lawman. As he crossed the street, one of the gang members opened fire and killed him.

J.H. Walker and Ed Bailey were arrested at Borger and held on suspicion of being involved in the murder of Buchanan. Ray Terrell and Matthew Kimes were also suspected of being involved in the incident.

Buchanan had been with the agency for two months and had just joined after serving fifteen years with the Waco Police Department. He was survived by his wife, Ada Owen, and five children. Buchanan is buried at the Greenwood Cemetery in Waco.

The Cotton Top Walker Gang was led by the Kimes brother and had murdered Deputy Perry Chuculate of the Sequoyah County, Oklahoma Sheriff's Office on 27 August 1926. Two of the brothers were convicted of manslaughter in connection with Chuculate's murder and sentenced to twenty-five years in prison. One of the brothers, Matthew Kimes, escaped from prison and continued his crime spree.

Matthew Kimes continued robbing banks with the Cotton Top Walker Gang. Along with the murder of Buchanan, the gang was also credited with killing Deputies D.P. Kenyon and Almer Terry of the Hutchinson County Sheriff's Department on 1 April 1927 and Chief W. J. McAnnally of the Beggs, Oklahoma Police Department on 18 May 1927. Matthew Kimes, one of the leaders of the gang, was eventually arrested in Flagstaff, Arizona, on 23 June 1927.

Related Case: Hutchinson County Sheriff's Office, D.P. Kenyon and Almer Terry

Hutson, Joseph Theophelus "Joe"
Born 12 March 1889—Died 10 February 1929

Chief of Police "Joe" Hutson was fatally wounded when a fellow officer named Tom Hughes discharged his pistol accidentally.

When the incident occurred, Hughes was attempting to holster his gun. He accidentally shoved the pistol into the loops of the holster. The gun fell and hit the floor, firing on impact. The accidental discharge took place just as Hutson was entering the room. The bullet entered Hughes's right ankle, broke a bone and then ricocheted, striking Hutson in the thigh. He bled to death.

Hutson was a pioneer peace officer in the community. He was survived by his wife, Mary Tina Landers, and four or five children. Hutson is buried at the Borger Cemetery in Hutchinson County. Hutson's brother Lee was also a member of the Borger Police Department.

Bosque County Constable's Office

Barnes, Jefferson Davis "Jeff"
Born 15 February 1866—Died 28 July 1911

Precinct 5 constable Jeff Barnes accidentally shot himself while cleaning his pistol. He died instantly.

Barnes was elected constable for Precinct 5 in Bosque County on 8 November 1910 and qualified on 5 December 1910.

Barnes was survived by his wife, Leona Elizabeth Johnston, and six children. He is buried at the Kopperl Cemetery in Bosque County.

Bowie County Constable's Office

Kennedy, James M.
Born 5 January 1880—Died 3 September 1907

Constable James Kennedy was stabbed to death by an eighteen-year-old man named Robert Terrell. According to reports, Kennedy was intoxicated at the time of the incident.

Terrell was tried, convicted and sentenced to serve two years for the murder of Kennedy. That sentence was later reversed.

Kennedy is buried at the West Bowie Cemetery.

Goodwin, Millard Thomas
Born 28 March 1889—Died 19 December 1927

On Monday afternoon, 19 December 1927, former deputy constable and Texarkana motorcycle officer Millard Goodwin and his brother-in-law, James Reynolds, got into an argument over money that Reynolds claimed was owed to him by Goodwin. The men were in the office of an oil company in Texarkana at the time. Reynolds fired six shots at Goodwin. The first two rounds missed as Goodwin tried to flee. The next four shots hit Goodwin, wounding him fatally.

Reynolds was arrested and charged with the murder. He was tried on 30 January 1928 and acquitted after entering a plea of self-defense.

Goodwin's death certificate indicated that he was a merchant and a county officer at the time of his death. He is buried at the Red Lick Cemetery. Goodwin was survived by his wife, Mayme, and two children.

Bowie County Sheriff's Office

Briley, Clifford F. "Cliff"
Born December 1877—Died 2 September 1909

Deputy Sheriff Cliff Briley was shot and killed on East Broad Street in Texarkana, Arkansas, by Bowie County Precinct 1 deputy constable Melvin Anderson at about 1:30 a.m. on Thursday, 2 September 1909. Anderson and Briley were said to have had a disagreement of some sort. Anderson claimed Briley pulled his gun. In response, Anderson shot Briley once in the right temple with his .45-caliber pistol. Briley fell to the ground dead.

Afterward, witnesses claimed that Briley's gun was lying by his right side. Anderson was charged with second-degree murder by the Miller County grand jury. He pleaded self-defense. The outcome of the charges is not known.

Briley's place of burial is unknown. He was living in Texarkana, Texas, with his grandfather, mother and two siblings at the time of the 1900 census.

Bryan, Joel Freeman
Born 26 June 1858—Died 24 August 1922

By means of background, the racial tensions in Bowie County once again surfaced on Friday, 2 September 1921, when Deputy Sheriff Will Jordan alleged that masked men held him up and took his black prisoner, Myra Wilson. Wilson was later dropped off outside the local newspaper office and fled the scene.

Wilson had been a defendant in police and state cases during the preceding few months. On Sunday, 11 February 1921, Jordan once again claimed that four masked men had stopped his car and, at the point of drawn revolvers, taken his black prisoner, P. Norman. Norman's body was found the next morning with two bullet wounds in the head and one in his body. The criminal district attorney stated that the masked men had probably been searching for another black man who was claimed to have murdered a white man.

On Monday, 12 September 1921, Jordan alleged that three carloads of men fired volleys of gunfire into his home. Jordan returned fire. Notices were sent to the local newspaper from the Ku Klux Klan, Lodge 104, at Texarkana, posting a $100 reward for the arrest and conviction of the persons who lynched Norman. The Klan denied any involvement in the incident.

Jordan was arrested, charged with the murder of Norman and tried in district court. He was acquitted on 24 March 1922.

On 24 August 1922, between 4:00 and 5:00 a.m., Deputy Sheriff Joel Bryan was shot to death in the driveway of his own home. Before he died, Bryan claimed that a "big, black Negro did it." Bryan went on to say that the man took his pistol and shoved it against him and fired. He was hit below the heart and died in the hospital about 7:00 p.m.

Officers reported that they believed Bryan was trying to arrest the man when the incident took place. A black man was arrested but later released. It does not appear that anyone else was ever arrested or charged with the killing of Bryan. Newspaper accounts of the day claim that suicide was a possible motive. Bryan was separated from his second wife and had left a note explaining how to dispose of his pistol if he were to die.

At the time of his death, Bryan was an unpaid deputy. The sheriff paid all of his deputies on a commission basis, and Bryan had not worked in some time.

Bryan was survived by his wife, Harriet Adelia Copeland, and eight children. He is buried at New Boston. At his burial, twenty four Ku Klux Klansmen placed a cross on each side of the coffin.

BOWIE POLICE DEPARTMENT

Hill, William H. "Jack"
Born 11 January 1888—Died 6 July 1932
Date of Incident: 15 June 1932

Officer Jack Hill was shot and killed while assisting other officers who were conducting a liquor raid at an automotive service station. The owner of the station, W.S. Farar, suddenly opened fire on the lawmen. Hill was hit during the exchange of gunfire. The other officers returned fire and killed the murderer.

Hill was taken to a local hospital. He died of his wounds three weeks later.

Hill had served with the Bowie Police Department for three years. He had previously been a deputy sheriff and was defeated as a candidate for sheriff in 1928.

Hill is buried at the Elmwood Cemetery in Bowie. He was survived by his wife and three children.

BRASHEAR CITY MARSHAL'S OFFICE

Bridges, William "Will"
Born 23 September 1874—Died 2 June 1917

City Marshal Will Bridges was shot and killed by a woman named Maude Mauney (Mooney).

On Saturday, 2 June 1917, a man entered the Jack Mauney grocery store and asked for a ham for Marshal Bridges. The owner's daughters, Allie Lee and Maude Mauney, were both waiting on customers in the store. Maude told the man that they did not have any ham, but if they did, Bridges could not have one at any price. At that moment, Bridges entered the store. He started to say something, but before he had an opportunity to do so, Maude ordered him out of the establishment as she simultaneously threatened to kill him.

Without hesitation, Maude reached for a pistol and fired one shot at Bridges before he had time to exit the store. She followed up with a second shot in his direction after he had left the establishment.

Both shots hit Bridges and proved fatal within twenty to twenty-five minutes. Maude telephoned the sheriff and confessed to having shot and killed Bridges.

Maude Mauney was indicted for murder by the Hopkins County grand jury. She pleaded insanity at the final trial and testified that she was at times subjected to spells of mental aberration. Ms. Mauney went on to say that she and her sister had, at different times, been grossly insulted by Bridges and that Bridges had at one time brutally assaulted her. She further claimed that Bridges constantly meddled in their affairs and that they had tried to avoid him at all times, going on to say that some of this conduct on the part of Bridges had occurred just a few days before the shooting. Ms. Mauney claimed that she became very much agitated when Bridges entered the store and thought that he had advanced toward her. She said that she remembered nothing that had transpired during the incident.

The court record contains evidence of prior grudges and threats having been made by Maude Mauney against Bridges. At the examining trial, Mauney's pleadings stated that Bridges had insulted her and her sister. The state met her claim with evidence to the contrary, arguing that when her reasons for shooting Bridges had been disproved, she adopted an insanity defense. Although Maude Mauney was tried for murder, she was convicted of manslaughter and sentenced to serve five years in prison. The conviction was confirmed on appeal.

Bridges was survived by his wife, Zula Mooney, and three children. He is buried at the Greenview Cemetery in Hopkins County.

BRAZORIA COUNTY CONSTABLE'S OFFICE

Juliussesn, L.P.
Born (Unknown)—Died 19 July 1906
Date of Incident: 18 July 1906

Constable Juliussesn was shot and killed by a man named Henry Perry Jr. at the Velasco community, located about sixteen miles south of Angleton.

On Wednesday, 18 July 1906, Juliussesn attempted to arrest Perry. Perry knocked Juliussesn to the ground with an iron bar, took his pistol away from him and shot him with it, hitting him three times in the face and neck. Perry fired one additional shot at Deputy Sheriff H. Blades. The bullet missed the mark, and Blades was uninjured.

Juliussesn died from the gunshot wounds the following day. Perry was captured by a posse, but in the process of taking him into custody, possemen shot him in the foot and side. He was charged with the killing of Juliussesn. The disposition of those charges is unknown.

Juliussesn's place of burial is unknown. A newspaper account of the day claimed that Juliussesn's wounds might not have been fatal had Juliussesn been a younger or more robust man.

Brazoria County Sheriff's Office

Jackson, John Harrison
Born 1 December 1840—Died 30 December 1906

Deputy Sheriff John Jackson died of a heart attack that was apparently brought on when he became overexcited about a fire that had taken place.

Jackson was survived by his wife, Elizabeth Jane Ream, and five children. He is said to have been a Mason and to have served in the Confederate army during the Civil War. Jackson's place of burial is unknown.

Munson, Hillen Armour
Born 31 July 1863—Died 15 September 1909

Charles Delaney and John Cooper escaped from the county jail in Angleton. They were armed and headed to the rail station to catch a train to Houston. At the depot, they encountered stationmaster J.T. "Tut" Hardin, whom they shot and killed. The sheriff and a posse of five men located Steve Hayes, a cousin of Delaney, at Sandy Point. Munson joined the posse because he had employed Hayes and knew him. Accordingly, Munson was selected as the one to approach Hayes's cabin.

As Munson approached the building, either Hayes or Delaney fired one blast from a shotgun from inside the building. The pellets hit Munson in the face and chest. Mortally wounded, Munson calmly turned his horse around and rode several feet before dismounting and falling to the ground dead.

Hayes and Delaney fled the scene. Other posse members accidentally shot and killed three innocent men whom they assumed were the escapees. Munson family genealogists have recorded that Hayes was killed soon after, and Delaney was arrested and sent to prison.

Munson was from a prominent family and was survived by his wife and three children. He is buried at the Munson Cemetery in Bailey's Prairie.

Snow, Joseph Hughes "Joe," Sr.
Born 13 May 1872—Died 15 September 1920

Sheriff Joe Snow was shot and killed by a black man named Oscar Beasley while he was attempting to arrest Beasley for theft of a horse.

Snow had been to Beasley's farm the day before the incident took place to investigate a fire. While he was there, he noticed his own saddle and a group of horses that had been stolen from his farm a few days earlier. The following day, Snow returned to arrest Beasley. As it turned out, the plan did not work out so well for him. Beasley shot Snow at close range with a shotgun. The wound was fatal. Snow died almost immediately.

After an extended manhunt that lasted almost two days, Beasley was captured near Danburry, five miles from Angleton. He was arrested and taken to jail. Before he could stand trial, a mob of about three hundred angry citizens took justice into their own hands and lynched him from a tree in front of the jailhouse. Beasley's body was left hanging in the tree all day in a grotesque display of vigilante justice.

Snow was elected sheriff on 5 November 1918 and had been with the agency for two years. He was survived by his wife and one child. He is buried at the Angleton Cemetery.

Cook, James William
Born 15 February 1888—Died 26 August 1925

Deputy James Cook was shot and killed while he was attempting to arrest bootleggers, one of whom was S.R. Owens of Texas City.

The incident took place at about 4:30 p.m. on Wednesday, 26 August 1925, at Bryan Beach near Freeport. Cook and Deputy Jimmy Martin Jr. from West Columbia had obtained a search warrant and had gone to Owens's home. Cook was attempting to arrest Owens for violating the liquor law when a scuffle began. During the course of the struggle, each man was shot in the back. Cook was put in an automobile and returned to town for medical treatment, but he died en route.

Cook is buried at the New Town Cemetery in Brazoria. He was married.

Harnest, Joseph Arthur
Born 21 May 1903—Died 14 December 1937

Deputy Joseph Harnest was shot and killed by an overzealous farmer who mistook him for an escaped convict. The shooting took place near West Columbia.

Harnest was survived by his wife, Fannie Jewel Hess, and three children. He is buried at the Angleton Cemetery.

McKinney, John Wesley
Born 2 March 1862—Died 22 October 1940
Date of Incident: 19 October 1940

On Saturday, 19 October 1940, Deputy Sheriff John McKinney was responding to a complaint call near Sweeney when he was involved in a major traffic accident. McKinney was seriously injured in the collision and died on 22 October 1940.

McKinney had served as sheriff of Brazoria County from 1928 to 1932. He was survived by his wife, Josephine McCulloch, and six children. McKinney is buried at the Columbia Cemetery in West Columbia.

BRAZOS, COUNTY OF

McMinn, Robert Patton
Born 15 May 1866—Died 4 November 1913

Robert P. McMinn had been a prison guard prior to being assigned as county road superintendent. He was responsible for the oversight of prisoner road gangs.

Superintendent McMinn was beaten to death by three prisoners at the town of Cawthon. His attackers were Ed Deere and Charley Webb. Nothing further is known about this incident or any charges against the assailants.

McMinn was survived by his wife, Nettie Catherine Johnson. He is buried at the Wellborn Cemetery.

BRAZOS COUNTY SHERIFF'S OFFICE

Barker, Sidney Hamilton
Born 5 May 1888—Died 24 March 1910

Some sources claim that Sidney Barker was a Brazos County deputy sheriff. Thus far, evidence to confirm his service remains undiscovered. Nonetheless, his story has been included in the interest of completeness.

Sidney Barker was shot and killed by a man named Van Millican. Van Millican alleged that Barker attempted to make an unlawful arrest and that he was forced to kill him in self-defense because Barker had fired at him first. The prosecution claimed that Van Millican waylaid Barker and shot him from ambush. The appeals court records do not indicate that Barker was a peace officer.

Van Millican was charged with the killing of Barker, convicted and sentenced to serve life in prison.

Barker was survived by his wife, Ira Curd, and two children. He is buried at the Peach Creek Cemetery.

Morehead, Leonard Edgar
Born 7 July 1880—Died 19 March 1924

Sheriff Leonard Morehead was shot and killed while he was attending a magic show at the Steep Hollow schoolhouse in the Kurten community of Brazos County.

Morehead was seated in the back row when a man named Commodore Bullock approached him and fired a shotgun at his head from close range through an open window. The shotgun was loaded with nails, screws and bolts. It goes without saying that the blast resulted in a spectacularly devastating wound.

Bullock was arrested for the murder of Morehead. As it turns out, Bullock had been confined to a Texas asylum for mental derangement ten or twelve years earlier but had been judged cured and was released. Not surprisingly, he was again judged to be insane and committed to Austin State Hospital.

Morehead had been elected on 5 November 1918 and reelected on 2 November 1920 and again on 7 November 1922. Morehead was survived by his wife and three children. He is buried at the Bryan City Cemetery.

Morehead's wife was appointed to complete his term in office on 30 March 1924. She served until 1 January 1925 and thus became the second female sheriff in Texas history.

BREWSTER COUNTY CONSTABLE'S OFFICE

Valenzuela, Felix R.
Born 2 February 1882—Died 19 June 1938

Precinct 2 constable Felix Valenzuela was shot and killed near the Mexican border. Valenzuela and the justice of the peace had stopped an automobile that was suspected of transporting illegal liquor. One of the three occupants grabbed the justice's pistol and shot Valenzuela. The man who did the shooting stole the officer's car and fled to Mexico, leaving his companions behind. They, too, headed for the sanctuary of Mexico but had to do so on foot.

Valenzuela was survived by his wife, Josefa Baeza, and ten children. He is buried at Terlingua.

BRISCOE COUNTY SHERIFF'S OFFICE

Long, James O.
Born 15 April 1875—Died 5 May 1915

Sheriff James Long was shot and killed by Silverton High School superintendent W.G. Sears. The exact nature of the disagreement and circumstance of the shooting is somewhat unclear.

At about 4:30 p.m. on Wednesday, 5 May 1915, Long was shot twice in the head by Sears. According to his death certificate, Long died instantly. The incident is said to have taken place at a local drugstore. One newspaper account alleged that the trouble between the two men had grown out of some school-related disagreement. According to reports, Sears boarded single teachers. One source claimed that the teachers had gone to Long and complained about some matter and that Long had spoken with Sears about the grievance. After the confrontation between the two men, Sears went home and retrieved his pistol, returned to the drugstore and shot Long fatally. After the shooting, Sears surrendered to authorities.

Sears was arrested and charged with Long's murder. On 29 October 1915, the case against Sears was transferred to Hale County for trial in district court. On 8 February 1916, a hung jury acquitted Sears of the murder, voting eight in favor of acquittal and two in favor of conviction.

Long had been elected sheriff on 3 November 1914. He served until his death. Long is buried at the Citizens Cemetery in Clarendon.

BROWNSVILLE POLICE DEPARTMENT

Crixell, Joseph L. "Joe"
Born May 1871—Died 9 August 1912

In the early 1900s, the political and racial climate in Cameron County, and particularly in the county seat of Brownsville, was extremely volatile. The Democrats, who were known as the "Blues," were predominately Anglos and controlled the county offices. Independents, who were known as the "Reds," were predominately Hispanic and controlled the Brownsville municipal offices.

At about 9:45 p.m. on Friday, 9 August 1912, City Marshal Joe Crixell had finished his patrol of the city. Crixell was on horseback and had returned to the downtown area, near Elizabeth Street between Twelfth and Thirteenth Streets. He tied up his horse outside a saloon owned by his brother, Teofilo Crixell. Deputy Sheriff Paul McAlister, a former Texas Ranger, was seated in a chair a short distance away in front of The Club saloon. Crixell approached him as he walked along the sidewalk. When he reached a point within five feet of McAlister, McAlister shot him six times with a .45-caliber semiautomatic pistol. Crixell died within ten minutes.

No words were exchanged between the two men, and Crixell's unfired pistol was still in his holster. Texas Ranger captain J.M. Fox and Private James B. Mercer were nearby and arrested McAlister.

McAlister was held without bail. He managed to receive a change of venue to Hallettsville in Lavaca County. On 11 November 1913, McAlister was acquitted. He based his self-defense argument on the fact that Crixell had previously threatened him.

Crixell was survived by his wife, Pilar, and four children. He is buried at the Brownsville City Cemetery.

Paul McAlister remained a deputy sheriff in Cameron County until 1915, when he became a deputy sheriff in Duval County. On 5 July 1925, McAlister, who was at the time a deputy state game warden, was involved in a shooting that resulted in his death. Also killed in the same incident were Nueces County Precinct 1 constable Carl M. Bisbee and his deputy, R.R. Bledsoe.

Related Case: Texas Department of Parks and Wildlife, Paul McAlister

Rodriguez, Toribio
Born 6 April 1890—Died 14 November 1912
Date of Incident: 10 November 1912

Three months after the death of City Marshal Joe Crixell, the political violence continued at Brownsville among city, county and state lawmen.

In the early morning hours of Sunday, 10 November 1912, Texas Ranger captain J.J. Sanders was asked to assist Cameron County deputy sheriff Pat Haley in the arrest of former city policeman Ignacio Trevino. Trevino was wanted on three felony warrants. Sanders summoned rangers Joe Jenkins and Red Hawkins, who joined Deputy Sheriffs Haley and Andres Uresti. Together, the lawmen found Trevino at his home and arrested him. The rangers and deputies placed Trevino in a horse-drawn hack (carriage) for the ride to the county jail.

Special Policemen Guadalupe Mata, Santos Garcia and Toribio Rodriguez were on horseback and on patrol. The officers came upon the hack in the dark and noticed that the carriage did not have any lights. The officers called out to the driver to light his lamp. In an instant, gunfire erupted in the darkness.

The mounted officers contend that the men in the hack had cursed them and opened fire. The state rangers and deputy sheriffs in the carriage alleged that the city policemen commenced firing first. In either case, when the smoke cleared, Ranger Joe Jenkins was wounded in the left arm and had to be transported to the hospital. Officer Rodriguez was shot in the right arm. The impact had knocked him from his horse. Rodriguez walked home and was later treated by a doctor who came to his residence. Both the doctor and city police lieutenant O.M. Puig later testified that Rodriguez was only wounded in his arm during the shooting incident involving the hack.

Sanders and unnamed rangers, together with Deputy Sheriffs Uresti and Manuel Saldana, arrived at Rodriguez's house and found him asleep. Rodriguez claimed that the officers took him outside and that Uresti shot him in the back. The bullet pierced his right lung. Rodriguez was placed in the county jail and received no medical treatment. Sanders later stated that he knew nothing about Rodriguez's second wound because he did not examine him when he arrested him at his home.

Rodriguez had become a special policeman only five days before the shooting. He gave a dying statement claiming that he and the other policemen did not know that the hack contained rangers and deputy sheriffs. He further stated that he and the other city policemen had not fired first. Rodriguez claimed that Uresti shot him in the back at the time he was arrested at his home.

Rodriguez never fully recovered from the gunshot wound. At 2:30 a.m. on Thursday, 14 November 1912, he died from pneumonia.

Rodriguez is buried in an unmarked grave at the Brownsville City Cemetery.

The grand jury found no evidence to indict anyone for the death of Rodriguez and cleared the rangers and deputy sheriffs of any wrongdoing, stating that they had a right to defend themselves.

Puig, Octavio Monico Luis
Born 4 May 1885—Died 19 September 1913

Lieutenant Octavio Puig was shot and killed when he and another officer went to investigate a report of gunfire at a local sporting house.

When the officers arrived at the brothel, they recognized the shooters as being the county sheriff and several of his deputies. Puig extended every professional courtesy possible to his fellow lawmen and told the group to come to the police station the next morning. Apparently, they had expected to be let off without consequences, so they opened fire on him. Puig was shot a total of nine times. His wounds were fatal. There is no information regarding any charges against the sheriff or any of his deputies ever having been filed.

Puig was survived by his wife, Maria, and one child. He is buried at the City Cemetery at Brownsville.

BROWNWOOD POLICE DEPARTMENT

Fuston, William Clarence "Jack"
Born 24 March 1912—Died 3 February 1939

Officer Jack Fuston and two other lawmen went to a local tourist camp located on the outskirts of Brownwood to search for a prisoner who had escaped from the Palo Pinto jail. When they confronted the suspect, a man named William Thomas Haley Jr., he denied that he was the person they were looking for. Pretending to reach for identification papers to prove his claim, Haley instead drew a gun and shot Fuston four times, killing him instantly. Haley dashed into the bathroom. The other officers returned fire, emptying their pistols into the closed door. They managed to wound Haley, who escaped through the window.

Haley was apprehended between Dublin and Stephenville about noon the following day after he leaped from an automobile that he had stolen at gunpoint from a man in Dublin. Haley was sporting gunshot wounds in both arms and legs from the outhouse encounter with officers at the Fuston shooting site.

Fuston was survived by his wife. He is buried at the Greenleaf Cemetery.

BRYAN POLICE DEPARTMENT

Neal, Levi
Born circa 1851—Died 24 February 1900

Deputy City Marshal Levi Neal was shot and killed while he was escorting a man named Dennis Calhoun to jail.

Neal had arrested Calhoun, and while he was walking the prisoner toward the jail, Calhoun pulled a pistol that he had concealed under his coat and shot him. Neal is one of the first black law enforcement officers in Texas to have been killed in the line of duty.

Calhoun was tried and convicted of the murder. He was sentenced to serve life in prison.

Neal had been in law enforcement for about twenty years. He is buried in an unmarked grave at the Bryan City Cemetery. Although later efforts to locate his grave site proved unsuccessful, a marker commemorating his service was erected at the cemetery.

The twice-lucky Neal had previously survived a shootout on 15 May 1885 that took the life of Bryan deputy city marshal Levin P. Smith Jr. On 2 December 1888, Neal was with Bryan city marshal M.M. Wilcox when Wilcox was killed attempting to serve a warrant.

BURKBURNETT POLICE DEPARTMENT

Garland, William Irvin
Born 27 April 1871—Died 18 May 1935

Chief William Garland drowned when a bridge over the Red River collapsed during a period of heavy flooding.

Garland had noticed that a number of people were congregating on the bridge watching the rising floodwaters. As he went onto the elevated structure to warn them of the danger, the bridge was struck by a timber from a railroad bridge that had collapsed upstream. The impact of the object caused the bridge to collapse. Garland and six citizens were thrown into the river and drowned.

Garland had served with the agency for fifteen years. He was survived by his wife, Theodosia Dosia Wilson, and seven children (although some sources have reported eight children). Garland is buried at the Burkburnett City Cemetery.

BURLESON COUNTY CONSTABLE'S OFFICE

White, Garrett Alphonso
Born 15 January 1894—Died 13 March 1926

A man named W. Sledge Houston fatally shot Constable Garrett White in the town of Somerville. White was transported by train to the hospital in Temple, where he died after surgery at 9:00 p.m. on Saturday, 13 March 1926.

Houston alleged that back in 1922, when he was serving as a constable and White was a National Guard captain, they had trouble. Houston claimed that he had told White there were reports of gambling, drinking and misconduct at the armory.

Although Houston had served as a constable for twenty years, in 1924 White defeated Houston in the election for that post. The adversity between the two men reignited when Houston was appointed a special agent for the Santa Fe Railroad and alleged that White caused him to be temporarily dismissed and charged with illegally carrying a firearm.

When the two men crossed paths for the final time on Saturday, 13 March 1926, Houston claimed that White started reaching for his pistol. Houston fired three times as the men grappled and fell to the ground. One witness claimed that White's pistol fell on the sidewalk. A second bystander said that Houston removed White's pistol from his belt and threw it on the ground after shooting him. All onlookers were undisputed in echoing that White was holding on to Houston's pistol barrel and calling out, "Pull him off! I'm dying." Houston allegedly rose to a stooped-over position and shot White two more times; then Houston stood and fired one more time. Houston picked up White's pistol and handed it to a witness, then reloaded his own gun.

Houston surrendered to the sheriff. In White's dying statement, he alleged that no words were exchanged before Houston opened fire.

The first trial in Bell County resulted in a hung jury. The result of the second trial in Robertson County is unknown, but the fact that Houston was still a special agent for the railroad in 1930 indicates that perhaps he avoided a jail term.

White was survived by his wife, Christine. He is buried at the Oaklawn Cemetery in Somersville.

BURNET COUNTY CONSTABLE'S OFFICE

Murray, James Wayland
Born 7 April 1857—Died 20 December 1901

Precinct 1 constable James Murray was shot and killed when he went to investigate gunshots he heard near his home.

Murray encountered a deranged man named Dr. E.M. Simcock. Simcock had a gun and used it to shoot Murray when Murray attempted to arrest him. Although mortally wounded, Murray was able to return fire and kill Simcock.

Murray was survived by his wife, Mary "Mollie" Caroline Hall, and, according to newspaper reports, seven children. Family genealogists list only five. He is buried at the Burnet Cemetery.

CALDWELL COUNTY CONSTABLE'S OFFICE

Teas, Samuel B.
Born 8 June 1866—Died 29 December 1907

Precinct 1 constable Samuel Teas was shot and killed when he and three deputy sheriffs went to the town of Dale to arrest a man for arson.

When the lawmen first attempted to enter the man's residence, he refused to open the door. The suspect lit a match, as if he needed the light to see to unlatch the door. As he did so, one of the deputies noticed that he had a pistol that was pointed at the officers. One shot was fired by the lawmen at the arson suspect. The officers broke down the door of the building, and as they entered, they found two occupants, Cicero Thompson and Will Hemphill, holding pistols that were pointed at them. Teas handed Deputy A.H. Gomillion his pistol. Gomillion was now holding two pistols on Thompson and Hemphill. As Teas was attempting to handcuff one of the men, he fell against Gomillion, causing one of the guns he was holding to discharge. The bullet hit Teas in the shoulder. He was killed instantly. Thompson and Hemphill fled but were arrested and placed in the county jail.

According to reports, Gomillion and Teas were close friends, and he grieved deeply over the accidental death of his friend.

Teas was survived by his wife, L.V. Stiles, and two children. He is buried at the Lockhart City Cemetery.

CALDWELL COUNTY SHERIFF'S OFFICE

Franks, John Henry
Born 9 November 1876—Died 12 May 1915

On Friday, 19 February 1915, Caldwell County sheriff J. Henry Franks and Lockhart city marshal John L. Smith were involved in a dispute at the county courthouse. Newspaper reports indicated that Smith was formerly a deputy sheriff under Franks and had run against him for the post of sheriff. Smith is said to have cursed and defamed Franks, who went to his office to get a shotgun and settle the matter once and for all. When he returned, the two men opened fire at each other. Smith was killed. Franks was released under a $3,000 bond after an examining trial. The case was referred to the spring grand jury.

At about 9:30 p.m. on Wednesday, 12 May 1915, Franks was returning to his place of residence in the county jail after having attended a motion picture show. An unknown assassin who had concealed himself beneath a cotton platform at the railway depot fired two shotgun blasts at him. The first shot missed and harmlessly struck a telegraph pole. The second shot found its mark. Franks was hit in the back, neck and shoulder with eight pellets of buckshot. His wounds were fatal.

Other county sheriffs, as well as Texas Rangers, came to Lockhart to investigate the assassination. Caldwell County commissioner's court and the Texas governor posted a reward of $750. Texas Rangers later arrested two men who were suspected of the shooting, but the charges were dropped. Franks's killer was never apprehended. The case remains unsolved.

Franks was elected sheriff on 3 November 1908. He was reelected on 8 November 1910, 5 November 1912 and 3 November 1914. He served until his death. Franks was survived by his wife, Daisy Abbot, and one daughter. He is buried at the Lockhart City Cemetery.

Related Case: Lockhart Police Department, John L. Smith

Valdez, Pedro, Jr.
Born circa 1892—Died 19 February 1928

Very little information is available about the murder of Deputy Pedro Valdez Jr.

At about 1:00 a.m. on Sunday, 19 February 1928, Deputy Sheriff Pedro Valdez is said to have arrested a thirty-three-year-old garage owner named Gregoria Mendoza at the town of Luling. Mendoza was wanted for unlawfully carrying a pistol. One newspaper account of Valdez's death claimed that the shooting occurred at a dance. Another conflicting report claimed that the incident had taken place in front of a Mexican restaurant on Fourth Street. Regardless of the exact venue, the outcome was the same. Mendoza shot and killed Valdez.

Mendoza was arrested and placed in the county jail. He was indicted by the Caldwell County grand jury on 30 March 1928 for unlawfully carrying a pistol. There is nothing further recorded concerning the disposition of the firearms violation case. Eight months later, on 25 October 1928, Mendoza was indicted for the murder of Valdez. On 15 November 1935, that murder charge was dismissed without comment.

Valdez was reported to have been married. He is buried at the Catholic Cemetery in Luling. Newspaper reports of the day claimed that he had been a deputy sheriff for many years.

CALHOUN COUNTY CONSTABLE'S OFFICE

Livingston, William
Born 25 October 1891—Died 16 August 1931

Constable William Livingston of Port Lavaca died when his horse fell on him. The weight of the animal inflicted serious injuries that proved fatal. He died at a doctor's office shortly after the accident.

Livingston is buried at the Linwood Cemetery. He was survived by his wife, Julia Griffith, and six children.

CAMERON COUNTY CONSTABLE'S OFFICE

Falcon, Pablo
Born circa 1876—Died 12 July 1915

On Sunday, 11 July 1915, Deputy Sheriff Encarnacion "Chon" Cuellar and Precinct 4 deputy constable Pablo Falcon were working a *baile* (Mexican dance) at the Magnolia Dance Resort, located two and a half miles southeast of Brownsville. At approximately 12:30 a.m., Cuellar and Falcon were standing near the gate with their backs to the outside when someone called to them. When both lawmen turned to investigate, four gunshots were fired. Falcon fell to the ground wounded. He lapsed into unconsciousness before he could draw his pistol.

Falcon died from his wounds within twenty minutes. Cuellar was shot in the left side, just below the heart. He fell to the ground wounded. Cuellar was able to draw his pistol and return fire, managing to get off two shots at the fleeing assailants. Witnesses also fired at Cuellar's attacker. Unable to recover from the effects of the gunshot wound he had suffered, Cuellar died later the same day.

Witnesses at the scene identified brothers Adelaide and Ignacio Cantu as the shooters. One of the Cantu brothers was firing two pistols at the deputies, while the other used one. The body of Adelaide Cantu was found the next day on the Mexico side of the Rio Grande River. He had died from the effects of the wounds he received during the gunfight that took place when he had ambushed Cuellar and Falcon. There is no record of Cantu ever having been arrested or prosecuted for his role in the double murder of these two lawmen.

Apparently, the motive for shooting was revenge over Falcon and Cuellar having arrested Ignacio Cantu for drunk and disorderedly conduct at the same resort the week preceding the double murder. He was found guilty of that charge and fined one dollar. Thus, two lawmen and one civilian died violently over something as trivial as a fine of one dollar for public intoxication.

No personal information or burial records for Falcon have been located.

Related Case: Cameron County Sheriff's Office, Encarnacion "Chon" Cuellar

Longoria, Daniel
Born 13 November 1894—Died 30 March 1924

Daniel Longoria was shot and killed while he was watching a Mexican dance near La Feria. The incident took place in the presence of hundreds of partygoers. Longoria was sitting in his automobile when his assailant shot him in the head at such close range that it left powder burns. He was a well-known border peace officer, but it appears he was not a deputy constable at the time of his death. Abram Longoria, a distant relative, was arrested and charged with his murder, as well as those of four other family members. Officers stated that the murder was the result of a long-standing feud between factions of the Longoria family. It is unknown if anyone was ever convicted of the murder.

Longoria is reported to have been buried at the Galveston Ranch in Mercedes. His grave site has not been located. Longoria's death certificate indicates that he was married.

Billings, John Clayton "Jess"
Born 13 May 1895—Died 11 October 1926

Precinct 7 constable John Billings was fatally shot by men firing automatic shotguns from ambush while he was returning from a motion picture theater.

Two men were seen fleeing the scene. Billings was hit five times in the head and body by the shotgun blasts that had been fired at close range. His head was virtually torn from his body. It goes without saying that Billings died almost immediately from his wounds.

Revenge was allegedly the motive, as Billings was waging a war against bootleggers. It is unknown if anyone was ever arrested or prosecuted for his murder.

Billings was survived by his wife, Florence E. Witten, and two children. He is buried at the Wrightsboro Cemetery in Gonzales County. Billings had served as a constable for two years.

Torres, Mercedes
Born circa 1896—Died 11 June 1930
Date of Incident: 10 June 1930

On Tuesday, 10 June 1930, Deputy Constable Mercedes Torres of La Feria was shot from ambush by an unknown assailant while he was traveling in his automobile.

Torres had stopped his car on the Radd Road near Santa Rosa, where he had land that was being cleared by laborers. The killer fired twice. Both bullets pierced the windshield and struck Torres in the chest. A farmer discovered the wounded Torres and called for an ambulance.

Upon examination, officers discovered that Torres's pistol had been fired and was lying by his side. Torres died at 2:30 a.m. the following day. It is not known if anyone was ever arrested or charged with his murder.

Torres was survived by his wife and four children. He is buried at the La Capiella Cemetery.

CAMERON COUNTY SHERIFF'S OFFICE

Lawrence, Henry Boomer
Born January 1873—Died 31 July 1910

James Darwin, a young engineer for the San Benito Land and Water Company, was murdered by Jacinto Trevino. The company posted a $500 reward. Trevino's cousin Pablo informed authorities that Jacinto intended to return from Mexico and kill the company's chief engineer. Pablo led Texas Ranger privates Q.B. Carnes and Pat Craighead and Cameron County deputy sheriffs Henry B. Lawrence and Earl West, along with six company employees, to a location near the Rio Grande River where Jacinto was supposed to cross. There the posse split into four groups.

Sometime after midnight, the officers heard a group of men approaching. One of the lawmen hailed the party to stop. A barrage of gunfire quickly erupted. Lawrence and Carnes were hit when they arose from a crouching position to return fire. Lawrence died instantly after being hit with seven buckshot pellets in the right side of his head. Carnes was hit with seven rifle bullets, one entering through the back of his head and exiting through his right eye. He expired at about 9:00 a.m. Craighead and West came to their assistance. West was shot and wounded. Craighead retreated to alert the remainder of the posse of their plight. When he located the lawmen, he fired a signal shot as arranged, but the posse mistook him for the outlaws and opened fire, wounding him.

Once daylight illuminated the gruesome scene, the posse found the body of Pablo Trevino. Jacinto Trevino was never arrested and disappeared into Mexico. Authorities believe Pablo had led the officers into an ambush.

Lawrence is buried at the Fraternal Cemetery in Alice in an unmarked grave next to his parents. He was thirty-seven years old and unmarried.

Ranger private Quirl B. Carnes and his brother, U.S. customs inspector Herff Carnes, a former Texas Ranger, were both killed in the line of duty.

Related Case: Texas Rangers, Quirl B. Carnes

Cuellar, Encarnacion "Chon"
Born 25 March 1879—Died 12 July 1915

See earlier entry for Pablo Falcon. Cuellar had served as a Brownsville policeman for two years and a deputy constable for one year and had been a deputy sheriff for four years. He was survived by his wife and four children. Cuellar is buried at the Buena Vista Burial Park in Brownsville.

Related Case: Cameron County Constable's Office, Pablo Falcon

Martin, Frank, Sr.
Born October 1867—Died 25 November 1917

Deputy Sheriff Frank Martin was shot and killed when he and another deputy went to a dance hall to investigate reports of a disturbance.

After arriving at the hall, the officers confronted two men, Juan and Jesus Guerrero, and told them to quiet down. The pair left the hall but returned a short time later after arming themselves with a shotgun and rifle. Without warning, Juan and Jesus Guerrero immediately opened fire on the two deputies. Martin was hit twice by rifle fire. The other deputy was wounded by a shotgun blast. Juan and Jesus Guerrero fled the scene, reportedly to Mexico. They were never apprehended.

Martin also served as a special Texas Ranger. He was survived by his wife and son. Martin is buried at the Raymondville Cemetery. Raymondville was within the boundaries of Cameron County until 1921.

Esparza, Carlos Lerma
Born 12 July 1877—Died 1 June 1919

At about 2:00 a.m. on Sunday, 1 June 1919, Deputy Sheriff Carlos Esparza was gambling at a small *jacal* (an adobe-style housing structure historically found throughout parts of the southwestern United States and Mexico) at Ranchita, which is located about fifteen miles up the Rio Grande River from Brownsville. Two men standing outside opened fire. Esparza was struck in the head with a .45-caliber bullet. The lights were shot out, and the men inside began to flee the scene. As they did so, Domingo Trevino had the top of his head blown off by a shot from a .30-30-caliber rifle bullet. Pedro Zepeda was shot in the hip and chest. He died about 4:00 p.m. Nicholas Esparza was shot and wounded.

The two killers entered the building and then rifled through the dead and dying men's pockets and took their money. Deputies who arrived at the scene found a trail to the river and assumed the killers had escaped into Mexico.

Authorities reported that Esparza was a well-known border lawman and had previously served as a U.S. mounted customs inspector. According to reports, he had many enemies, and officers believed that the robbery might not have been the motive but rather a revenge killing of Esparza. The recent arrest and extradition to the United States of Antonio Rocha and Pedro Paz, who were both wanted for committing a murder in the same vicinity, may have been a factor in Esparza's killing as well. Three years earlier, Esparza had been ambushed at Ranchita and had his horse shot dead under him. Several other attempts had been made on his life.

Esparza is buried at the Esparza Cemetery.

Carpenter, George Ramsey
Born 16 April 1904—Died 3 June 1922

Perez, Andres
Born circa 1903—Died 3 June 1922

Deputy Sheriff George Carpenter was shot and killed while attempting to disarm a man at a Mexican dance in Brownsville.

Carpenter had asked a man named Martine George to surrender his pistol. George stepped forward as if to comply and then shot Carpenter in the abdomen. Carpenter drew his gun. Both men grabbed each other by the shoulder and proceeded to empty their pistols into the other man's body from point-blank range as they struggled in mortal combat. The shooting continued until both combatants had emptied their pistols. The results were predictable. Both lay dead on the floor of the dance hall.

Deputized citizen Andres Perez, who is believed to have been assisting Carpenter preserve peace at the dance, was found dead, lying about one hundred yards from the scene with two empty shells in his pistol. He had one bullet hole through his throat.

Perez's killer remains unidentified. Benito Trevino was arrested for his role in the murder and tried in April 1924. He was found not guilty. A newspaper account stated that two more men would be tried in the next term of the court. The disposition of that action is unknown.

Carpenter was married. According to the 1900 census, Perez was about nineteen years old and was single, living with his mother and two siblings. Carpenter, Perez and George are all buried at the Los Indios Cemetery.

Dicken, Aaron Lee
Born 28 June 1868—Died 1 June 1926

At about midnight on Tuesday, 1 June 1926, Deputy Sheriffs Aaron Lee Dicken, Alex Champion, Ernest Garcia and Ray Driuilhat were attempting to stop a light truck suspected of hauling a load of liquor. The incident took place about four and a half miles from Brownsville, near the El Jardin pumping station. The deputies were waiting on the banks of the main canal when the truck appeared on the bridge. The driver was ordered to stop. Two men in the truck began shooting at the lawmen. Dicken was shot through the right shoulder, left ankle and under the arm. The suspects fled and were never captured.

Dicken had been engaged in law enforcement for most of his adult life. He had been a Texas Ranger, with a lengthy record of service along the Texas/Mexico border from El Paso to Brownsville. He had also been an Arizona Ranger and a government scout and had served in various other peace officer capacities. About one year before his death, he returned to Brownsville and joined the sheriff's department.

Dicken was survived by his wife, Fanny Samuel Harris, and two children. He is buried at the Buena Vista Cemetery in Brownsville.

Harrison, Claude J.
Born circa 1897—Died 12 December 1927

Deputy Sheriff Claude Harrison was shot and killed at Rio Hondo. He was found clutching his fully loaded revolver in his right hand.

Harrison had been shot once in the right shoulder. The bullet passed through his spinal column and exited through his back. One newspaper report stated that Harrison had left his home about 10:00 p.m. to answer a call involving a report of trouble at a religious service. He quieted the disturbance and issued summonses to two men to appear in court. Harrison had confiscated a knife from one of the men and was returning to his vehicle when he was shot. A second and conflicting newspaper report claimed that Harrison had gone to investigate a report of bootlegging at a dance hall and had made one arrest when he was shot. In either case, his killer is said to have escaped into Mexico.

Harrison was survived by his wife and an infant daughter. He is buried at the Mont Meta Memorial Park in San Benito.

Johnson, William Horace
Born 7 June 1899—Died 9 June 1928

Deputy Sheriff William Johnson was shot and killed while investigating bootleggers.

Johnson had received information that a consignment of liquor was to be smuggled across the Rio Grande River. Johnson, along with U.S. border patrolmen Roy Harrell of Mercedes and Ramon Longoria of Harlingen, made an attempt to intercept the shipment. The officers stationed themselves along the road that they expected the smugglers to travel. When the two outlaws appeared, they ordered them to stop. The men opened fire on the lawmen. Johnson was hit by three bullets. One passed through his right arm and another through his chest. The third struck him in the heart. Johnson managed to return fire and kill one of the smugglers before he died.

Johnson was survived by his wife and son. He is buried at the Harlingen City Cemetery. Johnson's father was the former sheriff of Fisher County and had also been a Texas Ranger.

Chaudoin, Louis Mackey
Born 18 December 1886—Died 19 February 1936
Date of Incident: 19 September 1935

Deputy Sheriff Louis Chaudoin died of injuries he received when he and another deputy stopped the occupants of a stolen electric company truck. One of the three juveniles in the vehicle opened fire on the deputies, hitting Chaudoin in the arm and groin. One of the bullets pierced his bladder. Chaudoin and his partner returned fire and killed the suspects. Chaudoin struggled to recover but died from the effects of his wounds on 19 February 1936.

Deputy Chaudoin had been with the agency for only two months at the time of the shooting. He was survived by his wife, May Wroten, and four of the couple's five children. Chaudoin was buried in Harlingen.

CAMERON POLICE DEPARTMENT

Richards, George Archer
Born 19 September 1879—Died 22 September 1935

Officer George Richards was shot and killed in a confrontation that took place during a routine traffic stop.

Richards had stopped a man named Hill for making an unlawful U-turn and for parking illegally. The incident occurred in front of a store owned by Hill's brother. The brother, Raby Hill, came out of the store and immediately launched into a heated argument with Richards. Raby Hill then shot Richards eight times.

Hill turned himself in to the county sheriff. He was tried and convicted of the murder and sentenced to serve ninety-nine years in prison.

Richards had been with the agency for fourteen years. He was survived by his wife and two daughters. Richards is buried at the North Elm Cemetery in Milam County.

CARBON CITY MARSHAL'S OFFICE

Walker, J.M.
Born (Unknown)—Died 23 December 1905

Former city marshal Walker was shot and killed during a disagreement with Deputy Sheriff John Findley and City Marshal E.P. Alvey. Walker was resisting arrest. The confrontation escalated and resulted in Walker being shot and killed.

Walker is buried at the City Cemetery in Carbon, Eastland County.

CASS COUNTY CONSTABLE'S OFFICE

Blackwell, L.F.
Born 14 February 1898—Died 31 July 1937

Precinct 5 constable L.F. Blackwell was shot and killed when he responded to a disturbance at a residence in McLeod. The incident involved an intoxicated man who was beating his wife. When Blackwell arrived at the scene, he tried to get the man to come outside. Instead, the man fired a shotgun through the screen door. The blast hit Blackwell full on in the chest.

Blackwell's wife, who was riding with him at the time, grabbed a gun and returned fire. The man was later arrested, tried and convicted of the murder of Blackwell and sentenced to serve ten years in prison.

Blackwell was survived by his wife and three children. He is buried at the Good Exchange Cemetery in McLeod.

CASS COUNTY SHERIFF'S OFFICE

Mason, James Harry
Born 27 June 1865—Died 11 March 1919
Date of Incident: 9 March 1919

Deputy Sheriff James Mason was killed in a railroad train accident. The incident occurred on Sunday, 9 March 1919. Mason died of his injuries two days later, on 11 March.

Mason was survived by his wife, Fannie Adelia Callaway, and one child. He is buried at the Hughes Springs Cemetery.

Alexander, Harper Lafayette "Doc"
Born 3 July 1884—Died 4 December 1937

Deputy Sheriff Harper Alexander was killed in an automobile accident that occurred about twenty miles south of Texarkana. Alexander's automobile collided with a truck. His injuries were fatal. Alexander was off duty at the time the incident took place.

Alexander was survived by his wife, Ollie Rebecca Lawrence, and four children. He is buried at the Beach Cemetery.

CHAMBERS COUNTY CONSTABLE'S OFFICE

Oliver, Levi E.
Born 7 February 1873—Died 5 March 1930

Precinct 5 deputy constable Levi Oliver covered the Barbers Hill community. While accounts of the incident that led to his death vary somewhat, all agree that a nineteen-year-old named "Buck" Wallace was involved in what was described as a "family affair"—presumably a family argument of some sort. Oliver attempted to intervene and resolve the dispute peacefully. Ultimately, he became involved in an argument with young Wallace. Wallace left, but the following afternoon he returned and resumed the previous day's quarrel with Oliver. The confrontation escalated. Wallace drew his pistol and fired six times at Oliver. One bullet hit Oliver in the eye. Oliver managed to fire back three times before he died, missing Wallace with all three shots.

Wallace fled the scene but was eventually arrested and charged with murder. He was indicted by a grand jury on 9 May 1931, but an order of dismissal was issued.

Oliver was a widower and had at least eight children. He is buried at the Cedar Crest Cemetery in Chambers County. No grave site or tombstone has been located.

CHAMBERS COUNTY SHERIFF'S OFFICE

Frost, John Lighter
Born 14 January 1862—Died 10 November 1900

Sheriff John Frost was shot and killed while he was attempting to serve sequestration papers (garnishment or lien papers) on a prominent citizen who managed a hunting preserve called Lake Surprise.

Frost had gone to Lake Surprise to serve papers. When he failed to return, a search party was sent out to look for him. Frost's body was discovered in a nearby lake with a gunshot wound. The man Frost was attempting to serve the warrant on, Captain William Kennedy, and three other men (two of Kennedy's sons and a man named Robert Heimann) were arrested and charged with Frost's murder. It is not known if any of the Kennedys, or anyone else, was ever tried or convicted of Frost's murder.

Frost had been sheriff for four years. He was survived by his wife, Mable, and one daughter. Frost is buried at the Wallisville Cemetery.

CHEROKEE COUNTY SHERIFF'S OFFICE

Brunt, William Jesse "Bill"
Born 1 November 1909—Died 3 August 1939

Sheriff Bill Brunt was shot and killed by a tavern owner named Isaiah "Red" Creel, proprietor of a local establishment called the Rock Inn, during a gun battle that occurred near Rusk.

At about 4:00 a.m. on Thursday, 3 August 1939, Brunt made several attempts to stop Creel's vehicle for suspicion of transporting beer through the county. Creel was traveling southbound from Kilgore at the time. Brunt sounded the patrol car's siren and passed Creel's automobile, shooting out one of the vehicle's tires, which forced Creel to the shoulder of the road. Brunt approached the right side of the car and ordered Creel out. He complied but came out shooting, hitting Brunt in the heart. Although mortally wounded, Brunt was able to return fire, killing Creel and wounding a female passenger named Myrtle Stanley, who was an employee of Creel's and worked at the Rock Inn. Stanley was unable to leave the scene and summon help. The bodies of Creel and Brunt lay alongside the highway for at least an hour before being discovered by a passerby.

Stanley recovered from her injuries and was released from the hospital at Jacksonville on 7 August. Stanley was charged with murder and was sent to jail awaiting arraignment and trial. On 12 August, Ms. Stanley was "no billed" and released after claiming that she had no role in the shooting.

Brunt had been with the agency for twenty months. He was survived by his wife, Mary J. Dear, who was appointed to complete his term in office. Brunt had first been elected on 3 November 1936. He was reelected on 8 November 1938. He is buried at the Old Palestine Cemetery in Alto.

CISCO POLICE DEPARTMENT

Bedford, George Emory Bit
Born 7 August 1868—Died 23 December 1927

Carmichael, George
Born 7 August 1867—Died 6 January 1928
Date of Incident: 23 December 1927

It all began about noon on Friday, 23 December 1927 when the foursome of Marshall Ratliff, Henry Helms, Robert Hill and Louis Davis held up the First National Bank of Cisco. All of the robbers except the unwitting Louis Davis, a relative of Helms, were ex-cons. Ratliff was by no means a novice stickup man. He and his brother Lee had been captured after the pair robbed the First State Bank in Valera in 1925. Each man served only a year of his sentence before being pardoned by Governor "Ma" Ferguson.

Ready for action, the would-be holdup men were said to have stolen a blue Buick sedan in Wichita Falls and driven the 123 miles to Cisco. Ratliff got out of the car several blocks from the bank and put on a Santa Claus suit. Once inside, he began to grab money from the tellers and shove it into a potato sack, while another robber stood guard at the entrance. While the holdup was in progress, Mrs. B.P. Blassengame and her six-year-old daughter, Francis, had entered the bank. Realizing the danger, and in spite of warnings from the robbers that they would shoot her, the undaunted Mrs. Blassengame did not panic. She quickly led her daughter through the bookkeeping department to the side door that emptied into the alley. She struggled with the door at first, not realizing that it opened in and not out. Next, she dashed across a vacant lot and made her way to the city hall, where she entered the police station and screamed for help, yelling, "The First National is being held up!"

Her announcement alerted Chief of Police George Emory "Bit" Bedford. Within minutes, practically the whole town had heard the news. Meanwhile, inside the bank, Ratliff had filled a sack with money and emerged from the vault. Bedford, who had grabbed a riot gun, positioned himself at the head of the alley alongside the bank that opened onto Main Street. Deputy Carmichael took up a position in the alley running behind the bank, which intersected the other escape route the chief was covering. Both were directing crossfire at the back door of the bank where one of the robbers had emerged with a semiautomatic pistol in each hand, blazing away at both lawmen as he rushed from the building. Almost immediately, a fusillade of gunfire erupted from the street and alley, as lawmen and armed citizens alike fired through the bank window and down the alley.

Ratliff and his accomplices forced bookkeeper Freda Stroebel, customer Marion Olson, employee Oscar Cliett and teller Vance Littleton out the back door and toward their car. The bandits also grabbed two girls, twelve-year-old LaVerne (Laverne) E. Comer and ten-year-old Emma Mae Robertson, to use as hostages in the escape. The group was met by more gunfire once outside the bank. Alex Spears was hit in the jaw, and Marion Olson received a gunshot wound in the leg. Oscar Cliett, who had decided to make a break and run for it, dashed down the alley and alerted Carmichael that the robbers had hostages. Marion Olson, who made it to the getaway car with the bandits, managed to escape. As he ran down the alley to safety, he passed the crumpled body of Deputy Carmichael lying mortally wounded in the street. After firing a shot from his riot gun, Chief Bedford slumped to the ground wounded. Citizen Charlie Nosek, who had been standing behind the chief, picked up his gun and fired a shot at Santa Claus that he later claimed found its mark.

Most of the bank employees and customers escaped, except for the two girls. With their young hostages loaded, the four holdup men leaped into their getaway car and sped out of the alley, turning south onto Main Street. Newspaper reports claim that more than one hundred shots had been fired. That estimate was later increased to over two hundred.

The robbers suddenly realized that they were almost out of gas. To make matters worse, one of their vehicle's tires had been shot out by a gun-toting postman during the gunfight in the bank alley.

Pursued by an angry mob that chased behind them on foot and then took to their automobiles, the bandits drove to the edge of town and attempted to commandeer an Oldsmobile belonging to the Harris family. The clever fourteen-year-old driver, Woodrow Wilson "Woody" Harris, gave the robbers the car but switched off the ignition and took the keys. Not realizing this, the robbers transferred their belongings to the Oldsmobile amidst a hail of gunfire only to realize that they could not start the vehicle.

Davis was unconscious from his injuries. The remaining three outlaws left him in the purloined Olds and moved back to their first getaway car with their two young hostages in tow. In the process of doing so, they neglected to take the bag of holdup money with them, leaving it lying on the seat alongside the now senseless Davis.

Citizens jumped into an automobile and pursued the bank robbers, firing wildly as they went. Eastland County sheriff John Hart had by now been alerted and, along with a score of deputies, had piled into automobiles and raced the dozen or so miles to where the getaway car had last been seen. More lawmen and citizens poured in. This had become a manhunt like no other.

The protracted chase lasted until Christmas Day. Bedford died, and Carmichael was in critical condition. Davis, who had been left behind by the bandits, was transported to Fort Worth, where he died Friday night. During the chase, another lawman had been injured. Sheriff Gib Abernathy of Palo Pinto County was wounded by the accidental discharge of someone's firearm.

The money, which had been left in the Oldsmobile the robbers had attempted to steal, was returned to the bank. Ratliff and his crew had almost made off with $12,400 in cash and $150,000 in nonnegotiable securities. Besides the two wounded police officers, there had been six townspeople shot during the gun battle.

The threesome was eventually ambushed by Sheriff J.B. Foster at South Bend in Young County. Foster intercepted the trio as the men were trying to cross the Brazos River. A car chase followed, which ended in a shootout in a field while the three bandits were trying to make their escape on foot. Eastland County deputy sheriff Cy Bradford, who was a seasoned Texas Ranger veteran and a participant in numerous mortal shootouts, was involved in the gunfight. According to most reports, Bradford bailed from his vehicle with a shotgun in hand and wounded all three holdup men. Ratliff was unable to continue his flight. The remaining two robbers were captured not long afterward.

Asked why they had fled, both holdup men responded that with the Texas Bankers Association reward of $5,000 for dead bank robbers, but nothing for live ones, they might as well get killed running as be gunned down in cold blood with their hands up.

Hill pleaded guilty to armed robbery and took the stand on his own behalf. In March 1928, he was sentenced to serve ninety-nine years in prison. Hill escaped from prison three times but was recaptured on each occasion. He was paroled in the mid-1940s, changed his name and experienced no further brushes with the law.

Helms was identified as the one who had gunned down both Bedford and Carmichael. The court took a much dimmer view of his actions and sentenced him to death. Once in prison awaiting execution, he refused to eat and slept in the corner of his cell in a crouched position. Although some believed he had gone insane, he was examined and found to be competent. The death sentence was carried out on 6 September 1929, when Helms was executed by electrocution at Huntsville. He became the fifty-fourth person to meet that fate in Texas.

Ratliff went on trial on 16 January 1928 in the court of Judge George L. Davenport. He was first convicted of armed robbery on 27 January 1928 and sentenced to serve ninety-nine years in prison. Although no one could testify to having seen him fire a gun in the bank, on 30 March 1928 Ratliff was sentenced to be executed for his role in the deaths of Bedford and Carmichael. He appealed his case and, when that failed, filed an insanity plea.

Ratliff attempted to escape from jail but failed after killing Eastland County deputy sheriff Tom Jones. He was lynched by a mob of angry citizens.

Bedford was a career lawman and the former Eastland County sheriff from 1902 to 1908. He was survived by his wife, Lela Leona McCleskey, and four children. Bedford is buried at the Oakwood Cemetery in Cisco.

Carmichael remained in a coma until his death approximately two weeks later. He was survived by his wife and one child. He is buried at the Oakwood Cemetery in Cisco.

Related Case: Eastland County Sheriff's Office, Tom Jones

CLARENDON POLICE DEPARTMENT

Slaughter, John Wilson
Born 2 December 1895—Died 12 March 1927

At about 1:15 a.m. on Saturday, 12 March 1927, night watchman John Slaughter was making his regular rounds in the downtown area of Clarendon when he was shot and killed by an unknown person. His assailant used a twelve-gauge shotgun. Slaughter's body was found the following morning, lying on Sully Street between city hall and Parson's Produce. Tire marks near the body indicated that someone had sped away in a vehicle. A filling station had been broken into during the night, and investigators suspected that Slaughter might have been attempting to stop the burglar.

The citizens of Clarendon raised $2,000 as a reward for the capture and conviction of Slaughter's killer. Over two years later, in July 1929, John Scott of Wichita Falls gave a statement implicating S.P. Scroggins (alias S.B. and O.B. Scroggins) as the killer. Scroggins was charged with the murder. He was arrested and released on bond. Scroggins died of a heart attack or stroke in September 1929, before he could be tried for the murder charge.

Slaughter, who was a widower, was survived by two children. He is buried at Citizens Cemetery in Clarendon, Donley County.

COCHRAN COUNTY SHERIFF'S OFFICE

Smith, DeWitt Talmage
Born 18 April 1893—Died 8 December 1939

Deputy Sheriff DeWitt Smith was shot and killed while he and Sheriff Tom C. Standefer were investigating a hit and run accident.

Smith and Standefer had received information concerning the whereabouts of a vehicle that had been involved in the accident. When they approached the automobile, one of the occupants opened fire, killing Smith. The officers returned fire. Howard Lackey, one of the vehicle's occupants, was also killed during the exchange of gunfire. The two remaining men, J.W. Martin and Raymond Davis, were arrested, tried and convicted. They were sentenced to serve life in prison.

Smith had been with the agency for just under four years. He was survived by his wife, Bessie May. Smith is buried at the Morton Memorial Cemetery in Cochran County.

COKE COUNTY SHERIFF'S OFFICE

Hickman, Will James
Born 6 December 1874—Died 9 February 1915
Date of the Incident: 7 February 1915

Griffith, Tate Abner
Born 27 February 1871—Died 28 April 1915

Will Hickman was elected sheriff of Coke County on 6 November 1906. He served until 3 November 1914.

On Sunday, 7 February 1915, Hickman was in his lawyer's office and was not armed when Deputy Sheriff Tate Griffith entered and shot him fives times with an automatic pistol. The reason for the shooting was not revealed.

Hickman died several days later at San Angelo. A newspaper account noted that Hickman was one of the most prominent officers in West Texas.

Griffin was released under a $10,000 bond and was under indictment in the death of former sheriff Will Hickman. At about 8:00 a.m. on Wednesday, 28 April 1915, Griffith was on Main Street in Bronte when Robert Hickman, brother of the slain lawman and a local merchant in the town, stepped out of his store and shot Griffith two times with a shotgun. Griffith fell to the sidewalk and died within minutes.

Robert Hickman was tried in January 1916 for the killing of Griffith but was acquitted.

Griffith was survived by his wife, Lela Frazer, and four children. Will Hickman was survived by his wife. Both men are buried at the Fairview Cemetery in Bronte.

COLEMAN COUNTY SHERIFF'S OFFICE

Griffith, Joseph Henry "Joe"
Born 30 May 1860—Died 17 February 1924

Late in the evening on Sunday, 17 February 1924, Deputy Sheriff Joseph
H. Griffith and Constable W.L. Connolly attempted to arrest a man named
Dave Rutherford at Santa Anna on the minor charge of drunkenness.
Rutherford, who was a farmer, had become intoxicated. When Griffith and
Connolly approached him to place him under arrest, Rutherford produced
a pistol and opened fire. One shot hit Griffith in the stomach. Connolly was
shot twice through the thigh. The officers were able to return fire, wounding
Rutherford in the jaw. Griffith died of his wounds. Both Connolly and
Rutherford recovered.

Rutherford was found guilty of the murder of Griffith and sentenced to
life in prison. He was stabbed to death while serving his sentence.

Griffith was survived by his wife, Mary Jane, and three children. He is
buried at the Santa Ana Cemetery.

Pauley, Richard Allen "Dick"
Born 26 March 1882—Died 16 May 1925
Date of Incident: 14 May 1925

Sheriff "Dick" Pauley was called to the railroad yard to assist in
apprehending two men who were riding on top of a freight car. The men,
John Smith and Arthur Tebo, had boarded the train at Brownwood and
had refused the conductor's order to leave. When the train stopped in
Santa Anna, the conductor telegraphed ahead to Coleman to ask for the
sheriff to meet him when the train arrived. As Pauley climbed the ladder
on the side of the boxcar, he was shot by Smith. Pauley died from the
gunshot wound two days later.

A posse of over one thousand men pursued the killer and eventually
apprehended him. Smith went to trial at Coleman later in May. A detachment
of four Texas Rangers was sent to the town to manage any potential violence
that might occur during the trial. Smith's case was later moved to Brown
County for trial.

One 1 June 1925, a mob comprising approximately one hundred angry
citizens stormed the jail at Brownwood in an attempt to lynch Smith and

Tebo. Their efforts were halted by armed lawmen. In a packed courtroom on 2 June 1925, the jury handed down a verdict of guilty in the case of Smith. It had deliberated just eighteen minutes. Smith was sentenced to death. On 16 April 1926, that sentence was carried out when John Smith was executed by electrocution at Huntsville. He became the twenty-fifth criminal to meet this fate.

Sheriff Pauley was survived by his wife, Susan Katherine "Kate" Dancer, and son, Russell. He is buried at Valera Cemetery in Coleman.

Some confusion exists regarding Pauley's date of birth. Two family genealogists have the date listed as 26 March 1882, while another has it recorded as 29 March 1882. His tombstone bears the date 23 March.

Collinsville Police Department

Brooks, James W.
Born circa 1844—Died 19 July 1905

At about noon on Wednesday, 19 July 1905, City Marshal James W. Brooks arrested Z.T. Trice for failure to pay a court fine that had been issued six weeks earlier. Trice was on his way to Fort Worth to have his foot treated and was traveling in his buggy with his wife when the incident occurred. After making the arrest, Brooks had Trice sit down in a chair. While Brooks was apologizing to Trice's wife, Trice came up behind him with a knife and cut him across the abdomen and stabbed him in the heart. Brooks fell to the sidewalk mortally injured. He was pronounced dead within two minutes.

Trice was arrested and charged with the murder. On 26 October 1906, a Grayson County jury acquitted him of the crime.

Brooks was survived by his wife, Nannie, and four children. No burial records have been located for Brooks.

Colorado County Sheriff's Office

Clements, William D. "Willie"
Born January 1876—Died 19 August 1911

The bitterness between the Townsend and Reese families came to a head on 16 March 1899. As former sheriff Sam Reese was tying up his horse near the town square, Sheriff Will Buford's deputies—Marc Townsend, Marion Hope and Willie Clements—opened fire on him. Reese and a farmer named Charles Boehm were killed in the barrage of gunfire. A stray bullet wounded a small boy. Although all three deputies were arrested, none was ever convicted of the killings.

On 18 May 1899, Sam Reese's brother, Dick, and another man were shot and killed by Deputies Step Yates and J.G. Townsend. The pair had been stopped at a bridge at the entrance to the county on suspicion of carrying a pistol. On 15 January 1900, J.G. "Jim" Townsend was tried at Bastrop on a change of venue for the killing of Dick Reese. Yates died of tuberculosis before the trial. A motion for continuance was granted. The parties were leaving the courthouse when gunfire erupted. There were three shooters involved in the affray: Walter Reese, son of the dead former sheriff; Jim Coleman, the alleged killer of Constable Larkin Hope; and Tom Daniels. All opened fire on Clements. Although Clements was their intended target and was seriously wounded during the exchange, they accidentally killed Sheriff Buford's son Arthur. Reese, Coleman and Daniels were never convicted of the killings.

On Tuesday, 31 July 1900, Jim Coleman and Walter Reese were involved in another shootout. This time, the incident took place on a train. Willie Clements, Marc Townsend, Frank Buford and A.B. Woolridge were all involved. On this occasion, Coleman and Reese were both badly wounded. Remarkably, on 30 June 1906, Marion Hope and Herbert Reese were involved in another shooting that resulted in the death of Hiram Clements.

Jim Coleman was later killed in San Antonio. Herbert Reese was killed with his own gun when he inadvertently dropped the pistol, causing it to discharge accidentally. Walter Reese died in an automobile accident.

The violent life of Will Clements came to an end on Saturday, 19 August 1911, in Matagorda County. Clements and a man named Frank Stelzig had a previous disagreement. Clements was riding a horse past a store near the Southern Pacific Railroad when Stelzig opened fire at him with a shotgun loaded with buckshot. Clements was in his shirtsleeves at the time, and his pistol was in his saddlebag. The pellets hit Clements in the head, killing him almost instantly.

Stelzig was arrested and charged with the murder. On 20 June 1912, he was acquitted in a courtroom guarded by state rangers who were on the lookout for more trouble.

Clements is buried at the Odd Fellows' Cemetery in Weimar. He was survived by his wife, Lyda Bishop, and three daughters.

For a more complete account of the feuds involving Clements and Will Buford, readers should consult C.L. Sonnichsen's *"I'll Die Before I'll Run": The Story of the Great Feuds of Texas.*

COMAL COUNTY SHERIFF'S OFFICE

Benoit, Heinrich "Henry"
Born 25 December 1874—Died 7 August 1916

Deputy Sheriff Heinrich "Henry" Benoit and Corporal Elmer E. Bromley, Third Illinois Infantry, were killed in a railroad train accident at New Braunfels. Two other men in the car, August Knetch and Gus Scholl, were injured.

Bromley was thirty years old and a veteran of the Spanish-American War. His home was in Aurora, Illinois. Bromley was survived by his wife.

Benoit was survived by his wife, Hermine, and one child. He is buried at the Comal Cemetery.

Fischer, Alfred Otto
Born 20 September 1880—Died 10 March 1917

Deputy Sheriff Alfred Fischer had detained a man named George Burkhardt in reference to a watch that had been stolen in a burglary. The owners of the watch were present at the time of the arrest and identified the timepiece as being the stolen property. Fischer called Sheriff W.H. Adams, who advised him to arrest Burkhardt but to release him if he could post bond. Fischer tried to assist Burkhardt with making bond, but his efforts failed. As Burkhardt began to walk away, Fischer placed his hand on his shoulder to stop him. Burkhardt pulled out a pistol, fired three shots at Fischer and then fled.

A volley of shots followed Burkhardt in his flight as Fischer and local citizens returned fire. He eventually fell with a bullet wound to the head. One of Fischer's brothers was at the scene of the incident and commented that Fischer may have killed Burkhardt. Fischer said, "No, he has killed me" as he pulled back his coat and revealed a bullet wound to his chest. Fischer collapsed and died at the scene. Burkhardt survived and was sentenced to fifty years in prison. The case was later overturned on appeal.

Fischer is buried at the Fischer Cemetery.

COOKE COUNTY CONSTABLE'S OFFICE

Clark, James Lemuel "Lem"
Born 1 March 1876—Died 28 July 1903

At about noon on Tuesday, 28 July 1903, James Clark, constable of the Gainesville precinct, was shot and killed while he was sitting in his office at the courthouse. A local liveryman named J.J. Tripp did the shooting. Both the *Galveston Daily News* and the *Dallas Morning News* of 29 July 1903 reported that "the tragedy was the result of a difficulty which took place between the men last evening over a sum of a few dollars." Tripp shot Clark in the heart with a .45-caliber revolver. He died at the scene.

Clark had previously been a Cooke County deputy sheriff. He was survived by his wife, Anne Basinger, and one child. Clark is buried at the Fairview Cemetery in Gainesville.

COOKE COUNTY SHERIFF'S OFFICE

Emerson, William Warner
Born 19 January 1887—Died 5 December 1927
Date of Incident: 4 December 1927

At about 3:00 a.m. on Sunday morning, 4 December 1927, Sheriff Jake Wright and Deputy William W. Emerson, along with a complainant named Autrey, went to a farm where Dave T. Wilson was living. The lawmen had a search warrant for stolen chickens and turkeys and suspected that the missing fowl were located on Wilson's farm. Wilson became enraged when he saw Mr. Autrey. He grabbed Emerson's pistol and shot him with it. Emerson died from his wounds at 4:30 p.m. on Monday, 5 December 1927.

Wilson was convicted and sentenced to life in prison for murdering Emerson. He was given an additional eight years for assault with intent to murder against Wright and one more year for various theft charges.

Emerson was survived by his wife of four months. He is buried at the Fairview Cemetery in Gainesville.

CORPUS CHRISTI POLICE DEPARTMENT

Prater, Luther B.
Born 21 December 1886—Died 14 September 1919

Officer Prater was killed in the aftermath of the hurricane that struck the Texas Gulf Coast in September 1919. He drowned while he and other officers were attempting to rescue citizens.

Prater had traveled across the Rincon Channel several times in an effort to bring victims back to the Nueces County Courthouse. He even housed some at his own home. According to newspaper reports of the day published by the *Caller Times*, the quick rise of water in Corpus Christi Bay sent Prater into the Rincon Channel, where he drowned trying to save the lives of more adults, as well as a small child.

Prater, along with other victims of the storm and its aftermath, was first buried in a mass grave near Portland. His remains were originally listed as unidentified, since most of the victims were covered in a black oil substance. Two days after being entombed, the burial site was washed out by the storm, and the bodies of the victims had to be reinterred. At that time, Prater's remains were identified and buried at the Rose Hill Cemetery in Corpus Christi. Some of the remaining victims of the incident were buried in a mass grave at Rose Hill Cemetery and others in Portland.

Although the precise death count is not known, it is estimated that as many as one thousand lives may have been lost during the course of this vicious hurricane.

Prater was survived by his wife, Olive.

This unnamed hurricane was the fourth most intense and deadly storm of the twentieth century. It passed near Key West, Florida, on 9–10 September. The slow-moving storm reached an intensity of 27.37 inches (927 millibars) as it passed the Dry Tortuga Islands near Florida, which are located about sixty-five miles from Key West. Ten vessels were lost at sea, accounting for more than 500 of the nearly 1,000 deaths. The hurricane progressed slowly westward, and on 14 September 1919, the center went inland just south of Corpus Christi. Tides rose sixteen feet above normal, and an additional 287 lives were lost.

Moon, Joseph Leroy
Born 4 January 1905—Died 10 June 1938
Date of Incident: 7 June 1938

Patrolman Moon was killed in a motorcycle accident while in pursuit of a speeding motorist.

On Tuesday, 7 June 1938, Moon was attempting to apprehend a motorist on Timon Boulevard. As he began to make the turn onto Market Street, the rear brakes on his vehicle jammed, causing the machine to hit the concrete curb. Moon's body struck the handlebars of the motorcycle with great force. He was transported to the hospital, where he died on 10 June 1938. Ironically, this was Moon's first day back on the job after having been on leave recovering from another motorcycle accident.

Moon had been employed with the Corpus Christi Police Department for one year and was survived by his wife and two children. He is buried in Swifton, Arkansas.

CORSICANA POLICE DEPARTMENT

Maddux, Charles D. "Charley"
Born circa 1874—Died 2 August 1904

Policeman Charley Maddux was shot and killed by a man named Walter Earles (Earl), whom he had just arrested for rape and a lesser charge of causing a disturbance.

Maddux had taken Earles into custody at the Union Depot on Beaton Street near Sixth Avenue and was walking him to jail. About two blocks from the arrest site, Earles suddenly jerked free from his grasp, pulled out a pistol and opened fire. Although Earles fired six or seven shots, Maddux was hit by only one bullet, which entered his left side and struck his spine. He collapsed and fell to the sidewalk, but in spite of being mortally wounded, he was able to return fire. His shot did not find its mark, however, and Earles escaped. Maddux got up, walked a few feet and then collapsed into the arms of friends. He was carried home, where, before slipping into a coma, he said, "I am done for."

Earles was arrested a short time later by Mounted Deputy Warren Bradley and charged with murder. He was tried and convicted of the crime and initially sentenced to twenty years in prison. That verdict was reversed. He was convicted a second time and sentenced to serve four years in prison.

Maddux had only served with the Corsicana Police Department for five days when he was killed. He was survived by his wife. Maddux's place of burial is unknown.

Newspaper reports, as well as some family genealogists, list his surname as Maddox, not Maddux, and the surname of his killer as Earl, not Earles.

Arp, Vess
Born 8 May 1897 (1898)—Died 10 January 1924
Date of Incident: 4 January 1924

G.C. McCain reported that a man named Roger Q. Grace approached him and several other men and asked if they would help him start his car. The men agreed to assist. When the group arrived at Grace's car, two men with guns robbed them of six to eight dollars and a .45-caliber pistol. Grace disappeared after the robbery.

After receiving a report from McCain regarding the incident, Officers Arp and Speed went to Grace's home near Post Oak Creek in the city to investigate. Speed went to the front door, and Arp covered the back door. The house was dark. Arp eventually made contact with Grace's wife, Maudie. She refused him admittance to the home. When Arp attempted to enter, Maudie Grace shot him in the abdomen. Someone else inside the home fired a weapon, but no one else was hit. Arp was transported to the hospital, where he died several days later.

Roger Grace took the gun from his wife and fled. Both husband and wife were arrested but released on a $7,500 bond. Maudie Grace claimed that some men had come to her house the night before and threatened her husband for having been involved in a whiskey robbery. She claimed that she thought Arp and Speed were the same men. The district attorney filed murder charges against both Roger and Maudie Grace. On 15 February 1926, the charges were dismissed because no witnesses were located.

Arp was not married. He is buried at the Oakwood Cemetery in Corsicana.

CORYELL COUNTY SHERIFF'S OFFICE

Hollingsworth, Walter Warren
Born 28 February 1874—Died 22 April 1934

Sheriff Walter Hollingsworth died from injuries he received when he was accidentally hit on the head with a pipe while struggling with a mentally ill prisoner in the county jail. A friend of Hollingsworth had come to his aid during the skirmish. While the men were trying to subdue the prisoner, Hollingsworth's friend accidentally hit him on the head with the pipe.

Hollingsworth had been sheriff for nineteen years. He was survived by his wife, Willie Birdie Ridens, and eight children. Some family genealogists have reported only seven children, however. Hollingsworth is buried at Gatesville.

CRANE COUNTY SHERIFF'S OFFICE

Allen, John Jefferson "Jack"
Born 12 February 1874—Died 31 May 1929

Sheriff "Jack" Allen was killed in an automobile accident.

Allen and Bill Cliffs were traveling in Allen's vehicle along the highway about three miles south of Wink in Winkler County. Allen's automobile plowed into a truck loaded with lumber. One of the timbers pierced Allen's chest. He was transported to the hospital, where he died shortly after arrival. Cliffs's injuries were not serious. It is not known why Allen was in Winkler County or whether he was in the official discharge of his duties at the time of the incident.

Crane County was created in 1887 from Tom Green County but was not organized until 1927. Allen was elected the county's first sheriff on 3 September 1927 and reelected on 6 November 1928.

Bud Blair was appointed to fill out the remainder of Allen's second term in office.

Allen was survived by his wife, Myrtle May Crawford, and two children. He is buried at the Elm Grove Cemetery in Alpine, Brewster County. According to several newspaper accounts, Allen had been a Texas Ranger. Records of his service have not been located.

CULBERSON COUNTY SHERIFF'S OFFICE

Feeley, John Henry
Born July 1871–Died 9 February 1914

Sheriff John Feeley was shot and killed when he responded to a call involving a disagreement between two well-known political officials.

The men, a judge and a citizen, were fighting in the street. Both men were armed. Feeley unwisely attempted to stop the fight by stepping between the pair. As he did so, the judge shot him in the head, killing him instantly.

The only punishment the judge received for murdering Feeley was a fifty-dollar fine for discharging a firearm. Such a gross miscarriage of justice simply leaves one speechless.

Feeley had served with the agency for six years. He was elected on 18 April 1911 and reelected on 5 November 1912.

Feeley was survived by his wife, Ida Mae Trammell, and six children. He is buried at the Van Horn Cemetery.

DALLAM COUNTY SHERIFF'S OFFICE

Boyking, William H.
Born 4 May 1879—Died 10 May 1925
Date of Incident: 5 May 1925

Deputy Sheriff Boyking was killed accidentally when a pitching horse bucked him off. The fall inflicted fatal injuries resulting in Boyking's death five days later.

Along with serving as a deputy sheriff, Boyking had also been a cattle inspector.

Boyking is buried at the Llano Cemetery in Amarillo. He was survived by his wife.

Alexander, George W.
Born 28 July 1876—Died 19 July 1930

Sheriff George Alexander had received a tip that a man wanted on a felony warrant was hiding out at a small home near Dalhart. Although Dalhart is the county seat of Dallam County, the city is divided by both Dallam and Hartley Counties.

Alexander's chief deputy, H.D. Foust, and Hartley County deputy sheriff Earl Damron accompanied Alexander to the home of Lon and Orrell Dillinger, who were brothers. It was their intent to arrest the pair for jumping bond on an illegal liquor charge. The home was located about five miles south of Dalhart. Alexander kicked in the front door of the residence, while Damron and Foust covered the back door. When Alexander entered the house, he was shot and killed. After hearing gunfire, Foust kicked in the back door of the dwelling. When Lon Dillinger lunged at him, he opened fire. Lon Dillinger was shot through the head. His death was instantaneous. Orrell Dillinger rushed through the front door and was shot through the throat and stomach by Foust. Orrell died a short time afterward.

Arleta Borger Dillinger, Lon's wife, was also slightly wounded in the wild exchange of gunfire.

Alexander's wounds were fatal. He died within forty minutes of the shooting incident.

Alexander had been with the agency for five years. He was elected on 2 November 1926 and reelected on 6 November 1928.

Alexander was survived by his wife, Bennie Lula Raborn, and four children. He is buried at the Dalhart City Cemetery (Memorial Park Cemetery).

On 22 July, Bennie Lula Alexander was appointed to serve out the remainder of her slain husband's term in office.

DALLAS COUNTY CONSTABLE'S OFFICE

Sparks, Benjamin Warden
Born 4 April 1881—Died 20 July 1924

At about 3:00 p.m. on Sunday, 20 July 1924, former deputy constable and private detective Benjamin Sparks was shot and killed by a man named J.H. Harper. The incident took place at the South Dallas residence of Harper. Harper shot Sparks five times in what was reported to have been a personal disagreement of some sort. Sparks had apparently been a boarder at the home of Mrs. Harper, who was separated from her husband. Harper, an oil well driller, made his way to the criminal courts building and surrendered without making a comment. He later claimed that he had shot Sparks "in defense of his home."

Sparks is buried in an unmarked grave at the Mount Auburn Cemetery. He was survived by his wife, Mattie Allen Walker, and two of the couple's three children.

Harris, Elijah James "Lige"
Born 12 May 1872—Died 4 September 1924

Precinct 3 constable Elijah Harris was shot and killed while investigating a burglary at a local business. As Harris approached the establishment, a suspect leaped from the bushes and shot him in the stomach. Harris was able to return fire and wound his assailant.

The case remained unsolved until Frank and Lorenzo Noel were charged with the rape of a woman named Mary Steer near Dallas. That incident took place on 12 April 1925. The pair also killed her companion, Ryan Adkins, at the same time. The Noel brothers were found guilty and sentenced to death. That sentence was carried out on 3 July 1925, when both were executed by electrocution at Huntsville. They were the sixteenth and seventeenth criminals to be electrocuted in Texas. Frank and Lorenzo Noel confessed to the murder of Harris during their last half hour of life.

Harris was survived by his wife, Nola Josephine, and ten children. He is buried at the Garland Cemetery.

James, Clarence Elmo
Born 21 June 1890—Died 28 July 1928
Date of Incident: 27 July 1928

At about 10:30 p.m. on Friday, 27 July 1928, Precinct 1 deputy constable Clarence James and Mrs. Charlie Anderson were on the grounds of the Lakewood Country Club. The constable was attempting to trap and arrest a hijacker who had robbed several couples in the area. James and Mrs. Anderson were sitting on a bench when the constable spotted a man crawling through a fence. The man suddenly trotted toward them and began shooting. During the exchange of gunfire that followed, James was hit in the abdomen and mortally wounded.

In his dying statement, James said that the man began firing without saying a word. Blood evidence at the scene indicated that the killer had been wounded during the shootout.

James died of his wounds the following day. The killer has never been identified.

James was survived by his wife, Wilson Lenore Driskill, and three children. He is buried at the Grove Hill Cemetery in Dallas.

Broome, James Leon
Born 4 November 1881—Died 15 December 1929
Date of Incident: 14 December 1929

Precinct 7 constable James Broome was beaten to death while guarding a pump house at the Oak Cliff Cemetery in Dallas.

On Saturday, 14 December 1929 Broome had been assigned by Constable Dancer to guard the facility after it had been broken into seven times over the preceding ten days. When Dancer returned at about 7:00 a.m. on Sunday to pick up Broome, he found that he had been assaulted near the cemetery storehouse and beaten with a car crank handle and wrench. Broome's shotgun had been discharged once and his pistol twice. The grass around the area where Broome was lying was covered with blood. Investigators concluded that Broome had surprised the robbers in the process of breaking in to the storehouse building. Broome died at 4:25 p.m.

Five people were arrested under suspicion of committing the deadly assault: two black men and three black women. The two men who were apprehended, Luther J. Whaley (Whatley) and L.W. Conway, admitted to killing Broome when the officer caught them breaking into the storehouse. They were indicted by a grand jury on 20 December 1929. One of the killers was subsequently sentenced to ninety-nine years in prison, and the other was sentenced to life.

Broome is buried at Laurel Land Memorial Park Cemetery in Dallas.

Davis, John Thomas
Born 23 October 1866—Died 1 July 1930

At about 5:00 p.m. on Tuesday, 1 July 1930, Precinct 4 constable John Davis and Deputy Constable T. Gardner Jones arrested four men whom they caught in the act of stealing accessories from a stolen automobile. The officers also found a pistol in the vehicle. En route to jail, the four men (Antonio Adamez, Arturo Sanchez, Lupe Martinez and Jesus Bustos) began fighting with the officers. During the struggle, they managed to disarm both Davis and Jones and used their guns to shoot them. Davis was shot in the chest and died instantly. Jones was wounded with powder burns from the gunfire.

All four men escaped. Three were later arrested. Antonio Adamez and Arturo Sanchez were sentenced to life in prison. Lupe Martinez received a thirty-five-year sentence. Jesus Bustos escaped prosecution.

Davis was survived by his wife and two children. He is buried at the Mesquite City Cemetery.

DALLAS COUNTY SHERIFF'S OFFICE

Woods, Thomas I.
Born 28 August 1884—Died 21 December 1922

Deputy Sheriff Thomas Woods was shot and killed near Rowlett in a gunfight that took place between deputies and three men who ran a whiskey still. One of the three moonshiners captured in connection with this incident was J. Henry Belcher

After his third trial on 29 May 1924, Belcher was acquitted of the murder of Woods.

Another moonshiner who was involved in the incident was Sidney Welk, who shot and killed Deputy Sheriff Willis Champion during an attempted jailbreak on 26 September 1923.

Woods had been employed with the Dallas County Sheriff's Department for ten years.

Woods was single. He is buried at the Cox's Cemetery in Dallas.

Related Case: Dallas County Sheriff's Office, Willis Champion

Champion, Willis Glover
Born 5 November 1877—Died 26 September 1923

Deputy Sheriff Willis Champion was shot and killed during a jailbreak attempt. One of the two prisoners involved in the episode was a convicted cop killer. During the exchange of gunfire, Champion was shot in the abdomen and knee. He later died from his injuries. One of the jailbreakers was also killed in the shootout. The other, Sidney Welk, was eventually captured. Welk was tried and convicted of the murder of Champion and sentenced to death. That sentence was carried out 3 April 1925, when Welk became the fourteenth criminal to be executed by electrocution at Huntsville. Welk had also shot and killed Deputy Sheriff Thomas Woods the previous year.

Champion was survived by his wife. He is buried at the Oakland Cemetery in Dallas.

Related Case: Dallas County Sheriff's Office, Thomas Woods

Wright, James C.
Born 31 August 1879—Died 28 September 1924
Date of Incident: 31 August 1924

On Sunday, 31 August 1924, Deputies James C. Wright, Lonnie Marshall and Edward Thompson were traveling by automobile to serve a search warrant for operating an illegal whiskey still in the Trinity River bottoms. Marshall was driving and Wright was the front seat passenger when their patrol car struck another vehicle. Wright was thrown from the automobile and suffered severe head injuries. Marshall received grave cuts to his head and arms. Thompson, who was in the back seat, was uninjured. Wright died from his injuries on Sunday, 28 September 1924.

Wright was survived by his wife, Bettie. He is buried at the Mesquite City Cemetery.

Noell, Thomas Lively "Tom"
Born 18 December 1882—Died 31 May 1928

At about 1:00 a.m. on Thursday, 31 May 1928, Deputy Sheriff Tom Noell was dispatched to a disturbance at the Bachman Dam. Noell never arrived. His lifeless body was found by a service station operator slumped over the steering wheel of his automobile at about 3:30 a.m. An inquest determined that Noell had died of apoplexy (more commonly called thrombosis, or stroke).

At the time of his death, Noell was serving as the bailiff in a state district court. He was survived by his wife, Emma Dee, and one son. Noell is buried at the Frankfort Cemetery in Collin County.

Fuller, James Willis
Born 12 August 1896—Died 13 June 1932
Date of Incident: 11 June 1932

On Saturday, 11 June 1932, Deputies James Fuller, Bill Large and others were investigating a burglary on a farm where firearms, whiskey and tires had been stolen. The investigation was taking place at the home of Mrs. Gus Williams, located south of the Dallas city limits. The lawmen arrested one man on their way to the house. That man, Jesse Warren, indicated that he was at the farmhouse when the five burglars arrived and that they were all armed.

While the deputies were inside the residence, the five men, including Roy Hardin and Roy James, returned. One of the men was heard to say, "Get ready to haul out that whiskey." The thieves began firing into the house. A shotgun blast hit Fuller in the head. Deputy Large and, according to some newspaper reports, Sheriff Hal Hood and Jesse Warren, returned fire and took five suspected thieves into custody.

Fuller had been with the agency for five months. He had previously been with the Dallas Police Department for thirteen years. Fuller was survived by his wife and two sons. He is buried at Grove Hill Cemetery in Dallas.

Chapman, Cecil Vincent
Born 14 May 1905—Died 9 September 1934

Deputy Sheriff Cecil Chapman was shot and killed while he and his partner were on a stakeout.

Chapman and his partner, W.J.B. Peck, were looking to capture a pair of robbers who had stolen eight dollars in cash and an automobile from citizens. The officers were sitting in their patrol car near Walnut Hill and Midway Road when the two men drove past them, turned around and returned to the officers' vehicle. They were driving an automobile that had been stolen from F.V. Richardson a few hours earlier. A man named Eugene Lane got out of the car and approached the officers with his gun drawn. A shootout quickly developed, during which Chapman and Eugene Lane were both fatally wounded. Chapman died shortly after the shooting affray. Eugene Lane died the following day at a local hospital. Peck was also wounded in the neck and ear but was able to take the second man, Leroy Lane, into custody.

Leroy Lane was tried and convicted of the murder of Chapman. He was executed by electrocution on 25 January 1935, thus becoming the 107th person to meet such a fate for committing murder in Texas.

Chapman was survived by his wife, Asha Odessa Walters. He is buried at the San Jose Cemetery in Dallas.

DALLAS POLICE DEPARTMENT

Patrick, Leslie N.
Born 10 March 1872—Died 13 June 1901

Officer Patrick was shot and killed while arresting a man for stealing a horse. During the struggle that occurred, the man, Jim Saussier, pulled out a handgun and struck Patrick on the head with it. The gun discharged accidentally, fatally wounding Patrick.

Saussier was initially sentenced to forty years in prison, but in a second trial, his sentence was reduced to five years for the shooting of Patrick and two years for stealing the horse, giving evidence to the fact that punishment for horse theft in Texas was half as severe as the penalty for murdering a lawman.

Patrick had been with the agency for one year. He is buried at the Edgewood Cemetery in Lancaster.

Tedford, Theodore Alonzo "Theo"
Born 22 September 1869—Died 26 July 1912

Officer Theo Tedford was shot and killed while responding to a disturbance call.

Tedford was on mounted patrol. When he arrived on the scene, the suspect, Mr. Potts, opened fire. A bullet from Potts's gun hit him in the side. Tedford fell from his horse. Potts shot Tedford again and then fled the scene.

Four days later, Potts shot and killed Red River County sheriff Charles Stephens, who was a member of a posse trying to arrest him for the shooting of Tedford. Potts was chased for several miles before eventually being shot and killed by possemen.

Tedford had served with the agency for seven years. He was survived by his wife, Frances J. "Fannie" Renfrow, and three sons. Tedford is buried at the Oak Cliff Cemetery in Dallas.

Tedford's brother Alex was killed in the line of duty fifteen years later while serving with the Dallas Police Department.

Related Case: Red River County Sheriff's Office, Charles Stephens

Wright, Jesse
Born circa 1873—Died 17 June 1914

Officer Jesse Wright was shot and killed by fellow Dallas police officer S.R. Trammell. The two men had been involved in a disagreement in a bar that centered on a woman. During the altercation, Trammell shot and killed Wright.

Wright was survived by his wife, Myrtle May Brittain. He is buried at the Oakland Cemetery in Dallas.

Wright's death certificate, along with newspaper accounts of the day, lists his month of death as June. However, family genealogists, as well as Wright's tombstone, record May as the correct month.

Thornton, W. Roy
Born 23 July 1888—Died 12 January 1916

Officer Roy Thornton was in the process of arresting a man named Frank Bonano for a misdemeanor. Another lawman, motorcycle officer Roy C. Booth, arrived at the scene and asked if Thornton needed any assistance. At the same instant, Veto Cortal, a friend of Bonano and a saloonkeeper, appeared and opened fire with a ten-gauge shotgun. The blast hit both officers. Thornton was killed, and Booth was wounded. Booth managed to draw his pistol and return fire.

Bonano escaped and was never captured.

Thornton had been with the agency for two years and was survived by his wife. He is buried in Ardmore, Oklahoma.

Wood, Leroy "Roy"
Born 19 September 1896—Died 7 February 1922
Date of Incident: 5 February 1922

On Sunday, 5 February 1922, Officer Leroy Wood was accidentally shot by his partner during a struggle with a suspect.

The officers had observed a man attempting to burglarize a business by using a butcher knife to pry open a window. When Wood confronted the burglar, a struggle took place. In an unwise but undoubtedly well-intentioned move, Wood's partner, J.J. Crawford, attempted to shoot the weapon out of the burglar's hand. Giving evidence to the fact that Hollywood motion picture scenes are often materially different from the real-life drama of police work, the bullet ricocheted and hit Wood.

Wood remained conscious with his parents, relatives, wife and three children in attendance at his hospital room. He called his partner to his bedside and said, "Go back to work and be careful, Jim. Take good care of yourself, and do not think that I blame you. I know it was an accident. Be sure and live right, be good and meet me in heaven." Crawford and Wood had been friends since childhood. Wood then addressed his wife, children, parents and relatives. He closed his eyes and died at 3:40 p.m. on Tuesday, 7 February 1922.

The shooting was ruled accidental. Wood had been employed with the Dallas Police Department for one year. He was survived by his wife, Willie Lois Shelton, and three children. Wood is buried at the Maypearl Cemetery in Waxahachie, Ellis County.

Gibson, Johnnie C. "Hoot"
Born 18 January 1901—Died 19 April 1923

At about 3:45 a.m. on Thursday, 19 April 1923, Officer "Hoot" Gibson and his partner observed a man standing in a drugstore. Presuming that the man was a burglar given the time of night, they approached the store with their guns drawn. As they did so, the man opened fire. One shot from the criminal's .38-caliber handgun hit Gibson in the neck. The thieves, Blaine Dyer and Earnest Lawson, escaped.

Both Dyer and Lawson were arrested one month later when they shot and killed Dallas officer John Crain under almost identical circumstances. Dyer and Lawson had used the same .38-caliber handgun in that crime that they had used to murder Gibson. Both men were charged, convicted and sentenced to death. They were executed by electrocution on 28 March 1924. They became the sixth and seventh Texas criminals to meet such a fate.

Gibson was survived by his parents and siblings. He had been with the agency for one year. Gibson is buried at the West Dallas Cemetery.

Gibson's nickname of "Hoot" no doubt came from that of the famous rodeo champion, actor, filmmaker and producer Edmund Richard "Hoot" Gibson, who was a major film attraction of the day.

Crain, John Richard
Born 15 September 1867—Died 24 May 1923

At approximately 3:30 a.m. on Thursday, 24 May 1923, Officer John Crain was on patrol and investigating suspicious activity at a local drugstore on Junius Road. He noticed that some lights were on in a pharmacy. As Crain looked through the window into the store, a burglar inside shot him in the head with a .38-caliber handgun.

Both burglars, Blaine Dyer and Earnest Lawson, were the same pair responsible for the murder of Officer Johnnie "Hoot" Gibson, which had occurred just one month earlier under almost identical circumstances. The killers used the same handgun.

Both men were charged, convicted and sentenced to death. They were executed by electrocution on 28 March 1924, becoming the sixth and seventh Texas criminals to meet such a fate.

Crain was survived by his wife, Lula, and four children. He is buried at the Sunny Point Cemetery in Cumby, Hopkins County.

Phillips, Dexter Clayton
Born 27 March 1895—Died 11 August 1923

Officer Dexter Phillips was killed when his motorcycle struck a pothole in the street, causing him to lose control of the machine. The motorcycle fell on him, inflicting serious injuries. He was taken to a local hospital, where he died.

Phillips was survived by his wife and three sons. He is buried at the Grove Hill Cemetery in Dallas.

Swinney, Charles S.
Born 9 February 1873—Died 21 June 1925

Officer Charles Swinney was shot and killed on Knox Street while patrolling the area's business district.

Swinney became involved in a deadly struggle when he confronted two suspicious men who were entering a store near a railroad crossing in northeast Dallas. One of the pair shot him through the abdomen and beat him severely with a pistol. Despite being mortally wounded, Swinney was able to identify the shooter and his accomplice before he died a few hours later.

The pair escaped in an automobile. One of the men was named Joe Brown, who was captured on 28 June. The other was William Jennings Bryant Goodman, an Oklahoma National Guard captain, who was later apprehended. Both men were charged and convicted of Swinney's murder. Goodman was convicted of manslaughter on 22 August 1925, and Brown received his sentence in September 1925.

Officer Swinney was survived by his wife, Emmie Lou Ely. He is buried in an unmarked grave at the Oakland Cemetery in Dallas.

Isbell, Clarence Marshall
Born 14 February 1900—Died 4 February 1926

Officer Clarence Isbell was shot and killed while attempting to stop a speeding automobile.

Isbell maneuvered his patrol car alongside the vehicle to tell the driver to pull over. A shot was fired from inside the car, hitting Isbell in the head. The wound was fatal.

The two men in the automobile, S.A. and Forest Robinson (Robins), were arrested. The Robinson brothers were charged with the murder of Isbell. S.A. Robinson was convicted and sentenced to be executed. Forest Robinson was charged with rape in a separate incident. He was also found guilty at his trial and sentenced to death. Both men were to be put to death on the same day. That sentence was carried out on 6 April 1926, when the Robinson (Robins) brothers were executed by electrocution at Huntsville. They became numbers twenty-three and twenty-four to be electrocuted by the State of Texas.

Isbell had been with the Dallas Police Department for one year. He was survived by his wife, parents and siblings. Isbell is buried at Grove Hill Cemetery in Dallas.

Tedford, Alex W.
Born 25 December 1873—Died 26 December 1927
Date of Incident: 4 October 1927

Officer Alex Tedford died from an infection in his leg that he contracted while conducting a Prohibition raid. During the raid, Tedford fell and tore ligaments in one of his legs. A blood clot and infection formed, eventually resulting in his death.

Tedford was survived by his wife, Katherine, and three children. He is buried at the Grove Hill Cemetery in Dallas.

Officer Tedford's brother, Theodore Alonzo Tedford, had been shot and killed in the line of duty fifteen years earlier while he was serving as a member of the Dallas Police Department.

Hale, W. Roy
Born 27 September 1903—Died 11 August 1931
Date of Incident: Circa 1929

Detective Hale apparently entered the hospital on about 8 August 1931 and was operated on for an intestinal obstruction. He died at 11:55 p.m. on 11 August 1931. Hale's death certificate indicates that the factor contributing to his death was an accident that had occurred two years earlier when his police motorcycle was struck by an automobile. The date of the event, and whether Hale was on duty at the time, has not been established. An incident that took place on 18 July 1928 involving Hale, during which he shot Jack Stewart in the foot as Stewart was fleeing, may be linked to the earlier-cited accident and Hale's death.

Hale was survived by his wife and two children. He is buried at Garland. Hale had been on the police department for five years.

In an unrelated incident, on 2 September 1930, Hale's father, James N. Hale, shot and killed Oscar Bell. Bell was a farmer and meat seller. James Hale stated that he saw Bell making eyes at his wife at a church meeting sometime earlier. When he saw Bell drive up in front of his house while making his rounds delivering beef, he took out his pistol and shot Bell in the forehead. James Hale then drove to his son's house and was later taken to the sheriff's office. Another one of Hale's sons told the district attorney that he thought Bell had "tried to date mama up."

Lanford, Samuel Griffin "Sam"
Born 26 January 1890—Died 29 June 1933

At daybreak on Thursday, 29 June 1933, Officer Sam Lanford was shot and killed by an assailant when he and his partner interrupted a burglary and trailed the suspect into the backyard of a nearby home. The burglar, a black man named R.T. Bennett, fatally shot Lanford, hitting him twice in the head and once in the chest. The other officer was able to wound Bennett, who was later arrested at about noon.

Bennett confessed to the killing and was subsequently convicted of Lanford's murder. He also confessed to the strangulation death of Mrs. H.K. "Smiley" Buchanan, a twenty-eight-year-old blond film executive, at her apartment during the winter of 1932 and the robbery of twenty dollars and shooting of George A. Coffee, Dallas wholesaler and manufacturer. The Buchanan murder had baffled police for months after they discovered her naked and beaten body, strangled about the neck with a silk stocking, at her residence. Bennet was executed by electrocution on 18 August 1933. He became the eighty-seventh person to meet this fate.

Lanford had been with the agency for six years. He was survived by his wife, daughter, three bothers and two sisters. Lanford is buried at the Lakeview Cemetery in Marietta, Oklahoma.

Griffin, Jesse Emmett
Born 15 March 1902—Died 28 December 1933
Date of Incident: 27 December 1933

Officer Jesse Griffin was responding to a stabbing call on his police motorcycle. While he was en route to the call, the driver of an automobile suddenly turned in front of him, causing a collision. Griffin died from the injuries he received in that accident the following day.

Griffin had been with the agency for four years. He was survived by his wife and daughter. Griffin is buried at the Garland Cemetery.

Bell, Luke James
Born 7 March 1899—Died 18 May 1934

Officer Luke Bell was shot and killed with his own handgun while recapturing a prisoner who escaped his custody.

Bell was transporting three prisoners to jail when one of them, Richard Charles Rhem, escaped and fled. Bell gave chase and caught up to Rhem. Rhem put up his hands as if to surrender and then grabbed Bell's handgun and shot him in the side with it.

After a protracted pursuit by officers, Rhem was shot and wounded. He recovered from his wounds and was eventually tried and convicted of killing Bell. Rhem was sentenced to thirty years in prison, but before completing his sentence, he was stabbed to death by a fellow inmate on 22 August 1938.

Bell had been employed by the Dallas Police Department for five years. He was survived by his wife, Birdie Mae Tuggle, and four siblings. Bell is buried at the Forest Lawn (American Legion) Cemetery in Dallas.

Leonard, Ernest E., Jr.
Born 13 January 1912—Died 28 May 1935

Officer Ernest Leonard was killed in a motorcycle accident while attempting to catch a vehicle that he was pursuing for having committed a speed limit violation.

Leonard was survived by his parents and five siblings. He is buried at the Grove Hill Cemetery in Dallas.

Dieken, John William
Born 26 February 1902—Died 10 August 1935
Date of Incident: 9 August 1935

Officer John Dieken was killed in a motorcycle accident while responding to a fire call.

At about 4:00 p.m. on Friday, 9 August 1935, Dieken was en route to the scene of the fire when a female motorist made an unlawful U-turn in front of him, causing a collision. The fuel tank of his motorcycle ruptured on impact, soaking his clothing with gasoline, which ignited and burned Dieken. The flames were quickly extinguished; however, the internal injuries Dieken suffered in the crash resulted in his death the following day.

An investigation revealed that the motorcycle Dieken was riding had previously been involved in two other accidents in which the rider was either injured or killed.

Dieken had served with the agency for one year. He was survived by his wife, Margaret Isabel Smith, and one son. Dieken, a former "China Marine," is buried at the Colfax Center Presbyterian Cemetery in Grundy Center, Iowa.

Roberts, John Rush
Born 25 October 1876—Died 23 December 1935

Former detective John Roberts was shot and killed when he attempted to stop a gas station robbery at the North Loop Garage in the Oak Cliff community in Dallas.

Roberts, who had recently retired from the police force, was employed by the garage. The robber, Dwight Beard, entered the establishment and walked straight to the office, telling those present to face the wall. The proprietor, C.C. Scott, and another man named Carson complied and turned toward the wall. Scott was relieved of the contents of the cash till. Roberts apparently decided to shoot it out with the holdup man and attempted to pull his service revolver. Beard, who was holding a gun on him at the time, obviously beat Roberts to the draw. Roberts was hit in the abdomen with one gunshot from Beard's pistol. The wound proved fatal. Beard escaped with his haul of eight dollars.

Beard fled but was eventually apprehended. He was charged and convicted of Roberts's murder. Beard was sentenced to death and was executed by electrocution on 4 June 1937. Beard was the 143rd criminal to be electrocuted by the State of Texas.

Roberts was survived by his wife, Margaret Hardwick, and four children. He is buried at the Laurel Land Memorial Cemetery in Dallas.

It is truly a sad testimonial that Roberts, who had served with the Dallas Police Department for thirty-one years before his retirement, was gunned down in a gas station holdup that netted eight dollars and resulted in the execution of his assailant.

Hoyt, Ralph Wendell
Born 22 August 1912—Died 20 February 1937
Date of Incident: 19 February 1937

Officer Ralph Hoyt died from injuries he received when his police motorcycle struck a depression in the roadway. He was thrown from the machine and suffered severe injuries. Hoyt died the following day, on Saturday, 20 February 1937.

Hoyt had been with the agency for one year. He was survived by his parents and three siblings. Hoyt is buried in Wichita, Kansas.

DEAF SMITH COUNTY SHERIFF'S OFFICE

Miller, John Benjamin
Born 5 November 1878—Died 6 January 1936

Sheriff John Miller was killed in an automobile accident in Randall County while he was returning to the county seat at Hereford from Amarillo.

Miller had been conducting an investigation concerning a stolen vehicle. His automobile overturned when it struck a patch of ice on the highway. Miller was thrown from the car and sustained fatal injuries.

Miller had served for eight years. He was elected on 6 November 1928 and reelected every two years thereafter until his death. Miller was survived by his wife, Susan Addye Vaughn, and six children. He is buried in West Park Cemetery.

Miller's wife was appointed to complete his term as sheriff.

DENISON POLICE DEPARTMENT

Crane, John Albert
Born 16 February 1870—Died 12 September 1907
Date of Incident: 9 January 1901

At about 1:00 a.m. on Wednesday, 9 January 1901, Officer John Crane responded to a call regarding a disturbance at a local sporting house. A nineteen-year-old client named George Puryear was complaining that he had been robbed by one of the ladies of the evening. Puryear and another man, who was from the Indian Territory (present-day Oklahoma), had been in town all day and were drinking heavily. As Crane approached the scene, Puryear, who was on horseback at the time, turned in his saddle and fired at Crane. The bullet hit Crane in the leg just above the knee. Puryear fled to the Indian Territory. He was shot and killed there on 11 November 1901 by a posse of officers from Denison, Sherman and Grayson Counties.

Crane recovered from his gunshot wound slowly and was eventually able to return to work on light duty as a police clerk. In May 1907, he became bedridden from the effects of the wound and had to leave the department. He died on 12 September 1907 as a result of the lingering injury.

Crane was survived by his wife and two children. He is buried in Fairview Cemetery, formerly Maple Grove Cemetery, in Denison.

DENTON COUNTY SHERIFF'S OFFICE

Parsons, Robert Bruce
Born 19 May 1864—Died 6 August 1925

On Thursday, 6 August 1925, Deputy Sheriff Robert Parsons was on East Hickory Street near the public square, about a block from the main business district in Denton, when the deadly incident that resulted in his death took place.

An automobile with two occupants pulled up to him, and according to some witnesses, one of the occupants said, "I heard you threatened to kill me." In an instant, gunfire rang out as Parsons was shot eleven times. His wounds were fatal.

A man named Webb A. Martin was suspected of being the killer. About fifty lawmen surrounded Martin's house, and after he refused to surrender except under his terms, the lawmen opened fire. In total, three separate barrages of gunfire were launched at the Martin home, none of which seemed to take effect. After a five-minute round of machine gun fire, however, Martin did capitulate. He had been grazed slightly by a bullet. Over three hundred shots had been fired into the Martin home.

Martin was charged, convicted and, on 12 October 1925, sentenced to serve ninety-nine years in prison. He was already under indictment for robbery at the time of the Parsons killing. Although his lawyers tried to introduce evidence that the killing was part of a feud that existed between Martin and Sheriff W.S. Fry, who was his political enemy during the recent election for that post, they failed to prove any connection.

Parsons had been in law enforcement for forty years. He is buried at the Odd Fellows Cemetery in Denton.

Garrett, Carl Edward
Born 19 May 1864—Died 3 July 1934
Date of Incident: 2 July 1934

Deputy Sheriff Carl Garrett died from a gunshot wound he received when he and several deputies raided a café in Justin.

Deputies had been to the café a week earlier and charged the co-operators, Jimmie Glasscock and Boyd Wilkerson, with illegal possession of beer in a dry-option county. During that incident, Wilkerson is said to have assaulted Deputy Garrett and his partner, Hugh Elliott, with a meat cleaver. This time, Glasscock, armed with a pistol, shot Garrett in the throat. Elliott returned fire and killed Glasscock. Garrett lived until the following day, when he died from the injury.

Wilkerson was indicted for murder and assault with intent to murder.

Garrett was survived by his wife and one daughter. He is buried at the Elizabeth Cemetery in Roanoke.

Dickens County Sheriff's Office

Arthur, William Bowen
Born 3 June 1886—Died 27 October 1934

Sheriff William Arthur was shot and killed with his own weapon during an escape attempt that occurred at the county jail.

Two prisoners, Virgil Stalcup and Clarence Brown, asked Sheriff Arthur to fix the stopped-up plumbing. As Arthur walked past their cell, Brown grabbed the sheriff's gun and shot him in the neck.

Both Stalcup and Brown escaped but were later apprehended. The pair was charged and convicted. Stalcup was sentenced to death and was executed by electrocution at Huntsville on 4 May 1936, thus becoming the 129th criminal to suffer this fate. Brown avoided execution but was sentenced to ninety-nine years in prison.

Arthur was elected on 4 November 1930 and reelected on 8 November 1932 and had been nominated for a third term when he was killed. He was survived by his wife, Nancy Vesta Stegall, and five children. Arthur is buried at the Dickens Cemetery.

DIMMIT COUNTY SHERIFF'S OFFICE

Tumlinson, Joel Maurice Walker "Walk"
Born 17 May 1853—Died 10 May 1903

Deputy Sheriff Joel "Walk" Tumlinson went to the county jail to take care of an insane prisoner. He remained there with the man for the night. While at the jail, Tumlinson was involved in a struggle with the man. When he returned home, his wife noticed that he looked rather pale. He indicated that his chest hurt and asked for a doctor. Several physicians were summoned to his aid, but his condition became more severe. Tumlinson died of an apparent heart attack within an hour.

Tumlinson was survived by his wife, Fenatty H. "Nate" Moseley, and two children. He is buried in Carrizo Springs.

Ortiz, Candelario
Born May 1860—Died 12 September 1913

Deputy Sheriff Candelario Ortiz was shot and killed when he and another deputy, Eugene Buck, were abducted by a band of gunrunners who were smuggling weapons into Mexico to start a revolution.

Ortiz and Buck were members of a posse that had gone to investigate a report of a group of men who were said to be smuggling guns into Mexico from the United States. The posse successfully intercepted fifteen men who were making their way from Carrizo Springs to the Mexican border. Predictably, a gunfight broke out. Hopelessly outnumbered and short of ammunition, the posse attempted to retreat. Ortiz and Buck were captured and taken to the smugglers' camp. Later, when the smugglers left their camp, they tied the two deputies' hands behind their backs and loaded them down like pack animals with guns and ammunition. Burdened in this manner, Ortiz and Buck were forced to walk for several miles. Hampered by the heavy load, Ortiz was unable to climb a hill, so the merciless smugglers shot and killed him on the spot.

After being involved in a shootout with lawmen and U.S. Army soldiers, the outlaw group of freebooters was finally captured. Smuggler Panfilo Vazquez was killed during the battle. Charles "Barney" Cline, the leader of the band, was the only American among the suspects to be captured. He was a member of the Industrial Workers of the World, commonly known as the "Wobblies."

The Wobblie group was organized because of the belief among many unionists, socialists, anarchists and radicals that the American Federation of Labor (AFL) had failed to organize the working people in America.

Cline was charged and went to trial. Jose and Alberto Ortiz, sons of the slain deputy, were quoted in the newspaper as asking to be appointed executioners if any of the suspects were sentenced to death. Sheriff Hess agreed that they could assist him. After a hung jury and a conviction that was appealed and remanded, Cline was finally convicted and sentenced to life in prison.

The other individuals captured included Jose Serrato, Lino Gonzales, Jesus Gonzales, Peonardo L. Vasquez, Pedro Perales, Abram Cisneros, Bernardino Mendoza, Engenio Alzide, Luz Mendoza, Miguel P. Martinez, D.R. Rosas, L.R. Ortiz, Jose M. Rangel and F. Sanchez. Newspaper reports of the day indicate that four received life sentences, nine were sentenced to between five and twenty-five years in prison and one was acquitted. Serrato was reported to have escaped from the state prison in 1914.

In 1926, the ill-famed Governor Miriam A. Ferguson granted full pardons to six of the convicted men, including the ringleader Cline.

Ortiz was survived by his wife and seven children. His place of burial is unknown but is most likely at the Guadalupe Cemetery in Carrizo Springs.

Buck had served as sheriff from 1904 to 1912 and stayed on as a deputy sheriff after being defeated for reelection.

Some family genealogists and a couple of newspaper articles list 11 September as Ortiz's date of death; however, most report it as 12 September.

DUVAL COUNTY CONSTABLE'S OFFICE

Burch, Joshua
Born 13 October 1874—Died 2 August 1939

According to newspaper reports, the Burch family was awakened by the sound of a gunshot around daybreak on Wednesday, 2 August 1939. Joshua Burch's son Albert ran outside and discovered his father lying dead from a single gunshot wound to the forehead. The incident took place in Freer.

Constable Burch is believed to have taken his own life. The circumstances surrounding the incident are unknown.

Burch was survived by his wife, Mentha Minty Ree Donahue, and twelve children. He is buried at the Montell Cemetery in Uvalde.

Duval County Sheriff's Office

McNeill, Archibald "Archie"
Born 13 May 1875—Died 2 July 1900

Deputy Sheriff Archie McNeill was shot and killed by a man named Luther Gillett in the town of San Diego. McNeill was able to return fire and wound Gillett during the shooting affray.

McNeill was survived by his wife, Ila B. Williams, and two children. He is believed to have been buried at San Diego, but no grave site has been located.

Anguiano, Antonio
Born circa 1873—Died 18 May 1912

Deputy Sheriff Antonio Anguiano was at the county courthouse monitoring an election. A dispute of some sort broke out. When Anguiano attempted to intervene, he was shot and killed by one of the members of the crowd. During the mêlée that followed, District Clerk Pedro Eznail and a farmer named Candelario Saenz were also killed.

Frank Robinson, Charles Gravis and Dr. S.A. Roberts were arrested. The disposition of any charges against them is not known at this time.

No personal information on Anguiano has been found. His place of burial is unknown.

Rossi, Frank
Born 11 February 1902—Died 21 July 1935
Date of Incident: 14 July 1935

Special Deputy Sheriff Frank Rossi died from a stab wound he received when he was attempting to arrest a man for drunkenness at a saloon in Realitos. During the arrest, a second man approached Rossi from behind and stabbed him twice in the chest and once in the arm. Rossi was transported to a hospital in Corpus Christi, where he died one week later.

The two men were arrested and convicted of murder. One of them was paroled after serving only one year. The second man was paroled after serving approximately eight years.

Rossi had been with the agency for two years. He was survived by his wife and two children. Rossi is buried at the Holy Cross Cemetery in Corpus Christi.

EAGLE LAKE POLICE DEPARTMENT

Kinard, William R.
Born 12 March 1868—Died 4 June 1903

City Marshal William Kinard was asked to respond to a disturbance at a local saloon. When he arrived at the bar, he disarmed an intoxicated man named W.L. McDow. Kinard told the inebriated McDow to go home. McDow complied but returned about one hour later. This time, he was armed with a Winchester rifle. McDow shot Kinard in the side. Although seriously wounded, Kinard was able to return fire and kill McDow.

City Marshal Kinard had been with the agency for five years. He was survived by his wife and seven children. Kinard's place of burial is unknown.

EAST BERNARD, CITY OF

Hargis, Joseph Leonard
Born 8 July 1890—Died 11 July 1935

Early on Thursday morning, 11 July 1935, night watchman Joseph Hargis apparently became involved in a disagreement of some sort with several men at a filling station. The argument turned violent. Hargis was shot by one of the men named Jimmie Boatwright. The bullet entered near Hargis's heart and inflicted a fatal wound. Witnesses to the disagreement that preceded the shooting indicate that Boatwright was intoxicated. Hargis's body was discovered after daylight. His pistol was missing, and there was evidence of a struggle.

Bloodhounds were brought in from the state prison farm at Sugar Land to aid in the search for the killer. Boatwright was discovered sleeping in a ditch about sixty yards from the scene of the murder. Boatwright was tried and convicted of the murder. He was sentenced to serve nine years in prison.

Hargis is buried in Mount Enterprise in Rusk County. He was survived by his wife, Ada E., and one child.

EASTLAND COUNTY SHERIFF'S OFFICE

Hennessee, John Walter
Born 15 November 1887—Died 23 July 1924

Deputy John Hennessee was shot and killed in the most unfortunate of incidents when a farmer mistook him for a thief. The farmer, C.Q. Davis, grabbed his shotgun and went outside to confront a person whom he believed to be a robber. Hennessee, presuming the farmer was one of the suspects he was searching for, ordered him to drop his weapon. Both men fired simultaneously. Both men were killed instantly.

Hennessee was survived by his wife, Olivia "Ollie" Sellers, and two children. He is buried at the Eastland Cemetery.

Jones, Thomas Alexander
Born 20 April 1874—Died 20 November 1929
Date of Incident: 19 November 1929

Deputy Sheriff Thomas Jones died from a gunshot wound he received when he tried to foil an escape attempt by a jailed criminal.

The prisoner, Marshal Ratliff, was in jail for the murder of two lawmen, Officer George Carmichael and Chief George Bedford of the Cisco Police Department. The crimes had taken place two years earlier. Ratliff, who was known as the "Santa Claus Bank Robber," had already been tried, convicted and sentenced to death for the murders of Carmichael and Bedford.

Ratliff had gone on trial on 16 January 1928 in the court of Judge George L. Davenport. He was first convicted of armed robbery on 27 January 1928 and sentenced to serve ninety-nine years in prison. Although no one could testify to having seen him fire a gun in the bank, on 30 March 1928 Ratliff was sentenced to be executed for his role in the deaths of Bedford and Carmichael. He appealed his case and, when that failed, filed an insanity plea.

Ratliff was taken to the Huntsville state prison in handcuffs and shackles by Sheriff T.P Hudson and three associates on 28 April 1928. Ratliff began his ruse of acting deranged. He managed to convince his jailers that he had gone mad. His mother, Rilla Carter, filed for a lunacy hearing in Huntsville. Citizens of Eastland County were infuriated that he had not yet been executed and that the he was attempting to dodge his guilt by pleading insanity. In retaliation, Eastland County judge George L. Davenport issued a bench warrant for theft to a vehicle and extradited Ratliff to the Eastland County jail. Once there, Ratliff managed to convince jailers Edward Paxton "Pack" Kilbourn and Tom Jones that he really was insane. They had to feed him by hand, bathe him and take him to the toilet.

On 18 November 1928, a quite lucid Ratliff attempted to escape from the county lockup, mortally wounding jailer Tom Jones with three shots from a pistol that he had taken from the desk drawer of the lockup while trying to gain his freedom. After Ratliff shot Jones, "Pack" Kilbourn grabbed him by the gun arm to prevent him from firing further. Kilbourn struggled with Ratliff down the stairs and through the door of the jail. Hearing the commotion, Kilbourn's married daughter, Malaquay Taylor, took her father's pistol from their home and pushed her way through the crowd, attempting to shoot Ratliff herself. The Kilbourn girl would surely have taken the shot were it not for her fear of accidentally hitting her father in the process. During the ruckus that followed, the pistol discharged harmlessly into the ceiling, marking the fifth and final shot. At that point, Jailer Kilbourn disarmed Ratliff, beating him senseless in the process, and returned him to his cell.

The following morning, a crowd began to gather. By nightfall, the mob had grown to over one thousand outraged citizens. The crowd demanded that Ratliff be handed over to them. Although Jailer Kilbourn refused, he was eventually overpowered as the horde of vigilantes rushed the jail and pulled Ratliff out into the street. They promptly tied his hands and feet and headed for a nearby utility pole to carry out the death sentence that the State of Texas had failed to complete. Their first attempt to lynch Ratliff failed when the amateur hangman's knot came loose, causing Ratliff to tumble to the ground. After a fifteen-minute wait for a second rope, the crowd made another attempt. This time, the noose did not come undone. Ratliff was pronounced dead at 9:55 p.m. on 19 November 1928. Jones died the same evening, bringing the total number of dead, including the three bank robbers, to six.

Although a grand jury was formed to investigate the incident, not surprisingly no one ever stood trial for the vigilante-style lynching of Ratliff. Such exercises of justice administered by the masses were not infrequent in Texas. Before Judge Garrett could order that the corpse of Ratliff be locked up, several thousand persons had already viewed the body, which had been placed on display at a local furniture store. Ratliff's family took possession of his remains and arranged for a funeral in Fort Worth. He is buried there at Olivet Cemetery.

Jones was a former police officer who was volunteering at the jail. He was survived by his wife. Jones is buried at the Eastland City Cemetery.

Related Cases: Cisco Police Department, George Carmichael and George Bedford

ECTOR COUNTY SHERIFF'S OFFICE

McMeans, I. George "Gee"
Born 11 June 1876—Died 1 October 1917

Texas is famous for its feuds. The Johnson-Sims feud was one of them.

The Johnson-Sims feud began when Ed Sims and Gladys Johnson Sims were divorced. Sims and Johnson came from prominent ranching families in Garza, Kent and Scurry Counties. After the divorce, Gladys and her brother Sid shot and killed an allegedly unarmed Ed Sims in Snyder when he came to get his daughters for Christmas 1916. The charges against Gladys were dismissed, but Sid's case was set for trial. Gladys married the famous Texas Ranger Frank Hamer shortly after the shooting.

On 1 October 1917, Frank and Gladys Hamer were returning from Sid's trial in Baird. They were traveling with Gus Hamer and Sid Johnson. When the group reached Sweetwater, they were ambushed in a garage by George McMeans and H.E. Phillips. McMeans shot Hamer twice with a .45-caliber pistol at close range, once in the shoulder and once in the thigh. Although seriously wounded, Hamer managed to shoot McMeans in the heart while they grappled. Phillips joined in and fired a shotgun at Hamer. All he managed to hit was Hamer's hat, however. In total, ten shots were fired by the combatants. Seven revolvers, three repeating rifles and two semiautomatic pistols were taken from the group when they were arrested by the police chief. The Nolan County grand jury, which was in session at the time, came outside to witness part of the shootout. They returned to the courtroom and no billed Hamer for acting in self-defense.

McMeans was married to Ed Sims's sister and was a former Texas Ranger (1903–05) in Company C. Newspaper accounts of the day indicated that he was a former sheriff of Ector County, but that has not been confirmed. He was survived by his wife and eleven-year-old son. McMeans is buried at the Aspermont Cemetery in Stonewall County.

EL CAMPO POLICE DEPARTMENT

Lee, James Otway
Born 27 June 1877—Died 11 August 1914

On the afternoon of Tuesday, 11 August 1914, City Marshal James Lee was shot through the chest when he attempted to quell a disturbance at a Mexican restaurant. A bystander named William Moreland also received a painful wound to the shoulder during the same shooting affray. While being pursued by a number of citizens, the two men who had done the shooting fled to a nearby thicket. During the shootout that followed, one suspect was killed, and the other was reported to have been mortally wounded in the shoulder by one of the citizens. Lee died the same night at 7:00 p.m.

Lee was survived by his wife, Millie Lollar, and three children. He is buried at the Gardens of Memories (Sons of Herman) Cemetery in El Campo. Some family genealogists report a fourth child, daughter Verna Lee, who was born on 12 May 1899. Based on the date of birth, Verna was apparently a twin of son Vernon Lee, who was born on the same day. The source does not list a date of death for Verna Lee or offer any source documents.

ELLIS COUNTY CONSTABLE'S OFFICE

Conger, Thomas David
Born 13 March 1868—Died 24 July 1908
Date of Incident: 6 June 1908

Precinct 4 constable Thomas Conger was attempting to serve a bond forfeiture warrant on a man named Milton Golden at Red Oak. During the arrest attempt, Golden was somehow able to gain control of Conger's service revolver. Golden shot Conger several times and then fled. He was eventually arrested in Oklahoma in 1909.

Conger had served with the agency for two years. He is buried at Bells Chapel Cemetery in Rocket. Conger was survived by his wife and three children.

Godfrey, Thomas Page, Jr.
Born circa 1867—Died 3 August 1938

At about 7:20 p.m. on Wednesday, 3 August 1938, Precinct 1 constable Thomas P. Godfrey Jr., who was at the time accompanied by Deputy Constable Emmett Hales, was walking across the highway to serve an arrest warrant at Fincher's tourist camp. The officers were acting on a request from the Fort Worth Police Department. Godfrey apparently did not see an oncoming vehicle driven by Clifford H. West. West tried to avoid a collision, but Godfrey was knocked down by the vehicle. West stopped to provide aid and took Godfrey to the hospital in Waxahachie. Godfrey died from his injuries about an hour later. No charges were filed against West.

Godfrey is buried with his wife, Mary Inez Godfrey, in unmarked graves at the Boren Cemetery in Reagor Springs. He had been a lawman for thirty-five years and had served the preceding ten years as an elected constable.

Ellis County Sheriff's Office

Warren, William Earl
Born 9 March 1891—Died 4 August 1931

Deputies William Warren and Albert Snipes were questioning a suspicious person near the railroad yards. During the interrogation, the suspect, G.W. Williams, opened fire on the deputies. Both lawmen were able to return fire and kill Williams, but unfortunately Warren was also killed during the exchange.

Warren had served with the Ellis County Sheriff's Department for one year. He was survived by his wife, Mary Elizabeth Watkins, and seven children. He is buried at the Myrtle Cemetery in Ennis.

El Paso County Constable's Office

Clements, Emanuel "Little Mannen" or "Mannie," Jr.
Born 16 January 1869—Died 29 December 1908

Emanuel Clements Jr. was called "Little Mannen" or "Mannie" to distinguish him from his father, Emanuel "Mannen" Clements.

Clements had been involved in the Frazer-Miller feud, based largely on his association with Sheriff Bud Frazer of Pecos, for whom he had been employed. Emanuel Clements's sister Sallie married the notorious Jim "Killing Jim" or "Deacon Jim" Miller. Miller got himself appointed Pecos City marshal and hired Clements to work for him as a deputy.

In 1894, Clements moved to El Paso and for the next fourteen years worked as a deputy constable, constable and deputy sheriff. During the 1890s, he was united in El Paso with his cousin John Wesley Hardin, who had just been released from prison. Clements also renewed his bonds with his murderous brother-in-law, Jim Miller, who was also in the city at the same time. In 1908, Clements was indicted for armed robbery. Although he was acquitted, his career as a lawman was over.

On Tuesday, 29 December 1908, Clements was shot and killed at the Coney Island Saloon in El Paso. Most historians claim that he was killed by a man named Joe Brown, who was a former constable of El Paso County. Rumors at the time of the killing suggested that Clements had been killed because he had tried to blackmail Albert Fall, threatening to provide proof of Fall's entanglement in a plot to murder Pat Garrett, the famous sheriff from New Mexico who killed Billy the Kid.

Clements's murderer has never been found. He was survived by his wife, Hellen Effie Bramlette. Clements is buried at the Evergreen Alameda Cemetery in El Paso.

Carpio, Carlos
Born September 1885—Died 4 December 1910
Date of Incident: 1 December 1910

On Wednesday, 30 November 1910, Carlos Carpio filed his bond and qualified to be the Precinct 3 constable.

In the early morning hours of Thursday, 1 December 1910, Constable Carpio was shot while he was attempting to break up a fight at a dance in Socorro. The bullet entered his left side, passing through his abdomen and perforating the intestines, and came out above the right hip. The same bullet wounded two other men. Carpio died three days later, on 4 December 1910.

Carpio's place of burial is unknown. No personal information has been located.

Stepp, Samuel Jones "Sam"
Born 14 March 1886—Died 2 January 1920
Date of Incident: 1 January 1920

Precinct 1 constable Sam Stepp and an El Paso County deputy sheriff were attempting to arrest two men suspected of robbing a citizen. The victim had immediately notified Stepp of the heist. As Stepp and the deputy, accompanied by the victim, returned to the place where the incident had taken place, they encountered two men named George R. Gaddy and R.H. Crie. The victim identified the pair as the men who held him up.

Stepp informed Gaddy and Crie that he was placing them under arrest. Gaddy protested. Crie produced a pistol and shot Stepp three times. In spite of being mortally wounded, Stepp returned fire and fatally shot Crie. The deputy transported Stepp to Providence Hospital, where he died the following day.

Gaddy and Crie were on active duty in the U.S. Army at the time of the incident. A military policeman took Gaddy into custody and charged him with murder. Nothing further is known concerning the outcome of any charges against Gaddy.

Stepp was survived by his wife. He is buried at the Evergreen Cemetery in El Paso.

EL PASO COUNTY SHERIFF'S OFFICE

Garlick, William Henry
Born 18 July 1868—Died 23 June 1913

Texas Ranger captain John R. Hughes assigned Private Scott Russell to accompany Deputy Sheriff William Garlick to serve an arrest warrant on a man named Manuel Guaderrama. Guaderrama was charged with cattle rustling. The Guaderrama clan were frequent offenders and as such were well known to local law enforcement.

The two lawmen went to an enterprise owned by Manuel and his brother Juan that consisted of a store and saloon. The business was located in an unincorporated industrial area called Smeltertown. To avoid arousing suspicion, the officers entered the store under the pretext of buying tobacco.

Juan and his mother, Marina, were the only people in the store when the lawmen entered. Without warning, Russell was struck in the head with an axe handle by Marina. Juan pulled a 9mm Luger semiautomatic pistol and opened fire, killing both Russell and Garlick. Juan then pulled down the curtains of the store and began to hack at the fallen officers' heads with a hatchet. Following this wild and grisly scene, Juan discovered that during his shooting spree he had accidentally shot and mortally wounded his mother. Juan's wife soon arrived and removed both officers' six guns and Russell's gun belt.

Juan Guaderrama fabricated a story that he thought would be convincing and called police, reporting that the two officers had come to the store intoxicated and had struck his mother. Lawmen did not buy his story and believed that the Guaderrama clan had planned the murders in revenge for the rustling investigation.

Thirteen members of the Guaderrama clan were arrested. A grand jury determined that they did not have sufficient evidence to charge seven of the family members. Six, including Juan, were indicted for murder. The Guaderramas hired the best legal representation available. Five of the family members were tried on 13 January 1914. The jury deadlocked. Rangers and deputies raised funds to aid the district attorney in a second trial. By the time the second trial date rolled around in June 1915, only Juan Guaderrama was convicted, and on a lesser charge of second-degree murder. Juan was sentenced to serve five years in prison.

Garlick had been with the agency for seven years. He was survived by his wife, Martha Jane Harris, and six children. Garlick is buried at the Valentine Cemetery in Jeff Davis County.

Related Case: Texas Ranger, Grover Scott Russell

Trice, Robert Alexander
Born 15 April 1877—Died 18 November 1931

Along with being a deputy sheriff, Robert Trice was a commercial night watchman for the community of Clint.

At about 2:15 a.m. on Wednesday, 18 November 1931, the fifty-four-year-old Trice was shot and killed in front of a store in Clint. It is believed that he had surprised burglars who were in the process of entering a store. Trice's body was not found until 6:00 a.m., when the owner of the business arrived to open the store. Trice had been shot three times at close range; one bullet entered his chest, a second his forehead and a third glanced off his brow. Powder burns on the sidewalk indicated that Trice had been on the ground when he was shot repeatedly at close range. Trice's watchman's clock indicated that he had rung in at 2:15 a.m., probably a few minutes before the shooting took place. The killers took Trice's pistol and ring of keys. The lock on the front door of the store had holes bored in it, indicating an attempted forced entry.

Newspaper reports of the day claimed that Trice had arrested two men about six months earlier who had been committing burglaries in the area. The men fled back into Mexico. The store that Trice was murdered in front of had been burglarized three times in the recent past.

Three men were arrested by Juarez, Mexico police with evidence from another store burglary and cartridges from the same caliber gun that was used to kill Trice. Fingerprints were lifted at the scene and compared to the three suspects. The men were later released. It is unknown if anyone was ever charged or convicted for the murder of Trice.

Trice was reported to have lived in and around Clint for twenty-three years. He was survived by his wife, Emma Foster Perkins, and eight children. Trice is buried at the Evergreen Cemetery in El Paso.

Wheeler, Shafter H.
Born 12 January 1899—Died 1 November 1933

Deputy Sheriff Shafter Wheeler was shot and killed when he responded to a disturbance at a café/bar in La Tuna.

As Wheeler approached the establishment, he asked W.H. Jenes, who was a night watchman at a local gin, if he had a gun. Jenes replied that he did and then promptly opened fire on Wheeler. Jenes fatally wounded Wheeler when one of the bullets he fired hit Wheeler in the head. Jenes was later arrested. The seventy-year-old killer offered no explanation for the shooting.

Wheeler had been with the agency for three years and had been in law enforcement for twelve years. Some family genealogists report his date of death as 5 March 1933.

White, V.O. "Bill"
Born 7 May 1903—Died 28 August 1934

Deputy Sheriff Bill White was killed when his departmental motorcycle struck the back of a vehicle driven by a drunk driver he was chasing. The intoxicated vehicle operator stopped his automobile suddenly, causing White's motorcycle to collide with it.

White had been with the agency for seven years. He was survived by his expectant wife, whom he had been visiting at the hospital prior to the accident. White is buried at the Restlawn Memorial Park in El Paso.

Cramer, John R.
Born 15 March 1884—Died 26 April 1940

Deputy Sheriff John Cramer had arrested a young Mexican man named Rosalio Ontiveros of Clint on undisclosed petty charges. Ontiveros was a local hooligan of some renown. Cramer, who was a veteran officer, attempted to find a justice of the peace but was unsuccessful in doing so. He then loaded Ontiveros into his patrol car and headed into the sand hills east of El Paso. Cramer's body was later discovered in his automobile about seventeen miles east of El Paso. He had been shot and had three knife slashes across his abdomen.

Several hours later and only a half hour before dark, Deputies Jack Bell, Jim Hicks and Bob Bailey found Ontiveros about three miles from where he had murdered Cramer. He immediately opened fire on the lawmen, who returned fire and killed him. They found the Smith & Wesson revolver belonging to Cramer and a folding pocketknife in Ontiveros's possession. According to his pursuers, had Ontiveros managed to stay out of sight for thirty minutes longer, he would have escaped.

Cramer was survived by his wife, Angela. He is buried at the Evergreen Alameda Cemetery in El Paso. Local citizens established a fund for Ms. Cramer in order that she might meet funeral expenses. There was no widow's pension for sheriff's department employees at the time.

Some sources have reported the spelling of Ontiveros's surname as Oativeras. Ontiveros is also buried at the Evergreen Alameda Cemetery in El Paso.

El Paso, City of

Garcia, Juan M. "Johnny," Jr.
Born circa 1886—Died 1 February 1918

Deputy Tax Collector Johnny Garcia and Patrolman Octaviano Perea were shot and killed during a gun battle with a man named Felipe Alvarez, who had just murdered a woman and her two infant children.

Perea was shot and killed when he directed a spotlight at Alvarez during the search. Garcia was fatally wounded during the final episode of the chase. A posse of lawmen had cornered Alvarez in an outhouse. Numerous possemen opened fire. Garcia was the only posse member to be injured. His wounds were fatal. The barrage of gunfire launched at the privy by lawmen that day was shocking. Reports indicate that Alvarez sustained over eighty bullet wounds.

As a tax collector, Garcia was considered to be a law enforcement officer and as such was required to assist the police department whenever needed. He had served with the City Tax Collector's Office for eight years. Garcia was survived by three siblings. He is buried at Evergreen Cemetery in El Paso.

Related Case: El Paso Police Department, Octaviano Perea

El Paso Police Department

Stewart, Newton "Newt"
Born 20 October 1872—Died 17 February 1900

Patrolman "Newt" Stewart was shot and killed by a group of soldiers who were attempting to break two fellow servicemen who had been arrested for drunkenness out of jail.

The troops were attached to Company E, Twenty-fifth Infantry, one of the all-black units popularly referred to as "Buffalo Soldiers." The soldiers had armed themselves with Krag-Jorgensen rifles and had lined up outside the station house at 5:00 a.m. Two of the soldiers entered the building and told Stewart to release and hand over their jailed companions. Stewart refused and ordered the servicemen out of the police station. They rebuffed the command and opened fire. Stewart was shot twice in the lungs. Jailer Richard Blacker, who was asleep inside the jail at the time the incident began, grabbed a pistol and confronted the soldiers. They opened fire at him but missed. Blacker returned fire and shot one of the soldiers.

A blood trail led officers to the wounded trooper, who was discovered lying dead just a few blocks away. Stewart died from his wounds about 7:00 a.m.

Three other soldiers who were involved in the incident received a court-martial. John Kipper, the trooper who killed Stewart, received a sentence of life in prison.

Stewart is buried at the Concordia Cemetery in El Paso.

Paschall, William L. "Billy"
Born 10 November 1879—Died 4 December 1914

Patrolman Billy Paschall was shot and killed while he was investigating the robbery of two citizens. One of the two men he was questioning, Dave Jones, alias Robert Grayson, shot him in the head. Witnesses say the two men fled the scene and ran toward a rail yard. Officers soon located Paschall's body.

Dave Jones was later shot and killed while in custody for the murder of El Paso patrolman Gus Chitwood.

Paschall was survived by his wife. He is buried at the Evergreen Alameda Cemetery in El Paso.

Related Case: El Paso Police Department, Gus C. Chitwood

Chitwood, Gus C.
Born 21 February 1874—Died 13 February 1915

Patrolman Gus Chitwood was investigating gunfire on a side street in El Paso. While he was shining his flashlight in an alley, a gunshot rang out. The bullet hit Chitwood, inflicting a fatal wound.

A suspect was apprehended and taken to the detectives' office for questioning. While in custody, Dave Jones, alias Robert Grayson, confessed to the murder of Patrolman William Paschall, which had occurred two months earlier. After the confession, he attempted to escape and grabbed an officer's pistol. His breakout attempt was foiled when he was shot and killed by other officers.

Chitwood was survived by his wife, Cordelia Watson, and two children. He is buried at the Evergreen Cemetery in El Paso.

Related Case: El Paso Police Department, William L. Paschall

Benson, Sidney J. Albert "Sid"
Born 16 September 1877—Died 28 June 1917

Patrolman Albert Benson was transporting a prisoner named Jose Garcia to jail in a jitney bus. Along the route to the lockup, Garcia, who was not handcuffed, reached over and grabbed Benson's handgun. He then shot Benson, twice in the head and twice in the torso.

The killer fled the scene and was never apprehended.

Benson had been with the agency for seven years. He was survived by his wife, Dorothy, and one child. Benson is buried at the Concordia Cemetery in El Paso.

Perea, Octaviano
Born January 1868—Died 1 February 1918

Patrolman Octaviano Perea and Deputy Tax Collector Juan M. "Johnny" Garcia were shot and killed during a gun battle with a man named Felipe Alvarez, who had just murdered a woman and her two infant children.

Perea directed a spotlight at the man during the search. The murderer opened fire, fatally wounding Perea.

The search for the multiple-murder suspect continued. Garcia was fatally wounded in what turned out to be the final shootout between officers and Alvarez. The incident took place alongside an outhouse where Alvarez had been cornered. Numerous members of the posse of lawmen who were searching for Alvarez opened fire. Garcia was the only member of the posse to be injured. His wounds were fatal. Newspaper reports of the day indicate that Alvarez sustained over eighty bullet wounds during the exchange. Needless to say, Alvarez was killed.

Perea had served with the El Paso Police Department for three years. He was survived by his wife, Teodoro Garcia, and children. Perea is buried at the Greenwood Cemetery in El Paso.

Related Case: City of El Paso, Juan M. "Johnny" Garcia

Drake, George Franklin
Born 31 December 1879—Died 22 September 1918

Officer George Drake was killed when a vehicle driven by a man who had just shot and wounded a detective collided with his motorcycle. The driver of the vehicle, Tom Davis, had shot Detective George Minturn during a dispute that had occurred earlier when officers ejected him from a party. During the chase by Drake and other lawmen, Drake's motorcycle was hit by the suspect, pinning Drake under the machine and causing fatal injuries. Minturn survived his wounds.

Drake's killer had worked with him in the past and had been a friend.

Drake had served with the agency for two years. He was survived by his wife, Nora May (Mae) Cranston, and two sons. Drake is buried at the Concordia Cemetery in El Paso.

Phoenix, Packard Harry
Born 17 April 1884—Died 13 June 1921

Captain Harry Phoenix and two other officers were questioning a pair of suspicious men. When the officers attempted to arrest the pair, a gun battle developed during which Phoenix was shot in the head. He died instantly. During the same shootout, Sergeant Schuyler Houston also suffered serious gunshot wounds. The two suspects fled to Mexico and were never apprehended.

Phoenix had served with the agency for ten years. He was survived by his wife and daughter. Phoenix is buried at the Concordia Cemetery in El Paso.

In spite of the lingering effects of his critical injuries, which required frequent trips to the hospital, Sergeant Schuyler Houston remained with the police department and was eventually promoted to captain. He ultimately died from the effects of his wounds on 4 October 1927.

Related Case: El Paso Police Department, Schuyler Houston
Burns, Frank J.
Born 23 February 1894—Died 12 April 1923
Date of Incident: 10 April 1923

Detective Frank Burns was shot and killed while assisting federal narcotics agents in breaking up a drug ring. While the officers were entering a store to arrest the drug dealer, a man opened fire from a concealed position inside the building. A bullet hit Burns, inflicting a serious injury. He was transported to a local hospital, where he died two days later.

Burns was survived by his wife. He is buried at the Evergreen Alameda Cemetery in El Paso.

Coleman, John Jack
Born circa 1867—Died 14 July 1924

Detective John Coleman was fatally shot from ambush while driving down a city street. As Coleman turned a corner, the shooter, Salvador Jacques, who was standing in a cluster of trees, opened fire.

Jacques was later arrested and sentenced to death. That sentence was commuted on 22 July 1925 to life in prison.

Coleman is buried at the Evergreen Alameda Cemetery in El Paso.

McClintock, Lynn Reed "Mack"
Born 21 July 1879—Died 3 October 1926

Officer Mack McClintock was killed in a motorcycle accident while pursuing a liquor smuggler. During the chase, McClintock attempted to leap from his motorcycle to the running board of the vehicle he was chasing. The driver of the vehicle intentionally swerved into the motorcycle and caused the two vehicles to collide. The driver of the automobile was later arrested.

McClintock had been with the agency for eighteen years, He was survived by his wife, Eunice, and three daughters. McClintock is buried at the Concordia Cemetery in El Paso.

Houston, Schuyler Colfax
Born 16 July 1878—Died 4 October 1927
Date of Incident: 13 June 1921

On Monday, 13 June 1921, Sergeant Schuyler Houston and two other officers were questioning a pair of suspicious men. When the officers attempted to arrest the duo, a gun battle broke out during which Captain Harry Phoenix was shot in the head and killed instantly. The two suspects fled to Mexico and were never apprehended. Houston suffered the lingering effects of his wounds for many years. He finally died from complications associated with those injuries on Tuesday, 4 October 1927.

Houston was survived by his wife and two children. He is buried at the Concordia Cemetery in El Paso.

Related Case: El Paso Police Department, Harry P. Phoenix

Rivera, Enrique "Yaqui"
Born circa 1895—Died 25 November 1923

Special Officer "Yaqui" Rivera was shot and killed when he attempted to break up a disturbance at a local dance hall.

Rivera was inside the establishment when he heard two gunshots fired outside. When he went downstairs to investigate, he was shot three times. Rivera's body was discovered lying in the street by a police captain sometime later. He was transported to the hospital, where he died later the same evening. Rivera is believed to have been a victim of members of a drug smuggling ring that officers had been working to break up.

The shooter, Arnulfo Valles, was captured several months later. He was tried, convicted and sentenced to death. On 30 July 1925, the death sentence was commuted to life in prison.

Rivera served as the driver of the city's chain gang truck and held a special police commission. He was a World War I veteran and was survived by his wife and young daughter. Rivera is buried at the Evergreen Alameda Cemetery in El Paso.

ERATH COUNTY CONSTABLE'S OFFICE

Purves, Vernon Compton
Born 25 April 1894—Died 16 December 1931

Precinct 1 constable Vernon Purves was accidentally shot and killed inside the Erath County Courthouse at Stephenville. The gunshot wound was to his lower stomach and passed through his body. Although he was reported to have been in poor health, it was believed he dropped his Colt pistol, and it discharged accidentally.

Purves is buried at the West End Cemetery in Stephenville. He was survived by his wife, Alice Thomas. Some sources have his surname spelled as Purvis.

FALLS COUNTY SHERIFF'S OFFICE

Ratliff, Jacob Anderson
Born August 1844—Died 3 June 1906
Date of Incident: 2 June 1906

Mack Bazee, also known as Mat Bazy, entered a saloon in the town of Perry and began to cause a disturbance. When ordered by the owner to stop, Bazee fired a shot at him. Deputy Sheriff Jacob Ratliff heard the gunfire and entered the saloon to investigate. As he stepped inside, Bazee shot him in the right hip and critically wounded him.

Bazee fled the scene but was shot and killed by citizens. Ratliff died from his wounds the following day.

Ratliff was survived by his wife, Marie Elizabeth Schwalbe, and, according to family genealogists, perhaps as many as six children. He is buried in an unmarked grave at the Riesel City Cemetery in McLennan County.

Sharp, Oscar B.
Born circa 1880—Died 4 November 1920

Deputy Sheriff Oscar Sharp was shot and killed at the county jail during an escape attempt.

Sharp had just opened the cell doors to give the inmates their lunch when he was attacked by two prisoners, Jordan Israel and Jose Flores. The inmates managed to gain control of Sharp's gun and used it to shoot him. Although mortally wounded, Sharp was able to prevent the escape by throwing the jail keys out an open window.

Israel and Flores were tried and convicted of the murder. They were both sentenced to death. That sentence was carried out on 21 July 1921, when both were executed by hanging. Pedro Sanches was also convicted and sentenced to death for the murder, but Israel made a confession just minutes before being hanged, indicating that Sanches was not guilty. Sanches's case was on appeal.

The pair was among the last ten criminals to be put to death by hanging in Texas. Execution by means of electrocution began in 1924. Nathan Lee was the last convict to swing from the hangman's rope when he was executed on 31 August 1923. Charles Reynolds was the first to meet his fate by electrocution on 8 February 1924.

Sharp was survived by his wife and four children. He is buried in an unmarked grave at the Chilton Cemetery.

Stuart, Leonard Fleet
Born 5 March 1880—Died 19 June 1933

Deputy Sheriff Leonard Stuart was shot and killed by a man named Roy Mears in retaliation for an incident that occurred twenty-one years earlier. On that occasion, Stuart had shot and killed Mears's half brother while he was attempting to arrest him.

Stuart was patrolling a festival in Durango when Mears approached him. Without speaking a word or warning, Mears opened fire and fatally wounded Stuart. Mears was sentenced to five years in prison but was pardoned by the governor on 21 August 1939.

Stuart had served with the agency for twenty-one years. He was survived by his wife. Stuart is buried at the Union Cemetery.

FANNIN COUNTY SHERIFF'S OFFICE

Fortenberry, George Forest
Born 23 September 1879—Died 16 May 1930

Frankly, some occurrences of lawlessness seem to defy logic and test the bounds of civilized behavior. The needless murder of Deputy Sheriff George Fortenberry was, unquestionably, a case of mala prohibita—wrong because it was against the law. The subsequent killing of Fortenberry's assassin, George Johnson, was a case of mala in se—an act that was wrong in itself. Absolutely no one could have possibly felt proud of him or herself for having been a participant in this gruesome act of mob violence or for having been a witness to the incident and idly standing by while the abomination unfolded.

Deputy Sheriff Fortenberry was shot and killed by a black man named George Johnson. The shooting affray took place at Honey Grove and had grown out of a personal dispute between Fortenberry and Johnson that turned fatal for both men.

Johnson was an employee on Fortenberry's farm. Fortenberry and a companion named Tom Hannard had gone to see Johnson about a debt that was owed to him. A disagreement resulted. Johnson shot Fortenberry three times and then took his gun and fled while threatening Hannard.

Johnson barricaded himself in a cabin that was soon surrounded by lawmen. The officers, estimated by one newspaper to have numbered in excess of three hundred (and by another source to have been just ten), opened fire. The lawmen maintained a steady barrage of gunfire for about four hours until the shooting from within the cabin had ceased. A crowd that had formed near the cabin made a rush for the building. Inside, they discovered Johnson's lifeless body on the floor, pierced by numerous bullets.

An angry mob tied Johnson's corpse to a truck and dragged him back to Honey Grove, a distance of about two miles. After circling the town with the body of Johnson in tow, the vehicle stopped in front of a black church where a mob hung the lifeless and mutilated remains from a tree. Next, the crowd dowsed the remains with gasoline and set the corpse on fire. The frenzied horde, estimated to have grown to two thousand in number by this point in the hideous pageant, was not dispersed until a rainstorm passed over sometime later in the day. Johnson's burned remains were finally handed over to a black undertaker for burial, which occurred at about 8:30 p.m. that evening.

Fortenberry was survived by his wife, Verna Elizabeth McDow, and eight children. He is buried at the Oakwood Cemetery in Honey Grove. Some family genealogists have spelled Fortenberry's middle name Forist.

Moore, Thomas Sidney "Tom"
Born 1 December 1888—Died 3 December 1931

Deputy Sheriff Tom Moore and another deputy were en route to pick up a prisoner at Denison when their patrol car had a flat tire. While Moore was changing the tire, a passing motorist hit him. Moore was transported to a local hospital, where he died four hours later.

Moore had served with the Fannin County Sheriff's Department for five years. He was survived by his wife, Grace Ione Richards, and four children. Moore is buried at the Forest Grove Cemetery in Telephone.

Fisher County Sheriff's Office

Smith, Robert Jefferson
Born 20 May 1896—Died 27 August 1927

Owens, Jake C.
Born 12 January 1889—Died 27 August 1927

Sheriff Robert Smith and Deputy Jake Owens were shot and killed when they attempted to arrest two men for stealing a bale of cotton.

The officers allowed the men, Bill Smith and Lloyd Karensky (Conaster), to go home and change before transporting them to jail. When the suspects exited their home, they had apparently picked up more than just a change of clothing. Bill Smith had picked up a pistol.

The officers placed Smith and Karensky in the patrol car, Karensky in the front seat with Sheriff Smith and Owens in the back with prisoner Bill Smith. The vehicle had traveled only about fifty feet when Bill Smith pulled a pistol and shot Sheriff Smith in the back. The bullet traveled through his body, piercing his heart. Owens leaped from the car to return fire but was hit by several bullets that pierced his heart. Both Bill Smith and Karensky fled the scene in an automobile and were accompanied by their wives. Authorities speculated that they were headed to Oklahoma.

Both murderers were eventually apprehended, tried and convicted of the killings. Bill Smith was sentenced to death but instead was sent to a state mental hospital. He was subsequently declared sane and returned to prison, where he was executed by electrocution on 17 October 1930 at Huntsville, becoming the sixty-third person to meet that fate. Karensky was apprehended and sentenced to life in prison. He was paroled after serving fourteen years.

Smith had served with the agency for eight months. According to newspaper reports of the day, he was survived by his wife, Blanch Ella Cox, and three children (although family genealogists report only one child). Smith is buried at Roby.

Owens was survived by his wife, Emma Green McClendon, and two children. He is also buried at Roby.

FORT BEND COUNTY SHERIFF'S OFFICE

McGee, Robert A.
Born circa 1870—Died 4 July 1901

On Thursday, 4 July 1901, Deputy Sheriff McGee arrived on a train at Duke to attend an outing at Clear Lake. After discovering the picnickers had departed, he went to the general store of Colonel John Fenn at about 7:30 p.m. to inquire about the departure time of the northbound number 8 passenger train. J.T. "Ed" Shields, the store clerk, also ran a small saloon there and was sitting on the windowsill. McGee asked Shields about the train schedule. Shields replied that he did not know the time, as he didn't keep track of the trains. McGee then asked to purchase a glass of beer. Shields informed him that he could not sell him the beer as he had temporarily transferred his liquor license for the picnic. Angered by his reply, McGee said, "What in the hell do you know?" Predictably, the two men became involved in an argument. McGee slapped Shields, knocking him out of the windowsill, and then drew his pistol.

McGee left and walked out to the train tracks in front of the store. An angry Shields retreated to the rear of the store and armed himself with a shotgun, then returned to the doorway and opened fire on McGee. When McGee saw Shields holding the shotgun and standing in the doorway of the store, he fired at him three times with his revolver. Shields emptied the shotgun at McGee, who was struck in the face and chest. He died almost instantly. McGee's body remained where he had fallen, near the railroad tracks, until about 7:30 a.m. the following day, when friends discovered him. He was placed in a coffin and returned to Richmond on the 9:30 a.m. train.

Shields rode out of town on horseback and headed to Houston, where he surrendered to Sheriff Anderson. At about 11:00 a.m. on 5 July 1901, Sheriff Briscoe of Fort Bend County went to Houston, returned with Shields and placed him in the jail at Richmond. The disposition of any charges against Shields is not known.

McGee is buried at the Morton Cemetery in Richmond. He was survived by his wife and one child.

Hardin, Edmond H.
Born 1 April 1880—Died 15 September 1927

Deputy Sheriff Edmond Hardin was escorting two prisoners from the local fairgrounds. He accidentally drove into the path of an airplane that was giving rides at the fair. The aircraft was in the process of taking off at the time. Hardin was killed in the collision. The status of the two prisoners is unknown.

According to reports of the day, Hardin was survived by his wife, Martha Josephine Davis, and ten children. Family genealogists have recorded only seven children. Hardin is buried at the Modessa Cemetery.

Bell, Frank Pleasants
Born 1 January 1874—Died 10 October 1930

Deputy Sheriff Frank Bell was assisting several citizens who had been injured in an automobile accident on the highway. As he stepped from behind a parked car, a passing automobile hit him. The driver of the vehicle was charged with negligent homicide.

Bell had been with the agency for three years. He was survived by his wife and two children. Bell is buried at the Morton Cemetery in Richmond.

On 27 July 1928, Deputies Bell and Tom Davis were wounded while attempting to arrest seven prison escapees who had killed state corrections sergeant Henry Ward. One of the inmates who escaped had killed state corrections guard William Rader on 22 July 1926 in a separate escape attempt.

FORT WORTH POLICE DEPARTMENT

Grimes, Andrew J.
Born circa 1863—Died 12 May 1902

Officer Andrew Grimes was shot and killed by a hack driver named Jeff Van in front of the Texas and Pacific Railroad Station.

Grimes was attempting to get the operator to comply with a city ordinance concerning where taxicabs could be staged at the passenger station. Angry words were exchanged. Van pulled out a .45-caliber handgun and fired at

Grimes, hitting him once in the abdomen. Grimes returned fire, but his shot did not find its mark.

Van was apprehended by other officers. He was tried, convicted and sentenced to death. Van appealed the ruling, arguing that Grimes had provoked the difficulty. He won a new trial. The outcome of that litigation is unknown.

Grimes was survived by his son. He is buried at the Oakwood Cemetery in Fort Worth.

Nichols, John Dee, Jr.
Born 6 August 1863—Died 22 December 1906

Special Officer John Nichols was shot and killed while he was investigating a disturbance at a local theater.

The disagreement involved the price of an admission ticket. While Nichols was speaking with an enraged patron named Barney Wise, Wise pulled out a handgun and hit Nichols on the head. As Nichols fell, Wise began shooting at him. Although mortally wounded, Nichols was able to return fire and kill Wise. Nichols was transported to a local hospital, where he died.

Nichols had been assigned to this patrol area for two years. He was survived by his wife, Kate Brown. Nichols is buried at the Oakwood Cemetery in Fort Worth. He died in a dispute over the price of a thirty-five-cent theater ticket.

Campbell, William Addison
Born 17 September 1878—Died 12 August 1909

Officer William Campbell and another officer were on patrol when Campbell was fatally shot from ambush.

The two lawmen were making a foot patrol in an area notorious for gambling, crime and prostitution. Someone opened fire on them with a shotgun from a balcony behind where they were standing. Campbell was hit in the back of the head and died instantly. The shooter, Stokes Clark, was later apprehended. Clark was also identified as the murderer of Texas Ranger Homer White. White's killing had taken place the previous year.

Campbell had been with the Fort Worth Police Department for just four months. He is buried at the Honey Grove Cemetery in Fort Worth.

Dodd, James Robert "Junior"
Born 13 December 1859—Died 27 January 1912
Date of Incident: 25 January 1912

During the months of January and February 1912, a minor epidemic of *Neisseria meningitidis* hit the city of Fort Worth. Several other Texas cities experienced the same scourge. The city quarantined citizens, refusing to allow train tickets to be sold for travel heading outbound. Police officers, who already worked twelve-hour shifts, were tasked with additional responsibilities, including the enforcement of quarantines and dealing with the sick and dying. In some cases, officers were called on to remove the bodies of the victims.

Officer Dodd was assigned to Police Beat #4, known as "Hell's Half Acre." The beat was located at the center of the outbreak. At about 9:00 p.m. on Thursday, 25 January 1912, Dodd became ill while at dinner. His symptoms included severe nausea. Dodd went home but reported for duty at 9:00 a.m. the following morning. Dodd worked until about 4:00 p.m., when he telephoned the desk sergeant to advise him that he was too sick to continue working.

Dodd's condition deteriorated, and a doctor was called in. The physician diagnosed Dodd's illness as meningitidis and began treating him for the disease. Dodd lapsed into unconsciousness at about 4:00 a.m. He died at 10:00 a.m. on Saturday, 27 January 1912.

Prior to this illness, Dodd had maintained a perfect attendance record for ten continuous years.

Dodd is buried at the Oakwood Cemetery in Fort Worth. He was survived by his wife Elizabeth "Lizzie" Dodd and six children.

Neisseria meningitidis is a bacterium that lives in the noses and throats of 5 to 10 percent of the population but rarely causes serious disease. Serious "invasive" disease occurs when meningitidis spreads through the body via the blood stream after penetrating the mucous membranes of the nose and throat. Viral infections, household crowding and chronic illnesses, as well as active and passive smoking, increase the risk of disease occurring. Those living in crowded environments have a slightly higher chance of getting meningococcal disease than people of the same age who do not.

Ogletree, John Asbury
Born 5 September 1876—Died 15 May 1913

Officer John Ogletree was shot and killed while attempting to arrest a man for firing a gun in public.

Ogletree confronted a man named Thomas "Tommie" Lee, who had discharged his firearm in public. Ogletree ordered Lee to drop the gun. Rather than complying with Ogletree's order, Lee opened fire, hitting Ogletree in the chest. In spite of being mortally wounded, Ogletree was able to return fire. His shots went wild and had no effect. Ogletree made it to the steps of a nearby saloon. He was then taken to the St. Joseph Infirmary, where he died from his injuries.

Lee was eventually arrested. He was never tried for Ogletree's murder but for that of another victim during the same shooting spree. Subsequent to that trial, Lee was convicted of the murder of Ogletree and was executed by hanging on 9 March 1914.

Ogletree was survived by his wife, Lona Ellen Dillon, and two children. He is buried at the Hawkins Cemetery in Arlington.

Hollowell, Robert P. "Bob"
Born circa 1873—Died 26 December 1914
Date of Incident: February 1914

Officer Bob Hollowell died from injuries he received in a motorcycle accident.

Hollowell was responding to a call when the accident occurred. His motorcycle collided with a dog at the intersection of Throckmorton and Third Streets. Hollowell was transported to a local hospital, where he remained. During the months following his accident, Hollowell drifted in and out of a coma. He finally died on 26 December 1914. No information was uncovered concerning the fate of the dog.

Prior to becoming a Fort Worth police officer, Hollowell had served ten years with the Waco Police Department. During that time, he had been shot or stabbed a total of ten times while on duty. The injuries he received during the motorcycle mishap, combined with a lung wound he received during a previous stabbing incident, resulted in his death.

Hollowell had been with the Fort Worth Police Department for just two years. He is buried at the Mount Olivet Cemetery in Fort Worth.

Coffey, George Frank
Born 6 July 1878—Died 26 June 1915

Captain George Coffey was shot and killed when he attempted to arrest a man named Ed Cooper, who had been involved in a fight earlier in the day. One of the man's relatives, Tom Cooper, opened fire on Coffey, hitting him three times. Tom Cooper was tried and acquitted by reasons of self-defense.

Coffey had served with the agency for two years. According to newspaper reports, Coffey was survived by his wife, Mary Fannie Card, and four children. Family genealogists report only three children, however. Coffey is buried at the Mount Olivet Cemetery in Fort Worth.

Howard, Peter
Born 15 March 1871—Died 16 August 1915

Officer Peter Howard was killed by a suspect who refused to be searched. While he was escorting the subject to jail, the man pulled a knife and stabbed Howard.

Howard had been with the agency for twenty-five years. He was survived by his wife, Pleasant Henrietta Boyd, and one child. Howard is buried at the Oakwood Cemetery in Fort Worth.

Conant, George Frances, Jr.
Born 24 November 1871—Died 27 October 1916

Captain George Conant died of pneumonia, which he contracted while on a stakeout searching for a stabbing suspect.

Conant was survived by his wife and two children. He is buried at the Oakwood Cemetery in Fort Worth.

Parsley, Claud Estes "Ed"
Born 12 March 1889—Died 28 September 1917

Yates, James Kidwell
Born 20 May 1867—Died 28 September 1917

On Friday, 28 September 1917, former police officer James Yates shot and killed Police Commissioner Claud Estes Parsley. The killing was the result of a personal disagreement between the two men. Yates had apparently harbored a grudge against Parsley over an incident that had occurred sometime earlier. After Yates shot and killed Parsley, other officers killed Yates.

Yates began his law enforcement career in Lancaster, where he served as "night marshal." In 1901, he shot and killed his first man. The victim, a twenty-three-year-old day laborer named Dick Whitworth, had previously been jailed by Yates for being drunk and disorderly. A few days after the incident, Whitworth was drinking again. He started bragging that he was going to kill Yates, who was alerted to the threat. Yates went looking for Whitworth. Before long, he located him and put four bullets into the unarmed Whitworth.

Yates turned himself in. Whitworth died two days later. Yates was allowed to remain free on a $2,500 bond. Although a grand jury no billed him, Yates apparently felt it was time to move on. He moved to Fort Worth in 1903 or 1904. By 1911, he had joined the Fort Worth Police Department.

On 25 April 1911, he was involved in a disagreement with a black Pullman car porter named J.B. Ballard. The next night, he confronted Ballard inside one of the Pullman cars and shot him three times. Ballard died on the spot. Yates turned himself in, explaining that Ballard had threatened him with a hammer and that he had to shoot him in self-defense.

Yates was taken before the justice of the peace and freed on $2,000 bond. A grand jury did not buy his self-defense plea, however, and he was indicted on 31 May.

Yates is buried in an unmarked grave next to his wife, who passed in 1908, at the Edgewood Cemetery in Lancaster.

Parsley was survived by his wife, Lillie Myrtle Rooker, and three children. He is buried at the Greenwood Memorial Cemetery in Fort Worth.

Daggett, Jeff
Born 31 January 1862—Died 23 October 1917

Special Officer Jeff Daggett was shot and killed by Tarrant County deputy sheriff J. Ben Leggett. Apparently, there had been some sort of disagreement between the two men that escalated to mortal gunplay.

Leggett was charged and convicted of Daggett's killing. The conviction was overturned in 1918.

Daggett is buried at the Old Trinity Cemetery in Tarrant County.

Warren, Sterling Price "Dick"
Born 31 January 1862—Died 7 May 1919

At approximately 6:00 a.m. on Wednesday, 7 May 1919, Officer Dick Warren was struck and killed by a streetcar at the intersection of Boaz and Front Streets. The incident took place during a heavy downpour. Warren had just used the police call box on the corner and was waiting for the streetcar to transport him (either back to the station or to his home for lunch break). When he saw the streetcar drawing near, he ran into the roadway to board. Unfortunately, he did not notice another streetcar approaching from the opposite direction. He was hit and killed instantly.

Warren had served with the Fort Worth Police Department in the past. He had just been reappointed as a regular officer the day preceding the incident. Warren is buried at Mount Olivet Cemetery in Fort Worth.

Gresham, George G.
Born 28 January 1878—Died 9 April 1920

Officer George Gresham was shot and killed out of revenge for an incident that had taken place the preceding night.

The killer had been chased out of the neighborhood by Gresham after he had fired several shots at the man. Gresham was on patrol and spotted the man crouching behind a pole. When he shined his flashlight at the partially concealed man, the suspect opened fire, fatally wounding Gresham.

One man was arrested for the Gresham killing but was never charged. Officially, the case is unsolved.

Gresham was survived by his wife and three daughters. He is buried at the Mount Olivet Cemetery in Fort Worth.

Loper, Joseph Birch
Born 22 June 1874—Died 21 October 1920
Date of Incident: 20 October 1920

At about 8:00 p.m. on Wednesday, 20 October 1920, Officer Joseph Loper was patrolling the Frisco railroad yard just west of the roundhouse when a would-be robber wearing khaki trousers, a cap and a dark coat, thinking Loper was a private citizen, pulled a gun on him. Some sources report the time of the incident as 10:00 p.m. Loper attempted to arrest the gun-wielding man, Thomas Vickers, telling him to "throw up his hands." Vickers replied, "I guess not" and shot Loper twice. Loper was taken to a local hospital, where he died of his wounds the following morning.

Loper's killer was convicted and sentenced to death. That sentence was overturned during a retrial. He eventually served about twenty years before receiving a parole.

Loper had been with the agency for two years. He was survived by his wife, Nettie Mathis, and one son. Loper's place of burial is not known.

Couch, Jeff C.
Born circa 1894—Died 20 December 1920

Officer Jeff Couch was shot and killed by a man named Thomas Vickery. Vickery, a service car driver, was arrested and charged with the murder. He claimed that the incident was the result of a disagreement between him and Couch over some money. Vickery apparently settled the score by shooting Couch five times.

Vickery was apprehended and confined in the jail. Later the same night, a mob of about twenty-five angry citizens forcibly removed him from the jail, lynched him from a tree and then shot him for good measure. Another case of Texas vigilante justice—swiftly administered.

Couch had been with the agency for just two months. He was survived by his wife, daughter and stepdaughter. Couch is buried at the Oakwood Cemetery in Fort Worth.

Bell, John DeWitt "Jack"
Born 24 April 1893—Died 13 August 1921

Officer Jack Bell was killed in a motorcycle accident while responding to a burglary call. The driver of a vehicle was attempting to yield the right of way to another police vehicle when he collided with Bell's motorcycle. The incident took place on Fourth Street. Bell died from his injuries the following day.

Bell is buried in Grapevine.

Gentry, Webster C.
Born February 1898—Died 25 April 1922
Date of Incident: 12 August 1921

Special Officer Webster Gentry drowned while attempting to rescue a family that had become stranded during a period of flooding in the city.

Gentry bravely dove into the floodwaters and succeeded in rescuing three of the family members. Unfortunately, he became entangled in submerged barbed wire when he was in the process of trying to rescue a child. His body was recovered the following day.

Due to the extreme flooding, Gentry had been appointed a special officer earlier in the day. He was issued a gun and a badge and assigned to one of the areas most affected by the flooding.

Gentry was survived by his wife and fifteen-month-old daughter. He is buried at the Greenwood Cemetery in Fort Worth.

Lewis, Lewis J., Jr.
Born 28 January 1897—Died 7 March 1923
Date of Incident: 6 March 1923

Officer Lewis Lewis died from injuries he received in a motorcycle accident.

Lewis's motorcycle collided with the back of a streetcar as passengers were disembarking on Houston Street. He was among a group of Motor Unit officers who were returning to the downtown police station after having worked at the Fat Stock Show. Lewis was transported to a local hospital, where he died the following morning from massive head and chest injuries.

Lewis had only served with the Fort Worth Police Department for two months. He was survived by his wife, Mona Marion Jobe, and infant son. Lewis is buried at the Oakwood Cemetery in Fort Worth.

The Fat Stock Show was formerly known as the National Feeders and Breeders Show. The event has since been renamed and is today called the Southwestern Exposition and Livestock Show.

Brewster, Bertram Fallis
Born 18 April 1898—Died 13 January 1925

Officer Bertram Brewster and his partner were on bicycle patrol. At approximately 1:30 p.m. on Tuesday, 13 January 1925, they stopped at a church located at the intersection of Hemphill and West Berry Streets to take their lunch break. As the two lawmen were eating, they observed a car drive down the street toward a grocery store that they knew had been burglarized several times recently. The officers quickly got up, grabbed their coats and rushed to the store to investigate. As Brewster picked up his coat, he knocked his service revolver out of its holster. The gun hit the ground and discharged accidentally. The bullet hit Brewster in the leg and traveled to the middle of his back. He was taken to All Saint Hospital, where he remained until he died at approximately 7:50 p.m.

Brewster had served with the Fort Worth Police Department for four years. He is buried at Mount Olivet Cemetery in Fort Worth.

Dearing, William R. "Bill"
Born about 1880—Died 21 April 1925

Special Officer Bill Dearing was shot and killed by Fort Worth police officer A.C. Macklin (Maclin).

Macklin had arrested Ethyl Dearing sometime in the evening on 20 April 1925. She was accused of using abusive language. Mrs. Dearing had come to the police station with her daughter, Mrs. Thelma Coffman, to file a complaint against Mr. Dearing. At about 11:00 a.m. on Tuesday, 21 April 1925, Mrs. Dearing and Macklin were standing near the corner of Third and Main when Dearing approached from Third Street about twelve feet away. Dearing flashed a gun and held it on Macklin. Mrs. Dearing positioned herself in front of Macklin in an effort to stop the gunplay. Dearing fired anyway, aiming high over the head of his wife. As he did, Macklin attempted to move Mrs. Dearing behind him to protect her. At the same time, she tried to grab his pistol. Dearing's first shot hit his wife in the head, killing her instantly. The bullet entered through her right jaw and lodged in her skull. She was hit a second time during this exchange, that bullet entering her abdomen.

Macklin returned fire. Dearing was hit five times. One bullet entered through his chin, two in the right side of the chest, one in the left side of his chest and one in the abdomen. According to newspaper reports, Macklin was said to have been seriously injured during the shootout with Dearing, and his wounds were expected to prove fatal.

Dearing was a former regular policeman, deputy sheriff and detective. He is buried at the Greenwood Cemetery in Fort Worth.

Maco, Tomaso Frank
Born 5 April 1883—Died 23 December 1926

Officer Tomaso Maco was killed when he was pushed from a moving car.

Maco was assisting in a traffic detail. He had ordered a man driving a vehicle to stop. The man refused and sped on. Maco jumped on to the running board of the vehicle in an attempt to halt the car. As the driver attempted to speed away, Maco fired a shot at him before being pushed from the vehicle's footboard. Maco was seriously injured in the fall and died from his injuries later the same day.

Maco had immigrated to the United States from Italy at age seventeen and had come to Tarrant County in 1920. He was survived by his wife, Rosa Miles, and two children. Maco is buried at the Greenwood Cemetery in Fort Worth.

Howell, Richard Daniel "Dick"
Born 3 January 1868—Died 30 September 1927
Date of Incident: 11 April 1908

Officer Dick Howell died from the effects of a gunshot wound that he had received on 11 April 1908 while he and North Fort Worth police chief Oscar Montgomery were investigating a shooting.

Howell had been in the city police station speaking with the chief when citizens alerted them to a shooting at Twelfth and Lake Streets. Howell and Montgomery responded.

The two officers attempted to arrest the man responsible for the gunfire, Ike Knight. Knight had just shot and killed his son-in-law, Ed Larmon. That incident took place at Knight's home, where Larmon and his bride of one week were boarders. After the event, the family was not able to offer any explanation as to what had caused the fatal disagreement that resulted in Larmon's death.

After shooting Larmon, Knight ran into the street with his shotgun and tried to hold a crowd that had gathered at bay. Knight then proceeded up the street with the crowd following close behind. When Montgomery, Howell and other officers attempted to arrest him, he opened fire. Montgomery was hit in the leg, abdomen and groin. His wounds were not fatal. Howell was hit in the thigh, causing a serious injury that shattered his femur. According to newspaper reports, more than forty gunshots were fired during the affray.

After the shooting, Knight calmly boarded a streetcar and went to the Panther City Creamery, where he was arrested by Officer Tom Grisso without incident.

Howell's leg wound was serious enough that it required amputation of the limb. During the years following the surgery, Howell suffered several strokes as a result. In spite of his handicap and medical condition, he was appointed night sergeant for North Fort Worth and continued in that position after the city was annexed by Fort Worth in 1910. He eventually died as a result of the injury on 30 September 1927.

Howell had been a law enforcement officer for a total twenty-five years. He had served with the North Fort Worth Police Department, Fort Worth and Denver Railroad Police and Fort Worth Police Department. He was survived by his wife, Mattie Harrison. Howell is buried at Mount Olivet Cemetery in Fort Worth.

Turner, George
Born 18 March 1895—Died 20 May 1928

Officer George Turner was shot and killed while he was attempting to stop a suspect who had tried to run him down with an automobile several days before.

On the night he was shot, Turner, a bicycle officer, was assigned to a patrol car with two other lawmen. He spotted the automobile, and the officers gave chase in the patrol car and overtook the vehicle. As the three policemen approached the car, which was occupied by two men and a woman, Turner was shot at point-blank range with a .45-caliber semiautomatic pistol in the hands of a man named Tenola Moore, one of the two male occupants.

Turner managed to fire once at Moore before he fell to the ground. He died thirty minutes later at a local hospital.

Moore fled on foot. After taking a moment to comfort Turner, the two other officers gave chase, firing at Moore while they pursued him. Unfortunately, Moore got away. Lawmen searched throughout Wise and Denton Counties, armed with shotguns, pistols, machine guns and tear gas grenades. They employed the use of an airplane to aid in the search, but Moore was not found. Eventually, the search extended into Oklahoma, where Moore had a brother. A $500 reward was eventually offered. After months of searching, Moore was apprehended in Chicago and brought back to Texas to stand trial. Moore was finally returned to the Tarrant County Jail on 5 August 1929, nearly one year after the killing. He was sentenced to life in prison but was pardoned after serving only twenty years. On 8 June 1928, charges were filed against Hubert Bratcher for being an accessory in the murder of Turner. Bratcher had apparently been the man who was driving the automobile when the incident took place.

Turner had served with the agency for only seven months. He was survived by his wife and one child. Turner is buried at the Big Spring Cemetery in Garland.

Graham, Joe V.
Born 19 August 1896—Died 10 May 1935
Date of Incident: 29 March 1935

Officer Joe Graham died as a result of an infection that developed when he was bitten by a man he was attempting to arrest.

Graham was on his way home when he was involved in an automobile accident at Twenty-fifth Street and Market Street. He was placing the driver of the automobile under arrest when the man began to resist and bit Graham on the tip of his right middle finger. The injury did not appear serious, and Graham was able to complete the apprehension.

Soon after, Graham's finger began to swell. He was admitted to the hospital on 11 April. After receiving emergency treatment, the finger had to be amputated. Unfortunately, the surgery failed to stop the infection, and Graham was readmitted to the hospital. Attempts to control the spread of the infection were unsuccessful, and Graham died on 10 May 1935.

Graham had served with the Fort Worth Police Department for nine years. He is buried at Mount Olivet Cemetery in Fort Worth.

Driskill, Isaac Green Parker
Born 29 September 1872—Died 11 November 1935
Date of Incident: 1931

Officer Isaac Driskill died as a result of injuries he received in 1931, when he had been struck by an automobile while on duty. The injuries caused him to take a medical retirement from the police department. He was given a pension by the city council. Driskill died on 11 November 1935.

Driskill had served with the Fort Worth Police Department for seventeen years. He was survived by his wife, Victoria Evangeline "Vick" Gray, and seven children. Driskill is buried at Mount Olivet Cemetery in Fort Worth.

Some family genealogists cite 1873, not 1872, as Driskill's birth year. They also cite his cause of death as carcinoma of the prostate, a disease seemingly unrelated to an automobile accident. However, newspaper reports of the day indicate that he never fully recovered from the accident and was unable to work again. Family members believe that the injury hastened his passing.

Courtney, William J.
Born 9 April 1884—Died 24 March 1938
Date of Incident: circa 1931

Officer William Courtney died from injuries he received when he was struck in the chest by a suspect in 1931.

Courtney had responded to a disturbance call at the local courthouse. During a struggle with a suspect, he was hit in the chest and injured seriously. The impairment forced Courtney to take a medical retirement, which he finally did just four months before his death.

Courtney had been with the agency for fifteen years. He was survived by his wife and two children. Courtney is buried at the Rosehill Burial Park in Fort Worth.

Bounds, Thomas Carroll
Born 17 March 1871—Died 8 December 1938

At about 3:45 a.m. on Thursday, 8 December 1938, Officer Thomas Bounds suffered a fatal heart attack while he was attempting to climb out of a deep ravine. Bounds was investigating loose livestock at the time. Bounds was the city's livestock officer and pound keeper and was on patrol when he spotted the animals wandering unattended. He suffered the heart attack while still in the ravine. His body was not located until the following day.

Bounds had served with the agency for seventeen years. He was survived by his wife, Floy Adela Leach. Bounds was also survived by between one and three children, depending on which set of family genealogy records one relies. The family also lists a conflicting birth date of November 1870. Bounds is buried at the Mount Olivet Cemetery in Fort Worth.

FREER POLICE DEPARTMENT

Etter, Edgar Levi "Ed"
Born 27 October 1893—Died 1 August 1936
Date of Incident: 28 July 1936

Deputy City Marshal Ed Etter was shot and killed by a man named Robert L. Grafft.

Grafft, who was formerly a night watchman in Fort Worth, owed a debt to his landlord, who lived in the town of Freer. The landlord brought Etter into the matter, attempting to favorably influence Grafft to pay the outstanding debt or face eviction. Apparently, the plan backfired. An argument developed when Etter attempted to evict Grafft, who by some newspaper reports was intoxicated at the time of the encounter. Grafft hit Etter over the head with his pistol and fractured his skull, then shot him in the abdomen. The incident took place on Tuesday, 28 July 1936.

Etter was flown by ambulance plane to the Nix Hospital in San Antonio on 29 July. He died on 1 August.

Grafft was apprehended in San Antonio on 3 August. He was tried and convicted of the killing of Etter and sentenced to serve five years in prison. That sentence was later reversed.

Etter was survived by his wife, Vera Elizabeth Emery, and eight children. He had also served as a Hidalgo County deputy sheriff before becoming a deputy city marshal at Freer. Etter is buried at the Weslaco Cemetery.

Freestone County Constable's Office

Dunbar, George Washington Bragg
Born 5 February 1870—Died 9 August 1918

Constable George Dunbar was shot and killed by two men he was attempting to arrest for burglarizing a home.

Dunbar and the homeowner chased the suspects, Frank Wallace and Alvin Henry, in their patrol car. When they finally overtook the pair, both Wallace and Henry opened fire with rifles while Dunbar was in the process of exiting his vehicle. Caught by surprise, Dunbar was killed, and the citizen was wounded.

Both Wallace and Henry were arrested and sentenced to death. Newly elected governor William P. Hobby reduced their sentences to life in prison, bowing to public pressure in opposition to the death penalty. Both Wallace and Henry died in prison.

Dunbar was survived by his wife, Lula B. Cornwell. He is buried at the Antioch Cemetery in Fairfield.

Gainesville Police Department

Clements, John Walter
Born 1 January 1888—Died 24 July 1931

Johns, William Edward
Born 19 November 1891—Died 2 August 1931
Date of Incident: 24 July 1931

Fire marshal and special policeman John Walter Clements and Motorcycle Officer William Johns had arrested a man named Frank Bracken a few days earlier. At the time of the apprehension, they confiscated Bracken's shotgun. When Bracken was released, he attempted to have his shotgun returned to him, but Johns refused.

Later the same day, Bracken returned. He had obtained another shotgun from an unknown source. Bracken managed to locate Clements and Johns on East California Street. According to witnesses, Bracken drove up to the curb in his automobile, got out and opened fire on Johns, who was seated on his motorcycle. Both Johns and Clements returned fire. A shotgun blast to the chest killed Clements almost instantly. Another blast from Bracken's shotgun hit Johns in the abdomen, inflicting thirty-nine wounds. The wounds proved fatal. Johns died nearly a week later.

During the exchange, Bracken was wounded by night watchman Charles Tune. Tune fired three times, hitting Bracken once in the hand. A bystander disarmed Bracken, and he was taken into custody.

Bracken was convicted and sentenced to serve ninety-nine years in prison.

Johns was buried at the Valley View Cemetery in Cooke County. He was survived by his wife, Mattie J. Little. Some family genealogists list his middle name as Eugene.

Clements is buried at the Fairview Cemetery in Cooke County. He was survived by his second wife, Alice Harris, and one son. Clements's first wife, Gertrude "Gertie" Hogan, preceded him in death. Clements had been a city policeman but had resigned to become the city fire marshal.

Tune, Charles Benjamin
Born 9 February 1882—Died 23 January 1935

Patrolman Charles Tune was accidentally shot and killed by a fellow officer.

One of Tune's fellow officers was reenacting a story that he had heard about hijackers in front of a group of fellow lawmen. The officer was using his .44-caliber pistol as a prop in the skit. During the course of the reenactment, the gun discharged accidentally. The bullet hit Tune in the chest. His injury proved fatal.

Tune had been with the agency for eight years. He is buried at the Valley View Cemetery in Cooke County. Tune was not married.

GALVESTON, CITY OF

White, James A.
Born (Unknown)—Died 25 December 1920

Night watchman James White was shot and killed by a man named J.C. Sears. According to reports, the incident took place at the aviation depot and developed out of a personal disagreement of some sort between the two men. After shooting White, Sears phoned the police station and informed the officers that he had shot White in self-defense. Apparently, there was a third man who was witness to the shooting, but his identity is unknown.

When officers arrived to investigate, they found three army revolvers lying on a table in the room.

No personal information has been located on White. His place of burial is unknown.

GALVESTON COUNTY CONSTABLE'S OFFICE

Ivanovich, Element Mitchell
Born circa 1888—Died 2 April 1927

Precinct 2 deputy constable Element Ivanovich was struck by a vehicle while directing traffic on the Galveston Causeway Bridge. He was taken to the Galveston Hospital, where he died later the same day.

Ivanovich had served with the agency for six years. He was survived by his wife. Ivanovich is buried at the Lakeview Cemetery in Galveston.

GALVESTON COUNTY SHERIFF'S OFFICE

Meyer, Joseph August
Born 30 May 1874—Died 2 January 1931

Deputy Sheriff Joseph Meyer was shot and killed while working in the county jail.

A man named Sam Rivett entered the jail and asked to see an inmate named Tommy Reis (alias Roy Britton). Reis was released from his cell to meet with Rivett. When Rivett turned to leave, he pulled out a concealed handgun. Jail trustee Claude Pond began to struggle with Rivett. During the fight, the pistol discharged, hitting Meyer in the abdomen. Pond was also wounded during the affray.

Rivett and Reis both escaped. Both were captured, tried and convicted of killing Meyer. Both were sentenced to serve ten years in prison.

Meyer had been with the agency for six years. He was survived by his wife, Dora Jensen, and seven children. Some family genealogists list eight children. Meyer is buried at the Galveston Memorial Park in Hitchcock.

Kirk, Robert Edgar
Born 22 October 1881—Died 27 December 1931
Date of Incident: 24 November 1931

Sheriff Robert Kirk died from injuries he received in an automobile accident one month earlier on 24 November 1931.

Kirk had served with the agency for twenty-three years. He was survived by his wife and two children. Kirk is buried at the Galveston Memorial Park Cemetery in Hitchcock.

Goode, Ernest Earl, Sr.
Born 2 September 1895—Died 12 June 1938

Deputy Sheriff Ernest Goode was shot and killed during an escape attempt that took place at the county jail.

Goode was removing an inmate from his cell when the man suddenly produced a semiautomatic pistol that had somehow been smuggled in to him by a friend. The man ordered Goode to release two other inmates. Goode did so. While Goode was pleading for his life, the inmate callously shot him in the chest. As the group of jailbreakers attempted to flee the building, they were confronted by the chief jailer, whom they beat severely before making good their escape.

All three of the inmates, Roland Tyler, Peter John Calandra and Edward F. Sutton, were eventually apprehended. Two were sentenced to life in prison, and the third was sentenced to serve fifty years.

Goode was survived by his wife, Mamie I. Moody, and three children. He is buried at the Galveston Memorial Park Cemetery in Hitchcock.

GALVESTON POLICE DEPARTMENT

Richards, Frederick L.
Born circa 1856—Died 8 September 1900

Howe, Adolph
Born circa 1854—Died 8 September 1900

Tovrea (Tivera), Samuel Eugene
Born circa 1866—Died 8 September 1900

Wolfe, Charles
Born circa 1852—Died 8 September 1900

Officers Richards, Howe, Wolfe and Tovrea were killed in the hurricane of 1900.

At the end of the nineteenth century, Galveston was known as the "Jewel of Texas." The town retained that distinction until the single deadliest natural disaster in U.S. history wiped away much of what had been a booming future. The buzzing island community had been the hub of the cotton trade and was at the time Texas's largest city. Progress bred complacency, however, which became apparent when city officials and residents decided against building a seawall to protect the town. When the category 4 hurricane, with winds speeds estimated at 135 miles per hour, made landfall in the early morning hours of Saturday, 8 September 1900, buildings crumbled under the force of fifteen-foot-high storm surges. By late afternoon, the entire island was submerged, destroying over 1,500 acres of property. An estimated eight thousand people perished. Although the city was successfully rebuilt, it never regained the prosperity that had earned it a reputation as the "New York of the South."

Richards had served with the agency for ten years. His wife, Louisia, and one son, Edward, also perished in the storm.

Howe's wife, Clara, and five of the couple's nine children also perished in the hurricane.

Tovrea had served with the agency for ten years. His wife, Addie, their four children and his mother-in-law were also killed in the hurricane. Tovrea was survived by his parents and eleven siblings. Family genealogists list only three children, however.

Wolfe had served with the agency for seven years. His wife, Johanna, and one son, Charles Jr., also perished in the storm.

Although the Galveston and Texas History Center at the Rosenberg Library lists the spouses and children of these officers as having been victims, as cited above, newspaper accounts of the day make reference to them as survivors in their articles; thus, some ambiguity remains.

Mayo, Martin
Born March 1859—Died 28 July 1905

Officer Martin Mayo was shot and killed when he responded to a domestic disturbance.

A man and woman were fighting over a jewelry box. When Mayo attempted to break up the fight, he was shot in the back by the man, Eugene Hull. Mayo died en route to the hospital.

Hull was sentenced to serve fifty years in prison for the murder of Mayo.

Mayo had been with the agency for two years. He was survived by his wife, Mary J., and five children. Some family genealogists cite six children from this union.

Burke, John J.
Born circa 1893—Died 11 January 1914

Detective John Burke was shot and killed during a raid on an illegal liquor establishment.

Burke was in the process of kicking in the door when a man inside opened fire, wounding him fatally.

Burke had served with the department for ten years. He was survived by his wife and two children. Burk's place of burial is unknown.

Burrell, Charles
Born circa 1881—Died 30 July 1914
Date of Incident: 23 July 1914

Detective Charles Burrell was in a restaurant at the corner of Twenty-eighth and Church Streets when two men approached him from behind. One of the men shot Burrell in the neck. The bullet traveled upward through his jaw and lodged in his head. Both men were quickly captured, and the weapon was recovered. Burrell was taken to a local hospital, where he was able to identify one of his assailants.

The investigation into the shooting revealed that Burrell, a black man, had been working to wipe out cocaine dealing in the segregated areas of Galveston. He had arrested the two assailants, both white males, several times in the recent past for dealing drugs. Burrell died from his wounds a week later, on 30 July 1914.

Burrell was survived by his wife, Landonia. The location of his burial is unknown.

Lawson, John B.
Born (Unknown)—Died 3 June 1919

On his second day of duty as a Galveston policeman, John Lawson was shot and killed by a disgruntled former officer named Ernest Brent.

Lawson had been hired to replace Brent, who had been fired by the police chief. Upon hearing that Lawson had been hired to replace him, Brent searched for Lawson, located him and then shot him several times.

Brent was convicted of the murder and sentenced to death. The court of appeals reversed the sentence and ordered a new trial. The disposition of that trial is unknown.

Before joining the police force, Brent had been arrested for assault to murder for the shooting of another man in January 1912. He was arrested again in March of the same year for carrying a pistol.

No personal information has been located on Lawson. His place of burial is also unknown.

Reegan, James Gene
Born 8 October 1900—Died 29 June 1927

Officer James Reegan was killed in a motorcycle accident while pursuing several suspects he was attempting to stop for a traffic violation. The men lost control of their automobile and struck a sign, knocking it into the roadway. Reegan was unable to stop his motorcycle in time to avoid hitting the object. He hit the sign and was thrown over the handlebars. Reegan suffered fatal injuries in the mishap.

Reegan had served with the agency for five years. He was survived by his wife and four children. Reegan is buried at Calvary Cemetery in Galveston.

Hawkins, Telephus T. "Tell"
Born 7 April 1859—Died 2 January 1930
Date of Incident: 4 May 1929

At about 9:00 a.m. on Saturday, 4 May, 1929, Patrolman Tell Hawkins was escorting a messenger for the Galveston Dry Dock Company who had just picked up the payroll from the Hutchings Sealy Bank. Two men confronted the messenger at Strand and Twenty-third Streets and attempted to rob him. One of the men yelled, "Stick 'em up!" Hawkins resisted and began to grapple with one of the pair. For his bravery, he was shot twice through the body during the struggle. He remained hospitalized until his death seven months later, on 2 January 1930.

The holdup men managed to escape in a waiting getaway car with the $6,000 they had wrestled away from the wounded messenger.

Hawkins had been with the agency for eleven years. He was survived by his wife, Louisa Cruz, and eight children. Some family genealogists cite ten children. Hawkins is buried at Kyle Cemetery in Hays County.

Hawkins had been a deputy sheriff in Hays County for fifteen years before becoming a special Texas Ranger in 1917 and a regular Texas Ranger in 1919–20.

Lera, Emmanuel
Born 23 August 1903—Died 22 June 1930

Patrolman Emmanuel Lera was killed, and Kenneth Martin of Texas City was seriously injured, when a monoplane piloted by Lera crashed about four miles west of the city near Fort Crockett. Witnesses say that the plane swooped down to within about twenty-five feet of the ground, straightened up for a moment and then plunged headfirst into the damp field. The strength of the impact caused the engine to be buried two feet in the muddy soil. Lera was transported to the hospital and died about an hour after the crash.

Lera was known by friends and acquaintances as the "flying policeman." He never married. Lera was survived by his parents, who had emigrated from Italy about 1889. Lera is buried at Calvary Cemetery in Galveston.

Fredrickson, Albert Bernard
Born 25 March 1904—Died 2 June 1933

Officer Albert Fredrickson was killed in a motorcycle accident at Seawall and Fifteenth Streets. The incident took place while he was responding to a report of an overturned vehicle. His motorcycle collided with a parked trailer.

Fredrickson had been with the agency for six years. He was survived by his wife and one child. Fredrickson is buried at the Old City Cemetery in Galveston.

GARZA COUNTY SHERIFF'S OFFICE

Dalton, Roy C.
Born 16 February 1893—Died 10 March 1925

Deputy Sheriff Roy Dalton, well-known local rancher and land man, was shot and killed about twelve miles north of Post, near Southland, by a man named Will Luman.

The circumstances surrounding his killing are unknown. Will Luman was by no means a stranger to the law, having logged numerous charges for liquor law violations, as well as for being involved in at least two prior murders. He surrendered to the sheriff after the incident.

Bond was granted soon after he was charged, and Luman was released on 10 March 1925. His outstanding bonds totaled $7,500, of which $5,000 was for the murder charge. The remainder was for an assortment of liquor offenses.

Luman had been charged with the 3 March 1916 murder of a man named J.F. Bostick. That incident occurred near Stamford, sixteen miles from Rotan. Bostick was traveling to town with his fifteen-year-old daughter in their wagon when the pair was jumped by two gun-wielding men, Will Luman and Alfred Raspberry. The incident occurred at the Red Creek crossing. Bostick jumped from the vehicle and pulled his gun in self-defense. Luman and Raspberry shot him. Bostick's feisty young daughter picked up her fallen father's gun and chased the assailants away. J.F. Bostick was scheduled to go to trial the following week for the killing of Lee Raspberry. That murder had occurred on 27 November 1915.

On 17 September 1916, Alfred Raspberry was found guilty of the Bostick murder. Raspberry was sentenced to serve twenty-five years in the penitentiary. On 15 December 1917, a jury failed to agree on a verdict on murder charges filed against Luman in the Bostick case. He was released. On 23 May 1919, a district court at Haskell found him guilty of manslaughter in the Bostick case and sentenced him to serve five years in the penitentiary. Luman had also been indicted by a special grand jury at Kent County for the fatal shooting of Judge Cullen C. Higgins in a hotel lobby at Clairemont. Luman and an accomplice named Bob Higdon had committed that murder.

On 27 April 1925, a charge of murder in the Dalton killing was brought against Luman in district court at Lubbock. The outcome of that trial is not known.

Dalton was survived by his wife, Clara V., and two children. He is buried at the City of Lubbock Cemetery in Lubbock.

GILLESPIE COUNTY SHERIFF'S OFFICE

Pape, William O. "Willie"
Born 9 May 1875—Died 6 June 1928
Date of Incident: 22 April 1928

Deputy Sheriff Willie Pape was shot and killed while he and several other officers were stopping cars and looking for illegal alcohol. Pape was shot in the back. He turned to return fire but was too weak from his injury to do so.

Pape suffered for fifty-seven days from the wound caused by the bullet, which had entered his abdomen, fractured two lower ribs and finally lodged in the spinal column, causing partial paralysis. Immediately after Pape's death, Walter Klein, who is suspected of having fired the shot and who was held under $5,000 bond, was charged with assault with intent to murder.

According to family genealogists, Pape's father carried his son's service revolver, always loaded, ready to kill the person whom he believed had murdered his only son. He maintained this ritual until the day he died.

Pape was survived by one son. His wife preceded him in death. Pape is buried at St. Anthony's Catholic Cemetery in Harper.

GONZALES COUNTY CONSTABLE'S OFFICE

Tomlinson, Thomas Jefferson "Jeff"
Born December 1872—Died 17 December 1910

Precinct 3 constable Jeff Tomlinson was investigating a group of drunken revelers who were shooting up the town.

Tomlinson left his home near the creek at about 9:00 p.m. on Saturday, 17 December 1910. He had reached a side street in the business section before the trouble started. According to local newspaper reports, the killing occurred near J.R. Martin's Saddle Shop. Witnesses stated that they heard two shots, followed by five more. When J.H. Martin investigated the shooting, he found the body of Tomlinson. He had been shot twice, just below the heart.

Sheriff Johnson was called to the site of Tomlinson's murder. Eugene Bowers, a young barber from Waelder, was arrested and charged with the murder. Bowers was transported to the county jail.

According to state election records, Tomlinson had been elected on 3 November 1896. He took office on 1 January 1897 and served in that capacity until his death on 7 December 1910.

Tomlinson was survived by his wife, Maggie Glover, and six children. His place of burial is uncertain, but his wife is buried at the Waelder City Cemetery. Local newspapers reported that Tomlinson had shot two men, killing Junis Fisher on 23 April 1903.

Brown, William Collins "Carl"
Born 22 February 1863—Died 18 August 1912

Precinct 7 constable Carl Brown was stabbed to death by a prisoner whom he and a sheriff's deputy were walking to jail in Harwood. As the three men paused for a moment, the prisoner, George Brown, suddenly pulled out a large knife and stabbed Carl Brown in the side. The knife wound caused severe damage to his right lung. George Brown also cut the deputy on the wrist.

Because of the large crowd standing nearby, neither officer drew his weapon. Constable Brown, with assistance from bystanders, was able to subdue George Brown and place him in jail.

Carl Brown had served Precinct 7 for fourteen years. He was survived by his wife, Fannie Redding, and eight children. Brown is buried at the Masonic Cemetery in Gonzales County.

GONZALES COUNTY SHERIFF'S OFFICE

Jones, William Earl
Born 25 April 1841—Died 1 March 1900

William Jones, the former sheriff of Gonzales County, owned a ranch about eight miles north of Medina in Bandera County. At about noon on Thursday, 1 March 1900, he was shot and killed near Medina by his neighbor, Captain A. Robinson. Robinson turned himself in to Deputy Sheriff Lee Humphries.

Robinson was a captain in the Third Regiment of the Texas Volunteers during the Spanish-American War. Jones was also referred to as "Captain" due to his service in the army of the Confederate states. Newspaper accounts of the day gave no particulars with regard to the cause of the shooting, except that the two men had an altercation of some sort.

Jones was first appointed sheriff on 10 November 1871. He served until 8 November 1872. Jones was elected on 4 November 1884 and again on 2 November 1886 and 6 November 1888. He served until 4 November 1890. After a brief gap in service, Jones was elected again on 6 November 1894 and served until 3 November 1896. He was reportedly a U.S. marshal for a period of time, as well.

Jones was survived by his wife, Emma Memefee, and two children. He is buried at the Odd Fellows Cemetery in Gonzales.

Schnabel, Henry J.
Born 26 February 1862—Died 14 June 1901

Glover Jr., Richard Martin "Dick"
Born 27 May 1862—Died 14 June 1901

Sheriff Dick Glover and posseman Henry Schnabel were shot and killed when they attempted to arrest a man named Gregorio Cortez for the murder of Karnes County sheriff W.T. Morris.

Morris had been killed two days earlier. Cortez was waiting in ambush for Glover and Schnabel. As the two lawmen approached, he opened fire. Both Glover and Schnabel were killed.

Cortez was arrested, convicted of the killing and subsequently sentenced to prison. He was later pardoned by the governor.

Glover was serving his second term as sheriff when he was killed. He had been with the agency for at least seven years. Glover was survived by his wife,

Margaret Alice "Maggie" Collie, and six children. He is buried at the Smiley Cemetery in Gonzales.

Schnabel was survived by his wife and several children. He is buried at the Belmont Cemetery in Gonzales County.

Although most historians have followed the party line on this case and noted Glover's given name as Robert, more recent research appears to establish conclusively that his name was actually Richard Martin Glover Jr., son of Richard Martin Glover and Delilah "Della" Bundick, who met and wed at Gonzales on 17 July 1861.

Related Case: Karnes County Sheriff's Office, William T. "Brack" Morris

Strickling, Arthur R.
Born 19 September 1884—Died 2 January 1930

Deputy Sheriff Arthur Strickling was shot and killed in a personal disagreement with Gonzales Police Department night watchman John Samuel Tate.

The incident took place in an alley behind a bank at Gonzales, late in the evening of Thursday, 2 January 1930. Strickling, who was reported to have been under the influence of alcohol at the time, approached his longtime friend Tate with his gun drawn and yelled, "Stick 'em up, damn you!" Strickling then opened fire, hitting Tate with five bullets. Tate fell to the ground and returned fire, hitting Strickling three times. Investigators believed that one of the gunshots wounds in Strickling's body may have been fired from a smaller-caliber pistol; thus, they began a search for a possible third shooter. The outcome of that search is unknown.

Strickling is buried at the IOOF Cemetery in Gonzales. He was married.

Related Case: Gonzales Police Department, John Samuel Tate

Gonzales Police Department

Tate, John Samuel "Sam"
Born 31 January 1855—Died 2 January 1930

As previously cited, night watchman Sam Tate was shot and killed in a personal disagreement with Gonzales County deputy sheriff Arthur Strickling. Both men were killed during this incident.

Tate is buried at the Masonic Cemetery in Gonzales. He was survived by his wife, Adelaide "Addie" W. Wilson, and four children.

Related Case: Gonzales County Sheriff's Department, Arthur Strickling

GRANGER POLICE DEPARTMENT

Lindsey, Henry Jackson
Born 3 March 1889—Died 15 February 1934

City Marshal Henry Lindsey and Williamson County Precinct 2 constable Sam Moore were shot and killed while placing a prisoner in a jail cell.

The prisoner, Lewis Cernock, had been arrested by Moore for failing to pay a fine for disturbing the peace and use of abusive language to a woman. His fines totaled $28.50. Moore had apparently failed to search Cernock thoroughly. As Lindsey and Moore were placing Cernock in the jail cell, he produced a .38-caliber semiautomatic pistol that he had apparently concealed on his person and fatally shot both lawmen. Lindsey was shot through the heart and died almost instantly. Moore was rushed to the hospital, suffering from wounds to the head, neck, chest and arms. He died soon after the incident. Witnesses claimed that Cernock calmly stood in the middle of the room, reloaded his pistol, lit his pipe and walked to town.

Cernock was later apprehended by a hastily assembled posse. When he was captured, one of the possemen, H.L. "Jack" Taylor, said, "You shouldn't have done this." Cernock replied, "They double-crossed me, and they are not going to put me in jail for not having [the] money to pay the fine." Maxie Goff, a member of the posse, hit Cernock over the head with an iron weight and disarmed him. He was taken to the county jail by Sheriff Louis Lowe.

Cernock was arrested and charged with double murder, as well as for shooting at Justice John W. Nunn and assistant county attorney B. Colbert. He was tried and convicted of killing Lindsey and Moore. He was sentenced to death. That sentence was carried out on Friday, 12 July 1935, when Cernock was executed by electrocution at Huntsville. Cernock was the 118th criminal to be electrocuted in Texas.

Lindsey also served as a constable and deputy sheriff in Williamson County. He is buried at the Granger City Cemetery.

Related Case: Williamson County Constable's Office, Sam Moore

GRAY COUNTY CONSTABLE'S OFFICE

Hendrix, Otis Howard
Born 18 January 1895—Died 30 January 1939

Precinct 2 constable Otis Hendrix, the county sheriff and several deputies were conducting inspections at several local bars. As the lawmen entered one of the establishments, they were confronted by the owner, J.D. White. White told the sheriff to leave. As the sheriff tried to speak with him, White pulled a gun from under his coat and began shooting. White missed the sheriff, but one of the bullets hit Hendrix. The wound was fatal. The other deputies returned fire, killing White.

Hendrix was survived by his wife and five children. He is buried at the Fairview Cemetery in Pampa.

GRAYSON COUNTY CONSTABLE'S OFFICE

Mounger, Thomas Frederick
Born circa 1872—Died 27 September 1911

Precinct 1 constable Thomas Mounger was shot and killed while he was responding to a report of a man trespassing in a boxcar.

When Mounger approached the man, Sellers Vines, the man drew a .45-caliber pistol and shot Mounger. The wound was fatal.

Vines was later arrested. He was tried and convicted of killing Mounger and sentenced to death. That sentence was carried out on Friday, 9 August 1912, when Vines was executed by hanging at Sherman.

Mounger was survived by his wife, Julia Rivers. Newspaper reports indicate that Mounger was survived by four children. Family genealogists seem to indicate only two children. Mounger is buried at the West Hill Cemetery.

GRAYSON COUNTY SHERIFF'S OFFICE

Burgess, Lee D.
Born circa 1870—Died 21 December 1906

At approximately 4:00 p.m. on Friday, 21 December 1906, Deputy Sheriff Lee Burgess arrested an intoxicated man named Percy Yeager. Burgess was taking Yeager to jail in Denison. On the way to the lockup, the men walked past Yeager's house. When they did so, Yeager attempted to break free from Burgess and make a run for his home. Burgess struggled with Yeager to prevent him from escaping custody, eventually knocking him to the ground with his nightstick. When Burgess leaned over to pick Yeager up, he fell over and died, apparently from a heart attack. An investigation was conducted to determine the cause of death. Doctors concluded that Burgess's death was the result of chronic heart problems. No death certificate was filled out.

Yeager was not prosecuted for the death of Burgess. Three years later, Yeager was charged with robbery. The case was dismissed several weeks after it was filed.

Burgess was survived by his wife and one daughter. He is buried at the Fairview Cemetery in Denison.

Gunter, Howard
Born 10 June 1883—Died 25 April 1934
Date of Incident: 24 April 1934

Special Deputy Sheriff Howard Gunter was killed in an automobile accident while driving a prisoner's car to the county jail.

Gunter and his partner had just arrested two escaped bank robbers. The partner was transporting the two suspects to the jail in the patrol car while Gunter followed in the holdup men's vehicle. The deputy driving the police vehicle applied the brakes suddenly, causing Gunter to crash into the rear end of the vehicle. The collision resulted in serious injuries. Gunter died the following day.

Gunter had been with the agency for six years. He was survived by his wife, Bessie Judd, and six children. Some family genealogists list as many as seven children. Gunter is buried at the Van Alstyne Cemetery in Grayson County.

GREENVILLE POLICE DEPARTMENT

Southall, John L.
Born 11 June 1869—Died 6 October 1912

Assistant Chief John L. Southall and Hunt County special deputy sheriff Richard Shipp were shot and killed while attempting to arrest an intoxicated man who was firing a pistol.

Sometime between 5:00 and 5:30 p.m. on Sunday, 6 October 1912, officers received a call concerning an intoxicated man on South Stone Street. Shipp and Southall, as well as Deputies Roy Harrington and George Duncan, quickly mounted up and responded. When the lawmen reached a point along the street about a block or two north of the Mineola branch of the MK&T Railroad, they overtook Sant Slimmons and John Cooper, both of Lone Oak, who were riding in a buggy. Slimmons immediately opened fire on the officers, hitting Southall in the forehead and the bowels and breaking one of his legs. He died instantly and fell in the backyard of W.M. McBride, whose house the men were in front of when the incident began.

The unarmed Shipp was the next to fall, shot through the heart. He fell in the yard of Erv Harrison, just a few feet from where Southall was lying dead. Harrington and Duncan returned fire, hitting Slimmons five times. He was taken to a hospital and died an hour and a quarter later. Cooper was arrested and taken to jail. His role in the shooting affray is unclear.

Southall was survived by his wife, Lillie Mae Coon, and three children. He is buried at the East Mount Cemetery in Greenville.

Related Case: Hunt County Sheriff's Office, Richard Emmett Shipp

GREGG COUNTY CONSTABLE'S OFFICE

Fambrough, G.A. "Andy"
Born 5 December 1877—Died 14 August 1914

Precinct 4 special deputy constable Andy Fambrough was assisting Constable Dave Whittington in arresting a man named John Daniels. Daniels was at his home in Elderville. As the two officers stepped on to Daniels's porch, he opened fire with a shotgun, killing Fambrough and wounding Whittington. In spite of being seriously wounded, Whittington was able to return fire and kill Daniels.

Fambrough is buried at the Peatown Cemetery. No personal information has been located.

Gregg County Sheriff's Office

Watson, H. Eugene
Born 8 March 1892—Died 3 July 1915

At about 4:30 p.m. on Saturday, 3 July 1915, Deputy Sheriff H.E. Watson was shot and killed while he was entering the office of county attorney F.A. Taylor at Longview. Taylor used a shotgun to commit the crime. He fired twice at Watson. Both blasts found their mark.

Taylor was arrested and released on bond. The nature of the dispute and the final disposition of the charges against Taylor are unknown.

Watson was to have been married to Miss Audra House of Ennis the following day. He is buried at the Clear Lake Cemetery in Collin County.

Killingsworth, James William "Buddy"
Born 28 September 1907—Died 29 December 1939
Date of Incident: 28 December 1939

Deputy "Buddy" Killingsworth and other officers were attempting to arrest a twenty-year-old man named J.R. "Buster" Mitchell, who was wanted for committing several robberies in Titus and Upshur Counties. Mitchell was also wanted for the 17 December kidnapping and robbery of J.B. Buford of Tyler.

When officers arrived at the Mitchell residence in Longview, Killingsworth entered the home and located "Buster" Mitchell, who was hiding beneath a bed that was at the time occupied by his mother. When Killingsworth ordered Mitchell to come out, he opened fire with a handgun, hitting Killingsworth in the arm and body. His wounds turned out to be fatal, and Killingsworth died the following day. State Patrolman E.C. Campbell, who was next to enter the residence, shot and killed Mitchell.

Newspaper reports indicate that Killingsworth was survived by his wife, Margaret Elizabeth Culver, and three children. Family genealogists only identify one child, however. He is buried at the Grace Hill Cemetery.

GRIMES COUNTY CONSTABLE'S OFFICE

Jones, Robert Harris
Born 4 January 1853—Died 28 January 1901

Constable Robert Jones was shot and killed under the most unfortunate of circumstances. His death occurred in connection with an incident of family violence that, for him, turned fatal.

At about 6:30 a.m. on Monday, 28 January 1901, Jones was shot and instantly killed by his son Robert. Constable Jones is said to have been beating his wife, Missouri Arsmus, unmercifully, using a large black snake whip. His son Robert Jones intervened. Newspaper reports claim that Constable Jones had been maligning his wife for quite some time that morning. Robert and a younger brother had attempted to interrupt their father's abuse, but each time they did so, they were struck several times by their father with the whip. At a point when the beatings were so severe that young Robert feared for his mother's life, he attempted to intervene but was hit on the forehead with the whip.

Undaunted, Robert stepped into an adjoining room, picked up a shotgun loaded with duck shot and opened fire at his father, hitting him in the head. Constable Jones died instantly in a gruesome scene. The force of the gunshot tore open his skull and scattered the contents on the floor.

According to reports, Robert, who was nineteen, was a quiet and unassuming young man. After the killing, he immediately surrendered himself to authorities.

Constable Jones is said to have been a large man who was a tyrannical ruler in his home. He had been involved in similar events of violence on quite a number of occasions over the years. Missouri Jones was a small, weakly woman. Due to her poor health, she was unable to perform the household duties. After suffering this forbidding thrashing at the hands of her spouse, her condition was reported to be serious, with one or two broken ribs and an array of severe bruises on her face and body as proof of the maltreatment.

Jones had been constable for eight years. He was survived by his wife, Missouri Arsmus, and eight children. He is buried at the Courtney Cemetery.

GUADALUPE COUNTY SHERIFF'S OFFICE

Porter, John Starling
Born February 1877—Died 3 or 4 November 1906
Date of Incident: 2 September 1906

Deputy Sheriff John S. Porter had gone to a Mexican dance near Redwood to keep the peace. Redwood is in the northern part of Guadalupe County, located about seven miles from San Marcos. Porter was attacked by two brothers named Torres. One of the men shot Porter in the abdomen, inflicting a reportedly fatal wound. In spite of the fact that his pistol only contained two cartridges, Porter returned fire, killing one of his attackers outright with his first shot and wounding the second. There has been no independent verification that Porter died from the wound.

Porter was not married. His place of burial is unknown.

HAMILTON COUNTY SHERIFF'S OFFICE

Knowles, Henry Clay
Born 20 June 1861—Died 28 July 1911

Deputy Sheriff Henry Knowles was killed when his automobile collided with a railroad train. His injuries were fatal. Knowles had just driven his wife to the train station in town and was returning home when the incident occurred.

Knowles was survived by his wife, Texana C. Teague, and seven children. He is buried at the Hurst Ranch Cemetery in Hamilton County.

Gibson, Audie Lee
Born 20 August 1891—Died 16 December 1932

At about 1:00 a.m. on Friday, 16 December 1932, G.L. Griffin was awakened when a burglar alarm sounded at his drugstore in Carlton. Griffin telephoned Deputy Sheriff Audie Gibson, who lived four blocks from the store. Not long after, Griffin and the sheriff discovered Gibson's body lying near the railroad station. Apparently, Gibson had been shot by one of the three burglars while they were fleeing the scene. He had been killed instantly.

The suspects, F.C. Blakely, Jack Foreman and a man named Watson, were arrested shortly thereafter and lodged in the county jail. Blakely and Foreman pleaded guilty to murder and were sentenced to life in prison. Watson, who was the driver of the car, was not charged with murder.

Gibson was survived by his wife, Clora Laura DeVolin, and one child. He is buried at the Carlton Cemetery in Hamilton County. Gibson had been a peace officer for about five years.

HANSFORD COUNTY SHERIFF'S OFFICE

Martin, Robert Eli "Bob"
Born 11 March 1868—Died 26 January 1911

Sheriff Robert Martin accompanied a U.S. deputy marshal to the ranch of a local man named Phil J. Fifer. Fifer had been instructed by the court to move all of his belongings off the property. When the lawmen came on the premises, Martin called out to Fifer. Fifer ran into the barn. Martin gave chase. When Martin entered the barn, Fifer shot and killed him.

Fifer was arrested, tried and convicted of murder. He was sentenced to life in prison but managed to escape after serving only five years. Fifer returned to his home, where he was later shot and killed by lawmen.

Martin was survived by his wife, Sophira Snowden, and eleven children. He is buried at the Hansford Cemetery in Spearman.

Martin's son, Clarence Martin, later became the police chief of the Las Animas, Colorado Police Department. On 20 April 1947, Chief Clarence Martin was killed when he was punched in the chest while trying to break up a fight at a local bar.

HARDIN COUNTY CONSTABLE'S OFFICE

Harris, Johnnie
Born circa 1881—Died 24 December 1905
Date of Incident: 22 December 1905

On Friday, 22 December 1905, twenty-four-year-old Deputy Constable Johnnie Harris went to a sawmill plant at Dearborn that was owned by the McShane Lumber Company, two and a half miles from Saratoga. He made the trip to collect fines due by some of the men in that area. While at the mill, he observed some men firing their guns and causing a disturbance. Harris disarmed two of the men and then turned them loose.

At about 10:45 a.m. Harris was standing near a saloon talking with several men. Suddenly, someone fired a shotgun. The blast came from outside the building and from the direction of a gate. Some of the pellets of buckshot struck Harris in the back. The remainder of the load traveled past Harris and lodged in the groin of an unidentified man standing near him. That man died in about two hours.

Harris was taken to the hospital in Beaumont, Jefferson County, where he underwent surgery. The physician indicated that there was little chance of Harris recovering from his wounds. At 4:00 a.m. on Sunday, 24 December 1905, Harris died. Before he expired, Harris told police that he suspected one of the men he had disarmed and released earlier was the shooter. A search was conducted, but no one was ever captured.

Harris is thought to have been William J. Harris from Travis County. However, sufficient data to verify that claim has not been located. Harris was unmarried. He is reported to have been buried in Saratoga; however, his place of burial has not been located.

Whitsitt, L.
Born (Unknown)—Died 18 December 1906

Constable L. Whitsitt was shot and killed by a man named John Anthony during a duel that took place in the streets of Saratoga on the evening of Tuesday, 18 December 1906. Whitsitt managed to hit Anthony with one shot, striking him in the abdomen.

Anthony, a local sawmill operator, is said to have refused medical treatment.

No further information is available about this incident. No burial location has been located for Whitsitt, nor has any personal information been found.

HARRIS COUNTY COMMUNITY SUPERVISION AND CORRECTIONS DEPARTMENT

McReynolds, David
Born 9 April 1868—Died 28 October 1928
Date of Incident: 26 October 1928

A witness observed three men in a coupe-style automobile pass him. One passenger in the vehicle fired a pistol into the air six or seven times. The car turned into an alley. Shortly afterward, Assistant Probation Officer David McReynolds came running up to the witness and inquired about the gunfire. The citizen directed him to the alley where he had last observed the automobile. About three minutes later, a man was seen hastily running out of the alley. He was soon followed by two other men, one of whom had a pistol in his hand.

Witnesses later found McReynolds shot through the body, lying facedown behind the coupe automobile in front of a house. McReynolds was transported to the hospital, where he died on Sunday, 28 October 1928.

Pablo Jazo and Enrique Magana were arrested in La Grange on Friday, 26 October 1928. Magana was in possession of a .45-caliber pistol and 136 rounds of ammunition. Both men were charged with the murder of McReynolds. Jazo and Magana claimed that McReynolds had entered the house and immediately opened fire on Magana. Magana then shot and killed McReynolds in what he asserted was self-defense. Witnesses claimed that McReynolds's pistol was in its holster when they discovered his body. A number of witnesses examined McReynolds's gun and testified, without contradiction, that it showed no evidence of having been fired recently. They also testified that the front door of the house was locked.

Both Pablo Jazo and Enrique Magana were convicted of the murder. Jazo received a fifteen-year sentence, and Magana received a ten-year sentence.

McReynolds was survived by his wife, Emma, and four children. He is buried in Granite City, Illinois.

HARRIS COUNTY CONSTABLE'S OFFICE

Reed, James S.
Born circa 1877—Died 6 September 1905
Date of Incident: 2 September 1905

Deputy Constable James Reed was shot in the abdomen as he was attempting to serve an arrest warrant on a man identified as Tenard Calhoun, alias Charles Johnson. Calhoun was wanted for highway robbery. Reed located him at the Chaneyville Community west of Houston. Reed managed to shoot Calhoun in the side with a .38-caliber revolver during the struggle. The bullet severed Calhoun's spinal cord. Reed died from his injuries four days later, on 6 September. Calhoun died on 13 September.

Reed had been with the agency for four months. He was survived by his wife and two small children. Reed is buried at the German Cemetery in Houston. Some sources list Reed's middle initial as "S."

Isgitt, Edgar Eugene
Born 6 February 1874—Died 15 June 1911
Date of Incident: 14 June 1911

At about 9:00 p.m. on Wednesday, 14 June 1911, Constable Edgar Isgitt was shot and killed when he attempted to arrest a man named Matthew Young for whipping his wife. Isgitt died from his wound the following day. Young was arrested, but the disposition of the charges is unknown.

Isgitt was the elected constable of the Harrisburg Precinct. He was survived by his wife and four children. Isgitt is buried at the Glendale Cemetery in Harris County.

Singleton, James N.
Born 8 March 1883—Died 8 June 1912
Date of Incident: 6 June 1912

Constable James Singleton was involved in a motorcycle accident while chasing a speeding automobile. He suffered severe internal injuries, as well as a broken arm and a mangled leg that was so severe the limb had to be amputated. Singleton died two days later.

Singleton is buried at the Sterling White Chapel and Cemetery in Harris County. He never married.

Grayson, James L.
Born 29 November 1888—Died 12 April 1915

Precinct 1 deputy constable James Grayson was shot and killed when he and another officer responded to a complaint call involving loud music at a local park. When the officers arrived at the recreational area, the suspect began physically assaulting Grayson and then shot him in the chest.

Grayson had been with the agency for eight years. He was survived by his wife and one child. Grayson is buried at the Holy Cross Cemetery in Harris County.

Harless, William Clinton
Born 24 October 1890—Died 15 April 1915
Date of Incident: 14 April 1915

Precinct 7 deputy constable William Harless died of a gunshot wound he received while attempting to serve a burglary arrest warrant.

The incident took place at about 5:00 p.m. on Wednesday, 14 April 1915, in Spring. The suspect, Louis Utley, fired a shot from a Winchester rifle through the front window of the house, hitting Harless in the neck. Harless died the following day.

Utley was arrested, tried, convicted and sentenced to death. That sentence was carried out on 1 February 1916, when he was executed by hanging at Huntsville.

Harless had been with the agency for two years. He held a dual role as a deputy sheriff for the Harris County Sheriff's Office. Harless is buried in Spring.

Hicks, W. Emory
Born April 1896—Died 14 September 1923

Deputy Constable Emory Hicks of the Harrisburg precinct was mistakenly shot and killed by a federal Prohibition agent named Kelly Hines.

Hicks and Thomas (Jimmy) Veal had been contacted by a messenger at about 7:00 p.m. on Friday, 14 September 1923, alerting them that a citizen had reported seeing men transferring a load of liquor from a broken-down automobile by the Sims Bayou Bridge on the Galveston Road near Houston.

As it turned out afterward, the men were federal agents, not bootleggers. When Hicks and Veal arrived at the scene, they observed two men transferring cases of liquor to two other men in another automobile. The two federal agents thought the two constables were the bootleggers. Before the two groups of lawmen were able to make their respective identities known, a shootout took place.

Veal fired a shot into the ground. A second shot was fired by Veal or Hicks, knocking the gun out of the hand of Frank C. Hines, brother of federal agent Keller Hines, who was also on the scene. Kelly Hines grabbed a Winchester rifle from his vehicle, and both Hines brothers dropped to the ground and returned fire. The other two men, S. Lockhart and G.C. Harris, ducked to avoid being hit. When the smoke cleared, Hicks had been fatally shot through the body, and Veal was hit in both ankles. Hicks died at the hospital the same day. Before lapsing into a coma, Hicks said, "They cold-blooded me. I don't want a doctor, I want an undertaker." Hicks was taken to St. Joseph Hospital, where he died later the same day.

Seventeen cases of whiskey were found at the scene. Hines's friends told officers that they had received a tip that a car was coming from Galveston with liquor and had told him about it. Hines, with the assistance of his brother, had gone to lay in wait for the car. Harris told officers that the first shots fired had come from Hicks's automobile.

A few days later, Agent Hines surrendered to authorities to face charges for the murder of Hicks. On 11 November, his trial was set. The outcome of those charges is unknown, but by 9 May 1924, Hines was back on the job, making a sizeable haul on 179 gallons of whiskey in his search for moonshiners in Jasper and Newton Counties.

A week after Hicks's death, on 20 September, indictments were entered in a Harris County grand jury charging Hicks and Veal with the assault of a prisoner named Ramsey Sam. A second indictment was filed charging the pair, along with John Phillips and O.A. Smith, with the assault of a man named Sam Bowden. Hicks's brother, B.C. Hicks, was also charged by the same grand jury with the illegal manufacture of alcohol.

Hicks is buried at the Hollywood Cemetery in Harris County. He was not married.

Weaver, John Monroe
Born 6 January 1889—Died 19 June 1929

Precinct 8 constable John Weaver was shot and killed when he and two other lawmen conducted a raid on a black dance hall on Yale Street seven miles west of Houston that was being used as an illegal bootleg establishment. As officers approached the building, approximately thirty people poured out, fleeing in every direction. During the mêlée, the constables were only able to apprehend the building owner's daughter. She led the officers to her uncle and directly into an ambush. Weaver was shot twice, once in the elbow and once in the stomach, with a .30-30-caliber rifle. He was rushed to the hospital but died less than half an hour later from the effects of his wounds.

The shooter escaped. A black man named Jack Martin was found dead on 21 June just a few miles from Houston, having committed suicide by cutting his own throat with a razor.

Weaver was the elected constable of Precinct 8 and had held that post for five months. He was survived by his wife, Maggie, and one son. Weaver is buried at the Forest Park Cemetery in Houston.

Winter, Marvin Alton
Born 30 October 1878—Died 4 December 1937
Date of Incident: 3 December 1937

Precinct 4 constable Marvin Winter was killed while he was directing traffic at the scene of a truck accident in North Harris County. Winter was accidentally hit by two different automobiles. He died from his injuries early the following morning.

Winter was survived by his wife, Willie D. Hastings, and two children. He is buried at the Rosewood Park Cemetery in Houston.

HARRIS COUNTY CONVICT CAMP

Taylor, William Isham
Born 6 February 1881—Died 18 February 1914

Bailey, Leroy "Roy"
Born circa 1891—Died 18 February 1914

Many Texas counties maintained convict camps and poor farms that were under the control of a county administrator. These operations housed prisoners who had been convicted of misdemeanor crimes. The facilities were generally not under the control of the sheriff. The convict guards were armed correctional officers.

At about 8:00 a.m. on Wednesday, 18 February 1914, four convict guards were in charge of a group of prisoners at the Harris County Convict Camp Number 2, which was located alongside the Houston Ship Channel. Several prisoners made an escape attempt by running toward the waterway. All except Sam Jones and Joe Brown stopped and surrendered when ordered by guards to do so.

Guards released their dogs to pursue the fleeing prisoners Jones and Brown. Brown managed to get away when, to his good fortune, the canines elected to pursue Jones instead of him. Jones attempted to escape into the ship channel. Bailey ran after him into the water, which was about three feet deep where Jones was standing. He began to shoot at the prisoner when Taylor said, "Don't do that. We can get him without having to shoot him." Bailey put his pistol in his belt and attempted to capture Jones. He eventually overtook Jones, at which point the two men began to struggle. The pair accidentally stepped off into a deep hole in the channel bottom and went under water. Bailey shouted for help. Taylor came to his rescue. Bailey allegedly grabbed Taylor, and both men drowned.

Jones swam to the distant shore with the dogs still in pursuit and managed to escape.

The bodies of Bailey and Taylor were recovered by sheriff's deputies and city police divers. County Commissioner W.H. Lloyd, who was in charge of the convict camp, said the two guards "died like heroes and showed their loyalty by not using their guns."

Jones was arrested at about 3:45 p.m. the same day. He was found hiding at his brother's house. Jones had been convicted on a charge of assault and fined $1.00 plus court costs, totaling $25.20. Being unable to pay his fine and costs, he was sentenced to county jail and sent on to the county convict camp. At the time of the incident, his bond had been made, but the paperwork had not yet reached the camp.

Newspaper reports indicated that the Harris County grand jury was investigating the deaths of the two county guards. The disposition of the case against Jones and Brown is unknown.

Controversy exists concerning Taylor's date of birth, as well as the location of his interment. According to cemetery records, he is buried at Prairie Lea in Washington County and was born on 6 February 1881. However, according to his death certificate, William Isham Taylor was born on 10 January 1882 and was thirty-two years of age and single. That file claims he was buried at Lyons, Burleson County. Inaccuracies of this nature are commonplace when examining period records. Unfortunately, this one is yet to be reconciled. In any case, Taylor was survived by his parents.

Leroy Bailey was twenty and was not married. He had worked for the county as a guard, off and on, for about eighteen months. Bailey is buried at the White Oak Cemetery in Houston.

Harris County Sheriff's Office

Menefee, DeWitt Clinton
Born 31 July 1875—Died 21 May 1914

Constable J.M. Kellett and his deputies, Guy Hahn and Ralph Ricketts, of the Harrisburg precinct were arrested and jailed for the murder of DeWitt Clinton Menefee. Menefee was a well-known rancher and special deputy sheriff living about twelve miles south of Houston.

At the time of the shooting, Menefee was in an automobile with his brother T.W. Menefee, four local ranchers and a well-known attorney. The lawmen approached Menefee and his party at a store where the group had stopped and shot him. He was hit two times in the back and died at the scene.

The lawmen claimed that they were trying to arrest Menefee and that he had resisted. Both were charged with his killing.

Kellett resigned as constable prior to the murder trial. Kellett testified that he had not fired his weapon. At his trial, Ricketts testified that he had only fired one time, in spite of the evidence that Menefee had been shot twice in the back. The jury acquitted Kellett and sentenced Ricketts to two years in prison with a recommendation that the sentence be suspended.

Menefee is buried at the Madisonville City Cemetery in Madisonville. He was survived by his wife and four children.

Taylor, Arthur
Born circa 1879—Died 24 May 1914

Between the hours of 9:00 and 10:00 p.m. on Saturday, 23 May 1914, Houston police chief Ben Davison assigned Officer John Richardson to team up with Officer Isaac Parsons to investigate a suspect who was terrorizing a neighborhood with a rifle. Parsons called in and said that he would not be there to meet Richardson since he had gone into the area alone to look around. Richardson assigned Officer Cordona to assist.

Neither Richardson nor Cordona knew that Arthur Taylor was in the vicinity of the incident doing an investigation. The pair rode the midnight trolley to the intersection of Nance and Schwartz and commenced a search for the individual with the gun. At about 12:35 a.m., they heard gunshots. Knowing that two other officers were in the area, they ran toward the gunfire. While en route, they heard two more shots. Unknown to all, Taylor and Parsons were working together. They also heard the gunshots and ran toward the area from where the sound had come. Richardson saw a black male running toward him with gun drawn. He commanded him to stop. When he did not do so, Richardson opened fire. The black man was Taylor. He was hit twice and died instantly.

Richardson and Cordona then opened fire on the other man, not knowing it was Parsons. They hit Parsons four times, killing him instantly.

Chief Davison ordered an investigation. Cardona and Richardson were both charged and indicted. Both were released on bail on 28 May 1914. After an investigation, it was determined that the shootings were the result of mistaken identity. Charges were dropped against both Cardona and Richardson.

Taylor had been deputized one day earlier, on 23 May. He was survived by his wife. Taylor is buried at the Olivet Cemetery in Houston.

Related Case: Houston Police Department, Isaac Parsons

Fuchs, Wilhelm William
Born 3 August 1869—Died 2 March 1930

Sixty-one-year-old Deputy Sheriff Wilhelm Fuchs had been assigned to work security at the White Oak Gun Club, a roadside dance hall near Houston. He and Deputy Sheriff Alee McDonald had just arrested a man named I.J.

Carroll after receiving complaints from the management that Carroll and another man had been quarreling. Fuchs and McDonald managed to take Carroll into custody and bring him outside when Fuchs dropped over dead, apparently from a heart attack brought on by the excitement. McDonald later described the scene at the establishment as "a free for all." Fuchs's body was covered with contusions, and McDonald's hands were bruised, although McDonald claimed that there had not been any fisticuffs at the scene.

Fuchs is buried at Spring Branch. He was survived by his wife, Betty Maria Rinkel, and two children.

Williams, William C. "Dubb," Jr.
Born 20 November 1907—Died 16 April 1930

Deputy Sheriff William Williams was accidentally shot and killed by an informant while the man and several deputies were conducting a liquor raid near Satsuma, located about twenty-five miles north of Houston.

When the officers arrived to investigate a barn where illegal activity was suspected to be taking place, Williams remained outside while the other deputies, and the informant, went inside to conduct a search. While the informant, A.T. Botkin, was searching for suspected bootleggers, he saw the silhouette of Williams outside. Thinking Williams was one of the bootleggers, Botkin ordered him to stop. When Williams shined his flashlight at Botkin, he opened fire, shooting him through the heart with a high-powered rifle. Williams died almost instantly.

Botkin was arrested and set free on a $1,000 bond. On 2 May 1930, Botkin was indicted on a charge of murder. Five other men, including Tony Palermo and Sam Solario, were indicted on charges of manufacturing and possession of liquor. Charlie Cash, Barney Petronella and John Cusha were also charged and indicted. The outcome of any of these charges is unknown.

Williams is buried at the Forest Park Cemetery in Harris County. He was not married.

Trapolino, Joseph A. "Joe"
Born 13 June 1894—Died 23 May 1936

Deputy Sheriff Joe Trapolino was shot and killed when he and another deputy attempted to serve a man with a warrant for insanity. When the deputies arrived at the man's home, they discovered that he was armed with a shotgun. Trapolino attempted to persuade the man to put the gun down by telling him they were only going to take him to a doctor. The man continued to menace the deputies with the gun. As the lawmen walked down the driveway, they both drew their weapons and took cover. The man shot Trapolino in the back. The deranged shooter was arrested a short time later.

Trapolino had been with the agency for eighteen years. He is buried at the Glenwood Cemetery in Houston. Trapolino was survived by his wife, Della Grace.

HARRISON COUNTY CONSTABLE'S OFFICE

Hays, Charles Lott
Born 15 September 1879—Died 1 October 1903

Precinct 4 constable Charles L. Hays and Deputy Constable Sid Keasler went to a farmhouse to arrest Mich Davis. Davis was wanted on a warrant they were holding. The officers were told by Davis's brother Walter that Mich was not there and that he was working in a nearby cotton field.

Hays and Keasler galloped their horses to the field to prevent Walter Davis from arriving ahead of them and warning his brother of their presence. Mich saw the officers coming and attempted to get his gun from a nearby building. Hays and Keasler beat him to the gun and made the arrest.

After Hays and Keasler had left the farmhouse, Walter took his shotgun and went to the road. When the lawmen approached with Mich in custody, Walter raised his shotgun and demanded that they release his brother. Walter Davis fired a load of buckshot into Hays's side. Keasler fired at Walter Davis, striking him in the side. Walter was only slightly injured. Hays fell from his horse, mortally wounded.

Walter Davis was arrested and placed in the jail at Marshall. Mich Davis and Nathan Hilton, the Davises' stepfather, were both arrested as well.

Later the same evening, a mob of angry citizens forced their way into the jail, overpowered the guards, removed Walter and lynched him.

Hays was survived by his wife, Janie M. Buchanan, and two children. He is buried at the Hallsville Cemetery in Hallsville.

Cunningham, John D.
Born 3 March 1865—Died 28 November 1916

Precinct 3 constable John Cunningham and two other officers were attempting to arrest two men who had robbed a mail carrier. During the arrest attempt, Cunningham was shot and killed by one of the thieves. Both robbers were arrested. One was convicted and sentenced to ninety-nine years in prison. The disposition of any charges against the second man is unknown.

    Cunningham was survived by his wife and five children. He is buried at the Greenwood Cemetery in Marshall.

Coon, Ernest Blain "Bilbo"
Born 23 February 1884—Died 22 May 1925
Date of Incident: 19 May 1925

At about 8:30 p.m. on Tuesday, 19 May 1925, Deputy Constable "Bilbo" Coon and another officer went to the cabin of a black man named Hal Hicks that was located a few blocks from Marshall. The lawmen went to investigate a knifing incident involving two black women. Coon sat down and put his leg over the man's chair. Apparently, this breach of etiquette was enough to cause Hicks to fatally shoot Coon. Coon was hit twice. He died at the Texas & Pacific Hospital three days later, on 22 May 1925.

    Hicks was arrested, but the grand jury conducted an investigation and refused to indict him.

    Coon is buried at the Greenwood Cemetery in Marshall. He was survived by his wife, Bessie, and six children.

Moore, Allen F.
Born 16 October 1909—Died 28 December 1934
Date of Incident: 26 December 1934

Precinct 2 constable Allen Moore died from gunshot wounds he received when he was attempting to arrest a man near Karnack at Caddo Lake.

    The man, Theodore "Hank" Mitchell, was wanted for the murder of his wife and a man in Houston. Officers received a tip that Mitchell was attending a Christmas party at the Buck Ridge schoolhouse. When Moore arrived, Mitchell opened fire and fled into the woods. The gunshot that killed Moore entered his body near his right kidney, ranged downward and emerged on his left side. Moore died two days later, on 28 December 1934.

Mitchell fled the scene. A search party scoured the Big Cypress Bayou area and eventually captured Mitchell. He was tried and convicted of murder. Mitchell was sentenced to life in prison, but that sentence was commuted on 19 May 1936.

Moore is buried at the Hope Cemetery in Karnack.

HARRISON COUNTY SHERIFF'S OFFICE

Rogers, William J.
Born 27 August 1862—Died 26 August 1908

Deputy Sheriff William Rogers was killed in a railroad train accident.

The Texas and Pacific Railroad train left Longview Junction in Gregg County at about 11:30 p.m. on Tuesday, 25 August 1908, bound for Marshall in Harrison County. Just as the train pulled out, several officers who had been attending a baseball game got aboard. When the train was about three miles west of Marshall, four rail cars left the tracks.

Rogers had been on the lookout for a man named Will Schmidt, who was wanted in a knifing incident. Rogers was riding on the train when the four boxcars left the rail and crashed into a ditch. He was crushed during the derailment. Two other men were injured. Rogers's watch and pistol were smashed to pieces during the collision. His timepiece had stopped at precisely 12:22 a.m., marking the exact moment of the incident.

Rogers is buried at the Greenwood Cemetery in Marshall. He was survived by his wife, Nora G., and six children. Mrs. Rogers died two months later. She was only thirty-two.

Readers should note the irony of the fact that there are two lawmen by the name of William J. Rogers in this book. Both men were born on the twenty-seventh day of the month. Both men died on 26 August, but in different years.

Huffman, Lewis Markham
Born 16 December 1881—Died 26 April 1909

Deputy Sheriff Lewis Huffman was shot and killed when he and another deputy went to a railroad camp to investigate a disturbance. Shots were fired at the lawmen as they approached the encampment. Both officers were hit. Huffman died at the scene. His partner survived.

Three suspects, "Creole" Mose, Hill Chase and Mat Chase, were apprehended. Four days later, a mob of angry citizens lynched all three.

Huffman is buried at the LaGrone Chapel Cemetery in Harrison County. No personal information has been found on Huffman. Based on family genealogy records, it is believed that he was not married.

Haskell County Sheriff's Office

Bischofshausen, Ralph George
Born 21 August 1892—Died 4 June 1921

H.J. Whitaker was a twenty-three-year-old veteran of the Great War. At about 9:00 a.m. on Saturday, 4 June 1921, Deputy Sheriff Ralph Bischofshausen was mending a fence by the roadside two miles southeast of Haskell when H.J. Whitaker and his brother Jess drove by in a wagon. According to reports, Bischofshausen and H.J. Whitaker had had a former difficulty of an unknown nature. H.J. Whitaker fired six times at Bischofshausen with a .44-caliber pistol, hitting him three times in the stomach and once in the shoulder. Bischofshausen died from his injuries at 3:20 p.m. that afternoon.

Both H.J. and Jess Whitaker were arrested and charged with the murder. Jess was later no billed and released. Bond for H.J. was set at $10,000. The outcome of any charges is unknown.

Bischofshausen was survived by his wife, Rose "Rosette" McGregor, and three children. He is buried in Haskell County.

HASKELL POLICE DEPARTMENT

Beauchamp, John Keifor
Born 24 December 1901—Died 23 October 1926

Twenty-four-year-old John Beauchamp was employed as the night watchman for the City of Haskell.

At about 10:00 p.m. on Saturday, 23 October 1926, Beauchamp confronted several men who were burglarizing the Davis Economy Store. When Beauchamp did not return home on Sunday morning, his wife called Chief of Police Welsh and friends to report his absence. Chief Welsh was already investigating the situation. The chief suspected that misfortune had befallen Beauchamp because the awning and show window lights in the business section of town were still illuminated. It was the night watchman's responsibility to turn them off at about 10:00 p.m. each night.

Upon examination, it seemed apparent that when Beauchamp confronted the burglars inside the Davis Economy Store, a gunfight had broken out. Beauchamp was shot through the left side of the heart and the top of his head. He had fallen in the doorway with his head and shoulders outside the building in the alleyway. His pistol was lying nearby. One round had been fired.

Two men, Walter King and Reuben Davis, were arrested in 1927 and charged with the murder. According to reports, both men were convicted and sentenced to serve forty years in prison.

Beauchamp is buried at the Rochester Cemetery in Rochester. He was survived by his wife, Daisy Irene Speck, and two children.

HAYS COUNTY SHERIFF'S OFFICE

Davis, John Springer
Born 21 April 1876—Died 8 June 1913
Date of Incident: 7 June 1913

On Saturday night, 7 June 1913, Special Deputy Sheriff John Davis was attempting to quiet a disturbance at a Mexican wedding celebration at the Perry Best farm near San Marcos. While doing so, he was attacked by two men. One of the men, Sabas Castillo, held Davis, while Sango Ybarra cut him repeatedly in the abdomen with a knife. Once they had finished their work with the cutlery, the pair shot Davis just for good measure.

Before he died, Davis told a witness, "These Mexicans have cut me all to pieces." A witness testified at the trial that Sabas Castillo was holding Davis while Sango Ybarra stabbed him. The witness called to Castillo to release Davis, and Castillo allegedly said, "Now you will see, you son of a bitch," as the fatal wound was being delivered by Ybarra.

Davis died at 5:00 a.m. on Sunday, 8 June 1913.

Pedro Ortego, Sabas Castillo and Sango Ybarra were arrested and held in connection with the death of Davis. Pedro Ortega testified against Castillo and Ybarra. Sango Ybarra was convicted and sentenced to death. His case was reversed and remanded. Yabarra was convicted a second time and sentenced to serve ninety-nine years in prison. Sabas Castillo was convicted and sentenced to serve ninety-nine years in prison.

Davis was the son of Hays County district clerk J.S. Davis. He was survived by his wife, Blanche, and four small children. Davis is buried at the San Marcos Cemetery.

HEMPSTEAD POLICE DEPARTMENT

Shelburne, J.D. "Dick"
Born 10 December 1893—Died 3 April 1937

At about 1:30 a.m. on Saturday, 3 April 1937, City Marshal Dick Shelburne was shot and killed by Waller County deputy sheriff Clyde Hutchins. The incident took place during a gun battle in front of a café in the center of the town of Hempstead. Hutchins was also wounded during this exchange of gunfire and died of his injuries the following day.

Newspaper accounts of the day provide little clue as to the nature of the disagreement between the two lawmen, other than that it must have been serious for it to have escalated to mortal gunplay.

Shelburne was survived by his wife and one child. He is buried at the Hempstead Cemetery.

Related Case: Waller County Sheriff's Office, Clyde Hutchins

Henderson County Constable's Office

Hopson, James W.
Born circa 1879—Died 10 December 1917

Precinct 1 constable James Hopson was shot and killed while attempting to serve a warrant on a man named George Davis. Davis was suspected of stealing several firearms, and other items, from a local hardware store.

As Hopson and the sheriff arrived at the man's home to serve the warrant, the sheriff approached from the rear while Hopson approached the front door. When Hopson entered the house, Davis opened fire, killing him. As Davis fled, he also shot and wounded the sheriff.

Davis was captured in Corsicana nine days later. He was convicted of Hopson's murder and sentenced to life in prison.

Hopson was survived by his mother and two brothers. He is buried in an unmarked grave at the Black Jack Cemetery in rural Henderson County.

Brown, Elvis Orval
Born 14 September 1911—Died 17 June 1937
Date of Incident: 16 June 1937

At approximately 11:00 p.m. on Wednesday, 16 June 1937, Precinct 8 deputy constable Elvis Brown was driving westbound on Texas Highway 31 between Malakoff and Trinidad. He was on duty at the time and riding his departmental motorcycle. Brown attempted to pass a small delivery truck that was stopped in the roadway, possibly without its lights on. Brown's motorcycle collided with the rear of the vehicle, causing Brown to be launched from his seat. He received fatal head and chest injuries during the incident. The driver of the truck took Brown to a Corsicana clinic, where he died the following morning at 7:00 a.m.

Brown was survived by his wife and one son. He is buried at the Oakwood Cemetery in Corsicana.

Two hours before his fatal motorcycle accident, Brown and Henderson County constable D.D. Billings had responded to a report of a disturbance at the residence of William Baker in Malakoff. As the two officers approached the residence, William Baker, age forty-seven, came out on the front porch and fired a shotgun at the two lawmen. As Baker was reloading his shotgun, Brown and Billings fired one shot each at Baker. One bullet struck Baker in the heart, and he was killed instantly. Justice of the Peace W.F. Young returned an inquest verdict that Baker had died while resisting arrest. The foregoing information leads one to believe that perhaps Brown was distracted while driving that evening, for good reason.

HENDERSON COUNTY SHERIFF'S OFFICE

Reeves, John Carlie
Born 9 July 1895—Died 17 September 1928

At about 1:15 a.m. on Monday, 17 September 1928, Deputy Sheriff John Reeves was on duty and working at a dance in Malakoff. He asked a man named Jose Hernandez, who had been causing a disturbance, to leave the dance platform. Without warning, Hernandez pulled a pistol and shot Reeves in the head, killing him instantly. Hernandez left the dance but returned a short time later and surrendered.

Using Mr. Melvin Dodd's automobile, Henderson County constable White and Dodd left the dance with Hernandez in custody to deliver him to the county jail in Athens. Before getting out of the city of Malakoff, the car was intercepted by a group of local citizens. White was pulled from the vehicle while two of the citizens shot Hernandez seven times, killing him instantly.

Neither White nor Dodd was injured by the gunfire. The local newspaper reported that the identity of the men who shot Hernandez was not known to either White or Dodd.

Reeves was survived by his wife, Nola Nima Ingram, and three small children. He is buried at the Restland Cemetery in Dallas.

HEREFORD POLICE DEPARTMENT

Rutherford, Ralph Jarrell
Born 18 October 1898—Died 29 March 1927

Officer Ralph Rutherford was killed when his motorcycle collided with another vehicle. The police motorcycle that Rutherford was riding would later be involved in another fatal accident. On that occasion, Officer Paul Jowell was killed.

Rutherford was survived by his wife, Effa Dodd Arterburn, and four children. He is buried at Hereford.

Jowell, Paul Horace
Born 24 September 1901—Died 28 May 1927

Officer Paul Jowell was killed when his motorcycle collided with another vehicle. Jowell was riding the same police motorcycle that Officer Ralph Rutherford had been riding when he was killed two months earlier.

Jowell was not married. He is buried at Hereford.

HIDALGO COUNTY CONSTABLE'S OFFICE

Hinojosa, Santiago
Born August 1874—Died 30 March 1912

Precinct 1 constable Santiago Hinojosa was shot and killed while trying to disarm several men during an altercation in Mercedes. His death certificate indicates that he was shot through the heart with a .32-caliber rifle and died at 10:30 p.m. on Saturday, 30 March 1912.

Two men suspected of being involved in the killing were captured. A posse was in pursuit of the others. The disposition of any charges is unknown.

Hinojosa is buried in Mercedes. He was reported to have been married. Hinojosa was elected constable on 8 November 1910.

Solis, Alejandro A.
Born circa 1905—Died 29 November 1927

At about 12:30 p.m. on Tuesday, 29 November 1927, Precinct 5 deputy constable Alejandro Solis was shot and killed while he was attempting to make an arrest. Solis was shot through the neck. The bullet severed his jugular vein.

One man was arrested and another was being sought, although he was believed to have escaped into Mexico. Solis had been responding to a reported robbery at the Missouri Pacific Railroad station. Witnesses reported that he had been fired on before he could defend himself.

Solis was not married. His mother was the postmistress at Sam Fordyce. Solis's place of burial is unknown.

Esparza, Manuel
Born May 1896—Died 1 July 1928

On Sunday, 1 July 1928, Sebastian Zuniga, J.A. Greer and Lorenzo Tagle were riding in a small coupe automobile just outside Edinburg when they turned a corner and were confronted by Deputy Constable Esparza. Esparza allegedly opened fire with a large-caliber rifle. Three bullets entered the vehicle, but none hit the occupants. Someone in the car returned fire, and Esparza was shot in the head. He died instantly. A witness standing by Esparza was hit in the hip and wounded.

Esparza is buried at the Esparza Cemetery in San Benito. He was married.

Hidalgo County Sheriff's Office

Cuellar, Filigonio
Born (Unknown)—Died April 1916

Sheriff's Deputy Filigonio Cuellar was shot and killed by two men named Antonio Rocha and Aniceto Ramos. The circumstances surrounding his death are unknown, as is the disposition of any charges against Rocha and Ramos.

Cuellar's place of burial is unknown.

Edwards, George Morgan
Born 17 February 1879—Died 29 July 1921

Deputy Sheriff George Edwards was killed instantly when his automobile ran off a canal bridge near Pharr. Edwards was a widely known Mexican border peace officer.

Edwards was survived by his wife and two children. He is buried at Edinburg.

Tidwell, Samuel Ralston "Sam"
Born 3 March 1889—Died 29 June 1935

Deputy Sheriff Sam Tidwell was killed when his motorcycle collided with another vehicle on the Donna–Mercedes highway near Edinburg.

Tidwell had served with the agency for five years and was assigned to traffic duty at the time of his death. He was survived by his wife, Josie Elvira Moore. Newspaper reports indicate that Tidwell was also survived by three children, although family genealogists do not list them. Tidwell is buried at the Weslaco Cemetery.

Dennett, George Marsten
Born 1 January 1890—Died 7 July 1935

Deputies George Dennett, N.K. Campbell and Ingram were on surveillance at a farm near the Rio Grande River located about fifteen miles west of Mission. They were on a stakeout, waiting for thieves to cross over from Mexico.

In time, the outlaws crossed the Rio Grande River in a small boat, as predicted, and attempted to sneak up on the deputies, but their presence was detected. When Dennett ordered the group to surrender, one of the men, Sam Fortuna, who was armed with a shotgun, turned and fired. Dennett's wounds were fatal. Deputy N.K. Campbell, who was with Dennett at the time of the shooting, said that he was certain they had wounded Fortuna before he managed to escape. The killer dropped his shotgun and fled, leaving a small trail of blood for the officers to follow.

Fortuna, an American citizen, was a known smuggler and outlaw and was wanted on both sides of the border.

A man and woman who were accomplices to the killing were arrested almost immediately and taken to Edinburg. As many as forty county and federal officers immediately began a manhunt on both sides of the border. Fortuna was finally captured on 10 July 1935 in the heavy brush country about thirty-five miles west of Reynosa, Mexico.

On 18 July 1935, authorities in the United States were still awaiting the extradition of Fortuna. No further information has been located concerning the outcome of any charges against him.

Dennett had been with the agency for seven months. He was survived by his wife, Enriqueta, and four children. Dennett is buried at Hidalgo.

Olivarez, Zacaris R., III
Born 15 August 1903—Died 29 May 1938

On Sunday morning, 29 May 1938, Deputy Sheriff Olivarez was crossing the highway north of Weslaco when he was struck by an automobile driven by Victor Reyes. Olivarez was killed almost instantly. Reyes was held in connection with the death, but no charges were filed.

Olivarez was survived by his wife, Rita, and three children. He is buried at the Garciaville Cemetery in Starr County. Olivarez's death certificate, as well as family genealogists, indicate that he died on 30 May. Newspaper reports of the day claim the twenty-ninth, however. His tombstone is inscribed with the twenty-ninth date.

HIGHLAND PARK POLICE DEPARTMENT

Tubre, Thomas Jasper "Jack"
Born 23 March 1895—Died 15 February 1938
Date of Incident: 13 February 1938

Patrolman Jack Tubre died from injuries he received in a motorcycle accident.

On Sunday, 13 February 1938, Tubre was driving across a trench that had been cut in the road for electrical repairs. The front wheel of his motorcycle was forced to the right, causing him to lose control of the machine. Tubre was thrown to the ground and suffered fatal injuries.

Tubre had been with the agency for one year. He was survived by his wife and one son. Tubre is buried at the Restland Memorial Park in Dallas.

HILLSBORO POLICE DEPARTMENT

Glasgow, Franklin "Frank"
Born 5 June 1867—Died 21 June 1911

Officer Frank Glasgow was shot and killed by a man named Jim Fox. Fox was lying in ambush for Glasgow and shot him as he was walking home from work at the end of his shift.

A local doctor had convinced Fox that Glasgow had made derogatory remarks about the man's wife. The physician, A.J. Menefee, held a grudge against Glasgow. Sometime earlier, Glasgow had charged Menefee with a murder that had resulted from an illegally performed abortion.

Fox was sentenced to five years in prison. Menefee was sentenced to life in prison, but that sentence was later overturned.

Glasgow had served with the agency for three years. He is buried at the Ridgepark Cemetery in Hillsboro, Hill County.

HOPKINS COUNTY SHERIFF'S OFFICE

Flippin, Nathan Asa
Born 24 October 1882—Died 29 August 1915

In a case where the hunter suddenly became the hunted, Chief Deputy Nathan Flippin and Sheriff J.B. Butler were ambushed by two suspects for whom the lawmen had been diligently searching. Among the charges against this pair was the burning of the sheriff's home, the shooting death of his wife and the theft of his horses. Making the crime all the more heinous, the pair had burned the sheriff's wife in the fire. Perhaps that fact alone helps explain the surprising and hideous outcome of their capture.

The two black men involved, King Richmond and his brother Joe, were wanted for having committed a variety of crimes, including murder, arson and horse theft. A man named Seawright Jones had tipped off the officers as to the whereabouts of the Richmond brothers. As Flippin and Butler approached the brothers' cabin near Tazwell, the pair hid out in an orchard near the home and waited. The two men ambushed the officers, rushed out from cover and shot Flippin in the head, sending a bullet through his brain and killing him instantly. Next, they shot Butler in the neck. A desperate hand-to-hand fight commenced between the Richmond brothers and Butler during which Butler was shot through the arm and grazed across the top of his head. The Richmond brothers then pistol-whipped and thrashed Butler, just for good measure, crushing his skull in three places.

Amazingly, Butler's injuries were not fatal. The killers grabbed Butler by the collar and were in the process of dragging him to a nearby wooded area, presumably to finish him off, when a neighbor named John Stribling intervened and rescued Butler from almost certain death.

Now having in their possession the pistols of both Flippin and Butler, the Richmond brothers fled. After being notified of the incident at about

8:35 a.m., Constable Sam Smith and Deputies Grover Williams and Bob Gafford headed for the scene. Crowds of armed citizens began to gather near the courthouse as word of the crime spread through the town like wildfire. Groups of twos and fours, heavily armed, took to the field and joined the chase. Word spread by wire. Soon, lawmen from Hunt, Delta, Franklin and Rains Counties joined the search. Makeshift posse members converged near Burks Creek, where the Richmond brothers were believed to be hiding. Before long, an estimated two thousand searchers had responded.

At around 11:00 a.m., King and Joe Richmond were surrounded in a pasture belonging to Don Campbell, located about two to three miles south of Tazwell. Bloodhounds struck the trail at about 11:30 a.m. and followed the escapees to a cabin near Jim Copelin's farm, where they continued the search to a sandy creek bottom area nearby, where the pair was found hiding in a clump of willows. When commanded to come out with their hands up, one of the men failed to comply. A barrage of gunfire immediately followed, resulting in the instantaneous death of one Richmond brother and the wounding of the other.

The two killers, one now dead and the other wounded and unconscious, were loaded into a wagon and brought to town at about 4:30 p.m. Almost at once, a crowd, estimated to number upward of 8,000 citizens, began to assemble near the bandstand. The mob of angry citizens then doused the pair with coal oil and burned their bodies, while an estimated 1,500 to 2,000 onlookers watched the hideous spectacle—another case of Texas-style vigilante justice swiftly administered. This time, however, no witness could possibly have felt good about the vile display that had unfolded before his or her eyes.

Although such acts of mob violence are clearly outside the bounds of the law, to say nothing of human decency, it is interesting to note the frequency with which the killers of Texas lawmen are sentenced to surprisingly short stays in prison, acquitted and even pardoned of their crimes. Statistically speaking, unless a "cop killer" was him or herself killed by lawmen at the time of the crime, the chances of the individual serving a life sentence—or being executed for his deeds—was remarkably small. Perhaps that is why history records so many such incidents. Without question, there was a racial component involved in some of the lynching activities that took place in the early 1900s. Historically speaking, there were as many as twenty-seven Jim Crow laws passed in Texas between 1866 and 1958, most between 1889 and 1926.

Flippin had been with the agency for seven years. He was survived by his wife, Lida C. Blansett, and one child. Flippin is buried at the Sulphur Springs City Cemetery in Hopkins County.

Butler eventually recovered from his severe thrashing.

HOUSTON COUNTY CONSTABLE'S OFFICE

Bobbitt, James J.
Born 31 October 1870—Died 30 April 1910

James J. Bobbitt was the elected constable for Precinct 7. Bobbitt discovered a group of men gambling. The group included a man named John Pugh. Bobbitt attempted to arrest Pugh, but Pugh refused to be taken into custody. Later, when a deputy sheriff tried to arrest Pugh, he fought with Pugh over the fine.

Pugh had, on several occasions after his arrest, used abusive language when speaking about Bobbitt. He also began carrying a shotgun at all times, claiming that he had as much right to carry the gun as the officers did their pistols. Pugh had become unruly on the grounds of the baseball park. When asked to stop, he used extremely offensive language and threatened to kill Bobbitt. Later the same day, Bobbitt was at the general store when he discovered that Pugh was there. He asked him if he had his gun. Pugh replied that he did not. As Bobbitt and his brother started to leave the establishment, Pugh reached behind the counter, grabbed a shotgun and shot Bobbitt.

Pugh was convicted and sentenced to five years in prison for the murder of Bobbitt.

Bobbitt was survived by his wife, Dolly K. Gage, and seven of the couple's eight children. He is buried at the Weches Cemetery in Houston County.

HOUSTON COUNTY SHERIFF'S OFFICE

English, Jesse Lawrence
Born 1 October 1887—Died 28 May 1923

Deputy Sheriff Jesse English, along with the Houston County sheriff and the Grapeland city marshal, was trying to capture two men who had escaped from a Texas state prison.

English had received word that the men, Tom Davis and R.L. Clark, would be in the area. Lawmen began a search. At about 11:00 p.m., English encountered the pair traveling along a dirt road. He ordered the men to stop three times. One of the pair opened fire with a shotgun, hitting English in the head. He died from his wounds approximately seven hours later.

Both Davis and Clark were apprehended soon after the shooting. Tom Davis, the shooter, was sentenced to serve ninety-nine years in prison.

English was survived by his wife, Myrtle, and three children. He is buried at the English Cemetery, ten miles east of Crockett.

HOUSTON POLICE DEPARTMENT

Weiss, William F.
Born 7 March 1870—Died 30 July 1901

On Monday, 29 July 1901, Officer Herman Youngst arrested J.T. Vaughn for discharging a firearm. Vaughn was released later that night. He immediately began looking for the officer who had arrested him, claiming that his watch and twenty-five dollars were missing. Vaughn solicited his brother Newt and his attorney, R.E Kahn, to aid in the search. They eventually located Officers Weiss and Youngst. Youngst told them to file a report at the police station. Vaughn accused Weiss of being involved in the alleged theft. An argument ensued. Vaughn drew his pistol and fired four times, striking Weiss twice in the chest. He died at the scene.

When Officers J.C. James and Henry Lee arrived at the scene of the shooting, Youngst told them that the killer was inside a nearby saloon. Vaughn fled. Lee and James caught up with him and fatally wounded him. That incident took place near where the dead body of Weiss was lying.

Weiss is buried at the Glenwood Cemetery in Houston. He was survived by his wife and two small children.

Youngst, Herman
Born circa 1843—Died 11 December 1901

James, John C.
Born August 1867—Died 11 December 1901

On Wednesday, 11 December 1901, two more Houston officers were murdered on the same corner, in front of the same saloon, where Officer William F. Weiss had been killed on 30 July 1901.

Sid Preacher, a strange name for a gambler, was arguing with several officers over the arrest of a friend. Preacher pulled a shotgun from a buggy and shot James. Youngst grabbed Preacher, but Preacher was able to break free. He shot Youngst in the back as he tried to flee the scene. Before leaving, however, he struck the dying Youngst in the head three times with the butt of the shotgun. In spite of the fact that he was mortally wounded, James rose up and shot Preacher several times as he fled. Now mortally wounded, Preacher started back toward James to finish the job. Citizens intervened and took away his shotgun. Several months earlier, Preacher and another man had viciously shot and killed two black men and a black woman, adding to the suspicion that the two incidents may have been somehow connected.

Youngst is believed to have been a widower with two daughters. He had served on the police force for twenty-eight years.

James was survived by his wife and is believed to have had four children. He had been on the police force for almost three years and had previously been a deputy constable. Both men are buried at the Washington Cemetery in Houston.

Simpson, J.S.
Born (Unknown)—Died 5 March 1908

Officer Simpson was shot and killed by his lifelong friend Mounted Police Officer J.H. Lee.

The incident took place at George Voss's Saloon at about 6:30 a.m. on Thursday, 5 March 1908. Simpson and Lee had become involved in a disagreement of some sort. Lee fired three times, hitting Simpson once in the chest and once in the stomach. Lee claimed self-defense, but that assertion seemed on its face to be a bit far-fetched when one considers the fact that Simpson was unarmed at the time. Simpson died at 1:30 p.m.

Lee was tried and convicted of murder in the second degree. He was sentenced to serve twenty-five years in prison. Lee had been one of the officers who shot and killed J.T.Vaughn, the murderer of Officer Weiss, in 1901.

Simpson's place of burial is unknown. The newspaper reported that he had joined the police force a year earlier and was working as a turnkey at the city jail. His wife had died a few months earlier. Simpson was from La Porte.

Murphy, William E.
Born 10 March 1862—Died 1 April 1910

Deputy Chief William Murphy was shot and killed by a former officer named Earl McFarlane.

McFarlane ambushed Murphy as he was eating his dinner at a local restaurant. Murphy had terminated McFarlane from the police force in late 1909 or early 1910, citing McFarlane's violent conduct as the reason for dismissal. Murphy, who was on duty as night chief, was seated at a stool at the Acme Restaurant when McFarlane entered the establishment. Without saying a word, McFarlane shot and killed Murphy.

McFarlane was apprehended but later acquitted due to a lack of a witness to the crime. McFarlane had been indicted for assault with intent to commit the murder of Chief of Detectives Kessler. On 13 January 1910, he had also pulled his pistol on Murphy but had been prevented from using it by other officers who were nearby. McFarlane had continued to threaten Murphy afterward and right up to the time of the killing.

Murphy served as a lawman for twenty-one years. He was survived by his wife, Caroline "Carrie" A. Blau, and three children. Murphy is buried at the Evergreen Cemetery in Houston.

Cain, John Morris
Born 4 March 1881—Died 3 August 1911

Officer John Cain was on patrol at the International & Great Northern Railroad yard at Nance Street when he observed Houston Sharp hop a freight train. Sharp was carrying a suitcase and a small grip. Cain approached him and asked where he was from. Sharp replied, "Conroe." Cain next asked where Sharp was going. He received no reply. Sharp turned and began to walk away. When Cain challenged him, Sharp pulled a pistol and fired one shot, hitting Cain in the chest. The bullet passed through his body and nearly severed his spinal cord. Cain had no chance to defend himself. The fatally wounded lawman collapsed in a heap and was unable to return fire.

Deputy Chief Heck and Sergeant Lomax arrived at the scene soon after and began a search. Sharp was later arrested, tried and convicted of the murder. He was set to be executed by hanging on 8 September 1916, but thus far proof of that sentence having been carried out has not been confirmed. Ill-famed Texas governor Miriam Amanda Wallace "Ma" Ferguson may have pardoned him in 1925.

Cain is buried at the Magnolia Cemetery in Houston. He was survived by his wife.

Free, Joseph Robert
Born January 1882—Died 18 October 1912
Date of Incident: 13 October 1912

Residents of a rooming house complained to the police chief that a boarder named Floyd Buckingham had been making insulting and rude remarks to female inhabitants. The chief dispatched Detectives Joseph Robert Free and T.N. Reneau to investigate. Two mounted officers had been there earlier, but Buckingham was not in his room.

When Free and Reneau arrived, several women told them that Buckingham was unbalanced, and that he had been acting that way for days. They neglected to tell the detectives that he was armed with a large-caliber pistol. When the two officers entered Buckingham's room, he shot and wounded Free. Reneau helped Free out of the room through the doorway, and both lawmen returned fire. Buckingham was hit in the chest and died at the scene.

Free was hit in the right side of the stomach. The bullet penetrated his liver. He died on 18 October.

Free was survived by his wife, Helen Butler, and four children. He is buried at the Prairie Lea Cemetery in Brenham, Washington County. Free had been on the police force for six years.

Parsons, Isaac
Born 29 September 1885—Died 24 May 1914

Between the hours of 9:00 and 10:00 p.m. on Saturday, 23 May 1914, Houston police chief Ben Davison assigned Officer John Richardson to team up with Officer Isaac Parsons to investigate a suspect who was terrorizing a neighborhood with a rifle. Parsons called in and said that he would not be there to meet Richardson since he had gone into the area alone to look around. Richardson assigned Officer Cordona to assist.

Neither Richardson nor Cordona knew that Taylor was in the vicinity of the incident and doing an investigation. The pair rode the midnight trolley to the intersection of Nance and Schwartz Streets and commenced a search for the individual with the gun. At about 12:35 a.m., they heard gunshots. Knowing that two other officers were in the area, they ran toward the gunfire. While en route, they heard two more shots. Unknown to all, Taylor and Parsons were working together. They also heard the gunshots and ran toward the area from which the sound had come. Richardson saw a black male running toward him with gun drawn. He commanded him to stop. When he did not, he opened fire. The black man was Taylor. He was hit twice and died instantly.

Richardson and Cordona then opened fire on the other man, not knowing it was Parsons. They hit Parsons four times, killing him instantly.

Chief Davison ordered an investigation. Edward Cardona and John Richardson were both charged and indicted. Both were released on bail on 28 May 1914. After an investigation, it was determined that the shootings were the result of mistaken identity. Charges were dropped against both Cardona and Richardson.

No personal information is available on Parsons. He is buried at the Evergreen Negro Cemetery in Houston.

Related Case: Harris County Sheriff's Office, Arthur Taylor

Daniels, Rufus E.
Born circa 1861—Died 23 August 1917

Meinke (Meineke/Meinecke), Edwin Gustav
Born 26 November 1893—Died 23 August 1917

Moody, Horace Clifton
Born 2 September 1869—Died 23 August 1917

Patton, D. Ross
Born 21 March 1888—Died 8 September 1917
Date of Incident: 23 August 1917

Raney, Ira Devoud
Born 19 April 1878—Died 23 August 1917

Officers Edwin Meinke, Ira Raney, Ross Patton, Horace Moody and Rufus Daniels were all shot and killed during race riots that were sparked by the arrest of several black soldiers assigned to Camp Logan. After an incident during which one soldier was arrested and reportedly harassed by local citizens and law enforcement officers, a large mob of the soldiers stole rifles from the base and went on a rampage, shooting and killing a total of sixteen people throughout the city of Houston.

The violence that occurred during the night of Thursday, 23 August 1917, is oftentimes referred to as the Camp Logan Riot, although the actions of the mutinous soldiers assigned to the camp took place away from the actual premises of the military base. Two locations were involved: the first along Buffalo Bayou in the suburban residential community of Brunner, which is on the north side of Buffalo Bayou and at the intersection of Washington Avenue and the modern Shepherd Drive; and the second on the south side of Buffalo Bayou, along San Felipe Road (now known as West Dallas Avenue) in a residential area of the Fourth Ward known as the San Felipe District.

The events began when army corporal Charles W. Baltimore, an off-duty military policeman from the Third Battalion, was arrested and reportedly treated roughly by a Houston policeman. Rumors circulated that Baltimore had been killed, provoking anger and frustration among the troops. The disquiet continued to build during the early evening. To avoid an armed confrontation, the commandant, Major Kneeland S. Snow, ordered all the rifles and ammunition collected. As the weapons were being gathered, troops sighted a mob that was advancing toward the camp. Someone fired a shot, and then chaos broke out. The soldiers raided the supply tent for their guns. They began firing indiscriminately into the residential neighborhood. A mob of over one hundred soldiers poured out of the camp and onto the streets of the Brunner community, determined to march to the Fourth Ward jail and release their imprisoned comrade

Officers Rufus Daniel, W.C. Wilson, Horace Moody and C.E. Carter had commandeered a vehicle to ride to the action. They stopped the car when they heard shots fired. Mob leader Sergeant Vida Henry ordered his men to take cover in the City Cemetery, located on the south side of the street. Officer Daniels unwisely decided to charge the troops in the cemetery armed only with his service revolver. He was instantly killed. Carter, Wilson and Moody took cover in a nearby garage. Moody was shot in the leg and severely injured. He later died while doctors were amputating his leg. The firing ceased, and the soldiers brutalized the corpse of Daniels, battering his face and bayoneting his body. Next, the frenzied mob advanced toward downtown Houston.

At Heiner Street, four blocks into their route, the throng encountered a seven-passenger touring car driven by James E. Lyon. The car had two civilian passengers, along with police officers John E. Richardson and Ira Raney, who had hitched a ride to get to the area where the violence was taking place. The mob disarmed the group in the vehicle and held them with their hands in the air. Richardson inadvertently let his hands down and was hit over the head by a soldier with the butt of a rifle. At that point, Officer Raney and civilian passenger Eli Smith decided to take off running in hopes of reaching safety. Smith was shot. His body was later found in the ditch at Heiner Street. Smith had also been bayoneted in the hip and the left armpit. Officer Raney was shot, too. His body was beaten and bayoneted as well. Asa Bland, the other civilian passenger in the touring car, was shot as well. The bullet grazed him just over his left eye.

A second car arrived at the Heiner Street intersection. That vehicle carried army captain Joseph Mattes from Camp Logan, three enlisted soldiers and Officer Edwin Meinke. When Captain Mattes stood up in the car to address the out-of-control horde, about forty of the soldiers took aim at the vehicle and opened fire. Both Mattes and Meinke were killed immediately.

During the mêlée, detective T.A. Binford received a minor wound to the knee. He later served as Harris County sheriff for twenty years.

In little more than two hours of violent rioting, the mob had killed its own captain and five Houston police officers.

The now deflated mob retreated a few blocks to the south and re-formed ranks near the railroad tracks on the eastern edge of the Fourth Ward. By that time, most of the soldiers had lost interest in their savage crusade and slowly drifted back to camp. No doubt fearing reprisal for his role in the affray, Sergeant Henry took his own life at about 2:05 a.m. the following day.

On 24 August 1917, Governor James E. Ferguson declared martial law in Houston and placed Brigadier General John A. Hulen, commander of the Texas National Guard, in charge of the city. In an effort to restore order, 350 U.S. Coast Guard servicemen were dispatched from Galveston, along with 600 infantrymen from San Antonio. By 9:30 a.m. on Saturday, 25 August 1917, all of the troops of the Third Battalion had been loaded on trains and sent to either San Antonio or New Mexico to await trial. Order was restored to the city on Monday, 27 August 1917.

A total of eleven citizens and five police officers were killed during this unspeakable disaster. Thirty citizens suffered severe wounds. Four of the rioting soldiers were killed. Two fell at the hands of their own men, who mistook them for citizens. One soldier who had been shot by a citizen died in a hospital, and Sergeant Vida Henry died by his own hand knowing reprisals were forthcoming.

Three separate courts-martial were convened at Fort Sam Houston in San Antonio in 1917. The court indicted 118 men of I Company, Twenty-fourth Infantry, Third Battalion. Seven of the soldiers who rioted testified against the others in exchange for clemency. Approximately 110 of the mutinous soldiers were found guilty of at least one charge; 19 of them were hanged, and 63 of them received life sentences. Two officers of Camp Logan faced courts-martial but were released.

Daniels was a widower. He is buried at the Glenwood Cemetery in Houston.

Meinke was survived by his wife. He is buried at the Pilgrim's Rest Cemetery in Bellville, Austin County.

Moody was survived by his wife and married children. He is buried at the Hollywood Cemetery in Houston.

Patton is buried at the Hart-Magee-Oates-Singleton Cemetery in Houston. He is believed to have been married.

Raney is buried at the Evergreen Cemetery in Houston. He was survived by his wife and nine children. Raney had been wounded in the line of duty only months earlier.

Davidson, John "Johnnie"
Born 26 February 1886—Died 19 February 1921

At about 10:00 p.m. on Saturday, 19 February 1921, Detectives John Davidson and Henry (Tony) Margiotta responded to a report of a prowler. The officers discovered the intruder, Joe Harrison, in the side yard of a house in the residential section of Houston. Harrison saw the officers approaching, dropped his gun and began walking. When Davidson and Margiotta attempted to stop Harrison, he started to run. Harrison picked up his gun and fired several times. Two bullets grazed Margiotta's head, burning part of the hair from the right side. Next, Harrison hit Margiotta over the head with the butt of his pistol, inflicting a deep gash. Harrison then turned his gun on Davidson, hitting him with two shots. Davidson died instantly.

Davidson had been with the agency for several years and had resigned to serve as a deputy constable and deputy sheriff. He had returned to the police force three years prior to his death. Davidson was survived by his wife, Pearl. He is buried at the South Park Cemetery in Pearland.

Some sources have identified the killer's surname as Harris, not Harrison.

Young, Jeter Q.
Born 14 March 1887—Died 19 June 1921

At about 3:40 p.m. on Sunday, 19 June 1921, Officers Wilbur E. Scearce and Jeter Young were on call and traveling in their patrol car when a dairy truck struck the vehicle. Scearce was driving, and Young was a passenger. The patrol car flipped over twice, crushing Young's head in the process. Scearce was also injured, but not seriously. Young was transported to St. Joseph's Hospital, where he died shortly after arriving without ever recovering consciousness. The driver of the dairy truck was arrested and charged with negligent homicide.

Young was survived by his wife, Annie Lou Shaw, and three children. He is buried at the Hollywood Cemetery.

Murdock, David Duncan "Dave"
Born 31 August 1882—Died 27 June 1921
Date of Incident: 22 June 1921

Officer Dave Murdock and other lawmen responded to a report of shooting in the Fourth Ward of the city. The individual involved in the gunplay, Will Alexander, was accused of having shot and killed a woman named Edna Phelps.

As the lawmen arrived at the residence where the gunfire had taken place, they were met by Alexander, who had barricaded himself in his home. Murdock attempted to rush the house and was met by a hail of bullets. He was hit in the jaw by one gunshot. A heated gun battle between officers and Alexander followed.

Murdock was transported to a local hospital and was expected to recover. Unfortunately, he died of complications from the wound five days later, on 27 June 1921.

Alexander was captured. The body of Ms. Phelps was discovered in the kitchen of Alexander's home after the Murdock shooting. Alexander faced charges of murder in the killings of both Murdock and Phelps. He was sentenced to serve ninety-nine years in prison for the murder of Phelps, but there is no record of his conviction for killing Murdock.

Murdock had been a convict guard, deputy constable and deputy sheriff in Brazos County and had joined the police force in 1920. He was survived by his wife and three children. Murdock is buried at the Oak Lawn Cemetery in Rockdale, Milam County.

Etheridge, John Clark
Born 12 July 1898—Died 23 August 1924

On Friday night, 22 August 1924, Motorcycle Officers John Clark Etheridge and W.E. Sammons were both on patrol south of the downtown area. Shortly after midnight, Etheridge was involved in the pursuit of a speeding automobile. While chasing the speeder, another vehicle pulled out in front of him, causing Etheridge to take evasive maneuvers that resulted in his motorcycle going into a skid and flipping over. Etheridge slid under the automobile and was fatally injured.

Etheridge was survived by his wife, Ruth Landers. He is buried at the Forest Lawndale Cemetery in Houston. Etheridge had been on the police force for only two years.

Corrales, Pete
Born 8 April 1876—Died 21 or 22 January 1925

Detective Pete Corrales was seated in an establishment belonging to Max Martinez on Congress Avenue that served as a barbershop and soft drink parlor. An elderly Mexican man named Jose Caceras was the only witness to the affray that was about to unfold who lived to tell about it.

According to newspaper reports, and Caceras's eyewitness testimony, Caceras was talking with Detective Corrales at the time the incident took place. Max Martinez, who had part interest in a nearby restaurant, had been wooing a girl named Juanita Guzman, who operated a rooming house at the same address. Guzman was seated at a cold drink stand behind a screen adjacent to the barbershop. Martinez had gone over to the stand and asked for a cold bottle of soda. Caceras claims that he overheard her tell him that she did not have any soda left. In a moment of anger, Martinez suddenly and unexpectedly shot the twenty-five-year-old Guzman to death. Seeing the incident unfold, Corrales drew his revolver and leaped behind the partition. There, he was confronted by Martinez standing across the dead body of Guzman. Martinez and Corrales fired at each other almost simultaneously. Both men fell to the floor, seriously wounded. Martinez and Corrales were transported to the hospital. Martinez died en route. Corrales died shortly thereafter.

Paul Diablo, the girl's uncle, claimed that there had been several recent disagreements between Guzman and Martinez.

Corrales was survived by nine children. He is buried at the Holy Cross Cemetery in Houston. Corrales had been employed by the police department for four years.

Chavez, E.C.
Born 13 October 1885—Died 17 September 1925

Detective E.C. Chavez and Pablino Ramirez had been socializing at a fiesta, and both had been drinking heavily. At about 2:30 a.m. on Thursday, 17 September 1925, Chavez left Pablino and went to the Ramirez house. He was inside with Ysabel Ramirez, Pablino's wife, when Pablino returned home. Seeing Chavez, Pablino went back outside and returned with a pistol. The two men started struggling for the gun. Pablino managed to pull free and shot Chavez in the stomach. Chavez was transported to the hospital, where he died at 3:30 a.m.

Pablino Ramirez was arrested on Congress Street at about 3:00 p.m. the same day. He was charged with murder. He was released on a $500 bond. The disposition of the charges is unknown.

Chavez was survived by his wife and one son. He is buried at the Washington Cemetery in Houston. Chavez had replaced Detective Pete Corrales, who had been killed in the line of duty on 21 or 22 January 1925. Some sources report Chavez's given name as Edward.

Jones, Perry Page
Born 3 July 1893—Died 30 January 1927

Officer Perry Jones was shot and killed while attempting to arrest a man he believed was intoxicated. The suspect, Pete Chester, shot Jones in the head as he attempted to make the arrest.

Chester was tried and convicted of manslaughter and sentenced to four years in prison.

Jones had served with the agency for four months. He was survived by four children. Jones's wife, Mary Simmons, preceded him in death six months earlier. He is buried at the Fields Store Cemetery in Waller County next to his wife.

After Chester was released from prison, he went to work as a cook. He started stalking former special officer Charlie Stewart, who had been an investigator gathering evidence against him. On Friday, 22 December 1933, Chester and Stewart passed each other on the street. Stewart shot Chester six times and killed him. Stewart claimed that Chester had been reaching for his pistol and that his actions were in self-defense.

Stewart was charged with murder, but no evidence has been found to indicate that he was ever prosecuted.

Wells, Rodney Quinn
Born 3 July 1893—Died 30 July 1927

Officer Rodney Wells and his partner, M.A. Gresham, were in the process of responding to a call involving an accidental shooting at the residence of W.L. Stallings on Arbor Street. They were riding in their police patrol car when they collided with an ice truck at La Branch Street and Elgin Avenue. The vehicle overturned, crushing Wells underneath. Wells suffered serious internal injuries, while Gresham escaped with minor wounds. Wells was taken to Jeff Davis Hospital, where he died at 8:30 a.m. the same day.

Wells was survived by his wife, Bessie, and two sons. He had been on the police force since 1921. Wells's body was transported via the Missouri Pacific Railroad to New Waverly, Walker County, where he was buried at the East Sandy Cemetery.

Greene, Carl
Born 27 May 1893—Died 14 March 1928

Detective Carl Greene and Sergeant Claude Beverly were assigned to the Harris County district attorney's office as liquor investigators. At 8:30 a.m. on Wednesday, 14 March 1928, the pair went to serve a search warrant for illegal liquor operations at the farm of Sam Maglitto.

Maglitto denied that he had an illegal still and invited the officers into his home. Greene followed Maglitto while Beverly went to the barn. Once inside the house, Maglitto drew a .38-caliber pistol and shot Greene in the stomach. Greene returned fire. Bevelry ran into the kitchen and saw Maglitto on his knees with the pistol in his hands. He fired three rounds and killed Maglitto.

An inquest reported that Maglitto was shot a total of six times. Maglitto's twenty-seven-year-old daughter was caught in the crossfire and was hit two times.

Locally, Greene was recognized as being a model officer and vigorous enforcer of the liquor laws. The Loyalty to Law League mounted a major fundraising effort to aid Greene's widow.

Sam Maglitto was a poor farmer who left behind a young widow, infant child and eleven stepchildren. His widow claimed that he had only turned to illegal liquor to put food on the table. There was ample evidence of the family's subpoverty-level existence.

Greene was survived by his wife. He is buried at the Forest Lawndale Cemetery in Houston.

Whitlock, Paul W.
Born 27 January 1901—Died 22 April 1928
Date of Incident: 17 April 1928

Traffic Officer Paul Whitlock was accidentally shot during a target practice session that took place on the sixth floor of the police station.

A fellow traffic officer named H.N. Howard had just raised his gun to fire when someone nearby him accidentally bumped into him, causing his shot to go wild and strike Whitlock in the abdomen. Whitlock was taken to the Baptist Hospital, where he died on 22 April.

Whitlock had just joined the police force in January 1928. He was survived by his wife. Whitlock is buried at the Forest Park Lawndale Cemetery in Houston.

Davis, Albert Worth
Born 17 October 1897—Died 17 June 1928

Detective Albert Davis was shot and killed while he was attempting to disperse a crowd in the early morning hours of Sunday, 17 June 1928.

A member of the rabble, a black man named Robert Powell, fled down Robin Street with Davis in hot pursuit. A running gun battle broke out between Davis and Powell during which Powell shot Davis in the head and shoulder. The wounds proved fatal. Davis died at the Baptist Hospital at about 11:45 a.m.

The wounded Powell was arrested and placed in custody. He refused to make a statement. On 20 June 1928, Powell was forcibly removed from the hospital by eight unidentified men; his hands and feet were bound, and then he was shot in the stomach and lynched. A witness, hospital orderly Jackson McCarter, testified that Powell's last words were, "Oh Lord, have mercy." Powell's lifeless body was discovered at about 6:30 a.m. by Detectives John Gambill and Ira Nix hanging from a bridge about eight miles from town. A reward of $1,250 was offered for information leading to the arrest of the person or persons who had lynched Powell. A $10,000 fund was raised to conduct a probe into the incident. Texas Ranger captain Frank Hamer was assigned to the case and came to Houston later in the day on 20 June.

Davis is buried in an unmarked grave at the Hollywood Cemetery in Houston. He was survived by his wife and two young sons. Davis had served for six years on the police force.

Hope, Oscar Emmett
Born 17 August 1897—Died 22 June 1929

Detective Oscar Hope was shot and killed when he responded to a disturbance call involving a man named Henry Charles (aka Mims). Charles had a weapon and had threatened to kill anyone who came near him.

The complaint had been filed by two women who had been living at the residence for the preceding several weeks. Hope's wife, Frankie, had driven their family automobile to the station to pick up her husband from work. Mrs. Hope drove her husband and his partner, Ira Nix, to the Charles residence. When they arrived at the scene, Hope entered the residence through the front door, while Nix went around to the back. When Hope stepped into the house, Charles shot him in the back of the head. Hope managed to get off three shots from his .38-caliber revolver before he died. Hearing the gunfire from within, Nix forced his way into the home through the back door and shot Charles twice in the chest with a .44-caliber pistol. Mrs. Hope had remained in the vehicle, only a few feet away, while the entire incident took place.

Hope was survived by his wife, Frankie, his parents and seven siblings. He is buried at the Forest Park Lawndale Cemetery in Houston.

Jones, Ed
Born circa 1880
Died 13 September 1929

At about 10:30 p.m. on Friday, 13 September 1929, Detective Jones was shot and killed in front of his home with his own weapon.

Jones had attempted to arrest his brother-in-law, Johnnie Wilson, at about 10:30 p.m. on Friday, 13 September 1929, at Jones's home on MacGregor Street. Wilson stole Jones's service revolver. When Jones chased Wilson outside, Wilson shot him in the chest and leg. The wounds were fatal.

Police described Wilson as demented and dangerous and armed with a pistol marked "Houston Police." He was arrested the following day.

Jones was survived by his common-law wife, Sylvia. He is buried at the Olivewood Cemetery in Houston.

Thomas, C.F. Osburn
Born 8 May 1906—Died 17 December 1929

Officer Thomas was killed when his motorcycle collided with a fire engine while he was responding to a two-alarm fire.

Thomas heard the fire engine approaching and was attempting to get to the next cross street to halt oncoming traffic. Thomas entered the intersection at the same time as the fire engine and hit the machine in the rear end.

Thomas was transported to a local hospital, where he died from his injuries ten hours later. He was survived by his wife, parents and four siblings. He is buried at the Forest Lawndale Cemetery in Houston.

Fitzgerald, Edward D.
Born 1 February 1903—Died 20 September 1930

Phares, William "Willie" Bonner
Born 29 February 1904—Died 30 September 1930
Date of Incident: 20 September 1930

On Saturday, 20 September 1930, Officers Willie Phares and Edward Fitzgerald approached a vehicle occupied by two men whom they suspected of being involved in the recent robbery of the Touchy Furniture Company. As the officers advanced toward the car to question the occupants, Jesse J. Maple and E.F. Grimes, Maple opened fire with a .45-caliber pistol. Fitzgerald was killed instantly. Phares was mortally wounded but managed to rise to his knees and fire three times at his assailant. Unable to fire again, the undaunted lawman told a bystander, "Here, take this pistol and load it up and let him have it." Phares managed to hang on for ten days. He died from the effects of his wounds on 30 September 1930.

Both of the criminals were captured a short time afterward. The gunman, Maple, went to trial on 30 September 1930. He was found guilty and sentenced to death. That sentence was carried out on 28 November 1930, when Maples was executed by electrocution at Huntsville. Maple became the sixty-fifth criminal to be electrocuted in Texas.

Phares was survived by his wife, Leona Kerr, and one son. He is buried at the Glendale Cemetery in Lufkin.

Fitzgerald was survived by his mother and two siblings. He is buried at the Mont Belvieu Methodist Cemetery in Chambers County.

Landry, Joseph D.
Born 23 November 1895—Died 3 December 1930
Date of Incident: 2 December 1930

On Tuesday, 2 December 1930, Motorcycle Officers Joseph Landry and A.O. Taylor were working traffic near downtown Houston. Landry was killed in a motorcycle accident while he was attempting to stop a vehicle on Tuam Avenue. As the driver of the automobile, Fred Soland, was pulling over, he slowed to turn into a parking lot. Landry's motorcycle collided with the rear end of the car as Soland was coming to a halt. Landry died at 6:00 p.m. the following day.

Landry was survived by his wife, Elia, his parents and four siblings. His body was shipped to New Iberia, Louisiana, for burial.

Mereness, Henry Talcott "Harry"
Born 15 September 1882—Died 18 October 1933
Date of Incident: 16 October 1933

On Monday, 16 October 1933, Officer Henry Mereness was killed in a motorcycle accident. The incident took place when Mereness was making a left turn onto Park Place. His motorcycle collided with another vehicle that was also making the turn, throwing Mereness to the ground and inflicting fatal injuries. The driver of the automobile was charged in juvenile court with negligent homicide.

Mereness was survived by his wife, Gertrude "Gertie" Cure, and two sons. His body was shipped to Ypsilanti, Michigan, for burial.

Sullivan, Rempsey Hayes "Rimps" or "Remps"
Born 8 July 1900—Died 9 March 1935

Detective Rempsey Sullivan was shot and killed at the scene of an assault.

Sullivan, who was at the time Houston mayor Oscar Holcombe's driver, was on his way home from the mayor's house when he stopped at a shoe repair shop on Dowling Street to drop off a friend named Steve Conroy. Conroy went inside the business and was physically assaulted by a store employee named Isaac Jones. Jones pushed Conroy out the door, still staggering from the blows. Just as Conroy managed to get to his feet, Jones grabbed him by the collar. Sullivan entered the shop, identified himself as an officer and yelled, "Let that man alone!" Jones ran behind the counter. As Sullivan pursued him, Jones grabbed a gun and shot him.

Jones claimed that an intoxicated Negro man had entered the store and Sullivan had gotten in the way of the gunfire. He held rescue workers at bay for thirty minutes before eventually giving himself up. Sullivan died en route to the hospital.

Jones was convicted of the murder of Sullivan and sentenced to death. He won a new trial on appeal and received a life sentence. Jones later received a full pardon on 1 July 1960.

Sullivan was survived by his wife and one child. He is buried at the Forest Park Lawndale Cemetery in Houston.

Gambill, James T.
Born 27 August 1887—Died 1 December 1936

Officer James Gambill suffered a fatal heart attack following a violent struggle with a suspect he was arresting.

Gambill and his partner, George Seber, had just arrested a man named Martin Holmes for threatening to murder his wife. They were transporting Holmes to jail in their patrol car when, at a point along Calhoun Street, Holmes attempted to grab Gambill's service revolver. A struggle ensued during which Gambill pulled Holmes out of the car. Gambill slumped down and collapsed. Seber ran around the vehicle to see what had happened to him. Holmes menaced Seber with Gambill's revolver, so he shot him five times, wounding him gravely. It was not until Holmes was wounded that he released his grip on Gambill. After the violent struggle, Gambill took two steps into the street and collapsed dead. Holmes died from his wounds at 4:05 a.m. the next day.

Gambill had been with the agency for fourteen years. He was survived by his wife and one daughter. Gambill is buried at the Resthaven Cemetery in Houston.

Martial, Adolph P.
Born 24 January 1883—Died 8 November 1937
Date of Incident: 6 November 1937

On Friday, 8 November 1937, Officer Adolph Martial died from injuries he received in an automobile accident that had taken place two days earlier.

Martial and his partner were on patrol when his partner swerved to avoid an oncoming car and struck the curb. The impact caused Martial to hit his head on a gun rack that was mounted above the windshield. After the incident, he complained of a headache. He took some aspirin and went home. Shortly after reaching his residence, he lapsed into a coma and died of a blood clot that had formed. The clot was a result of a concussion he had received from the impact of his head striking the gun rack.

Martial was survived by his wife, Alfreda, and one daughter. He is buried at the Hollywood Cemetery in Houston. Martial had risen to the rank of captain but had been demoted to patrol officer. This was customary when a new administration took charge during the political spoils system that was prevalent at the time.

Palmer, Marion Edward, Sr.
Born 20 March 1891—Died 24 March 1938

Officer Palmer was shot and killed when he and his partner, H.D. Roberts, responded to a domestic disturbance.

The call involved a crazed and apparently suicidal man named Light Zink, who had locked his wife out of their garage apartment and turned on the gas. Palmer walked to the back of the apartment to make sure that Zink did not escape while his partner turned off the gas at the supply valve located outside the building. As Palmer was watching the back window, a barrage of gunfire poured from the house. Palmer was fatally wounded.

The body of the gunman, Zink, was found inside the apartment, dead from apparent suicide. Zink had written a suicide note and left his Bible open to Jeremiah 15:14: "I will make you serve your enemies in a land that you do not know, for in my anger a fire is kindled that shall burn forever."

Palmer had been with the agency for eight years. He was survived by his wife, Christine, and two sons. Palmer is buried at the Forest Park Lawndale Cemetery in Houston.

Edwards, George Dewey
Born 25 April 1899—Died 30 June 1939

Officer George Edwards was shot and killed when he and two other lawmen were questioning a man named Carl Adams of El Campo, who was suspected of attempting to steal an automobile. Adams was a former Arizona convict.

The officers had located Adams at Fannin and Congress Streets. They had begun to question him when they discovered that Adams had a gun in his pocket. A struggle soon developed. In spite of the fact that the officers were beating Adams over the head with the butts of their guns, he was able to gain control of the weapon. Once in hand, Adams opened fire on the officers. Edwards was mortally wounded. One of the other officers, Sidney T. Roe, was wounded in the left arm. Adams was shot six times during the exchange. His wounds were fatal.

Edwards was survived by his wife, Audie Elsie Cowan, and two children. He is buried in Dialville at the Rock Springs Cemetery in Cherokee County.

HOWARD COUNTY SHERIFF'S OFFICE

Satterwhite, Walter Watson
Born 5 December 1868—Died 24 March 1925

Sheriff Walter Satterwhite was elected on 7 November 1922 and reelected on 4 November 1924. He served until his death.

Satterwhite and Taylor County constable George Reeves were shot and killed while attempting to arrest a murder suspect. The incident took place at the G.W. Richie farm about eleven miles from Merkel at about noon on Tuesday, 24 March 1925.

Satterwhite and Reeves approached the suspect, Lopez Morales, who was working on a grubbing crew. Morales recognized the pair to be lawmen. He grabbed his rifle and shot Reeves, killing him instantly. Sheriff Satterwhite ran to a nearby house for aid. He borrowed an automobile, but as he was about to speed off, Morales caught up with him and shot and killed him. The bullet went through the front seat of the vehicle and into Satterwhite's right side, then traveled upward and lodged near his heart. After being shot, Satterwhite drove the car about 150 yards before crashing into a fence.

Morales, who was now heavily armed with weapons he had taken from the fallen officers, fled to the rough country of Mulberry Canyon, southwest of Merkel. A posse of three to five hundred men gave chase in what newspapers called "the greatest manhunt in west Texas in many years." Morales was eventually located by the sheriff of Jones County on 26 March, hiding out in a freight car about four miles southeast of Sweetwater. Posse members laid down a barrage of gunfire followed by a dynamite blast, all in an effort to dislodge Morales from his hideout. After a second attempt, Morales burst forth from the railcar, firing as he appeared. Morales fell dead almost instantly from a hail of bullets fired by the hundreds of posse members who had his hideout surrounded.

Satterwhite was survived by his wife, Louise Lola "Lula" Campbell, and several children. He is buried at the Masonic Cemetery in Merkle.

Related Case: Taylor County Constable's Office, George Reeves

Howe Police Department

Jordan, Albert
Born 19 January 1881—Died 20 March 1903

Deputy City Marshal Albert Jordan was shot and killed while attempting to disarm a disorderly man named Jim Black.

Black had had an earlier disagreement with Jordan and Police Chief McCoy. On the morning of Friday, 20 March 1903, Black was observed walking into the town of Howe carrying a loaded double-barreled shotgun. At a restaurant in town, he told a bystander that he intended to kill both McCoy and Jordan. Later in the day, Black was observed dancing around and hollering, throwing gravel and rocks. Seeing this behavior, the town's mayor ordered Black's arrest. Black had the double-barreled shotgun with him, and it was leaning against a nearby building. When Jordan approached Black to arrest him, Black fired his shotgun, killing Jordan.

Black was apprehended, tried and sentenced to death. He was set to be executed on 26 August 1903. In July 1903, a clemency petition was filed. On 14 December 1903, further time was granted for his appeal. On 20 August 1904, Black's sentence was commuted by the Texas governor.

The twenty-two-year-old Jordan had been with the agency for only three months. He was survived by his mother. Jordan is buried at the Hall Cemetery in Howe, Grayson County.

Hunt County Constable's Office

Hardin, George William "Will"
Born January 1869—Died 2 July 1900
Date of Incident: 1 July 1900

At approximately 11:30 p.m. on Sunday, 1 July 1900, Deputy Constable Will Hardin and Greenville police officers Lee Howard and Tom Ingram were outside Bob Bolton's Saloon on the east side of the town square. The officers were there to determine if Bolton was selling liquor in violation of the Sunday closing law. Howard entered the saloon and was pushed out through a back window by Bolton. Angry to have been treated in such a way, Howard ran around the building, through the door and up to the bar to confront Bolton. Not surprisingly, the pair became engaged in a heated quarrel. Both men pulled their pistols and fired almost simultaneously. Remarkably, neither man was hit.

Hearing the gunfire, Hardin stepped into the doorway of the saloon and was shot in the stomach by Bolton. The injured Hardin drew his pistol and returned fire, hitting Bolton with several shots and killing him. Hardin fell mortally wounded. He died at 6:00 p.m. the following day.

Hardin was survived by his wife, Eva Viola Mason. He is buried in an unmarked grave in the Mason family plot at East Mount Cemetery.

Keith, William Eugene "Gene"
Born 31 March 1871—Died 26 July 1917

Former constable Gene Keith was fatally stabbed on the streets of Celeste by a man named Lowery Glascoe. During the struggle, Glascoe inflicted a deadly wound to Keith's neck. According to his death certificate, Keith bled to death.

Newspaper reports of the day claim that both Keith and Glascoe had served as constables.

Keith was survived by his wife, Docia Kennedy, and one son. He is buried at the Mount Carmel Cemetery in Celeste.

HUNT COUNTY SHERIFF'S OFFICE

Velvin, Robert Willis "Will"
Born February 1864—Died 13 September 1902

At about 7:30 p.m. on Saturday, 13 September 1902, Deputy Sheriff Will Velvin was shot and killed while attempting to arrest a man named Jim L. Beckman. Beckman was wanted for violating the local liquor laws. Velvin had sworn out three warrants against Beckman two days earlier.

Beckham was arrested for murder. Beckam's brother, along with Sam and Abe Goodman, were arrested as accessories to murder. The disposition of the charges is unknown.

Velvin had served with the agency for ten years. He was survived by his wife. Velvin is buried at East Mount Cemetery in Greenville.

Shipp, Richard Emmett
Born 23 November 1878—Died 6 October 1912

Greenville Police Department assistant chief John L. Southall and Special Deputy Sheriff Richard Shipp were shot and killed while attempting to arrest an intoxicated man who was firing a pistol.

Sometime between 5:00 and 5:30 p.m. on Sunday, 6 October 1912, officers received a call concerning an intoxicated man on South Stone Street. Shipp and Southall, as well as Deputies Roy Harrington and George Duncan, quickly mounted up and responded. When the lawmen reached a point along the street about a block or two north of the Mineola branch of the MK&T Railroad, they overtook Sant Slimmons and John Cooper, both of Lone Oak, who were riding in a buggy. Slimmons immediately opened fire on the officers, hitting Southall in the forehead and the bowels and breaking one of his legs. He died instantly and fell in the backyard of W.M. McBride, whose house the men were in front of when the incident began.

The unarmed Shipp was the next to fall, shot through the heart. He fell in the yard of Erv Harrison, just a few feet from where Southall was lying dead. Harrington and Duncan returned fire, hitting Slimmons five times. He was taken to a hospital and died an hour and a quarter later. Cooper was arrested and taken to jail. His role in the shooting affray is unclear.

Shipp was survived by his wife and three children. He is buried at the Concord Cemetery in Jacobia.

Related Case: Greenville Police Department, John L. Southall

HUNTSVILLE POLICE DEPARTMENT

Cates, Hill J.
Born 4 February 1850—Died 29 September 1901

Chief of Police Hill Cates had gone to the home of Granderson Allen to question the man regarding threats Allen was said to have made. During the questioning, Allen produced a pistol and shot Cates. The injuries were fatal.

Allen was charged with murder and sentenced to life in prison. That decision was reversed in January 1902. In April 1902, Allen pleaded guilty to manslaughter and was sentenced to five years in prison.

Cates is buried at the Oakwood Cemetery in Huntsville. No other personal information has been located.

Birmingham, Charles Braxton "Caps"
Born 26 January 1869—Died 13 October 1926
Date of Incident: 12 October 1926

Officer Caps Birmingham was shot and killed by Rollie Cansler, the brother of Henry Cansler, whom he and City Marshal T.R. Gaines had shot and killed earlier in the year. Birmingham was under bond for the death of Henry (Horace) Cansler at the time of his death.

Rollie Cansler was in a speeding automobile when he shot Birmingham, who was standing near the corner of the city square talking with friends. Cansler fired as he drove past, hitting Birmingham with nine pellets of buckshot. One of the pellets struck Birmingham in the groin, severing an artery in his leg. Dr. J.R. Martin, who was standing a few feet away from Birmingham when the incident took place, rushed to his aid and stopped the flow of blood from the wound. Birmingham bled to death the following afternoon at about 6:30 p.m.

Birmingham managed to get off five shots at the occupants of the automobile as it motored away. The killer's vehicle was found abandoned outside of town with a bullet hole in the fuel tank, presumably from Birmingham's gun.

Officers and citizens immediately gave chase. Rollie Cansler was arrested and charged with the murder of Birmingham. In 1927, he was convicted and sentenced to five years in prison, but the sentence was suspended.

Birmingham was survived by his wife, Ida Mae Aiken, and seven children. He is buried at the Oakwood Cemetery in Huntsville. Birmingham had been a law enforcement officer for more than thirty years.

HUTCHINSON COUNTY CONSTABLE'S OFFICE

Hutson, Willie Lee
Born 28 May 1891—Died 14 December 1937

Constable Willie Hutson was shot and killed by Borger police officer Ben Chapman.

Hutson, Chapman and Deputy Sheriff G.L. Warren were driving back from Wheeler, where they had been witnesses in a trial. The shooting occurred in Carson County. According to newspaper accounts of the incident, Hutson was intoxicated at the time of the shooting.

Chapman was tried and convicted of killing Hutson and was sentenced to life in prison, despite his plea of insanity.

Hutson is buried at the Highland Park Cemetery in Borger. He was married.

HUTCHINSON COUNTY SHERIFF'S OFFICE

Kenyon, Daniel Pratt
Born 22 May 1882—Died 1 April 1927

Terry, Almer Loin
Born 8 June 1882—Died 1 April 1927

Deputies Daniel Kenyon and Almer Terry were shot and killed by members of the Cotton Top Walker Gang immediately following a bank robbery that had been committed by the gang.

Kenyon and Terry had received a tip that the gang, comprising Matthew Kimes and Ray Terrill, would be robbing the National Bank of Pampa and went to stop it. As they saw the robbers' blue and black sedan approach on the Phillips Road near Whittenburg, they swerved and attempted to block the highway with their automobile. Both lawmen jumped from the car to halt the would-be robbers. Witnesses who discovered the bodies of Kenyon and Terry after the incident indicated that, based on the position of their corpses, the officers had apparently tried to capture the gang members. Their pistols were lying between them. Neither gun had been fired. Terry was shot in the eye and Kenyon in the left chest and back. Both are believed to have died instantly from their wounds.

After the bank robbery and killing of Kenyon and Terry, Kimes and Terrill hid out at the Archer farm between Pampa and Borger. There they parked their automobile in the garage and held the Archer family hostage until the following morning, when they drove off toward Borger. Kimes and Terrill were believed to be hiding out in a shack near Borger, but when officers stormed the building on 2 April, they found that it was empty.

Both Kenyon and Terry were commissioned on 3 January 1927, thus had served with the agency for only three months.

Kenyon was married and had seven children. He is buried in Kaw City, Kay County, Oklahoma.

Terry is buried at the White Deer Cemetery in Hutchinson County.

The Cotton Top Walker Gang was led by Matthew Kimes of the notorious Kimes Brothers Gang (Matthew and George Kimes). By the time of the Terry/Kenyon slayings, they had already murdered Deputy Perry Chuculate of the Sequoyah County, Oklahoma Sheriff's Office on 27 August 1926. The two brothers were convicted of manslaughter in connection with Deputy Chuculate's murder and sentenced to serve twenty-five years in prison. One of the brothers, Matthew Kimes, escaped from prison and continued his crime spree.

During the following year, the fugitive Matthew Kimes continued robbing banks, now having formed an alliance with the Cotton Top Walker Gang. The Walker bunch was responsible for the murders of Borger patrolman Coke Buchanan on 19 March 1927. The gang continued its killing spree, capping it off with the murder of Police Chief W.J. McAnally of the Beggs, Oklahoma Police Department on 18 May 1927.

Matthew Kimes, one of the leaders of the gang, was arrested in Flagstaff, Arizona, on 23 June 1927. He was tried for complicity in the murder of Chief McAnally and sentenced to death by electrocution. The sentence was later commuted to life, and in 1945, he was turned down for parole but given a brief leave. During the leave from prison, he robbed another bank in Morton, Texas. On 1 December 1945, Matthew Kimes's killing spree came to an unlikely end when he was struck by a truck in Little Rock, Arkansas.

JACK COUNTY SHERIFF'S OFFICE

Leftwich, George Madison
Born July 1855—Died 10 August 1901

Deputy Sheriff George Leftwich was shot and killed when he and several members of a posse came upon a group of suspected horse thieves. The incident took place about seven miles outside Jacksboro. A gunfight quickly developed, during which Leftwich was shot and fatally wounded. The suspected horse thieves all managed to escape.

Leftwich had been deputized earlier in the day to assist in the apprehension of this particular gang of rustlers.

He was survived by his wife, Jennie Rebecca Berry, and five children. Leftwich is buried at the Jacksboro Cemetery.

Jackson County Sheriff's Office

Brugh, Frank Wells
Born February 1859—Died 13 September 1903

Wharton, George Franklin, Jr.
Born 18 April 1862—Died 13 September 1903

Deputy Sheriff Frank Brugh and Sheriff George Wharton were shot and killed by a man named W. Grey Landers. Brugh and Wharton had just arrested Landers while he was traveling on a train between Victoria and Edna.

Landers was wanted for escaping from a prison in Billings, Montana. As Landers was being put in a cell at the jail, he was somehow able to obtain a gun. He opened fire, mortally wounding both Brugh and Wharton. Before he died from his wounds, Wharton was able to return fire and kill Landers.

Wharton was survived by his wife, Willie Allice Heard, and ten children. He is buried at Memory Gardens Cemetery of Edna in Jackson County. Wharton was appointed sheriff on 10 December 1900 and elected on 4 November 1902.

Brugh was survived by his wife, Anna Lee White, and seven children. He is buried at the Memory Gardens of Edna in Jackson County. Some family genealogists list his date of death as 14 September.

Milby, Franklin W. "Frank"
Born 5 October 1851—Died 6 December 1903

Deputy Sheriff Frank Milby accidentally shot and killed himself.

Milby's revolver fell from its holster. During the fall, the hammer struck a chair, causing the gun to discharge accidentally. The bullet entered his right side from the back. Milby walked down the stairs and collapsed dead on the sidewalk.

Milby was fifty-two years of age at the time of his death. He was survived by several siblings. Milby is buried at the Memory Gardens Cemetery of Edna in Jackson County.

Milby's deceased brother, Ben Milby, had served as sheriff. Ben Milby was elected on 4 November 1890 and served until he resigned for health reasons on 12 March 1896.

JACKSONVILLE POLICE DEPARTMENT

Hooker, Harry Floyd
Born 20 September 1879—Died 22 July 1913

Night policeman Harry Hooker had been notified that a stranger had robbed a drunken man. The suspect had headed out of town on foot by way of the Cotton Belt Railroad track.

Hooker boarded a freight train that was "doubling" the hill north of town and sighted a man standing by the track waiting for the train to pass. When the train stopped, Hooker disembarked and walked back to where the man was standing. The trainmen overheard Hooker ask the stranger to let him see what he had in a bundle he was carrying. The man pulled a gun and shot Hooker once in the left chest, then fled.

By the time the trainmen reached Hooker, he was lying in the center of the track dying. He reportedly said, "He got me" before he died. Hooker's pistol was lying on the track near his body, indicating that he had seen the stranger draw his gun and had attempted to shoot but was apparently too late.

A search by the sheriff and a posse failed to locate the killer. No one was ever arrested or prosecuted for the crime. Family oral history accounts claim that Hooker's killer was shot and killed near Houston a year later and that the man had confessed to the slaying of Hooker before he died.

Hooker had been made night watchman about six months prior to his death. He was survived by his wife, Betty Pearl Ward, and two sons. Jacksonville citizens donated $250 to his widow. Hooker is buried in the Kemp City Cemetery in Kaufman County

JASPER COUNTY CONSTABLE'S OFFICE

Abbott, Wesley A.
Born February 1854—Died 8 December 1902

At about 3:00 p.m. on Monday, 8 December 1902, Precinct 3 constable Wesley Abbott was inside W.J. Newton's store in Kirbyville warming himself from the cold when he became engaged in a dispute with an unidentified man. Abbott had had an earlier confrontation with this same individual. On this occasion, the man hit Abbott over the head with a stick. Bystanders were able to separate Abbott and his assailant. Dr. J.D. Yates was called to the scene and discovered that Abbott was dying from a brain hemorrhage. He passed at about 7:00 p.m. the same day.

Newspapers reported that no arrest was made. It is not known if the dispute was of a personal nature or if it was related to Abbott's law enforcement duties.

Abbott was survived by his wife, Nancy C. Matthews, and five children. He had been the elected constable about one year earlier. Abbott's place of burial is unknown.

Cooper, Daniel H. "Dan"
Born 2 September 1877—Died 16 November 1910

Constable Dan Cooper was shot and killed by Jasper County deputy sheriff J.J. Johnson. The killing was the result of a personal disagreement between the two men that turned fatal.

Johnson was tried and convicted of the killing. He was sentenced to serve seven years in prison.

Cooper was survived by his parents and four siblings. He is believed to be buried at Derbyville.

JEFF DAVIS COUNTY SHERIFF'S OFFICE

Sproul, Franklin Lee
Born 16 May 1885—Died 24 February 1933

Sheriff Franklin Sproul was shot and killed while he and two other officers were attempting to arrest three youths who had just looted the commissary at the ranch of Max Sproul, brother of the sheriff.

The Sproul Ranch is located in the wild open country south of Fort Davis. The youthful trio of robbers was composed of brothers Paul and Wilkert Steinberg and James Thomas Farmer. Their haul consisted of three rifles, food and about fifty rounds of ammunition. When the three officers surrounded seventeen-year-old James Thomas Farmer, the youth shot Sproul in the abdomen with one of the rifles he had stolen during the burglary. When Farmer was arrested, he stated that he thought he was shooting a cow. When asked why he was shooting a cow, he simply said that he was hungry.

The Steinberg brothers had drifted into town, having ridden a railcar from Alpine to Fort Davis. The pair said that they had been sentenced to serve six months in prison at Belton, Montana. After serving three months at the state facility at Deer Lodge, they were released on parole. The brothers had met Farmer recently at Wichita Falls and claimed that their association had been brief. Farmer confessed to robbing the Lacky Lumber Company in Brookston, Lamar County. Sheriff Clyde Shelton of Lamar County, who had been investigating the trio, stated that he believed Farmer's real name was Jimmy Murray and that the Steinberg brothers were actually named Reeder.

Sproul had been with the agency for eighteen years. He was survived by his wife, Alice, and young son. Sproul is buried at the Hillcrest Cemetery in Fort Davis.

JEFFERSON COUNTY CONSTABLE'S OFFICE

Reddick, William C. "Will"
Born September 1869—Died 26 April 1903

There was ongoing friction between the various drinking establishments of Jefferson County and local law enforcement over the City of Beaumont's mandated Sunday closing laws. In spite of the strife, the day preceding his death, Precinct 1 constable Will Reddick had announced that he intended to enforce the unpopular law.

Reddick and Deputy Constable Price were making their rounds and had closed several saloons when they entered a drinking establishment called the Metropolitan. It was about 10:00 p.m. on Sunday, 26 April 1903, as Reddick stepped through the doorway of the enterprise. Dr. J.M. "Doc" Harris opened fire and shot him. Reddick received a fatal wound to the chest. It is unclear if it was Reddick or Price who returned fire, but one of them certainly did. Harris, who was one of the proprietors of the Metropolitan saloon, was wounded in the exchange. Reddick's corpse lay where it fell for about an hour before the coroner arrived.

Harris was arrested, charged and indicted for the murder of Reddick and the attempt to murder Deputy Constable Price. He was granted a change of venue to Liberty County. His attorneys continued to seek delays. In 1904, he was tried. The jury could not reach a verdict. Harris was retried in 1905, but the result was the same. It is not known if Harris was ever convicted of the murder.

Reddick had served with the agency for two years. He was survived by his wife, Della Goldman, and one daughter. Reddick is buried at the Magnolia Cemetery in Beaumont.

Pevito, Elijah
Born 31 March 1870_Died 17 December 1905

Walter (also referred to as Henry) Powell, who was about nineteen years of age, was observed walking along the streetcar tracks in Beaumont with a pistol in each hand. Motorman Bryon Merritt, who still held his commission as a Beaumont police officer, brought his streetcar to a stop just in front of Powell. Merritt stepped to the right side of the vestibule and ordered Powell to consider himself under arrest. Powell spoke to Merritt and asked him if he had a gun. Merritt replied that he did not. Powell immediately raised one of his revolvers and fired a shot at close range, striking Merritt in the chest. The wounded Merritt ran about twenty steps, fell facedown at the side of the track and died.

Powell then proceeded to a nearby house and ordered the resident to take his wife and child and flee because he intended to kill the officers who would soon be coming after him. Powell also indicated that he intended to die with them.

Deputy Constable Pevito, Deputy Sheriff Reed Tevis and Beaumont policemen John Sheffield and Nott Smith soon arrived at the residence and began to surround the house. Pevito approached the dwelling from the front, while the other officers took up positions on each side and to the rear of the building. Without warning, a shot rang out. Pevito was seen staggering backward near a fence. He fell dead, shot through the heart.

Tevis remained at the rear of the building and ordered Powell to come out. Powell complied but emerged from the house holding a revolver in each hand. Tevis ordered him to drop the guns, but when Powell began to do so, he made a move to shoot. Tevis raised his Winchester rifle and fired one shot, hitting Powell in the temple and penetrating his head. The bullet, fired at close range, killed Powell instantly. As Powell fell to the ground, he discharged one of his revolvers. The bullet traveled through the air harmlessly and struck no one.

Pevito had come to Beaumont from Orange four or five years earlier and was a peace officer almost the entire time of his residence in Jefferson County. He had served on the Beaumont police force, as well as the Jefferson County Sheriff's Department.

Pevito had been appointed a deputy constable in Precinct 1 just a few months before he was killed. He was survived by his wife, Ida Allen, and four children. Pevito is buried at the Magnolia Cemetery in Beaumont.

Related Case: Beaumont Police Department, Bryon Merritt

Holder, George Russell
Born June 1869—Died 7 January 1906

Precinct 1 constable George Holder was shot and killed by a Jefferson County deputy sheriff. The shooting took place during an unfortunate incident that occurred at the county jail.

Holder's six-year-old daughter had been assaulted. The suspect, William Gregorson, was captured and taken to the jail. Holder was furious, as any father would be.

On 6 January 1906, Gregorson was convicted and sentenced to serve fifty years in prison. Holder was upset that Gregorson did not receive the death penalty. About 8:00 a.m. on Sunday, 7 January 1906, Holder went to a café owned by one of the jurors. He was heard to say, "I want to tell all you boys and friends goodbye, as I am going to hell with Gregorson." As Holder walked from the café down Pearl Street to the county jail, he told each person he passed the same thing. A witness called the sheriff's office and warned them that Holder was heavily armed and headed their way. Several officers confronted Holder about two blocks away from the jail, but he pointed his shotgun at them, and they let him pass. At the jailhouse, Holder demanded admission. When he was refused, he opened fire on Jailer Thomas, as well as other officers. Officers had no choice but to attempt to stop Holder from taking justice into his own hands, so they returned fire and fatally wounded him. Holder died at 9:30 a.m. from a rifle bullet through his bladder.

Holder is buried at the Magnolia Cemetery in Beaumont. He was survived by his wife and at least two children.

Landrum, John Perry
Born 12 December 1860—Died 17 May 1907

Precinct 4 constable John Landrum had arrested twenty-one-year-old Tom Jackson previously for assaulting an elderly man. He later arrested Jackson, and several other young men, for train riding without a ticket.

Jackson had complained that Landrum cursed him in front of several young ladies. He made threats to kill Landrum. On Friday, 17 May 1907, Landrum was traveling on horseback along a public road about three-fourths of a mile from Odelia, about fifteen miles from Beaumont, when he was shot and killed from ambush. Family historians claim that Jackson was hidden in the bushes along Landrum's intended path and assassinated him, using a shotgun to inflict the deadly wound to Landrum's chest.

Jackson surrendered to officers and admitted to the shooting. He was locked up in the county jail and charged with Landrum's murder. Jackson claimed self-defense, saying that he shot Landrum to save his own life. Jackson also said that Landrum had told him that both of them could not live in Odelia. The young Jackson went on to allege that Landrum had drawn his pistol and fired a shot at him at close range that left powder burns on his arm.

Jackson was indicted for murder on 22 May 1907. On 29 October 1907, he pleaded guilty to manslaughter and was sentenced to two years in the penitentiary. He was released just six months later.

Landrum was elected constable for Precinct 4 in Fannett on 6 November 1906. He was commissioned on 11 February 1907 and had been a constable for slightly over three months when he was killed. Local newspapers reported that he had been a deputy constable for a considerable time, as well. Landrum was also the postmaster in the Odelia community, located in western Jefferson County.

According to accounts in the local newspaper, Landrum had been married twice and was survived by his second wife and two children. The article went on to claim that Landrum had two grown children. He is buried in the Landrum Cemetery in Fannett. His tombstone incorrectly reflects his date of death as 13 May 1907.

Thornton, Robert Edward
Born 7 March 1873—Died 10 February 1917

On Saturday night, 10 February 1917, the bad blood that existed between Deputy Constable Robert Thornton and former Port Arthur policeman Josh Griffith boiled over. Griffith was a candidate for constable, running against Thornton's boss. The two men were in a bar and stepped outside, where the argument turned fatal for Thornton. Both men went for their guns, and a deadly dual commenced in the streets of Port Arthur.

According to varying reports, Thornton was shot four or five times through the body. He managed to get off two shots at Griffith, but both bullets missed their mark.

Griffith was jailed. The disposition of any changes is unknown. Griffith was still recovering from a wound suffered when he was shot in the arm by fellow Port Arthur policeman V. Pozzo on 13 June 1916. Griffith and Pozzo fought each other in a similar street-style duel.

Thornton was survived by his wife, Sophronia (Saphronia) Perkins, and five children. Some family genealogist's list as many as eight children, but it is unclear if the other three were offspring of Thornton's union with Sophronia or from an earlier marriage. He had been a deputy constable for four years. Thornton is buried at the City Cemetery (either in Port Arthur or Groves).

Foster, Joseph "Joe"
Born circa 1885—Died 23 August 1921

On Tuesday, 23 August 1921, Charles Blackwell, who was a former Texas Ranger captain and, at the time, the chief of the guards at the Gulf Refinery, was standing on the street speaking to Port Arthur night captain McAfee and two patrolmen when Deputy Constable Joe Foster approached them. Blackwell allegedly said, "Joe, what do you want?" Foster replied, "Not a ---- thing, you ----." Blackwell claimed that Foster reached for his pistol. In any case, Blackwell was quicker on the draw and shot Foster once through the heart. Afterward, Blackwell contended that Foster kept trying to pull his pistol, so he shot him three more times in the chest. He then handed his gun over to Captain McAfee.

Foster and Blackwell had quarreled during a recent strike. Foster had apparently boasted that he intended to get Blackwell. Blackwell claimed that he was in fear of his life and had shot Foster in self-defense, and only after he had cursed him and reached for his pistol.

Blackwell was arrested and released on a $5,000 bond. The disposition of the charges against him is unknown.

Foster is buried at Lockhart in Caldwell County. He was survived by his wife.

JEFFERSON COUNTY CONVICT CAMP

Carr, W.F.
Born circa 1878—Died 3 November 1906

W.F. Carr was employed as a night convict guard for the Jefferson County convict camp where inmates worked on public roads as a part of their punishment. On Saturday, 3 November 1906, the guards and convicts left the camp to go to work on the roads.

Harry Williams was a trustee and the camp cook. Carr, who slept during the day, had retired to his bed. Williams slipped into Carr's room and took Carr's Winchester shotgun, firing a blast into Carr's head while doing so. Williams left the shotgun behind and stole Carr's revolver as he fled. When guards returned that night, they discovered Carr dead, lying in his bed in a pool of blood. Local police were alerted, and Williams was arrested later that same night in Beaumont.

Williams confessed to shooting Carr, and on 24 January 1907, he was tried and convicted of the crime. He was sentenced to be hanged. Williams received several reprieves, and shortly before his scheduled execution date in August 1907, Governor Campbell commuted his sentence to life in prison, basing the commutation on Williams's diminished mental incapacity.

Very little is known about Carr. He was about twenty-three or twenty-five years old when he was killed. The newspaper reported that he was a widower with two children living in Tyler County while at the same time having a wife and four children he had abandoned to escape indebtedness in Caldwell County.

Carr's father is reported to have taken the body back to Lockhart, but no records have been located that indicate where he was buried. It is claimed that he is buried at the Bunton Cemetery in Dale, Caldwell County, but no grave site has been located.

JEFFERSON COUNTY SHERIFF'S OFFICE

Douglas, Ottawa
Born circa 1886—Died 5 September 1913
Date of Incident: 4 September 1913

Deputy Sheriff Douglas was shot and killed when he responded to reports of a man who was brandishing a pistol in the town of Nome.

When Douglas arrived at the scene, he placed his hand on the man's shoulder and told him he was under arrest. The man responded by striking Douglas in the face and pulling out his gun. Douglas drew his own gun and shot the fellow in the chest three times. The wounded man was able to return fire, shooting Douglas in the groin. Douglas fired three more times, killing his assailant.

Douglas succumbed to his wounds the following day during an operation. He had been with the agency for only sixteen months and had previously served with the Beaumont Police Department and Fire Department. He is buried at the Magnolia Cemetery in Beaumont.

Giles, Jake W.
Born 11 March 1866—Died 24 March 1916

Sheriff Jake Giles was shot and killed by Paul V. Hadley as he transported Hadley and his wife back to Texas to face felony charges.

On Friday, 24 March 1916, Hadley and his bride left Checotah, Oklahoma, on a southbound MK&T Railroad train bound for Beaumont, Texas, under the custody of Sheriff Jake Giles. According to witnesses, Hadley was handed a concealed pistol by his wife, who said, "Now use this and get clear of the crowd." He did so and shot Giles fatally, then stole his gun and fled.

The Hadleys were later arrested. Mrs. Hadley was acquitted of murder but sentenced to serve ten years in prison on an escape charge. Paul Hadley was convicted and sentenced to life in prison. He escaped four years later. Hadley returned to a life of crime, and on 23 April 1923, he was hanged in Arizona after a conviction on another murder charge.

Giles was a widower and was survived by his nine children. He is buried at the Magnolia Cemetery in Beaumont. Giles was elected sheriff on 3 November 1908 and reelected in 1910, 1912 and 1914. He served until his death.

At the time of his death, Giles was carrying the pistol that belonged to Douglas, which he had taken when he killed him.

Hutcheson, John E.
Born circa 1875—Died 28 June 1925

Deputy John Hutcheson was shot and killed with his own revolver by an unruly prisoner in the county jail.

The man, a Mexican named Rosa Neues, was serving time in jail for public drunkenness and was working off a twenty-one-dollar fine. At about 10:00 a.m. on Sunday, 28 June 1925, Neues became unruly and threw everything in reach at Hutcheson, including a piece of metal that grazed Hutcheson's head. Hutcheson reported the incident to the sheriff, who told him not to give Neues lunch without his assistance.

Hutcheson neglected the sheriff's warning and enlisted the help of Jailer King and an inmate named Clifton Lotela (Clifford Dochile) to serve lunch to Neues. Observing Neues's agitated state, he also released prisoners George McNeil and George Henry to aid in the meal service. As Hutcheson entered the cell, Neues leaped past him, vaulted over a banister and dropped to the lower floor. Hutcheson and the inmates followed. According to one report, Neues jumped on Hutcheson's back and hit him in the head with a broken cuspidor. One source reported that the metal object was an iron chamber pot. The impact knocked Hutcheson to the floor. Neues grabbed Hutcheson's .45-caliber service revolver and shot him in the left chest.

The three inmates who had been assisting Hutcheson serve lunch—George McNeil, George Henry and Clifton Lotela (Clifford Dochile)—immediately attacked the shooter. McNeil hit Neues over the head with an iron bar. A desperate struggle took place during which Neues was shot in the head and fatally wounded.

The inmates who assisted Hutcheson were released from the county jail for their heroic actions.

Hutcheson was survived by his wife and four daughters. He is buried at Magnolia Cemetery in Beaumont.

Both the *Mexia Daily News* and the *Galveston Daily News* of 29 June 1925 reported the killer's name as Rosa Neues. The *San Antonio Light* newspaper of 29 June 1925 claimed that the killer's name was Gross Rincon. It is unclear which account is correct.

Rogers, William J.
Born 27 May 1888—Died 26 August 1925
Date of Incident: 25 August 1925

At about 12:30 a.m. on Tuesday, 25 August 1925, Deputy Sheriff William Rogers was attending a dance at White's houseboat in Port Acres. A witness named Clyde Allen said that he was dancing with a young lady when another man started paying attention to her. Allen and the woman went to the porch, but the man, identified as Dennis Wood, followed. Wood instigated a squabble, and Allen hit him. Wood reached for his .22-caliber pistol. A man named Joe Valleaux grabbed Wood. During the struggle over control of the gun, it discharged accidentally, striking Rogers in the abdomen. He died the following day at Mary Gates Hospital in Port Arthur.

Wood and Valleaux were arrested and charged with assault with intent to murder. They were both given $500 bonds and bound over to the grand jury. Despite Rogers's death, the justice of the peace stated that the charges would not be upgraded to murder. The disposition of this case is unknown.

Rogers is buried at the Frost Cemetery in Kerens, Navarro County. He was not married.

As noted earlier, readers should note the irony of the fact that there are two lawmen in this book with the name William J. Rogers. Both men were born on the twenty-seventh day of the month. Both men died on 26 August, but of different years.

Durden, Cay
Born 12 February 1875—Died 6 June 1928
Date of Incident: 5 June 1928

On Tuesday, 5 June 1928, Deputy Sheriff Cay Durden was in the 400 block of Forsythe in Beaumont when he became involved in a quarrel with a man named A.N. Adams, who had approached him about a debt. Adams struck Durden. Durden drew his pistol and shot Adams in the thigh. Beaumont patrolman John Freeman arrested Durden and was in the process of escorting him across the street when Adams's two sons, Clarence and James, charged them. James Adams struck Durden in the head with a heavy length of pipe. Freeman attempted to arrest the Adams brothers, but they fled the scene. They were arrested later and released on bond.

The Adams brothers were indicted by the grand jury. James Adams was tried for the murder of Durden. The final disposition of that case is unknown.

Durden was survived by his wife, Hattie, and at least two children. He is buried at the Robinson's Cemetery.

KARNES COUNTY SHERIFF'S OFFICE

Morris, William T. "Brack"
Born 15 June 1860—Died 12 June 1901

Sheriff Brack Morris was shot and killed while he was questioning a man about a stolen horse. During the interrogation, the suspect's brother, Gregorio Cortez, rushed at Morris. Morris opened fire, wounding Cortez. Cortez then opened fire at Morris, hitting him four times. After the sheriff had already fallen to the ground, mortally wounded, Cortez shot him a fifth time.

Two days later, Cortez was involved in another incident with lawmen during which he shot and killed Gonzales County sheriff Richard Glover and a posseman named Henry Schnabel. The lawmen were in the process of arresting Cortez for the murder of Morris.

Cortez was charged and convicted but was eventually pardoned by the governor.

Morris had served with the Karnes County Sheriff's Office for five years. He was first elected on 3 November 1896 and reelected in 1898 and 1900.

Morris was survived by his wife, Dixie Harper. He is buried at the Rung City Cemetery.

Related Cases: Gonzales County Sheriff's Office, Richard Glover and Henry Schnabel

Lewallen, Elihu L.
Born 28 April 1885—Died 18 August 1926

Deputy Sheriff Elihu Lewallen was killed in a shootout that took place on the streets of Kenedy.

Lewallen had been having a disagreement with a man named Louis P. Pullin. The two had engaged in another shooting scrape at a dance near Kenedy some months earlier. During that encounter, Pullin was wounded several times by Lewallen. On this occasion, the men met on one of the side streets of Kenedy. According to eyewitnesses, both men got out of their cars the instant they saw each other. The pair began shooting at each other almost immediately. Both were armed with shotguns. Lewallen was hit, with several pellets of shot entering his head and body. He died almost instantly. Pullin received a flesh wound to the leg, a shattered finger and a nick on one ear. After the shooting, Pullin surrendered to Deputy Sheriff Shaw.

Pullin was charged with the murder of Lewallen, and on 20 August, his bond was set at $7,500. The outcome of the charges against Pullin is unknown.

Lewallen was survived by his wife, Bertha Viola Hood, and seven children. Some family genealogists show nine children. He is buried at the Kenedy Cemetery.

KAUFMAN COUNTY CONSTABLE'S OFFICE

Burk, John Dee
Born July–August 1872—Died 1 May 1905

On Monday, 1 May 1905, Precinct 8 constable John Burk was in the city of Kaufman conducting business. At about 3:30 p.m., he responded to a report of a disturbance at J.J. Patterson's billiard hall. Burk arrested an intoxicated man named M.B. Scott, who was at the root of the commotion. Scott resisted arrest, making it necessary for Burk to hit the man on the head with his pistol in order to make Scott comply. After the incident, Burk allowed Scott to wash his hands. Scott returned with not only clean hands but also a pistol, which he used to shoot Burk in the head. Burk died from the gunshot wound about two hours later.

On 15 July 1905, Scott was sentenced to serve twenty years in the state penitentiary for murder in the second degree. On 21 February 1906, the Court of Criminal Appeals of Texas reversed the decision and sent the case back to the lower court. On 9 January 1907, Scott pleaded guilty to manslaughter and was sentenced to three years and nine months in the state penitentiary for the murder of Burk.

Burk was survived by his wife, Maude. He is buried in Hill County. Some sources report his surname as Burke rather than Burk.

KERR COUNTY SHERIFF'S OFFICE

Butler, M.F. "Tom"
Born (Unknown)—Died 4 September 1909

Deputy Sheriff Tom Butler was shot and killed while assisting other officers in the arrest of a man named John Purdy.

On Saturday, 4 September 1909, Deputy Sheriff Henry Stout had responded to a report of a man making trouble with a woman named Polly Coleman in the black section of Kerrville. According to a witness, "He [John Purdy] was raising hell with Polly." As Stout approached the home of Ms. Coleman on horseback, Purdy grabbed a pistol from Coleman and fired at him. Purdy then ran toward Stout and, when he had come to within about twenty steps, fired again. Stout and Purdy exchanged several shots, and then Purdy ran off through a pasture. Stout telephoned Sheriff Moore to report the incident.

Sheriff Moore and Stout spotted Purdy near Mountain View Cemetery. At that point, Butler approached Moore on horseback and inquired about the chase. The pair spotted Purdy in the distance and tore down a wire fence in order to continue the hunt. Stout and Butler gave chase, splitting up in order to cover Purdy's possible escape routes up the side of a nearby hill. Stout had gone about 250 yards around a hill when he heard two gunshots fired in rapid succession. He rode to the spot where he had heard the report of the firearm and found Butler's horse standing and Butler seated and holding his side, wounded from a gunshot fired by Purdy. His leg was also broken near the middle of the thigh. Sheriff Moore had observed Butler from a distance and had seen him dismount and pull his pistol as he headed into the brush in search of Purdy. It was at that point that Moore heard the gunfire and headed to the spot where the incident took place.

Butler died from his wounds shortly after the shooting. Purdy, who was a repeat offender, was found guilty of killing Butler and was sentenced to life in prison. Purdy filed an appeal on 23 January 1910 and received a change of venue to Uvalde County. He contended that Butler had no right to arrest him and that he had fired in self-defense. On 26 October 1910, the appeal was heard and the conviction was upheld.

Butler's place of burial is unknown.

KILGORE POLICE DEPARTMENT

Scroggins, John Carter
Born circa 1890—Died 12 December 1927
Date of Incident: 11 December 1927

Officer John Scroggins died from injuries he received when he was struck by a hit-and-run driver.

Scroggins was directing traffic at the scene of an accident on the Longview–Kilgore Highway. A vehicle operated by a man named W.P. New hit Scroggins, inflicting serious injuries. New was arrested shortly after the incident. Scroggins died the following day.

New was charged with the murder of Scroggins.

Scroggins had served with the agency for five years. He was survived by his wife and one son. Scroggins is buried at Huntington Cemetery, near Lufkin.

KILLEEN POLICE DEPARTMENT

Blair, John Toliver
Born 19 February 1871—Died 4 April 1917

City Marshal John Blair was shot and killed while he was attempting to stop a shootout.

The incident involved a father and son pair, pitted against a man whom the father thought had stolen his wife. William C. "Will" Cannon had been absent from home for several years. When he returned, he discovered his wife had taken up with another man, Monteville B. Ray. The two men had had a confrontation days earlier.

On Wednesday, 4 April 1917, Cannon and his nineteen-year-old son, Floyd, went gunning for Ray. Blair warned Ray to get out of town. The Cannons were watching the garage where Ray kept his automobile. When the two men took a break at about 5:00 p.m., Blair and Ray went to get the car. Unfortunately, the Cannons arrived just as the automobile was being gassed up.

Will Cannon shot Blair. As the wounded Blair fell, he managed to return fire, hitting Cannon. The two men emptied their pistols at each other as they lay on the ground until both were mortally wounded. Next, Ray and Floyd started shooting. A reported twenty rounds were fired. Amazingly, neither man was injured. Blair's final words were: "I was only doing my duty."

Ray posted bond. Only Floyd Cannon was indicted. He was tried and found not guilty. Three years later, Will Cannon's son Floyd and Ray were involved in another shootout. Ray had returned to Killeen to visit his sick mother. He intended to be in town only for a brief time. When the afternoon train was late, he walked to the bank. While leaving the bank, Floyd called out to him and then opened fire. Ray was wounded but managed to pull his pistol and empty it at Floyd, eventually killing him. Ray survived and was never prosecuted.

Blair was survived by his wife, Florence A. Overton, and five children. He is buried at the Killeen City Cemetery. Blair had served two terms as city marshal and had been reelected to a third term.

KIMBLE, COUNTY OF

Cox, Jehu Thomas
Born 23 April 1862—Died 2 January 1914
Date of incident: December 1913

Sometime in December 1913, A.S. Etheridge shot and killed county sheep inspector Jehu Cox.

Etheridge was arrested and charged with the killing. He was tried in 1915 on a change of venue to Gillespie County and acquitted of the murder by a jury.

Cox is buried at the Junction City Cemetery. He was not married.

KIMBLE COUNTY SHERIFF'S OFFICE

James, Raymond Edison
Born 16 September 1887—Died 2 June 1917

Kimble County authorities received information that an army deserter had escaped from the county jail at Rock Springs and boarded a freight wagon that was headed toward Junction. Deputies Raymond James and J.W. Ragland, along with two freighters, were sent out to intercept the deserter.

When the runaway, Harrison S. McAlester, was located outside Junction, he was ordered to stop and surrender. McAlester stepped down from the wagon as if to comply. As he did so, he fired one shot at the lawmen from a .45-caliber Model 1911-A1 army semiautomatic pistol. The bullet hit James in the abdomen, inflicting a serious wound. McAlester was overpowered by Ragland and arrested. A posse transported McAlester to jail in Junction. James was also returned to Junction, where he died on the operating table from the wound.

McAlester claimed that he had deserted from the U.S. Army in San Antonio on 22 May 1917. Along with the killing of James, he was also suspected of being involved in two murders in the Bexar County that involved other deserters. Although McAlester was never charged in the Bexar County homicides, his accomplices were.

James was survived by his wife, Willie Vara Pickett, and two children. He is buried at the South Llano Cemetery.

KING COUNTY SHERIFF'S OFFICE

Mitchell, Joseph John "Red"
Born February 1868—Died 24 December 1916

At about 7:30 a.m. on Monday, 10 January 1916, former sheriff "Red" Mitchell shot and killed a man named S.H. Morton in the dining room of the Mitchell Hotel in Knox City, Knox County. Morton was shot four times. At the time of the incident, Morton was anticipating trouble and was carrying a .45-caliber pistol. The cause of the incident was reported as having been related to a domestic dispute between the two men that had resulted in the breakup of Morton's home. Afterward, Mitchell and his wife cross-filed for divorce.

Mitchell was charged with the murder of Morton and was released on a $5,000 bond. He was formally charged, but the indictment was later dismissed.

At about 9:00 p.m. on Sunday, 24 December 1916, Mitchell and Knox County deputy sheriff Joel Reed were standing in front of the drugstore in Knox City. An automobile pulled up, and a man named George Douglass got out with a Winchester rifle. Douglass opened fire and shot Mitchell in the back, then fired six rounds from his pistol into the already wounded Mitchell. When Reed and the city marshal later tried to arrest Douglass, he shot and killed Reed. Douglass fled in the automobile.

Douglass, who was Mitchell's brother-in-law, was arrested for the murders. On 6 March 1917, he was tried for the murder of Reed. A mistrial resulted when the jury was unable to reach a verdict, voting eight to four for acquittal. On 20 March 1917, Douglass was tried in the same court in Benjamin for the murder of Mitchell. The judge granted a continuance until the next term of court. Furious at the outcome, Mitchell's brother Bill Mitchell opened fire, killing Douglass and wounding his attorney and a witness. The disposition of any charges against Bill Mitchell is unknown.

Mitchell was survived by his wife, Ellen Lucinda Douglass, and three children. His place of burial is unknown. Mitchell had been elected sheriff on 3 November 1908 and served until 8 November 1910.

Related Case: Knox County Sheriff's Office, Joel Reed

KNOX COUNTY SHERIFF'S OFFICE

Reed, Joel Bailey
Born 21 April 1882—Died 24 December 1916

A personal feud developed between former King County sheriff Joseph John "Red" Mitchell and George Douglass. Mitchell was engaged in a divorce proceeding, and Douglass was his brother-in-law. Mitchell was walking down the street in Knox City on Christmas Eve when a car pulled over. Douglass stepped out of the vehicle armed with a Winchester rifle and shot Mitchell in the back. After Mitchell fell, Douglass drew a handgun, stood over Mitchell and continued to fire several more shots. Reed and the Knox City marshal ran to the scene and tried to arrest Douglass, but Douglass opened fire on them, hitting Reed three times and killing him. Douglass escaped from the scene but was later captured.

On 6 March 1917, Douglass was tried for the murder of Reed. The jury was hung at eight to four in favor of acquittal. On 20 March, Douglass was back in court facing charges of killing Mitchell. The judge granted a continuance until the next term of court. Furious at the outcome, J.J. Mitchell's brother Bill Mitchell opened fire, killing Douglass and wounding his attorney and a witness. The disposition of any charges against Bill Mitchell is unknown.

Reed was survived by his wife, Inez Elender Adaline Cone. He is buried at the Long Branch Cemetery in Eastland, Eastland County.

KYLE POLICE DEPARTMENT

Joslin, Henry Hampton
Born circa 1852—Died 31 January 1905

At about 12:40 a.m. on Tuesday, 31 January 1905, Kyle night watchman Henry Joslin was patrolling downtown near the train depot when he heard someone approaching from behind. As he turned around to see who it was, a man fired one shot from a .41-caliber pistol. The bullet struck Joslin in the chest and exited his body. The sound of the gunfire awoke the son of a woman who lived nearby. The boy woke his mother, who investigated the disturbance and the cries of a man calling for help.

Joslin was found lying near the train station. He was still conscious. Unfortunately, he was unable to identify his assassin because it was too dark to see the man. Joslin also claimed that he had no known enemies.

Joslin died about 2:40 a.m. No records have been located to indicate if anyone was ever arrested or if the case was solved.

Joslin's wife, Eliza W., preceded him in death. He was survived by six children. Joslin is probably buried at the San Marcos Cemetery in Hays County, but no record of that interment, or tombstone, has been located.

LAMAR COUNTY CONSTABLE'S OFFICE

Draper, William Robert
Born 30 April 1871—Died 5 February 1909

Deputy Constable William Draper was shot and killed when he and Constable Matthews attempted to serve a warrant on a man named Bill (Will) McIntosh.

At about 8:00 p.m. on Friday, 5 February 1909, Draper and Matthews went to the home of Bill McIntosh in Paris to place him under arrest for a charge of assault. When they arrived, McIntosh was not at home. The lawmen were talking with a woman at the home when McIntosh returned. Draper and Matthews told him that they had come to place him in custody. McIntosh grabbed a rifle from inside the back door of his home and shot Draper at point-blank range, killing him instantly. After the shooting, McIntosh fled.

McIntosh was captured in Wister, Oklahoma, on 9 February and returned to Paris. He was tried and convicted of Draper's murder and executed by hanging on 7 October 1909.

Draper was survived by his wife, Susan, and two children. He is buried at the Evergreen Cemetery.

LAMAR COUNTY SHERIFF'S OFFICE

Robertson, George Richardson
Born 28 October 1885—Died 10 September 1940

On Tuesday, 10 September 1940, Deputy Sheriff George Robertson went to a filling station in Paris to arrest two men, Turner Ross Fowler and Charles "Buddy" Acker, for suspicion of attempting to sell a stolen tire and wheel. Fowler and Acker were also wanted for committing robberies in Buffalo and Huntsville.

Robertson made the arrest and was transporting Fowler and Acker to jail. He was driving Fowler and Acker's vehicle to the lockup with the two prisoners in the back seat. He was following the sheriff, who was driving his automobile. Robertson and the two prisoners suddenly disappeared. Robertson's body was found near Powderly, north of Paris, late on the evening of Wednesday, 11 September. He had been shot, slashed and beaten unmercifully.

A manhunt began almost immediately for Fowler and Acker. Their vehicle was reported as having been a dark green or gray 1939 Ford or Chevrolet sedan. The suspects were sighted near Grant, Oklahoma, turning west on a gravel road. They were not captured.

Charges were filed against the pair on 14 September at Paris. On 13 October, the *San Antonio Light* newspaper reported that Fowler and Acker were still at large, hiding out in the woods of San Jacinto County. The following day, Acker was captured in the dense woods near Oakhurst, and Fowler was apprehended walking along the railroad tracks in New Waverly. Nothing is known about the outcome of the charges against Fowler or Acker.

Robertson had been with the agency for eight years and was survived by his wife, Margaret "Maggie" Gray. He is buried at the Evergreen Cemetery in Lamar County.

LAMB COUNTY SHERIFF'S OFFICE

Bolin, Harvey S. "Harve"
Born 25 October 1879—Died 20 August 1932

Deputy Sheriff Harve Bolin was shot and killed in Roosevelt County, New Mexico, while he was riding with a posse that was attempting to apprehend a gang of bank robbers.

The posse tracked the thieves to the Pegworth Ranch near Portales, New Mexico. The men took up positions nearby to observe activities. Posse member G.R. Crim, who was sheriff of Lamb County, spotted one of the wanted men, Ed "Pearchmouth" Stanton, and called out to him to put up his hands. Instead of complying with the sheriff's order, the man grabbed several weapons and opened fire on the posse. Bolin was hit in the head with one shot and killed instantly. Another deputy, R.L. Hollis, was seriously injured. One of the outlaws, Lee Pebsworth, was also injured in the shooting affray.

The gang fled. They remained on the run for some time and were responsible for the murders of three other law enforcement officers before one of the men, Glenn Hunsucker, was shot and killed. Jack Sullivan (the surname reported by one source was Hedrick) and Lee Pebsworth were intercepted in their automobile near the Dalmont Ranch, sixty-five miles from Portales. The two men gave themselves up and were transported to Portales. The other gang members, A.C. Hunsucker and Jack Williams (alias Sullivan), were also arrested.

Ed Stanton, who was responsible for the murder of Bolin, was tried and sentenced to death. Stanton was subsequently executed by electrocution at the Huntsville State Penitentiary on 28 September 1934. Stanton became the 104th criminal to be electrocuted in Texas.

Bolin had been in law enforcement for almost twenty-two years. He was survived by his wife and ten children. Bolin is buried at the Lockney Cemetery in Floyd County.

Bolin had been a game warden for two to three years before he was named a deputy sheriff in Floyd County in 1917. Until 1926, Bolin served as the Lockney night watchman and continued as a Floyd County deputy sheriff. In 1926, he moved to Plainview, where he served as a policeman until June 1927. Bolin was a Hale County deputy sheriff until January 1929, when he returned to the Plainview Police Department, where he served until April 1932. He was reportedly the night chief of police and chief of police in Plainview. In April 1932, Bolin became a "special officer" working for the Banker's Association and assigned to the Olton Bank robbery when he was killed. In all likelihood, he was employed by the Banker's Association and deputized by the Lamb County sheriff during this investigation.

Related Cases: Swisher County Sheriff's Office, John Moseley; Wise County Sheriff's Office, Joseph Brown; and Lincoln County, New Mexico Sheriff's Office, Thomas Jones

Loyd, Franklin Aubrey
Born 6 March 1888—Died 22 March 1937
Date of Incident: 20 March 1937

Franklin Loyd was appointed sheriff on 12 June 1935, when J. Len Irvin resigned. He was subsequently elected to the post on 3 November 1936. Loyd served until his death.

On Saturday, 20 March 1937, Loyd was shot and killed while attempting to arrest a drunken man named Leroy Kelly at the train station in Littlefield.

Kelly had been accused of shooting at a woman. When Loyd and Deputy Sam Hutson arrived at the depot, they encountered Kelley, who was standing next to a crowd of people holding a gun. Loyd ordered Kelley to drop his gun. He did not but instead chose to shoot Loyd. Loyd was hit once in the head and once in the shoulder. The two men grappled for a while before Loyd fell from the effects of the gunshot wounds. Loyd's deputy, Sam Hutson, who was unarmed, picked up Loyd's gun and returned fire. He managed to hit Kelly twice, wounding him in the arm. Huston was then able to arrest Kelly and transport him to jail.

Loyd died from his wounds at midnight on 22 March 1937.

Loyd's tombstone, as well as various memorials, lists his date of death as being the twenty-first. His death certificate lists the date as the twenty-second but notes that he died at midnight on the twenty-first.

Kelley was tried and convicted of murder. He was sentenced to death and subsequently executed by electrocution at the Huntsville State Penitentiary on 15 March 1938. Kelly became the 150th person to meet such a fate.

Loyd had been with the agency for two years and was survived by his wife, Grace Owen, and eight children. He is buried at the Littlefield Cemetery.

Loyd's wife was appointed to complete his term in office on 24 March 1937. She served until 1 January 1939. The *Amarillo Globe* of 25 March 1937 described Grace Loyd as being a pretty brunette who, in Mrs. Loyd's own words, has fired a six-shooter "only once, and that was a long time ago."

LAMPASAS COUNTY CONSTABLE'S OFFICE

Connell, John J.
Born 10 November 1860—Died 8 April 1915

Precinct 3 constable John Connell was shot and killed while he was chasing a suspect on horseback near Lometa.

Connell and another officer had arrested a man named F.W. (or W.F.) Bader for forgery. During questioning, Bader managed to escape. A gun battle followed during which Connell was fatally wounded.

Bader, who also used the alias H.S. McDonald, was tried and convicted of the murder. On 23 April, he was sentenced to serve fifty years in prison.

Connell had been with the agency for ten years. He was survived by his wife, Lena, and five children. Connell is buried at the Lometa Cemetery, IOOF section.

Lancaster Police Department

Solomon, Peter Monroe
Born 25 January 1856—Died 2 November 1912

At about 7:30 p.m. on Saturday, 2 November 1912, City Marshal Peter Solomon and Deputy Marshal Tom Ellis made an arrest at a point about a mile and half south of the interurban train line. The officers secured the prisoner and stationed themselves at the train stop at Valley View in order to flag down the northbound train on the Dallas–Waxahachie line. Solomon placed himself in position at the Valley View stop to flag the oncoming northbound train with his hat. He was struck and thrown with great force against the stationhouse. One arm was broken, and his skull was crushed.

Solomon was survived by his wife and at least nine children. He is buried at the Edgewood Cemetery in Lancaster, Dallas County.

Laredo Police Department

Garcia, Arturo
Born 23 May 1887—Died 6 November 1917

Shortly after 6:00 p.m. on 6 November 1917, Officer Arturo Garcia was walking when he met Francisco Hernandez at San Francisco Avenue between Jardin and Bruni Streets. Hernandez, a former section hand on the Texas-Mexican railroad, was riding on a wagon. When he saw Garcia, he jumped down and approached him. What was said prior to the shooting is unknown. Hernandez fired three times with his .38-caliber revolver, hitting

Garcia in the left backside. The bullet passed near his heart and exited on his right side. Garcia died instantly. One newspaper report stated that Garcia had stepped out of his vehicle and was standing against a fence near the home of Hernandez. Witnesses claimed that a few words were spoken, and then Hernandez opened fire, hitting Garcia one time in the side as he was turning away.

Officer Flavio Molina heard the shots and rushed to the scene. Hernandez was standing over Garcia with the pistol in his hand. He admitted that he had shot Garcia and surrendered himself peacefully to Molina. Hernandez was arrested and brought to the police station. He was later transferred to the county jail. On 8 December, Hernandez was indicted by the grand jury for the murder of Garcia, but it is unknown whether he was ever tried or convicted.

Garcia was survived by his wife and a small child. He is buried at the Catholic Cemetery, but his grave site has not been located. Newspaper reports of the day claimed that Garcia had become a member of the police force the preceding January and that he was "recognized as one of the best, most fearless and trustworthy members of the police department and his loss was keenly felt."

Ayala, Pedro
Born 28 February 1887—Died 11 June 1936
Date of Incident: 7 June 1936

Officer Pedro Ayala, who was investigating an accident at the time, was hit by a vehicle that was operated by a man named Charles Legay (Lagay) of Fort McIntosh. Legay, a sergeant in the army, was intoxicated at the time the incident took place and had four other soldiers with him in the car. Ayala was seriously injured in the mishap and died four days later.

Charges of murder, driving while intoxicated and failure to stop and render aid were filed against Legay. The outcome of those charges is unknown.

According to some sources, Ayala had been with the agency for twenty-eight years, although several newspaper accounts of the day claim only sixteen. He was survived by his wife, Crecencia Vargas, and one son. Ayala's place of burial is unknown.

Lavaca County Constable's Office

Manning, Benjamin
Born 31 October 1878—Died 3 November 1928

At about 8:00 a.m. on Saturday, 3 November 1928, Deputy Constable Benjamin Manning was shot and killed by a man named P.L. Hall. Hall shot Manning three times with a shotgun. The injuries were fatal, and Manning died instantly.

The exact circumstances surrounding this killing are unknown, but according to witnesses, Manning was on a ladder when Hall shot him. Manning was also a carpenter by trade. Both Manning and Hall were working on the same job site when the incident took place, giving rise to the belief that the shooting may have been the result of a personal disagreement between the two men. Hall was an employee of Hall & Morrow Plumbing, a plumber supply business at Yoakum.

The outcome of any charges against Hall is unknown.

Manning was survived by his wife, Josephine Goodson, and one daughter. He is buried at the St. Joseph's Catholic Cemetery in Yoakum (formerly the Yoakum Catholic Cemetery).

Lee County Sheriff's Office

Mundine, John Harmon
Born 6 November 1860—Died 18 April 1903
Date of Incident: 17 April 1903

Deputy Sheriff John Mundine was wounded when his pistol fell from his pocket and discharged accidentally. The mishap occurred while Mundine was disembarking from the Aransas Pass train in Lexington. The bullet entered his stomach.

Mundine died from the results of the gunshot wound at his home at about 8:30 p.m. the day following the accident. Mundine's cause of death was ruled as peritonitis, which is an inflammation or irritation of the tissue that lines the wall of the abdomen and covers the abdominal organs.

Mundine was survived by his wife, Alice Holman, and three children. He is buried at the Mundine Cemetery.

Leon County Constable's Office

Linson, Laurin Queston
Born 27 October 1872—Died 5 May 1900

On Thursday, 3 May 1900, Edgar Linson and J.W. Miller had an altercation at the Buffalo Trading Company where Miller worked as a clerk in the clothing department. The fight continued that night at the MacMillan & Lagrone saloon, where Miller cursed and verbally abused Linson. The following day, Edgar Linson and his father, Walter T. Linson, came to town armed with a shotgun. Miller was warned and retreated to the hotel, where he remained all day. The Linsons eventually were talked into putting away their guns and remained outside the building. Constable Laurin Q. Linson refused to disarm his father and brother. When Sheriff Reed finally arrived on the train at about 3:00 p.m., the situation quieted down.

On Saturday, 5 May 1900, Reed escorted Miller to his job at the Buffalo Trading Company. He later allowed Walter Linson to enter and try to settle the dispute. Miller was armed with a shotgun and a revolver. The argument got heated, and Reed took Walter outside. At about 8:00 a.m., Constable Linson entered the store, but when things got heated, he was escorted out by Reed. At about 9:00 a.m., Edgar Linson entered the office of the *Banner* newspaper and asked to write a few lines. He went to the Robinson & Richards store and was writing when Laurin Linson was seen walking toward the Rock store. When in front of the store, Miller shot him, emptying both barrels of his shotgun at close range. Linson walked about fifteen feet and fell over dead.

Walter Linson immediately ran toward his dead son. As he passed the store, Miller, who had by this time reloaded, shot him as well. As Walter reached the spot where his son was lying mortally wounded and knelt by his side, Miller fired again with the second barrel of his shotgun. Edgar Linson managed to borrow a .32-caliber Winchester rifle. Approaching Miller at an angle so as not to be shot himself, he fired one shot before Miller returned fire, hitting him in the leg. As Edgar fled, Miller shot him in the shoulder and neck. Miller fled into the Bryan's store.

A doctor dressed his wounds at the site, but Miller was not disarmed for more than an hour. The sheriff escorted him back to the hotel and allowed him to remain armed.

Miller was indicted for both deaths and posted bond in the amount of $1,000 for one and $3,000 for the other. On 17 May 1901, he was tried and found not guilty of killing Constable Linson.

Miller had taken the train from Houston to Palestine to stand trial for the murder of Walter Linson, but the trial was postponed, so he continued on to Buffalo to conduct some business. On Saturday, 17 May 1902, he boarded the train to depart. The conductor warned him that Edgar Linson was on the train. As Miller walked into the smoking car, Linson shot him in the back of head and then fired several more rounds into his body for good measure as he lay bleeding on the floor. Edgar Linson was arrested. The disposition of the case is unknown.

Laurin Linson is buried at the Buffalo Cemetery. He was survived by his wife, Cora Bennett Richardson, who was expecting the couple's first child at the time of Laurin's death. Linson had been elected constable in the last general election.

Some family genealogists have recorded that Edgar Linson died from gunfire on 19 March 1907, and his brother, Eugene, met a similar fate on 1 December 1906.

LIBERTY COUNTY CONSTABLE'S OFFICE

Duncan, William B.
Born May 1869—Died 16 March 1901

Constable William Duncan was shot and killed by his father-in-law, William K. Wall.

In an apparent personal disagreement that turned fatal, Wall and Duncan opened fire on each other inside a local saloon. Duncan was killed, and Wall was wounded. Another man named Wharton Branch, a well-known attorney, was also wounded in the deadly exchange of gunfire. Branch was charged with his role in the death of Duncan. Nothing further is known about the outcome of any charges against Branch.

Duncan was survived by his wife, Ella, and three children. His place of burial is unknown. Duncan was also serving as a deputy sheriff at the time of his death.

Limestone County Constable's Office

Gibson, Grover Cleveland
Born 1 August 1886—Died 23 September 1921

Precinct 4 constable Grover Gibson was shot down in an alley near the post office at Mexia at about 8:00 p.m. on Friday, 23 September 1921. His killer was a Mexia police officer named Scott "Scotty" Ferguson. Ferguson was immediately suspended from the force for thirty days pending an inquiry. No further information concerning the nature of this deadly incident is known.

Ferguson was charged with the killing of Gibson, found guilty and sentenced to five years. That decision was later reversed.

Gibson was survived by his wife, Abbie Stevenson, and one child. He is buried at the Lost Prairie Cemetery.

Smith, Rosie Lee "Ras"
Born 18 September 1871—Died 30 April 1933
Date of Incident: 8 April 1933

On Saturday, 8 April 1933, Precinct 5 constable Ras Smith was walking along a street in Kosse when, for no apparent reason, a man named Monroe Crisp attacked him with a knife. When a bystander attempted to intervene and stop the assault, Monroe's brother, Eugene Crisp, threatened the citizen with a hammer.

Smith received severe stab wounds during the attack. He died three weeks later, on 30 April.

Both Monroe and Eugene Crisp were charged with assault with intent to murder. Sometime later, murder charges were filed but were dismissed. Monroe and Eugene Crisp were each fined twenty-five dollars. Eugene was sentenced to serve three months in jail. Eugene's conviction was later reversed by a court of appeals.

Smith was survived by his wife. He is buried at the Eutaw Cemetery.

LIVE OAK COUNTY SHERIFF'S OFFICE

Hinton, Harry
Born 30 March 1874—Died 20 December 1914

Deputy Sheriff Harry Hinton died after being beaten and suffocated with bedclothes by two inmates during an escape attempt at the county jail in Oakville.

An accomplice had passed up an iron bar to two Mexican prisoners. The man had attached a length of fishing line to the piece of metal so the inmates could haul it up to their cell window from the street below.

The two men escaped. A reward of $500 was offered for their arrest.

Tensions ran high in the community as a result of the brutal killing. Hinton was a member of a prominent family in the area and was well liked in the community. A major manhunt was immediately organized involving hundreds of citizens, many of whom were provided by local rancher George West. Information provided by a local man led to the arrest of Ysidro Gonzales, one of the murderers. Gonzales was captured in the Mexican section of Oakville on Wednesday, 23 December, and immediately lynched by a mob of angry townspeople. He was strung up from a large tree and his body riddled with bullets. Four members of the man's family were taken into custody and given until nightfall to get out of the county or they would suffer the same fate.

Hinton had served with the agency for three years. He was survived by his wife, Ella Ferrell, and two sons. Hinton is buried at the Oakville Cemetery.

James, William P.
Born 5 August 1861—Died 6 October 1917

On Friday, 5 October 1917, Sheriff Charles L. Tullia went to the Loso home, which was located on a farm near Majeska, to arrest two of the Loso brothers for draft evasion. The brothers barricaded themselves in the home, but Tullia managed to gain entrance. The father, Serapio Loso, came into the room with a weapon and shot Tullia. Tullia returned fire and killed him.

Hearing the gunfire, the farm's owner responded and discovered the wounded Tullia fighting with the two brothers. He assisted him in breaking free. Tullia managed to shoot and kill one of the brothers. The other escaped.

At noon on Saturday, 6 October 1917, the brother who had escaped from the earlier incident with Sheriff Tullia arrived on a train at Live Oak, the county seat, accompanied by a third brother, who lived in Corpus Christi. The sheriff arrested the brother who was wanted for draft evasion but ignored the brother who was not wanted. The third brother reached into his boot for a weapon. When he did so, James shot him. Before he expired, he returned fire, fatally shooting James.

James had been with the agency for ten years. He is buried at the Gussettville Cemetery.

LOCKHART POLICE DEPARTMENT

Smith, John Leroy
Born 31 July 1866—Died 19 February 1915

At about 11:30 a.m. on Friday, 19 February 1915, City Marshal John Smith was shot and killed at the county courthouse by Caldwell County sheriff J.H. Franks. Newspapers reported that there had been no other witnesses to the murder.

Franks did not live long enough to be tried. He was assassinated several months later, on 12 May 1915.

Smith is buried at the Lockhart City Cemetery. He was survived by his wife, Lula Bell Magee, and one child.

Related Case: Caldwell County Sheriff's Office, J.H. Franks

LORENA POLICE DEPARTMENT

Witt, Mangrum Elmode "Mote"
Born 20 December 1880—Died 11 December 1917

The body of Lorena night watchman "Mote" Witt was discovered on the morning of Wednesday, 12 December 1917, lying along the railroad tracks of the Katy Railroad near the city. His head and limbs had been severed from his body, and the trunk was badly mutilated. A strap attached to his watchman's clock and a belt worn by Witt, to which his pistol holster was fastened, were found not far from the scene. The strap and belt had been cut in two with a knife. Witt's pistol was not found. The body showed evidence of two knife wounds to the left side of his neck.

Lawmen investigating the murder discovered that a pane of glass had been removed from the back door of a general merchandise store in town. Investigators surmised that Witt had come upon intruders robbing the store and that they had stabbed him to death. Apparently, the criminals had laid his body across the railroad tracks in the path of an oncoming train in an effort to conceal the evidence of their crime.

The following day, Sheriff S.S. Fleming and Deputy Lee Jenkins arrested three men for the murder of Witt. It appears these suspects were not charged since the case was still unsolved as of 9 February 1918, when the sheriff offered a $500 reward for any information concerning the death of Witt. It is unknown if anyone was ever arrested or prosecuted.

Witt had been employed as the night watchman for two months. He was survived by his wife, Myrtle Lee Watkins, and six children. Witt is buried at the Lorena Cemetery.

Lawson, Frederick Everett "Fred"
Born 18 July 1888—Died 9 February 1918

The body of Lorena night watchman Fred Lawson was discovered at around 3:00 a.m. on Saturday, 9 February 1918, at the town's cotton gin. The foreman of that enterprise found Lawson's corpse in the office of the Westbrook and Evans gin. A bullet wound was discovered in his right side, under the arm. Lawson's Colt .44-caliber six-shooter was found under a nearby chair with one chamber having been fired. His lunch, which he usually ate about midnight, was found spread out before him and untouched. The fatal pistol shot, which apparently had been fired at point-blank range, had ignited his vest. There was no evidence of mischief or an attempted burglary of the enterprise.

The coroner concluded that Lawson had met his death by accident or murder. Family historians claim that his death was the result of the most unfortunate accidental discharge of his own revolver and probably took place when it fell from its holster and struck the floor.

Lawson was survived by his wife and five small children. He is buried at the Lorena City Cemetery. Lawson had been employed as the town's night watchman for only two months, having replaced night watchman M.E. Witt, who was murdered while on duty on 11 December 1917.

LOTT POLICE DEPARTMENT

Daffin, Elias Jackson "Lash"
Born March 1868—Died 12 July 1925

City Marshal Lash Daffin was shot and killed when he attempted to arrest a man named Raymond Bailey for committing a minor offense. While Daffin was attempting to lead Bailey by the arm to jail, Bailey pulled out a .45-caliber pistol and shot him. The incident occurred so quickly that Daffin was not able to draw his weapon and defend himself.

The murderer was tried and, for some reason, found not guilty.

Daffin was survived by his wife, Anna Tululah "Tula" McClatchy, and three children. He is buried at the Clover Hill Cemetery in Lott.

LYNN COUNTY SHERIFF'S OFFICE

Redwine, Felix Edgar
Born 11 June 1877—Died 7 March 1936
Date of Incident: 6 March 1936

Deputy Sheriff Felix Redwine was shot and killed with his own weapon by a jail inmate named Elmo Banks. Banks was in the process of making an escape attempt at the time when he grabbed Redwine's gun and fired five shots into his body at close range. Redwine died from his injuries the following day.

Banks was captured near Tahoka. He was tried and found guilty of the murder of Redwine on 13 March. Newspapers reported that the trial of Banks was one of the speediest in Lynn County. Banks was sentenced to death, the first ever death penalty handed out by the 106th judicial district. He filed an appeal on 14 March, which was not successful. That sentence was carried out on 23 October 1936, when Banks was executed by electrocution at the Huntsville State Penitentiary. Banks became the 140th person to be executed by electrocution in Texas.

Redwine was survived by his wife, Lou Vesta Gray, and five children. He is buried at the Tahoka Cemetery.

MADISON COUNTY CONSTABLE'S OFFICE

Simonton, Eugene A.
Born 26 December 1872—Died 7 December 1900

Precinct 1 constable Eugene Simonton and a man named Henry Thomas Slaughter were both shot and killed by Seth Duncan at Evan's Saloon. Simonton and Slaughter were related. The cause of the shooting is unknown.

Duncan was tried and convicted of the crime and was sentenced to life in prison.

Simonton was survived by his wife, Elizabeth "Marian" Connor (or Conner), and three children. He is buried at the Burrows Cemetery in Conner, Madison County.

Simonton had been elected constable of Precinct 1 at Madisonville on 8 November 1898. F.E. Word was elected to that post on 6 November 1900. Since Simonton died a month after the election, he may have been out of office or serving until Word made his bond.

MARION COUNTY CONSTABLE'S OFFICE

Proctor, Charles H.
Born August 1870—Died 2 October 1908

At about 1:30 p.m. on Friday, 2 October 1908, Charles Proctor, constable of Precinct 3, was shot and killed by Marion County sheriff Will S. Terry. At the time of the incident, Proctor was resisting arrest.

Proctor was under a five-year sentence for killing a man named Harry Newman. That incident occurred at Cass County in July 1905. He was under bond waiting a decision of the court of appeals.

Proctor's bondsman had withdrawn his bond. Cass County sheriff W.C. Blalock and his deputy, Griffin, had come to Jefferson, the county seat of Marion, to arrest Proctor and transport him to the Cass County jail in Linden. Proctor said that he would rather die than go to jail. The lawmen did not want to use force, but Proctor advanced on Terry with an open knife. Terry fired over his head. When Proctor refused to surrender, he fired twice, hitting Proctor. Proctor remained where he had fallen, in an alley, until he died at 2:05 p.m. the same day.

Proctor's place of burial is unknown. He was survived by his wife, Eddie, and one child.

Proctor, William R. "Will"
Born 28 July 1866—Died 16 October 1923

There had been some trouble between Constable Will Proctor of the Jefferson precinct and Sheriff B.B. Rogers over the service of court papers. The sheriff had fined the constable. The two lawmen had a fierce disagreement that escalated to the point where "fighting words" were exchanged.

On Tuesday, 16 October 1923, the two men sighted each other just blocks from the courthouse on the main street in Jefferson, which is the county seat of Marion County. Not a word was spoken as Proctor shoved Rogers into a fire hydrant. When Rogers fell, he pulled his pistol and fired at Proctor, hitting him once in the hip and once in the heart. Proctor fired his pistol at the same moment, shooting Rogers in the head. Both men died at the scene.

Proctor was survived by his three children. He is buried at the New Prospect Cemetery in Jefferson. Proctor's brother, Charles B. Proctor, was a constable who was shot and killed by Sheriff Terry on 2 October 1908.

Related Case: Marion County Sheriff's Office, B.B. Rogers

Todd, Eddie Russel
Born 25 September 1896—Died 10 February 1940

Eddie R. Todd was the constable of Precinct 4 at Smithland, a community located east of Jefferson.

An oil field worker named Clyde Whatley had agreed to take a married woman to visit one of her sick relatives. Todd tried to discourage the woman from making the trip, knowing that the woman's husband was upset by the prospect of his wife undertaking the journey with Whatley. Nonetheless, she decided to proceed. Upon their return, Whatley stayed away from the husband.

On Saturday, 10 February 1940, Whatley, who was armed with a gun, went to the neighborhood store and asked the husband to step outside. According to Whatley, the pair had a friendly conversation. As the men were talking, Todd approached.

Precisely what took place next is a matter of some conjecture. Whatley alleged that he acted in self-defense, claiming that Todd drew his pistol first, and he believed the constable was going to kill him. The local newspaper reported that the husband said that Whatley drew his gun first and shot Todd through the sleeve. In any case, Whatley fired again; this time, the bullet struck Todd in the back. As the wounded Todd fell to the ground, he tried to draw his own gun and return fire but was unable to do so. Whatley fired two more shots at Todd and then drove away in an automobile.

Court records indicate that when Todd's body was examined, he had his pistol in a loose holster concealed under his shirt. After the shooting, the pistol, still in the holster, was lying near Todd's hand.

Clyde Whatley was convicted of murder without malice and sentenced to serve five years in the penitentiary. He appealed over being denied bail. The case was reversed and sent back to the lower court for a second trial. Whatley agreed to plead guilty and was assessed a two-year sentence in the penitentiary.

Todd was survived by his wife, Gertrude. He is buried at the Shiloh Cemetery in Cass County.

MARION COUNTY SHERIFF'S OFFICE

Griffith, William "Will"
Born February 1874—Died 6 July 1904

A.L. "Ab" Allen had a record of arrests for drunkenness, gambling, horse racing and fighting. On 15 April 1884, Allen was armed with a pistol and had been drinking when an argument took place during which he shot and killed Robert Pastian. Allen was tried, convicted and sentenced to the state penitentiary for sixty years. About 1900, he was pardoned and returned to Marion County.

Allen was again arrested for being drunk and for fighting. On one particular occasion, he was armed and threatened the sheriff and a deputy who had tried to arrest him. On another occasion, he allegedly disarmed Deputy Sheriff Will Griffith and then struck the deputy on the head with a pistol. Bystanders intervened to prevent further violence.

On Wednesday, 6 July 1904, Allen and Griffith had a chance encounter in front of the Star Saloon on Austin Street in Jefferson. After only a few words had been exchanged between the pair, Allen shot Griffith with a shotgun that he had borrowed for the expressed purpose of shooting either his son, Ernest Allen, or Griffith. According to oral reports at the time of the incident, Allen happened upon Griffith first; thus, Griffith was the one to be shot.

Griffith was able to pull his pistol and fire several shots at Allen, striking him in the groin. Allen went into the Star Saloon and fell to the floor, where he died moments later. Griffith, who was shot in the bowels, was taken to Dr. Armstrong's office, where he died at 7:30 p.m. the same day.

Griffith is buried in an unmarked grave at the Oakwood Cemetery in Jefferson. He was survived by his wife, Rebecca Jane Sroufeand, and at least one son.

Dugan, John Sidney
Born 29 November 1857—Died 29 November 1905
Date of Incident: 27 November 1905

On Monday, 27 November 1905, Deputies John Dugan and John W. Wilson went to arrest a man. The individual resisted, drew a gun and shot at the deputies six or seven times. In the midst of the tension and confusion of the moment, Wilson accidentally shot Dugan.

Newspaper accounts indicated that the man they had gone to arrest was taken into custody. Unfortunately, the man's name and the disposition of any charges against him are unknown.

Although the local newspaper claimed that Dugan's gunshot wound was not necessarily fatal, he died from the results of the injury on Wednesday, 29 November 1905. As was the custom of the time, Wilson was charged with murder and posted bond.

Dugan was survived by his wife, Alice Thacker, and seven children. He is buried next to his mother, Mary Ann, at the Kellyville Cemetery in Marion County.

Wilson, John W.
Born (Unknown)—Died 24 March 1906

On Monday, 27 November 1905, Deputies John Sydney Dugan and John W. Wilson went to arrest a man. The individual resisted, drew a gun and shot at the deputies six or seven times. In the midst of the tension and confusion of the moment, Wilson accidentally shot Dugan.

Dugan died from the results of the injury on Wednesday, 29 November 1905. As was the custom of the time, Wilson was charged with murder and posted bond.

Wilson was still on bond for the fatal shooting of Dugan when, on Saturday, 24 March 1906, he was shot and beaten to death near his home in the Comet community in Marion County. Wilson and his family were tenants on the farm of John Coffman. One of Coffman's sons had married one of Wilson's daughters. The Coffman boy had left his wife, resulting in strained relations between the families. John Coffman and his son Ben were convicted of the murder of Wilson. John Coffman received twenty years in prison. Ben Coffman was sentenced to forty years in prison.

No personal information is known about Wilson. The local newspapers reported that he was buried in the county and was a member of the Dick Taylor Camp UCV.

Rogers, Bennett Boggess "Bud"
Born 31 July 1869—Died 16 October 1923

There was trouble between Sheriff Bud Rogers and Constable W.R. Proctor of the Jefferson precinct over the service of court papers. The sheriff had fined the constable. The two lawmen had a disagreement that escalated into "fighting words" being exchanged.

On Tuesday, 16 October 1923, they sighted each other just blocks from the courthouse on the main street in Jefferson, the county seat of Marion County. No words were spoken as Proctor shoved Rogers into a fire hydrant. As Rogers fell, he pulled his pistol and shot Proctor once in the hip and once in the heart. Proctor fired his pistol at the same moment and shot Rogers in the head. Both men died at the scene.

Rogers was survived by his wife, Neppia "Neppie" Whitworth, and one child. He is buried at the Avinger Cemetery in Cass County. Rogers was elected sheriff on 7 November 1922. His predecessor, Sheriff Will Terry, shot and killed Constable Charles H. Proctor on 2 October 1908. Charles Proctor was the brother of W.R. Proctor.

Related Case: Marion County Constable's Office, W.R. Proctor

Brown, Jerry Alexander
Born 21 December 1891—Died 10 March 1937

Jerry Brown was appointed sheriff on 13 May 1936 to fill the job that had been vacated by Sheriff Thomas W. Taylor when he resigned on 12 May

1936. Brown was subsequently elected sheriff on 3 November 1936. He served until his death.

Brown was shot and killed in his bedroom while he was preparing to retire for the evening. Brown's apartment was attached to the county jail.

A man named Charlie Brooks, who had escaped from jail five days earlier, was later arrested and charged with the murder. Brooks confessed to killing Brown. He said that he killed Brown because he believed that Brown would have killed him if he captured him.

Brooks was tried, convicted and sentenced to death. That sentence was carried out on 31 May 1938, when Brooks was executed by electrocution at Huntsville. Brooks was the 157th criminal to meet such a fate in Texas.

Brown had been with the agency for just one year. He was survived by his wife and two children. Brown's wife, Ethel, was appointed to complete his term in office. He is buried at the Oakwood Cemetery in Marion County.

Marlin Police Department

Coleman, Marion Marcus
Born 2 February 1846—Died 18 September 1905

City Marshal Marion Coleman was shot and killed by a man named Holland Dillard. The murder was in retaliation for Coleman having testified against Dillard in a court case.

At about 3:55 p.m. on Monday, 18 September 1905, Coleman and Officer Stallworth were walking from the courthouse to the train station along Live Oak Street. Coleman was carrying a valise and was on his way to catch the 4:00 p.m. passenger train out of the city on official business. Dillard approached the lawmen from the rear. Without warning, he fired a single blast from a double-barreled shotgun into the back of Coleman. Coleman immediately sank to the pavement, and without ever moving a muscle, he died.

Stallworth immediately rushed Dillard, disarmed and arrested him. Dillard claimed that he had killed Marlin for good reason, saying, "I killed Major Coleman because he had thrown slurs at me. I had good cause to do what I did." Although Dillard was tried for the murder of Coleman, he was eventually acquitted on 13 February 1908.

Coleman is said to have been a veteran of the Confederate army and was called "Major," although no records to confirm his service have been located. He served with the Marlin Police Department for twenty years. Coleman's wife preceded him in death. He was survived by five children. Coleman is buried at the Calvary Cemetery in Marlin.

Mason County Sheriff's Office

Murray, Allen Thomas
Born 30 July 1881—Died 28 February 1929

Allen Murray was elected sheriff on 4 November 1924. He was reelected on 2 November 1936 and again on 6 November 1928. Murray served until his death.

Murray left the county seat at Mason on Thursday afternoon, 28 February 1929, headed toward San Antonio in response to a call he had received by J.G. Smith, a produce buyer, alerting him that his suitcase might have been found by two men near Loyal Valley. Murray's lifeless body was discovered later in the day with three bullet wounds. Murray had been shot and killed when he attempted to arrest the two men, Antonio Chavez and Ofilio Herrera, for possessing containers of illegal whiskey.

Both men escaped in a gray coupe automobile. Herrera was captured later the same day about eight miles north of Mason on the Brady highway. Chavez was apprehended near Santa Anna on Saturday, 2 March 1929. Murray's gun, bloodstained clothing and forty-five gallons of liquor were also recovered during the arrest.

The gunman, Ofilio Herrera, was tried and convicted of first-degree murder and was sentenced to death on 22 May 1930. That sentence was carried out when Herrera was executed by electrocution on 19 June 1931 in Huntsville. Herrera was the sixty-seventh criminal to be electrocuted in Texas.

Murray was survived by his wife, Alma Louise Schimdt, and two children. Alma was appointed to fulfill his term as sheriff. She served until R.W. White was elected on 4 November 1930.

Murray is buried at the Old Gooch Cemetery in Mason. Some family genealogists have reported Murray's year of birth as 1886.

Matagorda County Sheriff's Office

Mangum, Josiah Joseph "Joe"
Born 19 September 1875—Died 8 July 1931
Date of Incident: 7 July 1931

Joe Mangum was elected sheriff on 4 November 1924 and was reelected in 1926, 1928 and 1930. He served until his death.

Mangum had been seriously injured in an automobile accident two weeks earlier while chasing some boxcar thieves. On Tuesday, 7 July 1931, his daughter Thelma had to drive the still recovering sheriff to a funeral. While Mangum and his daughter were returning home, they were accidentally struck by a Gulf, Colorado and Santa Fe train. Mangum died the following day. His daughter, who was driving the car at the time of the incident, was injured but later recovered.

Mangum was survived by his wife, Pearl Lee, and at least five children; some family genealogists report as many as seven. He is buried at the Cedarvale Cemetery in Bay City.

McAllen Police Department

Saenz, Federico R.
Born 27 November 1895—Died 26 March 1933

At about 6:00 a.m. on Sunday, 26 March 1933, Officer Federico Saenz was shot and killed when he stopped a pickup truck containing six people. While he was speaking with the driver, one of the passengers opened fire on him. The bullet struck Saenz in the ribs. While Saenz was crawling along the ground wounded, struggling to regain control of his own gun, the brutal killer shot him again, this time in the forehead. The second shot was fatal.

Five of the suspects were apprehended, but the driver fled to Mexico.

Saenz was survived by his wife, Cantu, and three children. He is buried at the La Piedad Cemetery in McAllen.

McKinney Police Department

Burks, Samuel Perry
Born May 1857—Died 12 June 1902
Date of Incident: 11 June 1902

City Marshal Samuel Burks was accidentally shot and killed by a storeowner when he responded to a prowler call.

Burks and a night watchman had just arrested three prowlers at a McKinney business. The night watchman took two of the men, and Burks took the third. As Burks placed the prisoner in his vehicle, the storeowner, who mistakenly thought Burks was one of the prowlers, opened fire with a shotgun. Burks died from the wound the following day.

Burks had served with the agency for eleven years. He was survived by his wife and three children. Burks is buried at the Pecan Grove Cemetery in McKinney.

Taylor, Marion E.
Born 9 October 1903—Died 2 March 1938

Motorcycle Officer Marion Taylor was shot and killed when he stopped a taxicab that was occupied by a hijacker.

While Taylor was on patrol, he saw a cab driver who was waving him down. The cabbie had been abducted at gunpoint in Dallas and was being forced to drive to Denison. When Taylor stopped the vehicle, the hijacker, J.W. Rickman, shot him six times.

Rickman was tried and convicted of the murder and sentenced to death. That sentence was carried out on 18 March 1940, when Rickman was executed by electrocution at Huntsville. Rickman became the 179th criminal to meet this fate.

Taylor had served with the agency for ten years. He was survived by his wife, Beulah. Taylor is buried at the Princeton Cemetery in Collin County.

McLennan County Constable's Office

Sparks, Earl Evans "Early"
Born February 1881—Died 25 March 1910
Date of Incident: 19 March 1910

Precinct 1 deputy constable Early Sparks died from wounds he received when he was repeatedly cut and stabbed by a frenzied man who was attacking passersby on a sidewalk in Waco. When Sparks confronted the man, he was stabbed in the stomach. The sanguineous Sparks managed to fire one shot at his attacker, inflicting a fatal wound.

Sparks was taken to the hospital. The blade of his attacker's knife had penetrated his intestines and one kidney. Surgeons attempted to save his life, but he died from his wounds six days later.

Sparks's father, as well as his grandfather, was a peace officer who had been recognized for his courage. His uncle was Texas Ranger captain John C. Sparks, who had served with distinction as well.

Sparks was not married at the time of his death. He is buried at the Bosqueville Cemetery in McLennan County.

McLennan County Sheriff's Office

Harris, William T.
Born November 1844—Died 21 October 1901

William Harris was elected sheriff on 7 November 1882 and was reelected in 1884 and 1886.

After leaving office, the former Sheriff Harris was shot and killed by Dr. J.T. Lovelace. The shooting was the result of a personal disagreement between the two men that turned violent.

Harris and Lovelace were related by marriage. Harris and his son Will met Lovelace and his stepson Zack T. Reynolds at the Turf Saloon on Austin Avenue at about 1:00 p.m. on Monday, 21 October 1901, and the quarrel was renewed. Harris is said to have appeared with a shotgun and opened fire on Lovelace. During a scuffle that quickly broke out, Harris grabbed Lovelace and was hit in the back by a shotgun blast. Lovelace shook the elder Harris off his back and continued firing at Will Harris. In the meantime, Reynolds pumped a volley of shots into Harris with his revolver. In all, Harris was hit three times and his son Will Harris, eight times. Both men fell to the floor of the saloon dead.

Lovelace and his stepson Zack Reynolds, empty pistols in hand, walked down the street to the sheriff's office and surrendered.

Harris is buried at the Oakwood Cemetery in Waco. He was survived by his wife, Lena.

Woodall, Robert Henry "Bob"
Born 21 May 1866—Died 23 September 1925

Deputy Sheriff Glenn Wright and jailer Robert Woodall left Waco at 5:30 a.m. on Friday, 23 September 1925, to transport a prisoner to the insane asylum in Austin. While returning to Waco at about noon the same day, the automobile Wright was driving lost a wheel and overturned, coming to rest in a narrow ditch. Both men were pinned under the vehicle. Woodall died from a broken neck. Wright suffered a broken collarbone and four broken ribs. He managed to survive.

Woodall had been employed as a jailer for the past two years. He was survived by his wife, Flora Ellen Archer, and five children. Woodall is buried at the Oakwood Cemetery in Waco.

Russell, A.W. "Abe"
Born 22 September 1851—Died 2 August 1929

At about 8:30 p.m. on Friday, 2 August 1929, Abe Russell was driving his automobile in West when he was struck by a railroad train. He died while being transported to the hospital. One newspaper article indicated that his passenger, Tom Ellis, was uninjured during the mishap. Another article reported that Russell had dropped off Ellis and was alone at the time. Apparently, Russell had become confused in the dark and accidentally turned in front the train.

Russell was survived by his two sons and two daughters. He is buried at the Liberty Grove Cemetery. At the time of his death, Russell was an elected constable and a deputy sheriff at the surprisingly advanced age of seventy-seven. He had reportedly served as a law enforcement officer for fifty years.

Russell's death certificate indicates that his date of birth was 21 September 1851, but his tombstone has 22 September 1851.

Emmons, Edward D.
Born 13 March 1892—Died 12 January 1935

Deputy Sheriff Edward Emmons was dispatched to an accident on the Dallas Highway about six miles north of Waco. While crossing the highway on foot with a driver of one of the damaged vehicles, Emmons was struck by a passing automobile and fatally injured. The man who was walking with him was seriously injured. The driver of the vehicle that struck him, Aubrey Basham, was charged with negligent homicide.

Emmons had been a Waco police officer for seven years and had joined the sheriff's office just six months earlier. He was survived by his wife, Bettie, and one son. Emmons is buried at the Rosemound Cemetery in Waco.

McMullen County Sheriff's Office

Holland, William Tolbert "Will"
Born 22 October 1872—Died 12 November 1915

Will Holland was elected sheriff on 5 November 1912 and reelected on 5 November 1914. He served until his death.

Sheriff Holland was shot and killed by Beeville city marshal C.P. Edison. The incident was a result of a personal dispute between the two men.

Shortly before the fatal event took place, the two men had met cordially. They had been friends since boyhood. The deadly incident unfolded in the lobby of the Beeville Bank & Trust Company. Holland was in the lobby of the bank speaking with a cashier when Edison entered the establishment. After a friendly greeting, Holland told Edison, in a joking manner, to be careful lest he be arrested. Edison took offense to the comment. Pistols were quickly drawn, and both men fired two shots at the other. Edison's aim was apparently superior to that of Holland, as Holland was struck in the head with one of the two bullets that Edison launched in his direction. The wound was fatal. Holland collapsed on the bank floor dead.

Holland is buried at the Hilltop Cemetery in Tilden. He was survived by his wife, Virginia Ida Byrne, and four children. One daughter had preceded him in death.

Mercedes Police Department

January, Thomas Tomas "Tom"
Born 20 September 1892—Died 23 June 1924
Date of Incident: 21 June 1924

On Saturday, 21 June 1924, Special Officer Tom January was at a Mexican dance in Mercedes. A disturbance broke out, and January attempted to quell the ensuing fight. A man named Lino O. Cavillo shot and killed January. Cavillo was in turn killed during the shootout. Emil Gomez Encarnacion and Frederico Solis were wounded.

January was transported to the hospital, where he died two days later.

January is buried at Mercedes. He was survived by his wife, Virginia Templeton, and one child.

Merkel Police Department

Hutcheson, Chester C.
Born 11 February 1902—Died 12 April 1936
Date of Incident: 11 April 1936

City Marshal Chester Hutcheson was shot and killed when he was attempting to speak with the owner of a dance hall near the city limits.

Hutcheson had responded to calls of trouble at the dance hall twice that evening and asked the owner to step outside to talk. The owner, Lonnie Mitchell, refused to do so and shot Hutcheson in the left eye as the marshal stood in the doorway. Hutcheson died from the wound several hours later, on 12 April 1936.

Mitchell was arrested the following day. He was tried and convicted of the murder of Hutcheson and sentenced to death. The death sentence ruling was reversed.

Hutcheson had been with the agency for two years. He was survived by his wife, Abbie Ruth Darsey, and three children. Hutcheson is buried at the Rose Hill Cemetery in Merkel, Taylor County.

Mexia Police Department

Vandiver, Coy Carter, Sr.
Born 13 February 1892—Died 3 April 1922

Officer Coy Vandiver accidentally shot and killed himself while attempting to arrest a man on the Tehuacana highway in the west part of the city. The man refused to submit to arrest or raise his hands. Vandiver hit the man over the head with the butt of his revolver. The impact caused the gun to discharge. The bullet hit Vandiver in the right side, severed an artery and eventually lodged in his liver.

Vandiver was taken to the Mexia General Hospital, where he died from the wound at 7:10 p.m.

The local newspaper reported that Vandiver had been an officer for only a few days. He was survived by his wife and three children. Vandiver is buried at the Oakwood Cemetery in Waco.

MIDLAND POLICE DEPARTMENT

Wyrick, John Perry
Born 1 September 1884—Died 10 November 1935

Night watchmen John Wyrick and E.B. Patterson were investigating a disturbance involving a drunken man who was attacking another person. When the lawmen arrived at the scene, one of the pugilists, E.M. McMullen, opened fire with a shotgun. The bullet hit Wyrick in the chest. In spite of being mortally wounded, Wyrick was able to fire two rounds into the head of McMullen, fatally wounding him. Patterson also fired six shots into the assailant, emptying his revolver into McMullen apparently just for good measure.

Wyrick had served with the agency for five years. He was a longtime resident, cowboy and ranch foreman in the area. He was survived by his wife, daughter and five stepchildren. Wyrick is buried in an unmarked grave at the Fairview Cemetery.

MIDLOTHIAN POLICE DEPARTMENT

Blair, Josiah Clark
Born 4 March 1882—Died 1 May 1916

City Marshal Josiah Blair's death was ruled accidental. According to some reports, however, Blair may have taken his own life. In spite of diligent research, conclusive information regarding the circumstances and nature of Blair's death has not yet been uncovered.

Clark was not married. He was survived by eight siblings. Clark is buried at the Midlothian Cemetery.

MILAM COUNTY CONSTABLE'S OFFICE

Applin, John Marian
Born 19 May 1847—Died 29 August 1920
Date of Incident: 15 August 1920

Constable John Applin died from injuries he received in an automobile accident. It is unclear if his death was line of duty related.

Applin was survived by his wife, Mattie Drucilla Wilson, and their eight children. Applin also had six surviving children from an earlier marriage to Sarah Elizabeth Hanna, who passed away in 1887. He is buried at the Lilac Cemetery in Sharp.

Sens, Charles Henry
Born 3 May 1896—Died 23 December 1929

Precinct 1 constable Charles Sens was shot and killed when he responded to the scene of a shooting that had taken place at an automobile dealership on Main Street in Cameron.

Anton Hubner had been hit over the head with a large stick during an argument at the dealership two years earlier that involved a dispute over an eight-dollar tire. At about noon on Monday, 23 December 1929, Hubner, who held a long-standing grudge with the car lot, parked his vehicle across the street from the business, which was located on Main Street, walked into the agency and purchased some parts. Almost immediately, he returned to his automobile and retrieved his .38-55-caliber rifle and box of cartridges and then came back to the showroom and opened fire. The dealership's owner, Herbert Hefley, tried to borrow a gun and stop him. Hefley bravely walked in and confronted Hubner, saying, "I've got to take care of my men." Hubner shot and killed Hefley on site, hitting him twice, with one shot entering his brain. One bystander was also wounded during the exchange.

For thirty minutes, Hubner ruled the downtown streets, emptying and reloading his rifle three times as he fired at anyone he saw.

As Sens and Sheriff's Deputy Blaylock approached the body of Hefley, Hubner opened fire on them, killing Sens and wounding Blaylock in the leg. Hubner concealed himself behind automobiles in the showroom and continued firing. Eventually, he calmly walked outside, where he was met by an armed citizen, local café proprietor Gene Smith. Smith and Hubner were involved in a shootout that resulted in Smith fatally wounding Hubner.

Sens was survived by his wife and son. He is buried at the Oak Hill Cemetery.

MILAM COUNTY SHERIFF'S OFFICE

Avriett, Giles Croxton
Born 7 June 1857—Died 20 June 1905

Giles Avriett was elected sheriff on 4 November 1902 and served until 8 November 1904.

At about 9:00 a.m. on Tuesday, 20 June 1905, former Sheriff Avriett was shot and instantly killed in the corridor of the Milam County Courthouse. The current sheriff, Robert Todd, surrendered after the shooting and was charged with the crime.

According to reports, there was only one other person in the corridor of the courthouse at the time, and he fled immediately after the gunfire commenced.

Todd and Avriett met in the hallway. Apparently, there was a disagreement of some sort that led to both men pulling their guns and opening fire. Three shots were fired in all. It is not clear who fired first. The nature of their argument is unclear, and there was no evidence given regarding any previous ill feelings between the two men that may have entered into the deadly exchange that occurred. The fact that Todd had defeated Avriett in the election for sheriff in November 1904, and had been defeated by Avriett two years earlier, may well have played into the killing. The contest for sheriff between the two men had been heated on both occasions. Feelings ran high, but it was thought that their political differences were not so severe that they would have brought about this type of fatal result.

Avriett was survived by his wife, Ida Massengale, and six children. He is buried at the Oak Hill Cemetery in Cameron.

Alford, Nathaniel Jefferson "Nat"
Born 13 August 1861—Died 24 June 1921

Deputy Sheriff Nat Alford was killed in an automobile accident while he was returning to Cameron with several other men, one of whom was a federal immigration officer. A front wheel of the automobile he was traveling in somehow became detached from the vehicle, causing it to overturn. Alford was thrown from the car and pinned beneath it. He died from his injuries.

Alford was survived by his second wife, Izora E. Young, and one son. He is buried at the IOOF Cemetery in Rockdale.

Pope, Guy Austin "Dutch"
Born 26 November 1899—Died 29 October 1930

Chief Deputy "Dutch" Pope and Santa Fe Railroad Police Department special officer Jack Dunman were shot and killed while investigating the burglary of a freight depot warehouse.

Pope and Dunman, along with Deputy Sheriff Roy Robinson, went to the store of Reagan Brady to question him about stolen property. When Brady saw the lawmen, he ran into the store, grabbed a shotgun and began firing. A blast of shot struck Pope in the abdomen. Another hit Dunman in the neck. Both were killed instantly. Brady then shot and wounded Robinson, who returned fire and was able to get off four shots at the killer.

Other officers arrived at the scene and exchanged gunfire with Brady. The gunman eventually turned the shotgun on himself and committed suicide, blowing away a large portion of his head in the process.

After the bloody incident had drawn to a close, Sheriff L.L. Blaylock could offer no explanation as to what had triggered Brady to open fire on the officers. Blaylock commented, "He had no quarrel with the officers as far as we knew."

Pope had been with the agency for eight years. He was survived by his wife, Alice Lucille Henderson, and three children. Pope is buried at the Ben Arnold Cemetery.

Related Case: Santa Fe Railroad Police Department, Jack Dunman

MINEOLA POLICE DEPARTMENT

Cage, Marcus Tillman
Born 9 August 1869—Died 17 October 1903
Date of Incident: 14 October 1903

City Marshal Marcus Cage was accidentally shot and killed by a man named W.J. Schubert.

Schubert (or Shurbert), who was reported to have been some type of detective or deputy U.S. marshal from Grand Saline, had been involved in an argument with a man named W.D. Kitchens on Johnson Street in Mineola. The quarrel quickly escalated into a gunfight.

As the incident unfolded, at about 2:45 p.m., Cage was trying to assist Kitchens, who had fallen to the ground along Johnson Street. Schubert had previously filed papers alleging that Kitchens had violated liquor laws, which apparently led to the disagreement and subsequent gunfight. In the process of aiding Kitchens, who at the time was still lying on the ground, Cage was accidentally shot in the top of the head by Schubert. It does seem somewhat unclear why Schubert would have had a pistol drawn and pointed in the direction of Cage in the first place. Nonetheless, the incident was ruled an accident.

As one might predict with any gunshot wound to the head, the damage was serious. Kitchens immediately picked up a pistol and shot Schubert. His aim was accurate, and Schubert fell dead instantly. A bystander named N.M. Harpole was also wounded during the wild exchange of fire.

Cage died from the effects of the gunshot wound three days later, at 3:00 a.m. on Saturday, 17 October 1903.

Cage was survived by his wife, Laura. He is buried at the Cedars Memorial Gardens.

MONAHANS POLICE DEPARTMENT

Burkett, Earl Monroe
Born 8 June 1910—Died 17 May 1939

Deputy City Marshal Earl Burkett was shot and killed in the city jail while attempting to search and interrogate a man named C.W. (or O.W.) Ely Jr., who had just been arrested.

Ely was an eighteen-year-old from Jal, New Mexico. Local lawmen had been searching for one young man and two young women who were runaways from Hobbs. Ely, who along with another man named Glen Osburne had been hitchhiking, had been apprehended and confined in the jail at Monahans, where he was being questioned about the missing youths when the incident occurred. Ely had somehow managed to obtain a firearm. He began a struggle with Burkett and shot him in the left lung. Burkett died later the same day.

Ely and Osburne escaped with Burkett's automobile, which was later found near Winkler. Ely was eventually captured and was taken to the Reeves County jail in Pecos and charged with murder. Ely was sentenced to death, but that ruling was later reversed.

Burkett was survived by his wife, Hellen. He had been employed by the Monahans Police Department for only six months. Burkett is buried at the Sweetwater Cemetery in Nolan County.

Montgomery County Constable's Office

Beyette, Thomas Joseph.
Born 20 April 1888—Died 6 August 1931
Date of Incident: 1 August 1931

Precinct 3 constable Thomas Beyette was shot and killed while he was transporting two prisoners to jail.

Beyette and a local judge had arrested two young men, ages seventeen and nineteen, for stealing merchandise from a garage. During the drive to jail, one of the young men managed to gain control of Beyette's service revolver and shot him in the head with it. Both men fled the scene. The judge was able to drive Beyette to a local hospital, but he was pronounced dead upon arrival.

The two suspects were eventually apprehended. The nineteen-year-old who had done the shooting was convicted of first-degree murder and sentenced to death. He later escaped from confinement. There are conflicting stories about how the young killer managed to get out of the Montgomery County jail, but he did so. On 20 December 1931, he was shot and killed by a deputy sheriff in Chambers County.

The seventeen-year-old killer was convicted of first-degree murder and, on 26 May 1932, was sentenced to ninety-nine years in prison.

Beyette was survived by his wife, Janie Lulu Bradford and three children. He is buried at the Magnolia Cemetery in Montgomery County.

Morris County Constable's Office

Tucker, George W.
Born 28 March 1876—Died 26 November 1912

At about 5:00 a.m. on Tuesday, 26 November 1912, Constable George Tucker, along with a man named Ed Boozer, was attempting to serve a civil writ of sequestration on a man named Gus Finley, alias Will Taylor. The order included picking up a mule for which Finley had traded sometime earlier.

When Tucker approached Finley, Finley opened fire. Tucker was hit twice and died from his wounds. Boozer was not hit during the shooting exchange.

Kinley fled to Louisiana, where he was captured and transferred to the jail in Shreveport. The killer told lawmen that he had shot Tucker because Tucker was in the process of pulling a gun on him.

Kinley was tried and convicted of the murder of Tucker. He was sentenced to death and scheduled to be hanged on 6 May 1913. Governor Colquitt granted a thirty-day reprieve, after which he was transferred out of the Daingerfield jail when an angry mob burned two churches and a residence in that town on 5 May 1913. Finley was later lynched by a mob of angry citizens on 13 May 1913.

Tucker was survived by his wife, Zorada Calista Wood, and five children. Some family genealogists report seven children. He is buried at the Omaha Cemetery.

MORRIS COUNTY SHERIFF'S OFFICE

Henderson, Jesse S.
Born 15 September 1877—Died 23 January 1923
Date of Incident: 17 January 1923

Deputy Sheriff Jesse Henderson accidentally shot himself in the thigh in Mount Pleasant. He was transported to the hospital in Greenville, where physicians determined that the injured leg required amputation of the limb. Henderson's operation was not a success. He died at 9:00 a.m. on Tuesday, 23 January 1923.

Henderson was survived by his wife, Birdie Hall, and two children. Some family genealogists report only one child. He is buried at the Omaha City Cemetery.

MOTLEY COUNTY CONSTABLE'S OFFICE

Stegall, Leroy Franklin "Lee"
Born 25 February 1888—Died 28 November 1927

Precinct 5 constable Lee Stegall, who just two weeks earlier had been appointed constable for the Flomot precinct, was driving home when he was assassinated by four men.

Stegall's automobile was found parked along the road with the lights still on and the vehicle sitting at a forty-five-degree angle to the highway. Witnesses to the crime indicated that Stegall was sitting at the wheel of the automobile with one foot on the clutch and the other on the brake. His body was slumped over, and his hat was lying just to the rear of the vehicle. Stegall's pistol was lying between his legs, with the barrel protruding and still warm from having been recently fired. That fact gave rise to the hypothesis that some sort of shootout had occurred between Stegall and his assailants. Stegall had been shot through the head.

Quick work on the part of the newly appointed constable led to the arrest of Calvin Barnes, W.F. Allen, Harmon Mosely, Adolphus Mosely and Paul Allen. It seems that Stegall had arrested Harmon Mosely, who was W.F. Allen's son-in-law, one week before the shooting. When Stegall refused to take the specie circular, or form of bond that Allen offered for the release of Harmon Mosely, Allen became angry and threatened to kill Stegall. Stegall, in turn, filed a complaint against Allen.

The disposition of the charges against Barnes and the Mosely brothers is not known. Paul Allen was convicted of murder and sentenced to five years in prison.

Stegall was survived by his wife, Laura Alice Ash, and five children. Some family genealogists report six children. He is buried at Memorial Park Cemetery in Flomot.

Moulton Police Department

Riske, Charles Oscar
Born 26 July 1874—Died 2 March 1935

Night watchman Charles Riske was shot and killed when he interrupted a man in the process of committing a burglary at a saloon in Moulton. The bandit struck Riske over the head with a blunt object and then shot him as he lay unconscious on the floor. Riske's killer fled and was never identified.

After serving nine years as night watchman, Riske had just filed his retirement papers the previous Friday. He had agreed to work through the weekend until a replacement could be found.

Riske is buried at the Old Moulton Cemetery in Lavaca County. He was survived by his wife, Emma. Riske was a veteran of the Spanish-American War.

MOUNT CALM CITY MARSHAL'S OFFICE

Callaway, James Terrell
Born 3 November 1875—Died 25 October 1905
Date of Incident: 24 October 1905

Sometime after 11:30 p.m. on Tuesday, 24 October 1905, Deputy City Marshal James Callaway was attempting to arrest two drunken men, Jack Early and Harmie Horn. During the course of the struggle, both Early and Horn stabbed Callaway repeatedly. Callaway was carried into a livery stable, where he was reported to have died about 2:45 a.m. on Wednesday, 25 October 1905.

Early and Horn were tried three times for Callaway's murder. Early was sentenced to three years in prison. Horn was acquitted.

Callaway had served with the agency for over one year. He was survived by his wife and three children. Callaway is buried at the Mesquite Cemetery in Hill County.

NACOGDOCHES COUNTY CONSTABLE'S OFFICE

Wynne, Jones L.
Born 17 March 1866—Died 7 October 1924

Constable Jones Wynne and four white men had gone to a tenant house on the Tucker farm near Chireno, about twenty miles east of Nacogdoches. Wynne's purpose was to serve a warrant on a black woman for having used abusive language against a white woman from the Chireno community. As Wynne stepped into the home of the suspect, he was shot and killed by a black man named Louis Dennis. Dennis fled the scene and escaped.

A posse was formed to locate Dennis, along with one suspected accomplice. Eventually, five black men were jailed in connection with the shooting. Dennis was tried and convicted of the crime. He was sentenced to serve twenty years in prison. That sentence was reversed and sent back to the lower court. The disposition of any further proceedings against Dennis is unknown.

Wynne was survived by his wife, Exa Lula Speights. He is buried at the Chireno Community. Wynne was elected constable in 1922 and 1924. He served until his death.

Nacogdoches County Sheriff's Office

Moody, Norton R.
Born April 1870—Died 31 March 1906

A citizen named Dave Taylor held a dance at his home in the Woden community of southeast Nacogdoches County. Deputy Sheriff Will Alders deputized a private citizen, Norton R. Moody, to accompany him to the event and assist in maintaining the peace.

During the affair, a disturbance took place. Alders and Moody attempted to arrest a man who had been creating the commotion. The host, Dave Taylor, told the lawmen not to enter the yard, cautioning them that if they did, they would be killed. Alders tried to explain to Taylor that the men inside the house were creating a tumultuous situation and had to be arrested. Neglecting Taylor's warning, Alders entered the yard. Following through on his threat, Taylor produced a revolver and shot Alders in the chest. The seriously wounded Alders was able to draw his own gun, fire and hit Taylor twice. Taylor's wounds proved fatal.

Moody went to the aid of Alders. Dave Taylor's brother Farmer (given name also reported as Palmer) stepped forward and shot Moody. The wound was fatal, and Moody died almost instantly.

Farmer Taylor fled the Woden community but was soon arrested and jailed. In April 1907, he was tried in Nacogdoches County and found not guilty.

Local newspapers reported that Moody was buried at the cemetery in Pea Ridge, but thus far burial records have not been located. Moody was survived by his wife, Cora Bell Furlow, and five children.

Carnley, William Jackson
Born 6 August 1877—Died 16 May 1918

Deputy Sheriff William Carnley accompanied the sheriff to a local farm to arrest a man who had caused a disturbance at a Red Cross meeting. When they arrived at the residence, Carnley located the suspect, Orange Escow, hiding in the bushes. Escow immediately opened fire on Carnley with a double-barreled shotgun, hitting him in the face. Carnley was able to fire one shot before he died from his wounds. The sheriff also returned fire, but he was unsuccessful in hitting Escow.

Escow fled the scene. A manhunt was quickly organized. Among the possemen involved in the chase was D. Brown, a cousin of Carnley. Brown had apparently been deputized. During the course of the chase, Brown shot and killed Orange Escow's brother, Alex. Brown was convicted of manslaughter and sentenced to two years in prison. It is not known if Orange Escow was ever prosecuted for the murder of Carnley.

Carnley was survived by his daughter. He had been with the sheriff's department for four years. Carnley is buried at the Swift Cemetery in Nacogdoches County.

Martin, John Womack "Johnnie"
Born 15 January 1880—Died 28 March 1924

Deputy Sheriff Johnnie Martin was shot and killed when he and Sheriff T.G. Vaught stopped an automobile they suspected of transporting whiskey.

Bud Dixon drove the vehicle. I.V. Nobles and L.G. Hanks were passengers. The officers had stopped their patrol car on a bridge and were waiting for Dixon's car to approach. They planned to stop the automobile as it came closer to their position. The sheriff approached the vehicle as it drew near, with a pistol in one hand and a flashlight in the other. Martin followed and began to open a window curtain to the see if there was whiskey in the vehicle. As he did so, three shots were fired from inside the car. Martin returned fire, killing Dixon and wounding Hanks. The sheriff opened fire as well. He was wounded in both legs during the exchange of gunfire but did manage to hit Nobles in the head with one shot as the bootlegger attempted to escape. Not knowing Martin's condition, the sheriff called out to him to stop Hanks from escaping. The mortally wounded Martin replied, "I am shot through and through...I am killed."

Hanks was tried and convicted of killing Martin. He was sentenced to fifty years in prison, but the case was reversed on appeal.

Martin was survived by his wife, Mamie "Nannie" E. Hargis, and three children. He is buried at the Blackjack Cemetery in Nacogdoches County.

Vaught, Thomas Garrett
Born 16 August 1862—Died 6 January 1928
Date of Incident: 3 January 1928

On Tuesday, 3 January 1928, Sheriff T.G. Vaught was shot and killed by his own deputy, Carl Butler. The incident stemmed from a disagreement of some sort between the two men. Butler had called at Vaught's home early in the morning and woke him up. The pair was headed out on a raid of some sort at an undisclosed location about three miles from Nacogdoches. The incident was probably related to illegal alcohol.

The two officers drove past Butler's home on the way to their destination. Within about a half mile of the Butler residence, a disagreement of some sort took place. Butler shot Vaught through the abdomen with a .45-caliber revolver. He died of his injuries at about 11:00 a.m. on Friday, 6 January. The mortally wounded Vaught managed to return fire, shooting Butler and wounding him in the right forearm. Vaught also used a .45-caliber revolver. The bullet that hit Butler shattered a bone in his arm, but the wound was not fatal.

Butler had originally been charged with assault to murder as a result of the affray. He was released on $5,000 bond. On 8 March 1928, a Nacogdoches County grand jury exonerated Butler of any guilt in the death of Vaught.

Butler had served as a deputy under Vaught for about three years.

Vaught is buried at the Greenwood Cemetery at Garrison. He was survived by his wife, Dora Pounds, and five children.

Hargis, John Arlington
Born 12 July 1883—Died 23 August 1928

Deputy Sheriff John Hargis was shot and killed when he and two other deputies went to investigate a report of a man selling illegal liquor on Shawnee Street.

Hargis confronted the whiskey peddler, who immediately opened fire on the deputies. Hargis was hit and mortally wounded. The Nacogdoches police chief arrested his killer the following day.

Hargis was survived by his wife, Vera May Booth, and five children. He is buried at the Blackjack Cemetery.

King, Claud S.
Born 29 September 1894—Died 6 October 1929

Deputy Sheriff Claud King and U.S. Bureau of Prohibition officer James L. Chance killed each other in a shootout that was reminiscent of an Old West duel. The shooting affray took place in the courthouse at Nacogdoches.

A disagreement existed between King and Chance that stemmed from their involvement in a recent Prohibition raid. King had also been defeated in a recent election for sheriff, which perhaps played a role in the strife between the two men. Both officers had been working with federal Prohibition agents J.W. Hammonds of Lufkin and J. Calloway of Beaumont during the preceding week. Chance claimed that King had tipped off the alleged bootleggers about an impending raid. King was furious, believing that his honor had been placed in question.

The two lawmen met on Sunday morning, 6 October 1929, in the office of Sheriff Eugene Turner at the courthouse. Turner was seated, talking with Chance, when King walked in. The quarrel between the two men was quickly renewed. King struck Chance with his fist. Chance dodged the blow, drew his revolver and fired one shot in King's direction at close range. The bullet hit King in the abdomen, inflicting a fatal injury. The mortally wounded King returned fire, hitting Chance in the head and killing him instantly.

King walked the fifty feet to an automobile and was taken to a local hospital, where he died of what was reported to have been "a ghastly wound" soon after arrival.

King was survived by his wife and two children. He is buried at the Douglass Cemetery.

Related Case: U.S. Bureau of Prohibition, James L. Chance

Wyers, Hiriam W. "Bud"
Born 2 January 1885—Died 25 June 1933

Former deputy sheriff "Bud" Wyers was shot and killed by Constable Ollie Strode.

Strode and Sheriff Carl Butler were in the process of searching Wyers's vehicle on Main Street in Nacogdoches when Wyers suddenly drew a gun and pointed it at the lawmen. Strode quickly responded, drew his own revolver and shot Wyers in the neck.

No further information regarding Wyers's reason for pulling a pistol on the officers, or the circumstances that led to this incident, has been uncovered.

Wyers was survived by his wife, Johnnie Mae Sparks. He is buried at the Old North Church Cemetery at Nacogdoches.

NAVARRO COUNTY CONSTABLE'S OFFICE

Hanks, Elbert Norton
Born 16 December 1858—Died 25 June 1912

Deputy Constable Elbert Hanks was shot and killed by a fourteen-year-old boy who had just escaped from the Navarro County Prison Farm.

The fugitive, Boyd White, saw Hanks approaching him along the railroad tracks and fled into a nearby restaurant. The establishment's owner told White to escape through the back door. White took the man's advice, and as he headed out the back, he also grabbed the restaurant owner's pistol from behind the counter. When the young man reached the back door, he found that it was locked. Having no other avenue of exit, he concealed himself behind a door in the cleaning room. When Hanks entered the darkened room, he lit a match. White fired a shot at Hanks, causing him to drop the match. White then fired a second shot, hitting Hanks in the chest.

White dashed out of the restaurant, this time through the front door. He was eventually apprehended, tried and convicted of the murder of Hanks. White was sentenced to life in prison. On 21 June 1927, the Texas governor pardoned White and released him from custody.

Hanks had served in law enforcement for at least two years and had worked for the Corsicana Police Department before becoming a deputy constable. He was survived by his wife and four children. Hanks is buried at the Oakwood Cemetery in Corsicana.

Henderson, Samuel Chapman "Chap"
Born 2 October 1870—Died 28 July 1913

Samuel Henderson was shot and killed. Although it was reported that he was a constable, thus far documentation verifying that Henderson was a lawman at the time of his death has proved elusive. No information concerning the circumstances of his death has been uncovered. Henderson ran the Witherspoon Grocery Store in Chatfield. Henderson was survived by his wife, Lula Caroline Weems, and eight children. Two of Henderson's children were from his previous marriage to Nora Minford. He is buried at the Old Chatfield Cemetery.

NEVADA CITY MARSHAL'S OFFICE

Cotner, James Robert
Born 29 February 1852—Died 15 March 1930

At approximately 2:00 a.m. on Saturday, 15 March 1930, City Marshal James Cotner was investigating a robbery at a hardware store in Nevada. Cotner had received a telephone call from K.A. Taylor of the Taylor Drugstore alerting him to the presence of the three holdup men at the nearby hardware store. When Cotner arrived at the scene, he ran into the thieves, who were by then on their way out. The bandits opened fire at once, hitting Cotner in the abdomen and hip.

The mortally wounded Cotner apparently tried to give chase, as he was found lying in the street bleeding and unconscious by Deputy City Marshal H.G. Rodgers, who, when he heard the gunshots, had rushed to the scene. Cotner was taken to St. Paul's Hospital in Dallas, where he died from his injuries three hours later. Before he died, he told friends that he had fired five times at the holdup men. "They got me…but I believe I wounded one or two of three," Cotner said.

The holdup men fled in an automobile, exchanging gunshots with Rodgers as they made their way out of town and headed toward Wiley. From Wiley, their trail was lost. In total, the robbers had hit five business establishments in Nevada and made off with ten dollars. In the process, they had gunned down a lawman.

The three men who were involved in this string of holdups were arrested several days later. Charles Kinkhead and George McDowell were apprehended in Oklahoma and charged with Cotner's killing. The outcome of any charges against them is unknown.

Cotner was survived by his wife, Mary Susan Dale, and four children. He is buried at the Thompson Cemetery in Copeville, Collin County.

Having passed his seventy-eighth birthday at the time of his death, Nevada city marshal James Robert Cotner holds the distinction of being the oldest Texas lawman to be killed in the line of duty. Given modern-day age limitations on service, that is a claim that he will no doubt hold in perpetuity.

Newton County Sheriff's Office

Humphreys, David Cicero
Born 15 March 1887—Died 8 February 1932

David Humphreys had been elected sheriff on 7 November 1922 and was reelected on 4 November 1924, 2 November 1926, 6 November 1928 and 4 November 1930.

Former sheriff David Humphreys was shot and killed while he was assisting Constable Recy Hamilton with a would-be escapee.

Hamilton was struggling with a prisoner named Caesar Powell. Powell was in the process of attempting to escape. He had been jailed the previous night for the knife murder of his wife. Two other men were in the cell with Powell—a roustabout from the carnival who had hijacked a bootlegger and a man from Kirbyville.

The three prisoners had managed to maneuver a keg of confiscated whiskey that was stored at the jailhouse into a position where they were able to access the contents. According to local newspaper reports, by the time the jailbreak attempt took place, the three had become quite intoxicated and boisterous.

Hamilton was the first lawman to respond to the disturbance. One of the inmates grabbed his key ring away from him and began to beat him relentlessly with it. Another prisoner grabbed Hamilton's gun. Humphreys, who was sitting with his wife on the front porch of their home across the street from the courthouse, heard the racket and rushed to the jail to investigate. Two local men, B.A. "Boldy" Meadows and Bob Collins, joined Humphreys, all making a dash to the courthouse building and up the stairs to the jail area.

As Humphreys stepped through the doorway, he was met by Powell and a blaze of gunfire. Humphreys was killed instantly. Next to fall was citizen Meadows, also fatally shot by Powell. Citizen Collins wrestled with Powell, attempting to disarm the crazed man while Powell struggled to get out of the courthouse through a locked back door.

While this desperate skirmish was taking place, Humphreys's son Curtis, who had recently replaced his father as sheriff, heard the gunfire from the street below. He rushed into the courthouse, unlocked the gun cabinet and grabbed a .30-30-caliber Winchester rifle. Curtis Humphreys then unlocked the jail door. At the instant he did so, Collins rushed past him to freedom, with Powell following close behind in hot pursuit. Collins grabbed the Winchester from Humphreys as he sprinted past him and used the gun to shoot Powell in the neck, inflicting a fatal wound.

This bloody episode, which unfolded in a matter of minutes, left former Sheriff Humphreys and citizen Meadows lying dead on the courthouse floor. Hamilton was severely beaten and had his nose bitten off by one of the escapees.

Humphreys was survived by his wife, Maude Hamilton, and seven children. He is buried at the Newton Cemetery.

NEWTON POLICE DEPARTMENT

Gibson, Charles
Born 3 September 1888—Died 18 October 1940

Officer Charles Gibson was shot and killed when he interrupted a burglary at a local filling station. The robber opened fire on Gibson, mortally wounding him. Gibson's killer escaped. He had managed to steal thirty-five cents during the holdup. The man was later apprehended and brought to justice.

Gibson had been with the agency for five years. He was survived by his wife, Ida Jane Jones, and six children. Gibson is buried at the Bleakwood Cemetery in Bleakwood.

NILES CITY POLICE DEPARTMENT

Finch, Thomas Edward "Tom"
Born July 1877—Died 27 November 1917

At about 2:00 p.m. on Tuesday, 27 November 1917, Officer Tom Finch was shot and killed by a millwright named W.A. Jobe. At the time the incident took place, Finch was standing at the corner of Main and Twelfth Streets talking with Jobe's wife.

Jobe was arrested and taken to the city jail. He was formally charged with the murder of Finch and was released on a $7,500 bond. During her testimony in criminal district court, Jobe's wife admitted that she had had an improper relationship with Finch. Although on the night before Finch's murder, Mrs. Jobe said that she had revealed to her husband that she had met with Finch, she claimed that she had not told him that the liaison was an affaire d'amour.

Jobe's trial date was set and postponed a number of times. Jobe was eventually convicted of the murder of Finch, but a sympathetic jury sentenced him to serve only a five-year suspended sentence.

Finch was survived by his wife, Edna Leona Helm, and the couple's four children. He is buried at the Mount Olivet Cemetery in Fort Worth. Niles City was annexed into the city of Fort Worth in 1921. Finch's tombstone shows his year of birth as 1876; however, family genealogists claim July 1877 as the correct date.

NOCONA POLICE DEPARTMENT

Gooch, Albert R.
Born 26 January 1881—Died 13 January 1929

City Marshal Albert Gooch was shot and killed while he was attempting to serve a search warrant for possession of illegal liquor at a residence in Nocona.

At the time of the incident, Gooch was accompanied by another officer. The killer, Carl Goodspeed, fled but was arrested at Montague a few hours later. He was tried and convicted of the murder of Gooch. Goodspeed was sentenced to serve twenty-five years in prison. His conviction was later reversed.

Gooch was not married. Both of his parents had preceded him in death. Gooch is buried at the Barr Springs Cemetery in Westport.

Gooch's successor, Edward C. Powell, was shot and killed in the line of duty nine months later.

Powell, Edward C. "Ed"
Born 31 January 1893—Died 12 October 1929
Date of Incident: 9 October 1929

City Marshal Ed Powell died from a gunshot wound he received when he was involved in a desperate struggle with a man named Walter W. Reagan.

Powell was attempting to arrest Reagan for a liquor law violation. During the struggle that took place between the two men, Powell drew his pistol. He dropped the gun, which accidentally discharged. The bullet struck Powell in the left chest. Powell hung on for three days before he finally died from the results of the gunshot wound.

Reagan was arrested after the shooting incident. He was tried, convicted and sentenced to serve ten years in prison.

Powell had served as a city marshal for nine months. He had been appointed after the previous marshal, Albert Gooch, was shot and killed. Powell is buried at the Odd Fellows Cemetery in Denton.

NOLAN COUNTY SHERIFF'S OFFICE

Newman, James Franklin
Born 20 December 1849—Died 30 December 1914
Date of Incident: 29 January 1891

Former sheriff James Newman died as a result of gunshot wounds that he had received twenty-two years earlier when he was ambushed and shot at close range by Arch and Dick English.

The shooting incident occurred on Thursday, 29 January 1891. Newman had recently testified against Arch and Dick English. The court had released the two men on bond. Soon after, the pair shot Newman in the back with a shotgun from a distance of twenty feet. Newman never recovered from the wounds and lingered for more than two decades before finally expiring.

Newman's father swore out a complaint against Arch and Dick English. The two men were subsequently arrested. The outcome of any charges is unknown.

Newman had served with the agency for six years. He had been elected sheriff on 4 November 1890.

Newman was survived by his wife, Josephine Rushing, and five children. He is buried at the Sweetwater Cemetery.

Lamkin, John Harvey
Born 13 April 1876—Died 15 June 1933
Date of Incident: 1 June 1933

Deputy Sheriff John Lamkin died from gunshot wounds he had received when, while on patrol, he came upon a burglary in progress at the Magnolia warehouse. One of the criminals, Luke Trammell, immediately opened fire. A shot from Trammell's pistol hit Lamkin in the back, near the right shoulder. The bullet traveled through his lungs and came out near the collarbone on his left side. As he fled the scene, Trammell intentionally ran into Lamkin with his vehicle.

Lamkin was taken to the Sweetwater Hospital, where he lingered in pain until his death on Thursday, 15 June. According to Sheriff Lambeth, the only loot the robbers made off with that evening was a tank full of gasoline.

Trammell was sentenced to fifty years in prison for the murder of Lamkin. On 19 June 1936, he and another inmate murdered state prison guard Felix Smith as they made good their escape from the penitentiary. Both men were recaptured. Trammell was sentenced to death for murdering the prison guard. That sentence was carried out on 20 August 1937, when Trammell was executed by electrocution at Huntsville, becoming the 148th criminal to meet such a fate.

The other inmate involved in the murder of Smith was sentenced to sixty years in prison.

Lamkin was survived by his wife and five children. He is buried at the Blackwell Cemetery.

Related Case: Texas Department of Criminal Justice, Felix Smith

NUECES COUNTY CONSTABLE'S OFFICE

Feely, Patrick William
Born 28 February 1868—Died 25 March 1917

Precinct 1 constable Patrick Feely was shot and killed by a former deputy sheriff named Raymond Bellamy.

Feely had responded to a disturbance call. A group of men were driving around in an automobile with one man perched on the vehicle's hood. Bellamy was hiding in the bushes. When Feely walked past Bellamy, he shot him from ambush. Feely was able to return fire, wounding Bellamy. Feely's wound proved to be fatal.

Bellamy was arrested and charged with murder. Those charges were dismissed.

Feely was survived by his wife, Alma Mary Gosling, and several children (perhaps as many as eight). Some family genealogists report Alma's middle name as Gertrude, not Mary. Feely is buried at the Holy Cross Cemetery.

Bledsoe, Richard Ross
Born 18 March 1898—Died 5 July 1925

Bisbee, Carl M.
Born 27 November 1896—Died 5 July 1925

Precinct 1 constable Carl Bisbee and Deputy Constable R.R. Bledsoe were shot and killed in a five-man gun battle while they were questioning several men who, some sources claim, had been observed drinking in public.

Although there are several accounts of this incident given by participants, eyewitnesses and the local newspapers, it appears that when the lawmen attempted to place the threesome under arrest, the shooting began.

Bisbee and Bledsoe were said to have been members of a rival political faction whose views differed from those of George Ryder, Rufus McMurray and Paul McAlister. McAlister was a deputy state game, fish and oyster commissioner and a former Cameron County deputy sheriff with a checkered past. Bisbee and Bledsoe were seated in Bledsoe's automobile when the shooting started. Apparently, McMurray and Bledsoe got into a heated disagreement of some sort. The quarrel quickly escalated into deadly gunplay. McMurray was the first to fall. He was shot a second time after he collapsed on the ground. McMurray claims that Bledsoe fired the first volley and that Bisbee tried to intervene.

George Ryder's brother Lee related a slightly different story afterward, claiming that George had told him how the incident unfolded before he died. Ryder claimed that he and McAlister had left Bessie Miller's sporting house on Sam Rankin Street together and had walked to his automobile. McAlister had entered the vehicle, and Ryder was about to do so, when Bledsoe and Bisbee pulled up. Either Bisbee or Bledsoe asked where the men were going. Ryder responded, "San Diego" (meaning the town of San Diego in Duval County). Bledsoe then said, "No you are not," and told them that they were under arrest. When Ryder asked why, Bledsoe told him that it made no difference, just: "Hands up."

Ryder claimed that he was still standing by the fender of his automobile when Bledsoe fired first. Bisbee then let loose with one shot that hit McAlister, who leaped from the car and was struck by a second bullet from Bisbee's gun. Ryder said he followed Bledsoe, who had chased McAlister, and fired three shots at him while the women from the sporting house watched the whole gruesome scene unfold on the street below.

By the time the smoke had cleared, Ryder, Bisbee, Bledsoe and McAlister were all either dead or mortally wounded. Bisbee and McAlister both died a few hours after the fight. According to one report, Bledsoe and Ryder died the following day. Ryder went on to claim that he did not know who had fired the fatal shot that downed Bisbee. McMurray recovered and died in 1936.

Bledsoe had been with the agency for seven months. He is buried at the Forest Hill Cemetery in Petty. Bledsoe had also served as a Texas Ranger, having enlisted in Company B at Corpus Christi on 8 August 1923. He was not married.

Bisbee was survived by his wife, Buelah Ehlers. He is buried at the Rose Hill Cemetery in Corpus Christi.

Related Case: Texas Department of Parks and Wildlife, Paul McAlister

Nueces County Sheriff's Office

Downs, Alexander Stevens, Jr.
Born 2 February 1907—Died 16 October 1932

Deputy Sheriff Alexander Downs Jr. was working at a dance when he confronted an intoxicated man named Liborio Garza, who was creating a disturbance. Downs told Garza to "cut out the racket." As Downs walked away, Garza pulled out a pistol and shot him. Stray gunfire from Garza's gun also hit three innocent bystanders: Francisco Villarreal, Jose Rodriguez and Andres Garcia.

Downs was taken to a doctor's home, where he died within a few minutes of his arrival. Villarreal died as well. Jose Rodriguez and Andres Garcia survived their wounds.

Garza pleaded not guilty based on insanity from having been intoxicated and smoking marijuana. He was convicted and sentenced to ninety-nine years in prison.

Downs was survived by his wife and infant son. He is buried at the Robstown Cemetery in Nueces County.

ORANGE COUNTY CONSTABLE'S OFFICE

Chesson, John Joseph
Born 6 December 1877—Died 26 June 1922

Precinct 3 constable John Chesson was shot and killed in an unusual incident involving a justice of the peace named Lon Garrison and a barber named Simon Johnson.

In testimony given by Johnson, he indicated that Chesson shot him in the mouth while he was in the process of unlocking the door to his home. Considering that he knew both Chesson and Garrison, he was caught completely off guard by their actions. Johnson wheeled and fired three shots at Chesson and saw him fall. He next claimed that Garrison fired at him, as well, so he returned fire but missed. After the gunfight had ended, the seriously wounded Johnson ran to a neighboring home for help.

Johnson claimed that Chesson's daughter, Mrs. Melba Mae "Maude" Herrington, had told him that Chesson was going to kill him. The truth of the matter remains a mystery.

Chesson was survived by his wife, Allie Pearl Barron, and eight children. Various family genealogists claim anywhere from four to nine children, while newspaper accounts of the day indicate eight. Chesson is buried at the Walles Cemetery in Orange County.

ORANGE COUNTY SHERIFF'S OFFICE

Boykin, John
Born July 1878—Died 6 May 1907

On 20 April 1907, Deputy Sheriff John Boykin shot and wounded a bartender he was attempting to arrest for having ambushed a woman at a saloon in the city of Orange. A constable arrested Boykin, who in turn posted a $500 bond pending an examining trial, which was the customary process at the time.

On the night of Monday, 6 May 1907, two men, Baily Hudson and O.F. Woodfin, were shot and wounded from ambush while they were riding in a hack in the downtown area. A third man who was with them escaped injury.

Later that evening, at about 11:10 p.m., Boykin was socializing with friends at the same saloon where he had shot the bartender on 20 April. Suddenly, someone from outside the saloon shot him. The wounded Boykin walked outside, where he was shot two more times. Now suffering from the effects of three bullet wounds, he fell to the ground. Unbelievably, his merciless assailant shot him three more times. As one might imagine, the wounds were fatal.

The sheriff and a local lawman arrested seven men and women as material witnesses in the murder. The sheriff claimed that the witnesses knew who had killed Boykin and wounded the two other men. Newspaper reports alleged that Boykin's killing was done in revenge for the shooting death of the bartender in April.

A grand jury investigated the death of Boykin and the wounding of Hudson and Woodfin. It is not known if anyone was indicted, tried or convicted for Boykin's murder.

Almost no personal information has been uncovered about Boykin. His place of burial is unknown, although he may have been buried in one of the local black cemeteries.

Haley, Charley Erwin "Luke"
Born 31 January 1880—Died 7 March 1922

Deputy Sheriff Luke Hailey died in a shootout that took place on Fifth Street in the business district of Orange. Apparently, Haley and a boatman named Henry Griffith were involved in a disagreement of some sort. The quarrel turned violent. Both men pulled their pistols and fired. According to witnesses, there were as many as nine shots exchanged during this gory street battle. Both of their crumpled bodies dropped to the street wounded and bleeding.

At first it was thought that each man had killed the other. Upon investigation, however, Orange County sheriff J.W. Helton believed that the shot that killed Haley had come from someone in the crowd of bystanders watching the affray between Haley and Griffith unfold.

Former deputy sheriff Columbus Canter and his brother-in-law, John Ratliff, who was a dairyman, were charged with the killing. Apparently, Sheriff Helton's suspicions concerning the pair's involvement in the killing proved correct. On 11 May 1922, an Orange County grand jury issued a joint bill of indictment against Canter and Ratliff for the murder of Haley. The outcome of the charges is unknown.

Griffith died of his wounds the following day. Haley died at the scene of the altercation.

No personal information on Haley has been uncovered. His body was shipped to San Angelo for burial.

Stakes, Basil S. "Shorty"
Born 22 March 1895—Died 14 February 1925

Two local meat markets were involved in a business feud, competing over territory. A confrontation between the warring factions occurred, during which two employees of one firm were shot and killed by two employees of the rival company.

Deputies W.C. Woods, "Shorty" Stakes and a citizen named Arthur Sanders attempted to arrest the two survivors of the bloody mêlée. While accounts vary, the two men, Frank Wilkes and Herbert Batchan, resisted arrest. One of them was armed with a pistol and the other with a rifle. Stakes took the rifle away from the man who was so armed and was using it to subdue the pair when the gun accidentally discharged. When that occurred, either Wilkes or Batchan shot Stakes with a .38-caliber revolver. Stakes was hit in the face just under his left eye. He died at the scene.

The grand jury met two days later and indicted both Wilkes and Batchan. They were tried, convicted and sentenced to death for killing their two business rivals. Both men appealed. In a second trial, Wilkes was sentenced to fifteen years in prison for the murder of Stakes, but that case was reversed and sent back to the lower court in 1926. Wilkes died in prison on 1 March 1926 while awaiting the outcome of his appeal. Batchan's death sentence was reversed and sent back to the lower court. There is no appeals court record of a second trial.

Stakes was twenty-nine years old at the time of his death. He was a widower and was survived by his parents. Stakes is buried at the Evergreen Cemetery in Orange. Stakes's death certificate lists his name as Samuel Basel Stakes; however, his tombstone is inscribed "Basil S. Stakes." Other records show his name as Bosie S. or Basell Stakes.

ORANGE POLICE DEPARTMENT

Jett, James A.
Born 13 July 1858—Died 12 May 1902

James Jett was shot and killed during a personal dispute. His killer, a man named George Pool, was tried and convicted, but that conviction was overturned.

By means of background, Texas Rangers had been sent to Orange to quell what were described as riotous disturbances. On 21 December 1899, Texas Ranger T.L. Fuller arrested a man named Denny Moore, who was causing trouble. Fuller was trying to get Moore to jail when another man named Oscar Poole jumped him. Either Poole was part of Moore's gang or the man just hated authority—it is unclear. In either case, Fuller was attacked by the knife-wielding assailant and had to shoot Poole in self-defense.

Poole was the son of Orange County judge George F. Poole. Fuller was arrested and jailed without bail. He was, however, cleared in the Poole shooting.

The Poole family filed a complaint of false arrest in Orange County against Fuller. Ranger captain Bill McDonald protested, claiming that the charge was nothing more than a ploy to get Fuller back in Orange. His superiors overruled McDonald.

McDonald and ranger private A.L. Saxon were in Orange as witnesses in the case involving Fuller, who had just been promoted to the rank of lieutenant. During a break in the trial, Fuller and Saxon decided to get a shave.

At 5:30 p.m., Fuller was standing in Adams's Barbershop washing his face at a basin in the center of the room when a gunshot was fired. The bullet from a Winchester rifle hit Fuller in the back of the head and exited through his eye. He fell to the floor and died within a few minutes. Tom Poole, brother of Oscar, ran into the adjoining butcher shop with a Winchester rifle in hand. He was placed under arrest.

Thomas Poole was tried for the murder of Fuller and was acquitted on 4 May, 1901.

In March 1902, City Marshal James A. Jett shot and killed Tom Poole. On 12 May 1902, Jett became engaged in a personal dispute with George H. Poole. George, Claude and Grover Poole shot and killed Jett in a gun battle that unfolded on the streets of Orange.

Jett was survived by his wife, Agnes Roger, and one child. He is buried at the Evergreen Cemetery in Orange.

Jordan, Josiah Joseph "Joe"
Born 14 April 1840—Died 5 November 1902

City Marshal Joe Jordan was shot and killed while he was walking a prisoner named Will Harris to the city jail.

Jordan had just arrested Harris for murdering a man during a personal dispute. As the two walked to the jail, Jordan was shot by Harris's brother, Doug (Dug), in an attempt to free his kinsman. Doug Harris was arrested and charged with Jordan's murder. He was subsequently convicted and sentenced to five years in prison.

Jordan had served with the agency for six months. He was survived by his wife, Mary Elizabeth Shaver, and one child. Jordan is buried at the Evergreen Cemetery in Orange. His tombstone reads, "He died as He Lived, a Pure Upright Man."

Combs, Samuel N.
Born circa 1872—Died 18 April 1910

A local hotel manager had been experiencing repeated thefts of linen for a period of about two weeks. At about midnight on Monday, 18 April 1910, the innkeeper was on the lookout for the criminals in an effort to spot the "linen bandits." Believing that he had spotted the culprits, he called Deputy City Marshal Ben Stokes and asked that he arrest two men.

Stokes arrested one of the men and asked Deputy City Marshal Sam Combs to assist him in locating the second. While searching a residential neighborhood for the thief, Combs noticed a man escorting a woman to a house and walking away. Stokes was tying up his horse as Combs approached the man, Jackson White, and asked for his identification. White pulled out a large knife and slashed Combs across the throat. The laceration nearly severed his head. Combs fell to the pavement and died.

White fled, but a posse later surrounded his house. While in the process of attempting to arrest White, Stokes claimed that the man made a movement as if to go for a weapon. Predictably, Stokes shot him. The bullet hit White in the neck. He survived the injury and denied his guilt. Officers, however, had found a large knife covered with bloodstains in his overcoat. Rather incriminating, to say the least.

White was tried twice. The first hearing ended in a mistrial. He was convicted and sentenced to death in the second trial. It appears as though White's sentence was never carried out.

Combs was survived by three sisters. He is buried at the Evergreen Cemetery in Orange, but no record seems to exist as to the specific location.

White, William C. "Will"
Born 4 March 1880—Died 25 March 1930

Officer William White was shot and killed by a former Texas Ranger and Prohibition agent named N.E. Perkins.

According to period newspaper reports and appeals court records, Officers White and Leonard Carr had gone to Perkins's store to investigate a report of some loud talking. Perkins lived in the store and was in bed when the officers knocked. Perkins asked Carr to go across the street and get some cigarettes. When he returned, he found White lying on the ground with two bullet holes in his body. Based on the locations of the wounds, one of the shots had been fired into his back. The second shot, which appeared to have been fired from a large-caliber pistol, entered below the left collarbone.

Perkins claimed that he shot White in self-defense and that he had fired when White shot at him. The records indicated that there were bullet holes in the building, which supported Perkins's claim.

Both N.E. Perkins and his wife, Fannie, were arrested. N.E. Perkins was convicted of killing White and sentenced to serve ninety-nine years in prison.

White is buried at the Jett Cemetery in Orange.

O'Reilly, Edward James
Born 25 May 1894—Died 29 May 1935

Chief Edward O'Reilly was shot and killed by a local preacher named Edgar Eskridge. Eskridge had been arrested the previous day for impersonating a Texas Ranger.

At the time of the arrest, Eskridge, who was the pastor of the Orange First Baptist Church, was carrying two pistols, which O'Reilly took away from him. He claimed that he held a commission as a special Texas Ranger. According to reports, Eskridge had led a raid on a nightclub on the Orange–Port Arthur highway on Sunday, 26 May 1935, during which he had brandished a Texas Ranger badge. He was known locally as a fierce enemy of vice and corruption.

Once O'Reilly confirmed that Eskridge was not a sworn peace officer, he arrested him and brought him before the county attorney. The preacher was released without any charges being filed. According to friends, Eskridge was very upset about the incident and spent the night driving around in his automobile.

The following day, O'Reilly was standing in front of Ingram's Café on the corner of Fifth and Main, in the heart of downtown Orange, when Reverend Eskridge rounded the corner at Fifth onto Main in his brown Oldsmobile coupe and fired a shotgun directly at O'Reilly. The blast hit him in the face, inflicting a fatal injury. Pellets struck O'Reilly in the right eye, mouth and neck. He fell to the pavement dead. C.C. Ledy, chief accountant for the Lutcher Moore Lumber Company, was an eyewitness to the incident and claimed that Eskridge had stopped the automobile briefly and, without getting out, opened fire with his shotgun.

Eskridge sped away down Main Street toward the Sabine River Bridge, narrowly avoiding collisions with two other automobiles as he made his way from the scene of the shooting. Mayor W.L. Blanchard, who was standing at the same corner at the time, was an eyewitness to incident and claimed that Eskridge had driven around the block twice before opening fire on O'Reilly.

Eskridge was arrested about two hours after the incident and jailed in De Ridder, Louisiana. He claimed that he feared for his life being locked up there. Eskridge indicated that he was willing to be returned to Sheriff Richardson of Beaumont but that he would not submit to Orange County sheriff W.P. Brown, a man of whom he had been openly critical for allowing widespread vice to take over the county. Eskridge believed that the county law enforcement organization was rife with corruption and had been outspoken about that on a number of occasions.

Eskridge and O'Reilly had been friends prior to this incident, and O'Reilly had been a parishioner at the pastor's church. An investigation into Eskridge's background revealed that he had been a federal Prohibition agent stationed at Tyler about ten years earlier. He was known there as a "two-gun marksman" and was able to write his named on a target with bullets fired from two six-shooters simultaneously.

On 4 June 1935, Eskridge was extradited to Texas to stand trial for the killing of O'Reilly. On 21 June, he received a change of venue, moving his trial to Houston. Throughout the trial process, Eskridge was portrayed as a legal crusader. He received boundless support from his congregation. His lawyers claimed that he was insane when he killed O'Reilly. On 19 November 1935, a mistrial was declared over an improper juror. On 14 June 1936, the district court handed down a verdict of guilty of murder without malice and sentenced Eskridge to serve five years in prison for the murder of O'Reilly.

O'Reilly was survived by his wife and one child. He is buried at the Evergreen Cemetery in Orange.

Godwin Jr., John Delaney "Johnny"
Born 4 March 1904—Died 11 August 1935

Acting chief of police Johnny Godwin was shot and killed when he attempted to arrest two escaped convicts, Clyde Dawson and B.L. Thompson, who were fleeing from San Antonio.

The two hoodlums had been given medical treatment after their arrest at a San Antonio hospital. During their escape from lawmen, who were in the process of transporting the pair to the county jail, Dawson managed to snatch Bexar County deputy sheriff Ernest Macla's pistol from the officer's shoulder holster on their way out of the building. Initially, the pair had stolen Macla's vehicle but quickly made a switch a few minutes later at Buena Vista Street, near Leona, when, at the point of a cocked pistol, they forced a man named R.C. McNee to give up his automobile.

Godwin had taken over the role of police chief after the recent slaying of Edward O'Reilly by preacher Edgar Eskridge. He and Officer George Lafitte were waiting near the Beaumont–Orange highway for the pair, who had committed an armed robbery of taxicab driver Fred Thomas in Orange. The thieves had also taken Thomas's automobile.

The officers stopped the vehicle, which had been stolen from Thomas. Lafitte held a shotgun on the pair as Godwin ordered the men to exit the automobile. The men complied, but as they did so, one began a scuffle with Godwin. The thief drew his gun, fired twice and hit Godwin with one bullet in the abdomen. A conflicting report claimed that the two lawmen had gotten into the stolen vehicle with Dawson and Thompson when the shooting incident occurred.

After the gunplay, the convicts ran from Green Street down toward Front Street. Thompson was arrested shortly after the shooting affray. Dawson managed to slip away. He kidnapped an Orange couple named Jesse Webb and Rosa Lee Patterson, robbed them of sixteen dollars and commandeered their automobile.

Dawson was arrested near Lake Charles, Louisiana, not long after the incident. He confessed to killing Godwin. On 23 September 1935, Dawson and Thompson bluffed their way out of the Orange County jail using a pistol carved from a bar of soap. They attempted to steal the automobile of a one-armed war veteran, but the man threw away his keys and began struggling with them. The sheriff heard the noise and arrested the pair of escapees.

The disposition of the case against Thompson is unknown. Dawson was tried, convicted and sentenced to serve life in prison.

Godwin had been with the agency for only five months. He was survived by his two children. Godwin is buried at the Evergreen Cemetery in Orange.

Panola County Constable's Office

Wyatt, Marcus M. "Mark"
Born 25 December 1859—Died 6 January 1901

Constable Mark Wyatt was shot and killed by a man named Walter W. White. According to reports, Wyatt was intoxicated when the incident occurred and had been involved in a personal disagreement with his killer.

The incident took place at White's saloon business, which was located on Main Street in Tatum. Wyatt was one of his customers and had run up an account at the bar. Wyatt was a violent, argumentative, overbearing and dangerous man when under the influence of liquor. Wyatt and White had had a quarrel at some point the previous night, during which Wyatt had drawn his pistol and attempted to shoot White. The pair had apparently settled their differences, however, shaking hands and exchanging pleasantries afterward.

The shooting occurred in the barroom at about 1:00 p.m. on Sunday, 6 January 1901. Wyatt had been drinking at White's bar the preceding evening and into the night. He would not allow the bartender to close the saloon until 1:00 or 2:00 a.m. Wyatt was at the saloon again on Sunday morning.

Wyatt would not allow the barroom to be closed that morning. White, hearing of this, tried to get mutual friends to coax Wyatt away from the bar. They failed.

While White was waiting for someone to cajole Wyatt to leave, a man named Shivers drove up in a wagon and handed him a shotgun. The gun was the property of a third party named John Fort, and Shivers wanted White to deliver it to the owner. After taking the gun, White testified that he loaded it with shells he had in his pocket. The shells were loaded with squirrel shot. He then went into the saloon with the gun; walked passed Wyatt, who was standing in front of the counter; and said, "Boys, here is a gun Shivers left with me for John Fort. It is Sunday, and the doors ought to be closed." Wyatt turned from the counter and said, "There's the son of a bitch" and, according to some witnesses, drew his pistol. At that point, White fired the shotgun, blowing the top of Wyatt's head off. As one might imagine, Wyatt was dead at the scene.

One eyewitness to the crime was the esteemed ex-slave Lum Barker, who was employed as a porter at White's drinking establishment. Although Barker was called upon by the grand jury to testify, he refused to offer any insight into the crime, simply answering with a terse, "Tatum don't talk."

White was tried and convicted of the murder of Wyatt. He was sentenced to serve ten years in prison. That sentence was later reversed.

Wyatt was not married. He was survived by his mother and six siblings. Wyatt is buried at the Harmony Hill Cemetery in Rusk.

Fleming, John Johnson
Born 16 August 1892—Died 8 September 1929

A black church was having its annual revival, and several hundred people were gathered. Precinct 8 constable John Fleming lived about 250 yards from the house of worship. Since the revival was to run all week, at about 6:00 p.m., Fleming and two friends went to the church to see if it needed any beef. A man named Andrew Castleberry began speaking loudly and appeared to be intoxicated. Fleming noticed that Castleberry was carrying a pistol. Fleming asked Castleberry to come over and said, "You seem to be feeling pretty good, but you had better give me that gun." As Fleming reached out his left hand to grab the handle of the pistol, Castleberry stepped backward, wrenching the weapon from Fleming's hand. Castleberry raised the pistol and attempted to fire. Fleming was faster on the draw and pulled his pistol first, shooting Castleberry twice in the head. The wounded Castleberry lived about an hour.

Andrew Castlberry's brother Walter walked up and shot Fleming through the forearm. The bullet traveled down into Fleming's lower bowels. A man named Charley Thompson then shot the constable from behind. That bullet went through Fleming's shoulder and into his heart. Fleming emptied his pistol at his assailants as he fell, wounding two bystanders. A man named Albert McDowell grabbed a board and struck Fleming with it several times as he fell to the ground. Fleming died at the scene.

The sheriff arrested Robert Castleberry, the father of Andrew and Walter, and his other sons, David, Ned and Will. He also arrested Charley Thompson. Walter Castleberry and Albert McDowell fled the scene. Thompson was charged, found guilty and sentenced to ninety-nine years in prison. McDowell was not apprehended until 1940. He was convicted and sentenced to forty years in prison. Walter Castleberry was never apprehended.

Fleming was survived by his wife and three children. He is buried at the Clayton Cemetery.

Matthews, Jesse P.
Born 6 March 1882—Died 4 September 1937

Precinct 2 constable Jesse Matthews was on duty and responsible for maintaining order at a singing convention that was taking place about one mile east of Beckville. While there, two vehicles collided, and the drivers began quarreling. Matthews was attempting to settle the dispute when one of the men shot and killed him.

The killer fled the scene. Texas Rangers had to be sent to Panola County to restrain vigilantes, who were searching for the killer. No information has been located indicating whether anyone was ever arrested or tried for the murder.

Matthews was first elected constable of Precinct 2 in November 1914 and was serving his twelfth term. He was survived by his son and two daughters. Matthews's wife, Nettie Sparks, had preceded him in death. He is buried in Tatum.

PANOLA COUNTY SHERIFF'S OFFICE

Alford, Julius Charles "Charley"
Born 25 February 1878—Died 22 December 1905

On Friday, 22 December 1905, Deputy Sheriff Charley Alford was at his home in Ragley. When he stooped over to place some phonograph records into a trunk, his pistol fell from his side pocket and discharged. The bullet entered his stomach and passed through his body, killing him.

Alford was survived by his wife and five children. He is buried at the Woodlawn Cemetery in Shelby County.

Langley, J. Willis A.
Born 10 May 1868—Died 10 July 1906

Deputy Sheriff Langley was struck by lightning and killed while working in the fields plowing near his home in Fair Play.

Langley was survived by his wife, Jetta Bowen. He is buried at the Pinehill Baptist Cemetery in Pinehill in Rusk County.

PARIS POLICE DEPARTMENT

Schultz, William Cluff
Born 17 November 1872—Died 3 March 1904
Date of Incident: 21 February 1904

Officer Schultz died from a gunshot wound when his pistol fell from his pocket and discharged accidentally. The bullet struck him in the body, and based on the location of the projectile, physicians were unable to remove it. He died two weeks later.

Schultz had been with the agency for ten months. According to some accounts, he was survived by his wife, Mary Ellen Warren, and four children. Most family genealogists report only one child. He is buried at the Evergreen Cemetery in Paris.

Cross, Duain Sheb "Mann"
Born 26 September 1876—Died 20 July 1920
Date of Incident: 19 July 1920

Officer Duain Cross was shot and killed by a mentally ill man named Miles Bowie.

According to newspaper reports, Bowie had reportedly threatened to kill some children earlier in the day after they had teased him. Bowie had just shot a man named J.F. Massey, who was a bill collector for a Dallas furniture house. Massey had gone to the home of Bowie's neighbor, an elderly woman, to make a collection. The woman was not home at the time, so Massey took a seat on the front porch. Seeing the stranger, Bowie grabbed his shotgun and opened fire without saying a word.

At about 6:00 p.m., Cross and a fellow patrol officer named R.S. Rodgers went to Bowie's home on North Walls Street and attempted to disarm him. While doing so, Bowie shot Cross with a shotgun, hitting him in the left hip and the stomach. Rodgers returned fire with his pistol, killing Bowie and saying, "I got him" as he did so. Cross, who was Rodgers's friend and fellow officer, was lying wounded on the ground and was heard to say, "Yeah, but he got me."

Cross was taken to the hospital. Despite the efforts of Paris surgeons, he died the following day.

Cross was survived by his wife, Lillian B. Kimball, who gave birth to the couple's only child three weeks after his death. Cross is buried at the Evergreen Cemetery in Paris.

PECOS POLICE DEPARTMENT

Moorhead, Thomas Yowell
Born 10 November 1870—Died 8 February 1914

City Marshal Thomas Moorhead was shot and killed when he responded to a call at a location where several officers were investigating a street disturbance.

The officers had stopped two men for questioning. One of the men, Fernando Subia, pulled out a handgun and fired at them. A bullet from Subia's gun hit Moorhead in the face. The wound proved fatal.

Moorhead had been with the agency for five years. He was survived by his wife and six children. Moorhead is buried at the Fairview Cemetery.

Roddy, Marion Lee
Born 19 February 1875—Died 30 January 1923

City Marshal Marion Roddy was shot in the heart and killed by a man named Arthur Hayes.

At about 6:00 p.m. on Tuesday, 30 January 1923, Roddy and another man were drinking in front of the Motor Service Company garage when Roddy and Hayes got into an argument of an unknown nature. Hayes pulled a gun and fatally shot Roddy.

Roddy's death certificate indicates that he died in a duel. Hayes was arrested, tried and convicted of the murder. He was sentenced to serve seven years in prison. That sentence was later reversed.

Roddy is buried at Pecos in Reeves County. He was survived by his wife and son.

PITTSBURG POLICE DEPARTMENT

Newsom, Charles Washington
Born 12 November 1875—Died 5 December 1920

At about 2:00 a.m. on Sunday, 5 December 1920, night watchman Charles Newsom was called to the kitchen of the Owl Café to investigate a disturbance of some sort. When he arrived there, a man named Carl Norvell stabbed him in the neck so severely that the jagged cut almost severed his head. A second attacker, Kern Norvell, the brother of Carl, shot Newsom four times. Newsom died at the scene.

Apparently, Newsom had been killed out of revenge for the arrest of Roger Kesterson, which had occurred a few days earlier. Kesterson's arrest had been for some minor charge.

Carl Norvell was tried, convicted and sentenced to twenty-five years in prison for stabbing Newsom. Kern Norvell committed suicide before he could be arrested. Roger Kesterson was tried at Mount Vernon, in Franklin County, on a change of venue and was found not guilty.

Newsom was survived by his wife, Ida Inez Orr, and nine children. He is buried at the Rose Hill Cemetery in Pittsburg.

PLANO POLICE DEPARTMENT

Rye, Green Wesley
Born 2 February 1871—Died 28 February 1920

At about 5:00 a.m. on Saturday, 28 February 1920, Deputy City Marshal Green Rye was shot and killed when he interrupted a burglary at the Plano National Bank. Rye was wounded once in the abdomen. The thieves managed to escape with Liberty savings bonds valued at several thousand dollars. Early estimates placed their haul at a whopping $250,000. Authorities believed that one of the burglars was a woman who was dressed up in overalls.

The sneak thieves escaped and fled a few miles south before turning their automobile in a westerly direction and making good their getaway. Lawmen scoured north Texas counties and eventually apprehended one of the burglars. No one was ever charged with Rye's murder.

Rye had served with the agency for eighteen months. He was survived by his wife, Minnie, and three children. Rye is buried at the Odd Fellows Cemetery (Old San Saba Cemetery) in San Saba.

PORT ARTHUR POLICE DEPARTMENT

Smith, Ed G.
Born May 1870—Died 24 September 1902
Date of Incident: 23 September 1902

Deputy City Marshal Ed Smith was shot and killed while responding to a disturbance call near the Sabine Hotel.

Smith's killer and another Mexican man had both worked at the Sabine Hotel. They were discharged at noon and immediately began drinking to celebrate their termination of employment. Smith and an unnamed deputy responded to the disturbance call. When the lawmen tried to take the unruly pair into custody, one of the men pulled a pistol and shot Smith. The bullet entered the left side of his chest. Smith and the deputy were able to return fire, killing one of the two men, but not the one who had shot Smith. The other man fled, presumably to Mexico. Smith died at about 10:10 a.m. the following day. No information has been discovered regarding the capture of Smith's killer.

Very little personal information about Smith has been uncovered. He came to Texas from Tennessee and was living in a boardinghouse in Port Arthur. His place of burial is unknown.

Carlin, James "Jim"
Born circa 1871—Died 9 September 1907

On Monday, 9 September 1907, Officer Jim Carlin was shot and killed by his wife, Ella (Brown). Ella was arrested and charged with murder. Jim had walked out to the porch for some water, and as he returned, she shot him with a pistol. Ella claimed that the shooting was an accident, but Jim made a dying declaration that it was not.

Ella Carlin was indicted, but a jury acquitted her in February 1908. According to newspaper reports, when the verdict was read, she went into violent hysterics. She screamed and shouted, fell to the floor and rolled in a paroxysm of passion. It was impossible to control her until she had exhausted herself.

Jim Carlin's place of burial is unknown. He and Ella Brown had been married in the Orleans Parish of Louisiana on 10 December 1894. Carlin was reported to have been from New Orleans.

Grimes, Roy
Born 22 April 1880—Died 30 December 1919

At about 12:30 p.m. on Tuesday, 30 December 1919, Chief Roy Grimes was shot and instantly killed by a man named Jack Hyde.

The deadly incident took place in the back of city hall. Hyde had been waiting for Grimes in ambush and fired twice when he appeared. One bullet hit Grimes in the head and the other in the chest. Grimes drew his pistol and shot at Hyde but missed.

Hyde, who was a former Port Arthur and Beaumont police officer, was later arrested and charged with Grimes's murder. He was tried and acquitted. He claimed that Grimes had attacked him. According to newspaper reports, the two men were involved in a personal feud. The report went on to claim that Hyde's wife had filed for divorce, giving the impression that perhaps Grimes and Mrs. Hyde had been involved in an affaire d'amour.

Grimes is buried at the Fairview Cemetery in Bastrop County. He was survived by his wife, Johne Mae Roberts (Robertson), and one child. Grimes had been chief for one year. He was planning to announce that he was going to run for sheriff when he was killed.

Hamilton, Richard D. "Dick"
Born 18 November 1882—Died 11 December 1920

Dick Hamilton worked at the Gulf Refinery as a foreman. He was appointed a special police officer by Chief Pete Williams.

On Wednesday, 3 November 1920, Hamilton went to Oscar Spence's electrical shop to arrest Spence on a warrant for burglary. Hamilton claimed that when he informed Spence that he had come to arrest him, Spence opened a desk drawer and drew a pistol. Seeing the gun, Hamilton fired six shots in rapid succession. Spence ran into the street and collapsed. He died shortly afterward at the hospital.

At about 8:00 p.m. on Saturday, 11 December 1920, while Hamilton was driving home from a motion picture show with his wife and family, two men in an automobile pulled alongside them. One of the men leaned out through the car's window and fired a blast from a twelve-gauge shotgun at Hamilton. Hamilton, who was driving the family automobile at the time, fell over dead into his wife's arms. A load of No. 6 shot, which had been fired at close range, entered Hamilton's body in the back, under the left shoulder blade.

Some of the shot exited through his right chest. Hamilton's clothing was burned from the almost point-blank gunshot blast. A large hole was torn in his back.

Hamilton's car swerved into the curb, smashing the right front wheel as the vehicle nearly overturned.

Ralph F. Spence, the twenty-one-year-old brother of Oscar Spence, was arrested in Beaumont shortly after the incident. Spence had rented the automobile that he used in the assassination of Hamilton. The owner, who was driving the car at the time of the incident, was later released, claiming he had no idea what Spence intended to use the vehicle for. Spence was charged with the murder, but it is not known if he was ever tried or convicted.

Hamilton is buried at the Greenlawn Cemetery in Port Arthur. He was survived by his wife, Josie E. Gossett, and three children.

Harris, Ben A.
Born 3 April 1869—Died 16 August 1923

Detective Ben Harris had been targeted for assassination by criminals who disdained him. Several weeks prior to this incident, Harris had been involved in an incident with local grocer R.A. Brown during which Harris was accused of brutally thrashing the man. Harris had been suspended pending investigation and had just been reinstated on the morning of Thursday, 16 August.

Harris was reported to have been one of the most active officers in the war on bootlegging. Less than an hour before his murder, Harris had led a raid on a local soft drink parlor where a quantity of liquor was seized.

The shooting incident took place on Houston Avenue while Harris was driving a police vehicle. He was accompanied by other officers when the assassination occurred. A passing vehicle with two occupants fired a blast from a shotgun that hit Harris in the left chest. The wound was serious, tearing away a portion of Harris's body. The mortally injured Harris lost control of the police car and crashed it into a curb, causing the vehicle to overturn.

Not long after the incident, four Texas Rangers were dispatched to Port Arthur to assist in quelling the disturbance that was caused by the assassination of Harris and the subsequent beatings of Clay and Carl Dunn and Lonnie Davis.

The outcome of any charges against Harris's killer is unknown.

Harris is buried at the Upton Church of Christ Cemetery in Upton. Prior to joining the Port Arthur Police Department, Harris had served as a Texas Ranger. He enlisted in Company C at Marshall on 12 August 1922 and was discharged 11 April 1923.

Bradley, Albert Richard
Born 29 January 1904—Died 13 December 1936
Date of Incident: 12 December 1936

Superintendent of Police Albert Bradley died about midnight at St. Mary's Hospital from gunshot wounds he had received in a shootout earlier in the evening. Bullets penetrated his right lung and thigh. Bradley's killer, C.W. Rogers, died at the same hospital a few minutes after Bradley. Rogers had been shot four times, including a fatal wound in the abdomen, by James McWilliams, shipmaster for the Atlantic Oil Company. The bloody incident had taken place just outside a local Port Arthur sporting house.

Bradley, along with James McWilliams and Houston police officer F.M. Sallee, left the police station at about 10:40 p.m. on Saturday, 12 December 1936, to investigate a report of trouble at a sporting house operated by Grace Woodyard that was located on Eighth Street. Some accounts of the incident claim that Ms. Woodyard's establishment was a "beer house." It seems that term may have been the politically correct form of speech for a brothel at the time.

When the group arrived, a woman who was standing in the door of the house pointed toward two men who were standing on the sidewalk claiming that they were the ones responsible for the trouble. McWilliams and Bradley walked up to the pair and asked for identification. Bradley and Rogers began to quarrel, questioning each other's authority. A gun battle quickly developed. McWilliams claimed that during the scuffle Rogers had jerked away from him and shot Bradley. McWilliams then pulled his pistol and shot Rogers. Bradley's bloodstained nickel-plated .45-caliber revolver contained two empty cartridges, giving evidence to the fact that he had managed to get off at least a couple shots at his killer.

Chief H.F. Baker later said that the entire unfortunate incident was the result of mistaken identity.

Bradley had been with the agency for six years. He was not married. He was survived by his parents and ten siblings. Bradley is buried at the Greenlawn Cemetery in Port Arthur.

Some sources reported that Bradley was married; however, no evidence has been found to confirm that assertion.

PRESIDIO COUNTY SHERIFF'S OFFICE

Speed, Robert Eustis "Bob"
Born 7 December 1878—Died 1 January 1940

On Monday, 1 January 1940, Deputy Sheriff Bob Speed was said to have been drinking. Speed apparently claimed that he was going to kill William B. "Bill" Howell, who owned a local package liquor store in Shafter. Speed entered the establishment armed with a .45-caliber pistol. Howell had heard about the threats and had two .32-caliber pistols behind the bar. Gunfire erupted, and when the smoke cleared, Speed had been shot in the head and chest and lay dead on the floor.

Howell was arrested and charged with murder. He was tried, convicted and sentenced to serve five years in prison. However, the jury recommended that his sentence be suspended. It is claimed that Speed had been feuding with Howell over arrests that Speed had made at Howell's bar and that Speed had shot and wounded Howell the previous year.

Speed was survived by his wife, Ida May Brooks, and two children. He is buried at the Brooks-Fuentes Cemetery in Shafter.

Speed was a former Texas Ranger. He enlisted in Company B on 31 October 1911 in Kenedy and again on 31 October 1913 in Del Rio. His last commission expired on 31 October 1915. Speed reenlisted in Company A in Presidio on 16 March 1921 and again on 16 March 1923. He resigned on 10 December 1923. He had served as a deputy sheriff for thirteen years.

PROSPER POLICE DEPARTMENT

Hayes, Amos
Born 24 June 1879—Died 28 July 1917

City Marshal Amos Hayes was shot and killed by a man named T.E. Watson. Hayes and Watson had been involved in some sort of business deal that went bad. Their disagreement turned violent, leaving Hayes dead from a gunshot wound.

Hayes is buried at the Walnut Grove Cemetery. He was survived by his wife, Mary Jane Greenwood, and seven children.

Ranger Police Department

Jordan, Alfred Devaun "Alf"
Born 25 April 1877—Died 16 November 1919

Officer Alf Jordan was shot and killed during an encounter with a known illegal-liquor smuggler.

Jordan was returning from the local railroad station after having conducted an inspection for illegal liquor when the unfortunate and fatal encounter with Bill Shamblin occurred. After exchanging words, Shamblin produced a handgun and shot Jordan several times. The mortally wounded Jordan was able to return fire and wound his assailant.

Shamblin was taken into custody and charged with murder. He was sentenced to serve fifteen years in prison, but that sentence was eventually overturned.

Jordan had only worked for the Ranger Police Department for three days. He had previously served as a Texas Ranger, having enlisted at Texarkana on 20 July 1901. Jordan is buried at Texarkana, but records noting the specific details and location have not been uncovered.

Daniel, James Henry "Jimmie"
Born 9 May 1881—Died 8 February 1925

Policeman Jimmie Daniel was shot and killed while attempting to arrest several men who were in possession of a stolen automobile.

Daniel had been alerted about the stolen vehicle and had been searching for it during his overnight shift. He finally located the automobile and its occupants while he was driving home at about 6:00 a.m. When he attempted to arrest the men in the car, they opened fire. Daniel was hit several times. Although he was seriously wounded, he managed to return fire. His shots hit the vehicle but none of its occupants.

Other officers soon discovered Daniel's body lying in the street with his service revolver by his side. A suspect, Herve (or Harve) Wells, was eventually apprehended and charged with murder. He was indicted. Wells then sued the sheriff, one deputy and the chief of police for false imprisonment and malicious prosecution. A jury rendered a verdict in favor of the officers. The disposition of the murder charge is unknown.

Daniel was survived by his parents and several siblings. He is buried at the Evergreen Cemetery in Ranger.

REAGAN COUNTY CONSTABLE'S OFFICE

Hays, George A.
Born 10 February 1868—Died 12 November 1926

Shortly before midnight on Friday, 12 November 1926, Precinct 5 constable George Hays ejected a thirty-four-year-old man named W.L. "Billie" Coats from a dance at the Santa Rita Hotel in Best. The revengeful Coats soon returned to the ball, this time with a .45-caliber pistol, which he used to shoot Hays. Gunfire from Coats's pistol hit Hays in the head twice, killing him instantly.

Coats also shot a man named C.A. Jones, who was a rig boss for the Texon Oil Company, wounding him in the right wrist. Apparently not yet finished with the shooting spree, Coats continued on his rampage by shooting a local telephone operator named Miss Alva Beam. That bullet struck Miss Beam in the temple, killing her instantly. Panic filled the dance hall as the frenzied patrons plunged through windows to escape the crazed gunman.

Coats managed to flee. He committed suicide in a hotel room on 14 November 1926.

Hays had been a peace officer for less than three months. He was appointed constable for Precinct 5 on 9 August 1926 and elected to the position on 2 November 1926. Prior to becoming a lawman, Hays had spent the preceding twenty years as a general foreman on numerous West Texas ranches.

Hays was survived by his wife, Mary Elizabeth Ray, and one son. He is buried at the Fairmont Cemetery in San Angelo, Tom Green County.

RED RIVER COUNTY SHERIFF'S OFFICE

Stephens, Charles S.
Born 28 April 1880—Died 30 July 1912

At about 9:30 p.m. on Tuesday, 30 July 1912, Sheriff Charles Stephens, City Marshal Tom Ferguson and Constable Enos Elder went to a residence in Detroit in search of a man named Leonard Potts. Potts was wanted for the murder of a Dallas police officer named T.A. Tedford. That incident had occurred two days earlier.

Potts was sitting on the front porch of the house when the officers approached. He began firing almost immediately, using two semiautomatic pistols. Stephens was killed, and Elder was slightly wounded.

Potts managed to escape into the river bottoms. A posse located him five days later. Potts was killed by posse members during their attempt to take him into custody.

Stephens was survived by his young bride, Mary Della "Mollie" Lawson. He is buried at the Old Shamrock Cemetery in Bagwell.

Related Case: Dallas Police Department, T.A. Tedford

Puckett, Algie Rufus
Born 19 March 1885—Died 21 July 1920

Deputy Sheriff Algie Puckett and two other men went to the Lawson farm, located south of Annona, with a warrant for the arrest of a black man named Fox Belcher. The warrant was for stealing a pair of trousers.

A struggle occurred during which Belcher managed to grab Puckett's pistol from its holster and disarm the other two men. Puckett attempted to rush Belcher and reclaim his gun. As he did so, Belcher fired at him four or five times, killing Puckett almost instantly.

Belcher escaped from the scene of the shooting. Several hundred men from Red River, Bowie and surrounding counties scoured the area for Belcher. At about 1:00 p.m. the following day, he was shot and killed near Talco by a Titus County constable and his son, who were attempting to arrest him.

Puckett had married Sibyl Bishop two years earlier, in July 1918. They had no children. He was survived by a number of siblings. Puckett is buried at the Garland Cemetery in Red River County.

ROBERTSON COUNTY SHERIFF'S OFFICE

Rushing, Charles Thomas "Tom"
Born 23 November 1873—Died 21 September 1913

Several men were playing cards at a house in Petteway, a community located about eight miles from the county seat in Bremond. Some sort of quarrel took place during which a man named Will Davis shot and killed Luther

Hodge. As Davis fled the scene, he shot and wounded another man named Tom Maxwell.

Deputy Sheriff Tom Rushing, who was riding his horse nearby and heard the gunfire, rode to the home and ordered Davis to surrender his gun. Rather than surrender, Davis shot Rushing in the stomach. The wounded Rushing dismounted, pulled his pistol and tried to return fire. Before he was able to shoot, Davis fired again, this time hitting him in the heart and killing him instantly.

A large posse of citizens located Davis. After he admitted to having murdered Rushing and Hodge, the citizens lynched him from a nearby tree.

Rushing was survived by his brother, Will, who was at the time the Robertson County sheriff. He is buried at the Walnut Creek Cemetery in Bremond.

RUNNELS COUNTY SHERIFF'S OFFICE

Kuhn, Florence Jessie
Born 4 June 1878—Died 23 August 1923

Deputy Sheriff Florence Kuhn was shot and killed by a black man named John Smith during a dispute regarding crop cultivation.

Smith was a tenant on Kuhn's farm. Kuhn had taken two Mexican workers into the field, which was located about three miles from town. After he arrived, an argument broke out between Kuhn and three black workers over the amount of the settlement due for crops on the farm. What began as a quarrel quickly turned into a desperate struggle. The trio overpowered Kuhn. Smith took Kuhn's revolver and shot him in the head with it. The wound was fatal. Kuhn died instantly.

Smith fled. A posse of several hundred men was immediately formed. Smith and his two accomplices were captured about twenty hours later while walking along a road near Sweetwater. They were carrying Kuhn's bloodstained revolver. The disposition of any charges against Smith is unknown.

Kuhn is buried at the Rowena Protestant Cemetery.

RUSK COUNTY CONSTABLE'S OFFICE

Grigsby, James Elbert
Born 4 October 1908—Died 23 November 1937

At about noon on Tuesday, 23 November 1937, Precinct 3 constable James Elbert Grigsby of Tatum had gone to question Angus Williams about a recent burglary in nearby Panola County. Williams and another man named Pegues had been drinking and were standing together as Grigsby approached. Williams was holding a single-barreled shotgun at the time. Grigsby disarmed Williams and told him to quiet down or he would have to take him to jail. After the admonition, Grigsby returned the empty gun to Williams and went back to his automobile. Williams took a shotgun shell loaded with No. 4 shot from his pocket, reloaded and fired one blast at Grigsby, hitting him in the arm. Grigsby turned and fired, emptying his revolver at Williams, but his shots went wild, missing his assailant. Williams pursued the now seriously injured Grigsby, hitting him with seven more pellets in the back and side, mortally wounding him.

Williams fled to his home. Pegues also fled but was arrested as a witness several hours later. A large posse mounted a three-county search for Williams that lasted through the night, but a snowstorm and heavy rain obliterated his trail. According to some reports, somewhere between 50 and 150 angry citizens joined the hunt for Williams. The following day, Williams, apparently determined that he could not escape the lawmen, committed suicide by shooting himself in the head with his shotgun. He calmly placed the gun between his legs and held it with his feet while he tripped the trigger with a toe. Williams was an ex-convict who had been sentenced to serve ninety-nine years in prison for the 1923 killing of his wife. Amazingly, after completing only four years of that sentence, he had been released on parole.

Grigsby, who was twenty-nine at the time of his death, had served only nine months as a constable. He was survived by his wife, parents and numerous siblings. Grigsby is buried in the Harmony Hills Cemetery in Rusk County.

County and Municipal Agencies

SABINE COUNTY SHERIFF'S OFFICE

Bright, Carl Bosco
Born 5 September 1872—Died 15 January 1918

Carl Bright had been elected sheriff on 7 November 1916 and served until his death. Sheriff Bright had received information that a man named Time Battle had killed two men in Louisiana and that he was hiding out in a cabin near Hemphill in Sabine County. Bright gathered a posse and surrounded the cabin. When the lawmen attempted to arrest Battle, a gunfight broke out, during which Bright was shot and killed. The fugitive Battle was also killed during the exchange of gunfire.

Bright is buried at the Hemphill Cemetery in Sabine County. He was survived by his wife, Nettie Florence Williams, and six children.

SAN ANGELO POLICE DEPARTMENT

Anderson, Charles Wallace
Born 15 January 1883—Died 26 October 1919

Patrolman Charles Anderson was killed in the most unfortunate of mishaps when he was electrocuted while attempting to light an arc lamp on South Oakes Street at the Orient Railway tracks. An arc lamp is the term generally used to describe a category of lighting devices that produce illumination by electric arc, or voltaic arc. The device consists of two electrodes that are typically made of tungsten and are separated by a gas.

Anderson was on motorcycle patrol at the time of the incident, with the chief of police riding in his sidecar. When Anderson noticed that the lamp was not illuminated, he attempted to reignite the device. He was immediately electrocuted when he accidentally grabbed the wire on the lamp.

Anderson had served with the agency for four years. He was survived by his wife, Hattie Daugherty, and one son. He is buried at the Fairmount Cemetery in San Angelo.

SAN ANTONIO POLICE DEPARTMENT

Lacey, William Madison
Born 23 January 1862—Died 29 November 1900

Patrolman William Lacey was accidentally shot and killed during a labor dispute.

Lacey had been assigned to guard non-union workers during a strike. He was escorting one of the laborers on a repair job when the man was attacked. When Lacy came to the man's aid, the assailant shot him.

Lacy had been with the agency for only two days. He was survived by his wife, Elizabeth Isabel Gandine, and four children. Lacy is buried at City Cemetery No. 4 in San Antonio.

Cantu, Miguel
Born circa 1843—Died 30 November 1907

Special Officer Miguel Cantu was shot and killed by a man named Ira Brown.

Brown, who was known by the nickname "Bum," had repeatedly made threats that he wanted to kill a policeman. At about 4:30 p.m. on Saturday, 30 November 1907, "Bum" Brown made good on that fulmination when, in front of more than one hundred witnesses, he shot and killed Cantu.

The murder took place at Durango and Leona Streets at a vacant lot where a merry-go-round was set up and operating. Over one hundred women and children had gathered to enjoy the music and entertainment when gunfire interrupted the gala proceedings. Witnesses claimed that when Brown emerged from his house with the weapon, he announced that he was going to kill a merry-go-round operator and a policeman.

Brown shot Cantu while Cantu's back was turned toward him. Brown's first shot proved fatal, hitting Cantu in the right side and striking his spinal column. As the mortally injured Cantu was falling face-forward, he managed to pull his revolver and get off one shot in his defense. The bullet went wild and was harmless. Brown continued to fire at the downed officer, hitting him with another shot that tore an ugly hole in his back. A final shot punched a hole in Cantu's helmet. To the shock and horror of the witnesses, Brown then turned his gun on himself and fired a fatal shot into his own head. The merry-go-round operator escaped unscathed.

Police Chief Mauermann was one of the first officers to arrive at the scene. Cantu told Mauermann, "I am done for, Chief." Mauermann replied, "You are a brave man and will live through it." "There is no need to talk that way," gasped Cantu. "I know how hurt I am and that I can't live but a little while." Cantu was taken to the hospital and remained conscious almost to the time of his death at 11:10 p.m.

Cantu had arrived in San Antonio several years earlier from Wilson County and worked as a special officer. The chief had assigned him to work at the merry-go-round and said he often filled in for regular officers.

The trouble between Cantu and Brown had started at about 4:00 p.m. when Cantu warned Brown not to annoy a Mexican street vendor who was set up on the corner of the lot. Cantu had apparently told Brown that it was obvious that he had been drinking and that if he did not go home, he would arrest him. Brown did go home but quickly returned with revolver in hand. A black woman named Sarah Stoggens tried to warn Cantu, but the music from the organ and the loud voices drowned out her signal.

Cantu was survived by his wife and children. In a 7 December 1907 edition of a local San Antonio newspaper, a brief article indicated that the fund that had been set up by local police officers for Cantu's widow had already surpassed $200. Cantu is buried at the San Fernando Cemetery in San Antonio, but the grave site has not been located.

East, Frank
Born circa 1893—Died 10 June 1917

Officer Frank East was killed when a man on a bicycle pulled out in front of his motorcycle. East was forced to swerve out of the path of the cyclist, causing him to lose control of his machine. East suffered head injuries during the accident, resulting in his death.

East was not married. He is reported to have been buried in Hinton, West Virginia.

Pedraza, Joseph J.
Born 7 May 1880—Died 7 October 1924
Date of Incident: 6 October 1924

Officer Joseph Pedraza and a military police officer were dispatched to a dance hall in the 500 block of East Commerce Street to investigate a disturbance. During the course of the investigation, the military police officer, Private Charles R. Jennings, fired a bullet that killed Pedraza.

There were conflicting reports of the shooting from eyewitnesses. Some who saw the incident claim that Jennings fired his pistol when he drew the gun from his holster and wheeled around suddenly. Others said that he fired a shot at the ground. Some, however, alleged that he fired the gun directly at Pedraza. One witness testified that Jennings had been frightened by the black men at the dance and had fired a shot into the pavement in the hope of dispelling the crowd. A black policeman named C.C. Mells carefully examined the pavement and could find no evidence of a ricocheted bullet imprint.

Physicians later dispelled the allegation that the bullet had ricocheted off the pavement and hit Pedraza, citing the fact that the bullet's path of entry was not consistent with that scenario.

Jennings was arrested and charged with murder. It is not known if Jennings was ever convicted.

Pedraza died while en route to Santa Rosa Hospital. He was survived by his wife and six children. Pedraza is buried at the San Fernando Cemetery No. 2 in San Antonio. He had been on the police force since 1912. His wife was ill when he was killed, and the couple had a newborn child who had not yet been named. Soldiers at Fort Sam Houston raised $1,500 to pay off her mortgage and all debts. She also received a $50-per-month police pension.

Street, Samuel A. "Sam"
Born 27 November 1866—Died 11 September 1927
Date of Incident: 10 September 1927

Chief of Detectives Sam Street was shot and killed when he confronted a bandit in front of the Piggly Wiggly Store at the corner of San Pedro Street and Myrtle Street.

Street, along with other detectives, was on a stakeout of the location when the suspect, John McKenzie, entered the store to commit a robbery. When Street stepped forward and confronted McKenzie, asking him, "What are you doing here, boy?" he turned, pulled out two pistols and began shooting. Street was fatally wounded in the barrage of gunfire. The two-gun bandit McKenzie, who was dressed partially in a military uniform, fled. Officers Tate and Stendebach, who were with Street at the time, returned fire. McKenzie collapsed once when hit; then he arose and ran again, eventually falling a second time. McKenzie somehow managed to get away. Street died at the hospital the following day.

After authorities received a tip from a citizen, McKenzie was arrested at about midnight. He was charged with the murder of Street, tried and convicted of the crime. McKenzie was sentenced to death, but the sentence was later reduced to life in prison. On 13 September 1957, McKenzie was paroled.

Street had served with the agency for ten years and was said to have been one of the most respected and feared lawmen in Texas. He was survived by his wife, Mary Rather Goodsell, and three children. Street is buried at the Mission Burial Park in San Antonio.

White, Robert "Bob"
Born 25 December 1895—Died 9 November 1927
Date of Incident: 7 November 1927

On Monday, 7 November 1927, Detective Bob White was shot and killed by a man named Sol Grant.

White had been called to investigate reports of a man with a gun who had run amok and seemed to be looking for someone. He stopped Grant for acting suspiciously. Grant had been arguing with several black men over a parking space. Grant, who had emerged from an alley near East Commerce and Cherry Streets, claimed that he had just chased two black men who had cursed him. White, who was also black, approached with his gun drawn. Grant said that he was chased by White and immediately ran into a store. He opened the door to the enterprise and peeked outside. As he did so, White fired a shot at him. Grant returned fire, hitting White with at least two bullets and fatally wounded him. In spite of his serious wounds, White held Grant at gunpoint until other officers could arrive and take him into custody.

White was transported to the Robert B. Green Hospital with a bullet wound to the arm and abdomen. He died at about 4:30 a.m. on 9 November 1927.

Grant was arrested and charged with the murder. On 9 January 1928, his trial was postponed until 6 February. No other information has been uncovered regarding the outcome of the trial.

White was survived by his wife, Lena. He is buried at Floresville in Wilson County.

Grobe, Louis Carol
Born 6 June 1903—Died 22 March 1930

Officer Louis Grobe was killed in a motorcycle accident. He was off duty at the time the incident took place.

Grobe had attached a sidecar to his motorcycle and was headed home. At about 7:05 p.m., he turned off Roma Street onto Flores Street when his motorcycle hit the front fender of George Bauderer's automobile. The force of the head-on collision was so extreme that Grobe was thrown through the automobile's windshield and out onto the pavement. His skull was fractured, and his facial injuries were so severe that he was unrecognizable. Grobe died at the Santa Rosa hospital about one hour after the incident.

George Bauderer was charged with assault with an automobile. Another source claimed that he was charged with negligent homicide. The outcome of that charge is not known.

Grobe had been with the agency for only six months. He was survived by his wife, Anna, and one child. Grobe is buried at the Mission Burial Park in San Antonio.

Boynton, Theodore Richard "Dick"
Born 18 October 1895—Died 29 July 1930
Date of Incident: 24 July 1930

Patrolman Dick Boynton died from gunshot wounds he received while attempting to stop a robbery on a city bus. At the time of the incident, he was assigned as the night switchboard operator.

Boynton was in uniform and riding to work when a sixteen-year-old juvenile boarded the Culebra Road bus and pointed a gun at the driver. Boynton jumped out of his seat and began struggling with the youth. During the course of the battle, both men fell through the open doors of the bus and into the street. Boynton struck his head on the curb and was stunned from the impact. The young man shot him three times and fled the scene.

The shooter was apprehended a short time later. Boynton died from the effects of the gunshot wounds, and the fall, five days later. The disposition of the charges against the youth is unknown.

Boynton had been with the agency for three years and served in World War I as a sergeant in the U.S. Marine Corps. He was survived by his wife, Myrtle Burke. Boynton is buried at the San Antonio National Cemetery.

County and Municipal Agencies

Taylor, Raleigh Walter
Born 11 February 1900—Died 25 December 1930
Date of Incident: 12 December 1930

Officer Raleigh Taylor died as a result of the injuries he received in a motorcycle accident while on duty. After the accident, he was admitted to a hospital and released a week later. Two weeks afterward, Taylor collapsed and died at home, after having spent Christmas with his family. Upon examination, he was found to have died from a blood clot in the brain.

Taylor had been with the agency for one year. He was survived by his wife, Lucile. He is buried at the San Jose Cemetery in San Antonio.

Scrivano, Peter J. "Pete"
Born 29 June 1891—Died 28 May 1931

Officer Pete Scrivano was shot and killed while investigating an automobile accident at the corner of Pecos Street and Produce Row.

The incident took place at about 10:00 p.m. on Thursday, 28 May 1931. Ascencio Campa was the driver of one of the vehicles that had been involved in the collision, and Ramon Gonzales was the driver of the other. While Scrivano was speaking with Gonzales, Campa approached him. Campa was intoxicated; he swaggered up to Scrivano and exclaimed, "Well, what are you going to do with me?" Scrivano replied that he would be with him in a minute, just as soon as he had finished speaking with Gonzales. As Scrivano turned to continue his discussion with Gonzales, Campa produced a .38-caliber revolver and jabbed it into Scrivano's side, ordering, "Stick 'em up!"

Scrivano was astonished and replied, "What's the matter with you, man?" as Campa continued to push him toward the sidewalk with the pistol. When Scrivano reached the curb, he fell over backward. As he collapsed to the pavement, Campa opened fire. Five shots tore into Scrivano's body as he desperately attempted to draw his own gun and return fire. Witnesses to the incident claimed that with blood pouring from his wounds, Scrivano managed to fire five shots into Campa at close range.

Scrivano was rushed to the hospital with gunshot wounds to the chest near his heart, abdomen, left leg, right arm and right breast. Scrivano died forty-five minutes later at the hospital.

Campa attempted to conceal his identity by telling investigating officers at the scene that his name was Joe Martinez. It was not until later that relatives disclosed his real name. Campa died from his wounds the following day.

Scrivano had been with the agency for three years. He had come to San Antonio from Italy as a youth in 1901. Scrivano was survived by his wife, Julia. He is buried at the San Fernando Cemetery #2 in San Antonio.

Goodman, Alexander "Alex," Jr.
Born 14 February 1904—1 September 1931

Milstead, Aubrey S.
Born 19 September 1890—1 September 1931

Detective Alex Goodman and Lieutenant Aubrey Milstead were both killed in an automobile accident. Special Investigator Hay S. Tate and Motorcycle Officer Homer Long were injured in the same incident, which took place near Bowling Green, Ohio.

The officers who composed the department's pistol team were returning home from the annual competition at Camp Perry in Ohio. The automobile they were traveling in overturned about eight miles from the camp. Tate, who was driving, said the car went off the road when the headlights of an oncoming vehicle confused him. Before he could right the car, Milstead got excited and grabbed the steering wheel, causing the car to overturn. Milstead was pinned under the vehicle and suffered a crushed chest. Goodman died of a broken neck. Before other San Antonio lawmen who were part of the group reached the scene of the accident, heartless thieves had stolen Milstead's competition pistol and wallet and the entire group's traveling expense money.

Goodman is buried at the San Jose Burial Park. He was survived by his wife, Stella Elizabeth Spahn, whom he had married less than two months earlier.

Milstead was survived by his wife and had also recently married. He had apparently been divorced. He is buried at Austin.

Perrow, Henry Carrington
Born 18 February 1877—Died 11 December 1933

Detective Henry Perrow had been alerted to the fact that a member of the notorious Dillinger Gang might be in the city. After trailing a suspicious stranger who was traveling in a taxicab, Perrow and his partner pulled up alongside the vehicle at a busy intersection. When they tried to approach the man, he fled down the street on foot and disappeared into a dark alley. Perrow and his partner followed. When they cornered the man in the alley, he produced two pistols and opened fire. Perrow was hit in the temple. His partner was hit as well. During the confusion, the two-gun shooter managed to escape.

It is believed that Perrow's killer was a man named Tommy Carroll, a member of the Dillinger Gang, who was killed in an unrelated shootout in Waterloo, Iowa, on 7 June 1934.

Perrow had served with the agency for fifteen years. He was survived by his wife, Mayme E., and one child. Perrow is buried at the San Fernando Cemetery #3 in San Antonio.

Stowe, John William
Born 26 August 1879—Died 2 December 1936

Patrolman John Stowe was shot and killed while attempting to disarm a young Mexican man who had a gun in a bar.

Stowe was off duty at the time the incident occurred. He was seated in the Kentucky Club, a bar on East Commerce Street, where he was working while off duty in order to obtain some additional Christmas money. The bartender, Arthur Lopez, informed him that a patron named Carlos Fernandez had a gun in his belt. Stowe went to the booth where Fernandez was seated and grabbed him by the arm, attempting to disarm him. Fernandez pushed Stowe back and then pulled his pistol and opened fire. Fernandez shot five times in rapid succession—two after Stowe had dropped to the floor gravely wounded. Stowe died almost instantly. Fernandez fled the establishment.

A bar patron named Betty Cummings, who had witnessed the bloody incident unfold, rushed over to the fallen lawman, grabbed his pistol and rushed to the door, where she bravely fired one shot at the fleeing killer. Fernandez turned and fired back at her, missing. The bartender, Arthur

Lopez, then took the gun from Ms. Cummings and fired at Fernandez as well. He also missed.

Fernandez, a nineteen-year-old beet field worker from Michigan, was taken into custody and confessed to police that he had been drinking beer and gin at the time of the shooting and did not recall where he had obtained the pistol he used to shoot Stowe.

Fernandez was indicted for the murder of Stowe on 15 December. After a forty-one-hour debate by jurors on 28 February 1937, Fernandez was found guilty and sentenced to death by electrocution. Lawyers for Fernandez had entered a plea of insanity based on the youth's intoxicated state at the time of the murder. All but one juror did not buy that excuse. The final juror, a law student who was no doubt trying to impress the others with his grasp of jurisprudence, finally concurred.

On 25 March 1937, lawyers entered a plea for retrial on behalf of Fernandez, citing jury misconduct as the reason. On 7 April, his death sentence was reaffirmed by a criminal court in Austin. Another motion was filed by those opposing the death penalty, and on 16 September 1938, the sentence was commuted and reduced to life in prison.

Stowe had been with the agency for twenty-six years. He was survived by his wife, Callie Clark Stewart. Stowe is buried at the San Jose Burial Park in San Antonio. As an aside, city officials reported that Stowe's widow would not be receiving her meager fifty-dollars-a-month survivor's pension for a while because the city was eleven months in arrears on other payments.

Edwards, Agnal Aubray "Bill"
Born 28 February 1903—Died 16 January 1937

Motorcycle Officer Bill Edwards was shot and killed when he stopped an automobile on East Jones Avenue that was wanted in connection with two filling station robberies. The occupant, John W. Vaughn, shot him as he approached the vehicle during the stop.

Vaughn was tried and convicted of killing Edwards. He was sentenced to death. That sentence was carried out on 30 April 1938, when John Vaughn was executed by electrocution at Huntsville. He became the 153rd criminal to be electrocuted in Texas.

Edwards had been with the agency for twelve years. He was survived by his wife, Mary Lee. Edwards is buried at the Salem Cemetery in Bexar County. Edwards's death certificate had his middle name spelled Aubrey. Other sources, as well as family genealogists, seem to agree on Aubray.

Sinclair, Arthur
Born 15 September 1903—Died 16 November 1937

Special Officer Arthur Sinclair was shot and killed in the parking lot of the Crystal Bar in San Antonio by Claude (Claud) E. "Cowboy" Henry.

Sinclair and Henry had been drinking together when an argument of some sort occurred. Henry used a .38-caliber pistol to commit the crime. Three shots were fired. Sinclair was hit twice, once in the stomach and a second fatal shot in the left breast. He staggered into the crowded tavern and collapsed dead in front of the bar.

Henry, who was a former prizefighter, claimed that he shot Sinclair in self-defense. Special Officer J.P. Palmer, who was in the bar at the time the incident occurred, disarmed him. Henry was tried, convicted and sentenced to fifty years in prison for killing Sinclair.

Henry's wife, "Toni Jo" Henry, whose maiden name was Annie Beatrice McQuiston, was jailed on narcotics charges not long after "Cowboy" went to the penitentiary for the Sinclair killing. She was convicted of the murder of a man named J.P. Calloway. That killing had taken place in Houston on Valentine's Day 1940. McQuiston was executed by electrocution on 28 November 1942, the Saturday after Thanksgiving, at the courthouse in Lake Charles, Louisiana. She is the only woman ever to have been executed by electrocution in Louisiana.

Sinclair was survived by his wife, Gladys Marion Siler. He is buried at the Mission Cemetery in San Antonio.

Kanning, Earl William.
Born 7 August 1907—Died 23 December 1938
Date of Incident: 22 December 1938

Officer Earl Kanning died from injuries he received when he was involved in a motorcycle accident.

Kanning's police motorcycle skidded on wet pavement at St. Mary's and Pereida Streets. Kanning, who had been involved in a remarkable three accidents in three months, suffered a fractured skull and lacerations to the head. Witnesses said that his motorcycle skidded seventy-five feet before coming to rest, hurling him to the pavement. He died from his injuries at 7:45 a.m. the following day.

Kanning had been with the agency for two years. He was survived by his wife, Lottie. Kanning is buried at the San Jose Burial Park in San Antonio.

San Augustine County Sheriff's Office

Wall, George W.
Born 12 June 1854—Died 21 April 1900

The Border-Wall feud had divided San Augustine County into two warring factions. The patriarch of the Wall family was W.A. "Uncle Buck" Wall, who declared himself pro-Union during the Civil War. That was an unpopular position in East Texas. Four of Wall's five sons became embroiled in the feud with the Border-Broock families, who were pro-Confederacy Democrats.

Lycurgus "Curg" Border and the four Wall brothers were all men who had been involved in shooting scrapes. Each had been acquitted, claiming self-defense. In 1894, the feud deepened when the People's Party, also called the Populists, swept the county elections. The party had its base among poor white cotton farmers in Texas and the South and distressed wheat farmers in the plains states. It represented a radical faction that was hostile toward banks, railroads and the elite in general.

"Uncle Buck" Wall was elected county commissioner, and his son George was elected sheriff.

The feud reached its zenith when Curg Border shot Sheriff George W. Wall in the back with a shotgun in front of witnesses in downtown San Augustine on Saturday, 21 April 1900. Wall was shot through the lungs and bowels. His wounds proved fatal. Wall had arrested Border for disorderly conduct a few months earlier and had refused to allow Border's friends to make his bond.

George W. Wall was elected sheriff on 6 November 1894 and reelected on 3 November 1896 and again on 8 November 1898. He was survived by his wife, Jane, and one daughter. He is buried at the McMahan Chapel Cemetery in Milam County.

Curg Border was indicted but never tried for the murder of Wall. One month later, Eugene Wall, George Wall's brother, shot and killed Border's cousin Ben Broock. On 4 June 1900, Border and three of Broock's brothers wounded Sheriff Noel Roberts, Wall's nephew, and killed his two brothers at the courthouse.

Border was never tried for those two murders. Eugene Wall was acquitted for killing Ben Broock but was assassinated by unknown persons on 25 October 1901. In November 1902, Border was elected sheriff but was removed in March 1903 for stealing tax money. On 7 May 1904, Border threatened to kill then-sheriff Sneed Noble. Sheriff Noble shot Border in the head and killed him.

Watts, Robert Lee "Rob"
Born 1 December 1875—Died 1 November 1919

J. Anthony "Tony" Miller owned a grocery store in town. Tony's brother, Johnny B. Miller, stopped by the store and noticed that Tony was already drinking. He advised his brother to stop and reminded him that Sheriff Rob Watts had warned him that he was not going to put up with his drinking any longer. Tony was nineteen days short of his forty-first birthday at the time.

Drew "Chuck" Davis Jr., sixteen years old, worked at Tony Miller's store and asked for his pay. Davis told Miller he had been shorted twenty-five cents. Miller and Davis got into an argument over the sum in dispute. Miller grabbed a loaded pistol. The frightened Davis ran into the street. Ed Burleson was the only other person in the store at the time. Thankfully, he was able to successfully prevent Miller from pursuing Davis.

The seventy-eight-year-old constable Noel G. "Node" Thomas, son of a former sheriff, was summoned to the store. When he arrived, Thomas discovered that the situation had calmed down and went outside. When he looked back, however, he saw Miller pointing a pistol at him. Thomas drew his gun, pointed it at Miller and told him he was a constable. Miller lowered his pistol. Thomas went to get Sheriff Watts. Watts quickly approached Miller's store, on the run, and saw that the door was closed. He drew his pistol. Deputy Sheriff Wiley Parker and Thomas followed Watts into the building with pistols cocked and ready. Watts rammed the door with his shoulder and broke it open. He charged into the store and opened fire as he entered. A total of eight shots rang out in the dark interior of the market. When the smoke cleared, Watts lay dead on the floor.

In the aftermath, bystanders confiscated Miller's pistol. Parker ordered Miller to surrender, but Miller had armed himself with a butcher knife and refused, telling Parker to "go to hell." Parker shot Miller in the chest, killing him.

Watts was elected on 7 November 1916 and reelected on 5 November 1918. He was survived by his wife, Sallie B. Sossaman, and five children. Watts is buried at the City Cemetery in San Augustine.

Watts had gained statewide attention when Texas Ranger John Dudley White Sr. was shot and killed on 12 July 1918 while attempting to arrest draft evaders in San Augustine County.

Carroll, John
Born (Unknown)—Died 20 June 1921

Deputy Chief John Carroll was shot and killed by a man named Lum Williams at White City. Williams was arrested and placed in the county jail. He refused to make a statement about why he had killed Carroll.

No further information about this incident has been uncovered or any personal information about Carroll. A World War I draft registration does list a "John Monroe Carroll" from San Augustine County who was born on 4 August 1896.

Chandler, Henry Isom
Born 7 July 1874—Died 11 January 1932

Deputy Sheriff Henry Isom Chandler lived in the lodging house at the Camp Worth logging camp, which was owned by the Frost-Johnson Lumber Company. The camp was located about twenty-five miles east of Nacogdoches.

In the early morning hours of 11 January 1932, a black man came to the door of his residence and shot him with a .38-55-caliber Winchester rifle. The killer fled. Texas Rangers were sent to search for him, but he was never located.

Chandler had been called earlier to settle a quarrel between the killer and his wife. It is not known if the unidentified suspect was ever arrested or convicted of the murder.

Chandler was survived by his wife, Elvira Vira Cuerton, and three children. He is buried at the Swift Cemetery in Nacogdoches. Chandler had served with the agency for seven years.

SAN JACINTO COUNTY CONSTABLE'S OFFICE

Palmer, Augustus Henry "Gus"
Born 5 June 1864—Died 13 October 1906

Sometime between 8:00 and 9:00 a.m. on Saturday, 13 October 1906, Constable Gus Palmer of the Oakhurst Precinct in San Jacinto County was shot and killed on the streets of Huntsville.

Palmer was making his way back home to San Jacinto County and had planned on boarding the mixed train. Palmer was walking near the depot when he had a chance encounter with a man named M.W. Bryan. Bryan had previously lived in San Jacinto County and, while there, had a disagreement with Palmer. Bryan was now a merchant in Huntsville, and on this day he was armed with a double-barreled shotgun. Bryan fired one barrel of the scattergun at Palmer, striking him in the left chest and shoulder area. The wound proved fatal, and Palmer died later the same day.

Bryan was given an immediate examining trial and posted a $2,500 bond. It is unknown if he was ever charged or convicted of the murder.

Palmer's body was returned to Oakhurst for burial. He was survived by his wife, Nancy Elizabeth Currie, and ten children (two of the couple's twelve offspring preceded Gus in death). Palmer is buried at the Center Hill Cemetery in Oakhurst.

Sprott, John F.
Born 28 October 1876—Died 25 December 1910
Date of Incident: 24 December 1910

John Sprott was the constable for Precinct 6 at Point Blank. He was elected on 8 November 1910 and qualified on 16 November 1910. According to reports, on Saturday, 24 December 1910, Dr. Polk was killed near the Trinity River at Oakhurst. Constable John Sprott went to the scene and was shot. Apparently, he died on Sunday, 25 December. No further information has been located.

Sprott was survived by his wife, Jennie Ferrell, and four children. He is buried at the Sprott Cemetery in San Jacinto County.

San Juan Police Department

Garza, Jose T.
Born circa 1887—Died 2 March 1930

At about 10:30 p.m. on Sunday, 2 March 1930, Deputy City Marshal Jose Garza stumbled into a shop mumbling incoherently. He died within minutes. Garza had four bullet wounds in his abdomen, inflicted by a .45-caliber semiautomatic pistol.

An inquest determined that Garza's murder had been a "death by gunshot wounds inflicted by persons unknown." There were no witnesses to the shooting. Residents, however, told police they heard about ten shots. Police found seven empty cartridges at the scene. The justice of the peace who conducted the inquest indicated that Garza had not drawn his pistol. The newspapers reported that Garza had had several recent personal difficulties, which involved bootleggers, and that several arrests were expected to be made. No further information is known at this time.

Garza was married. He is buried in San Juan in Hidalgo County.

SAN PATRICIO COUNTY CONSTABLE'S OFFICE

Chisholm, Richard Truman
Born 9 September 1889—Died 15 February 1938

Precinct 2 constable Richard Chisholm was fatally shot from ambush by a vegetable picker named Genaro Lugo. Chisholm had arrested Lugo for public intoxication three weeks earlier while he and a friend were on their way to San Antonio in a truck. Lugo claimed that Chisholm had struck him several times during the arrest.

Chisholm was on foot patrol in Odem. Lugo, who had been lingering behind a barbershop near Main Street, spotted him. He approached Chisholm and told him that they both had to die. It was Lugo's plan for each man to shoot and kill the other. Lugo fired three shots in all. Chisholm did not return fire. Chisholm's wounds were fatal. Lugo's plan did not work out.

Lugo made off with Chisholm's pistol and either eight or fifteen dollars cash, depending on which report one believes.

The killer and his associate were initially believed to have been the pair who earlier had held up a man named J.P. Craig near Elemendorf, Bexar County, and had taken fifty-five dollars cash and some clothing from him. The men used a .32-caliber pistol to commit that crime. They threatened to kill Craig and then decided better of it but bound him tightly and left him in a rural area. Police had thrown up blockades in the surrounding area in an effort to seize the criminals.

Lugo confessed to the killing the following day. Sheriff Frank Hunt had become suspicious of Lugo's absence from Odem. Lugo led officers to a house at Mussett and White where he had hidden Chisholm's pistol under a pillow on the bed.

Lugo was charged and convicted of Chisholm's murder. He was sentenced to death. Lugo's sentence was carried out on 23 April 1939, when he was executed by electrocution at Huntsville, becoming the 170th person to die this way in Texas.

Chisholm was survived by his wife, Bessie Ruth Hightower, and three children. He is buried at the Odom Cemetery.

SAN PATRICIO COUNTY SHERIFF'S OFFICE

Beasley, John
Born January 1867—Died 30 January 1910

Before midnight on Saturday, 29 January 1910, Deputy Sheriff Martin arrested Garza Rodriguez and placed him in the county jail at Aransas Pass. Garza's brother, Manual Rodriguez, came to the jail and demanded his release. Manual Rodriguez's request was refused, so he went home and got a shotgun.

Shortly after midnight, Manual Rodriguez walked back to the jail with the shotgun concealed alongside his leg. John Beasley had been deputized to assist Martin in lodging Garza Rodriguez in the jail and was standing nearby as Manual approached. Manual fired a shotgun blast directly into Beasley's stomach. Beasley died before he could be carried to his home a block away.

An angry mob quickly formed and surrounded the Mexican section of Aransas Pass. Calls for assistance went out to Aransas County sheriff Henry T. Bailey in Rockport and San Patricio County sheriff Dave Odem. Sheriff Bailey arrived with a posse at daylight on the thirtieth. Manual Rodriguez was arrested by Deputy John Barber at his father's house and transported to Rockport, the county seat of Aransas County, for safekeeping. The city of Aransas Pass is located just inside San Patricio County. It is unknown if Rodriguez was convicted of Beasley's murder.

Beasley was survived by his wife, America Echols. His place of burial is unknown.

Willis, Thomas T. "Tom"
Born January 1880—Died 26 September 1915

Deputy Sheriff Tom Willis was accidentally shot and killed when he and another officer became involved in a deadly struggle with an unruly knife-wielding man at a dance near Odem.

Willis and Deputies Newt Hurst, Bob Parker and Will Miller had been called to a dance at the Bailey Ranch to maintain order. A man at the dance began creating a disturbance. When Hurst attempted to intervene, the mischief-maker pulled a knife on him. Hurst pulled his gun. During the skirmish that quickly took place, the firearm discharged accidentally. One bullet hit Willis, who was standing near a wagon at the time. The shot proved fatal.

In one account of the deadly affray, Willis is claimed to have died within minutes while another stated that he expired several hours later at his home.

According to reports of this incident, the killer is said to have attempted to flee but was shot and killed by Miller while doing so. Another account claims that Hurst and Miller arrested the man and were transporting him to the county jail when he drew a knife and attacked them. The lawmen promptly killed him during the fight.

Willis is buried at the Bethel Cemetery in Odem. He was a junior partner in a mercantile store and worked part time as a deputy sheriff. Willis was not married at the time of the 1910 census. The newspaper reports of the day make no mention of a wife or children.

SCURRY COUNTY SHERIFF'S OFFICE

Stewart, John Y.
Born 28 June 1884—Died 20 January 1914

Deputy Sheriff John Stewart was shot and killed by a woman named Minnie Latham.

Stewart and Ms. Latham had a personal relationship. According to reports, Latham decided to shoot and kill Stewart when she discovered that he was having an affair with another woman. Latham was convicted of killing Stewart and was sentenced to serve five years in prison.

Stewart was not married. He was survived by his mother and eight siblings. Stewart is buried in Snyder.

Narrell, James G.
Born 25 June 1871—Died 6 February 1914

Deputy Sheriff James Narrell was killed in an automobile accident near Hermleigh. Narrell was traveling with another man named Howell at the time. Their vehicle overturned on the highway. Both men were dead by the time passersby discovered the accident.

Narrell was survived by his wife, Fenton, and eight children. He is buried at the Lone Wolf Cemetery in Hermleigh.

SHELBY COUNTY CONSTABLE'S OFFICE

Chapman, Daniel Edward
Born 27 November 1878—Died 13 November 1936
Date of Incident: 11 November 1936

Precinct 8 constable Daniel Chapman was shot and killed at an Armistice Day school dance in Stockman, sixteen miles southwest of Center.

A man named Alcus Lilly (Altus Lillie) came to a dance at the high school gymnasium of the school in Stockman. Outside the hall, Lilly became involved in a disagreement with two people who were attending the festivities. The confrontation turned violent. One of the men struck the other with a gun and knocked him to the ground.

The victim of the incident left the dance and informed Chapman and Justice of the Peace Alvin Gillespie about what had happened. All three returned to the site of the incident, where they found Lilly. Chapman asked Lilly to surrender his gun. Lilly replied that he did not have a gun. When Chapman began to search Lilly, the matter turned violent. Lilly jerked away and then produced a .38-caliber semiautomatic pistol from his hip pocket and shot Chapman twice in the chest, twice in the right shoulder and once in the nose.

Alcus Lilly was not done using his firearm just yet. Next, he shot and killed Gillespie. The mortally wounded Chapman struggled to return fire, letting loose two shots at Lilly and hitting him once in the chest, inflicting a fatal wound. Lilly died en route to the hospital. Chapman died of his wounds two days later.

Chapman had been appointed constable seven months earlier when the previous constable resigned. He was survived by his wife, Annis Ida Prince, and four children. Chapman is buried at the Mount Olive Cemetery.

SHELBY COUNTY SHERIFF'S OFFICE

McCarver, Oscar Julian
Born 25 October 1883—Died 11 February 1927

Deputy Sheriff Oscar McCarver was shot and killed by Constable George Hillen at Tenaha.

McCarver had been the resident deputy for a number of years and had been charged in the justice of the peace court with assault and battery on a man named Preston Conway. Hillen had an arrest warrant for McCarver. When Hillen informed McCarver of the warrant, he reportedly told Hillen that he could not arrest him and said, "You are pushing this damned business." McCarver is also reported to have said that he would kill the complainant, Preston Conway.

Hillen claimed that he tried to reason with McCarver and that he retreated twenty or thirty steps as McCarver advanced on him menacingly. As McCarver came closer, Hillen pulled his pistol. McCarver told him he would make him "eat that damned thing" as he allegedly reached into his pocket as if he were going for a gun. Seeing this, Hillen shot McCarver in the heart, killing him instantly.

After the incident, it was discovered that McCarver was unarmed. Hillen was arrested and charged with McCarver's murder. He was found guilty and sentenced to serve five years in prison. That sentence was later reversed due to errors during the trial.

McCarver was survived by his third wife, Anna Hooker, and five children. He was buried at the Old Tenaha Cemetery.

Jackson, James Walter
Born 26 March 1889—Died 9 May 1927
Date of Incident: 5 May 1927

On Thursday, 5 May 1927, Deputy Sheriff Walter Jackson was getting out of his car in front of his father's store in Center when his pistol fell to the running board and accidentally discharged. The bullet pierced his stomach. Jackson died on Monday morning, 9 May 1927, in a Center sanitarium.

Jackson was buried at the Jackson Cemetery in Shelby County. He was survived by his wife, Ollie Bell Ryans, and four children.

SIMONTON POLICE DEPARTMENT

Cornelius, Elbridge C.
Born 5 May 1871—Died 21 June 1929
Date of Incident: 20 June 1929

The town of Simonton is located in Fort Bend County. In the early morning hours of Thursday, 20 June 1929, a group of black men were returning from a Juneteenth celebration and were sitting in a parked automobile creating a disturbance. When night watchman E.C. Cornelius intervened, he was shot and mortally wounded. After undergoing an unsuccessful operation, Cornelius died at 12:54 p.m. the following day.

A man named Monty Jackson was arrested for the murder of Cornelius. He was later tried, convicted and sentenced to death. On 23 October 1930, that sentence was commuted and reduced to life in prison. Governor Dan Moody had commuted Jackson's sentence based on evidence that another man had actually fired the fatal shot. That man died in jail while awaiting trial. He had confessed to his relatives, who signed affidavits to that effect, that he had murdered Cornelius.

Cornelius was survived by ten children. His wife, Ella Marie Reynolds, preceded him in death. Cornelius is buried in Baird in Callahan County.

SOUR LAKE POLICE DEPARTMENT

Ray, Ben Foret
Born 23 January 1862—Died 26 December 1920
Date of Incident: 25 December 1920

Officer Ben Ray was shot and killed while on patrol at about 2:00 a.m. on Christmas Day.

Ray, a night policeman, was standing in the vestibule of a new building that was being erected on the main street when Sidney Oliver shot him several times with a pump shotgun. Ray was transported to Hotel Dieu Hospital in Beaumont but died the next day.

Oliver argued at his trial that as he came down the street past the Sharpstein Building, which was under construction at the time, he was fired upon by someone who was standing in the darkness near the building's entrance. He claimed that he raised his shotgun and fired, emptying all the shells in the magazine before he quit shooting. The appeals court noted that Ray was a peace officer who was discharging his duties at the time and that he was shot in the back in two places at close range. When challenged about why he was carrying a shotgun through town, Oliver claimed that he was on his way to go duck hunting at the time.

Ray made a dying declaration that his pistol was empty and that Oliver had tried to flee. The state put witnesses on the stand that testified that Oliver had told people he got even with Ray, who had beaten him up.

Oliver was convicted and sentenced to life in prison. That decision was later reversed. The outcome of the case is unknown.

Ray had been with the agency for seven years. He was survived by his wife and three children. Ray is buried in Sour Lake in Hardin County.

STARR COUNTY CONSTABLE'S OFFICE

Cantu, Jose
Born 17 December 1881—Died 6 March 1938

On Sunday, 6 March 1938, Justice of the Peace A.P. Vera Jr. deputized five men to serve a warrant on Eulalio Elizando on a charge of disturbing the peace the night before in the town of Lagruilla, near Rio Grande City. The deputies claimed that they observed Elizando leaving Rio Grande City in a truck accompanied by Ramon de la Cruz, so they followed the vehicle. The officers eventually overtook the truck and ordered the men to pull over and stop.

Someone opened fire. It is unclear if it was one of the deputies or one of the men in the truck that they had pulled over. In any case, when the smoke cleared the list of dead included former Starr County deputy sheriff Eulalio Elizando, former deputy constable Jose Cantu and Starr County deputy sheriff Ramon de la Cruz.

Elizando was to go on trial on Monday, 7 March 1938, in the town of Alice. Elizando was charged with the murder of a man named David Gomez. Gomez was killed in Rio Grande City on Memorial Day 1934. Cantu was also scheduled to go to trial in Alice for his role in the killing of Pablo Salis. Salis was also murdered on Memorial Day 1934.

Elizando had been tried once before for the murder of Gomez. That action had resulted in a conviction and a sentence of twenty-five years followed by a reversal for retrial.

Cantu was survived by his wife, Preciliana, and one child. He is buried at La Grulla Cemetery in Rio Grande City.

Related Case: Starr County Sheriff's Office, Eulalio Elizando and Ramon de la Cruz

STARR COUNTY SHERIFF'S OFFICE

Elizando, Eulalio
Born 19 June 1898—Died 6 March 1938

de la Cruz, Ramon
Born 14 January 1905—Died 6 March 1938

See Jose Cantu summary.
   Elizando was survived by his wife, Creseucia Salis. He is buried at La Grulla Cemetery in Rio Grande City.
   De la Cruz was survived by his wife, Siveana Rivera. He is buried at the La Grulla Cemetery in Rio Grande City.

Related Case: Starr County Constable's Office, Jose Cantu

STEPHENS COUNTY CONSTABLE'S OFFICE

Park, Oliver "Ollie"
Born circa 1898—Died 17 March 1932

Precinct 1 deputy constable Ollie Park was shot and killed while working at a dance in Breckenridge.
   Park observed a man named W.H. Bybee, who was from Pampa, drop a pistol on the dance hall floor. When he approached Bybee and attempted to arrest him, a struggle took place during which another man named Harry Roberts from Throckmorton opened fire on Park. Park was hit four times. His wounds proved fatal.
   Park was able to return fire and launch a fusillade of bullets at Roberts and Bybee before he expired. He hit Roberts in the right leg, above the knee. The bullet shattered the bone. Roberts survived. Bybee was also hit in the little finger of his left hand.

Jack Ellington, nephew of Park and a night watchman at the dance hall, arrested Roberts. He was tried, convicted and sentenced to life in prison.

The day following the shooting, Bybee was arrested in South Bend in Young County, where two pistols were taken from him. He had already been convicted in Albany in Shackelford County on a charge of robbery and given a sentence of twenty years in prison. That indictment resulted from his holdup of the Hill Top service station in Albany. It is not known if Bybee was ever convicted of Park's murder.

Park is buried at the Evergreen Cemetery in Paris. Numerous sources list his surname as Parks, and there remains some confusion as to which is the correct spelling.

SWISHER COUNTY SHERIFF'S OFFICE

Moseley, John C.
Born 28 August 1883—Died 23 January 1933

John Moseley was elected sheriff on 6 November 1928 and reelected in 1930 and 1932. Moseley was killed during a shootout with three men.

The trio of killers arrived in Happy in a new Ford eight-cylinder coupe at about 2:00 p.m. on Sunday afternoon, 22 January 1933. Deputy Sheriff Goen saw the men acting suspiciously and reported them to Moseley.

The incident occurred in the main business district of Tulia on Monday evening, 23 January 1933. Moseley had managed to apprehend the three dubious men, but only after a running gun battle that circled the town. He had persuaded the trio to go to his office for questioning when the men fired a final barrage of bullets, one of which hit Moseley in the head. The wound was fatal.

Moseley's wife watched the gun battle through her window as her husband chased the men around the town. After the slaying of Moseley, the killers held up a filling station directly in front of where the shooting had occurred. The men forced the attendant, Floyd "Jake" Ward, to service their automobile and not turn in an alarm. Ward complied at the point of a gun. Before the threesome left, they took twenty-five dollars from the till and pulled loose the telephone wires to the filling station. Next, they removed a rifle and six-shooter from the dead sheriff's car and fled Tulia.

An area-wide search began, based on what limited description of the killers could be provided by Deputy Groen and Floyd Ward. Eventually, one of the three men, Ed Stanton, was apprehended.

Stanton, who went by the somewhat uncomplimentary nickname "Perchmouth," was tried and convicted of Moseley's murder. He was sentenced to death. That sentence was carried out on 28 September 1934, when Stanton was executed by electrocution at Huntsville, becoming the 104th to meet such a fate. Another of the killers, Frank Wallace, was shot and killed in New Mexico during a shooting incident involving the death of Lincoln County chief deputy Thomas Jones.

Ed Stanton and his accomplice, Frank Wallace, were responsible for the murders of three other law enforcement officers before Stanton's sidekick was shot and killed in Swisher County and Stanton wound up on death row. The other officers killed were: Deputy Sheriff Harvey Bolin of Lamb County, Texas; Chief Deputy Sheriff Thomas W. Jones of Lincoln County, New Mexico; and Deputy Sheriff Joseph Brown of Wise County, Texas. As an aside, after the murder of Chief Deputy Sheriff Jones, the department purchased a Thompson submachine gun to better defend itself.

Moseley's wife, Ola E., was appointed to fulfill his remaining term. He is buried at the Rose Hill Cemetery in Tulia.

Related Case: Lamb County Sheriff's Office, Harvey Bolin; Wise County Sheriff's Office, Joseph Brown; Lincoln County Sheriff's Office, New Mexico, Tom Jones

TARRANT COUNTY CONSTABLE'S OFFICE

Morison, Robert Emmett
Born 15 June 1855—Died 8 November 1916

Precinct 8 constable Robert Morison was shot and killed while he was sitting in front of a store talking with friends.

A man walked up to Morison with a shotgun and shot him in the back, killing him instantly. The killer then entered the store and surrendered to the city marshal, who was inside.

It is believed that bootleggers had planned the murder of Morison because of his unwavering enforcement of the Prohibition law.

John Lamb and Claude "Wampus" Patterson were tried and convicted of the murder. Lamb was sentenced to five years in prison and Patterson to twenty-five years.

Morison was survived by his wife, Florence Moody, and two sons. He is buried at the Mansfield Cemetery. Several family genealogists show his surname as Morrison. Some confusion remains as to which is the correct spelling.

Poe, Robert Franklin
Born 9 January 1882—Died 23 December 1925

Precinct 1 constable Robert Poe was shot and killed while he was attempting to arrest an automobile garage owner named Manuel Carson for the theft of tires.

During the arrest, Carson indicated that he needed to tell his wife something and began to walk away. He suddenly wheeled around and fired twice at Poe with a .38-caliber pistol. Poe's partner, Deputy Constable G.E. Finch, struggled with Carson to gain control of the weapon and arrest him. During the skirmish, Poe shot Carson twice. Carson managed to get off one more shot at Poe, but the bullet went wild and had no effect.

Poe was survived by his wife and three sons. He is buried at the Greenwood Cemetery in Fort Worth. On 29 December 1925, the county commissioners voted to appoint his widow to fill out his remaining term.

Hurdleston, Mordica W.
Born 22 April 1869—Died 9 October 1927

Precinct 1 deputy constable Mordica Hurdleston was shot and killed while investigating the sounds of gunfire near the intersection of East Seventeenth and Terry Streets.

Hurdleston had been out with his family serving court papers in the area when he heard the shots. He exited his automobile and walked to the place where he had heard the gunfire. The man who had fired the shots, Matthew Carter, immediately shot Hurdleston twice in the chest. The wounds were fatal, and Hurdleston died immediately. Carter fled the scene but was arrested at his home a short time later.

Hurdleston had previously served as police commissioner of the Fort Worth Police Department. He was survived by his wife and two children. Hurdleston is buried at the Oakwood Cemetery.

County and Municipal Agencies

Barton, Bernell Looney
Born 12 June 1903—Died 25 April 1931
Date of Incident: 23 April 1931

Precinct 5 special deputy constable Bernell Barton was hit by an automobile while investigating a disturbance on Hemphill Street in Fort Worth.

While on patrol, Barton came upon a motor vehicle collision that had just taken place. Controversy over the cause of the accident quickly resulted in a fight between the drivers of the two vehicles who had been involved in the wreck. Barton stepped in to mediate and broke up the fight, instructing the men to return to their cars. While Barton was gathering more information about the accident, a passing automobile hit him.

Barton was transported to a local hospital, where he died two days later.

Barton is buried at the Mount Olive Cemetery. He was survived by his wife, Mary.

Pollock, John "Johnnie"
Born 13 June 1892—Died 20 June 1933
Date of Incident: 19 June 1933

Precinct 8 deputy constable John Pollock and another officer had gone to a Juneteenth Emancipation Day celebration dance to aid in maintaining order. The crowd was large, and the dance floor was overcrowded. While Pollock was attempting to clear the dangerously packed dance platform, he was slashed across the chest and stabbed in the left leg by one of the patrons. His wounds were serious. Pollock was taken to a hospital, where he died on Tuesday, 20 June 1933.

The assailant was identified as Sherell Davis. Davis admitted to having been drinking when the incident occurred. Davis was charged with the murder of Pollock on 21 June. No further information has been uncovered regarding the outcome of those charges.

Pollock had been with the agency for ten years. He was survived by his wife, Bettie Amber Lewis, and three children. He was buried at the Midlothian Cemetery in Ellis County.

TARRANT COUNTY SHERIFF'S OFFICE

Scott, Hamil Poston
Born 21 October 1865—Died 1 May 1907
Date of Incident: 22 March 1907

At about 5:00 p.m. on Friday, 22 March 1907, county attorney Jefferson D. McLean and Sheriff Wood led a large force of deputies on a raid at a gambling hall that was located over a saloon. Five men were found to be playing poker and faro. They were arrested and hauled away in a wagon. The posse was about to depart on another raid when McLean walked across the street to tell his wife, who was seated in a buggy, to remain there until he returned. As he retraced his steps to the front of the saloon, William Thomason accosted him with an oath. Although Thomason had been running the games, he was not present during the raid. Thomason shot McLean in the Adam's apple; the bullet passed through his neck and caused his death in ten minutes.

Thomason fled the scene and was pursued by Special Deputy Sheriff Scott, a former deputy sheriff who was deputized for the raid. Thomason shot him three times, inflicting fatal wounds. Thomason seized Scott's pistol, which had not been fired. A crowd reported that twenty police officers and deputies surrounded Thomason. Thomason refused to surrender and was shot three times and mortally wounded. The police had to pull their weapons to keep Thomason from being lynched.

Scott remained paralyzed until his death on Wednesday, 1 May 1907.

Scott had been with the agency for ten years, but he had resigned to become a Denver Railway claim agent. He was survived by his wife, Margaret "Maggie." Scott is buried at the Oakwood Cemetery in Fort Worth.

There is some controversy regarding the spelling of his given name. Most family genealogists have listed it as Hamill. His tombstone is inscribed Hamil, with only one "l." It is unclear which is correct.

Master, Walter Adrian
Born 2 March 1885—Died 10 February 1922

Special Officer Walter Master, night watchman at Mistletoe Heights, took his own life shortly after his home was raided by Fort Worth police officers and federal officers in search of narcotics.

Officers had been working to break up a drug ring operating between Texas and Mexico. Masters played a role of sorts in that group. At about 7:00 p.m. on Friday, 10 February 1922, federal agent W.M. Beresnack and city narcotics detective J.A. Riley conducted a raid at the Master home on Davis Street, where they discovered about forty quarts of bonded whiskey and an ounce and a half of cocaine. Master was on patrol at Mistletoe Heights at the time of the incident. His wife telephoned him at about 9:30 p.m. and informed him of the raid and the fact that "the house was full of police," as she put it.

Master is said to have left the police vehicle to get his own car when a single gunshot was heard in the darkness. Master's body was discovered lying in the roadway dead by his partner, A.L. Eastman, soon after his wife's call.

Master was survived by his wife, Fannie Louella Brooks, and four children. He is buried at the Mount Olivet Cemetery in Fort Worth.

Davis, Malcolm Simmons
Born 7 July 1881—Died 6 January 1933

Deputy Sheriff Malcolm Davis was shot and killed by the notorious Clyde Barrow while he and other deputies were staking out a house, waiting for members of the Bonnie and Clyde Gang.

Davis and other officers were staked out near the Dallas home of Odell Chandler. Chandler was wanted in connection with the holdup of the Grapevine Home Bank on 29 December. Robbers had made off with $2,850 during that heist. Two men showed up at the residence, and a gunfight with officers soon developed. Davis had been positioned at the rear of the cottage and came around to the front when he heard the shooting. One of the shooters, later identified as Clyde Barrow, made a dash for a small automobile. As he did so, Barrow opened fire with a shotgun, hitting Davis with two rounds of buckshot from point-blank range. The blast killed Davis almost instantly. Barrow and his accomplice, Odell Chandler, escaped in the small coupe automobile.

Three women were also arrested after the incident, two of whom were held on charges in connection with the Grapevine bank robbery. They were Lucile Hilburn and Lilly McBride.

Between 1932 and 1934, the Bonnie Elizabeth Parker and Clyde Chestnut Barrow Gang, which included Clyde's brother Marvin "Buck" Barrow, Buck's wife Blanche, Henry Methvin, W.D. Jones, Joe Palmer and Raymond Hamilton, was responsible for the murder of law enforcement officers in four states:

Arkansas, Missouri, Oklahoma and Texas. Bonnie Parker and Clyde Barrow started their criminal career by robbing banks. They quickly became notorious killers and were wanted for the murders of nine law enforcement officers and three citizens. As fate would have it, Bonnie and Clyde rose to the stature of folk heroes and often willingly received shelter, food and aid from ordinary citizens.

The two criminals were ambushed and killed on 23 May 1934 while slowly driving up a desolate road to their hideout in Bienville Parish, Louisiana. They were gunned down by a posse of six lawmen, including former Texas Ranger captain Frank Hamer. Other members of the posse included Bob Alcorn and Ted Hinton, who were Dallas County sheriff's deputies; Bienville Parish sheriff Henderson Jordan and his deputy, Prentiss Oakley; and former Texas Ranger B.M. Gault.

Davis was not married. He was preceded in death by his parents. He is buried at the Grapevine Cemetery in Tarrant County

TAYLOR COUNTY CONSTABLE'S OFFICE

Chapman, J.A. (J.M.)
Born (Unknown)—Died 15 September 1906
Date of Incident: 14 September 1906

On the afternoon of Friday, 14 September 1906, former constable J.A. Chapman was gunned down on the streets of Abilene by a man named Mat Shelley. Shelley used a double-barreled shotgun to do the work, inflicting a fatal wound that resulted in Chapman's death the following day.

Shelley is said to have been a longtime resident of Abilene. No reason for the killing was given by local newspaper accounts of the day.

Chapman is buried at the Abilene Municipal Cemetery. No personal information about Chapman has been found.

Reeves, George L.
Born 7 May 1877—Died 24 March 1925

Constable George Reeves and Howard County sheriff W.W. Satterwhite were shot and killed while attempting to arrest a murder suspect named Lopez Morales. As the two officers approached Morales, he grabbed a rifle and shot Reeves, killing him instantly.

Satterwhite ran to a nearby house for help and borrowed an automobile. He was about to speed off to get assistance when Morales caught up with him and shot and killed him.

Morales, accompanied by his brother, fled the scene. A posse of about three hundred men pursued him. They finally cornered Morales in a freight car near the town of Lawn, forty miles southeast of Sweetwater in Nolan County. The posse placed a charge of dynamite under the car to dislodge Morales, but the blast failed to flush the fugitive from his lair. Possemen placed a second charge, which provided the desired result. Morales burst forth from the railcar, firing as he appeared. As one might imagine, the posse of roughly three hundred launched a storm of bullets that cut down Morales in an instant.

Reeves was survived by his wife, Sarah F. He is buried at the Rosehill Cemetery in Merkel.

Related Case: Howard County Sheriff's Office, W.W. Satterwhite

TEMPLE POLICE DEPARTMENT

Fisher, Wiley Vick
Born 25 November 1874—Died 20 August 1926

Chief of Police Wiley Fisher was shot and killed at Belton by former sheriff Albert W. Bonds.

The two lawmen had been bitter political enemies for many years. Fisher was active in the 4 November 1924 sheriff's election against Bonds, which led to his defeat by a challenger. Bonds filed a criminal libel complaint against Fisher. Their hostility finally boiled over into violence. Bonds shot and killed Fisher shortly before noon on Friday, 20 August 1926, while Fisher was standing with his wife and the three small children of a man who had been killed in an automobile accident several days earlier. Bonds drove slowly past Fisher in his car and fired three shots in all. Witnesses to the incident claimed that as Fisher saw Bonds approach, he shouted a warning to his wife, saying, "Look out!" as he shoved her out of the way. Other witnesses claim that no words were spoken by either Fisher or Bonds.

Fisher died en route to the hospital. Bonds fled and abandoned his automobile about fifteen miles south of Belton. A $1,000 reward was offered for his capture.

Bonds eventually crossed the Rio Grande into Mexico on 19 September 1926 at a point known as Cow Creek, which is located about twenty-five miles south of Del Rio. By 30 September, Bonds was reported to have sought refuge deep in the interior of Mexico. He was eventually brought back to Belton and released on a $10,000 bond.

On Thursday, 2 December 1926, Bonds was shot and severely wounded while seated in his automobile in the public square. Monroe Fisher, the chief's son, was arrested and released on a $2,500 bond. Bonds recovered, and his trial for the murder of Fisher was set for 20 June 1927. However, no trial ever took place. At about 11:40 a.m. on Wednesday, 11 May 1927, Bonds was walking by the Belton National Bank when an unknown person shot him five times with a rifle. He died an hour later at the Belton Sanitarium.

Fisher was survived by his wife, Sarah Elizabeth "Sallie" Monroe, and ten children. He is buried at Hillcrest Cemetery. He had been with the agency for ten years.

Related Case: Bell County Sheriff's Office, Albert W. Bonds

TERRELL COUNTY SHERIFF'S OFFICE

Anderson, David L. "Doc"
Born 23 November 1861—Died 4 June 1918

Sheriff David Anderson was shot and killed when he responded to a disturbance call at a saloon in Sanderson.

Anderson was warned that a man named Ed Valentine, who was inside the bar at the time, was armed. Anderson, however, did not believe that Valentine was a threat. As it turns out, he was fatally wrong.

As Anderson entered the saloon, Valentine shot him three times, killing him instantly. A crowd of irate citizens gathered and began firing their guns into the saloon. Dr. F.W. Reeve entered the establishment and found Anderson slumped in a chair. He and a citizen removed Anderson's body.

Constable R.M. "Bob" Gatlin rushed to the scene, armed with a .30-30-caliber rifle, and positioned himself at a window inside the pool hall east of the saloon. As Valentine stepped outside, Gatlin shot him dead.

There remains some confusion regarding Anderson's background. Some reliable sources claim that Anderson, who was using the name "Buffalo Bill" or "Billie" Wilson at the time, was arrested by Lincoln County, New

Mexico sheriff Pat Garrett at Pete Maxwell's stable near Fort Sumner on 19 December 1880, along with Henry McCarty (Billy the Kid), Charlie Bowdre, Tom Folliard and Tom Pickett. On 30 March 1881, Wilson escaped from jail in Mesilla, New Mexico, and returned to Texas. Wilson, along with other Lincoln County war participants, received a pardon from President Grover Cleveland on 2 August 1896. He changed his name to Dave Anderson and later became sheriff of Terrell County.

Tise's book *Texas County Sheriffs* indicates that D.L. Anderson was appointed sheriff on 7 July 1915 and then elected on 7 November 1916. He served until he died sometime in 1917. Tise also indicates that Billie Wilson was appointed sheriff in early 1918 and served until 14 June 1918, when he was killed. This notation was not in the state election records but in county records. Anderson had also served as a U.S. customs inspector.

Anderson was survived by his wife, Margaret "Maggie" Fitzmaurice, and one daughter, Ella Mae. He is buried at the Saint Mary Magdalene Catholic Cemetery in Brackettville.

Cook, Lee Andrew
Born 1 September 1890—Died 13 April 1938

Lee Cook was elected sheriff on 4 November 1930 and reelected in 1932, 1934 and 1936. He served until February 1938, when he resigned.

On 13 April 1938, Cook was found in the stairwell of the courthouse with a pistol wound to his head. His death was held to be an accidental self-inflicted wound.

Cook married Alma McDonald on 9 July 1917. The couple had three children. They were divorced in 1936. Cook married Neil Nance Davis in February 1938, only two months before his death. Cook is buried at the Cedar Grove Cemetery in Sanderson.

TERRELL POLICE DEPARTMENT

Keller, Joseph Henry "Joe"
Born 2 November 1853—Died 27 October 1913

At about 9:30 a.m. on Monday, 27 October 1913, City Marshal Joe Keller was shot and killed by Constable J.B. Warren.

The two lawmen had met on the street an hour earlier and had a dispute during which Warren was disarmed by Keller. One shot was fired during that incident. Later, the two men again crossed paths, this time at the Candy Kitchen restaurant on Moore Avenue. This time, they opened fire on each other. It is not known who fired first, but Keller was hit in the center of the chest, left shoulder, right leg and left thigh. He died at the scene. Warren, who was apparently the superior marksman, was not injured.

Warren was charged with the killing of Keller. He was tried and found not guilty on 10 April 1915.

Keller had served as city marshal for twenty years. Prior to that, he served as a deputy constable and deputy sheriff. His brother, James Keller, had served as sheriff and had died in office.

Keller was survived by his wife. He is buried at the Oakland Memorial Park Cemetery

In 1898, City Marshal Keller shot and killed a hack driver named James Salmons in a dispute over fare. He was arrested but apparently was never convicted.

TEXARKANA POLICE DEPARTMENT

Walraven, James Richard, Sr.
Born 2 April 1877—Died 23 July 1929

Officer James Walraven was shot and killed by a man he had arrested two days earlier for being drunk in public.

Walraven was walking his beat and had stopped for a moment to sit down on a bench in front of a local filling station. A gasoline salesman named James D. Reynolds, whom Walraven had previously arrested, approached him in his automobile. Reynolds pulled a handgun and attempted to open fire on Walraven. After several misfires, Reynolds finally managed to get his pistol to function properly. Multiple bullets from Reynolds's gun hit Walraven, who, in spite of being mortally wounded, managed to return fire and mortally wound the suspect. Reynolds died the following day. Walraven died at the scene.

Walraven had served with the agency for seventeen years. He was survived by his wife, Ethel Sellman, and six children. Walraven is buried at the Hillcrest Memorial Cemetery.

Texas City Police Department

Evans, John Edward
Born 13 June 1875—Died 13 February 1928

Officer John Evans was shot and killed when he surprised two men who were robbing a grocery store.

A night watchman had driven two suspected burglars away from Lay's Drugstore earlier in the night. Evans was at home at the time but responded to the call and encountered the burglars when he entered the back door of the establishment. He was shot through the heart and killed. Nothing was taken from the store, but Evans's pistol and some money from his wallet had been removed from his body.

Evans's body was discovered at about 5:00 a.m. by night watchman Lashaweay and P.D. Harlow, who had become suspicious when they found his personal car abandoned at city hall.

A number of businesses in Texas City had been broken into in recent weeks, including a soft drink stand near Virginia Point, a grocery store at the outskirts of town and a dry goods store near Lay's Drugs. A reward of $350 was offered for Evans's killer. One of the murderers, William Curtis, was apprehended on 20 February. Curtis was a seaman and had been traveling between Texas City and New York on the Standard Oil tanker *A.C. Bedford*. When the ship docked in New York, Curtis, along with two accomplices, was taken into custody.

Evans was survived by his wife, Charles Bernice "Bennie" Scroggins, and three children. He is buried at the Burkburnett Cemetery in Wichita County. Although family genealogists list Evans's given name as John and his middle name as Edward, his tombstone has been engraved as O.E. Evans.

Throckmorton County Sheriff's Office

Spurlock, Joseph Gurney "Joe"
Born 21 October 1875—Died 3 October 1910
Date of Incident: 1 October 1910

Joe Spurlock was elected sheriff on 6 November 1906 and reelected on 3 November 1908.

Spurlock died on Monday, 3 October 1910, from gunshot wounds he had received two days earlier when he was attempting to serve a warrant on a man named Albert Condron.

Spurlock had gone to a wagon yard and feedhouse where some shooting had been heard. There, he encountered Condron. Condron resisted arrest, and a gunfight soon followed. Spurlock was wounded in the wrist, and Condron was shot through the leg. Just as the affray appeared to be over, someone fired a blast from a shotgun into Spurlock's abdomen. The wound was fatal. Spurlock died two days later.

A man named J.W. Overcash was arrested and housed in the jail at Throckmorton under suspicion of killing Spurlock. No information regarding the outcome of any charge is known.

Spurlock was survived by his wife and son. He is buried at the Throckmorton Cemetery.

TITUS COUNTY CONSTABLE'S OFFICE

Price, Edward
Born 20 July 1891—Died 22 March 1933

Precinct 8 constable Edward Price asked Bill Herron to stop shooting dice at the Winfield Train Depot. Arthur Sanders, the stepfather of Bill Herron, moved to position himself behind Price. When he had done so, Sanders cut, stabbed and almost decapitated Price with a long jagged-edged knife. Price died at the scene within minutes.

Sanders was tried, convicted and sentenced to thirty-eight years in prison for the murder. Herron was sentenced to eight years in prison for his part in the affair.

Price was survived by his wife, Claudie, and one adopted son. He is buried at the Talco City Cemetery.

TITUS COUNTY SHERIFF'S OFFICE

Gray, George Clem
Born 1 December 1884—Died 7 August 1925

Former Titus County deputy sheriff and federal Prohibition officer Clem Gray had been involved in, and charged with, a violation of the Prohibition act and had been brought to justice by federal Prohibition officer Manuel T. "Lone Wolf" Gonzaullas. Not long after, Gray was charged with robbing a bank in Upsher County.

Following the bank robbery incident, Gray was accused of the murder of a man named Ottice Stanley Ballard. Ballard had disappeared on Monday, 24 September 1923. Four days later, Ballard's body, stripped clean of clothing and weighted down with irons, was discovered in Cypress Creek. Gray was tried and convicted of Ballard's murder, and on 19 October 1923, he was sentenced to death by electrocution.

Gray was transported to the Dallas County jail, where he was held during his appeal process. The conviction was upheld, and Gray was scheduled to be executed on 7 August 1925.

During Gray's prosecution, the state charged that Ballard was murdered because he possessed knowledge of a bank robbery in Upsher County in which Gray had taken part. A black man named Burl Kemp testified that he had taken part in the murder of Ballard but that Gray had done the killing by beating Ballard with an iron bar. Gray's lawyers contended that Kemp had killed Ballard because of his loyalty to Gray. The appeals court judge ruled that it did not matter which man had struck the fatal blow and that Gray's conviction and death sentence were to be upheld. Kemp was also convicted for his role in the killing of Ballard and sentenced to serve thirty years in prison.

Many persons who knew Gray vouched for his character and sought clemency on his behalf, including federal Prohibition officer Lone Wolf Gonzaullas. Their efforts proved fruitless.

After a failed attempt on Gray's part to take his own life by cutting an artery in his left arm with a razor blade while awaiting his execution, Gray was forcibly strapped into the electric chair at Huntsville Penitentiary at about midnight on 6 August 1925. At 12:05 a.m. on 7 August 1925, Gray's sentence was carried out, and he became the nineteenth person to meet his fate by electrocution in Texas.

Gray was survived by his wife, Minnie Ola Ryan, and two children. He is buried at the Grove Hill Memorial Park at Dallas.

During his service as a federal Prohibition officer, Gray was assigned to the headquarters office in Little Rock, Arkansas. Much of his work was done in Texas, however. After leaving the federal service, he served as a deputy in Tutus County under Sheriff John Reeves.

TOM GREEN COUNTY SHERIFF'S OFFICE

Carruth, Charles Edwin
Born 16 September 1901—Died 1 June 1934

Deputy Sheriff Charles Carruth was shot and killed when he and another officer attempted to serve papers on a man for his commitment to a mental institution.

Carruth had gone to a local refinery near San Angelo to serve papers on a man named Jesse Barnett, who was the night watchman at the facility. Zeko Bates, special officer for the Santa Fe Railroad, accompanied him. Carruth and Bates had not disclosed the fact that they were officers, hoping to take Barnett into custody peacefully. Barnett, who was armed with a shotgun, suddenly opened fire, killing Carruth with one shot in the chest and wounding Bates.

Refinery employee's persuaded Barnett to give up the gun and then handcuffed him and held him for police. He was subsequently committed to a mental institution, where he died sometime later. Fellow employees indicated that Barnett's wife had died two months before the incident and that one of his three children had been ill in the hospital for two months.

The new Sheriff's Department headquarters, built in Tom Green County in 1998, was named in honor of Deputy Carruth.

Carruth had served with the agency for two years; however, newspaper reports of the day indicated that he had been an officer for seventeen months. He was survived by his wife, Thelma Valree Joiner, and three children. Carruth is buried at the Fairmount Cemetery in San Angelo.

TRAVIS COUNTY CONSTABLE'S OFFICE

Wilson, Jesse Rolland
Born 12 December 1868—Died 15 February 1918

Precinct 3 deputy constable Jesse Wilson was shot and killed by state game warden John W. Hill. This deadly incident was the result of a personal disagreement between the two men that ended after a mortal duel on the streets of Austin. During the fatal shootout, a total of five shots were fired. Two bullets hit Wilson. The other three went wild, striking electric light globes overhead or piercing signs in store windows.

Wilson was survived by his wife, Rella Gregory Belnap, and three children. He is buried at the Oakwood Cemetery in Austin.

TRAVIS COUNTY SHERIFF'S OFFICE

Duncan, George Lemuel
Born 3 February 1877—Died 23 September 1911

Deputy Sheriff George Duncan was shot and killed by a horse trader named John Teague.

Teague had just successfully murdered a saloonkeeper named John Guest with a shotgun blast to the head. Guest was Teague's brother-in-law. He had also tried to kill the bartender. Duncan heard the shots from his home and immediately went to investigate. When he arrived at the tavern, he was met by Teague, holding his shotgun. Teague immediately opened fire on Duncan, hitting him in the head with a shotgun blast. The wound was fatal. Teague took Duncan's pistol and fled.

An all-night chase by lawmen culminated in the eventual capture of Teague, who had fallen down a bluff not far from the scene of the crime. Teague was tried and convicted of the murder of saloonkeeper John Guest. He was sentenced to life in prison.

Duncan had been with the agency for one month. He was survived by his wife, Rosa A. Gagnon, and five children. Duncan is buried at the Live Oak Cemetery. Duncan's death certificate lists his date of birth as 4 June 1860, while family genealogists list it as 3 February 1877.

TRINITY COUNTY CONSTABLE'S OFFICE

Washburn, George W.
Born November 1853—Died 24 February 1901
Date of Incident: 23 February 1901

At 7:30 p.m. on Saturday, 23 February 1901, Precinct 1 constable George Washburn was shot in a personal disagreement with Robb Stevenson. He died from his wounds at 1:00 a.m. the following day.

Washburn also served as the city marshal of Groveton, the county seat.

The dispute had started a year earlier, at 1:00 p.m. on Tuesday, 29 January 1900, when Washburn and brothers Robb and Aaron Mack Stevenson were in W.L. Avery's saloon. The Stevenson brothers were both attorneys. Mack Stevenson was shot through the heart and killed. Washburn was shot through the left arm, making a painful flesh wound. Robb Stevenson was fired at three times but was not hit. Mack Stevenson and Washburn had quarreled earlier and had to be separated by Sheriff Collins. It was reported that the feud had been going on for some time. The disposition of charges against Robb Stevenson is unknown. He died on 4 June 1910.

Washburn was survived by his wife, Martha, and six children. His place of burial is unknown.

TRINITY COUNTY SHERIFF'S OFFICE

Kelley, Wade Hamilton
Born 8 April 1872—Died 24 April 1911

Deputy Sheriff Wade Kelley was asked by a man living near the lumber mill about one mile north of the city of Trinity to come to his residence and investigate some illegal activity that he had observed. As Kelley approached the man's home, he was shot and killed. When his body was later discovered, he was unarmed, but none of his personal effects had been taken.

Three Mexican men and one black man were arrested for the murder. The disposition of any charges against the foursome is unknown.

Kelley was survived by his wife and four children. He is buried at the Cedar Grove Cemetery in Trinity. Newspaper accounts of the day claim that Kelley was buried at the Trinity Cemetery and that he was a Royal Arch Mason. Some sources list his surname as Kelly.

TYLER COUNTY CONSTABLE'S OFFICE

Walker, Leonard Newman
Born 31 July 1873—Died 22 September 1928

Lawmen from Tyler County received information that Joe Cobb (alias John Jackson), who was an escaped convict from a Louisiana penitentiary, was hiding near Woodville. Cobb had been sentenced to serve twenty years in prison on 14 December 1915. He escaped on 3 September 1916 and had been living in Tyler County ever since, using the assumed name John Jackson.

On Saturday, 22 September 1928, Sheriff A.C. Ogden, Deputy Sheriff A.C. Walker, Game Warden Ernest La Roe and Precinct 5 constable Leonard N. Walker (A.C. Walker's brother) all went to arrest Cobb. Ogden and La Roe stationed themselves at the front gate, while the Walker brothers went around to the back of the house. La Roe called for Cobb to surrender. Cobb ran out the back door past the two Walker brothers, who ordered him to surrender. Cobb fired one shot from a double-barreled shotgun at Leonard Walker. Walker was struck in the side and died instantly. Cobb kept firing until the shotgun was empty. He then took his pistol and began shooting with it, wounding A.C. Walker in the right arm. Although the lawmen returned fire, Cobb managed to escape the shootout without so much as a scrape.

After engaging a posse in a brief gun battle, Cobb was captured near Spurger later that afternoon. On 4 December 1929, Joe Cobb, alias John Jackson, was convicted of the murder of Leonard Walker and sentenced to serve five years in prison. The charge of assault to murder against A.C. Walker was dismissed, citing "insufficient evidence to convict."

Leonard Walker was survived by his wife, Eula A. Clawson, and three children. He is buried in the Mount Pisgah Cemetery in Tyler County.

Walker had been appointed constable of Precinct 5 sometime in 1926. He was on the ballot on 6 November 1928 and was elected six weeks after his death.

TYLER COUNTY SHERIFF'S OFFICE

Parsons, John Wheat
Born 1 August 1849—Died 23 January 1904
Date of Incident: 22 January 1904

While seated in the lobby of the Griffin Hotel in Woodville, Special Deputy Sheriff John Parsons was killed when his Colt .38-caliber semiautomatic pistol fell from his pocket, discharged accidentally and fatally wounded him. The bullet entered above his hip and passed through his abdomen. He died the following morning.

Parsons is buried at the Segrest Cemetery in Tyler County. He was survived by his wife, Amanda Goode, and one son.

UPTON COUNTY CONSTABLE'S OFFICE

Miner, S.C.
Born (Unknown)—Died 8 May 1912

Constable S.C. Miner was shot and killed by a man named H. Crowden about three miles from Ore City. Eyewitnesses claim that Miner rushed at Crowden with his pistol in his hand. Crowden, it is claimed, grabbed a shotgun from a rack on the wall and fired in self-defense, killing Miner.

Nothing further is known about this incident or about Miner.

UVALDE COUNTY SHERIFF'S OFFICE

Haygood, John Wesley
Born 26 September 1873—Died 28 February 1935

Chief Deputy John Haygood was shot and killed while he was attempting to arrest a man who was wanted for murdering his estranged wife.

Haygood and Uvalde city marshal J.A. Couser had been on a daylong search for a man named John Trapper. They located Trapper just outside the city limits. As Haygood stepped from his car, Trapper opened fire with a shotgun, hitting him full on in the chest and fatally wounding him. Couser, who was with Haygood, returned fire and wounded Trapper in the leg.

In a speedy trial that concluded on 14 March, Trapper was tried and convicted of murdering both his wife and Haygood. He was sentenced to death, the first such ruling to be handed down in Uvalde County in fifty years. That sentence was carried out on 1 August 1935, when Trapper was executed by electrocution at Huntsville, becoming the 119th criminal to meet such a fate.

Haygood was survived by his wife. He is buried at the Uvalde Cemetery.

UVALDE POLICE DEPARTMENT

Connor, John Frank
Born 9 July 1883—Died 20 December 1930

Chief John Connor was shot and killed during an attack that was carried out by a man named B.H. Hunter and his three sons, Jamie, Bert and Lester.

Connor had arrested B.H. Hunter for a traffic violation a few months earlier. The two men had been involved in a quarrel at that time. The aftermath of that disagreement continued until the inevitable showdown, which occurred on Saturday, 20 December 1930. The incident took place in the alley alongside the Strand Confectionery in the heart of Uvalde at about 9:00 p.m. That business was owned by Hunter and his three sons. The Hunter family also operated a motion picture theater at the same site. Witnesses claimed that Connor had attempted to enter the theater without a ticket. The elder Hunter enlisted the aid of his three sons to eject Connor. A violent struggle occurred, during which Connor received a severe beating. Along with cuts and bruises he suffered in the bloody contest, Connor also had an injury to his spine that physicians later reported would probably have caused his death. During the affray, one of the Hunter brothers managed to gain control of Connor's pistol. He used it to shoot the lawman in the head. That wound was most definitely fatal.

Most local newspapers reported that Bert and Lester Hunter were responsible for the beating, as well as the gunplay. Hunter and all three of his sons were charged with the killing, however. The outcome of those charges is not known.

Connor had been with the agency for two years. He was survived by his wife and two children. He is buried at the Uvalde Cemetery.

VAL VERDE COUNTY SHERIFF'S OFFICE

Andrada, Sapario (Serapio)
Born September 1848—Died 28 November 1906

At about 10:00 p.m. on Wednesday, 28 November 1906, a group of five telegraph linemen who had been working near the town of Del Rio for the preceding week or more were drinking and partying at a local billiard hall in the Mexican section of town. Members of the group became unruly and began to fire their revolvers, shooting up the town. Deputy Sheriff Andrada arrested the group and placed the men in custody. He had begun to transport the men to jail in a hack when one or more opened fire on him. Andrada was struck by three bullets, killing him almost instantly.

The five men scattered and ran. A citizen caught one of them almost immediately. The remaining four were captured later by Sheriff John F.

Robinson and ranger captain John H. Rogers when they were discovered hiding out in a railroad car, where they had been living.

Andrada, who was born in Mexico, was survived by his second wife, Pioquinta, and nine children. His place of burial is unknown.

Bean, Sam
Born circa 1875—Died 5 May 1907

Deputy Sheriff Sam Bean was killed during a short but brutal gunfight that unfolded in the streets of Del Rio.

The incident came on the heels of a quarrel between the two men. Bean was armed with a pistol. His adversary, a painter named Gleceri Orasco, chose a knife for his weapon. Bean fired five shots. He hit Orasco once, inflicting a slight wound. While the trusted old adage "Never bring a knife to a gunfight" is generally good advice, in this case Orasco managed to cut and stab Bean about eight or ten times, depending on which newspaper report one relies on for such information.

Sam was the son of the notorious and colorful judge Phantley Roy Bean of Langtry. Following in his footsteps, Bean was also a saloonkeeper at the time of his death.

Most records indicate that Bean was not married; however, some family genealogists list his wife's name as Manuela Velasco. He is believed by most family genealogists to have been born in San Antonio. Bean was survived by his mother, Maria Anastacia Virginia Chavez. Some genealogists claim that Roy Bean had as many as nine children; however, most sources seem to report four. His year of birth ranges from 1858 to 1875, depending on the source. Bean is buried at the Whitehead Memorial Museum in Del Rio.

There is some inconsistency with regard to the date of this incident. Bean's death certificate indicated that his occupation was a deputy sheriff and that he died on Sunday, 5 May 1907. Newspaper accounts of the day claim that Bean was a saloonkeeper and that he died on Tuesday, 7 May.

VAN ALSTYNE POLICE DEPARTMENT

Echols, William Larkin "Will"
Born 4 January 1863—Died 23 March 1929
Date of Incident: 19 March 1929

On Tuesday, 19 March 1929, Chief Will Echols was making his normal rounds in the business district of the city when he came across several men who were preparing to rob two banks. Surprised by Echols, the would-be robbers drew their guns and opened fire. Echols's pistol misfired. The defenseless Echols was shot and killed by the pair, who quickly sped out of town in an automobile. Echols's body was discovered a short while after the shooting by night watchman J.T. Sheldon, who had heard the gunfire and ran to investigate.

Echols was hit in the abdomen and the leg. He was taken to the local hospital, where he died on Saturday, 23 March 1929.

The gang of robbers was believed to have been the same duo who entered the bank at Pottsboro, eight miles west of Denison, but was frightened away by citizens.

A reward of $1,250 was offered for the capture of the murderers and would-be bank robbers. On 27 March, Dennis M. Dixon and Robert Mason were captured in Coleman. Dixon confessed to being the one who had emptied his pistol into Echols and committed the murder. The third man, Clifford Harris, was arrested in Dallas. Dixon and Mason already faced charges of holding up a filling station at Coleman. During that incident, they had shot and seriously wounded a man named Elgie Leslie. Leslie was not expected to survive.

On 5 May, two other youths were apprehended in connection with the Echols murder. James E. Jones and Charles Baker had fled Texas and were captured at Salt Lake City, Utah. Nothing came of those charges

On 7 May 1929, Dixon was found guilty and sentenced to forty years in prison for the murder of Echols. On 10 May 1929, Mason and Dixon pleaded guilty to robbery charges and received sentences of six years in prison. Based on testimony by Mason and Dixon that he had nothing to do with the Echols murder, Clifford Harris was set free on 30 May 1929.

Echols had been with the agency for forty-six years. He was survived by his wife and two children. He is buried at the Van Alstyne Cemetery.

Some confusion exists regarding Echols's date of death. Although his death certificate is dated 21 March, several newspaper articles and other sources reflect an assortment of dates between 21 and 24 March.

VAN ZANDT COUNTY CONSTABLE'S OFFICE

Covert, John Eli
Born 16 February 1883—Died 24 December 1921
Date of Incident: 23 December 1921

Precinct 1 constable John Covert was shot and killed while he was raiding an illegal moonshine still.

At about 3:00 a.m. on Friday, 23 December 1921, Covert, along with Sheriff Ollie Osborne and Constable Clay Hollifield, conducted a raid on an illegal whiskey still near Pine Bluff in the eastern part of Van Zandt County. As they approached the site, they observed two or four men, at least one of whom was armed with a gun. While one of the officers was placing one man under arrest, a shot rang out. Covert was hit in the upper arm by a shotgun blast, close to his shoulder. The impact of the buckshot pellets nearly severed his arm. He was transported to Baylor Hospital in Dallas, where he died from his wound the following day.

On 6 January, Texas governor Pat Morris Neff offered a $150 reward for the capture of Covert's killer. The murderer was eventually arrested and taken to Canton, where he was charged with killing. No information concerning the outcome of those charges has been found.

Covert was not married. He is buried in Quinlan.

Tipps, William Leander
Born 24 July 1867—Died 28 November 1926

Precinct 7 constable William Tipps was shot and killed when he attempted to arrest a man for concealing stolen property.

At about midnight on Sunday, 28 November 1926, Tipps and three other constables went to the home of Bob Taylor with an arrest warrant. When they approached Taylor and informed him that he was being taken into custody, he appeared initially to comply. Apparently, Taylor changed his mind and drew a .32-caliber pistol with which he shot Tipps, mortally wounding him. Tipps was taken to Baylor Hospital in Dallas, where he died later that same day.

Taylor was charged with murder and tried in Van Zandt County. On 4 February 1927, a jury found him guilty and sentenced him to the state penitentiary for a term of ninety-nine years.

Tipps was survived by his wife, Mamie Kate Wells, and seven children. He is buried at the Prairie Springs Cemetery between Ben Wheeler and Canton.

VAN ZANDT COUNTY SHERIFF'S OFFICE

Vickery, Thomas B.
Born 24 May 1854—Died 22 December 1916

Former sheriff Thomas Vickery was killed in an automobile accident in Van Zandt County on 22 December 1916.

Vickery had been elected on 6 November 1894 and served until 3 November 1896.

Vickery was survived by his wife, Henrietta S. Norman. He is buried at the Myrtle Springs Cemetery.

Burnett, Ira
Born 4 February 1885—Died 26 April 1934

Sheriff Ira Burnett was killed in an automobile accident while he was returning from Canton after having served several warrants.

Burnett was traveling in his department vehicle when he collided with an oil truck driven by a man named W.D. Ashmore of Dallas. The incident took place about nine miles east of Terrell in Kaufman County. After the accident, Ashmore said that Burnett had sideswiped his truck and had been thrown clear of the wreckage. He was already dead by the time Ashmore reached him. Both vehicles were completely demolished. The truck was entirely consumed by flames. Burnett died at the scene of the incident.

Burnett was elected on 8 November 1932. He was survived by his wife, Ethel E. Williamson, and five children. His wife was appointed to serve out his term as sheriff. Burnett is buried at the Haven of Memories Cemetery in Canton.

VICTORIA COUNTY SHERIFF'S OFFICE

Kibbe, Walter Murray
Born 28 August 1878—Died 24 July 1911

Deputy Sheriff Walter Kibbe was shot and killed while he was questioning a man named Sidney Davis, who was wanted for murder.

Davis had threatened to kill any officer who tried to arrest him. Davis made good on his sullen pledge, as Kibbe was found seriously wounded by two rifle shots from Davis's weapon. Although gravely injured, Kibbe was able to return fire.

Davis was apprehended and charged with murder and lunacy.

Kibbe was survived by his wife, Beulah Eliza Nichols, and four children. He is buried at the Hillside Cemetery in Cuero, Dewitt County.

WACO POLICE DEPARTMENT

Mitchell, William Davis
Born August 1865—Died 27 October 1900

Officer Mitchell was shot and killed when he responded to a disturbance at a local saloon owned by L.P. Hanna. A man named Will King had been causing a drunken disturbance there. While Mitchell was dismounting from his horse, King shot him several times with a pistol, hitting him with at least three shots. One shot entered his chest, another hit him in the stomach and the third landed in the shoulder. The wounds were fatal. King was drunk at the time of the incident and had threatened to shoot the first officer who tried to arrest him. Mitchell fired several times at King and struck him once in the leg. A basket of grapes Mitchell was carrying home to his family fell on the ground. Mitchell's body was brought across the street, and his wife and children were summoned. He died about an hour later with them by his side.

King was apprehended, tried and convicted of Mitchell's murder. He was sentenced to be executed. At 1:45 p.m. on Friday, 25 October 1901, that sentence was carried out in McLennan County. King was the 277th person to be executed by hanging in Texas. When asked prior to hanging how he was doing, King replied, "Oh, I am as well as could be expected under the circumstances."

In spite of eyewitness reports to the contrary, all the way to the gallows King adamantly maintained that he did not shoot Mitchell, nor did he even know him. He also maintained that it had been a man named Will Cook who had shot him in the leg at the time of the Mitchell killing, not Mitchell.

Mitchell had been with the agency for six months. He was survived by his wife, Mary Virginia "Mamie" Copeland, and three children. He is buried at the Oakwood Cemetery.

Gantz, Charles May
Born 21 August 1886—Died 8 August 1923

Sergeant Charles Gantz died from being exposed to a mixture of carbon dioxide and nitrogen. While involved in an illegal liquor raid, Gantz was lowered into a dry well in search of illegal moonshine. While descending into the well, he was overcome by the fumes and asphyxiated. His lifeless body was recovered forty-five minutes later.

Gantz had served with the agency for two years. He was survived by his wife and seven children. Gantz is buried at the Oakwood Cemetery.

Thompson, Urby Joe "Sunshine"
Born 11 June 1895—Died 25 July 1933

Officer Urby Thompson was shot and killed while investigating a disturbance in a parking lot.

At about 11:15 p.m. on Monday, 24 July 1933, Thompson had just left the central station and driven his radio police patrol car into the parking lot of a café near Washington Avenue and Second Street. While ordering a cup of coffee at the establishment, he was told that an armed man who was creating a disturbance had just left. Thompson left the café to find the man. He first went to Perry Allen's filling station, located across the street, where he attempted to "collar" the man, a truck driver named Joseph Guy Mitchell, but Mitchell broke free. Thompson moved his patrol car back across the street near the café, stepped from his vehicle to look for Mitchell and was immediately confronted by him.

Mitchell launched into an attack with his fists, beating Thompson brutally and then shooting him fatally with a Colt .32-20-caliber revolver. The bullet entered behind Thompson's left ear and killed him almost instantly. Not satisfied that his pistol had done the job, Mitchell ran over to the body of Thompson, pulled the officer's pistol from the holster and shot him again with his own gun. Officer Hull, who was nearby, heard the shot, responded to the scene and arrested the killer. Thompson was pronounced dead at 12:15 a.m. on 25 July.

Mitchell was charged with the murder the following day. He was convicted and sentenced to ninety-nine years in prison.

Thompson had served with the agency for ten years. He was survived by his wife, Lennie Ola Ward, and four children. Thompson is buried in Italy in Ellis County. According to newspaper reports of the day, his widow received a pension of $51.75 per month, roughly half of Thompson's $103.50 monthly salary.

Baskin, James Monroe
Born 10 December 1889—Died 28 August 1936
Date of Incident: 18 August 1936

Patrolman James Baskin was dispatched to investigate a disturbance that had occurred on Colcord Avenue. The disagreement involved an intoxicated man by the name of I.W. Friedsam, who had refused to pay a one-dollar taxi fare. Friedsam opened fire with a shotgun, mortally wounding Baskin.

Friedsam was apprehended a short time after the incident. He was convicted and sentenced to fifty years in prison.

Baskin was taken to a local hospital, where he died of his wounds ten days later.

Baskin was survived by his wife, Nell Lala Peatree, and four children, one of whom was from a previous marriage to Rebecca Charlotte Allison. Some family genealogists report five children. He is buried at Osago Cemetery in Coryell County.

Huddleston, Elmer W.
Born 10 March 1900—Died 2 July 1940

Officer Elmer Huddleston was shot and killed when he and a rookie officer named Ira Royals stopped a vehicle at the intersection of South Third Street and La Salle Avenue.

Huddleston was teaching rookie officer Ira Royals "the ropes" on his first day on the job. He stopped an automobile to question the three occupants and ordered them to get out of the car. When the men emerged, they stepped to the curb with guns blazing. Huddleston and Royals exchanged shots with two of the men, Elmer Faulks and Ethmer Forrest. Huddleston shot Forrest in the head, and Royals shot Faulks in the abdomen. All three of the attackers, who hailed from Peoria, Arizona, were wounded. Unfortunately, Huddleston was seriously wounded during the exchange by one of the shooters. Royals was uninjured but had received an important lesson about the fragility of life when one pins on the badge and takes the pledge to uphold law and order.

Huddleston was taken to a local hospital, where he died from his wounds. All three suspects were arrested. Forrest and Faulks were charged with murder. The third man, who had not taken part in the shooting, was released. Forrest died two days later. Faulks was convicted of robbery and sentenced to serve ten years in prison. It is not known if he was ever convicted of the murder of Huddleston.

Huddleston had been with the agency for five years. He was not married, and both of his parents had preceded him in death. Huddleston is buried at the Oakwood Cemetery.

Anderson, Holly Ray
Born 21 August 1909—Died 8 October 1940
Date of Incident: 7 October 1940

Patrolman Holly Anderson died from injuries he received on 7 October 1940, when he collided with a vehicle at Austin Avenue and Eleventh Street on his police motorcycle. At the time, Anderson was responding to a fire. The vehicle that struck Anderson had failed to yield the right of way. He was transported to Providence Hospital, where he died the following night.

Anderson had been with the agency for six years. He was survived by his wife, Ida May Smith. He is buried at the Oakwood Cemetery.

Waller County Constable's Office

Cabeen, Daniel A. "Dan"
Born January 1860—Died 18 November 1900

According to one newspaper account of the day on Sunday, 18 November 1900, J.W. Gallion, E.E. Umland, Henry Sanders, John Seber, Tom Seber and Precinct 6 constable Dan Cabeen were on a hunting trip when Cabeen was accidentally shot and killed. Conflicting reports indicate that Cabeen was shot and killed by unknown persons, who fled in a buggy on the road to Brookshire, four miles south of the city of Waller. The circumstances surrounding the incident remain unknown.

Gallion surrendered to a deputy sheriff. He and the four other men were charged with murder. Tom Seber went to trial in November 1901. The jury deadlocked at eleven to one for conviction. He had a second trial in August 1902. The jury was once again deadlocked. In 1910, all charges were dismissed against the remaining four defendants.

Cabeen was survived by his wife, Mary. His place of burial is unknown.

Thompkins, John Clark
Born circa 1835—Died 18 February 1903

Constable John Thompkins was shot and killed by a man named C.W. LaGrand. Both men were from prominent families in the county. Nothing further is known about Thompkins or about the incident. He is buried at the Kirby Chapel Cemetery in Waller County, near Hempstead.

State election records do not indicate that he was elected; thus, he was likely appointed to the position.

Brode, Walter N.
Born 13 March 1899—Died 19 June 1934

Precinct 4 constable Walter Brode, who was also a farmer and lived in the town of Sunny Side, was shot and killed by a man named Jim McKenzie.

Brode had gone alone to a celebration at a black schoolhouse located about sixteen miles south of Hempstead. When he attempted to stop a fight between two men there, he was shot once in the head with a .38-caliber pistol and killed instantly. An unidentified bystander shot McKenzie in the back as he tried to flee. McKenzie died at the scene.

Brode was survived by his wife, Mary, and three children. He is buried in Waller County. State election records do not indicate that he was elected; thus, he was likely appointed to the position.

WALLER COUNTY SHERIFF'S OFFICE

Moore, Lewis Melvin
Born 27 September 1887—Died 8 May 1927

On Sunday, 8 May 1927, Sheriff Lewis Moore and H.D. Wheeler, a local confectioner, were driving on a highway about twelve miles north of Houston when Moore's automobile collided with a small coupe driven by a woman. Moore's vehicle rolled over several times, pinning him beneath the car. Moore was taken to the hospital in Hempstead, where he was pronounced dead. Wheeler was transported to a Houston hospital in critical condition. The driver of the other car was not injured.

Moore was survived by his wife and a small child. He is buried at the Hempstead Cemetery. Moore was elected sheriff on 4 November 1924 and reelected on 2 November 1926.

Hutchins, Clyde C.
Born 3 March 1902—Died 4 April 1937
Date of Incident: 3 April 1937

Deputy Sheriff Clyde Hutchins was shot and killed by Hempstead city marshal J.D. "Dick" Shelburne during a gun battle that took place in front of a café in the center of the town of Hempstead at about 1:30 a.m. He died of his injuries the following day. Shelburne was fatally wounded and died at the scene.

Newspaper accounts of the day provide little clue as to the nature of the disagreement between the two lawmen, other than that it must have been serious for it to have escalated into mortal gunplay.

Hutchins was not married. He was survived by his parents and numerous siblings. Hutchins is buried at the Hempstead Cemetery.

Related Case: Hempstead Police Department, J.D. Shelburne

WARD COUNTY SHERIFF'S OFFICE

Horn, Dan
Born circa 1883—Died 25 March 1928

At about 1:00 a.m. on Sunday, 25 March 1928, Deputy Sheriff Dan Horn was killed when he responded to a disturbance call at a rooming house in Monahans.

The establishment was owned and operated by Miss Leah Bailey. Horn had been keeping the peace at a dance hall when three men who were attending that function informed him about the commotion. When Horn arrived at the rooming house and stepped onto the porch, he was shot four times and stabbed twice. Two shots were fired from behind him. Other officers in the area heard the gunshots and went to investigate. Horn's lifeless body was found on the porch, where he had fallen.

Miss Bailey was arrested and charged with murder. Despite her self-defense argument, claiming that Horn had pistol-whipped her, a jury sentenced her to life in prison.

Horn had been with the agency for ten years. He is believed to have been buried in Monahans.

WASHINGTON COUNTY CONSTABLE'S OFFICE

Burch, Robert Hardin
Born 9 August 1871—Died 22 January 1914

Precinct 3 constable Robert Burch was shot and killed by Brenham night watchman John M. Lockett.

Burch was shot in the back of the head, and the bullet exited his right jaw. The fatal shooting grew out of a disagreement that had occurred between the two men.

Burch was survived by his wife, Ida Lee Petty, and one child. He is buried at the Prairie Lea Cemetery in Brenham.

On 10 October 1897, Burch's brother, Jim Burch, who was serving as the assistant superintendent of the county poor farm at the time, was killed in downtown Brenham by a former inmate. The murderer surrendered and was being escorted to jail when Constable Bob Burch shot and killed him. Burch was not convicted of that murder and continued as constable until his death.

WHARTON COUNTY CONSTABLE'S OFFICE

Townsend, James Gaither "Jim"
Born 23 October 1851—Died 29 August 1911

Precinct 7 constable Jim Townsend was shot and killed on 29 August 1911 during an argument with a saloonkeeper in the town of Louise. Nothing further is known about this deadly incident.

Townsend was survived by his wife, Marguerite Ella Downing, and three children. He is buried at the Columbus City Cemetery in Colorado County.

Townsend's father, Spencer Burton Townsend, was a veteran of the Texas Revolution and served with Captain William H. Smith's company of cavalry in San Jacinto. Another relative, J.L. "Light" Townsend, served as the sheriff of Colorado County from 1880 to 1894. A feud started between Sheriff "Light" Townsend and Sam Houston Reese, his cousin by marriage, who served as sheriff from 1894 to 1898. While serving as a deputy sheriff under Sheriff Will Buford, Jim Townsend participated in the shooting death of two men on 18 May 1899, one of whom was Dick Reese, the brother of former sheriff Sam Houston Reese. Jim Townsend was never convicted of the murders. The Reese-Townsend feud was one of the most violent in Texas.

For a detailed account of these feuds, see C.L. Sonnichsen's *I'll Die Before I'll Run: The Story of the Great Feuds of Texas*. *Texas Lawmen 1835–1899, The Good and the Bad* also has a summary of the deaths prior to 1900.

WHARTON COUNTY SHERIFF'S OFFICE

McCain, Henry Ross
Born 17 June 1871—Died 19 July 1908
Date of Incident: 17 July 1908

Deputy Jailer Henry McCain died from stab wounds he received when a lunatic prisoner attacked him. McCain was able to break free from his assailant, but not until after he had been stabbed numerous times. He was then taken by train to St. Joseph Hospital in Houston, where he died two days later.

McCain's killer was arrested and confined to jail immediately following the incident. He managed to escape but was recaptured the following day.

There is no further information concerning the disposition of any charges brought against McCain's killer.

McCain had served with the agency for seven years. He was not married and was survived by his brother. McCain is buried at the Normanee Cemetery in Bee County.

McCormick, Harry Charles
Born 3 March 1884—Died 26 June 1920

Deputy Sheriff Harry McCormick was shot and killed when he went to help Constable Walter Pitman serve a warrant on a man named Washington Giles.

Giles had first agreed to go along quietly with the officers but then began to resist. During a struggle that took place, Giles was able to gain control of Pitman's pistol. In the midst of the struggle, Osborne Giles, the brother of the suspect, emerged with a Winchester rifle in hand. While McCormick tried to assist the other officer, Osborne Giles shot him in the head and killed him.

The following week, the two Giles brothers were surrounded by a posse and shot and killed. Two other men who had aided in the original escape, Jodie Gordon and Elijah Anderson, were lynched by a mob of angry citizens. Washington Giles's wife, Lottie, was tried, convicted and sentenced to twenty-five years in prison. The case was reversed on appeal.

McCormick was survived by his wife, Mabel Lena Wescott, and two children. He is buried in Lakeside.

Related Case: Wharton Police Department, Walter W. Pitman

Simmons, Tipton M. "Tip"
Born 14 July 1893—Died 17 June 1936

On Wednesday, 17 June 1936, Special Deputy Sheriff Tip Simmons attempted to quiet a disturbance at a bonus-bond celebration dance at a café in El Campo that was attended largely by blacks. Trouble started when he escorted a woman outside to the sidewalk. He was quickly surrounded and fired his pistol in an attempt to hold back the crowd. His maneuver was not a success, and Simmons was overpowered, stabbed with knives and slashed with razors. He died from his wounds at about 12:20 a.m.

Five men and four women were originally arrested. A mob of 250 or more gathered outside the county jail in Wharton and demanded that the prisoners be released. Sheriff E.J. Koehl had deputies move the prisoners to five different county jails in the area in order to stay ahead of the mob. The killers were eventually placed in the Nueces County jail in Corpus Christi. The Wharton County sheriff went to the extreme of allowing mob representatives to search his jail, as did the sheriff of Matagorda County, to satisfy the rabble that the prisoners were not in their custody. Even though the owner had not been involved in the incident, the angry crowd then burned down the café where Simmons had been stabbed.

One of the killers, Willie Caesar, was tried, convicted and sentenced to death. That punishment was set to be carried out by means of the electric chair on 7 July 1938. The Board of Pardons thought Caesar's sentence too harsh and commuted it to life imprisonment. One woman who was involved received forty years in prison. Three other men who participated were sentenced to life in prison.

Simmons was not married. He is buried in the Garden of Memories Cemetery in Wharton.

Heyne, Otto H.
Born 30 July 1869—Died 31 July 1936

Just one day after turning sixty-seven years old, Deputy Sheriff Otto H. Heyne and Sheriff E.J. Koehl were involved in a fatal automobile accident. The incident occurred near Arcola, in Fort Bend County. Heyne died from his injuries at 3:00 p.m. the same day.

Heyne was a widower. He is buried at the Garden of Memories Cemetery in Wharton.

WHARTON POLICE DEPARTMENT

Pitman, Walter Wright
Born 14 January 1884—Died 9 November 1935

Walter Pitman was reported to have been one of the luckiest lawmen to ever wear a badge. In 1916, Pitman ran for constable of Precinct 1 in Wharton County. He won. Pitman cut a deal with the sheriff to live in the jail in exchange for helping run the facility.

Pitman's precinct covered the county seat of Wharton. He policed the city, as well. On Saturday, 15 September 1917, Pitman tried to arrest Francisco Lopez for being intoxicated in public. Lopez drew a Colt .38-caliber pistol and fired two shots. Pitman drew his Colt single-action .45-caliber revolver and fired back. His first bullet went down the muzzle of Lopez's gun, rendering his assailant's weapon useless. The lead bullet broke in half on impact. One fragment hit Lopez in the hand, causing him to drop the pistol. Pitman's second shot hit Lopez in the shoulder. At that point, Lopez took off running. Pitman arrested him shortly afterward. Lopez was fined $200 and sentenced to one year in jail for unlawfully carrying a weapon and a five-year suspended sentence for assault with intent to murder.

On Saturday, 26 June 1920, Pitman and Deputy Sheriff Harry McCormick went to arrest a man for tying a piece of paper that had been saturated with gasoline to a dog's tail and setting it on fire. The type of person who would conceive of doing such a thing, let alone follow through with the action, is baffling to most civilized persons. McCormick was unarmed. The suspect fled inside. The man's wife and brother became upset. Pitman was able to get the man to the front porch, where he knocked him to the ground with his pistol. At that point, the wife charged him, and the brother came out of the house with a .30-30 rifle. He grabbed Pitman's pistol and shot McCormick in the head with it. Pitman fled and narrowly avoided being hit by three pistol shots and seven rifle bullets that the man's brother fired at him as he escaped.

A manhunt for the shooter followed, during which a posse member killed the suspect and his brother. Just for good measure, a mob of angry citizens lynched a couple of the man's cousins. The fellow's wife was spared but received a twenty-five-year prison sentence. No information regarding the fate of the dog has been uncovered.

After serving two terms as constable, Pitman worked as a carpenter and grocery clerk before winning the city marshal position in Wharton. In 1932, Pitman was recognized by *Ripley's Believe It or Not!* for the "jammed gun shoot-out" affray and won a trip to Cuba.

Later the same summer, Pitman and another lawman had a run-in with Bonnie Parker and Clyde Barrow. When the lawmen attempted to stop the vehicle the pair was traveling in, someone inside opened fire just as the car made a quick U-turn and escaped.

On Saturday, 9 November 1935, the "thrice lucky" Pitman had a massive heart attack after dragging an intoxicated man to the jail.

Pitman had been a lawman for sixteen years and was only fifty-one years of age. Pitman is buried at the Wharton City Cemetery. He was survived by his wife, Mary Ella, and two daughters.

Related Case: Wharton County Sheriff's Office, Harry McCormick

WHITESBORO POLICE DEPARTMENT

Estes, Ches H.
Born 28 February 1900—Died 4 February 1935

City Marshal Ches Estes was shot and killed while attempting to arrest a man named Harold "Tommy" Locke.

Locke had outraged a young woman only moments earlier in an alley near the Depot Café. When Estes entered the café looking for Locke, he found the young man seated near the back of the room. Locke leveled a shotgun at Estes and opened fire, hitting him in the chest, just under the heart, with a blast of lead shot. The mortally wounded Estes drew his pistol as he was falling to the floor and fired five shots at Locke. None of the bullets found its mark.

Frank Stearns, an employee of the café and a witness to the incident, gave his statement to officers afterward.

Locke was tried and found guilty of killing Estes. He admitted to having used county relief money to purchase liquor and to being intoxicated at the time of the incident. After a jury deliberated for only twenty-two minutes, Locke was sentenced to death by electrocution. A second trial took place during which his sentence was reversed and reduced to ninety-nine years in prison.

Estes was survived by his wife. He is buried at the Oakwood Cemetery in Grayson.

Miller, William Thomas "Will"
Born 7 February 1885—Died 27 December 1940
Date of Incident: 25 December 1940

An accident occurred east of Whitesboro on Highway 82 on Christmas Day 1940. The mishap claimed the life of Chief of Police Will Miller.

Miller and other officers were investigating a collision that had occurred earlier. Hampered by fog, the lawmen were attempting to slow down passing vehicles. An oncoming automobile skidded and ran into Miller, inflicting serious injuries. He was taken to a Sherman hospital for treatment. At first, his condition was not considered serious. Unfortunately, his health grew worse. Miller died from the injuries he received in the mishap at 9:30 a.m. on Friday, 27 December 1940.

Miller had served as chief of police since the creation of the department in 1935. He was survived by his wife, Myram Matilda Sparks, and four children. Miller is buried at the Basin Cemetery in Grayson County.

Whitesboro chief of police William Thomas "Will" Miller has the distinction of being the last Texas lawman to die in the line of duty during the period covered by this book, from 1900 to 1940.

WICHITA COUNTY CONSTABLE'S OFFICE

Caple, William Marvin
Born 16 May 1885—Died 30 September 1920

Toney, William Sherrod
Born 15 September 1895—Died 30 September 1920

Special Deputies William Caple and William Toney were both shot and killed by a man named H.C. "Doc" Snow. Caple and Toney were wealthy Wichita Falls businessmen and were acting as posse members in a raid on a Kemp City gambling house. Both officers died at the scene. Eight men were arrested at the establishment afterward, but Snow escaped.

Snow was captured three days later by Sheriff McFall, about thirty miles southwest of Wichita Falls. He was tried and convicted of the murders. He was sentenced to serve twenty years in prison.

Caple was survived by his wife. He is buried at the Riverside Cemetery.

Toney was survived by his wife. He is also buried at the Riverside Cemetery.

WICHITA COUNTY SHERIFF'S OFFICE

Staley, John Albert
Born February 1874—Died 6 December 1910

Deputy Sheriff John Staley was shot and killed when he responded to a domestic dispute.

A man named L.G. "Al" Hard was beating his wife. The woman claimed that Hard had shot her father, Harry Brown. The incident was reported to the sheriff's office, and Staley responded. When Staley searched the Hard residence, he entered a shed where the man was hiding. Hard opened fire with a shotgun, killing Staley instantly. Afterward, it was confirmed that Hard had in fact killed the elderly Wichita Falls resident Harry Brown, Mrs. Hard's father.

Hard was tried and convicted of second-degree murder and sentenced to five years in prison.

Staley had been with the agency for one month and was survived by his wife, Almead Pierce, and five children. Staley is buried at the Riverside Cemetery.

WICHITA FALLS POLICE DEPARTMENT

Morris, Sterling Beck
Born 14 January 1877—Died 11 August 1913

At about 10:00 p.m. on Monday, 11 August 1913, Officer Sterling Morris was shot and killed by Officer E.D. Cox. Morris was off duty when the shooting took place and, according to reports, was intoxicated.

Cox was charged with killing Morris but was acquitted.

Morris was survived by his wife, Mary Etta Viney, and five children. He is buried at the Riverside Cemetery.

Fuller, Hugh Sevier
Born 20 August 1905—Died 22 October 1927

At about 2:00 p.m. on Saturday, 22 October 1927, Motorcycle Officer Hugh Fuller was en route to a vehicle accident at Ninth and Broad Streets. Just one block from the accident scene, he struck the side of a motorist making a turn in the intersection of Ninth and Bluff Streets. The motorist, who was traveling to the hospital to see his seriously ill wife, accompanied the injured Fuller to the hospital. Fuller died one hour later, at 3:00 p.m.

Fuller had been a night patrolman and had transferred to the motorcycle unit several weeks earlier. He was a well-known motorcycle racer, having pursued that avocation since he was a teenager and winning numerous awards for his skill. Fuller's wrecked motorcycle was placed in the lobby of the police station, where it occupied a place of honor for many years.

Fuller was survived by his wife, Sallie Emma Files. He is buried at the Riverside Cemetery.

Carlisle, Charles Sleigh
Born 2 June 1908—Died 29 June 1933
Date of Incident: 27 June 1933

Motorcycle Officers Charles Carlisle and his partner, E.M. McCord, were involved in a gunfight with a robber when they surprised a man who was attempting hold up a bakery in Wichita Falls.

Carlisle and McCord were on patrol in a police car when they were alerted by a taxi driver about a possible burglary at a bakery in the residential area of the city. As the lawmen approached the establishment, the thief, Milton Furr, opened fire from a taxicab in which he was seated. McCord was shot through the neck and survived. Carlisle was shot in the head. He died two days later. The shooter, Milton Furr, was wounded in the leg. A third man who had summoned the officers to the scene, Henry Hughes, was also injured in the gun battle when a bullet fired by the thief grazed his abdomen.

The thief, and now "cop killer," was arrested soon after as he attempted to limp away. He was charged with Carlisle's murder. Information regarding the outcome of those charges is unknown.

Carlisle was survived by his wife, Sybilyne Estelle Smith. He is buried at the Riverside Cemetery.

WILBARGER COUNTY CONSTABLE'S OFFICE

Holloway, Charles A.
Born 22 November 1874—Died 26 November 1911

Precinct 7 constable Charles Holloway was shot and killed when he and Deputy Constable Doyle attempted to arrest two men whom they suspected of robbing the Bank of Odell, blowing the safe and making off with $3,000. That robbery had taken place several days earlier.

The lawmen caught up with the suspected thieves, the Nichols brothers, in a farmer's field twenty miles northeast of Vernon. The pair was attempting to cross the Red River into Oklahoma. Holloway and Doyle jumped from their buggy and covered the Nichols brothers with their guns. While Doyle searched one of the brothers, the other one somehow managed to gain control of Holloway's gun and opened fire. Both Holloway and Doyle were hit by the gunfire. Doyle leaped aboard the buggy. The startled horse charged off with him aboard. When Doyle looked back, he saw one of the Nichols brothers fire another shot at Holloway and then turn and make a run for the river.

Holloway had been hit a total of four times, twice in the stomach and twice in the lungs. He was already dead by the time Doyle made it back to him.

The Nichols brothers fled to Oklahoma. They were arrested on 27 November and returned to Texas. Sheriff Carter of Tillman County, Oklahoma, and former sheriff John Williams of Vernon assisted in the capture. One of the brothers was acquitted. The other, who had done the shooting, was found guilty of manslaughter and sentenced to two years in prison. All charges against both men were later dropped.

Holloway was survived by his wife and child. He is buried at the Bell Cemetery in Odell.

WILBARGER COUNTY SHERIFF'S OFFICE

Coffee, James Daniel "Dan"
Born 26 January 1873—Died 16 February 1918

Deputy Sheriff Dan Coffee died from a gunshot wound that he received when he stopped an automobile he believed was being operated by smugglers of illegal liquor.

Coffee and a local constable from Fargo had gone to the Oklahoma side of the Red River at the Webb Crossing to stop, and arrest, bootleggers reported to be bringing whiskey into Oklahoma from Wichita Falls. Soon after the officers arrived, an automobile with the curtains drawn stopped to pay the toll. When Coffee drew back the draperies to look inside, two male occupants of the vehicle opened fire. Coffee was shot in the abdomen with a sawed-off double-barreled shotgun. His wounds were fatal.

The shooter, who had been released on bond after the killing of Cleveland County undersheriff Grover Fulkerson in Oklahoma on 24 August 1917, was later captured. He confessed to Coffee's murder and was sentenced to ninety-nine years in prison. The other men in the car were also arrested. There is no information regarding any charges against them

Coffee was survived by his wife, Louisa Jane Stafford, and seven children. He is buried at the Fargo Cemetery.

Gillespie, William Arthur
Born 28 February 1885—Died 11 March 1927
Date of Incident: 9 March 1927

At about 9:30 p.m. on Wednesday, 9 March 1927, deputy sheriff and motor traffic officer William Gillespie spotted a Chrysler automobile that fit the description of a vehicle that was wanted in connection with an armed robbery and shootout. That incident had taken place at a Gulf service station earlier that evening in Wichita Falls.

Gillespie gave chase on his police motorcycle. When he attempted to pass the vehicle, he was struck head-on by a truck. Gillespie was transported to a Vernon hospital, where he died two days later, on 9 March 1927.

As it turned out, the vehicle he was chasing was not the one that had been involved in the robbery.

Frank "Jack" Carter, the man who had been wounded in the Wichita Falls shootout, was arrested several days later in Oklahoma City, Oklahoma. Carter was also charged with the robbery of three service stations in Dallas. He was convicted and sentenced to ninety-nine years in prison for the Dallas holdups. Robbery charges were also filed against Carter in Fort Worth.

Gillespie was survived by his wife, Bessie, and two daughters. He is buried in the Harrold Cemetery in Wilbarger County.

WILLACY COUNTY CONSTABLE'S OFFICE

Shaw, Leslie Eugene "Red"
Born 17 January 1895—Died 5 September 1926

Deputy Sheriff Louis "Slim" May, Precinct 1 deputy constable "Red" Shaw and four other lawmen were assigned to keep peace at and around several Mexican dances. Sometime between 2:00 and 3:00 a.m. on Sunday, 5 September 1926, a shot was fired near where one of the dances had been held. The six lawmen split up into groups of three each and went to investigate the shooting.

The officers had not gone very far when one lawman told May and Shaw that he had seen a gun pointed at them. Soon after, the shooting began. Shaw was shot between the eyes and died instantly. May was shot in the heart and suffered a fatal injury. The third lawman in the group was slightly wounded in the stomach.

Local officers theorized that the first shots had been fired to lure the lawmen into a fatal trap in retaliation for a previous arrest they had made. Sheriff Teller and his deputies rounded up twenty to twenty-four persons who were in and around the area and placed them in custody for questioning.

On Tuesday, 7 September 1926, the father of a man named Jose Nuñez, who was one of the suspects being held in the shooting, was allowed to talk with his son at the jail. After doing so, the father told the sheriff that his son had confessed and would assist in locating the weapons that were used in the murder of Mays and Shaw.

Later that afternoon, five deputies took Jose and Delancio Nuñez, Cinco Gonzalez, Matt Zaller and Tomas Nuñez from the jail to a brushy area eight miles west of Raymondville. Reportedly, Jose Nuñez pointed out to the deputies where they would find the weapons that had been used in the murders of May and Shaw. The officers claim that when they led the prisoners into the underbrush, they were ambushed and met with a hail of gunfire. According to this extraordinary chronicle given by the lawmen, all of the officers ducked, returned fire and accidentally killed all five prisoners in the crossfire. For most, this seemed to be a feat simply too astonishing to believe!

Not surprisingly, there were many in the community who did not accept the lawmen's far-fetched narrative. On its face, it appeared as though the officers had simply marched the group out of town at gunpoint and, in an act of unspeakable vengeance, summarily executed them.

The Nuñez family made claims to the Mexican consul general that the body of Tomas Nuñez had been beheaded during the incident. At the request of the U.S. State Department, the governor ordered the Texas Rangers to investigate the shooting. The beheading rumors turned out to be false, but Sheriff Teller was accused of allowing a mob into the jail, thus permitting the group to remove the five prisoners and execute them.

A Willacy County grand jury investigated the case and indicted Teller and others, charging them with the murders of the five men. Teller was tried in 1927 as an accessory to the murders but was acquitted.

The reason for the murders of the May and Shaw may never be known. The motive for the execution of the five prisoners seemed clearly to be revenge. Their actions are reminiscent of two quotations, one by Stephen Vincent Benet, who wrote, "We thought that because we had power, we had wisdom." The other passage, by Sir Francis Bacon, may be the most stinging and should be carefully heeded by all who wear the badge: "In taking revenge, a man is but even with his enemy."

Shaw had been a deputy constable for only two months. He is buried at the Raymondville Memorial Cemetery. Shaw was survived by his wife, Etta LaGrande, and two daughters. The couple's third child was born soon after Shaw's death, on 21 December 1926.

Related Case: Willacy County Sheriff's Office, Louis "Slim" May

Cisneros, Francisco Asis
Born 6 October 1907—Died 26 July 1931

Haygood, Franklin William
Born circa 1867—Died 26 July 1931

Precinct 2 constable William Haygood and his deputy, Francisco A. Cisneros, were shot to death on Sunday morning, 26 July 1931. County jailer Jose Guzman was also shot in the same incident, but he managed to survive.

Haygood, Cisneros and Guzman were investigating a suspicious vehicle that was parked on the side of the road near a cemetery. There were two occupants, a man and a woman. The lawmen thought the car contained bootleggers. As the officers slowed their vehicle to speak with the occupants, the man and woman got out of the car and approached the lawmen, who were still seated in their automobile. As the man,

Pancho Chamberlain, walked up to the officers' car, he opened fire. One bullet hit Cisneros in the right wrist. Haygood leaped from the vehicle to return fire. As he did so, he was shot in the back and died instantly. Chamberlain then turned back toward the wounded Cisneros and shot him several more times. The bullets entered his left side and heart, inflicting fatal wounds. Guzman, who was crouching on the floor of the car, received a bullet wound to the mouth.

After the shooting, Chamberlain fled into brush, abandoning his vehicle and his paramour, Domlaga Bueno.

Guzman fled to Raymondville to get assistance. Willacy County deputies A.I. Pytle and John Nolen investigated the scene and searched for the killer, but without success. They believed that he had fled across the border into Mexico.

Willacy County justice of the peace J.B. Huffer held an inquest. He stated that he found Cisneros slumped in the front seat of the car, dead, with his gun lying in the road. The weapon had been fired once. Haygood was lying on his back on the right side of the car, his gun still in the holster. Officers felt the shootings were done in retaliation for a bootlegging arrest that Cisneros had made weeks earlier.

Cisneros was survived by his wife, Juana Gonzaba. He is buried at the La Piedad #1 Cemetery in Raymondville.

Haygood was elected constable of Precinct 2 on 4 November 1930. He assumed the office on 1 January 1931.

Haygood is buried at the Raymondville City Cemetery. He was survived by his wife, Lena Alice Cagle, and six children. Some family genealogists list his given name as William and his middle name as Franklin.

WILLACY COUNTY SHERIFF'S OFFICE

May, Louis A. "Slim"
Born 28 February 1906—Died 5 September 1926

For the complete account of the murder of Deputy May, please see Willacy County Precinct 1 deputy constable Leslie Eugene "Red" Shaw.

Deputy Sheriff Louis "Slim" May and Precinct 1 deputy constable Leslie Eugene "Red" Shaw were shot and killed during an ambush that occurred after a Mexican dance. Shaw was shot between the eyes and died instantly. May was shot in the heart and suffered a fatal injury. A third lawman in the group was slightly wounded in the stomach. Local officers theorized that the first shots had been fired to lure the lawmen into a fatal trap in retaliation for a previous arrest the officers had made.

May was just twenty years of age at the time of his death. He was not married. May was survived by his parents and sister. He is buried at Raymondville.

Related Case: Willacy County Constable's Office, Leslie Eugene "Red" Shaw

WILLIAMSON COUNTY CONSTABLE'S OFFICE

McBride, John C., Jr.
Born 13 November 1872—Died 24 December 1908

Precinct 8 constable John McBride was shot and killed when he attempted to arrest a man named Luis Guerra, who had been accused of stealing provisions from a local farm.

The farmer had driven his wagon to the constable's office in Round Rock and reported the theft to McBride. McBride and the farmer embarked on their fateful return trip to the man's farm in Duval on Christmas Eve. During the course of the journey, they encountered Guerra, who was armed with a .22-caliber rifle. McBride informed him that he was under arrest and instructed him to drop the gun. Guerra resisted, and a struggle occurred. During the skirmish between the two men, McBride was shot in the right eye, killing him.

Guerra fled the scene while the farmer was firing at him. The farmer returned to town and alerted the authorities. Travis County constable Lem King began tracking Guerra. He located him in a cabin near Merrilltown and attempted to arrest him. Guerra, who had stolen McBride's service revolver, pointed the weapon at King and pulled the trigger. As fate would have it, McBride's weapon was not loaded; thus, it did not fire. Undaunted, Guerra began to grapple with King. King managed to overpower Guerra and shot him fatally during the struggle.

McBride had served as the elected constable for two years. He was survived by his wife and two children. McBride is buried at the Bagdad Cemetery in Leander.

Hennech, John Otto
Born circa 1880—Died 5 February 1912
Date of Incident: 1 February 1912

On Sunday, 1 February 1912, Edmund Thomas stabbed a man named Aaron Moore. According to reports, Moore had struck Thomas with a stick. Moore was severely wounded in the incident, but his injuries were not fatal.

Precinct 6 deputy constable Otto Hennech and a man named Ike Campbell, who was reported to be Hennech's deputy, went to the Thomas home near the Circleville community in Williamson County. Hennech attempted to arrest Thomas. When he did so, Ike's blind brother Austin Thomas, along with four or five other family members, grabbed him. The family, collectively, stabbed Hennech repeatedly with knives and cut him with razors in a most barbarous assault.

Hennech suffered a total of sixteen wounds. His injuries were forbidding. Hennech's chest and stomach were laid open and his intestines exposed. Apparently, his assistant, Ike Campbell, had done nothing to come to his aid. That fact gives rise to a hypothesis held by some that Campbell was a deputized citizen and not a regular peace officer.

In any case, the Thomas family members fled. They were soon arrested by Constable Lee Allen of the Granger precinct.

Remarkably, Hennech survived the gruesome injuries he had received in the attack until Monday, 5 February 1912, when he finally expired.

Edmund Thomas was tried and convicted of the assault on Moore. He was sentenced to five years in prison. Edmund and Austin Thomas were tried and convicted of second-degree murder. They were sentenced to twenty-two years in prison.

Hennech was survived by his wife, Mattie, and three children. A fourth child was born after his death. Hennech is buried at the Taylor City Cemetery.

Hennech's surname is spelled differently in court documents, newspaper accounts, on his tombstone, in probate and census records and in cemetery records. One can find it as Hennech, Hennich, Hennck, Henek, Hencke, Hanneck, Hennick and Heneke. However, using the spelling on his tombstone and that used by his children after his death, the family apparently decided that "Hennech" was to be the proper spelling.

Moore, Samuel Martin
Born 12 July 1882–Died 16 February 1934

Precinct 2 constable Sam Moore and Granger city marshal Henry Lindsey were shot and killed while placing a prisoner named Lewis Cernoch in a jail cell.

Cernock had been arrested by Moore for failing to pay a fine for disturbing the peace and use of abusive language to a woman. His fines totaled $28.50. Moore had apparently failed to search Cernock thoroughly. As Lindsey and Moore were placing Cernock in the jail cell, he produced a .38-caliber semiautomatic pistol that he had apparently concealed on his person and fatally shot both lawmen. Lindsey was shot through the heart and died almost instantly. Moore was rushed to the hospital suffering from wounds to the head, neck, chest and arms. He died soon after the incident. Witnesses claimed that Cernock calmly stood in the middle of the room, reloaded his pistol, lit his pipe and walked to town.

Cernock was later apprehended by a hastily assembled posse of men. When he was captured, one of the possemen, H.L. "Jack" Taylor, said, "You shouldn't have done this." Cernock replied, "They double-crossed me, and they are not going to put me in jail for not having [the] money to pay the fine." Maxie Goff, a member of the posse, hit Cernock over the head with an iron weight and disarmed him. He was taken to the jail by Sheriff Louis Lowe.

Cernock was arrested and charged with the double murder, as well as for shooting at Justice John W. Nunn and assistant county attorney B. Colbert. He was tried and convicted of killing Lindsey and Moore. He was sentenced to death. That sentence was carried out on Friday, 12 July 1935, when Cernock was executed by electrocution in Huntsville. Cernock was the 118th criminal to be electrocuted in Texas.

Moore had been elected constable in 1932. He was survived by his wife, Mattie Odessa Fikes, and three children. Moore is buried at the Macedonia Cemetery in Granger.

Related Case: Granger Police Department, Henry Lindsey

Wink Police Department

Gilbreath, Rufus Nicholson
Born 4 October 1875—Died 1 June 1929

Chief of Police Rufus Gilbreath had relieved the desk sergeant and had gone into an empty cell in the city jail to repair a chain that was used to lock down unruly prisoners. Apparently, the chief's pistol fell from his holster. When it hit the floor, the gun discharged accidentally. The bullet passed through Gilbreath's left wrist and entered his skull near his nose. Hearing the sound of gunfire, the desk sergeant rushed to investigate and discovered Gilbreath lying in the cell gravely wounded.

Gilbreath was taken to the hospital, where he died at 12:11 p.m. the same day. The coroner held an inquest and ruled that Gilbreath's death was accidental.

Gilbreath is buried at the Middleton Chapel Cemetery in Wainwright, Muskogee County, Oklahoma. He was survived by his wife and four children. Gilbreath had come to Wink about fifteen months earlier. He had been employed as the chief of police for about one year.

Wise County Sheriff's Office

Brown, Joseph Hamilton "Joe," Jr.
Born 14 March 1882—Died 27 January 1933

Deputy Sheriff Joe Brown was shot and killed when he attempted to arrest a group of men wanted for stealing an oil drum.

Brown, who was also a barber by trade and operated a shop in Decatur, observed the men driving through the area and motioned for them to stop their vehicle. He brought all three individuals into his barbershop and sat them down while he called for backup. Unfortunately, he had not searched the threesome. One of the robbers, Ed Stanton, pulled out a pistol and tried to force Brown to come with him and his two accomplices. Brown refused and resisted. He pushed Stanton out the door. Stanton fell and hit the sidewalk and then fired six shots. One bullet hit Brown in the neck. Stanton and his associates managed to escape.

One of Stanton's accomplices during the Brown killing was Frank Wallace. Wallace was shot and killed in New Mexico during a shooting incident that involved the death of Lincoln County chief deputy Thomas Jones. Before finally being apprehended and brought to justice, Stanton would be responsible for the murders of three other law enforcement officers. Stanton, who went by the somewhat peculiar nickname "Perchmouth," was tried and convicted of the murder of Swisher County deputy sheriff John C. Moseley. He was sentenced to death. That sentence was carried out on 28 September 1934, when Stanton was executed by electrocution in Huntsville, becoming the 104th person to meet such a fate.

Brown was survived by his wife, Ruth Pope, and three children. He is buried at the Deep Creek Cemetery in Aurora.

Related Cases: Swisher County Sheriff's Office, John C. Moseley; Lamb County Sheriff's Office, Harvey Bolin; and Lincoln County New, Mexico Sheriff's Office, Thomas Jones

WOOD COUNTY CONSTABLE'S OFFICE

Wofford, John S.
Born 26 February 1874—Died 4 February 1907
Date of Incident: 2 February 1907

At about 5:30 p.m. on Saturday, 2 February 1907, Wood County Precinct 3 constable John S. Wofford and his brother, Wood County deputy sheriff Amos Wofford, were on Elm Street in downtown Winnsboro. R.O. "Dick" Milam, age fifty, was the operator of an illegal liquor operation known as a blind tiger. Milam's twenty-three-year-old son, W.A. Milam, who was a Dallas fireman, approached the Wofford brothers. Harsh words were exchanged, and the Wofford brothers attempted to arrest Milam and his son for liquor violations. A shootout followed, during which all four men were wounded.

Dick Milam died at the scene. John Wofford and his brother Amos both died two days later, on 4 February 1907. Milam's son died on 11 February 1907.

John Wofford was survived by his wife, Dove, and two children. He is buried at Shooks Chapel Cemetery in rural Hopkins County.

Related Case: Wood County Sheriff's Office, Amos Wofford

WOOD COUNTY SHERIFF'S OFFICE

Mattox, Reuben T.
Born December 1847—Died 2 June 1900

Deputy Sheriff Reuben T. Mattox and a small posse headed out in pursuit of a man named Shelby Fowler. They located Fowler four miles south of Winnsboro. Fowler was charged with assaulting a Winnsboro merchant named R.G. Andrews and cutting him with a knife earlier in the day.

The posse split up, and Mattox came upon Fowler alone. He attempted to arrest Fowler by himself and was shot and killed by the wanted man's father, Frank Fowler. Since the posse had scattered, Mattox's body was not discovered until the following day.

Frank Fowler was indicted by a grand jury and tried for the murder of Mattox. Remarkably, on 1 December 1900, the jury returned a verdict of not guilty.

Mattox was survived by his wife, Nancy M. "Fannie" Jones, and six children. He is buried at the Winnsboro City Cemetery. Some family genealogists report seven children.

Howard, Julian E.
Born July 1883—Died 10 July 1905

Deputy Sheriff Julian Howard responded to a report of a shot being fired at a billiard hall in Alba.

Deputy Sheriff Jim Shoemaker was already at the billiard hall, which was owned by W.F. "Fletcher or Fletch" Holmes. Shoemaker was serving papers when the gunshot was heard. Not long after Howard entered the establishment, a shootout occurred. Howard was shot in the chest with a bullet from a rifle. The wound was fatal. Before he died, the mortally wounded Howard managed to shoot Fletcher Holmes in the thigh.

Holmes and C.C. "Kit" Holmes were charged with Howard's murder. Their trial on 15 December 1906 resulted in a hung jury. On 8 December 1908, the cases against both men were dismissed on a motion made by the Wood County district attorney.

Howard was survived by his wife, Jennie B. Murdock, and two children. No records of his burial location have been uncovered.

Wofford, Amos Richard
Born 5 September 1871—Died 4 February 1907
Date of Incident: 2 February 1907

Deputy Sheriff Wofford and his brother, Constable John Wofford of the Wood County Constable's Office, Precinct 3, were shot and killed when they attempted to arrest a father and son for liquor violations. One of the suspects produced a handgun and opened fire, fatally wounding both lawmen. Both suspects were shot and killed by return fire in the incident.

Wofford had been with the agency for ten years. He was survived by his wife, Sally Dea Tramel, and three children. Wofford is buried at the Union Cemetery in Sulphur Springs, Hopkins County. He had also served as city marshal for Winnsboro.

Related Case: Wood County Constable's Office, John Wofford

YOUNG COUNTY CONSTABLE'S OFFICE

Lankford, Edward Clark
Born 25 July 1887—Died 18 November 1929

Precinct 3 constable Edward Lankford was shot and killed in his office by the husband of a woman who had come to him seeking protection from the man. Lankford saw the husband walking past the office and asked him to come in. When Lankford asked him if he had any weapons, the man began backing toward the doorway and then drew a pistol and started shooting. Lankford was fatally wounded.

Lankford was survived by his wife, Lona Nancy Jane Garner, and six sons. He is buried at the Restland Cemetery in Olney.

YOUNG COUNTY SHERIFF'S OFFICE

Cherryhomes, George Thomas
Born 8 November 1870—Died 24 February 1915

Deputy Sheriff George Cherryhomes and Riley Dollins had been charged with guarding the courthouse at night until after the district court convened.

At about 3:30 a.m. on Wednesday, 24 February 1915, the men had just finished their lunch when they heard sounds that drew their attention coming from near the cistern house. They stepped outside the courthouse building and had gone no more than about fifty feet when they were met by four armed men, who rushed them and demanded that they throw up their hands. According to reports, Cherryhomes replied, "I will never throw up my hands." At that point, the shooting commenced.

Cherryhomes emptied his two pistols at the burglars while Dollins fired six shots from a Winchester shotgun that was loaded with buckshot. The intruders, who had the advantage since Cherryhomes and Dollins were illuminated by the exterior lights of the courthouse, returned fire and then retreated toward the wagon gate at the east side of the courthouse. Cherryhomes informed Dollins that he had been hit during the battle and believed that he was fatally wounded. Dollins assisted Cherryhomes to the office of the Independent Telephone Exchange, where he was laid on a cot until a physician arrived. Shortly afterward, he was carried home. Some sources report that he was carried to a sanitarium. In either case, he died soon after.

The bullet that caused Cherryhomes's death struck him in front, in the lower part of the abdomen, and did not pass through his body.

Officers and citizens took up the trail of the assaulting parties. They followed the path to the Presbyterian Church, where bloodstains were found, along with the tracks of a buggy, giving evidence that a wounded man had been carried away. A wounded man named Pat Carlton was soon discovered at the home of Judge G.W. Fry. The bullet that struck him had passed through his body just over the hips. Along with Carlton, Pete Fry was also found at the home of Judge Fry. Pete was sporting a fresh scalp wound, obviously inflicted by a gunshot.

Pat Carlton was taken to the sanitarium, where he died later that day. Pete Fry was arrested and placed in jail, along with John Linsky, a stranger from Fort Worth, and R.M. Todd. G.W. Fry was the former county judge. The group of men trying to get into the courthouse was attempting to destroy records of Fry's wrongdoing.

Cherryhomes was survived by his wife, Ida May Baker, and five children. Some genealogists report Ida's middle name as Bell. Cherryhomes was buried at the Oak Grove Cemetery in Graham.

2

Texas Rangers

Fuller, T. Lawrence
Born (Unknown)—Died 15 October 1900

Texas Rangers had been sent to Orange to quell what were described as riotous disturbances. On Thursday, 21 December 1899, Fuller arrested a man named Denny Moore, who was causing trouble. Fuller was trying to get him to jail when another man named Oscar Poole jumped him. Either Poole was part of Moore's gang or the man just hated authority. In either case, Fuller was attacked by the knife-wielding Poole and had to shoot him in self-defense.

Subsequent to the killing, Poole was identified as one of the gang leaders. Poole was the son of Orange County judge George F. Poole. Fuller was arrested and jailed without bail. He was, however, cleared of any wrongdoing in the shooting. The Poole family filed a complaint of false arrest against Fuller in Orange County. Ranger captain Bill McDonald protested, claiming that the charge was nothing more than a ploy to get Fuller back in Orange. McDonald was overruled by his superiors.

McDonald and ranger private A.L. Saxon were in Orange as witnesses in the case involving Fuller. Fuller had just been promoted to the rank of lieutenant. During a break in the trial, Fuller and Saxon decided to get a shave. At 5:30 p.m., Fuller was standing in Adams' Barbershop washing his face at a basin in the center of the room when a shot was fired. The bullet from a Winchester rifle hit Fuller in the back of the head and exited through an eye. He fell to the floor and died within a few minutes. Saxon was in the chair being shaved at the time. There was no one else in the shop except the barber, Adams. Immediately after the shooting, Tom Poole, brother of Oscar, ran into an adjoining butcher shop with a Winchester rifle in hand. He was placed under arrest.

Thomas Poole was tried for the murder of Fuller and was acquitted on 4 May 1901. In March 1902, Orange city marshal James A. Jett shot and killed Tom Poole. On 12 May 1902, Jett became engaged in a personal dispute with George H. Poole. George, Claude and Grover Poole shot and killed Jett in a gun battle that unfolded on the streets of Orange.

Very little is known about Fuller. He had enlisted in Company B of the Frontier Battalion on 19 June 1899. According to some reports, he had completed his freshman year at the University of Texas. His remains were shipped to Fulshear in Brazoria County, but no grave site has been located. Fuller was the last member of the Frontier Battalion of the Texas Rangers to be killed in the line of duty. In 1901, the Texas legislature abolished the Frontier Battalion and established the Texas Rangers as a state police force.

Robuck, W. Emmett
Born 12 January 1877—Died 9 September 1902

Rancher and suspected cattle thief Alfredo de la Cerda and his brother Ramón owned the Francisco de Asís Ranch. Their land bordered the expansive King Ranch. Alfredo's father was killed in 1900 by a Brownsville policeman. In 1901, Alfredo and Ramón de la Cerda were arrested and charged with rustling cattle from the King Ranch.

Texas Ranger sergeant A.Y. Baker and Privates W.E. Robuck and Harry Wallis were investigating cattle rustling when they came upon Ramón de la Cerda, who was at the time in the process of branding cattle on the King Ranch property. Baker reported that de la Cerda fired at him and killed his horse, so he returned fire and shot de la Cerda in the head, killing him. All three rangers were arrested, charged with murder and released on $10,000 bond each. Miller, an employee of Mrs. M.H. King, was charged as an accessory. He was also released on a $10,000 bond.

The rangers were supported financially and legally by Richard King, former ranger captain John B. Armstrong and the Lyman brothers. The results of an inquest into the incident determined that Baker had acted in self-defense.

At about 10:00 p.m. on Tuesday, 9 September 1902, Baker, Robuck and a man named Jesse Miller, who has been reported as a ranger private, were riding their horses back to the Texas Ranger camp near Brownsville when several men ambushed them. Shots were fired from concealment. The assailants used shotguns loaded with buckshot. Robuck was struck and mortally wounded. He rode about 150 yards before he collapsed and died. Baker was slightly wounded. Miller was unscathed, although he had had his horse shot out from under him. The attackers escaped.

After an investigation by ranger captain John A. Brooks, Alfredo de la Cerda and five other men who were suspected of the ambush were arrested. A man named Heroulano Berbier, who was scheduled to testify against de la Cerda, was killed before he could do so.

Robuck was buried by the Knights of Honor at the cemetery next to the Episcopal Church in Brownsville. His remains were later reportedly moved to the Bunton Cemetery in Dale, Caldwell County. Robuck was not married and was survived by seven siblings. In some newspaper accounts, his surname is spelled Robuck or Roebuck, but his ranger enlistment papers indicate that his name was Robuck.

Alfredo de la Cerda was released on bond. He swore that he would kill Baker or pay $1,000 to anyone who would do it for him. Baker was a tough lawman. Rather than spend the remainder of his days looking over his shoulder, he acted first.

Shortly before 5:00 p.m. on Saturday, 3 October 1902, Baker caught Alfredo de la Cerda trying on a pair of gloves at a Brownsville store. He shot him through the store window with a Winchester rifle. Predictably, the rifle shot at close range did the job. Baker contended that Alfredo was reaching for his pistol at the time and that he had acted self-defense. Using money provided by the King family and others, Baker was soon free on bond. On Tuesday, 13 October 1903, Baker was acquitted of the killings of Ramón and Alfredo de la Cerda. The jury was out for deliberation for only twenty minutes. Baker later served as a U.S. customs inspector and sheriff of Hidalgo County. He died in 1930.

Goff, Thomas Jefferson "Tom"
Born 11 March 1870—Died 14 September 1905
Date of Incident: 13 September 1905

On Wednesday evening, 13 September 1905, ranger private Tom Goff arrested Augustine Garcia for creating a disturbance in a saloon in Terlingua. The small community of Terlingua is located in the Big Bend area of Brewster County. There was no jail in the town at the time, so Goff took Garcia on horseback up a steep mountainside back to the ranger camp. Garcia began to head down a different trail, so Goff tried to maneuver his horse in front of Garcia's to block the escape path. As he did so, the animal fell on him. Garcia grabbed Goff's Winchester rifle from the scabbard and began shooting. He missed with the first shot. Goff rose to his feet and reached for his pistol. Garcia fired a second shot that hit Goff in the spine. The impact from the bullet caused Goff to roll down the mountainside.

Goff was later rescued but died the following day. Garcia escaped into Mexico and was never prosecuted.

Goff had been with Company C for twelve years. He was survived by his wife, Ruby. Goff is buried at the Throckmorton Cemetery in Throckmorton County.

Some confusion exists regarding the precise date of Goff's death. The Texas Ranger marker at his grave site shows the date as 13 September. The Texas Ranger Hall of Fame and Museum lists his date of death as 13 September. The biography of Texas Ranger captain John H. Rogers lists the incident as having occurred on 14 September. In Rogers's original report, he stated that it occurred on 15 September. Family genealogists list his date of death as the fifteenth. Various newspaper articles indicate that Goff was shot on the thirteenth and died on the fourteenth. Such inconsistencies are not at all uncommon when researching records that are a century old. Debate as to which piece of data is the most correct can become heated, even between authors!

White, Homer
Born 18 August 1884—Died 4 February 1908

Mamie Ledford and Myrtle King took the train from Fort Worth to Weatherford in Parker County. Mrs. Ledford had left her husband for a man named E.S. "Stoke" Clark. Mamie called Clark in Fort Worth and told him they were in Weatherford. He said he would follow and arrive on the next train.

Mrs. Ledford approached Texas Ranger private Homer White and asked him to accompany them because she expected a confrontation with her estranged husband. Clark arrived in Weatherford and confronted Mr. Ledford. As predicted, an argument took place at the train depot. Several citizens approached White and requested that he intervene and arrest

Clark. White refused, but the witnesses persisted. White acquiesced and acknowledged that he was going to arrest Clark. White approached Clark and told him to put up his hands, he was under arrest. Clark resisted. Pistols were soon drawn, and a gun battle commenced.

Both men opened fire at close range. White collapsed on the depot platform, wounded twice. He died within minutes. Clark was seriously wounded and was arrested.

Clark and Ledford contended that they were not arguing and that White never identified himself as a lawman. They went on to claim that White had opened fire first, and Clark returned fire to protect himself.

Clark was tried in Parker County on 18 November 1908 and convicted of second-degree murder. He was sentenced to serve seven years in the state penitentiary. Clark appealed on 26 May 1909. His case was reversed; thus, Clark was never convicted of the murder of White. Clark had also been implicated, but never charged, in the murder of Fort Worth policeman William Campbell on 12 August 1909.

White was single. He had been appointed to Company A of the Texas Rangers on 1 December 1907 and had arrived in Weatherford only thirty days prior to his death. He is buried at the Graves-Gentry Cemetery in Hamilton, Hamilton County.

Thomas, Nathanial Pendergrass "Doc"
Born 5 March 1859—Died 5 January 1909

Between 1907 and 1909, the Texas Rangers were requested to enforce the Prohibition laws in the Texas Panhandle. That decision was made because officials felt the local police and sheriffs' departments were not being diligent enough.

A force of rangers, including ranger private "Doc" Thomas, shut down the section of Amarillo noted for its cheap hotels and bars, frequented by vagrants and drunks, and arrested hundreds of bootleggers. This caused bad feelings between the rangers and the local police and sheriffs' departments. The rangers were eventually assigned other duties, but Thomas remained in Amarillo. Thomas had told several people that he was a marked man because of his actions during the Prohibition law enforcement period and that he thought he would never get out of Amarillo alive.

Soon after the rangers departed, the bootleggers, predictably, were once again open for business. At about 10:00 a.m. on Tuesday, 5 January 1909,

Thomas was sitting in a chair in the county attorney's office in Amarillo with his leg up on a table talking with a local attorney about representing him in a dispute with the Potter County Sheriff's Department. A man who was wanted for murder in Arkansas had been taken out of the county jail by Thomas and released to a deputy sheriff from Arkansas. The lawman took the prisoner back to Arkansas but without any legal proceedings. Sheriff J.E. Hughes and his chief jailer, Deputy Sheriff James W. "Jim" Keeton, were upset over the incident and confronted Thomas. Both Hughes and Keeton accused Thomas of involvement in the "kidnapping" of the prisoner. The local attorney left the room. As he did so, he overheard Keeton call Thomas a liar.

In an instant, Keeton drew his pistol and shot Thomas. The bullet struck his head just above the right eye. Thomas was found with his hands in his lap and his head hanging back over the chair. Thomas's .45-caliber pistol was still in the holster. When Hughes, who had just walked out of the room, returned, Keeton surrendered to him. Thomas lingered for one hour before dying from the wound. There were no eyewitnesses to the actual shooting.

Keeton was indicted for the murder of the Thomas. At the trial, Hughes testified that he had fled the room when Keeton accused Thomas of being a liar and that he saw Thomas sit up in the chair and reach for his pistol. Keeton's testimony mirrored that of Hughes, with both claiming that Thomas had made earlier threats against them. Keeton was convicted and sentenced to five years in the penitentiary for second-degree murder. He appealed, but the conviction was affirmed.

Thomas is buried at the Springtown Cemetery in Wise County. He had been a deputy sheriff in Parker County before joining Company A of the Texas Rangers. Thomas rejoined the Parker County Sheriff's Department and then reenlisted in the Texas Rangers for the last time in January 1908. Thomas was not married.

Carnes, Quirl Bailey
Born 1 June 1884—Died 31 July 1910

Jacinto Trevino had murdered James Darwin, a young engineer for the San Benito Land and Water Company. The company posted a $500 reward. Trevino's cousin, Pablo, informed authorities that Jacinto intended to return from Mexico and kill the company's chief engineer. Pablo led a group of lawmen, including Texas Ranger privates Quirl Carnes and Pat Craighead,

Cameron County deputy sheriffs Henry B. Lawrence and Earl West and six San Benito Land and Water Company employees, to a location near the Rio Grande River where Jacinto was supposed to cross. The men split into four groups and waited.

After midnight, they heard a party of men approaching. One of the officers hailed the group to stop. Gunfire immediately broke out. Lawrence and Carnes were cut down as they rose from concealment to return fire. Lawrence died instantly from seven buck shot pellets in the right side of his head. Carnes was mortally wounded, with seven rifle wounds. One of the bullets entered through the back of his head and exited through his right eye. Carnes lived until 9:00 a.m.

Craighead and West came to the assistance of the ambushed lawmen. West was shot and wounded. Craighead left to get assistance. He fired a signal shot as had been prearranged, but the relief party mistook him for outlaws and opened fire, wounding him.

After daylight that morning, a posse discovered the body. Pablo Trevino was never arrested and disappeared into Mexico. Authorities believe Pablo had led the lawmen into an ambush.

Carnes is buried at Floresville in Wilson County. He had enlisted in Company B on 4 December 1908. His brother, U.S. customs inspector Herff Carnes, who was a former Texas Ranger, was shot in the line of duty on 1 December 1932 and died three days later.

Related Case: Cameron County Sheriffs Office, Henry B. Lawrence

Rountree, Oscar James
Born 1 September 1877—Died 19 August 1910
Date of Incident: 18 August 1910

Former ranger Rountree was shot and killed at Breen's saloon in San Antonio by D.B. Chapin. Chapin was arrested. One bullet from a .44-caliber pistol had hit Rountree almost exactly in the middle of the forehead, passing through the brain and coming out under the right ear.

The shooting occurred at about 9:30 a.m. and followed a quarrel between the two men. Although shot through the brain, Rountree retained his consciousness until after he was put under the influence of drugs at the hospital.

Chapin arrived in San Antonio on Wednesday night, 17 August. He owned the Chapin townsite and several thousand acres surrounding it.

Chapin served as county judge of Hidalgo County for several years and had recently been nominated for the legislature without opposition.

Rountree had served as a regular ranger between 1907 and 1910 in Captain Hughes's company, where he earned a good reputation. He resigned in January 1910 and had been residing in San Antonio for about four months preceding his death.

Chapin accredited the shooting to trouble that he had previously had with Edward Roos, a business partner, who came there from Houston several years ago and engaged in the real estate business. Rountree apparently was commissioned as a deputy sheriff in Cameron County and was acting as Roos's bodyguard.

"Rountree was hired to murder me," said Chapin, who went on to say, "I know what I am speaking about, because I have copies of cipher telegrams, translated, which he sent to his employer while spying on my actions."

Apparently, the jury believed Chapin's story. On 15 December 1911, Chapin was acquitted after the jury deliberated for only twenty minutes.

Rountree is buried at the Sonora Cemetery at Sonora. He was not married.

Russell, Grover Scott
Born 2 December 1887—Died 23 June 1913

Captain John R. Hughes assigned Private Scott Russell to accompany El Paso County deputy sheriff W.H. Garlick while Garlick was serving a warrant for rustling on Manuel Guaderrama. Members of the Guaderrama family were well known to law enforcement.

The two lawmen went to a store and saloon business owned by Manuel and his brother Juan. The enterprise was located in an unincorporated industrial area called Smeltertown. To avoid arousing suspicion, the officers entered under the pretext of buying tobacco.

Juan and his mother, Marina, were the only people in the store. Without warning, Russell was hit in the head by Marina, who used an axe handle to administer the blow. Juan pulled a 9mm Luger semiautomatic pistol and killed both Russell and Garlick. Next, he lowered the curtains of the store and began to hack at the fallen officers' heads with a hatchet. During the gruesome mêlée, Juan discovered, quite to his horror, that he had accidentally shot and mortally wounded his mother. Juan's wife arrived and removed both officers' guns and Russell's gun belt. The

Guaderramas called police and reported that the officers were drunk and had hit their mother.

Rangers believed the Guaderrama clan had planned the murders in revenge for the rustling investigation. Thirteen members of the family were arrested. Seven were no billed by the grand jury due to insufficient evidence, and six, including Juan, were indicted for murder. The family retained top legal talent. Five were tried on 13 January 1914, but the jury deadlocked. Rangers and deputies raised funds to aid the district attorney in the second trial. At the June 1915 trial, only Juan Guaderrama was convicted. He was found guilty of second-degree murder and sentenced to serve five years in prison.

Russell was single. He is buried at the East Memorial Cemetery in Stephenville, Erath County. Russell had been a Texas Ranger for only eight months.

Related Case: El Paso County Sheriff's Office, W.H. Garlick

Hulen, Eugene B.
Born March 1878—Died 24 May 1915

In 1912, U.S. customs inspector Joe Sitter arrested Francisco "Chico" Cano and members of his gang for the theft of horses and mules. On Monday, 10 February 1913, Inspectors Sitter and John Simpson "Jack" Howard, along with brand inspector J.A. Harvick, once again arrested Cano. As they transported him through the rugged mountains of the Pilares Canyon region, Cano's brothers and friends ambushed the lawmen. Howard was killed. Sitter and Harvick were wounded.

On Monday, 24 May 1915, Sitter gathered a posse that included fellow inspector and former Texas Ranger Charles Craighead and Texas Ranger privates Eugene B. Hulen, Harry Trollinger and A.P. Cummings. Sitter was intent on capturing Cano and his gang. When the posse arrived in Pilares Canyon, they could see stolen horses in the canyon. Some of the posseemen believed that the horses were part of an ambush plan by Cano. Others disagreed. Sitter decided to split the posse into two groups and enter the canyon.

Trollinger, Craighead and Cummings started up one side of the canyon but were met by heavy fire and were forced to retreat. They could see Sitter and Hulen pinned down across the canyon and claimed to have made five unsuccessful attempts to reach them. When the firing stopped, they believed that Sitter and Hulen were dead.

The three remaining lawmen walked four miles to a ranch and summoned help. The next day, a posse arrived and found Sitter and Hulen stripped naked and shot scores of times. Their faces had been beaten so badly that they were practically unrecognizable.

Hulen was not married. He had joined the service less than two months earlier. His brother was the former adjutant general of the rangers. Hulen is buried at the Fairview Cemetery in Gainesville, Cooke County.

Chico Cano was indicted for the murder of Sitter and Hulen but was never prosecuted. He became a captain in the Mexican revolutionary army. Cano retired to his ranch in Mexico and died peacefully on 28 August 1943.

Related Case: U.S. Customs Service, Joseph Russell "Joe" Sitter

Burdett (Burdette), Robert Lee
Born June 1881—Died 7 June 1915

Privates Robert Lee Burdett and Charles Beall were members of Company B and were stationed at Fabens, in El Paso County. A group of Mexican men had been drinking and had been warned by the rangers to stop making a disturbance. When the men began shouting once again, Burdett and Beall went into an alley to arrest them. A gun battle quickly erupted during which Burdett was shot just below the throat. The wound proved fatal. Beall returned fire, wounding two of the three men seriously. All three escaped into Mexico. According to newspaper reports, the two wounded assailants were not expected to live.

Captain Fox requested that the Mexican authorities return the killers. They refused. The infamous bandit and, to many, hero of the Mexican Revolution José Doroteo Arango Arámbula, better known as Pancho Villa, controlled the Chihuahua region of Mexico that lay across the border from El Paso. He executed the three killers for crimes they had also committed in Mexico.

Burdett was survived by his mother and at least one sibling. He is buried at the Mount Cavalry Cemetery in Austin in an unmarked grave. His surname has also been reported as Burdette.

Burdett served in Company C from 6 October 1911 to June 1912. He reenlisted in Company B on 1 February 1915.

Goodwin, Oscar W. "Doc"
Born August 1874—Died 10 February 1916

"Doc" Goodwin enlisted as a ranger private on 4 April 1914 and served until 10 February 1916 when he died at an El Paso hospital during an operation. He had served in Company A and later transferred to Company B.

Goodwin had been a druggist at the smelter in 1910 and had previously served as an El Paso County deputy sheriff. He is buried in an unmarked grave at Evergreen Alameda Cemetery in El Paso. Goodwin was not married. His middle initial is reported as "W" and "C" in various documents.

Ransom, Henry Lee
Born 29 December 1870—Died 1 April 1918

Captain Henry L. Ransom was shot and killed while investigating a shooting.

Ransom and ranger private William Koon were in Sweetwater, Nolan County, on business and were staying at a local hotel. Two other hotel guests named Marion Long and W.C. Miller began shouting at each other in the hallway. Shots were fired. Both Ransom and Koon, who were in their nightclothes at the time, stepped into the hallway to investigate. Ransom was shot instantly. Koon returned fire. Long was shot in the right hand and Miller in the left leg, below the knee.

Miller fled the scene in an automobile but was apprehended about twenty-five miles from Sweetwater and was returned. Long was arrested at the scene. Both were jailed and charged with Ransom's killing.

Ransom was survived by his wife, Martha Ella Cole, and two children. He is buried at the Hempstead Cemetery in Waller County.

Ransom was one of the most controversial lawmen in Texas history. He served in the U.S. Army during the Spanish-American War and later served during the Philippines Insurrection. He was a deputy sheriff, city marshal and ranger from 1902 until his death. Ransom was involved in scores of shooting affrays, especially while serving as a ranger during the Bandit Wars along the Mexican border.

Ransom and Jules Baker were retained as special officers in Houston to crack down on rowdy elements. On 25 October 1910, they shot and killed criminal defense attorney J.B. Brockman. Ransom was acquitted of the death and, in 1912, was appointed chief of police. He was later removed; however, he and Baker remained special officers. Not long afterward, the two men assaulted Robert Higgins, a newspaper reporter, whom they believed had written unfavorable articles about them. Ransom and Baker surrendered at the police station. The pair attempted to leave without posting bond. Officer C.E. Horton tried to stop them. Baker shot and wounded Horton in the neck. Baker was acquitted of the shooting. Ransom was convicted of carrying a weapon, but the case was reversed. In spite of all the controversy surrounding his background, Ransom reenlisted as a ranger captain on 29 July 1915.

A *Houston Post* article stated, "Ransom was known as one of the most fearless men in Texas. He was a man who lived by the sword but not to the sense that the law prohibited. And having lived by the sword he also died by the sword. His life was largely one of service to nation, state and community." A *Houston Chronicle* article stated, "The gun fighters all go the same route, sooner or later."

Adjutant General Bill Sterling wrote, "Ransom's early life around the Brazos bottom prison farms and his service in the Philippines had caused him to place a small value on the life of a lawbreaker. Captain Ransom held the belief that he was an instrument of justice, and that he had a definite mission to perform." Sterling quoted Ransom as saying, "A bad disease calls for bitter medicine."

Stillwell, William P. "Will"
Born 24 February 1870—Died 3 April 1918

Private Will Stillwell was shot and killed when he and U.S. customs inspectors confronted smugglers at the Rio Grande River near Santa Helena.

A group of smugglers headed up by Pabalo Dominguez had driven off four horses from a pen near Santa Helena the previous night. A group of Texas Rangers, including Stillwell, under the command of Captain Carroll Bates, crossed the Rio Grande River and made their way into Mexico, where they surrounded Dominguez and his men, who were barricaded in a house. During the shootout that followed, Stillwell, as well as the outlaw Dominguez, was killed.

Stillwell was survived by his wife, Meddie Christiana Bennett, and two children. He is buried in Alpine. Stillwell had enlisted in Company F on 15 February 1918.

Hyde, Thomas Carlyle "Carlie"
Born 26 May 1889—Died 30 April 1918

Carlie Hyde joined Company L of the Texas Rangers on 25 March 1918. He was stationed in Clint, in El Paso County.

Hyde, as well as his wife, two daughters and several other rangers stationed at the Clint camp, contracted amoebic dysentery from a contaminated well that the families used. Hyde and one of his daughters died. His wife and one daughter survived.

Captain W.W. Davis requested that the State of Texas pay for Hyde's funeral expenses. The state agreed to do so. Although life insurance policies were offered as early as 1844, their popularity was still limited. At the time, healthcare, or "sickness," insurance was new, having first been offered in 1890. It was not until the 1920s that any form of widespread coverage was available. Davis and the rangers used their own meager funds to bury Hyde's daughter and send his wife and surviving child back to her family in Kerr County.

Hyde had been a Texas Ranger for slightly over one month at the time of his death. He is buried in Marfa in Presidio County.

White, John Dudley, Sr.
Born 25 June 1879—Died 12 July 1918

Privates John Dudley White and Walter Rowe went to the home of Bose (or Boze) Williams. The Williams residence was located near White City, in San Augustine County. The lawmen intended to arrest two of the Williams boys who were deserters from the U.S. Army.

Once the rangers arrived, they searched the home but were unable to find the two young men. They decided to wait for them to return and took a seat on the porch. At about 2:00 a.m., Rowe heard a noise. Soon after, a shot rang out in the darkness. The first gunshot was quickly followed by another, which hit Rowe in the right thigh. Rowe fell wounded on the porch. White stood and fired, emptying his pistol in the direction from which the gunfire had come. A third shot fired from the darkness hit White in the back, killing him instantly. After the incident, Rowe claimed that he had seen one of the boys, Sam Williams, shooting at White.

Mrs. Williams, the mother of the boys, came out of the house and refused to assist Rowe. She claimed that Rowe had come to kill her boys and that they needed her. Rowe lay on the ground wounded for seven hours before officers arrived and transported him to the hospital at Beaumont.

Samuel M. Williams and Daniel H. Evans were tried and convicted of killing White. They were sentenced to death. Their sentences were later commuted to life in prison.

White came from a family of lawmen. His father served as Travis County sheriff, county judge, Austin mayor and Travis County road commissioner. His three brothers were all Texas Rangers.

White had been a Texas Ranger, off and on, from 1907 to 1913 and had reenlisted in 1916. While not a ranger, he was a Houston policeman and a U.S. mounted customs inspector serving along the Mexican border. White is buried at the Masonic Cemetery in the Oak Hill area of Austin. He was survived by his wife and three children. One of the White children, John Dudley White Jr., also served as a Texas Ranger.

Shaw, Joseph R. "Joe"
Born 10 June 1889—Died 21 August 1918

Private Joe Shaw was shot and killed between eleven and twelve o'clock in the morning on Wednesday, 21 August 1918, along the banks of the Rio Grande River below Fort Brown at a place known as Tomates Bend. The killing occurred when Shaw and his partner, ranger private S.T. Chavez, rode into a party of smugglers.

Shaw had been a ranger for a little over two months. He and Chavez were patrolling Tomates Bend, long notorious as a smuggling point. According to Chavez's account of the story, they saw men slipping through the brush ahead of them. The two rangers separated in order to keep the men from escaping back to the main road or across the Rio Grande River. Apparently, the smugglers saw the officers coming and remained concealed in the brush until the lawmen were within gunshot range; then they opened fire. Shaw was shot through the left breast and the back. Both rangers returned fire. Shaw, who was a novice lawman, was armed with a shotgun but had loaded it with birdshot rather than buckshot. When Shaw was hit, Chavez also fell from the saddle, acting as though he, too, had been killed. Chavez remained still until he was certain that the smugglers had left. He then mounted his horse and rode to Brownsville for assistance. A number of peace officers formed an impromptu posse and headed to the scene.

When the posse arrived at the location of Shaw's body, they discovered a path trampled smooth by the feet of the smugglers. The lawmen spread out and began beating the brush in search of the assailants. In the wall of a house nearby, they discovered a number of high-powered rifles that had been concealed there. Inside the house, officers found Manuel Solis. Solis had a wound to the head that had been recently inflicted. He told the lawmen a rather confusing story of how he had received the injury. Judge Kirk ordered his arrest. Upon searching the riverbank, officers uncovered a quantity of merchandise and three pairs of men's shoes believed to have belonged to members of the smuggling band who had escaped across the Rio Grande.

Ranger captain George W. Stevens, who was in Mercedes at the time of the incident, was notified and returned to Brownsville immediately, arriving at about 2:30 a.m. He filed a murder complaint against Manuel, Francisco and Telesforo Solis and ordered their arrest. The men were kept in Mercedes until the date for an examining trial was set.

It is not known if the Solises (Telifio, Manuel or Francisco) were ever charged with the murder. Two months after the killing of Shaw, ranger sergeant Delbert Timberlake was shot and killed. In a report of the Timberlake death, it is claimed that Encarnacion Delgado was Shaw's murderer. Delgado was killed in the Timberlake incident.

Shaw's body was brought to the Morris undertaking establishment in Brownsville. His remains were sent to his family in Harlingen for interment. Shaw is buried at the Harlingen City Cemetery on F Street. Other sources claim that he is buried at the Old Knoxville Cemetery in Troup, Smith County. Yet another source cites the Knoxville Cemetery in Cherokee County as his final resting place.

Shaw's date of birth is unclear. The 1900 census indicated that he was born in January 1891, which would have made him twenty-seven years old at the time of his death, not twenty-six, as was reported by the newspaper. The Texas Ranger enlistment oath of Joe R. Shaw, dated 5 July 1918, lists his age as twenty-eight years and seven months old, which would have made his date of birth December 1889. Shaw's enlistment oath indicates that he was married, but there is no mention of his wife in any of the newspaper accounts.

Sadler, Leonard Tillman
Born 23 July 1884—Died 16 September 1918
Date of Incident: 15 September 1918

Leonard T. Sadler enlisted in the Texas Rangers on 27 May 1918. Two of his brothers and one cousin served with him in Company G, which was at the time posted in South Texas. Another brother served in 1917.

The Texas-Mexico border was rife with bandits and smugglers. German spies, gathering information for the war effort in Europe, were a concern as well, since the United States had joined that conflict on 6 April 1917. Several rangers and federal customs inspectors had already been killed near Brownsville during the short period of time that Sadler had been a ranger.

Sadler and two other rangers had arrested a man whom they reported as an alleged smuggler. The lawmen claimed that they had released the man. When his body was discovered months later, the rangers were charged with murder.

A grand jury failed to find sufficient information to charge Sadler and the others with any crime. Not long after this incident, Sadler and four other rangers, including his brothers and cousin, were involved in a shootout on the Rio Grande River. Four or five bandits were reported to have been killed.

On Sunday, 15 September 1918, Sadler and a detachment of rangers were assigned to search for smugglers along the Devil's River in Val Verde County. One of the rangers in camp, A.P. Lock, was cleaning his pistol. Sadler had the misfortune of approaching the man from behind just as he test fired the six-gun over his shoulder, without looking to make certain that no one was downrange. The bullet wounded Sadler seriously. Sadler was transported to the hospital in Del Rio, where he died the next day.

Sadler was reported to have been married. His place of burial has not been confirmed, although the funeral was reported to have been held in San Antonio and the burial near Devine, in Frio County.

Timberlake, Delbert "Tim"
Born 12 September 1884—Died 11 October 1918
Date of Incident: 10 October 1918

Sergeant Delbert Timberlake was shot and killed when he and several other lawmen attempted to arrest a well-known smuggler named Incarnacion

Delgado. Delgado was believed to have been responsible for the murder of ranger private Joe Shaw, which had taken place four months earlier.

Rangers, deputies and U.S. customs inspectors had set up an ambush for Delgado on a path along the Rio Grande River near Brownsville. When the officers saw Delgado approaching along the trail, they ordered him to surrender. Delgado immediately spun around and opened fire. One shot hit Timberlake, inflicting a serious wound. The other lawmen returned fire, hitting Delgado five times. His wounds were fatal. Timberlake was rushed to a hospital in Brownsville, where he died the following morning.

Timberlake had served in law enforcement for six years. During that time, he had been a deputy sheriff for Galveston County, city marshal of Del Rio, policeman in Laredo and a ranger for Company A, Company F and Company I. He was assigned to Company I at the time of his murder.

Timberlake was survived by his father. He is buried at Uvalde.

Pennington, Benjamin L. "Ben"
Born May 1861—Died 12 October 1918
Date of Incident: 7 October 1918

Ben Pennington had been a lawman for twenty years. He had served twelve years as city marshal of Holland in Bell County and eight years as an elected Precinct 3 Bell County constable.

On 4 October 1917, Pennington enlisted as a Texas Ranger private in Company L and was posted in Brewster County in far West Texas. When the Spanish influenza epidemic killed millions throughout the world, officials in El Paso requested assistance from the Texas Rangers. Pennington was dispatched to keep order. He contracted influenza. Pennington became ill on 7 October and died on Sunday, 12 October 1918.

Pennington was a well-known officer and over his career had been shot sixteen times. He had lost one eye in a gun battle. Pennington was survived by his wife. He is buried at the Jackson Cemetery in Bell County, but his grave site has not been located.

Hunt, Robert Ernest
Born 1 May 1882—Died 15 October 1918

When the outbreak of Spanish influenza hit El Paso, Private Robert E. Hunt was dispatched to help maintain order. He contracted influenza.

Hunt became ill sometime in early October. He died on Tuesday, 15 October 1918.

Hunt had enlisted as a ranger in Company B on 8 June 1915 and served until 11 April 1916, when he resigned. He reenlisted in Company L on 20 August 1918 and served until his death. Hunt was not married. His body was shipped to Denver, Colorado, for burial.

Perkins, T.E. Paul "Ellzey"
Born 12 March 1884—Died 7 November 1918

"Ellzey" Perkins joined Company L of the Texas Rangers on 1 September 1918. Company L was stationed in El Paso County. Perkins's brother, James Clarke Perkins, had joined the rangers on 25 August 1917 and was the company sergeant. The rangers were investigating a man named Ben Anaya, who was a rancher on the island in the Rio Grande River near Fabens in El Paso County. They believed that Anaya was a supporter of Pancho Villa and was assisting the *Villistas* in getting arms and ammunition across the border into Mexico. The island is on the international border.

On Thursday night, 7 November 1918, ranger private Ellzey Perkins and special ranger Joe T. Place, a farmer from Fabens, left the ranger camp in Clint and drove to within a mile of the Anaya Ranch. It is thought that they wanted to see if there was any suspicious activity taking place.

Place later claimed that their vehicle had run out of water and that they were in the process of repairing a hose when they were ambushed. Place's report indicated that Perkins spotted riflemen in the brush and called to Place to take cover. The sniper opened fire. Ben Anaya approached the car with his pistol drawn, but Perkins fired first and killed him with three bullets to the chest. Almost immediately, Perkins was hit in the stomach by a gunshot. With nothing more than his pistol and two remaining cartridges, Perkins wandered off into the darkness.

Place was captured, put on a horse and rode back to Fabens for assistance. He arrived at about 8:30 p.m. A posse found Perkins the following day near the Anaya Ranch. He had been clubbed to death, and his body had been mutilated.

Anaya's father was reported to have tracked Perkins and beaten him to death. The elder Anaya fled to Mexico. Captain Will W. Davis offered Mexican river guards a $100 reward for his capture and return. The reward was never claimed, and Anaya was never captured.

Perkins was buried at the North Elm Cemetery in Milam County. He was not married. Perkins was survived by his parents and three siblings. He had been a Texas Ranger for slightly over two months when he was killed.

Hall, Bryant M.
Born 1 January 1860—Died 11 December 1918

Former ranger Bryant Hall was shot and killed in front of the courthouse in San Antonio. He had just appeared before a grand jury. Brothers Charles and Anson Hazlewood of Mineral Wells were arrested shortly after the shooting. Both men had semiautomatic pistols in their possession that had been fired several times.

The *Fort Worth Star Telegram* reported that there was trouble between Hall and the Hazlewood brothers over a note for $1,500 that had been given by Hall to another brother of the Hazlewoods' concerning the sale of some oil land. The Hazlewood brothers pleaded self-defense, contending that Hall had threatened to kill them. The final disposition of any charges is unknown.

Hall is buried at the Mission Burial Park in San Antonio. He was reported to be divorced. Newspapers claimed that Hall was a former ranger captain and a cousin of famed ranger captain Lee Hall; however, no evidence of his service has been located.

Moran, John August
Born 22 January 1886—Died 12 December 1918

John A. Moran died of influenza. Newspaper accounts of his death indicate that he had contracted the flu while on duty in Falfurrias in Brooks County and returned home, where he developed pneumonia and died.

Moran had enlisted in Company A of the Texas Rangers on 1 November 1918. He was assigned to the ranger camp in Alice in Jim Wells County.

Moran was not married. He is buried at the Crosby Cemetery in Mason County. Moran was survived by his father and siblings.

Veale, Bertram Clinton "Bert"
Born 13 September 1889—Died 7 February 1919

Private Bert Veale was shot and killed by ranger captain K.F. Cunningham. The shooting affray took place near Austin and had grown out of a personal disagreement between the two men, both of whom had been drinking. Veale managed to nick Cunningham in the neck during the shootout.

Lucky for Cunningham, his wallet stopped another bullet that would have penetrated his stomach. Afterward, Cunningham claimed that Veale had fired at him three times with a .45-caliber revolver before he returned fire. Cunningham used a .45-caliber semiautomatic pistol. Sergeant Walter Mayberry and Captain Harry M. Johnson, the ranger quartermaster, were with Cunningham and Veale when the incident took place.

This incident occurred while the Texas legislature was holding public hearings regarding improper ranger activities. The adjutant general reported that he refused to pay for Veale's casket and that Cunningham, Mayberry and Johnson were dismissed. Cunningham was charged with murder but was no billed by the Travis County grand jury. Mayberry was quietly reinstated on 25 November 1919.

Veale had enlisted in Company D on 31 July 1915 and resigned at some later date. He was a deputy sheriff in Harris County in 1917. Veale reenlisted in Company D on 24 October 1918. Cunningham had enlisted as a captain in Company M on 10 December 1917.

Veale was from Caldwell County and is buried in Houston. He was a convict guard prior to his enlistment. Veale was not married.

Alsobrook, William M. "Will"
Born 23 August 1883—Died 9 December 1919
Date of Incident: 8 December 1919

Private Will Alsobrook was a loyalty ranger from June 1918 until February 1919. During World War I, the loyalty rangers served as volunteers to seek out disloyal citizens. On 16 June 1919, Alsobrook enlisted in Company D of the regular rangers.

On Monday, 8 December 1919, Alsobrook was traveling by train in South Texas when he was accidentally shot and wounded. The unidentified shooter used a .45-caliber revolver. The incident took place near the tiny hamlet of Crestonia, in Duval County. Alsobrook was taken by a special train to Laredo, where he died at Mercy Hospital the following day.

Alsobrook was a popular lawman. He was the elected constable of Precinct 1 in Red River County from 1913 to 1917. The people of Hebbronville were said to be desirous of electing him to the post of sheriff of Jim Hogg County at the next election. He is buried at the Clarksville Cemetery in Red River County. Alsobrook was not married.

Buchanan, Joseph Benjamin "Joe"
Born 1 May 1890—Died 26 December 1921
Date of Incident: 25 December 1921

Joe Buchanan was appointed a special ranger in December 1917. His appointment covered an unspecified period of time. On 1 March 1921, Buchanan was appointed a regular ranger in Company A and was stationed in Presidio County.

At about midnight on Sunday, 25 December 1921, Buchanan was at a Mexican dance in the mining town of Polvo. Two strange men entered the ball. Buchanan approached the pair and asked for their identification. Rather than pulling out their papers, the duo drew pistols. Buchanan was shot in the right shoulder, rendering him unable to use his gun hand. The men shot Buchanan nine more times, killing him instantly. The unidentified murderers fled to Mexico and were never captured.

Buchanan is buried at the Marfa Cemetery in Presidio County. He was survived by his wife, Lucille Nord.

Majors, Norman Jacob "Jake"
Born 13 August 1901—Died 21 July 1922

Special ranger Jake Majors was discharged from the ranger service on Thursday, 20 July 1922. The following day, Majors and deputy U.S. marshal Walter H. Hill were on the Cotton Belt passenger train near Mount Pleasant in Titus County when Majors objected to Hill taking a suitcase from a man. Majors ejected Hill from the train twice, and after the second time, he shot Hill in the leg. Hill followed Majors back onto the train and shot him three times, killing him instantly.

Majors had been dismissed from the ranger force after being found asleep at the Cotton Belt roundhouse and ordered to surrender his commission; he failed to do so. During this period, special rangers were commissioned by the state and the salaries paid by companies like the railroads.

Majors is buried at the Mount Vernon Cemetery in Franklin County. He was not married. Majors was survived by his parents and two siblings.

Sherman, S.F.
Born January 1871—Died 7 November 1922

Special ranger private S.F. Sherman was struck by an International–Great Northern Railroad switch engine and killed almost instantly. Sherman's body was cut in two by the locomotive. The incident took place while he was on duty at the rail yards in Palestine in Anderson County. Ranger W. Rutledge, who was with Sherman at the time, said that he had become confused by the lights and accidentally stepped off one switch track onto another and into the path of the train.

Sherman had enlisted as a private on 5 September 1922 in the special ranger force (railroad rangers) under Captain Jerry Gray of Company A.

Sherman was survived by his wife. He is buried at Greenwood, Louisiana. Sherman was a rancher at Winona in Smith County.

Watson, James Aaron "Dick"
Born 28 August 1895—Died 21 February 1924

Governor Pat Neff had made Prohibition a top priority and wanted the Texas Rangers to decrease the number of liquor stills operating in the state. Neff ordered that Dick Watson, an undercover agent, be sent to Somervell County to work toward that end.

Watson was acting as a special Prohibition enforcement officer under the direction of Texas Rangers. By August 1923, he had enough evidence to proceed with arrests. Rangers organized a posse of area lawmen and made a series of raids, destroying twenty-three stills and arresting fifty men. One moonshiner was killed in a shootout.

Rangers organized another undercover operation in the Corsicana oil fields of Navarro County in an effort to shut down vice dens located there. Watson acted as the undercover officer. In February 1924, lawmen arrested scores of gamblers and bootleggers. The trial of the county attorney in Somervell County started in February 1924, and Watson was the state's principal witness.

During the proceedings, Rangers Marvin "Red" Burton and R.D. Shumate were staying with Watson at a Cleburne hotel. After giving his testimony, the rangers decided to take Watson to a Glen Rose boardinghouse for his safety. While in Cleburne, Watson went to visit a friend nearby. Burton was talking to a man in the town square and heard a shotgun blast. He found Watson lying dead on the floor of the hotel. Two assailants had fired a shotgun through the closed window. The blast struck Watson in the face and neck, killing him instantly.

Fifteen or more people were arrested. Six men were charged with the murder of Watson. No one was ever indicted. Although later disputed by local officials, Burton's personal notes indicate that Watson had started to work as a plainclothes detective for the Corsicana Police Department about two weeks before his death.

Watson is buried at the Marystown Cemetery in Johnson County. He was survived by his wife, Linnie Ida Sparkman, and one son.

Willard, Timothy Samuel "Tim"
Born 10 October 1895—Died 19 April 1928

Special ranger Tim Willard was shot and killed while he was raiding an illegal moonshine still.

Willard had been commissioned by the state governor as a special ranger to assist with Prohibition enforcement. While in the process of conducting a raid, he was shot and fatally wounded. Willard was able to identify his killer, W.J. Fagan, before he died. The seventy-year-old Fagan was sentenced to ninety-nine years in prison.

Willard had been with the agency for one year. He was survived by his father and several siblings. Willard is buried at the Lakes Chapel Cemetery in Fairfield.

McDuffie, Dan Lafayette
Born 16 February 1881—Died 7 July 1931

Private Dan McDuffie was shot and killed by a man named Jeff Johnson. Johnson was a veteran member of the Gladewater police force who had been dismissed recently.

McDuffie was at the Gladewater police station when a report came in of a man with a rifle who was threatening to kill the chief of police, J.A. Dial. McDuffie knew Johnson and volunteered to negotiate with him. When McDuffie arrived at the scene where Johnson had been indiscriminately shooting, friends of Johnson had gathered around him and were trying to convince him to put down the gun and go home.

Seeing the police car full of officers pull up, Johnson, from the darkened doorway in which he was standing, announced, "Stand back everybody, I am going to shoot." He then trained his rifle on the police car and fired one shot. Johnson's bullet hit the steering wheel, ricocheted off McDuffie's wristwatch and hit him in the leg, severing an artery. Dial returned fire, hitting Johnson with seven bullets fired from close range. Johnson died instantly.

McDuffie was survived by his wife, Willie Lemuel McCright, and one child. He had been with the agency for thirty years. McDuffie is buried at the Reed Cemetery in New Boston.

Turner, Henry Ross, Jr.
Born 17 January 1881—Died 11 July 1933

On Friday, 16 June 16 1933, Miss Elizabeth Hammond of Kosse and her fiancé, Mr. Erwin Conway of Bryan, both students at Baylor University in Waco, were driving to the home of Conway's parents to announce their engagement. The couple was allegedly held up by two men and a woman about five miles from Bryan. Conway reported that one of the men shot Miss Hammond through the heart. After robbing Conway of his watch, the assailants then shot Conway, inflicting a wound in his shoulder. The trio fled in a light-colored automobile. Conway said that he drove on to Bryan, where Miss Hammond was declared dead.

Miss Hammond was the niece of Captain E.H. Hammond of Texas Ranger Company C. Captain Hammond assigned Privates H.R. "Luck" Turner and Slim Taylor to the case. Several men and women were arrested and investigated for the murder. While in Kosse investigating the case on Tuesday, 11 July 1933, Private Turner suffered a stroke of apoplexy. On 22 August 1933, Texas Rangers exhumed the body of Miss Hammond and, based on the evidence the discovered, arrested Erwin Conway and charged him with her murder.

Turner was survived by his wife. He is buried in Tyler. Turner was elected sheriff of Smith County on 3 November 1914, reelected 7 November 1916 and served until 5 November 1918. He was appointed a regular ranger on 19 January 1933 and served five months.

White, Emmett (Emmet)
Born 16 August 1896—Died 8 August 1933

Private Emmett White was killed when he was struck by an oil truck on the Kilgore–Henderson highway in Rusk County.

White and two Rusk County deputies had been conducting an investigation and were returning to Henderson when they stopped to speak with two men sitting in a car on the side of the highway. As the officers and men were standing outside the vehicles, an oil truck came over a hill and hit White and one of the citizens, killing both of them.

White had been appointed a Texas Ranger in Company C on 19 January 1933. He was survived by his wife and four children. White is buried at the Oakwood Cemetery in Travis County. White was the last regular Texas Ranger (paid by the state) to die in the line of duty prior to the merger of the Texas Rangers into the Texas Department of Public Safety in 1935.

Franklin, Robert Lee
Born 26 May 1886—Died 9 September 1933
Date of Incident: 5 September 1933

Special ranger Robert Lee Franklin was responding to a call involving a woman who had been assaulted in Conroe in Montgomery County when his automobile left the roadway and collided with a telephone pole. Franklin was taken to the hospital with a broken leg, broken ribs and other injuries. Although he was reported to be doing well, he died suddenly four days later, on Saturday, 9 September 1933.

Franklin had been appointed a special ranger on 15 March 1933 and had served almost five months. He had previously been an officer in Nacogdoches County, a constable in Trinity County and a city policeman in Conroe. Franklin was survived by his wife, Safronie Azelea Burks, and four children. He is buried at the Alazan Cemetery in Nacogdoches County. Although Franklin was a special Texas Ranger (unpaid by the state), he did die in the line of duty prior to the merger of the Texas Rangers into the Texas Department of Public Safety in 1935.

3
State Agencies

TEXAS DEPARTMENT OF CRIMINAL JUSTICE

Unknown Guard
Born (Unknown)—Died 8 September 1900

An unknown guard lost his life during the hurricane that hit Galveston in September 1900. Over a century later, there are still over 180 unidentified victims of this epic disaster.

One of the deadliest hurricanes in U.S. history hit Galveston on Saturday, 8 September 1900. Over six thousand souls lost their lives before the storm subsided. The storm caused so much destruction along the Texas coast that reliable estimates of the number of victims are difficult to make. Some believe that as many as twelve thousand people may have perished, which would make it the most deadly day in American history.

Galveston Island lies just off the Texas coast. It is a long and narrow body of land about twenty-eight miles in length and two miles in width. The landmass is barely above sea level. As a major hub for trade, thousands of people settled on the island at the end of the nineteenth century.

It was Friday afternoon, 7 September 1900, before residents of Galveston had any indication that a storm, which had been bearing down on Texas for several days, was approaching. The Category 4 hurricane hit Galveston with sustained winds of at least 115 miles per hour. The town's wind gauge blew away; thus, an accurate determination of the maximum wind speed is not known. By 3:00 p.m., water had covered nearly the entire island, sweeping across the narrow landmass with tides fifteen feet higher than normal. Buildings crumbled and fell from the force of the water, and the high winds ripped the roofs off nearly every building in town.

Cupstead, D.M.
Born (Unknown)—Died 12 February 1905

Guard D.M. Cupstead was involved in a fight of some sort with fellow guard Archie Holt. The convict guards were traveling on the Trinity and Brazos Valley Railroad, a state convict train, near Hubbard in Hill County. Holt and Cupstead were joking with each other in the camp car and got into a bout of fisticuffs. During the fight, guard C.C. Holt, Archie's brother, shot and killed Cupstead.

C.C. Holt surrendered to authorities and was booked in the county jail. Archie was also arrested. An examining trial was set, but the final disposition of the case is unknown.

Cupstead's place of burial is unknown. No personal information has been found on Cupstead.

Wilkerson, Joseph Faulkner "Joe"
Born 12 March 1852—Died 23 April 1906

The Texas Prison System operated a railroad between an iron ore deposit and a smelter furnace that was located at the prison in Rusk in Cherokee County.

At about 6:30 a.m. on Monday, 23 April 1906, the train left the prison with 24 guards and 149 convicts. Shortly after leaving the penitentiary, one of the convicts uncoupled the two rear cars. The detached railcars began to quickly drop behind the rest of the train. The engineer was ordered to stop the locomotive. When he did so, two convicts jumped from a railcar and ran toward the woods.

Fifteen or twenty guards opened fire at the escaping prisoners. When the smoke cleared, the guards discovered that Wilkerson had been killed, and another officer, Will Lloyd, was slightly wounded by the barrage of bullets. Both had been victims of friendly fire. One convict was killed, and one was wounded.

Justice T.H. Findley conducted an inquest. The findings revealed that while trying to prevent the escape of a state convict, Wilkerson had come to his death from a pistol shot wound that was inflicted by a prison guard named Jim Bell. The findings further confirmed that Wilkerson's killing was accidental. Bell, however, was discharged by the prison system.

Wilkerson was survived by his wife, Lizzie May Jernigan, and four small children. He is buried at the Cedar Hill Cemetery in Rusk.

Millican, Wilbur Ashby "Will"
Born 25 September 1858—Died 15 November 1906

Wilbur Ashby "Will" Millican, who by some accounts had reportedly killed several men, was a guard at the convict farm in Brazos. Millican had also served as a Texas Ranger, having enlisted in Company B in Alice, Texas, on 21 July 1905. After leaving the Texas Rangers, Millican remained in Alice until the spring of 1906. He then returned to Brazos County.

On Thursday, 15 November 1906, Millican was shot and killed by fellow guard Sergeant Henry S. South. Millican's killing is believed by most to have been a continuation of the long-standing feud involving the Millican family.

Will's brother, Brazos County Precinct 1 constable Marcellus Randall "Pet" Milligan, was assassinated on Saturday, 14 December 1889, by Charles (Charlie) Campbell. Zeke and Poker Curd, brothers, enticed Campbell to kill Millican. The jury acquitted the Curd brothers even though Campbell testified against them. No reason was determined as to why the Curds wanted to kill Millican.

Millican had told the Curd brothers to leave the Millican community or he would kill them both. Acting against Millican's advice, Zeke Curd returned. As promised, Millican killed him in June 1890.

Millican was not married. He is buried at the Weaver Cemetery in Millican. All but three of his eleven siblings preceded him in death.

Wilbur Millican's father, Elliot McNeal Millican, had eight sons. Robert died while still in his teens. Jasper died of yellow fever in 1867. Of the remaining six sons, five were killed while serving as Texas lawmen. The only one to survive was Leander Randon "L.R." Millican, who initially followed the path of so many of his family members when he pinned on a lawman's badge and became a Lampasas County deputy sheriff. He left law enforcement and became a Baptist circuit rider. L.R., who had become a lifelong friend of Bill Wren and Pink Higgins, died in 1938, outliving all his siblings.

Sims, W.P.
Born (Unknown)—Died 24 December 1907

Sims was a convict guard on duty at the lignite mines in Hoyt, located about a half mile from Alba, in Rains County. Between 8:00 and 8:30 a.m. on Tuesday, 24 December 1907, Sims was smoking a cigarette too close to a powder keg while he was in the process of making a cartridge for use in the mine. The convicts were not allowed to handle powder except in small quantities. Any larger amounts were handled by the guards. Sims was found terribly mangled. It was reported he could not recover.

Sims was reported to have had a brother, R.F. Sims, living in Dallas. No other information is known about him.

McKnight, G.W.
Born (Unknown)—Died 13 May 1908

Guard G.W. McKnight was hit by lightning while supervising a prisoner on the Burleson and Johns convict farm. The farm is situated in the west side of Hill County, four miles from Kopperl in Bosque County. Both McKnight and the prisoner were killed in the incident.

Nothing further is known about McKnight or this unfortunate incident.

Elliot, James
Born circa 1878—Died 17 July 1908

On Friday, 17 July 1908, convicts at the Dewalt Farm in Fort Bend County and the Clemens Unit in Brazoria County carried out a concerted escape plan. A gang of ten to twelve convicts at the Clemens Unit attacked guard James Elliot, took his gun away from him and beat him with a garden hoe. Next, Elliot's attackers, Will Howard, Will Westphal, Austin St. Louis and Will Dow, kidnapped a man named George Johnson. Fearing he would give information that would lead to their capture, they shot and killed him. Austin St. Louis, who was at the time about twenty-two years old, is credited with killing both Elliot and Johnson.

On Saturday, 25 July 1908, the badly decomposed body of Austin St. Louis was found near Hinkle's Ferry in Brazoria County, not far from the prison. An inquest determined that he died from gunshot wounds received during the escape. When St. Louis was found, he was wearing a suit taken from Johnson. He also had a handkerchief containing four dollars that had belonged to Johnson and twenty-six dollars that he had taken from Elliot.

Elliot is buried at the Cheetham Cemetery in Colorado County. His surname was reported as "Elliott" by all the newspaper accounts of the day. However, it is spelled "Elliot" on his tombstone and in the State of Texas death records.

Wylie, John L.
Born circa 1870—Died 22 April 1909

John Wylie was a prison guard at the Steiner Valley state convict farm in Hill County. At about 9:00 p.m. on Thursday, 22 April 1909, Wylie and two other guards were attempting to locate an escaping convict named Joe Yates. Wylie was riding a mule along the Texas Central Railroad right of way near Fowler when the animal stumbled and fell. Wylie was killed instantly when his shotgun discharged accidentally. The load of shot hit him in the stomach. One of the other guards hurried to the nearest residence for assistance. By the time he returned with help, Wylie was already dead.

Wylie was survived by his wife, Mary. His place of burial is unknown.

Claiborne, Charles E.
Born circa 1893—Died 9 August 1915

Guard Charles Claiborne and a convict named Frank Dale were struck by lightning and killed while at work in a cotton field at the state prison farm in Sugar Land in Fort Bend County. Apparently, the bolt of lightning traveled along the ground, since the guard and Dale were twenty feet apart when they were hit. Claiborne was in charge of a squad of twenty-three men at the time of the incident.

Claiborne is buried at the Harriman Farm in Fort Bend County.

Vandorn, Walter Isaac
Born 18 February 1887—Died 12 August 1916

Sergeant Walter Vandorn was stabbed and killed while counting prisoners at the lunch break prior to their return to work. Vandorn had his back turned when a convict, armed with an improvised knife, rushed forward and plunged the weapon into his chest. The mortally wounded Vandorn was able to take a few steps backward, draw his pistol and kill his assailant. After shooting the knife-wielding killer, Vandorn dropped to the floor and died.

Vandorn was not married. His place of burial has not been located.

The Clemens State Farm, located in Brazoria County, was established in 1883 as a part of the Texas State Penitentiary System. It is still an active prison unit today and is a part of the Texas Department of Criminal Justice.

Massey, G.W.
Born 28 December 1874—Died 5 May 1918
Date of Incident: 1 May 1918

Guard Massey was shot by a fellow guard named Sam McMichael.

On Wednesday, 1 May 1918, Massey and McMichael got into a heated debate at the convict camp about two miles north of Arlington in Tarrant County. McMichael was arrested and charged with assault to murder and released on a $750 bond. Massey died at the hospital on Sunday, 5 May, at 11:00 p.m. McMichael was rearrested and charged with murder but later released on a $1,000 bond. He alleged that Massey started toward him with a pistol in one hand and a shotgun in the other. McMichael contended that he shot Massey in the abdomen in self-defense. The disposition of the case is unknown.

Massey is buried at the Mount Olivet Cemetery in Fort Worth. He was a widower.

Oliver, Dewitt Frisby
Born 23 December 1877—Died 17 September 1921
Date of Incident: 1 September 1921

At twelve noon on Thursday, 1 September 1921, Assistant Warden Dewitt F. Oliver was working at the Walls Unit in Huntsville, Walker County. He was standing on the east wall when convicts Maximo Vega and Ernest Conner approached him from behind. The men were armed with knives and slashed Oliver's throat. They next bound his hands and used him as a shield, threatening to kill him if any of the guards fired at them.

Vega and Conner seized the picket guard's guns and then pushed Oliver off the wall and escaped through the railway gate. Oliver fractured his left leg and suffered internal injuries. Early reports indicated that he was recovering rapidly; however, he died from his injuries on Saturday, 17 September 1921, at the local hospital.

Vega and Conner were chased by bloodhounds. They stole a horse and later boarded a train. Both were captured on 3 September 1921 while onboard a train as it arrived in Houston. The pair was returned to the prison.

On 12 September 1921, Vega allegedly tried to escape from a prison work gang and was shot and killed. The justice of the peace held an inquest and determined that the killing was justified. Vega was from El Paso and considered one of the most dangerous prisoners in the system. Conner was serving two years for burglary and was reportedly charged with the murder. The disposition of the case against him is unknown.

Oliver was survived by his father and two siblings. His body was shipped to Henderson for burial, but the actual cemetery is not known.

Lott, Early Alabama
Born 2 December 1867—Died 25 March 1926

Guard Early A. Lott was in charge of a squad of convicts at the Ramsey State Farm near Angleton in Brazoria County who were shocking and shelling corn. Convict Colley Underwood, who had been in prison for just two months of his two-year sentence, overpowered Lott and took his pistol. Underwood shot Lott twice. He died instantly. Underwood then took Lott's horse and fled.

Underwood was soon captured and confessed to the crime. He was sentenced to death for the murder of Lott. On appeal, the case was reversed and sent back to the lower court. Underwood received a ninety-nine-year prison sentence.

Lott is buried at the Holland Cemetery in Bell County. He was survived by his wife, Mary Atlas Armstrong, and three children.

Rader, William M. "Will"
Born May 1871—Died 22 July 1926

Guard Will Rader was shot and killed during a prison break at the Ferguson State Farm in Madison County.

Several men who had previously escaped from the farm drove up to the cell building in an automobile a short time after midnight. They entered the building and shot Rader with a shotgun, killing him.

Other guards immediately responded and exchanged shots with the fugitives. The two shooters, along with six inmates, were able to flee the prison farm and escape.

One of the escaped convicts was eventually recaptured when he participated in another prison escape on 27 July 1928. During that incident, dog sergeant Joseph Henry Ward was shot and killed, and Fort Bend County deputies Frank Bell and Tom Davis were wounded.

The twice-widowed Rader was survived by his nine children, four from a previous marriage. He is buried at the Midway Cemetery in Midway.

Related Case: Texas Department of Criminal Justice, Joseph Henry Ward

Wells, Thomas J.
Born 22 June 1866—Died 30 September 1926

Guard Thomas Wells was shot and killed at the Blue Ridge convict camp in Fort Bend County.

Fellow guard Forest Gaither Jr. and Wells got involved in an argument. Gaither cursed Wells. Wells went to the guard tower, retrieved his shotgun and then returned to the scene making threats to kill Gaither. Gaither attempted to avoid trouble, but Wells approached him in the dark with his gun raised. Gaither alleged that he shot Wells in self-defense. Wells's shotgun was found at the scene loaded with buckshot and the hammer cocked.

Gaither was tried, convicted and sentenced to forty years in prison. The case was reversed and remanded on appeal.

Wells is buried at the Harmony Cemetery in Walker County. He was a widower.

Long, Deb Edward
Born 26 February 1901—Died 2 February 1928

At about 1:00 a.m. on Thursday, 2 February 1928, sixteen convicts at the Eastham State Prison in Lovelady escaped by cutting through a wall of the wooden building in which they were locked up for the night. Their only tool was a pocketknife. During the escape, guard Deb Long was accidentally shot and killed by guard Tom Bozeman. Bozeman mistook Long for one of the convicts. The guards were in the woods at the time and were surrounded by escapees. Long was wearing white trousers similar to those issued to prisoners, further adding to the confusion.

By 4:00 p.m., all sixteen prisoners had been captured and returned to their cells.

Long is buried at the Salem Cemetery in Weldon. He was not married and was survived by his father.

Ward, Joseph Henry
Born 14 October 1897—Died 27 July 1928

Sergeant Henry Ward was shot and killed during an escape at the Imperial State Farm Number 2 near Sugar Land in Fort Bend County.

Several prisoners had attacked another guard and disarmed him of his pistol and shotgun. As the weaponless guard retreated on horseback, the convicts began firing at him. Hearing the shooting, Ward immediately went to his fellow guard's aid. When he did so, he was hit by a shotgun blast and fell from his horse. The already injured Ward was then shot through the throat with a pistol by one of the heartless escapees. He died within minutes.

A total of eight inmates had escaped from the farm that day. All were eventually apprehended by a posse. Seven of them were charged with involvement in Ward's murder and of wounding two deputies who were posse members. Ultimately, Raymond Hall and R.R. Carter were convicted. Both were sentenced to life in prison.

One of the inmates who had participated in this escape, a man named Alvin Ireland, was involved in another breakout attempt on 22 July 1926. During that incident, guard William Rader was shot and killed.

Ward was survived by his parents, four siblings and one son. His wife preceded him in death. Ward is buried at the McAdams Cemetery in Crabbs Prairie, Walker County.

Related Case: Texas Department of Criminal Justice, William M. "Will" Rader

Syms, Sidney Albert
Born 30 December 1876—Died 29 September 1928

Sydney Syms was a convict guard at the Retrieve State Prison Farm in Brazoria County. Lee Davis and Willie Davis were convicts there. Lee Davis was serving a sentence of ninety-nine years, and Willie Davis was serving twenty-five years. Both convictions were for robbery with firearms.

Lee and Willie Davis were part of a squad of ten convicts under the supervision of Syms. The pair made a plan to accomplish their escape. Syms was armed with a pistol that he carried in a holster and a shotgun that he carried in his hand. According to Lee Davis, their plan was to go for a drink of water and, as they passed Syms, Lee Davis was to grab him.

According to his testimony, Lee Davis grabbed Syms, who was sitting on a block with a shotgun in his lap. Lee Davis grabbed the shotgun from the left side of Syms. Simultaneously, Willie Davis attacked Syms from the right and grabbed his pistol. Willie Davis fired two shots at Syms, one of which proved fatal. Both Lee and Willie Davis fled but were captured the next day.

Both were charged in the murder of Syms. Lee Davis was convicted on 11 July 1929. He was sentenced to be executed. That sentence was carried out on 22 August 1930, when Lee Davis was executed by electrocution at the state prison in Huntsville. He was the sixty-first person to be electrocuted in Texas.

As fate would have it, Willie Davis was too sick to be tried. He died of tuberculosis on 15 July 1929 at the age of nineteen.

Syms was survived by his wife, Rena. He had one child from his first marriage and seven children from his second marriage. He is buried at the Peach Creek Cemetery in Brazos County.

There is considerable confusion regarding Syms's surname and given name. There is no death certificate on file for Syms. World War I draft registration has his name as "Sidney Albert Syms." The genealogy records have Sims, Symns, Symms and Syms—all from the same family. Cemetery records are Sidney A. Symns, but his parents are buried with the surname Syms. The 1880 census taker recorded his name as Sydney Syms. The Texas Court of Appeals record indicates his name as Sidney Symms. The death warrant for Lee Davis lists the deceased as Sydney Sims. The most consistent and probably most accurate spelling is Sidney Albert Syms.

Holmes, Wood Eli "Ely"
Born 22 September 1879—Died 9 December 1928

Sam Stapleton and his sons Henry, Dodd and Ab, along with a man named Roma Duke, got into an altercation at a sporting house with W.E. "Ely" Holmes and his friends. Holmes was a state prison guard at the Ramsey Prison Farm in Brazoria County. The parties separated, but Stapleton and his group lay in wait for Holmes. Several hours later, Holmes and some fellow guards were walking to the state prison when they saw an automobile stuck in the mud. When they went to investigate, Stapleton fired a shotgun at Holmes and killed him.

Stapleton argued self-defense, claiming Holmes had hit him with a pistol during the altercation and that he thought Holmes was reaching for his gun when he shot him. State witnesses testified that Holmes had struck Stapleton and Duke with his fist, and Holmes was unarmed when he was killed.

Stapleton was tried and convicted of the killing of Holmes. He was sentenced to serve thirty years in prison. Roma Duke was convicted and sentenced to ten years in prison, but the case was reversed and remanded.

Holmes is buried at the Lockhart Municipal Burial Park in Caldwell County.

Starnes, Tommy Mellie
Born 30 September 1906—Died 11 June 1931

Corrections officer Tommy Starnes served at the Ferguson State Prison Farm near Midway in Madison County. He was on duty at the state ferry crossing of the Trinity River between the prisons in Eastham and Ferguson. Starnes went into the ferryman's shack and placed his shotgun on the table. The weapon fell from the table and discharged accidentally. Fifteen pellets of shot hit Starnes, passing through his body. He died before aid could arrive from camp headquarters.

Starnes was survived by his parents and six siblings. He is buried at the Harmony Cemetery in Huntsville, Walker County.

Sneed, James Bostic "Jim"
Born 4 March 1892—Died 6 July 1931

Guard James Sneed was shot and killed by two prisoners using smuggled handguns during an escape attempt from the Retrieve Prison Farm (modern-day Wayne Scott Unit) in Brazoria County.

The two inmates, Jack Perry and Jim Rye (alias Merriman), were being punished for wrongdoing. Sneed was on guard duty at the west end of the main building at the prison facility. At about 10:15 p.m. on Monday, 6 July 1931, Perry and Rye came up behind him and demanded, "Put up your hands." The two men, who were brandishing pistols, demanded that Sneed hand over his keys. When Sneed began to reach for his gun rather than his keys, they opened fire on him. Sneed was hit by four bullets, two from each gun. He was killed instantly. One newspaper reported that only three shots had been fired.

After the incident, Rye and Perry surrendered, after being told that if they did not give up, "we will shoot you out." The pair was taken into custody. Afterward, the officers discovered a .45-caliber army semiautomatic pistol and a .32-caliber revolver in the men's possession. Rye Merriman was sentenced to life in prison for the murder of Sneed on 25 July 1931. Perry was to be tried a few weeks later, but this disposition is unknown.

Sneed was survived by his mother and one sibling. He is buried at the Sweeney Cemetery in Brazoria County. Family genealogists show Sneed's date of death as 5 July 1931.

Hinson, John Robert
Born 8 February 1871—Died 3 November 1932
Date of Incident: 15 October 1932

John R. Hinson was employed as a convict guard at the Eastham State Prison Farm, which is located thirteen miles west of Trinity in Houston County. On Saturday, 15 October 1932, Hinson was struck in the head with a pitchfork and knocked from his horse by three convicts: H.G. Daniels, Buchanan Sloan and Charley "Chuck" Wilson. His shotgun and pistol were taken. Once on the ground, the convicts beat Hinson viciously with the handle of the pitchfork. The threesome made a dash for freedom.

The remainder of the work detail carried Hinson to the hospital. A posse with bloodhounds cornered Wilson at about 8:00 p.m. Believed to be armed with the weapons he had taken from Hinson, when he refused to surrender, he was shot to death by guards. The posse caught Sloan and Daniels near Madisonville the following day, but only after an all-night pursuit. Hinson's pistol and shotgun was recovered from the two convicts.

At the time of the incident, Charley "Chuck" Wilson was serving a twenty-year sentence for robbery, Buchanan Sloan was serving a fifteen-year sentence for robbery and H. G. Daniels was serving twenty years for robbery.

Hinson died at a Huntsville hospital on Thursday, 3 November 1932. He was survived by his wife, Ellie Smith, and at least two children. Hinson is buried at the Weldon Cemetery in Houston County.

H.G. Daniels and Buchanan Sloan signed confessions admitting to the beating death of Hinson. There is no information about the sentences they received.

McCall, J.R.
Born 2 June 1890—Died 27 August 1933

Guard J.R. McCall was on duty in a dormitory with 120 convicts at the Central State Prison near Sugar Land in Fort Bend County. During the early morning hours of Sunday, 27 August 1933, he heard inmate Beaumont King shouting that he needed medicine immediately and that the McCall should wake up the druggist at once to come to his aid. McCall approached King to assist him. Somehow, King had come to possess a pistol, which he produced at that moment and pointed at McCall, ordering him to raise his hands. Before McCall could comply, King shot him once in the chest. McCall returned fire, wounding King in the chest.

King was transported to the prison hospital and survived. McCall was transported to a Sugar Land hospital and died later the same day.

Prison officials later learned that someone had smuggled the 9mm semiautomatic Luger pistol onto the prison grounds and hid it in a cotton sack just outside the walls.

King was serving a fifteen-year sentence at the time and was not considered a dangerous inmate. An informant later told investigators that a group of fifteen desperate "lifers" had convinced King to lead the escape attempt. King was unfamiliar with the operation of the 9mm semiautomatic Luger pistol, which resulted in the gun going off accidentally before he intended to fire.

McCall had worked at the prison three years. He was survived by two siblings. McCall is buried in Stonewall, Mississippi.

Crowson, Major Joseph "Joe"
Born 14 September 1900—Died 27 January 1934
Date of Incident: 16 January 1934

Joe Crowson was shot and killed by members of the Bonnie Parker and Clyde Barrow Gang while several constituents of that crowd were making a prison escape. (See the earlier case on Malcolm Simmons Davis for more information on the Bonnie and Clyde gang.)

Weapons had been smuggled into the prison by gang members, who were waiting outside with Thompson submachine guns. On Tuesday, 16 January 1934, the inmates made their escape attempt. As Crowson rode up on horseback, he was shot and mortally wounded. He died from his wounds on Saturday, 27 January.

Raymond Hamilton and Joe Palmer were tried and convicted of killing Crowson. They were sentenced to death. Both men were executed by electrocution in Huntsville on 10 May 1935. They became the number 113th and 114th criminals to meet that fate in Texas.

Crowson was not married. He is buried at the Evergreen Cemetery in Lovelady. Some authors have mistakenly reported Crowson as having the rank of major, but Major was his first name.

Welch, Virgil
Born 16 February 1878—Died 10 May 1935

Guard Virgil Welch was shot and killed during a breakout from the Eastham State Prison Farm, which is located about five miles southwest of Weldon in Houston County. The incident took place less than eighteen hours after Raymond Hamilton and Joe Palmer were executed for the murder of guard Joe Crowson.

On Friday, 10 May 1934, a fistfight between two prisoners led to an all-out brawl that broke out in the central prison yard. A prisoner named Ernest Young was stabbed to death before guards could intervene.

After that incident had settled, an inmate named Jack Peddy slipped up behind guard Tom Stephens while Stephens was checking prisoners before letting them back into the dormitory. Stephens turned and grabbed Peddy and started shooting. Peddy pushed the gun away as Stephens continued to shoot, but Peddy was able to take the gun away from him. Peddy pumped four shots into a convict turnkey guard named Parker. Peddy resumed the beating of Stephens until he was practically insensible.

Welch was sleeping upstairs in the guard shack. Hearing the sound of gunfire, he came running down the stairway to assist. Peddy shot him as he reached the midpoint on the staircase. Welch toppled down the remainder of the stairs and suffered serious head injuries. He was dead at the scene of the incident.

At that point, the remainder of the prisoners spilled out of the barracks room and broke into the weapons locker. They took two six-shooters, one double-barreled shotgun and two Winchester rifles. In the midst of the confusion, inmate Jack Peddy led a prison break. He joined the now well-armed Sam Grant, R.C. Tipton and Harry Ludlow and made a sprint across the open field toward the Trinity River. Guards shot Peddy down and left him behind, thinking he was dead, as they continued their chase after the other three escapees. When they returned later, they found Peddy gone. He suddenly materialized soon after, leaping from a clump of trees, armed with two pistols. Guards shot him again, this time fatally.

Of the four prisoners who made good their escape, two were shot and killed and two were captured. Reese Tipton was tried for the murder of Welch. The outcome of that trial is not known.

Welch was survived by his wife, Gertrude Levert Hill, and five children. He is buried at the Hendrick Cemetery in Cherokee County.

Smith, Felix
Born 6 April 1892—Died 19 June 1936

Guard Felix Smith was shot and killed during a prison break that took place at the Retrieve Prison Farm in Brazoria County. Inmates Luke Trammell and Forest Gibson were responsible for Smith's murder.

A group of prisoners were being supervised by guards and were making their way single file to the fields on horseback. One of the inmates dismounted from his mule and hid in the tall grass. He remained there while the other prisoners plowed fields. When the last guard in line passed his location, Gibson attacked him and, with the help of Trammell, managed to disarm him. Gibson took the guard's pistol, and Trammell took the guard's shotgun and horse.

Trammell raced on horseback along the line of prisoners and fired a shotgun blast into the back of Smith, who was at the time on horseback at the front of the line. The would-be fugitives took Smith's two pistols and made good their escape.

Trammell and Gibson were captured two weeks later. Both were tried for Smith's murder. Trammell, who had done the shooting, was found guilty and sentenced to death. He was executed by electrocution on 20 August 1937 in Huntsville. Trammell was the 148th person to be electrocuted in Texas. Trammel had been in prison for the June 1933 murder of Nolan County sheriff's deputy John H. Lamkin.

Gibson was convicted and sentenced to serve sixty years in prison for his role in Smith's murder. On 3 October 1937, Gibson was shot and mortally wounded by a prison guard when he, once again, attempted to escape. That incident took place at the Eastham Prison Farm. Gibson died two weeks later.

Smith is buried at the Oliver-Powell Cemetery in Smithville in Bastrop County. He was not married.

Shiflett, George Washington
Born circa 1888—Died 8 December 1936

Guard George Shiflett suffered a freakish and fatal accident while he was on horseback guarding a squad of inmates at the Blue Ridge State Farm. The Blue Ridge facility is located about sixteen miles east of Richmond, on a ridge overlooking Oyster Creek in northeastern Fort Bend County. The sound of a passing truck spooked his horse. The animal bolted and threw Shiflett to the ground. When he fell, his weapon discharged. A bullet entered his abdomen. Shiflett died at 9:45 a.m. the same day. Adding to the drama of the incident, the driver of the passing truck hit Shiflett's fleeing horse, killing the animal.

Shiflett was survived by his wife, Nola Charlotta Wiggins, and nine children. He is buried at the Weldon Cemetery in Houston County. Shiflett's death certificate lists his year of birth as 1889. His tombstone reflects 1888, as do family genealogists.

Wheeler, Sid J.
Born 31 October 1889—Died 14 August 1937

Darrington state prison guard Sid Wheeler was shot and killed by a man named Shep Harris during an argument over gas money for driving a truck to Houston in which Wheeler was a passenger. Wheeler had engaged

Harris to make the trip after Wheeler's automobile had been damaged in an accident. Wheeler's bullet-riddled body was found alongside the highway by passersby at dawn on 15 August 1937.

Harris was arrested on 16 August by Sheriff Norfleet Hall and charged with the crime. He admitted to having knocked Wheeler down; he then grabbed Wheeler's gun and "shot him three or four times."

Wheeler was survived by his wife, Clara E. He is buried at the Forest Park Cemetery in Houston.

Ford, John Cleophus "Johnnie"
Born 31 August 1901—Died 4 October 1937

Guard Johnnie Ford drowned while searching for two escaped prisoners.

Ford was a guard at the Central State Farm in Sugar Land in Fort Bend County. At about 2:45 p.m. on Thursday, 4 October 1937, he had taken a squad of convicts to cut wood at a location about seven miles from the prison farm near the Brazos River. Two of the convicts escaped into the woods and river bottoms. Ford and several other guards pursued them on horseback. They located a spot on the river where they thought the prisoners had crossed. When Ford started to ford the stream, his horse struggled, causing him to tumble into the river. Ford went under, surfaced once and then disappeared. The horse eventually made it across the stream. Guards dragged the river and eventually recovered Ford's lifeless body.

Ford had served with the Texas Department of Criminal Justice for approximately nine years. He was survived by his wife. Ford is buried at the Rayburn Cemetery in Madisonville, Madison County.

Greer, John R.
Born 4 January 1897—Died 27 August 1938
Date of Incident: 16 August 1938

Guard John Greer died from stab wounds that were inflicted by an escaping prisoner during a jailbreak attempt at the Eastham State Prison Farm, Number 2 Camp, in Houston County.

Greer and guard Starnes were attacked by a gang of thirteen prisoners who had decided to attempt a breakout. Starnes's horse kicked off his attacker, and he fired his rifle, causing five of the would-be escapees to give up their attempt. Prisoner Jack Kinsley jumped Greer and held him down, while prisoner Leonard Smith stabbed him in the stomach. The eight convicts took Greer's shotgun and pistol and escaped into the Trinity River bottoms.

The group of fugitives included W.E. Garner, John Hendrix Frazier, Charles Aaron, Leonard Smith, Raymond Wilkerson, Frank Johnson, Roy King and Jack Kinsley. This was King's second prison break.

Kinsley and Aaron were shot and killed by a posse on 16 August. The following day, posse members shot Frazier and Wilkerson to death. Smith and Johnson were discovered to have drowned in the Trinity River at some point during the chase. Garner, who was the alleged leader of the ill-fated escape, and King were the only two to eventually be captured.

Greer was a U.S. Army veteran. He was survived by his wife and two children. Greer is buried at the Weldon Cemetery in Houston County.

Owen (Owens), Albert Neill
Born 22 November 1888—Died 8 August 1940

Harlem State Prison Farm captain Albert Owen was involved in an automobile accident on Thursday, 8 August 1940. He died as a result of the injuries he received in that incident later the same day at the St. Joseph's Infirmary in Houston. It is unclear if his death was line of duty related.

Owen was survived by his wife, Ella Lawson, and three daughters. He is buried at the Morton Cemetery in Richmond, Fort Bend County. Owen's tombstone shows his date of birth as 25 November; however, family genealogists all seem to agree on 22 November.

TEXAS DEPARTMENT OF PARKS AND WILDLIFE: LAW ENFORCEMENT DIVISION

Armstrong, Sternberg "Berge"
Born August 1886—Died December 1915

Game Warden Berge Armstrong was shot and killed by two soldiers in Maverick County. No further details are known about this incident or Armstrong.

Roe, Robert Edward "Bun"
Born 10 March 1868—Died 1 July 1919

"Bun" Roe was a deputy fish and game warden, and Carl Griffith was a Marion County deputy sheriff. At about 7:00 p.m. on Tuesday, 1 July 1919, Roe went across Caddo Lake to Ames Springs to have a boat repaired and ran into Griffith. The two lawmen started arguing. The disagreement became so heated that Griffith left to get a shotgun. As he returned, Roe stepped out of a house with his pistol. Roe stumbled, and Griffith emptied the shotgun at him. Roe was hit in the head and died instantly.

Griffith surrendered to the sheriff. His bond was set at $1,000. The final disposition of any charges is not known.

Roe was survived by his wife, Minnie Lee Bruner, and six children. He is buried at the Ashland Cemetery in Gilmer, Upshur County.

About 1908, Roe was a member of a Marion County posse and was involved in the death of a man named Dave Rabb. The incident occurred while Roe was attempting to arrest a burglary suspect and mistakenly shot Rabb. The deputy leading the posse, D.J. Paris, was acquitted. Roe, however, was convicted and sentenced to serve five years in prison. He appealed, but the sentence was affirmed. Apparently, that conviction did not stop him from being appointed a deputy game warden.

The Texas Game, Fish and Oyster Commission existed between 1907 and 1950. The name was changed to the Texas Game and Fish Commission in 1951, and in 1963, the name was changed to the Texas Department of Parks and Wildlife.

Williams, John Josiah "Joe"
Born July 1845—Died 14 September 1919

Raymond, Harry
Born 17 July 1882—Died 14 September 1919

Game Warden Harry Raymond and Captain John Williams drowned when they were swept overboard while in the process of trying to anchor their Game, Fish and Oyster Commission watercraft. The officers were attempting to secure the boat for protection in advance of an impending hurricane when a large wave knocked them both into the water. Both of their bodies were recovered two days later.

On 15 September, the hurricane for which Williams and Raymond had tried to prepare hit Corpus Christi. The savage storm claimed 125 lives. Approximately 4,000 people were left homeless, and the city courthouse was pressed into service as a morgue. The hospital was laid to ruin, and many residential districts were almost obliterated. Damage from the storm, which raged for more than twenty hours, was in excess of $4 million.

Williams was survived by his wife, Nancy A. Verser, and one daughter. He is buried at the Rose Hill Cemetery in Corpus Christi.

Raymond was survived by his wife and two children. His place of burial is unknown.

Related Case: Corpus Christi Police Department, Luther Prater

Coward, Erastus Athelone
Born 28 January 1889—Died 15 January 1922

Deputy Game Warden Erastus Coward was shot and killed by a man named Augie Bader. Nothing further is known about this shooting incident or about any charges against Bader.

Coward was also postmaster. He was not married. Coward was survived by his parents and nine of his eleven brothers. He is buried in Poteet in Atascosa County.

McAlister, Paul Jerome
Born 30 May 1884—Died 5 July 1925

At the time of his death, Paul McAlister was a deputy state game, fish and oyster commissioner (deputy game warden today). On Sunday, 5 July 1925, McAlister and his friends George Ryder and Rufus McMurray were involved in a gun battle with Nueces County constable Carl M. Bisbee and his deputy, R.R. Bledsoe. Accounts vary about what happened that day and whether Bisbee and Bledsoe were enforcing the law concerning drinking in public or simply seeking political revenge.

Bisbee and Bledsoe were said to have been members of a rival political faction whose views differed from those of George Ryder, Rufus McMurray and Paul McAlister. According to one account, Constable Bisbee and Deputy Constable Bledsoe were seated in Bledsoe's automobile when the shooting began. Apparently, McMurray and Bledsoe got into a heated disagreement of some sort. The quarrel quickly escalated into deadly gunplay. McMurray was the first to fall. He was shot a second time after he collapsed on the ground. McMurray claims that Bledsoe fired the first volley and that Bisbee had tried to intervene.

George Ryder's brother Lee related a slightly different story afterward, claiming that George had told him how the incident unfolded before he died. Ryder claimed that he and McAlister had left Bessie Miller's sporting house on Sam Rankin Street together and had walked to his automobile. McAlister had entered the vehicle, and Ryder was about to do so, when Bledsoe and Bisbee pulled up. Either Bisbee or Bledsoe asked where the pair was going. Ryder responded, "San Diego" (meaning the town of San Diego in Duval County). Bledsoe then said, "No, you are not" and told them that they were under arrest. When Ryder asked why, Bledsoe told him that it made no difference and ordered, "Hands up!"

Ryder claimed that he was still standing by the fender of his automobile when Bledsoe fired first. Bisbee then fired one shot that hit McAlister, who leaped from the car and was struck by a second bullet from Bisbee's gun. Ryder said that he followed Bledsoe, who had chased McAlister, and fired three shots at him while the girls from the sporting house watched the whole gruesome scene unfold on the street below.

By the time the smoke cleared, Ryder, Bisbee, Bledsoe and McAlister were all either dead or mortally wounded. Bisbee, Bledsoe and McAlister both died a few hours after the fight. Ryder died the following day, but he claimed in his dying statement that he did not know who had fired the fatal shot that downed Bisbee. McMurray recovered and died in 1936.

McAlister was preceded in death by his wife, Olive Lynn Watson. He was survived by three children. McAlister is buried at the Aberdeen Cemetery in Corpus Christi. McAlister's surname is frequently spelled incorrectly as McAllister in various documents, newspaper articles and genealogy records.

McAlister had previously served as a Texas Ranger, a federal border officer, a Corpus Christi policeman, a Cameron County deputy sheriff and a Duval County deputy sheriff. On 9 August 1912, McAlister was serving as a deputy sheriff in Cameron County when he killed Brownsville city marshal Joe Crixell in a political dispute. He was tried and acquitted.

Related Cases: Nueces County Constable's Office, Carl M. Bisbee and R.R. Bledsoe; and Brownsville Police Department, Joe Crixell

Isom, Emerald Waymon
Born 15 May 1909—Died 29 January 1937

Game Warden Emerald Isom was shot and killed by a man named Jimmie Ragsdale in Hebron, Denton County.

Isom was in a drugstore in Hebron at the time the incident took place. According to the store's owner, Isom and Ragsdale became involved in a heated quarrel that was initiated by Ragsdale, whom Isom did not know prior to the encounter. Ragsdale, who was a drug addict and known to police as such, is believed to have instigated the gunplay that resulted in the death of Isom.

Ragsdale was tried and convicted of Isom's killing and was sentenced to serve ninety-nine years in prison.

Isom was not married. He was survived by his parents and one sibling. Isom is buried at the Furneaux Cemetery in Carrolton.

Murchison, Dawson Richard
Born 11 February 1887—Died 20 December 1938

Game Warden Dawson Murchison was shot and killed while patrolling the Ben Bolt area on the King Ranch looking for illegal poachers.

The incident occurred on the Concho Game Preserve of the King Ranch, near the boundary line that separates Kleberg and Jim Wells Counties. Murchison and Game Warden J.L. Robinson of Alice were looking for headlight hunters who had been reported in the area. The lawmen located the suspects, spotting their lights in the distance. Murchison shined his flashlight in the direction of the beam of light and called to the men to "Halt!" He was immediately met with a reply of gunfire. One bullet hit Murchison in the arm, and another struck him in the left chest. Murchison fell into Robinson, who caught him but in so doing was prevented from returning fire.

One newspaper reported that some speculate the killing may have been in retaliation for the shooting death of another Mexican poacher several years ago by Murchison.

Soon after the shooting, lawmen arrested three Mexican men who were suspected of being responsible for Murchison's murder. By Christmas, a $500 reward had been offered for the identity of the killer. The killer fled to Mexico and was never apprehended or prosecuted.

Murchison was survived by his wife, Mattie B. Some sources indicate that

Murchison was survived by three children, while others list only two. He is buried at the Chamberlain Cemetery in Kingsville. Murchison had been with the agency for ten years.

TEXAS DEPARTMENT OF PUBLIC SAFETY: HIGHWAY PATROL

Fischer, Arthur William
Born 18 January 1907—Died 18 January 1932

On his twenty-fifth birthday, Patrolman Arthur Fischer was killed in a motorcycle accident while on duty.

His motorcycle ran into soft dirt about nine miles from Houston. According to some reports, Fischer struck a horse. Fischer lost control of the vehicle and crashed.

Fischer had been with the agency for four months. He is buried at the Saint John Lutheran Cemetery in Bartlett, Bell County.

In 1927, the Texas legislature created the License and Weights section to regulate truck traffic. In 1929, the License and Weight section was moved into the Texas Highway Department and named the State Highway Patrol. In 1931, the agency was renamed the Texas Highway Patrol as a part of the Texas Highway Department.

Fischer graduated from the first class of the newly created Texas Highway Patrol on 14 October 1931. He would be the first highway patrolman to die in the line of duty.

Moore, Aubrey Lee, Sr.
Born 2 February 1902—Died 16 April 1932

Patrolman Aubrey Moore was killed in a motorcycle accident when his vehicle collided with an automobile three miles west of Arlington on the Fort Worth–Dallas pike. The incident took place at about 7:40 a.m. on Saturday, 16 April 1932. A large automobile pulled out of a filling station along the roadway just as Moore emerged from a dip in the highway. Neither driver saw the other until it was too late for evasive action.

Moore was taken to a hospital immediately after the wreck and declared to be dead on arrival. He suffered numerous broken bones in the collision.

Moore had been with the agency for eight months. He was survived by his wife. Moore is buried at the Oakwood Cemetery Annex in Austin. He graduated from the first Texas Highway Patrol class on 14 October 1931. He was the second member of that academy class to be killed in the line of duty.

Wheeler, Edward Bryan
Born 30 June 1907—Died 1 April 1934

Murphy, Holloway Daniel
Born 27 November 1911—Died 1 April 1934

Patrolmen Edward Wheeler and Holloway Murphy were shot and killed on Easter Sunday by members of the notorious outlaw gang headed up by Bonnie Parker and Clyde Barrow.

The two patrolmen had stopped their motorcycles near Grapevine thinking that a motorist needed assistance. As they approached the vehicle, the two outlaws opened fire, using a shotgun and a handgun. Both Wheeler and Murphy were killed.

Wheeler had served with the agency for four years. He was survived by his wife, Dorris. He is buried at the Grove Hill Memorial Park in Dallas. Wheeler joined the State Highway Patrol on 8 January 1930.

Murphy is buried at the Old Palestine Cemetery in Alto, Cherokee County. Murphy was survived by his wife, Maree Tullis. He joined the Texas Highway Patrol on 18 September 1933.

Avary, Joseph Newton
Born 1 July 1905—Died 17 May 1935

Patrolman Joseph Avary was killed in a motorcycle accident while on patrol near Barstow in Ward County.

Avary was chasing a speeding automobile when a state highway truck entered the main road from a side street. He did not see it approach and was unable to stop or take evasive action. Avary crashed his motorcycle into the rear of the truck. He died at the scene of the collision.

Avary had served with the agency for four years. He was survived by his wife, Cloyce Alice Leonard, and three children. There is a state monument that has been erected at Barstow in Avary's honor. His place of burial is unknown but is presumed to be in Ward County. He had joined the Texas Highway Patrol on 14 October 1931. Avary was the third member of that academy class to die in the line of duty.

Freese, Guy Albert
Born 20 July 1903—Died 11 July 1935

Patrolman Guy Freese was killed when he crashed his motorcycle into a tramway bus in downtown Fort Worth. Freese and other officers were escorting a caravan of Dallas newsboys on the return leg of an excursion to Lake Worth. He suffered a fractured skull and internal injuries when the bus dragged him fifty feet down the street. Freese died at the scene of the accident before an ambulance could arrive.

Freese had been with the agency for five years, having joined on 18 January 1930. He was not married and is buried in Crestline, Ohio.

Tarrant, Mart Dennis
Born 24 December 1896—Died 4 November 1935

Patrolman Mart Tarrant was killed when his police motorcycle was struck by an automobile near Waco.

Tarrant had been with the agency for four years and had served in the navy during World War I. He was survived by his wife, Marie Louise Braly, and two children. Tarrant is buried at the Old Larissa Cemetery in Mount Selman, Cherokee County. He joined the Texas Highway Patrol on 14 October 1931 and became the fourth member of that academy class to die in the line of duty.

McGonagill, David Alex
Born 26 February 1907—Died 4 September 1940

Patrolman David McGonagill was killed when he was struck by lightning while riding his motorcycle on patrol.

In the early evening hours of 4 September 1940, McGonagill and his partner, Patrolman Tom Majors, were returning to Plainview at the end of their watch. The two officers were riding their police motorcycles in a light rain east of Lockney in Floyd County when a bolt of lightning hit McGonagill.

Majors later said, "I was riding about one hundred feet ahead of McGonagill when there was a heavy clap of thunder and a blinding flash. I looked back, and McGonagill was still on his motorcycle, but it was headed for a ditch." The impact threw him from the machine. He was burned about the face, and the metal frames of his glasses had been melted away. Majors said that by the time he reached McGonagill, there were no signs of life.

McGonagill had been with the Texas Department of Public Safety for two years, having joined on 18 April 1938. He was survived by his wife. McGonagill is buried in Marathon in Brewster County.

TEXAS STATE HOSPITALS

Simpson, Benjaman Ogliesby "Oge"
Born 4 December 1880—Died 1 January 1933

Superintendent Benjaman Simpson was shot and killed by two men named James Donnell and James McCreary. Both were former guards at the state facility in Bexar County.

Donnell and McCreary we charged with the murder of Simpson. The outcome of those charges is not known.

Simpson was survived by his wife, Clara Meyers. He is buried at the Mission Burial Park at San Antonio.

4
Federal Agencies

UNITED STATES ARMY

Longoria, Damacio Loya
Born 11 December 1875—Died 23 October 1920

On Saturday, 23 October 1920, U.S. Army river guard Damacio Longoria was shot and killed and his son and another man wounded in a pistol fight near Santa Maria, about eighteen miles from Brownsville in Cameron County. The unidentified assailants were near a Mexican dance when they opened fire. Longoria's saddle, guns and horse were stolen by the killers, who fled into Mexico. It was reported that Longoria was assassinated because of his activities against smugglers and other law violators.

Longoria was employed by the U.S. Army as a scout and river guard to work in cooperation with the federal border and customs officers.

Longoria was survived by his wife, Josefita Solis, and at least five children. He is buried at the Longoria Family Cemetery in Bluetown-Iglesia Antigua, Cameron County.

UNITED STATES DEPARTMENT OF JUSTICE: BORDER PATROL

The Border Patrol was under the U.S. Immigration Service as early as 1904. Mounted watchmen were based in El Paso and patrolled the border to stop illegal crossings. About seventy-five federal officers had responsibility for the U.S. border from Texas to California. In 1915, Congress authorized a separate group of mounted guards, often referred to as mounted inspectors. They traveled by horseback, car and boat.

Today, the agency has been merged into the U.S. Department of Homeland Security as Customs and Border Protection (CBP).

Childress, Clarence Meek
Born 21 January 1877—Died 16 April 1919
Date of Incident: 13 April 1919

Mounted watchman Clarence Childress was shot and killed when he and his partner attempted to apprehend seven smugglers who were trying to cross into the United States from Mexico near the town of El Paso.

As the smugglers crossed through a barbed-wire fence, the watchmen approached. They were met by gunfire. Both officers returned fire, but the outlaws managed to flee back into Mexico. Childress was hit by the gunfire and told his partner that he was going to telephone for help. He was taken to a hospital, where he died from his wounds three days later.

Childress had been employed by the Border Patrol for one year. He is buried at the Clear Creek Cemetery in Bangs, Brown County.

Hopkins, Charles Lloyd
Born 22 February 1880—Died 9 May 1919
Date of Incident: 8 May 1919

At about 10:15 p.m. on Thursday, 8 May 1919, a group of mounted immigration, customs and public health officers were on patrol along the Rio Grande River, about seven miles from Laredo in Webb County. The group included customs inspectors Robert Rumsey and John Chamberlain; Border Patrol mounted watchmen Charles Hopkins, James Dunnoway and Mal Petty; and quarantine guard Ira Hill of the U.S. Public Health Service.

The officers witnessed four Mexican men in a boat land on the American side of the border. They disembarked near where Rumsey and Hopkins were hiding in the chaparral. The other officers were about fifteen feet away from them when Rumsey called out to the Mexican men to "Halt!" The men opened fire on the officers with rifles and revolvers. Hopkins was hit in the right side with a bullet that exited through his back. Rumsey shot the suspect who had mortally wounded Hopkins. That man was later identified as Jose Valdez.

Hill, Dunnoway and Chamberlain were involved in a gun battle with two other smugglers who were still in the boat. The officers managed to kill both of them. Rumsey killed the fourth man, who was in the water. During the wild exchange of gunfire, Dunnoway had his thumbs shot off, and Hill received a serious wound to the stomach. Valdez was captured.

Hopkins was brought to Mercy Hospital in Laredo and died at 1:00 a.m. on Friday, 9 May 1919.

Hopkins had been with the agency for seven years. He was survived by his wife. Hopkins is buried in Exchange, West Virginia.

Quarantine Guard Hill died from his wounds on 1 June 1919.

Three years later, on 19 August 1922, U.S. Customs inspector Robert Rumsey Jr. was killed in the line of duty near Laredo.

Related Case: U.S. Public Health Service, Ira Trueman Hill

Gardiner, Charles
Born 5 February 1882—Died 21 October 1922
Date of Incident: 20 October 1922

Shortly after daybreak on Friday, 20 October 1922, mounted officers Charles Gardiner, Charles T. Birchfield and A.R. Green were on duty in the Upper Valley area of El Paso County. They noticed a suspicious wagon being driven along a road by two men. The officers stopped the cart, and as they advanced, the occupants opened fire and fled. Officers Birchfield and Gardiner were wounded in the initial round of gunfire. The lawmen returned fire, with Green using his rifle. Birchfield believed that he had wounded one of the men in the shoulder. All the suspects waded across the river and escaped into Mexico.

Several sacks containing twelve bottles of tequila were found in the wagon. Both wounded officers were taken to the hospital. Birchfield was shot in the hip and jaw. Gardiner was shot once through both lungs. Gardiner died in the hospital on Saturday, 21 October 1922, at 5:00 a.m.

Gardiner was survived by his wife, Mattie New, and six children, two from a previous marriage. He had entered the immigration service four years earlier. Gardiner is buried at the Concordia Cemetery in El Paso.

A man named Adolpho Chavez, age twenty-five, who was suspected of having been involved in the shooting death of Gardiner, was discovered in Rodey, New Mexico. He was seriously wounded and had been lying in a cornfield near El Paso. Chavez was transported to New Mexico by his partner. He refused to disclose how he was wounded. It is not known if Chavez, or anyone, was ever charged with the murder of Gardiner.

Mankin, James Floyd
Born 5 April 1902—Died 14 September 1924

Inspector James Mankin was accidentally shot and killed when a rifle he had stored in the rear of his patrol vehicle discharged and the bullet struck him in the head.

Mankin and two other inspectors were on patrol, inspecting a riverbank near Laredo. When they got back into the truck, the two inspectors who were seated in the back tried to rearrange items, including the two rifles. One of the rifles fell from the truck and discharged when it hit the ground. The bullet struck Mankin in the head. He was taken to a local hospital, where he died from the wound.

Mankin had been employed with the Border Patrol for only two months. He is buried at the Forest Park Cemetery in Fort Smith, Arkansas. Mankin was not married.

Clark, Frank Horace
Born 4 January 1873—Died 13 December 1924

Inspector Frank Clark was shot and killed when he attempted to apprehend several smugglers near Cordova Island in El Paso County.

Clark and Inspector Herbert Brown confronted a smuggler and four spotters who were positioned to observe and protect the smuggler. One of them opened fire from ambush and fatally wounded Clark in the stomach.

One of the smugglers was arrested, tried and convicted. He was sentenced to ten years in prison.

Clark had been with the agency for six months. He was survived by his wife, Margarita Whitmore, and two children. Clark is buried in Las Vegas, New Mexico.

de La Pena, Augustine D.
Born 4 October 1882—Died 3 August 1925
Date of Incident: 2 August 1925

At about 7:00 p.m. on Sunday, 2 August 1925, Inspector Augustine De La Pena was shot and killed when he intervened in an assault at a restaurant in Rio Grande City, Starr County.

De La Pena and another inspector were at dinner when a mentally ill man entered the restaurant and began arguing with the establishment's owner. As the man attempted to leave, he was confronted by De La Pena. A struggle took place during which De La Pena was shot in the stomach. He continued to battle with the man as he grew progressively weaker from loss of blood. Finally, De La Pena managed to shoot and kill his attacker. De La Pena was transported to the hospital in Fort Ringgold, where he died at 1:00 a.m. on Monday, 3 August.

De La Pena had been with the agency for two years. He was survived by his wife and nine children. De La Pena is buried in Rio Grande City.

Pippin, Thaddeus "Thad"
Born 16 October 1889—Died 21 April 1927

Inspector Thad Pippin was shot and killed while tracking suspected smugglers along the Rio Grande River, about one mile west of El Paso.

A team of four inspectors had begun tracking a pack train but were uncertain which trail the smugglers had taken. The group split up into two teams, one to guard each of the trails. Before long, Pippin and his partner, Egbert Crossett, found themselves engaged in a gunfight with the outlaws. Pippin was fatally wounded, and Crossett was also seriously hurt. The other team of inspectors rushed to their aid and was able to confiscate a shipment of liquor and two pack animals, but they came up emptyhanded so far as capturing the smugglers was concerned.

Pippin had been with the agency for eleven months. He was unmarried and was survived by his mother. Pippin is buried in Bryan, Brazos County.

Hill, Benjamin Thomas "Bennie"
Born 23 October 1901—Died 30 May 1929

Inspector Bennie Hill was shot and killed while pursuing a suspected illegal alien near El Paso.

Hill had observed the man cross the Rio Grande River and began to chase after him. Hill overtook the man as he entered an alley at Findley and Latta Streets. The man suddenly turned and shot Hill in the chest.

Hill had been with the agency for two weeks. He was not married. Hill is buried at the Wheeler Cemetery in Wheeler County.

Scotten, Ivan E.
Born 17 June 1903—Died 20 July 1929

The Border Patrol office had received a tip that there would be heavy movement across the border by liquor smugglers and aliens before daybreak on Saturday, 20 July 1929. The crossings were planned to occur at the upper Las Pomas portage near Clint in El Paso County.

It was raining hard that morning, and there was little visibility. Three officers confronted a lone man on horseback. He immediately opened fire on them. The officers returned fire as the rider fled into Mexico. It was later discovered that the man had been wounded during the exchange of gunfire and had died.

The lawmen regrouped and were joined by three additional officers, including Inspector Ivan Scotten. This time, they returned to the scene in automobiles. Unbeknownst to the lawmen, smugglers had concealed themselves along both sides of the road. As the officers approached, they were ambushed and caught in crossfire.

Scotten was wounded in the thigh and fell to the ground. The five remaining officers retreated under heavy fire. The outlaws continued to advance. When the attackers reached the officers' automobiles, they found the wounded Scotten under the vehicle. The outlaws pulled him from under the car and, in typical execution style, shot him in the back of the head at point-blank range. Next, the bandits took Scotten's pistols, ring, watch and badge. The remaining lawmen made a desperate charge at the band of outlaws and were successful at driving them back into Mexico.

The Scotten killing remained unsolved until 1933, when a Border Patrol officer interrogated two brothers in a separate case and learned the identity of the killer. The brothers indicated that a man named Ramiro Galvan, alias Raul Galvan, had bragged about murdering Scotten and that Galvan had Scotten's pistols and other possessions.

Galvan was captured in 1934. He was tried and convicted of Scotten's murder and sentenced to death. On 13 February 1936, that sentence was commuted to life in prison.

Scotten was survived by his parents and three siblings. He had been with the agency for nine months. Scotten is buried at the Concordia Cemetery in El Paso.

Scannell, Miles Joseph
Born 10 December 1895—Died 9 September 1929

Inspectors Miles Scannell and Charles Holmes were patrolling along the Rio Grande River near El Polvo (present-day Redford) in Presidio County. The officers were traveling about six hundred yards apart when Holmes heard two muffled gunshots. He believed that the shots had come from a long distance and thought nothing further of it.

At about 8:00 a.m., he found Scannell's body. The officer's corpse had five bullet holes and fifteen stab wounds. More heinous yet, Scannell appeared to have been beaten with a club.

There was evidence of a struggle. Scannell had apparently been overpowered. His handcuffs and weapon were missing, leading investigators to postulate that Scannell had possibly handcuffed one of his attackers before he was attacked. Officers theorized that Scannell had probably intercepted a group of illegal aliens who were crossing the border to pick cotton. No one was ever apprehended or charged with Scannell's murder.

Scannell was survived by his wife and a two-year-old son. He had served with the agency for eight years. Scannell is buried in Alpine in Brewster County.

McCalib, William Douglas "Dock"
Born 20 December 1895—Died 7 January 1930

Inspector William D. McCalib was shot and killed when he and Inspector Buck West arrested a suspected illegal alien in Alice.

The man in question, Pedro Rendon, claimed to be a legal citizen and that a restaurant owner could vouch for him. The officers took Rendon to the eating establishment to interview the owner. McCalib remained in the patrol car with Rendon. While waiting in the vehicle, Rendon produced a concealed pistol and shot McCalib in the back of the head. When West returned to the automobile, he became engaged in a gunfight with Rendon and managed to wound him three times.

Rendon committed suicide in the Jim Wells County jail on 7 February 1930.

McCalib had served with the agency for one year. He was survived by his son, mother and five siblings. McCalib is buried in the Masonic section of the Laredo City Cemetery in Webb County.

Kelsay, Robert William
Born 23 January 1899—Died 25 June 1930

Senior Border Patrol inspector Robert Kelsay and Patrolman Edwin M. Brown had received a tip that a contraband liquor shipment would be put on the American side of the Rio Grande River near Laredo in Webb County. The lawmen went to the specified location to wait.

Just before dawn, Kelsay was making his way through the chaparral brush toward the river. As he climbed the side of a hill, a man lifted his head up at a distance of about ten feet and shot at him. According to Brown, the first bullet fired by the smugglers from the ambush hit Kelsay. Although critically wounded, Kelsay returned fire.

Officers followed a trail of blood left by the attackers all the way to the Rio Grande River, giving legitimacy to the belief that Kelsay had wounded one or more of the outlaws. A quantity of liquor was found nearby, along with a revolver and a semiautomatic pistol. Both were empty and had been abandoned by the fleeing smugglers.

Mexican police reported that a dead man named Juan Espinosa had been found on their side of the river with a loaded pistol in his hand. Espinosa was one of the smugglers who had been engaged in the shootout with Kelsay. Mexican officers also arrested three other members of the same group, all of whom were seriously wounded. One of the men, Jesus Cantu, died soon afterward.

Kelsay was survived by his wife, Helen Temple. He is buried in Denton. Kelsay had served three years with the agency.

Melton, Doyne C.
Born 16 January 1902—Died 7 December 1933

On 28 November 1933, U.S. Customs inspector Rollin Culberson Nichols was shot and killed by rum smugglers in East El Paso. Nine days later, on Thursday, 7 December 1933, six U.S. Border Patrol inspectors—Doyne C.

Melton, J.T. Love, Pedro Torres, Bert G. Walthall, Lester I. Copenbarger and Robert Clance—challenged thirteen smugglers as they waded ashore in El Paso with 150 cases of illegal liquor. One smuggler, who was hidden on the American side, opened fire on the officers. The others quickly followed. Melton was hit in the heart during the opening volley. He died at the scene. The other officers shot and killed two of the smugglers and wounded another. The remainder of the group fled back into Mexico.

Melton was survived by his wife, Lucille Mann. He is buried in Conyers, Georgia. Melton was a U.S. Marine Corps veteran and had served in Haiti. He was a sergeant in the U.S. Marine Corps Reserve.

Walthall, Bert G.
Born 27 February 1900—Died 27 December 1933

Inspector Bert Walthall was shot and killed when he and two other officers attempted to apprehend two illegal aliens in the slums of south El Paso.

After a short pursuit, a vehicle driven by the illegals came to a stop near the international boundary. Inspectors Walthall, Louis Smith and Curtis D. Mosley pulled up alongside in their patrol car. When they got out of their vehicle to investigate, the occupants of the car opened fire, fatally wounding Walthall. Smith was also hit with a bullet that grazed his head during the exchange of gunfire. Smith and Mosley returned fire, sending a hail of bullets at the Mexicans' car as it made a speedy escape. The vehicle was found a few blocks away. In it was one of the smugglers, Jose Estrada, who had been killed when the lawmen returned fire.

A chase that involved fifty lawmen followed. Officers captured three other Mexican men, two of whom had been wounded. One was injured so seriously that he required hospitalization. An elderly man in the house near where the gunfight occurred was also taken into custody.

Walthall had been with the agency for two years. He was survived by his wife and one child. Walthall is buried in Thatcher, Arizona.

Sills, William Leslie
Born 21 August 1909—Died 17 January 1940

Inspector William Sills was shot and killed while he was attempting to arrest a smuggler near McAllen in Hidalgo County.

At about 10:30 p.m. on Wednesday evening, 17 January 1940, Inspectors Sills, Albin Ulrickson and Leslie Buchanon surprised a group of three smugglers in La Grulia, located between Mission and Rio Grande City. The outlaws were attempting to bring goats across the border from Mexico illegally. Two of the men were arrested. Sills was shot once in the abdomen with a .38-caliber revolver by Moises "El Mocho" Alvarado, whom he was attempting to stop from escaping at the time. Sills was able to return fire, shooting five or six times in rapid succession at Alvarado. Alvarado slumped to the ground dead. Sills died from the wound while en route to the McAllen Municipal Hospital.

The other two smugglers, Felipe Solis and Guillermo Benecia, surrendered to Ulrickson and Buchanon. Friends of "El Mocho" Alvarado, who had observed the incident from across the river in Mexico, retrieved his body before investigators could return to the scene. Officers later found a wagon and a team of two mules, along with about twenty goats and a canvas boat that the smugglers had used to bring the animals across the river, near the scene.

Sills had been with the agency for three years. He was survived by his wife, Jeanette Evans. Sills is buried at the American Cemetery in Natchitoches, Natchitoches Parish, Louisiana.

UNITED STATES DEPARTMENT OF JUSTICE: BUREAU OF INVESTIGATION

What later became the Federal Bureau of Investigation (FBI) originated from a force of special agents created in 1908. It had neither a name nor an officially designated leader, other than the attorney general. The establishment of this kind of agency at a national level was highly controversial. The U.S. Constitution is based on "federalism"—a national government with jurisdiction over matters that crossed boundaries, like interstate commerce and foreign affairs, with all other powers reserved to the states.

When the bureau was established, there were few federal crimes. The organization primarily investigated violations of laws involving national banking, bankruptcy, naturalization, antitrust, peonage and land fraud. Because the early bureau provided no formal training, previous law enforcement experience or a background in the law was considered desirable.

Most field offices were located in major cities. However, several were located near the Mexican border, where they concentrated on smuggling, neutrality violations and intelligence collection, often in connection with the Mexican revolution.

With the April 1917 entry of the United States into World War I, the bureau acquired responsibility for the Espionage, Selective Service and Sabotage Acts and assisted the Department of Labor by investigating enemy aliens. During these years, special agents with general investigative experience and facility in certain languages augmented the bureau.

The period from 1921 to 1933 was sometimes called the "lawless years" because of gangsterism and the public disregard for Prohibition, which made it illegal to sell or import intoxicating beverages. Prohibition created a new federal medium for fighting crime, but the Department of the Treasury, not the Department of Justice, had jurisdiction for these violations.

In 1925, Agent Edwin C. Shanahan became the first agent to be killed in the line of duty when a car thief murdered him in Chicago, Illinois.

The Bureau of Investigation was renamed the United States Bureau of Investigation on 1 July 1932. Then, beginning 1 July 1933, the Department of Justice experimented for almost two years with a Division of Investigation that included the Bureau of Prohibition. Public confusion between Bureau of Investigation special agents and Prohibition agents led to a permanent name change in 1935 for the agency composed of Department of Justice investigators; thus, the Federal Bureau of Investigation was born.

Beverly, Thomas Houghston
Born 6 July 1886—Died 26 October 1918

The 1918 Spanish flu pandemic was an unusually severe and deadly influenza epidemic that spread across the world. Unlike most similar occurrences that affect primarily juveniles, elderly or weakened patients, this one most severely impacted victims who were healthy young adults. The epidemic lasted from June 1917 to December 1920 and even spread to the Arctic and remote Pacific islands. Between 50 and 100 million people died, about 3 percent of the world's population at the time, making it one of the deadliest natural disasters in human history.

Beverly was an attorney in McKinney in Collin County when he enlisted in Texas Ranger Company M on 29 December 1917. He was stationed in Eagle Pass. On 31 March 1918, Beverly resigned and accepted a position in Eagle Pass as a special employee of the Department of Justice's Bureau of Justice (BOI), known today as the Federal Bureau of Investigation (FBI).

He contracted Spanish influenza and died in Deming, New Mexico, on Saturday, 26 October 1918.

Beverly was not married and was survived by his mother. He was buried in McKinney.

UNITED STATES DEPARTMENT OF JUSTICE: BUREAU OF PROHIBITION

Prohibition in the United States, called by some the "Noble Experiment," took place between 1920 and 1933. During that time, the sale, manufacture and transportation of alcohol for human consumption was banned nationally. This unpopular ruling grew out of substantial pressure that was applied by members of the equally unpopular temperance movement. The efforts of the sobriety group resulted in the Eighteenth Amendment to the United States Constitution being passed on 18 December 1917. Ultimately approved by thirty-six states, the amendment was ratified on 16 January 1919 and took effect one year later, on 16 January 1920. Prohibition became increasingly unpopular during the Great Depression, a period in American history when libation appeared to be one of the few remaining pleasures. On 5 December 1933, Prohibition was repealed by the ratification of the Twenty-first Amendment (which cancelled the Eighteenth Amendment).

Ezzell, Raymond Levi
Born circa 1901—Died 27 July 1931

At about 8:30 p.m. on Monday, 27 July 1931, Prohibition agents Raymond L. Ezzell and J.W. Boyd were in Fort Worth waiting for a suspect to drive into the alley with a load of liquor. When the man arrived, Ezzell walked to the side of the automobile. The driver of the car fired a shot at Ezzell, wounding him in the hand. According to Boyd, who was on the other side of the automobile at the time, Ezzell and the suspect both shot each other simultaneously. Ezzell hit the man in the heart. He, in turn, was hit in the head. Ezzell slumped forward and dropped his pistol inside the car.

Ezzell was taken to a hospital, where he died at 10:10 p.m. His killer died at the scene.

Ezzell was survived by his wife, Emmie, and one daughter. He is reportedly buried at the Oakhill Cemetery in Buckholts, Milam County. Ezzell had been employed as a Temple city policeman in 1930 and a federal Prohibition officer with the agency for about ten months.

UNITED STATES DEPARTMENT OF THE TREASURY: BUREAU OF NARCOTICS

Stafford, Spencer Leverett
Born 11 February 1898—Died 7 February 1935

Inspector Spencer Stafford was shot and killed by a corrupt sheriff in Post, Garza County.

Local veterinarians had been charged with federal drug violations. Stafford and Dallas narcotics agent V.C. McCullough had gone to the office of one such firm to examine its records. As Stafford exited a veterinary clinic, Sheriff W.F. Cato opened fire on him with a machine gun. Stafford was killed instantly. Cato claimed that he had acted in self-defense.

Unidentified sources provided a slightly different account of the incident in a local newspaper story. According to those sources, Sheriff Cato had received a call that two armed men were at a local veterinary clinic. He deputized a local farmer named Tom Morgan and rushed to the location. When he arrived, he saw a man and woman seated in the narcotics agent's automobile. Cato questioned the pair and was told that the armed men inside were federal agents. Next, the man who was being questioned shouted to Stafford, who exited the building and saw Cato with the machine gun. As he did so, Stafford is quoted as having said, "Don't do that, we are officers." Stafford grabbed the barrel of Cato's machine gun and began to pull his pistol. Cato disarmed him. Stafford broke and ran between two automobiles just as McCullough emerged from the clinic. McCullough was not holding a gun and, according to witnesses, did not make a move to draw his pistol. McCullough yelled, "My God, man, don't do that! We are officers!" Cato opened fire, and in an instant Stafford fell to the ground dead, clutching his badge.

On 15 February, Cato and Morgan were formally charged with the murder of Stafford. Dr. L.W. Kitchen, DVM, and Dr. V.A. Hartman, MD, faced charges of complicity. On 21 February, Cato's attorney, N.O. Outlaw, was charged with conspiracy to obstruct justice. Outlaw was also put under indictment for perjury. He was charged with conspiring with a postman named C.M. Loe to give false testimony at a grand jury hearing.

On 3 June 1935, Cato and Morgan were acquitted of the machine gun slaying of Stafford.

On 12 June, Kitchen was sentenced to two years and Hartman to fourteen months; both sentences were to be served at the federal penitentiary in Leavenworth, Kansas.

Stafford was from New York and had graduated from pharmacy school. He had been living in Florida with his wife and parents until after 1930. Stafford was survived by his wife, Constance. He is reportedly buried in Fort Worth.

UNITED STATES DEPARTMENT OF THE TREASURY: CUSTOMS SERVICE

The newly formed United States of America needed revenue, and the First Congress passed the Tariff Act of 4 July 1789 authorizing the collection of duties on imported goods. Four weeks later, on 31 July, the fifth act of Congress established customs and its ports of entry.

For nearly 125 years, customs funded virtually the entire government and paid for the nation's early growth and infrastructure. The new nation that had once teetered on the edge of bankruptcy was now solvent. By 1835, customs revenues alone had reduced the national debt to zero.

With the passage of the Homeland Security Act, the U.S. Customs Service passed from the jurisdiction of the Treasury Department to that of the Department of Homeland Security.

On 1 March 2003, parts of the U.S. Customs Service combined with the Inspections Program of the Immigration and Naturalization Service, Plant Protection and Quarantine from the USDA and the Border Patrol of the Immigration and Naturalization Service to form U.S. Customs and Border Protection. The Federal Protective Service, along with the investigative arms of the U.S. Customs Service and the Immigration and Naturalization Service, combined to form U.S. Immigration and Customs Enforcement.

Levy, Alphonse
Born 1 January 1840—Died 13 December 1901

At about 10:30 a.m. on Friday, 13 December 1901, Inspector Alphonse Levy was on duty at Pier 20 at the Port of Galveston. Levy was checking a load of railroad iron from the steamer *Northwestern* when he attempted to pass between two railroad cars. He was caught in the drawheads and mortally injured. A drawhead is a device adapted to assist in the alignment of a railroad car coupling.

An ambulance surgeon and police officers came to his aid almost immediately. After his injuries were assessed, Levy was administered painkillers. He died of his injuries within fifteen minutes. An inquest into Levy's death was held, during which witnesses testified that the accident had not been the result of Levy's negligence.

Levy had resided in Galveston for forty years and had only recently joined the agency. He was survived by his wife

Chapman, Frank
Born 24 September 1854—Died 23 September 1906

At about daylight on Sunday, 23 September 1906, mounted customs inspector Frank Chapman was shot and killed by a Mexican smuggler in the town of Lajitas.

Lajitas is located about halfway between El Paso and Eagle Pass in the Big Bend country of Brewster County. Texas Ranger captain John Rogers reported that the murderer was under arrest. Later, newspaper reports claimed that fourteen Mexicans had been arrested. Chapman was under the jurisdiction of the customs office in Eagle Pass. Collector of customs R.W. Dowe reported that smugglers had shot up the town of Lajitas and that he had sent Inspectors Chapman and Donaldson to investigate. Chapman had been in the lead when he was shot from ambush and fell back into Donaldson's arms.

Chapman is said to have seen much service as a lawman on the Texas frontier. Seventeen years earlier, Chapman and Dowe had been scouts together and had numerous sensational encounters with smugglers. Dowe reported that Chapman was an excellent officer and an astonishingly brave man.

Chapman is believed to have been a deputy U.S. marshal around 1893, a Texas Ranger from 1880 to 1881 and a customs inspector since about 1900.

Chapman was survived by his wife, Sara Torres, and five children. Although unconfirmed as yet, some reports indicate that he is buried in Lajitas. Some family genealogists have his date of birth listed as 3 July 1853.

Duffy, Gregorio
Born March 1866—Died 27 January 1907
Date of Incident: 26 January 1907

The political parties in South Texas were known as the *Colorados y Azules* (Reds and Blues). The color system was used to assist Spanish-speaking voters who could not read the English ballot. These designations lasted from the 1870s to about 1920. In Starr County, Manuel Guerra was the Democratic (Reds) political boss, and Ed Lasater was the political boss of the Republicans (Blues). Republican sheriff W.W. Shely became ill and did not seek reelection in November 1906. Manuel Guerra ran his cousin, Deodoro Guerra, and Ed Lasater put up Gregorio Duffy, the chief deputy sheriff under Shely.

State District Court judge Stanley Welch, a Democrat aligned with Manuel Guerra, was found murdered on election day. Deodoro Guerra defeated Gregorio Duffy by sixty-three votes. A Republican supporter named Alberto Cabrera, a barber, was eventually arrested and convicted of the murder. He escaped from prison in 1912 and disappeared into Mexico.

On 1 January 1907, Duffy was appointed as a United States mounted customs inspector. This was allegedly a Republican favor, as the Blues still controlled the federal offices locally.

At about 11:00 p.m. on Saturday, 26 January 1907, Sheriff Guerra and Inspector Duffy were acting friendly toward each other. Duffy suggested that they go outside the saloon into the yard to talk. Guerra reportedly stated, "You were against me last fall, but that's all right; we will fix it up tomorrow." As they turned to go back into the saloon, they saw two men in the dark, one of whom was former deputy Juan Morales. Duffy struck Morales. A fight ensued. Guerra took Duffy inside the saloon and went back outside to arrest Morales. Gabriel Morales, who was a deputy sheriff and Juan's brother, was also present. Apparently, a gunfight erupted outside the saloon. Duffy was mortally wounded, and Juan Morales was slightly injured.

Gabriel and Juan Morales were charged in the conspiracy to murder Duffy while he was in the discharge of his duties. They were indicted by a grand jury and lodged in jail but released on bond. Gabriel Morales fled the scene and was later extradited from Mexico. In May 1907, the *Laredo Times* reported that a federal grand jury in Brownsville indicted Sheriff Desordo Guerra, County Commissioner Manuel Guerra and Deputy Sheriffs Gabriel Morales and Desidero Perez (a Texas Ranger who was present at the scene but resigned afterward to become a deputy sheriff). Juan Morales was tried separately in January 1908 on a change of venue from Starr County to Webb

County; his trial resulted in a hung jury. A second trial was held at Beeville for Juan Morales, but it is unclear if he was convicted a second time. In May 1909, it was reported that all of the defendants were acquitted. Deodoro Guerra was reelected sheriff on 3 November 1908 and served out his term on November 8, 1910.

Duffy was married to his second wife, Paulina, and had six children. Paulina had a child about three months after Duffy's death. Duffy's place of burial is unknown, but most likely it is in Starr County since his family members were pioneer settlers.

Jones, Charles E.
Born circa 1866—Died 19 March 1908

Logan, Charles R.
Born 21 January 1866—Died 19 March 1908

On Friday, 20 March 1908, U.S. Mounted Customs inspectors Charles R. Logan and Charles E. Jones were found dead at an isolated spot along the abandoned riverbed of the Rio Grande River, a short distance from El Paso.

The previous night had been especially dark, and the inspectors had been traversing the riverbank searching for smugglers. The officers had been sent out from the local station as border riders. Logan's body had one bullet hole through the heart. Jones's body had a bullet through the right side of his chest. Their horses were tied to a single bush, about sixty feet from the place where the bodies lay. The bullet that killed Logan was fired at such close range that there was a powder burn on his shirt where it had entered his body. The shirt had actually ignited and burned a dark spot, highlighting the wound with a black circle. People in the vicinity had heard three shots at about 9:00 p.m. the preceding night. It is believed that in the dark of the night, the two inspectors had mistaken each other for smugglers and killed each other accidentally.

Jones was born in England and had resided in El Paso for seven years. He is buried at the Evergreen Cemetery in El Paso in an unmarked grave. He was survived by his wife, Sina D. Smith, and three children. Jones had been a railroad man and had lived in San Antonio and Houston before entering the customs service.

Logan was survived by his wife and one child. He is buried at the family plot at Concordia Cemetery in El Paso.

O'Connor, Thomas L.
Born 24 August 1884—Died 30 January 1911

On Wednesday, 11 January 1911, two railroad officers from the Atchison, Topeka and Santa Fe Railroad were sent by train to investigate thefts at Abo Pass in New Mexico. One officer got off at a flagstop to send a telegram before they reached the pass, and Officer J.A. McClure continued on alone. He was never seen alive again.

A posse of lawmen suspected that a nearby homesteader named Frank B. Howe and his two sons, Robert and Guy, were involved in McClure's disappearance. The Howes were leading members of a loosely organized gang known as the Abo Pass Gang. On Friday, 27 January 1911, the posse discovered McClure's body in a well on the Howes' property. The investigation concluded that McClure had been shot from ambush after he had caught the Howes stealing and began to track them.

The Howes had boarded a southbound freight train to Fort Hancock on the Texas-Mexico border in Hudspeth County, about fifty miles south of El Paso. On Monday, 30 January 1911, between 11:00 a.m. and noon, the Howes were put off that train. They began walking in the direction of the riverfront. Their presence attracted the attention of U.S. Mounted Customs inspector Thomas L. O'Connor. He asked Justice of the Peace Myron R. Hemly to accompany him and investigate. O'Connor and Hemly overtook the three Howe men and asked where they were going. The men replied that they were looking for work. Suspicious of their answer, O'Connor and Hemly dismounted and drew their weapons, ordering the threesome to raise their hands. Hemly searched Frank Howe, and O'Connor searched Guy Howe; thus, both were fully occupied and did not notice Robert Howe drawing his pistol. Robert Howe shot O'Connor in the mouth and chest. O'Connor managed to return fire, getting off three shots in all. In a blaze of gunfire, the other combatants emptied their pistols.

Hemly was wounded in the wrist, and Robert Howe was wounded in the leg and shoulder. O'Connor suffered a total of four wounds in all, which proved fatal. Hemly fled to gather a posse. On their return, they found that O'Connor's pistol and cartridge belt had been taken.

The Howe gang first crossed into Mexico and then back into Texas, where they left the wounded Robert Howe. A posse of Texas Rangers and New Mexico lawmen overtook Frank and Guy Howe at about 9:00 p.m. that same day. Predictably, a gunfight quickly broke out. Also predictably, the exchange of gunfire resulted in the deaths of Guy and Frank Howe. Robert Howe was arrested and jailed in El Paso. He said that his brother, Guy, was the one who had killed McClure. Robert did testify to being the one who had shot and killed O'Connor.

Robert Howe was charged with the murder of O'Connor and bound over to the grand jury. He was held on a $25,000 bond. It is not known if Robert Howe was ever convicted.

O'Connor was survived by his wife, Mary Wafer, and two children. He is buried at the Concordia Cemetery in El Paso.

Howard, John Simpson "Jack"
Born 13 May 1871—Died 12 February 1913

In February 1913, mounted customs inspectors Jack Howard and Joe Sitter, who was a former Texas Ranger, along with a brand inspector for the cattlemen's association named J.A. Harvick, were scouting along the Rio Grande River near the settlement of Pilares in Presidio County. There they found Francisco "Chico" Cano, one of a band of Mexicans who had been smuggling horses and mules. The officers arrested Cano and left the next morning to take him to Marfa to appear before the U.S. commissioner.

The group was riding single file through a deep canyon and had gone about a mile and a half from Pilares when they were ambushed. Five or six members of the gang of smugglers were concealed behind some large boulders along the trail. Two of the members of the gang were brothers of Cano. As Howard reached a point directly below the hidden outlaws, they opened fire, at a range of about fifty yards. Howard was hit in the chest, and his horse was killed. Harvick and Sitter were shot off their horses. Harvick suffered a wound to his left thigh, and Sitter was shot through the left temple. The bullet exited behind his ear. In spite of their wounds, the officers drew their weapons and returned fire. Howard grabbed his rifle from his dead horse, but he was already too badly injured to use it. Sitter and Harvick were able to return fire, although they had difficulty spotting their attackers among the boulders.

For half an hour, the Mexicans did their level best to execute the lawmen. Frustrated, they finally left. Cano was long gone, having bolted to freedom when the shooting commenced. The three lawmen lay wounded at the ambush site in the mountains for fifteen hours before they were finally discovered and transported to a general store in Pilares. A posse and a doctor arrived the following day. Howard died on the night of 12 February. Sitter and Harvick survived the ordeal.

Howard was survived by his wife, Mary. He is buried at the Howard Cemetery in Boerne.

Sitter, Joseph Russell "Joe"
Born 13 January 1863—Died 24 May 1915

Joe Sitter was a veteran lawman on the Texas-Mexico border. He had served as a mounted inspector for the U.S. Customs Service for many years, resigned and joined the Texas Rangers on 1 August 1893. He next left the ranger service on 25 October 1896 and shortly afterward returned to the U.S. Customs Service.

In 1912, Sitter had arrested Francisco "Chico" Cano and other members of his gang for stealing horses and mules. Cano escaped. On 10 February 1913, Inspectors Sitter and John Simpson "Jack" Howard, along with Brand Inspector J.A. Harvick, had again arrested Cano. As they were transporting Cano through the rugged mountains near Pilares Canyon, a gang of outlaws that included Cano's brothers ambushed them. Howard was killed. Sitter and Harvick were wounded.

On Monday, 24 May 1915, Sitter gathered a posse that included fellow inspector and former ranger Charles Craighead, along with three Texas Rangers—Eugene B. Hulen, Harry Trollinger and A.P. Cummings. The group was intent on the capture of Cano and his gang. When the posse arrived at Pilares Canyon, they could see some stolen horses in the canyon. A disagreement arose as to whether the animals had been placed there as a part of an ambush. Sitter decided to split the posse into two groups and enter the canyon.

Trollinger, Craighead and Cummings had just started up one side of the canyon when they came under heavy fire and had to retreat. They could see Sitter and Hulen pinned down across the canyon and claimed to have tried unsuccessfully five times to reach them. When the gunfire stopped, they thought Sitter and Hulen were dead. Trollinger, Craighead and Cummings walked four miles to a ranch and summoned help. The following day, a posse arrived to reinforce them. They soon discovered Sitter and Hulen stripped naked and shot scores of times. Their faces were practically unrecognizable from having been beaten with large stones.

Sitter is buried in the Valentine Cemetery in Jeff Davis County. He was survived by his wife, Margarita Eugencia Hinckley, and several children. According to some sources, the surname Sitter was originally spelled Sitters.

Related Case: Texas Rangers, Eugene B. Hulen

Tate, Fred
Born 24 August 1860—Died 31 August 1918

U.S. Customs officers Fred Tate, Clint Adkins and Will Neale were in an automobile patrolling for smugglers along the Rio Grande River in Brownsville.

Paulino Alvarez and Emelia Parra were driving a wagon containing one thousand pounds of lard that was to be smuggled across the Rio Grande River into Mexico. Another smuggler from Mexico was driving a buggy that was preceding the wagon. When the headlights from the officers' vehicle illuminated the wagon, the man driving the buggy panicked and ran, escaping into a nearby pasture. By the time the lawmen's vehicle was brought to a stop and turned around, Paulino Alvarez and Emelia Parra had leaped from the wagon and crawled through a fence. The driver of the buggy soon joined the pair.

As the officers got out of their car, the smugglers opened fire on them. Tate was hit. In all, six or seven shots were then fired at the lawmen, who themselves managed to return fire. The smugglers escaped in the darkness.

After unloading the illegal cargo from the wagon, the horses were turned loose. The animals intuitively walked home, to a house near the freight depot. Cameron County sheriff W.T. Vann and deputies surrounded the building. Soon, a buggy with a man and woman in it approached the residence. When the officers stepped from hiding and ordered the couple to halt, Paulino Alvarez, driver of the horse-drawn carriage, appeared to be fumbling for a pistol in his belt. One of the deputies shot and killed him. Emelia Parra was arrested and was charged with the murder of Tate. Several other men were arrested soon afterward and charged with conspiracy to smuggle contraband into the United States. It is not known if Parra, or anyone else, was ever prosecuted for the murder.

Tate's body was shipped to Flatonia for burial. His place of burial has not been located. Tate was survived by his wife, Alice Hopper, and three children.

Tate was a veteran of the U.S. Customs Service and had served for approximately thirty years. He had also served as a special Texas Ranger from 25 April 1917 until December 1917. Tate had also been a city policeman in La Grange.

Rumsey, Robert Stuart, Jr.
Born 19 October 1880—Died 19 August 1922

U.S. Customs inspectors Robert Rumsey Jr., Frank Smith and Bill Musgrave were patrolling the Corpus Christi Road about thirty miles east of Laredo. The inspectors met two trucks carrying tequila, which they stopped and seized. Rumsey placed Frank Smith in one truck and Bill Musgrave in the other. He ordered them to drive to Laredo while he followed in his car.

Rumsey, who was a former Texas Ranger, was a border veteran and knew that rifles were essential in brush fighting and six-shooters were worthless at long ranges. Unfortunately, the two inspectors' Winchester rifles were in the back of his automobile. About three miles from Mirando City, the procession came upon a vehicle containing four or five heavily armed smugglers who were supposed to be the escort for the two trucks the lawmen had seized. Rumsey had stopped his car and gotten out to halt the smugglers' vehicle when they opened fire and killed him. The smugglers took Rumsey's car, leaving the two inspectors armed with only their pistols for defense. Smith and Musgrave emptied their guns at the attackers, used up all their ammunition and were forced to escape into the brush.

One local newspaper reported that Elias Torres had been arrested and charged with the murder of Rumsey. Another claimed that Jose Casanova was the man charged with the killing. Casanova's case was dismissed. It is not known if anyone was ever prosecuted.

Rumsey was survived by his wife, Maria H. He is buried at the Catholic Cemetery in Laredo.

Jones, Jot Gunter
Born 25 November 1892—Died 1 October 1922

Inspectors Barter and Jot Jones had obtained information that Jose Garza had liquor in his possession. Garza was a notorious criminal and had served time in prison in Texas or Louisiana for a murder several years earlier.

At about midnight, the lawmen went to Mercedes in Hidalgo County to arrest him. They managed to apprehend Garza at a dance hall, but in the process of doing so, Garza managed to knock a revolver from Jones's hand. Garza snatched the weapon from the ground and opened fire. Three shots were fired, all of which hit Jones. Two bullets struck him in the leg, and one pierced his chest. Jones lived about fifteen minutes.

Barter opened fire at Garza. He managed to wound him before Garza escaped and fled into Mexico. A posse was formed, and a search for Garza was mounted. While trying to enter a house in search of the escapee, the lawmen frightened a young girl. She ran from the building and was accidentally shot and killed by an overzealous posse member.

Jones had been in the customs service since February. His parents' home was in San Antonio, and his body was shipped there for burial at the Mission Burial Park. Jones was survived by his wife, Frances H. Harden, and two children. Mrs. Jones died just one month after her husband.

Wallen, James August
Born 20 August 1877—Died 6 March 1923

Inspector James Wallen was stationed in Del Rio on the Texas-Mexico border. Between 10:30 and 11:00 p.m., shortly before the closing of the International Bridge for the night, Wallen allowed two Ford automobiles to pass from the Mexican side. I.B. Baker, who was accompanied by his wife, drove the first car. The second car was driven by Mrs. C.O. Carruthers, Baker's mother-in-law. In that vehicle were Mrs. Carruthers's two children, ages five and ten.

The automobiles parked a short distance from the ferry. Wallen and Watkins left the bridge and had begun to drive to town when they had a flat tire and pulled to the side of the road. The vehicle driven by Baker passed them. The second car, driven by Mrs. Carruthers, turned around and started back toward the border. That seemed suspicious, so Wallen went to investigate on foot. Watkins was unarmed and remained behind to repair the flat tire. Within minutes, Watkins heard a volley of gunfire and saw muzzle flashes. Next, he heard the children who were with Mrs. Carruthers start crying. He heard a woman shout, "I told you so!" At that point, Mrs. Carruthers drove past the disabled customs vehicle at a high rate of speed. Wallen was found bleeding profusely from a bullet wound to the chest. He died at about 11:15 p.m. Officers from Del Rio arrested Baker and Mrs. Carruthers. Mrs. Carruthers claimed that two rumrunners had done the shooting when Wallen came upon them in the act of loading illegal liquor. Wallen had fired four shots at the smugglers, one of whom was later identified as Bob Bates. He managed to hit Bates twice.

Bates was later arrested, tried and convicted of murder and sentenced to five years in prison. He appealed, alleging that he should have been charged with manslaughter considering he had used self-defense as his argument. Bates claimed that Wallen had fired first, but witnesses testified that Bates shot Wallen first. The appeals court reversed the conviction and ordered a new trial, citing that Bates had not been allowed to make the argument of self-defense. It is not known if Bates was ever convicted of Wallen's murder.

Wallen had been with the customs service for just six months. He had previous experience as a law enforcement officer with the Border Patrol, Texas Rangers, Immigration Service and Val Verde County Sheriff's Office and as deputy city marshal of Del Rio. Wallen was a widower and was survived by five children. He is buried at the Masonic Cemetery in Del Rio, Val Verde County.

Ironically, Wallen was the grandfather of Inspector Richard Latham, who was shot and killed while on duty near the same spot on 27 January 1984.

Criss, Lloyd Parks
Born 17 December 1859—Died 13 January 1924

Inspector Lloyd P. Criss was walking on the gangplank of a steamer docked in the Houston Ship Channel when he slipped and fell, striking his head on a timber on the pier. Within minutes, several crew members dove into the water and brought him ashore, but they were unable to revive him.

Criss had served with the customs service for twenty years. He was survived by his wife and five children. Criss is buried at the Lakeview Cemetery in Galveston.

Parrott, John W.
Born 27 March 1856—Died 7 January 1927
Date of Incident: 30 December 1926

At about 7:00 p.m. on Thursday, 30 December 1926, U.S. Customs inspectors John W. Parrott and Leon L. Gemoets were on patrol in their automobile in the Upper Valley area of El Paso County and were on the lookout for smugglers. A short distance from the Rio Grande River, the lawmen signaled a truck that was occupied by three men to stop. The officers approached the truck with their flashlights to see what was in the vehicle. Gemoets opened a toolbox on the side of the vehicle but found no contraband. He then saw a bag of bottles on the back seat and reached into the car to retrieve it. At that point, one of the vehicle's occupants opened fire.

Gemoets was hit in the shoulder and fell to the ground. Seriously wounded, he managed to pull two pistols and began to return fire. In all, he got off three shots from one gun and four shots from the other. The driver, Victor Arriola, was wounded and fled the scene with Parrott in pursuit.

Parrott soon returned. He had fired five shots at the fleeing Arriola but had been hit in the stomach by a bullet from the outlaw's gun. Parrott staggered to the truck and managed to handcuff Franelsco Rodriguez to the seat. Alejandro Anaya was found dead in the truck with a shot through the head.

County motorcycle officer N.I. Chamberlain arrived and had both officers taken to the hospital. Customs and Border Patrol agents pursued Arriola to Bowen, New Mexico, where he was arrested. Arriola was tried and convicted of the murder of Parrott and sentenced to life in prison. The disposition of any charges against Rodriguez is unknown.

Parrott died in the hospital at about 5:00 p.m. on Friday, 7 January 1927. He had been employed as a customs inspector for only a few weeks. Parrott was survived by his wife, Olive Myrtle Bennett, and three children. Some family genealogists list four children. He is buried in the Masonic Section of Concordia Cemetery in El Paso.

Dawson, Stephen S.
Born 12 July 1872—Died 28 February 1928
Date of Incident: 27 February 1928

Inspector Stephen S. Dawson was one of the most highly regarded officers serving on the Mexican border. He had been involved in countless gun battles and had killed a number of smugglers. Outlaws had offered a standing reward of $500 to anyone who could kill him.

At about 7:30 p.m. on Monday, 27 February 1928, Inspectors Dawson and T.S. Rhode received information that liquor smugglers would be bringing a load across the Rio Grande River in the Smelter District of El

Paso County. The two officers went to investigate and observed two men cross the river and ordered them to halt. When they started to approach the pair, the outlaws dropped out of sight behind an embankment.

In total, six to eight smugglers were believed to have been hiding behind that earthwork. They opened fire on the officers. Dawson was hit in the chest and thigh. Rhode returned fire and wounded one smuggler, but other outlaws dragged the wounded man's body back across the river. Although Dawson had lost considerable strength from the bullet wound to his left lung, he did not fall and managed to return fire, emptying his pistol at the outlaws as he made his way to the roadside and sat down. Rhode stopped an automobile and asked the driver to transport Dawson to the hospital. Dawson died at 4:10 a.m. the following day.

Dawson was survived by his wife, Nora Mary, and three children. He is buried in the Masonic section of Concordia Cemetery in El Paso. Local newspapers reported that Dawson had been an officer for the customs service, immigration service and city health department for the past twenty years.

Morris, Thomas Sampson "Tom"
Born 3 November 1888—Died 23 December 1928

At about 5:00 a.m. on Sunday, 23 December 1928, U.S. Customs inspectors Tom Morris and M.R. Rogers stopped an automobile carrying two men about four miles southwest of Fabens in El Paso County. The vehicle had crossed the boundary line near the Fabens "hole-in-the-wall" on San Elizario Island in the Rio Grande River. The hole-in-the-wall district of Fabens was a well-known spot for illegal activity during the Prohibition era and a haven for prostitution.

Morris and Rogers had the two vehicles' occupants outside the car and were about to handcuff them when one of the men asked Morris if he could roll himself a cigarette. Morris said he could. Rather than retrieving the requisite tobacco and paper from his trousers pocket, the man pulled a .38 automatic pistol. He used it to shoot Morris, hitting him three times in the abdomen. The man then fired at Rogers. The shot passed through Rogers's leather jacket, a sweater and two shirts. Although Rogers was knocked backward from the impact, the small-caliber bullet was not powerful enough to reach his body and inflict a wound.

Both inspectors fired at the fleeing man as he escaped into Mexico. The driver was captured and charged with liquor violations.

Morris was taken to the Masonic Hospital in El Paso. He died from his wounds at about 4:30 p.m. The disposition of any case against Morris's murderer is unknown.

Earlier, on 19 May 1922, customs chief Grover Webb and Inspector Morris were attacked and wounded just a short distance from where the fatal attack on Morris would eventually take place. During this earlier incident, the two lawmen had stopped an automobile that was coming over the Lee Moore Bridge. Both Webb and Morris were shot through the jaw. Their attackers escaped into Mexico.

One local newspaper reported that Morris was survived by his father, mother and one sibling. Another claimed that he was survived by his widowed mother. In spite of diligent research, the correct information remains a mystery. Morris is buried in the Masonic section of the Concordia Cemetery in El Paso.

Morris's surname is spelled Morriss on various documents. His date of birth is also reported as having been 1886, 1887, 1889 and 1890.

Ellison, Egbert Lowry "Bert"
Born 30 December 1899—Died 9 August 1930

Margarito Rodriguez was upset over the deportation of his wife to Mexico. Knowing that federal officers would be in the area, Margarito and his brother Victor, along with Nicandro Munoz and Jose Maria Lopez, decided to hide in the brush about two hundred yards from a Mexican dance that was taking place in Hidalgo County and kill the first lawman they could capture.

Mounted inspector Bert Ellison and other officers were in the vicinity of the baile, keeping watch to make sure that no violations of the law were being committed. Ellison and Inspector Clark separated, following different trails into the brush. Shortly after the men split up, eight or more gunshots were heard. Clark called out to Ellison and received no response. Inspector Coy joined Clark. The pair soon found Ellison's lifeless body. His pistol holster was still in his pocket, but the gun and his belt were missing, along with a flashlight he had been carrying. Some empty .32-caliber cartridges were found near his body. Ellison had been shot a number of times.

A posse of lawmen caught Margarito and Victor Rodriquez the following day. A gun battle broke out during which Margarito was killed. Victor was captured. Nicandro Munoz and Jose Maria Lopez were also arrested. All three men confessed to the murder of Ellison.

The disposition of the case against Lopez is unknown. Munoz and Rodriguez were tried and convicted. They were sentenced to death. That sentence was carried out on 30 October 1931, when both murderers were executed by electrocution in Huntsville.

In total, there were three executions in Huntsville on 30 October 1931. Munoz was the seventy-first person to meet his fate in the electric chair. Rodriguez was number seventy-two. A Native American named Edward Red Wing rounded out the threesome.

Although listed as number seventy-two chronologically, twenty-year-old Victor Rodriguez was the first to die that day and went to his death with a shrug of his shoulders. He said, "I am dying unjustly." Fifteen minutes later, Nicandro Munoz, age twenty-six, followed. Unable to speak English, he addressed the warden in Spanish, saying, "They are going to kill me without my doing anything."

Ellison was survived by his wife, Ollie Boyd, and one child. He is buried in Mission, Hidalgo County.

Bowden, Ralph E.
Born 3 April 1883—Died 19 March 1932

Inspector Ralph E. Bowden died of a heart attack just before midnight on Saturday, 19 March 1932.

Bowden and two other inspectors were chasing four liquor smugglers who had been attempting to slip four sacks of liquor across the Rio Grande near Collingsworth addition. The inspectors saw the outlaws and gave chase on foot. During the pursuit, Bowden was observed to be acting in an unusual manner. Suddenly, he collapsed to the ground and died almost immediately. The smugglers were captured and were lodged in the city jail.

Bowden was survived by his wife, Margaret, and two children. He is buried in the Masonic section of Concordia Cemetery in El Paso.

Heard, John Henry
Born 27 February 1882—Died 2 May 1932

Mounted inspectors John Henry Heard and A.J. McKinney were both stationed in El Paso. The officers drove to the Tom Boles Ranch, located about sixty miles south of Hachita, New Mexico. Their purpose was to speak to the ranch owner about illegal crossing of horses and cattle from Mexico into the United States.

Claude Gatlin, a cowhand on the Boles place, had spent the preceding night at the ranch. When the inspectors stepped from their car, Gatlin walked out of the house armed with an automatic rifle. Mr. Boles was standing in the yard. Gatlin questioned the officers, saying, "What are you doing here?" Before Heard could reply, Gatlin fired four shots. All four bullets hit Heard. Three shots struck him in the chest and one in the side of the jaw. His right thumb was also shot off by one of the flying projectiles launched during Gatlin's barrage.

Heard fired twice at Gatlin before he collapsed. Neither bullet found its mark. Gatlin ran into the house, where Mrs. Boles and some other women were working. He dared McKinney to fire at him. Boles and McKinney immediately took Heard to Hachita and placed him on the eastbound passenger train to El Paso, where he could receive medical treatment. Heard died that night at a hospital in El Paso.

Three posses were organized to search for Gatlin, who had instantly fled to Mexico when McKinney left the Boles Ranch. The disposition of any charges against Gatlin is unknown at this time.

Heard's body was shipped to his hometown of Pecos for burial. The local newspaper reported that Heard had been employed in the customs service for ten years and had been stationed in El Paso for nine years. He was said to have been divorced and was survived by one son. Heard is buried at the Fairview Cemetery in Pecos.

Carnes, Herff Alexander
Born 23 May 1879—Died 4 December 1932
Date of Incident: 1 December 1932

Herff Carnes was a legendary lawman along the Texas-Mexico border. His brother, Texas Ranger private Quirl Carnes, was shot and killed in the line of duty on 31 July 1910. Another brother, A.B. Carnes, was sheriff of Wilson County, Texas, from 1917 to 1937.

Carnes joined the Texas Rangers in 1903 and rose through the ranks to sergeant. He resigned in 1911 and became a mounted inspector with the United States Customs Service. During his twenty-nine years of policing the border, he was involved in countless gun battles.

Carnes and three other mounted inspectors received information from an informant that smugglers were going to be transporting illegal liquor across the Rio Grande River near Ysleta, about thirteen miles downriver from El Paso. The federal agents went to investigate. They hid out near the crossing point. The lawmen were so well concealed that two of the smugglers who were traveling in advance of their companions began to walk between the lawmen.

Rather than allow a dangerous crossfire situation to develop, Carnes arose and ordered the smugglers to surrender. One of the men opened fire. The smuggler's bullet hit Carnes's pistol. The projectile split into two pieces, with both fragments entering his abdomen. Carnes and the other inspectors opened fire, but the smugglers escaped into Mexico.

Carnes was taken to a hospital in El Paso, where he died from his wounds on Sunday, 4 December, at 3:20 a.m. He was survived by his wife, Letha Lenora Lux, and three children. Carnes is buried at the Restlawn Cemetery in El Paso. His tombstone has his date of death inscribed as 4 December, which coincides with his death certificate and other records of his passing. In spite of this evidence, some family genealogists have listed the date as 3 December.

Nichols, Rollin Culberson
Born 1 August 1894—Died 28 November 1933
Date of Incident: 24 November 1933

On Friday, 24 November 1933, U.S. Customs mounted inspectors Rollin C. Nichols, J.H. Shaffer and L.R. Porter went to the foot of Glenwood Drive in El Paso in search of liquor smugglers. The inspectors had seized illegal liquor valued at $1,000 one week earlier near San Elizario. As Nichols was getting out of his car, which was parked near another vehicle believed to belong to the liquor runners, a smuggler fired one shot from a shotgun that hit him in the face. Three of the shot pellets lodged in Nichols's brain.

The other two lawmen dragged Nichols's body behind a river levee. An intense gun battle broke out during which an estimated one hundred gunshots were exchanged between the two inspectors and an estimated fifteen smugglers. The officers later postulated that they had been led into a trap out of revenge for the earlier San Elizario seizure.

By the time Nichols was taken to the hospital, he was unconscious and paralyzed. He died at 9:05 a.m. on Tuesday, 28 November 1933.

Nichols was survived by his wife, Allie Dee Russell, and one child. He is buried in Kenedy in Karnes County.

Henry, Loy Cash
Born 24 August 1896—Died 20 June 1934
Date of Incident: 19 June 1934

Inspector Loy C. Henry was at his home at 902 Avenue C in Del Rio on Tuesday, 19 June 1934, when a Mexican man came to the door and asked the location of a person's residence. The man acted as though he could not understand Henry, so Henry decided to drive the man to the address. En route to the home, the man shot Henry, inflicting a serious wound.

Henry died at 12:30 a.m. on Wednesday, 20 June 1934. Before dying, he was able to identify his killer as Rafael Dominguez from a photograph. Henry claimed that Dominguez was probably sent by smugglers to execute him.

Mexican army forces numbering more than one thousand men conducted a house-to-house search for the killer throughout northern Mexico. Dominguez was eventually captured on a ranch near Piedras Negras, across the Rio Grande River from Eagle Pass. He had been hiding there at the ranchero since his release by municipal authorities from the Villa Acuna, a Mexico jail. The United States government started the extradition proceeding to have Dominguez returned to the United States. It is unknown if he ever stood trial.

Henry was survived by his wife, Ewin Tennessee Neely, and one child. He is buried at the Westlawn Cemetery in Del Rio, Val Verde County. According to some reports, Henry had been a customs inspector for ten years.

Brown, Joseph Turner
Born 17 April 1897—Died 9 April 1940
Date of Incident: 3 April 1940

At about 12:30 a.m. on Wednesday, 3 April 1940, Inspectors Joseph T. Brown and C.B. Sills were on a county road near San Sebastian in Cameron County, where they confronted two men suspected of being smugglers. One of the men, Emeterio Chaso Corona, managed to jerk Sills's pistol from the holster and opened fire. Corona wounded both Sills and Brown. Sills was hit in the head, inflicting a serious scalp wound. Brown suffered a bullet wound to the abdomen, one through the left forearm and a scalp wound. Sills returned fire and wounded Corona. He was shot through both hips. Sills then managed to overpower and subdue him.

Sills loaded Brown into their vehicle, along with the handcuffed and wounded Corona, and rushed to the hospital for medical treatment. The other suspect, Isador Cruz, managed to get away. Officers were sent to the scene to begin a search.

Sills remained in the hospital until 8 April. Brown died at Valley Baptist Hospital in Harlingen at 9:35 a.m. on Tuesday, 9 April 1940.

On 25 April 1940, murder charges were filed against Corona and Cruz. On Tuesday, 7 June 1940, a jury found Corona guilty of Brown's murder. He was sentenced to life in prison. Cruz was acquitted of the murder but found guilty of smuggling liquor and received a sentence of thirteen months in jail.

Brown was survived by his wife and four children. He is buried in Denton.

UNITED STATES DEPARTMENT OF THE TREASURY: PROHIBITION, ALCOHOL AND TAX UNITS

In its present configuration, the Bureau of Alcohol, Tobacco and Firearms (ATF) is only twenty-seven years old. In a functional way, however, some of the agency's responsibilities can be traced back more than two hundred years. The duty to collect alcohol and tobacco taxes, for example, goes back to the Revenue Act of 1789. During the Civil War, the revenue realized from excise taxes imposed on alcoholic beverages was a significant source of income for the vast Federal war effort.

Another major milestone in the organization's long history was America's post–World War I attempt to drastically reduce the consumption of alcohol. Under the Eighteenth Amendment to the Constitution, ratified in early 1919, an ATF predecessor agency played a major role in the federal campaign to eliminate the commercial sale of beer, wine and whiskey. Prohibition, however, was extraordinarily controversial and came to an end with the ratification of the Twenty-first Amendment on 5 December 1933.

One of the unfortunate consequences of Prohibition was the development of a number of violent gangs that served up illegal booze to all Americans who desired it. The turf wars of these gangs was a major factor in making the homicide rates of the early 1930s among the highest in the nation's history. In both periods, one result was the passage by Congress of a long series of gun laws beginning with the National Firearms Act of 1934.

The ATF was formerly part of the United States Department of the Treasury, having been formed in 1886 as the "Revenue Laboratory" within the Treasury Department's Bureau of Internal Revenue. The history of the ATF can be subsequently traced to the time of the revenuers, or "revenoors," and the Bureau of Prohibition. That organization was formed as a unit of the Bureau of Internal Revenue in 1920 and was made an independent agency within the Treasury Department in 1927. It was transferred to the Justice Department in 1930 and became, briefly, a subordinate division of the FBI in 1933.

When the Volstead Act was repealed in December 1933, the unit was transferred from the Department of Justice back to the Department of the Treasury, where it became the Alcohol Tax Unit of the Bureau of Internal Revenue. Special Agent Eliot Ness and several members of the "Untouchables," who had worked for the Prohibition Bureau while the Volstead Act was still in force, were transferred to the ATU. In 1942, responsibility for enforcing federal firearms laws was given to the ATU.

In the early 1950s, the name of the Bureau of Internal Revenue was changed to Internal Revenue Service (IRS), and the ATU was given the additional responsibility of enforcing federal tobacco tax laws. At this time, the name of the ATU was changed to the Alcohol and Tobacco Tax Division (ATTD).

In 1968, with the passage of the Gun Control Act, the agency changed its name again, this time to the Alcohol, Tobacco and Firearms Division of the IRS, and first began to be referred to by the initials ATF. In 1972, President Richard Nixon signed an executive order creating a separate Bureau of Alcohol, Tobacco and Firearms within the Treasury Department.

Walker, Ernest W.
Born August 1885—Died 5 March 1921
Date of Incident: 2 March 1921

Prohibition officer Ernest Walker died from a gunshot wound he received when he and a group of federal agents and provost guards were searching for a cache of hidden liquor in El Paso.

Two local deputies had encountered several smugglers earlier in the day and pursued them across the border. The deputies returned to the station and informed the Prohibition officers of the encounter. When the Prohibition officers arrived at the scene, they encountered the smugglers, who had by that time returned. This time, they had reinforcements and were attempting to move the liquor back into Mexico.

An incredible shootout that lasted almost two hours soon commenced. Walker was wounded in the abdomen during the wild exchange of gunfire. He was taken to a local hotel, where he died three days later, on Saturday, 5 March 1921.

Walker had served with the U.S. Department of the Treasury, Bureau of Internal Revenue, Prohibition Unit, for eighteen months. He was survived by his wife, Bonnie M. Speer, and one child. Walker is buried at the Greenwood Cemetery in Fort Worth. Some sources cite Walker's year of birth as about 1889.

Beckett, Stafford E.
Born 21 February 1890—Died 21 March 1921

Wood, Charles Archibold "Arch"
Born 5 March 1886—Died 21 March 1921

Federal officers had received a tip that a load of twenty-three cases of liquor was to be sent across the border to the Neil Shearman hog ranch in the lower Rio Grande Valley, about five miles from El Paso.

On Monday night, 21 March 1921, Prohibition agents Stafford E. Beckett, Charles A. "Arch" Wood, J.F. Parker and W.C. Guinn approached the ranch and stopped a car driven by C.P. Shearman, the father of Neil Shearman. They found no liquor. Next, the officers headed to the ranch house in their vehicles. Shearman started for the house as well but returned to his automobile for his shotgun. The officers allowed him to do so. As the group started toward the house with Shearman in the lead, a volley of gunshots rang out. Beckett and Wood were mortally wounded. The remaining officers returned fire. By the time the agents were able to enter the house, the gunmen had already disappeared into the darkness.

C.P. Shearman and his sons Neil, John and Allen (who was an invalid) were all indicted and charged with the murders of Beckett and Wood. During the trial, the Shearmans testified that the federal officers had fired first. There was a mistrial in June 1921. In September 1921, C.P., Neil and John Shearman were reindicted for resisting federal officers. They were found not guilty. On 24 April 1922, U.S. District Court judge Duval West dismissed the indictment against the Shearmans on the grounds that it failed to state on what authority Prohibition agents had invaded the Shearman Ranch.

Beckett was survived by his wife, Rose Ruth Arfaten, and two children. He is buried at the Evergreen Cemetery in El Paso.

Beckett began his federal service in March 1916 as a temporary mounted watchman in El Paso with the U.S. Immigration Service, which at the time was part of the Department of Labor. He was promoted to immigration inspector in December 1918. Beckett enlisted as a Texas Ranger in Company B on 4 October 1919. He returned to federal service with the Border Department as a federal Prohibition agent a year prior to his death.

Wood was survived by his wife, Mabel (May Bell) Gray, and one daughter. He is buried in Abilene. Wood had been in the federal service for twelve years. He was reported to have been the first federal narcotics inspector stationed in Dallas after the enactment of the Harrison Anti-Narcotic Act in 1914. His brother, Will S. Wood, was also a federal narcotics inspector.

Floyd, Joseph William "Joe"
Born July 1876—Died 17 May 1922

Federal Prohibition agents Joseph Floyd and W.W. Edwards had received a tip that a truckload of whiskey was to be delivered to a residence in Houston that same morning. The officers went to the location, arrested a man who was leaving the house and discovered twelve quarts of whiskey in his possession. The officers obtained a search warrant and returned to the house, where they attempted to arrest the owner, Leon Briggs. Briggs tried to drive away. After resisting arrest, he fled back into the residence. Armed with a warrant, Edwards kicked in the front door and entered the home. Floyd went to the back door. Edwards heard the sound of a gunshot blast coming from the rear of the building and saw Briggs rushing through the back of the house. Briggs shot at Edwards, who quickly returned fire. Briggs was eventually arrested while hiding in the ceiling. Edwards discovered the lifeless body of Floyd lying facedown in the breezeway connecting the house to the garage.

Briggs argued self-defense during his trial and complained that he had been assaulted by the officers in his yard and had managed to get away from them, running into his home for safety. He claimed that he had shot Floyd when the agent pointed a gun at him. Briggs was convicted and sentenced to five years in prison. He appealed based on self-defense, and his conviction was reversed and sent back to the lower court. It is unknown whether Briggs was ever retried and/or convicted for the murder of Agent Floyd.

Floyd was survived by his wife and four children. He is buried in Madisonville, Madison County. Floyd had been appointed as a federal Prohibition agent with the U.S. Department of the Treasury on 18 November 1921 in Houston.

Sharp, Patrick Cleburne
Born 5 June 1885—Died 5 December 1928

Officer Patrick Sharp died from being exposed to lethal fumes in a room that had contained an old whiskey still.

Sharp and four other agents had gone to a Texas farm and located the still behind a trapdoor in the barn. The basement of the building was filled with toxic fumes know as "blackdamp." Blackdamp, also known as stythe or choke damp, is a mixture of unbreathable gases that form when oxygen is removed from an enclosed atmosphere and is largely replaced by nitrogen, argon, carbon dioxide and water vapor. These fumes, which produce no obvious odor, had apparently formed in the cellar of the barn. Sharp was overcome by the gases and died.

Sharp had been in law enforcement for fifteen years, serving as a San Antonio policeman and special railroad agent before joining the U.S. Department of the Treasury, Internal Revenue Service, Bureau of Prohibition, as a special agent three years earlier. He was survived by his wife and four children. Sharp is buried at the Hollywood Cemetery in Houston.

Stevens, Charles F.
Born 16 March 1868—Died 25 September 1929

Prohibition agents Charles F. Stevens, Pat Murphy and R.H. Hirzel were returning to San Antonio from a raid in Atascosa County when they were ambushed.

Stevens and Murphy had two prisoners and were being followed by Hirzel with another man in his vehicle. Hirzel stopped his automobile when he saw a woman sitting on the running board of a car waving a flashlight toward the embankment and culvert on the side of the road. She claimed that her husband had run off the road, but the agent doubted the veracity of her claim and arrested her. As Stevens and Murphy got out of their vehicle to investigate, shots rang out. Murphy heard Stevens yell, "Pat, they got me!"

Stevens continued firing although he had been hit in the chest by a rifle bullet. After the assailants had exhausted their supply of ammunition, they fled the scene.

Several of the attackers had been wounded during the exchange and had to seek medial attention. A number of people were charged with the murder of Stevens. One of the group died from his wounds shortly after being arraigned.

Stevens began his law enforcement career at the age of eighteen as a jailer, working for his father, Bexar County sheriff Edward A. Stevens. At twenty-three, he was elected and served three terms as a Bexar County constable. Stevens was appointed a deputy sheriff in 1898. In 1908, he ran for sheriff but was defeated. He was later appointed chief deputy. In 1910, he joined the Texas Rangers as captain of Company B. In 1912, he was appointed captain in the San Antonio Police Department. In 1921, he served as supervisor for the U.S. Bureau of Prohibition agents with the U.S. Department of the Treasury, Internal Revenue Service.

Stevens was survived by his wife, Trixie Cross. He is buried at the San Jose Cemetery in San Antonio.

Chance, James L.
Born 7 October 1884—Died 6 October 1929

Deputy Sheriff Claud King and Prohibition officer James Chance killed each other in a shootout that was reminiscent of an Old West duel. The deadly affray took place at the courthouse in Nacogdoches.

A disagreement existed between King and Chance that stemmed from their involvement in a recent Prohibition raid. King had also been defeated in a recent election for sheriff, which perhaps played a role in the strife between the two men. Both officers had been working with federal Prohibition agents J.W. Hammonds of Lufkin and J. Calloway of Beaumont during the preceding week. Chance claimed that King had tipped off the alleged bootleggers about an impending raid. King was furious, believing that his honor had been placed in question.

The two lawmen met on Sunday morning, 6 October 1929, in the office of Sheriff Eugene Turner at the courthouse. Turner was seated, talking with Chance, when King walked in. The quarrel between the two men was quickly renewed. King struck Chance with his fist. Chance dodged the blow and then drew his revolver and fired one shot in King's direction at close range. The bullet hit King in the abdomen, inflicting a fatal injury. The mortally wounded King returned fire, hitting Chance in the head and killing him instantly.

King walked fifty feet to an automobile and was taken to a local hospital, where he died of what was reported to have been "a ghastly wound" soon after arrival.

Chance was survived by his wife, Maggie Mae Sturrock, and nine children. He was employed by the U.S. Department of the Treasury, Internal Revenue Service, Bureau of Prohibition. Chance is buried at the Sacul Cemetery.

Related Case: Nacogdoches County Sheriff's Office, Claud S. King

Thomasson, Wilford Winn
Born 2 December 1900—Died 14 February 1937

State and federal liquor control agents had a sixty-gallon whiskey still under surveillance and were waiting for it to begin operations. At about 6:15 p.m. on Sunday, 14 February 1937, Special Agents Marty Mitchell and Wilford Thomasson, along with Texas Liquor Control Board inspector M.E. Carter, rowed a boat across the Colorado River near Mount Bonnell just outside the Austin city limits. The lawmen arrested Ike Young and Hazel Hamilton. Mitchell was watching the prisoners while Carter and Thomasson began searching the area, each in a different direction. Mitchell saw Thomasson walk up a hill and cross over into a ravine. He then saw Thomasson raise two fingers indicating that he saw two men near the creek.

Thomasson approached the pair, Pete Martinez and Hucel Hamilton, and reportedly said, "How are you?" When he saw Martinez draw a .38-caliber pistol, Thomasson shouted, "Drop it!" The first bullet from Martinez's gun hit Thomasson in the hand. The second shot struck him in the chest. Thomasson fell to his knees and leaned against a sapling, drew his own gun and returned fire. In all, the wounded lawman managed to get off seven shots, killing his assailant Martinez. Apparently not knowing that he had fatally wounded Martinez, Thomasson reportedly groaned, "Oh, Mitch, get him. He got me."

Agent Mitchell saw gun flashes and heard someone shout. Unfortunately, he could not investigate because he was guarding the prisoners. Carter also saw the gun flashes and began chasing a boy, later identified as Hamilton, from the scene. Carter fired three times at the fleeing Hamilton, but he managed to escape in a boat.

Officers made a sweep of the area and arrested more than a dozen people. Hucel Hamilton, age fifteen, had taken Martinez's pistol and given it to his sister, Beulah, to hide. The gun was later recovered by officers. The pistol belonged to Ike Young, who had allegedly ordered Martinez to shoot anyone who raided the still.

Under a new federal law applying to the death of federal agents in the line of duty, Ike Young, Beulah Hamilton and Hucel Hamilton were all charged with murder. Six others were charged with conspiracy: Augustine Garza, Pete Ancira, Tony Arevealo, Charley Rivera, Ysidro Saldana and Hazel Hamilton. Young was convicted of first-degree murder and sentenced to life in prison. He appealed his case. Young was granted a new trial but was once again convicted and sentenced to life in prison.

Thomasson was survived by his wife, May Larue Harp, and one daughter. He is buried at the Memorial Park Cemetery in Austin. Thomasson had been stationed in Austin as a Prohibition officer for more than four years, and after the repeal of Prohibition, he served in the federal liquor tax enforcement unit. During that period, there is some confusion concerning the various federal agencies. Newspaper articles refer to Thomasson as an agent of the Internal Revenue Service and a federal liquor agent. The Bureau of Alcohol, Tobacco and Firearms claims Thomasson as one of its own.

UNITED STATES PUBLIC HEALTH SERVICE

Hill, Ira Trueman
Born 24 February 1884—Died 1 June 1919
Date of Incident: 8 May 1919

Refer to U.S. Border Patrol agent Charles Hopkins's case above. Hopkins was brought to Mercy Hospital in Laredo and died at 1:00 a.m. on Friday, 9 May 1919.

Ira Hill died from an infection caused by the gunshot wounds on 1 June 1919. He was survived by his wife, Angela Eliza Lewis, and at least two children (possibly as many as five depending on which family genealogy source one relies on). Hill is buried at the Laredo City Cemetery.

Related Case: U.S. Border Patrol, Charles Hopkins

5

Other Agencies

RAILROAD POLICE

Since the late 1800s, the role of the railroad police has been to protect
the railroad's resources, passengers and cargo from vandalism, theft
and robbery. That role has not changed much since the inception of
the various forces. Chief Engineer Benjamin Latrobe of the Baltimore
and Ohio Railroad (B&O) established one of the earliest known railroad
police forces in 1849. By 1853, the B&O had a police force that numbered
roughly sixty. Many of these men moved to western railroads as their jobs
ended with the completion of construction of the railroad in this area.

Most railroads prior to the Civil War did not have their own police
forces, however, and most officers were not experienced in undercover
work and investigations. Contractors like Allen Pinkerton were hired to
look into the losses of freight and luggage that were mounting into the
millions of dollars. Pinkerton used his officers in a variety of ways to solve
the mounting epidemic of thefts from the railroads. He placed them in
undercover capacity as passengers or employees to watch for employees
who were stealing from the company or from passengers and tramps.

From the time of the first successful chartered railroad in Texas,
the Buffalo Bayou, Brazos and Colorado Railway Company, which
was launched on 11 February 1850, lawmen traveled the rails. Many
of the railroad police were recruited from the ranks of the Texas
Rangers, as well as various federal, state, county and municipal law
enforcement agencies.

Scores of railroads operated in Texas between 1850 and 1940, most of which have long since been sold, merged with others or are now defunct. Thus, the roster of lawmen in this category is arranged chronologically, beginning with the earliest officer to be killed in the line of duty during the period from 1900 to 1940. The railroad for which each respective officer worked is noted.

Gentry, George
Missouri-Kansas-Texas Railroad Police Department
Born (Unknown)—Died 5 January 1905

Special Officer George Gentry was shot and killed by an unknown assailant in Hillsboro, Hill County, while in the discharge of his duties. No further details concerning the incident, or Gentry, have been uncovered.

Gentry was a former Smithville, Bastrop County constable in 1898.

Etheridge, John Wesley "J.W."
International and Great Northern Railroad Police Department
Born 18 December 1853—Died 19 October 1905

Special agent and special Texas Ranger John Etheridge was shot and killed by a man named Charles D. Mitchell. The shooting occurred at the train depot in Troupe, located on Smith-Cherokee county lines, on Wednesday night, 19 October 1905. Mitchell reportedly used a pistol belonging to a deputy sheriff.

Mitchell was tried and convicted of the slaying and entered prison on 4 December 1906 to begin serving his ten-year sentence. He was discharged on 13 August 1914, after having served less than eight years for the murder of Etheridge.

Etheridge was elected constable of Precinct 3 in Marshall, Harrison County. He had also been appointed a special Texas Ranger on 27 May 1899. His appointment indicates that he served as a deputy sheriff and constable in Harrison County for approximately eight years. He was also reported to have served as a policeman in Marshall.

Etheridge was survived by his wife, Sarah Adriana "Addie" Leete, and six children. He is buried at the Palestine City Cemetery in Anderson County.

Other Agencies

Taylor, John Lafayette
El Paso and Southwestern Railroad Police Department
Born 10 March 1868—Died 3 May 1907

Special policeman John Taylor was shot and killed during a confrontation with ward politicians Pat and Sam Dwyer. The incident took place at the opening of The Lobby saloon in El Paso. Sam Dwyer admitted to shooting Taylor but claimed that Taylor had gone for his gun first. The fatal bullet from Dwyer's gun struck Taylor in the head. Another Dwyer brother, James, was under indictment for murder in the death of a man at the Coney Island saloon a year earlier. The fourth brother was the district judge for San Antonio.

Taylor is buried at the Evergreen Cemetery in El Paso.

Stewart, Charles Lee
Atchison, Topeka and Santa Fe Railroad Police Department
Born 17 February 1881—Died 13 August 1908

On 13 August 1908, Detective Charles Stewart was on duty at the Santa Fe rail yard at Amarillo when an unknown assailant, who was apparently hiding in a boxcar, stepped from around the corner and shoved a .45-caliber Colt pistol into Stewart's face and pulled the trigger. The bullet struck Stewart just over the left eye, passed through his head and lodged at the base of his skull. When Stewart's body was discovered by Ed Hurd sometime after the incident, he was lying in a pool of blood. His face was powder burned from the effects of the killer's weapon having been discharged at close range. One of the buttons on Stewart's suspenders was unfastened, indicating that he had probably attempted to pull his service revolver and defend himself.

A Mexican man was arrested under suspicion of having murdered Stewart, but he was later released. Stewart's killer has never been located.

Charles Stewart's father, William A. "Bill" Stewart, was one of the most fearless and well-respected sheriffs of Johnson County. Charles had served for several years under his father as a deputy sheriff, county guard and deputy constable. He had joined the Santa Fe Railroad as a detective in May 1907.

Stewart was engaged to be married. He is buried at the Cleburne Memorial Cemetery.

Bennett, Thomas Henry
Texas and Pacific Railroad Police Department
Born 18 December 1878—Died 11 September 1910
Date of Incident: 10 September 1910

Officer Thomas Bennett was shot and killed while investigating a railroad boxcar burglary at Dallas.

Bennett came upon three suspicious men whom he believed to be burglars. One of the men shot him in the chest. Bennett died from the gunshot wound the following day.

His murderers were apprehended, tried and convicted. All three were sentenced to death. However, based on Texas execution records, it does not appear that any of the threesome was ever actually executed.

Bennett had been with the agency for two months. He had previously been with the Dallas County Sheriff's Office. Bennett was survived by his parents and five siblings. He is buried at the Mesquite Cemetery.

Pipes, James Jeptha "J.J."
Southern Pacific Railroad Police Department
Born 27 September 1871—Died 2 November 1911

The Southern Pacific Railroad Company sent several special officers to Houston to assist during a strike by the railroad's union employees. The four officers sent were J.J. Pipes, Gordon Knight, H.S. Sisk and S.B. Crockett. They arrived on the No. 9 train from Athens.

Just after midnight, as the lawmen were being escorted into the railroad shop enclosure, a crowd of about one hundred strikers swarmed around them. The mob thought that the lawmen were strikebreakers and that they were headed to work in the facility. Railroad special officers were stationed inside and outside the shop. As Pipes passed through the building yard gate, gunfire erupted from the mob of angry strikers. Pipes was shot and instantly killed. Crockett was hit in the left chest and seriously wounded, Captain Sisk was struck by a rock and a club and Special Officer Knight was cut in the face with a knife. The knife-wielding assailant nearly severed his nose.

Crockett said that the shots had come from inside the rail yard and had been fired by guards who mistook the officers for strikers trying to enter the yard.

The Southern Pacific Railroad Company's official report stated that the guns used by the special officers were of a larger caliber than the .32-caliber bullets that killed Pipes and wounded Crockett. Justice of the Peace Crooker conducted an investigation. It was his opinion that the shots most likely came from company guards inside the yard.

Pipes was survived by his wife, Ella Holsomback, and two children. He is buried at the Athens City Cemetery in Henderson County.

McGee, Virgil Arthur
Texas and Pacific Railroad Police Department
Born 3 January 1883—Died 5 July 1916

On Wednesday, 5 July 1916, bridge guard Virgil McGee died in a railroad train accident near Abilene. A month earlier, Mexican bandits had attacked the bridge over the Medina River about twenty miles southwest of San Antonio. U.S. Army soldiers assigned as bridge guards routed the attackers, but two soldiers were wounded. The Texas and Pacific Railroad announced it would be placing guards at every bridge.

McGee was survived by his wife, Mary L., and three children. McGee also had four additional children from a previous union with Lonnie Staton. McGee's place of burial is unknown. Some family genealogists cite 6 July as his date of death.

Price, W.P.
The Katy Railroad
Born circa 1841—Died 8 July 1916

W.P. Price was a track walker and bridge guard for the Katy Railroad. On Saturday, 8 July 1916, he was struck by a train while walking the tracks about a half mile north of Argyle. Employees on the train that ran over him transported him by rail to Denton, where he died from his injuries.

Price was married. He was buried in Argyle, Denton County. Price had been employed by the railroad since the U.S. Army started moving troops to the Texas-Mexican border because of the bandit raids into Texas.

Dillon, Henry Labon
Texas and Pacific Railroad Police Department
Born 11 July 1880—Died 19 August 1922

Guard Henry Dillon was shot and killed by a fellow guard named Walter P. Petty. This fatal incident took place at the Texas and Pacific yard and was the result of a disagreement between the two men.

Petty fled the scene and vowed that he would not be taken alive. He had a change of heart and surrendered to the sheriff in El Paso the following day.

Dillon is buried at the Kopperl Cemetery in Bosque County. Newspaper reports of the day claim that Dillon was a deputy U.S. marshal.

Gross, James Alvis
St. Louis Southwestern Railroad Police Department
Born October 1894—Died 3 September 1922

Guard James Gross was killed when a railroad train hit him. Gross had fallen asleep on the tracks and somehow did not hear the oncoming train. As one can imagine, the accident was fatal.

Gross is buried at the Masonic Cemetery in Mount Pleasant, Titus County. He was survived by his wife, Lucille E. Hardin Campbell, and one child.

Torres, Migeril V.
Texas and Pacific Railroad Police Department
Born circa 1868—Died 6 September 1922

Special Officer Migeril Torres was shot and killed while patrolling the railroad yard in Mingus, Palo Pinto County. The incident took place during a labor dispute.

Torres was transported to a hospital in Fort Worth, where he was able to give a statement about the shooting, and the shooter, before he died. No one was ever arrested for his murder.

Torres was survived by his wife, Juanna, and three children. He is buried in San Antonio.

Other Agencies

Malone, James Nathaniel
Southern Pacific Railroad Police Department
Born 10 August 1894—Died 9 July 1924
Date of Incident: 8 July 1924

Apprehending liquor smugglers traveling on Southern Pacific trains between the Mexican border and San Antonio had been a particular target of Special Agent Malone for several months.

Malone was riding a northbound train near Uvalde when he discovered a smuggler hiding between two railroad cars. The man immediately opened fire, hitting Malone three times. Malone drew his revolver and returned fire, hitting the man five times. As the smuggler fell from the train, he fired at Malone again, this time hitting him in the leg. The train stopped and picked up the smuggler. Malone's gunfire, and the fall from the train, had proven fatal for the man.

The wounded Malone was taken to San Antonio, where he died from his wounds just after midnight on 9 July 1924.

Malone was survived by his wife, Ruby Estell Langley, and one child. A Texas Ranger honor guard accompanied his body to Del Rio, where he is buried. Malone had joined the Texas Rangers in 1916 and served five years. He also worked for the U.S. Customs Service before joining the Southern Pacific Railroad Police.

Garrett, William Walter
Fort Worth and Denver Railroad Police Department
Born 29 January 1879—Died 12 September 1927
Date of Incident: 10 September 1927

Special Officer William Garrett was involved in a fatal automobile accident.

Garrett's vehicle was hit by a motor car operated by seventeen-year-old George Mewborn. After hitting Garrett, Mewborn left the scene of the accident and made no attempt to render aid to the severely injured Garrett.

Garrett died of his injuries two days after the accident, on 12 September 1927.

Garrett was survived by his wife, Artie Britton, and one child. He is buried at the Rosemont Cemetery in Wichita Falls.

Varnon, Princess Jackson
Southern Pacific Railroad Police Department
Born 24 September 1892—Died 7 March 1928

Special Agent Princess Varnon was shot and killed when he attempted to stop two men in the rail yards in Yoakum, located on the Dewitt and Lavaca County lines.

The two men appeared to have been living in a railcar or perhaps passing through the facility after having jumped a train. Newspapers reported that one of the men opened fire on Varnon with a shotgun. The blast hit him in the neck and inflicted a serious injury. Later, ballistics information confirmed that the murder weapon had been a revolver. The mortally wounded Varnon managed to return fire as the killers, one of them with a one-hundred-pound sack of corn on his back, fled the scene.

Officers from the Yoakum Police Department heard the shots and quickly made their way to the source of the shooting. Varnon was able to describe his assassins before he died from his wounds. The lawmen found several sacks of corn and flower that had recently been stolen from a local mill lying near the open door to a boxcar.

On 25 March 1928, a $250 reward was offered by Yoakum residents for the killers. On 12 April 1928, the identity of the murderers was confirmed, and the pair was arrested. The killer was captured and held at the Lavaca County Jail. Both men were tried and convicted of murder.

Varnon was survived by his wife. He is buried in Stockdale, Wilson County.

Dunman, James Edward "Jack"
Atchison Topeka and Santa Fe Railroad Police Department
Born 13 June 1873—Died 29 October 1930

Milam County chief deputy Guy Pope and Santa Fe Railroad Police Department special officer Jack Dunman were shot and killed while investigating the burglary of a freight depot warehouse.

Pope and Dunman, along with Deputy Sheriff Roy Dunman, went to the store of Reagan Brady to question him about stolen property. When Brady saw the lawmen, he ran into the store, grabbed a shotgun and began firing. A blast of shot struck Pope in the abdomen. Another hit Dunman in the neck. Both were killed instantly. Brady then shot and wounded Robinson, who returned fire and was able to get off four shots at the killer.

Other officers arrived at the scene and exchanged gunfire with Brady. The gunman eventually turned a shotgun on himself and committed suicide, blowing away a large portion of his head in the process.

After the bloody incident had drawn to a close, Sheriff L.L. Blaylock could offer no explanation as to what had triggered Brady to open fire on the officers. Blaylock commented that "he had no quarrel with the officers as far as he knew."

Dunman was not married. He is buried at the Glendale Cemetery in Goliad. Before becoming a special officer in 1926, Dunman was a veteran law enforcement officer, having served as a deputy sheriff in Goliad County, a regular Texas Ranger private in Company C from 1901 to 1903, a mounted police officer and night chief in Houston about 1909 and a policeman in Beaumont about 1921. On 22 March 1928, he was commissioned as a special railroad Texas Ranger.

Related Case: Milam County Sheriff's Office, Guy Austin Pope

PRIVATE DETECTIVE AGENCIES: GALNAY DETECTIVE AND WATCH SERVICE

Meyer, Ferdinand Robert
Born 14 October 1877—Died 10 October 1906
Date of Incident: 9 October 1906

Private Detective Ferdinand Meyer was on his way home from the courthouse in Groveton when he was shot and killed by four assailants. He was hit by three bullets from his attackers' guns. The wounds proved fatal. It was later discovered that H.O. Parks and Virgil Winslow had done the shooting, while Ernest Swinney and Paul Meadows looked on.

Meyer had been employed by the Groveton citizens to find evidence and secure convictions against bootleggers and gambling houses operating in and around the city. He had filed several complaints against such criminals and was in town to attend the trial that day, at which he had testified. The court adjourned at about 9:00 p.m. Meyer had begun his walk home when he rounded a corner next to the depot and came upon his killers. Three shots were fired, one of which hit Meyer in the abdomen. Meyer managed to return fire, but his effort was to no avail. The attackers escaped. Meyer lived through the night but died from the effects of his wounds at about

6:00 a.m. the following morning. He was able to identify his assailants in a deathbed statement.

A $1,000 reward was offered by town citizens for the capture of Mayer's killers. H.O. Parks, Virgil Winslow, Ernest Swinney and Paul Meadows, all of Groveton, were arrested and charged with the murder.

On 17 November, charges against Meadows and Swinney were dropped. The state also introduced the dying testimony of Meyer that Park had shot him first and then Winslow. Meyer was the last man to shoot. The outcome of the trial of Park and Winslow is not known.

On 23 October 1906, the citizens of Groveton assembled at the courthouse and began a march on local drinking and gambling establishments. Business leaders, lawyers, county officials and the pastor of the First Methodist Church all joined the ranks. By the end of the day, all of the illegal operations had been closed down and had their doors and windows nailed shut.

Meyer was survived by his wife, Fannie S. Bowen. He is buried at the Sandy Point Cemetery in Brazoria County.

6

Texas & Southwestern Cattle Raisers Association

The Texas & Southwestern Cattle Raisers Association is the oldest and largest organization of its kind in the United States. The alliance was established in Graham, Texas, on 15 February 1877 under its original name, Stock Raisers' Association of North-West Texas. Cattlemen in Oklahoma, New Mexico and the Indian Territory were invited to join. In the fall of 1876, the initial meeting was called by a few leading cattlemen, including James C. Loving and C.C. Slaughter. The chief objective was to systematize the "spring work" and to curb cattle rustling. The association was incorporated in 1882. By 1893, the distribution of its membership had spread to such an extent that the name was changed to Cattle Raisers Association of Texas. In 1921, the organization merged with the only other cattlemen's group remaining in Texas, the Panhandle and Southwestern Stockman's Association, which had been founded in 1880. At that juncture, the group's name was changed to the Texas & Southwestern Cattle Raisers Association.

Beginning in 1883, inspectors for the association were located along the trails, at shipping points and at terminal markets. The practice resulted in the recovery of many cattle that, by accident or design, had become intermingled with herds in which they did not belong. As specially commissioned Texas Rangers, the organization's inspectors combined their cattle-industry knowledge with legal authority and detective skills.

Mayes, William Martin "Bill"
Born 16 December 1866—Died 14 May 1919

Field Inspector Bill Mayes and a federal Prohibition agent, Will Miller, were shot and killed while raiding a still in northern McCurtain County, Oklahoma. The killer, Wes Henry, was tried and acquitted.

Field inspectors for the Texas & Southwestern Cattle Raisers Association are commissioned as special Texas Rangers and have full law enforcement authority.

Mayes was survived by his wife, Jeanette "Nettie" Toby, and four children. He is buried at the Holly Creek Cemetery in Holly Creek, McCurtain County, Oklahoma.

Allison, William Davis "Dave"
Born 21 June 1861—Died 1 April 1923

Roberson, Horace Lorenzo "Hod"
Born 30 November 1875—Died 1 April 1923

Field inspectors Dave Allison and Hod Roberson were shot and killed by two men whom they were scheduled to testify against.

Allison and Roberson were sitting in the lobby of a hotel in Seminole, Gaines County, when the two suspected cattle thieves, Milton Good (alias Hill Loftis) and Tom Ross, entered the establishment. The pair immediately opened fire using a pistol and a shotgun. Allison was fatally wounded by a pistol shot. Roberson was felled by a shotgun blast.

Roberson's wife, Martha Kirk, came down the hotel staircase and saw what had just happened. She quickly snatched up her husband's .25-caliber semiautomatic pistol and boldly returned fire. The courageous woman managed to wound both Good and Ross. One bullet ricocheted off the belt buckle of Ross and hit him in the stomach. Another bullet from Martha's pistol struck Good in the arm.

The injured and bleeding pair fled but was soon apprehended when their automobile ran out of gasoline just a few miles from Seminole. Both Ross and Good were tried and convicted. Both were sentenced to serve more than fifty years for their crime. The duo subsequently escaped from prison on 29 November 1929.

Good was recaptured in Antlers, Oklahoma, and returned to prison. He was pardoned by the Texas governor soon after. Tom Ross assumed the name Charles Gannon and went to work for the Frye Cattle Company on the Blackfoot Indian Reservation near Browning, Montana.

On 2 February 1929, Ross was involved in an argument with the ranch foreman, Ralph Haywood, and shot and killed him. Ross then walked over to the bunkhouse and committed suicide.

Allison was survived by his wife, Lena Lee Johnston, and one child. He is buried at the South Park Cemetery in Roswell, New Mexico.

Roberson was survived by his wife, Martha Kirk. He is buried at the Confederate Cemetery in San Antonio. Some documents, including his military service registration, list his middle name as Lawrence.

Moseley, William Thomas "Tom"
Born, 12 December 1884—Died 2 February 1940

Special Officer Tom Moseley was quietly sitting at a table inside the White Star Café in Kingsville at about 6:00 p.m. on Friday, 2 February 1940, with Lon Allen and Rogers Word. A farmer named William "Bill" Bolin entered. Without saying a word, Bolin shot Moseley with a twenty-gauge shotgun. The charge struck him in the left side of the head.

Bolin immediately surrendered to Deputy Sheriff P.S. Parker. An investigation by the sheriff and county attorney could not ascertain the reason for the murder. Bolin did confess to the killing but refused to state a cause. One newspaper account claimed that Bolin was upset over an old feud dating to when Moseley had been sheriff. Bolin was indicted for murder. The trial was transferred to Refugio County, but the final disposition is unknown.

Moseley was survived by his wife, Beulah Viola Stark, and two sons. He is buried at the Chamberlain Cemetery in Kingsville, Kleberg County. Moseley had a long law enforcement career. He was a brand inspector for the Texas & Southwestern Cattle Raisers Association and a special Texas Ranger from 23 July 1915 to 15 January 1919. On 7 November 1922, he was elected sheriff of Kleberg County and served until August 1935, when he resigned. Moseley apparently returned as a special officer, but the Texas & Southwestern Cattle Raisers Association records indicate that he may have been a "market inspector," which was not a law enforcement position. All other records and accounts refer to Moseley as a law enforcement officer.

Appendix

Memorials

The criteria for inclusion on the national, state, sheriffs' and numerous local memorials vary. Some names may be enrolled on one or more of the memorials and not on others. Some of the cases listed in this book have not yet been thoroughly researched or may lack sufficient information to be included at this time. Other cases may qualify for inclusion on one or more of the memorials in the future.

A notation of "On File" means that the case has been submitted to the memorial for action but that no action has been taken yet. "Ineligible" means that for some reason the memorial has not accepted the lawman's case. A "Deferred" notation means that the memorial has considered the case but that it has been held because it does not meet that memorial's criteria.

(N)=National Law Enforcement Officers' Memorial (NLEOMF)

The National Law Enforcement Officers' Memorial Foundation, Inc., manages the national memorial in Washington, D.C. The NLEOMF does not accept cases from Texas during the republic period (prior to statehood in 1846). The names of the fallen officers are engraved on the memorial walls each year, for the most part in random order. To help visitors find the names of specific officers, directories are placed at each of the four entrance points. The directory lists names in alphabetical order, by state or by federal and U.S. territory agencies. Each name is associated with a panel and line number. Panels on the west are marked (W), and those on the east are marked (E). The walls are numbered from one to sixty-four. The panel number is engraved at the bottom of each panel. Line one is at the top of each panel, so you must count down to locate the line you are looking for. For example, Panel 20-W, Line 16, refers to the sixteenth line from the top on the twentieth panel of the west wall.

(T)=Texas Peace Officers Memorial

The Texas Commission on Law Enforcement Officer Standards and Education manages the state memorial, which is located at the state capitol in Austin. The location identifier system works as follows: The first number indicates the row number. The letter indicates the row, and the last number indicates the line. For example, location 07, C, 12, means column seven, row C and line twelve. When facing the memorial, the north elevation is on the left of the center columns, and the south, on the right.

(S)=Lost Lawman Memorial

The Sheriffs' Association of Texas manages the Lost Lawman Memorial located at its office at 1601 South IH 35 in Austin, Texas. The location identifier system is similar to that of the Texas Peace Officers' Memorial. The letter indicates the row, and the last number indicates the line. For example, location 3, A, 2, would be panel three, column A and line two.

A	National	Texas	Sheriff's
Ackerman, Frank B.	2-W: 8	05,C,13	4,A,03
Alexander, George W.	22-E: 27	34,C,17	3,A,10
Alford, Nathaniel J. "Nat"	24-W: 24	38,D,13	1,B,08
Allen, Tom	20-E: 21	11,C,04	N/A
Allison, William Davis "Dave"	22-W: 25	26,D,13	N/A
Alsobrook, William M. "Will"	11-E: 26	05,B,19	N/A
Anderson, Charles Wallace	7-W: 25	11,D,12	N/A
Anderson, David L.	27-E: 25	09,B,03	6,A,08
Anderson, Holly Ray	24-W: 13	15,B,08	N/A
Anguiano, Antonio	23-W: 10	37,C,15	6,B,01
Applestell, William	33-E: 11	N/A	N/A
Arp, Vess	4-E:27	31,A,05	N/A
Arthur, William Bowen	25-W: 14	02,C,12	6,B,13
Avary, Joseph Newton	25-W: 14	32,C,02	N/A
Ayala, Pedro	64-E: 9	26,C,07	N/A

B	National	Texas	Sheriff's
Bailey, Leroy	62-W: 27	17,A,06	On File
Barnes, Jefferson Davis "Jeff"	32-W: 26	18,A,04	N/A
Barton, Bernell Looney	63-E: 24	26,D,10	N/A
Baskin, James Monroe	42-W: 6	06,C,07	N/A
Beam, William Samuel	49-W: 28	11,D,09	N/A

Memorials

Beauchamp, John Keifor	12-E:27	19,A,14	N/A
Beckett, Stafford E.	33-E: 9	25,A,16	N/A
Bedford, George E. "Bit"	20-E: 18	38,B,04	N/A
Bell, Frank Pleasants	50-W: 23	13,B,16	0,A,17
Bell, John D. "Jack"	25-W: 13	24,B,05	N/A
Bell, Luke J.	30-W: 11	22,B,03	N/A
Bennett, Thomas Henry	22-E: 22	09,B,09	N/A
Benson, Sidney J. "Sid"	12-E: 5	38,B,14	N/A
Beyett, Thomas J.	22-E: 26	30,B,18	N/A
Birmingham, Charles Braxton "Caps"	50-W: 14	13,C,16	N/A
Bisbee, Carl M.	23-W: 2	08,C,17	N/A
Blackwell, L.F.	28-E: 24	30,B,19	N/A
Blair, John Toliver	35-W: 20	07,B,03	N/A
Bledsoe, Richard Ross	22-E: 59	34,B,13	N/A
Board, Abner Leonard	34-W: 26	23,A,03	N/A
Bobbitt, James J.	60-E: 26	26,A,03	N/A
Bolin, Harvey Samuel "Harve"	33-E: 26	07,B,16	12,B,07
Bounds, Thomas C.	5-E: 23	01,D,14	N/A
Bowden, Ralph E.	57-W: 17	13,A,04	N/A
Boykin, John	On File	14,A,16	On File
Boynton, Theodore T.	15-E: 14	02,C,16	N/A
Bradley, A.R.	22-E: 63	13,B,18	N/A
Brammer, Clarence Adam	25-W: 11	32,B,17	N/A
Brewster, Bertram F.	20-E: 24	05,D,12	N/A
Bright, Carl Bosco	26-W: 25	17,D,02	0,A,04
Brooks, James W.	41-E: 25	24,D,15	N/A
Broome, James Leon	45-W: 21	36,B,02	N/A
Brown, Elvis Orval	12-E: 25	31,C,19	N/A
Brown, Jerry Alexander	31-E: 21	04,C,13	5,B,04
Brown, Joseph Hamilton "Joe," Jr.	33-E: 21	01,C,13	10,A,09
Brown, Joseph Turner	38-E: 4	21,A,06	N/A
Brown, William Collins "Carl"	On File	13,D,16	N/A
Brugh, Frank Wells	27-E: 26	03,B,03	0,A,12
Brunt, Bill	30-W: 16	38,D,12	4,B,07
Buchanan, Joseph Benjamin	54-E: 26	34,B,03	N/A
Buchanan, Richard Coke	22-E: 14	33,C,12	N/A
Burch, Robert E. "Bob"	34-W: 28	On File	N/A
Burdett, Robert Lee	61-E: 26	34,B,16	N/A
Burgess, Lee D.	53-E: 25	15,D,18	0,D,01
Burk, James P. "Jim"	34-W: 27	10,A,9	N/A
Burke, John D.	28-W: 25	15,D,02	N/A
Burke, John J.	15-E: 2	03,B,02	N/A

Burkett, Earl Monroe	11-E: 18	09,B,06	N/A
Burks, Samuel Perry	35-E: 24	09,D,17	N/A
Burnam, Preston George	12-E:13	18,C,14	N/A
Burnett, Ira	22-E: 53	07,B,04	1,B,11
Burns, Frank	24-W: 9	01,C,18	N/A
Burrell, Charles	On File	14,A,04	N/A
Butler, M.F.	On File	17,B,12	11,A,16

C	National	Texas	Sheriff's
Cage, Marcus Tillman	62-E: 26	14,A,15	N/A
Cain, John Morris	42-W: 15	06,C,08	N/A
Callaway, James Terrell	30-W: 24	34,D,04	N/A
Campbell, W.A.	61-W: 22	03,C,03	N/A
Caple, William M.	24-W: 23	36,D,18	N/A
Carlisle, Charles Sleigh	60-E: 7	14,C,02	N/A
Carmichael, George W.	24-W: 22	37,C,09	N/A
Carnes, Herff Alexander	34-E: 7	08,C,18	N/A
Carnes, Quirl Bailey	14-E: 7	05,C,10	N/A
Carnley, William Jackson	44-E: 26	30,B,06	12,B,11
Carr, W.F.	4-W: 27	15,D,06	On File
Carruth, Charles E.	6-W: 19	38,D,14	8,B,06
Cass, Elijah James "Eli"	62-W: 7	03,C,04	N/A
Cates, Hill J.	26-W: 10	11,C,12	N/A
Champion, Willis Glover	56-W: 19	17,B,03	9,A,13
Chandler, Henry Isom	On File	10,A,16	On File
Chapman, Cecil Vincent	60-W: 21	38,B,01	9,B,15
Chapman, Daniel Edward	59-W: 13	01,D,11	N/A
Chapman, Frank	13-W: 2	16,A,02	N/A
Chaudoin, Louis Mackey	48-E: 1	10,C,01	5,B,11
Chavez, E.C.	59-W: 2	08,C,11	N/A
Cherryhomes, George T.	21-W: 21	11,C,17	8,B,03
Childress, Clarence Meek	9-E: 9	25,A,12	N/A
Chisholm, R.T.	23-W: 6	26,B,16	N/A
Chitwood, Gus	61-W: 11	13,B,01	N/A
Cisneros, Francisco A.	On File	30,D,09	N/A
Claiborne, Charles E.	61-E: 26	14,A,03	N/A
Clark, Frank H.	17-W: 10	27,A,08	N/A
Clements, John Walter	19-W: 19	05,C,16	N/A
Coffee, James Daniel "Dan"	36-W: 23	32,B,03	1,A,11
Coffey, G. Frank	61-W: 14	15,C,01	N/A
Coleman, John J. "Jack"	2-E: 13	04,C,17	N/A
Coleman, Marion Marcus	2-E: 24	09,D,07	N/A

Memorials

	National	Texas	Sheriff's
Combs, Samuel N.	21-W: 26	12,A,05	N/A
Conant, George Francis	On File	05,C,14	N/A
Conger, Thomas D.	1-E: 24	05,D,17	N/A
Connell, John J.	15-W: 22	36,B,18	N/A
Conner, John F.	22-E: 45	28,B,10	N/A
Cook, James William	54-E: 2	03,D,15	6,B,17
Corrales, Pete	13-E: 6	09,C,01	N/A
Cotner, JamesRobert	4-E: 21	38,C,12	N/A
Couch, J.C.	22-E: 37	29,C,19	N/A
Courtney, WilliamJ.	22-E: 62	11,B,15	N/A
Covert, John E.	40-W: 25	20,B,13	N/A
Cox, Floyd Carl	22-E: 52	05,B,17	N/A
Crain, John Richard	58-W: 23	07,B,08	N/A
Cramer, John R.	29-W: 19	37,C,14	10,B,04
Crane, John A.	55-W: 26	12,A,06	N/A
Criss, Lloyd Parks	On File	17,A,13	N/A
Crixell, Joseph L. "Joe"	On File	25,A,08	N/A
Cross, Duain S.	40-W: 5	35,C,10	N/A
Crowson, Major Joseph "Joe"	59-W: 21	05,B,05	N/A
Cuellar, Encarnacion "Chon"	On File	30,D,03	11,B,13
Cummings, James Redford	40-W: 12	27,C,03	N/A
Cunningham, John D.	43-E: 21	01,B,07	N/A

D	**National**	**Texas**	**Sheriff's**
Daffin, Elias J.	47-E: 21	37,C,07	N/A
Daniel, James Henry "Jimmie"	On File	13,D,11	N/A
Daniels, Rufus E.	32-W: 12	15,C,11	N/A
Davidson, Johnnie	24-W: 10	10,C,16	N/A
Davis, Albert Worth	62-W: 16	07,C,04	N/A
Davis, James A.	48-W: 7	24,B,09	N/A
Davis, John S.	44-E: 25	20,D,02	0,C,13
Davis, John Thomas	47-E: 24	22,B,18	N/A
Davis, Malcolm S.	59-W: 18	37,C,19	7,B,09
Dawson, Stephen S.	2-W: 18	21,A,15	N/A
De La Pena, Augustin D.	38-E: 2	13,A,13	N/A
Dennett, George Marsten	27-W: 7	18,C,13	7,B,04
Dicken, Lee	43-W: 27	19,D,06	0,C,05
Dieken, JohnW.	42-W: 5	16,C,14	N/A
Dodd, James R.	Deferred	20,D,03	N/A
Douglas, Ottawa	52-E: 23	28,B,19	12,A,07
Downs, Alexander Stephen, Jr.	58-E: 24	28,D,05	0,A,05
Drake, George Franklin	50-W: 17	21,C,01	N/A

	National	Texas	Sheriff's
Draper, William Robert	22-W: 22	37,C,03	N/A
Dugan, John Sidney	40-E: 25	09,C,19	0,B,11
Dunbar, George Washington Bragg	59-W: 4	22,C,16	N/A
Duncan, George L.	34-E: 20	10,C,02	9,A,16
Dunman, James Edward	45-W: 28	09,D,19	N/A

E	National	Texas	Sheriff's
East, Frank	25-E: 21	06,C,19	N/A
Echols, W.L. "Will"	25-W: 22	03,B,16	N/A
Edwards, Agnal Aubrey	12-E: 4	37,C,11	N/A
Edwards, George Dewey	11-E: 16	16,C,11	N/A
Elliot, James	47-E: 25	20,D,08	N/A
Ellis, William Louis	34-W: 26	17,A,01	On File
Ellison, Egbert Lowry	32-E: 14	26,A,08	N/A
Emerson, William Wagner	32-W: 25	13,D,07	12,B,01
Emmons, Edward D.	63-E: 26	17,D,07	0,C,03
English, Jesse Lawrence	16-W: 25	13,D,01	12,B,09
Estes, Ches H.	2-E: 22	37,C,04	N/A
Etheridge, John Clark	11-E: 2	09,C,10	N/A
Etheridge, John Wesley	39-W: 28	DeLord	N/A
Etter, Edgar L.	On File	24,B,17	N/A
Evans, John Edward	35-W: 2	03,C,08	N/A
Ezzell, Raymond Levi	10-W: 4	13,A,17	N/A

F	National	Texas	Sheriff's
Fambrough, G.A. "Andy"	On File	21,A,09	N/A
Feeley, John Henry	44-W: 22	38,C,15	10,B,06
Feely, Patrick William	23-W: 20	09,D,12	N/A
Fischer, Alfred Otto	19-E: 26	24,A,07	0,D,10
Fischer, Arthur William	13-E: 4	11,C,10	N/A
Fisher, A.L. "Bud"	Deferred	Deferred	N/A
Fitzgerald, Edward D.	40-W: 10	23,C,14	N/A
Fleming, John Johnson	On File	20,A,09	N/A
Flippin, Nathan Asa	22-E: 46	38,D,18	4,B,09
Floyd, Joseph William "Joe"	31-W: 17	14,A,11	N/A
Ford, John Cleophus	31-E: 25	17,D,11	N/A
Franklin, Robert Lee	On File	10,A,05	N/A
Franks, John Henry	14-E: 25	09,D,08	11,A,13
Fredrickson, Albert Bernard	12-E: 13	36,D,12	N/A
Free, Joseph Robert	37-W: 27	08,A,01	N/A
Freese, Guy Albert	62-W: 6	27,C,11	N/A
Frost, John Lighter	On File	08,C,06	3,B,05

Memorials

	National	Texas	Sheriff's
Fuller, Hugh Sevier	44-W: 27	30,A,04	N/A
Fuller, James Willis	30-W: 21	35,C,18	10,A,10
Fuller, T.L.	40-E: 24	34,B,14	N/A
Fuston, William C. "Jack"	25-W: 23	03,B,15	N/A

G	National	Texas	Sheriff's
Gaines, John	62-E: 21	15,C,05	N/A
Gambill, James T.	2-E: 8	25,C,06	N/A
Gantz, Charles May	13-E: 25	19,D,07	N/A
Garcia, Juan N. "Johnny," Jr.	38-E: 24	22,B,12	N/A
Gardiner, Charles	62-E: 16	12,A,14	N/A
Garland, William Irvin "Bill"	45-W: 24	07,D,12	N/A
Garlick, William Henry	22-E: 39	36,C,15	9,A,02
Garrett, Carl Edward	58-E: 25	15,D,09	0,B,03
Garrett, William Walter	4-W: 28	13,D,18	N/A
Gentry, Webster C.	21-E: 24	32,D,01	N/A
Gibson, Audie Lee	30-W: 22	03,B,13	2,B,07
Gibson, Charles	5-E: 23	26,B,11	N/A
Gibson, Johnnie C. "Hoot"	32-W: 16	17,C,01	N/A
Gilbreath, Rufus Nicholson	24-E: 25	17,D,01	N/A
Giles, W. Jake	58-W: 15	22,C,01	8,B,05
Gillispie, William A.	5-E: 26	26,A,04	On File
Glasgow, Franklin "Frank"	On File	26,D,12	N/A
Glover, Robert Martin	53-W: 24	34,D,10	4,B,15
Godfrey, Thomas Page, Jr.	22-E: 26	15,A,16	N/A
Godwin, John Delaney, Jr.	22-E: 48	05,C,12	N/A
Goff, Thomas Jefferson "Tom"	23-E: 26	32,C,15	N/A
Gooch, Albert R.	On File	11,D,02	N/A
Goode, Ernest Earle, Sr.	53-E: 21	01,D,19	10,B,13
Graham, Joe V.	26-E: 23	34,D,06	N/A
Gray, Robert W. "Bob"	46-E: 24	01,D,05	0,A,11
Grayson, James L.	60-W: 22	36,C,10	N/A
Greene, Carl	11-E: 1	20,C,10	N/A
Greer, John R.	59-W: 25	22,B,15	N/A
Gresham, George G.	26-W: 14	27,C,12	N/A
Griffin, Jesse Emmitt	42-W: 3	27,C,16	N/A
Griffin, William "Will"	44-W: 27	27,A,02	On File
Griffith, Joe Henry	55-E:16	04,C,19	6,A,02
Grigsby, James Elbert	On File	19,A,12	N/A
Grimes, Andrew J.	1-E: 24	36,D,02	N/A
Grobe, Louis Carol	12-E: 15	Deferred	N/A
Gross, James Alvis	On File	Deferred	N/A

	National	Texas	Sheriff's
Grounds, Chester Lewis	50-W:3	26,B,06	N/A
Grubbs, Isaac B.	22-E: 23	09,B,18	On File
Gunter, Howard	4-E: 23	11,B,12	1,A,07
H	**National**	**Texas**	**Sheriff's**
Hamilton, Richard D.	31-E: 25	24,D,17	N/A
Hanks, Elbert Norton	44-E: 24	26,D,17	N/A
Hardin, Edmond H.	17-E: 18	20,C,09	3,B,11
Hardin, George William "Will"	49-E: 26	17,A,07	N/A
Hargis, John Arlington	On File	38,C,14	0,B,04
Harless, William Clinton	56-W: 22	04,C,09	N/A
Harnest, Joseph Arthur	54-E: 2	07,C,17	3,B,16
Harris, Ben A.	22-E: 44	13,B,11	N/A
Harris, Elijah J. "Lige"	3-E: 21	28,C,11	N/A
Harris, Johnnie	49-W: 26	20,D,11	N/A
Hawkins, Alfred L.	3-W: 12	Deferred	N/A
Hawkins, Telephus T. "Tell"	22-E: 7	09,B,08	N/A
Hayes, Charles L.	17-E: 26	23,A,09	N/A
Haygood, John Wesley	41-W: 24	11,B,11	11,A,04
Haygood, William Franklin	On File	24,D,01	N/A
Hays, George E.	37-W: 26	23,A,16	N/A
Heard, John Henry	33-E: 11	14,A,08	N/A
Henderson, Jess S.	63-E: 26	18,A,16	On File
Hendrix, Otis Howard	61-E: 24	26,D,15	N/A
Henneck, Otto	On File	19,B,14	N/A
Hennessee, John W.	15-E: 25	05,D,02	12,B,03
Henry, Loy Cash	47-E: 2	16,A,17	N/A
Heyne, Otto H.	2-W: 27	28,A,02	On File
Hicks, Elvious	58-E: 25	30,B,09	5,A,08
Hicks, W. Emory	22-E: 13	33,C,18	N/A
Hill, Benjamin Joseph	7-W: 22	38,C,16	N/A
Hill, Benjamin Thomas	13-W: 9	15,A,12	N/A
Hill, Ira Trueman	On File	16,A,11	N/A
Hill, William H. "Jack"	On File	26,D,19	N/A
Hinson, John R.	43-W: 26	20,D,16	N/A
Hinton, Harry	22-E: 42	05,B,03	On File
Hollingsworth, Walter Warren	53-W: 18	06,C,17	4,B,17
Holloway, Charles A.	15-W: 25	17,B,17	N/A
Holloway, John Thomas "Bud"	9-W: 27	28,B,12	On File
Hollowell, R.P. "Bob"	22-E: 38	34,B,15	N/A
Hooker, Harry Floyd	60-E: 25	17,D,06	N/A
Hope, Oscar Emmett	60-W: 14	26,C,03	N/A

Memorials

Name	National	Texas	Sheriff's
Hopkins, Charles Lloyd	41-E: 8	26,A,01	N/A
Hopson, James W.	35-W: 25	15,D,10	N/A
Horn, Dan	22-E: 14	07,B,01	10,B,09
Houston, Schuyler Colfax	On File	32,D,16	N/A
Howard, John Simpson Howard	33-E: 9	26,A,16	N/A
Howard, Julian E.	14-E: 25	19,D,10	0,C,12
Howard, Peter	36-W: 22	36,B,19	N/A
Howe, Adolph	22-E: 47	32,C,19	N/A
Howell, Richard D.	Deferred	07,D,16	N/A
Howie, Henry Franklin	2-E: 8	29,C,12	N/A
Hoyt, Ralph Wendell	35-W: 5	19,C,06	N/A
Huddleston, Elmer W.	61-W: 17	14,C,06	N/A
Huffman, Lewis Markham	28-W: 23	30,B,02	1,A,04
Hulen, Eugene B.	20-E: 26	31,C,17	N/A
Humphreys, David C.	22-E: 25	30,B,14	8,B,04
Hunt, Robert Ernest	Deferred	34,C,13	N/A
Hurdleston, Mordica W.	6-E: 24	07,D,04	N/A
Hutcheson, Chester C.	59-W: 18	06,C,14	N/A
Hutcheson, John E.	16-E: 25	24,B,12	11,B,08
Hutson, Joseph Theophelus "Joe"	36-E: 26	21,A,10	N/A
Hyde, Thomas Carlyle "Carlie"	49-E: 26	13,D,05	N/A

I	**National**	**Texas**	**Sheriff's**
Ikard, Elijah Harrison	11-E: 11	01,B,05	4,B,11
Isbell, Clarence Marshall	59-W: 2	17,C,14	N/A
Isgitt, Edgar Eugene	5-W: 21	15,C,10	N/A
Ivanovich, Element Mitchell	52-W: 24	32,D,12	N/A

J	**National**	**Texas**	**Sheriff's**
Jackson, James Walter	15-E: 25	19,D,01	0,B,10
James, Clarence Elmo	24-W: 26	28,A,10	N/A
James, John C.	5-E: 4	27,C,15	N/A
James, Raymond Edison	7-W: 28	34,D,05	9,A,06
James, William P.	22-E: 28	07,B,10	1,B,16
Jenkins, Daniel "Dan"	On File	On File	N/A
Johns, William Edward	5-W: 19	05,B,07	N/A
Johnson, James Evan	30-W: 3	30,B,13	N/A
Johnson, William Horace	61-W: 27	19,D,17	0,B,13
Jones, Charles E.	Federal	12,A,08	N/A
Jones, Ed	26-W: 10	32,C,08	N/A
Jones, James Edgar	45-E: 20	01,B,02	N/A
Jones, Jot Gunter	54-E: 9	23,A,07	N/A

	National	Texas	Sheriff's
Jones, Perry Page	31-W: 2	21,C,05	N/A
Jones, Thomas Alexander	31-W: 22	04,C,01	3,B,07
Jordan, Albert	62-W: 23	32,B,13	N/A
Jordan, Alfred Devaun	On File	26,D,08	N/A
Jordan, Joseph J. "Joe"	6-W: 25	26,D,09	N/A
Joslin, Henry Hampton	60-W: 26	22,D,05	N/A
Jowell, Paul Horace	26-E: 19	26,B,19	N/A
K	**National**	**Texas**	**Sheriff's**
Kanning, Earl William	11-E: 12	20,C,13	N/A
Kelley, Wade Hamilton	6-W: 27	22,A,06	On File
Kelsay, Robert William	49-E: 3	22,A,04	N/A
Kenyon, Daniel Pratt	41-E: 25	14,C,12	9,A,10
Kibbe, Walter Murray	51-E: 26	14,C,18	5,A,07
Killingsworth, James W.	49-E: 9	19,C,03	5,A,02
Kinard, William R.	33-W: 22	01,C,07	N/A
Kirk, Robert Edgar	22-E: 32	03,D,14	1,B,02
L	**National**	**Texas**	**Sheriff's**
Lacey, William Madison	62-W: 10	07,C,06	N/A
Lamkin, John H.	22-E: 28	34,B,07	10,B,10
Landrum, J. Perry	29-E: 25	30,C,17	N/A
Landry, J.D.	12-E: 17	10,C,08	N/A
Lanford, Samuel Griffin "Sam"	10-E: 12	06,C,03	N/A
Lankford, Edd C.	3-E: 5	24,C,18	N/A
Lawrence, Henry B.	12-E: 25	34,B,08	0,B,08
Lawson, Fredrick Everett "Fred"	42-E:27	16,A,05	N/A
Lawson, John B.	27-W: 24	09,B,16	N/A
Ledwith, Charles	32-W: 26	18,A,06	On File
Lee, James Otway	On File	32,C,17	N/A
Leftwich, George M.	34-E: 26	13,D,04	12,B,17
Leonard, Ernest E., Jr.	10-E: 13	34,C,02	N/A
Levy Alphonse,	On File	16,A,12	N/A
Lewis, Lewis J., Jr.	6-W: 25	11,D,05	N/A
Lindsey, Henry Jackson	44-W: 18	34,C,09	N/A
Littlepage, James N.	59-W: 13	25,C,03	N/A
Logan, Charles R.	On File	27,A,14	N/A
Long, Deb Edward	On File	12,A,09	N/A
Long, James Glover	31-W: 25	11,D,10	N/A
Loper, Joseph Burch	63-W: 23	32,B,11	N/A
Lott, Early Alabama	55-W: 25	13,D,02	N/A
Loyd, Franklin Aubrey	58-W: 2	05,C,04	4,A,03

Memorials

M	National	Texas	Sheriff's
Maco, Frank	32-W: 16	11,C,16	N/A
Maddux, Charles D. "Charley"	42-E: 24	13,D,13	N/A
Malone, James Nathaniel	61-E: 26	22,B,11	N/A
Mangold, George L.	25-E: 23	09,B,13	5,A,15
Mankin, James F.	58-E: 8	26,A,02	N/A
Martial, Adolph P.	32-W: 14	29,C,11	N/A
Martin, Frank, Sr.	44-W: 25	13,D,14	0,A,08
Martin, John W. "Johnnie"	45-E: 26	38,D,01	12,B,02
Martin, Robert Eli "Bob"	49-W: 17	09,C,13	3,B,14
Matlock, Abner	On File	34,D,07	12,B,08
Matthews, Jesse P.	26-W: 26	22,D,11	N/A
Mattox, Rube T.	3-E: 25	24,D,09	0,C,07
May, Louis A. "Slim"	64-W: 27	20,A,02	0,C,04
Mayes, William	60-W: 25	26,D,09	N/A
Mayo, Martin	61-W: 23	03,D,09	N/A
McBride, John C., Jr.	33-W: 25	11,D,17	N/A
McCain, Henry Ross	13-E: 24	32,D,15	12,A,17
McCalib, William Douglas "Dock"	32-E: 16	22,A,03	N/A
McCall, J.R.	45-E: 24	28,D,03	N/A
McClintock, Lynn Reed "Mack"	60-W: 15	01,B,14	N/A
McCormick, Harry Charles	22-E: 48	34,B,01	2,B,05
McDavid, Dock	On File	17,D,13	N/A
McDuffie, Dan LaFayette	29-W: 2	29,C,07	N/A
McGonagill, David Alex	49-W: 3	16,C,16	N/A
McKinney, John Wesley	22-E: 59	38,D,08	10,B,07
McReynolds, David	On File	28,A,12	N/A
Meinke, Edwin Gustav	60-W: 9	15,B,02	N/A
Melton, Doyne C.	17-W: 11	21,A,16	N/A
Mereness, Henry Talcott "Harry"	3-E: 11	20,C,11	N/A
Merritt, Bryon	56-E: 25	20,D,15	N/A
Meyer, Joseph A.	22-E: 61	26,B,18	1,B,19
Milby, Frank W.	49-E: 26	11,A,10	On File
Miller, John B.	60-W: 27	07,D,02	6,B,08
Miller, William Thomas "Will"	48-W: 27	26,A,11	N/A
Mitchell, James W.	7-W: 20	36,C,16	N/A
Mitchell, William Davis	21-W: 22	38,C,03	N/A
Moody, Horace Clifton	32-W: 16	25,C,08	N/A
Moody, Norton R.	2-E: 27	22,A,08	On File
Moon, Joseph Leroy	23-W: 5	07,B,15	N/A
Moore, Aubrey Lee	3-E: 6	19,C,05	N/A
Moore, F. Allen	33-W: 25	28,D,13	N/A

	National	Texas	Sheriff's
Moore, Samuel Martin	30-W: 18	34,B,06	N/A
Moore, Thomas Sidney "Tom"	49-E: 23	34,D,16	11,B,04
Moorhead, Thomas Yowell	33-W: 22	36,C,04	N/A
Moran, John August	Deferred	19,B,15	N/A
Morehead, Leonard Edgar	18-E: 26	09,B,14	7,A,10
Morison, Robert Emmett	42-E: 21	38,C,08	N/A
Morris, Thomas Sampson	19-W: 4	18,A,02	N/A
Morris, W.T. "Brack"	16-W: 19	05,D,13	4,B,14
Morrison, Elkins Pond	35-W: 12	16,C,19	N/A
Moseley, John C.	49-W: 5	27,C,13	6,A,11
Mounger, Thomas Frederick	55-E: 21	02,C,19	N/A
Mundine, John Harmon	39-E: 26	17,A,08	On File
Munson, Hillen Armour	9-E:27	10,A,03	On File
Murchison, Dawson R.	22-E: 15	20,C,05	N/A
Murdock, David Duncan "Dave"	24-W: 8	30,C,01	N/A
Murphy, Holloway Daniel	55-E: 10	24,C,02	N/A
Murphy, William E.	40-W: 7	04,C,14	N/A
Murray, Allen Thomas	26-W: 6	09,C,08	6,A,06
Murray, James W.	14-E: 23	03,D,19	N/A

N	National	Texas	Sheriff's
Neal, Levi	22-E: 7	06,C,16	N/A
Newman, James Franklin	43-E: 26	Deferred	On File
Newsom, Charles Washington	47-E: 26	27,A,04	N/A
Nichols, John D.	22-E: 37	02,C,15	N/A
Nichols, Rollin Culberson	23-W: 13	26,A,15	N/A
Noell, Thomas L.	31-W: 26	25,A,10	0,C,06

O	National	Texas	Sheriff's
O'Connor, Thomas L.	On File	24,A,17	N/A
Ogletree, John A.	22-E: 62	30,C,16	N/A
O'Leary, William Joseph	7-E: 14	25,C,07	N/A
Oliver, Dewitt Frisby	46-W: 27	30,A,12	N/A
Oliver, Levi E.	On File	30,A,03	N/A
O'Reilly, Edward James	23-W: 3	05,C,18	N/A
Ortiz, Candelario	55-W: 21	01,B,19	9,B,07
Owens, Jake C.	24-W: 4	38,C,10	4,A,02

P	National	Texas	Sheriff's
Palmer, Marion Edward, Sr.	14-E: 4	15,C,07	N/A
Pape, William O. "Willie"	22-E: 38	01,D,01	2,B,11
Park, Ollie	On File	28,D,07	N/A

Parrott, John W.	28-E: 9	12,A,11	N/A
Parsley, C.E. "Ed"	22-E: 26	05,C,19	N/A
Parsons, Isaac "Ike"	23-W: 5	03,D,03	N/A
Parsons, John Wheat	62-W: 27	21,A,08	On File
Parsons, Robert Bruce	63-E: 21	03,B,07	9,B,11
Paschal, William L. "Billy"	32-W: 4	05,C,17	N/A
Patrick, Leslie N.	28-E: 2	21,C,07	N/A
Patton, D. Ross	62-W: 7	25,C,11	N/A
Pauley, Richard Allen "Dick"	55-E: 16	01,C,05	6,B,16
Pedraza, Joseph J.	59-W: 4	17,B,10	N/A
Pennington, Ben L.	Deferred	34,B,09	N/A
Perea, Octaviano	34-W: 6	36,C,07	N/A
Perkins, T.E. Paul "Elzey"	52-E: 26	28,D,08	N/A
Perrow, Henry C.	10-E: 17	28,B,02	N/A
Pevito, Elisha	On File	08,C,19	N/A
Phares, Willie Bonner	58-W: 1	06,C,09	N/A
Phillips, Dexter Clayton	7-E: 3	15,C,08	N/A
Phoenix, Packard Harry	40-W: 9	38,B,05	N/A
Pierce, Dave	14-E: 25	19,A,09	N/A
Pipes, James Jebty "J.J."	30-W: 27	18,A,08	N/A
Pippen, Thaddeus "Thad"	47-E: 3	13,A,12	N/A
Pitman, Walter Wright	On File	09,A,09	N/A
Poe, Robert Franklin	41-W: 19	37,C,16	N/A
Pollock, John	22-E: 27	07,C,18	N/A
Pope, Guy Austin "Dutch"	39-E: 23	07,B,18	9,B,09
Powell, Edward C. "Ed"	On File	11,D,01	N/A
Prater, Luther B.	34-W: 23	07,B,17	N/A
Price, Edward	46-E: 25	24,D,06	N/A
Puckett, Algie R.	53-E: 21	36,B,09	2,B,12
Puig, Octavio Monico	22-E: 34	34,C,18	N/A
Q-R	**National**	**Texas**	**Sheriff's**
Rader, William M. "Will"	22-E: 26	34,D,08	N/A
Raney, Ira Devoud	62-W: 9	14,C,01	N/A
Ransom, Henry Lee	28-E: 24	03,D,04	N/A
Ratliff, Jacob Anderson	4-W: 26	11,A,03	0,D,06
Ray, Ben Foret	33-W: 23	28,B,16	N/A
Raymond, Harry	22-E: 60	38,D,03	N/A
Reddick, W.G. "Will"	54-W: 24	17,B,16	N/A
Redwine, Felix Edgar	22-E: 20	32,C,14	10,A,16
Reed, James S.	62-W: 22	03,C,13	N/A
Reed, Joel Baylor	On File	19,A,19	0,A,07

Reegan, James Gene	58-W: 4	36,D,17	N/A
Reeves, George L.	19-E: 18	03,D,01	N/A
Reeves, John Carlie	47-E: 25	19,D,13	0,A,01
Richards, Frederick L.	22-E: 48	33,C,11	N/A
Richards, George Archer	On File	30,B,11	N/A
Rigney, Irl Wilkenson	22-E: 45	32,C,18	N/A
Riske, Charles Oscar	8-W: 21	03,C,09	N/A
Rivera, Enrique "Yaqui"	14-E: 24	36,D,08	N/A
Roberson, Horace Lorenzo "Hod"	35-W: 25	28,D,15	N/A
Roberts, John R.	42-W: 11	Deferred	N/A
Robertson, George R.	43-W: 22	38,C,11	2,B,14
Robuck, W. Emmett	27-E: 26	22,D,13	N/A
Rodriguez, Toribio	34-E: 24	09,D,14	N/A
Rogers, William J.	On File	On File	On File
Rossi, Frank	31-E: 21	36,B,05	9,A,17
Rumsey, Robert Stuart, Jr.	16-W: 3	17,D,15	N/A
Rushing, Charles Thomas "Tom"	22-E: 26	34,D,15	11,B,07
Russell, Grover Scott	61-E: 26	34,B,11	N/A
Rutherford, Ralph Jarrell	4-E: 23	38,D,06	N/A
Rye, Green Wesley	22-W: 24	38,D,19	N/A

S	National	Texas	Sheriff's
Sadler, Leonard Tillman	Deferred	17,D,10	N/A
Saenz, Federico R.	31-W: 11	18,C,06	N/A
Satterwhite, Walter Watson	45-W: 18	26,B,10	1,A,08
Scannell, Miles Joseph	60-E: 2	24,A,08	N/A
Schnabel, Henry J.	On File	24,B,19	On File
Scott, Hamill Poston	22-E: 49	05,B,06	10,B,25
Scotten, Ivan E.	19-W: 10	28,A,17	N/A
Scrivano, Peter J.	7-E: 4	24,B,04	N/A
Scroggins, John Carter	On File	36,D,04	N/A
Sens, Charles Henry	45-E: 23	26,B,17	N/A
Sharp, Oscar B.	37-E: 24	01,D,04	11,A,06
Sharp, Patrick Cleburne	11-E: 23	11,A,13	N/A
Shaw, Joe R.	2-W: 27	34,B,19	N/A
Shaw, Leslie Eugene "Red"	On File	24,D,12	N/A
Sherman, S.F.	On File	28,A,11	N/A
Shiflett, George Washington	16-W: 25	11,D,03	N/A
Shipp, Richard Emmett	12-E: 21	03,C,07	2,B,14
Shultz, William Cluff	22-E: 29	38,B,02	N/A
Sills, William L.	25-E: 17	16,A,04	N/A
Simmons, Tipton M.	On File	On File	On File

Memorials

Singleton, James	17-E: 23	30,B,17	N/A
Sitter, Joseph Russell "Joe"	43-E: 9	15,D,07	N/A
Slaughter, John Wilson	21-E: 26	23,A,13	N/A
Smith, Alexander S.	20-W: 1	N/A	N/A
Smith, Dewitt Talmage	53-E: 6	24,B,03	5,B,14
Smith, Ed	31-W: 23	26,B,12	N/A
Smith, Felix	63-E: 26	34,D,14	N/A
Smith, Robert Jefferson	58-W: 4	03,B,10	3,B,02
Smith, Rosie Lee "Ras"	5-W: 26	28,A,06	N/A
Sneed, James B. "Jim"	55-E: 24	09,D,03	N/A
Snow, Joseph Hughes, Sr.	54-E: 2	28,B,13	3,A,14
Solomon, Peter Monroe	On File	On File	N/A
Southall, John L.	9-E: 21	38,B,17	N/A
Sparks, Early Evans	61-W: 25	20,D,19	N/A
Sproul, Franklin Lee	48-W: 28	04,C,06	0,A,02
Spurlock, Joseph Gurney	27-W: 23	03,D,02	1,B,13
Stafford, Spencer L.	13-E: 1	22,D,19	N/A
Stakes, Samuel Basil "Shorty"	On File	15,D,13	0,C,15
Staley, John Albert	25-W: 19	30,D,16	9,B,17
Stansbury, Walter W.	37-W: 27	14,A,10	N/A
Starnes, Tommy Mellie	47-E: 26	27,A,12	N/A
Stegall, Lee	6-W: 26	20,A,05	N/A
Stephens, Charles	26-E: 21	35,C,04	2,B,15
Stepp, Samuel J.	37-W: 25	19,B,19	N/A
Stevens, Charles F.	21-W: 3	On File	N/A
Stewart, Charles L.	21-W: 28	19,A,18	N/A
Stewart, Newton "Newt"	14-E: 15	22,C,02	N/A
Stillwell, Will P.	33-E: 18	28,B,11	N/A
Stowe, John William	35-W: 1	17,C,04	N/A
Street, Samuel A. "Sam"	10-E: 17	34,C,12	N/A
Stuart, Leonard Fleet	33-E: 24	30,D,10	11,B,09
Stuart, William Murray	24-W: 7	20,C,14	N/A
Sullivan, Rempsey Hays	27-W: 6	25,C,02	N/A
Swinney, Charles S.	4-W: 25	28,D,12	N/A
Syms, Sydney Albert	60-E: 26	13,A,01	N/A

T	National	Texas	Sheriff's
Tarrant, Mart Dennis	26-W: 11	24,B,06	N/A
Tate, Fred	18-E: 12	19,D,09	N/A
Taylor, Arthur	22-E: 19	01,D,07	10,B,14
Taylor, Marion E.	61-E: 19	35,C,11	N/A
Taylor, Raleigh Walter	7-E: 2	19,C,18	N/A

	National	Texas	Sheriff's
Taylor, William Ishom	56-W: 27	17,A,09	On File
Teas, Sam B.	On File	28,D,19	N/A
Tedford, Alex W.	30-W: 2	13,C,02	N/A
Tedford, T.A.	30-W: 1	20,C,16	N/A
Terry, Almer Loin	55-E: 25	23,C,06	9,A,09
Thomas, C.F.	62-W: 10	19,C,16	N/A
Thomas, N.P. "Doc"	14-E: 6	28,D,01	N/A
Thomasson, Wilford Winn	47-E: 1	17,D,12	N/A
Thompson, Urby Joe	25-W: 1	13,C,09	N/A
Thornton, W. Roy	24-W: 4	11,B,02	N/A
Tidwell, Sam R.	22-E: 51	15,B,10	3,A,13
Timberlake, Delbert "Tim"	51-W: 25	15,D,01	N/A
Tipps, William L.	3-W: 25	13,D,19	N/A
Todd, Eddie Russel	33-E: 25	22,D,06	N/A
Tomlinson, Thomas Jefferson "Jeff"	On File	24,D,03	N/A
Toney, William Sherrod	39-W: 23	30,B,07	N/A
Torres, Migeril V.	27-W: 27	20,D,07	N/A
Tovrea, Samuel Eugene	22-E: 51	28,B,14	N/A
Trapolino, Joseph A. "Joe"	15-E: 6	37,C,10	8,A,02
Trice, Robert Alexander	29-W: 27	22,A,05	On File
Tubre, Thomas Jack	50-W: 8	08,C,09	N/A
Tucker, George W.	48-W: 20	13,B,15	N/A
Tumlinson, Joel M.W. "Walk"	On File	15,D,15	0,D,02
Tune, Charles Benjamin	58-W: 20	33,C,19	N/A
Turner, George	62-W: 17	16,C,18	N/A
Turner, Henry Ross, Jr.	On File	13,A,10	N/A
U-V	**National**	**Texas**	**Sheriff's**
Valdez, Pedro, Jr.	64-E: 26	22,D,09	0,C,02
Valenzuela, Felix R.	22-E: 11	05,B,14	N/A
Vandiver, Coy Carter, Sr.	On File	30,A,11	N/A
Vandorn, Walter Isaac	30-W: 26	20,D,18	N/A
Varnon, Printess Jackson	25-W: 27	15,A,09	N/A
Velvin, W.R. "Will"	60-W: 24	05,D,15	11,B,02
WXYZ	**National**	**Texas**	**Sheriff's**
Walker, Ernest W.	20-W: 10	16,A,09	N/A
Walker, Leonard N.	On File	17,A,17	N/A
Wall, George W.	On File	17,D,14	5,B,03
Wallen, James August	64-E: 4	14,A,13	N/A
Walraven, James R., Sr.	18-W: 25	11,D,14	N/A
Walthall, Bert G.	24-E: 17	25,A,01	N/A

Memorials

Ward, Joseph Henry	56-E: 24	15,D,08	N/A
Warren, Sterling Price "Dick"	41-E: 23	24,B,14	N/A
Warren, William Earl	7-W: 24	05,D,19	11,B,15
Watson, James Aaron "Dick"	On File	29,A,13	N/A
Watson, John	58-E: 12	27,A,10	N/A
Watts, Robert Lee	38-E: 26	11,D,18	On File
Weaver, John Monroe	63-E: 20	32,C,01	N/A
Weiss, William A. "Willie"	On File	03,C,18	N/A
Welch, Virgil	40-W: 25	05,D,11	N/A
Wells, Rodney Quinn	12-E: 15	28,B,04	N/A
Wharton, George Franklin	46-E: 26	04,C,15	8,B,13
Wheeler, Edward Bryan	55-E: 10	26,C,12	N/A
Wheeler, Shafter H.	37-W: 19	02,C,10	2,B,16
White, Emmett	52-W: 24	07,D,13	N/A
White, Homer	35-E: 26	07,D,17	N/A
White, John Dudley, Sr.	52-W: 18	26,D,11	N/A
White, Robert	42-W: 4	03,B,08	N/A
White, V.O. "Bill"	22-E: 11	38,B,07	2,B,10
Whitlock, Paul W.	On File	26,A,06	N/A
Wilkerson, Joseph F. "Joe"	50-E: 26	27,A,06	N/A
Willard, Timothy Samuel	3-E: 3	33,C,13	N/A
Williams, Joe	22-E: 39	01,D,03	N/A
Williams, William C. "Dubb," Jr.	2-E: 5	09,C,05	5,B,08
Willis, Tom	1-E: 27	22,B,19	On File
Wilmoth, W.D.	22-E: 60	N/A	N/A
Winter, Marvin Alton	22-E: 35	34,B,04	N/A
Witt, Mangrum Elmode "Mote"	34-E:27	21,A,07	N/A
Wofford, Amos R.	22-E: 16	01,B,12	2,B,08
Wofford, John S.	22-E: 54	38,B,03	N/A
Wolfe, Charles	22-E: 11	31,C,18	N/A
Wood, Charles Archibold	62-W: 2	26,A,17	N/A
Wood, Leroy	24-W: 3	05,C,08	N/A
Woodall, Robert H. "Bob"	2-E: 26	24,D,14	0,C,17
Woods, Thomas I.	10-E: 19	26,C,09	9,A,07
Wright, James C.	45-W: 26	15,A,13	0,B,15
Wylie, John L.	28-E: 26	24,A,01	N/A
Wyrick, John Perry	31-W: 26	16,A,16	N/A
Young, Jeter	11-E: 17	28,B,06	N/A
Youngst, Herman	62-W: 12	26,C,06	N/A

Bibliography

BOOKS

Adams, Verdon R. *Tom White: The Life of a Lawman.* El Paso: University of Texas at El Paso, 1972.

Alexander, Bob. *Lawmen, Outlaws, and S.O.B.s: Gunfighters of the Old Southwest.* Silver City, NM: High-Lonesome Books, 2004.

———. *Lawmen, Outlaws, and S.O.B.s: Gunfighters of the Old Southwest. Vol. 2.* Silver City, NM: High-Lonesome Books, 2007.

———. *Rawhide Ranger, Ira Aten: Enforcing Law on the Texas Frontier.* Denton: University of North Texas Press, 2011.

Cano, Tony, and Ann Sochat. *Bandido: The True Story of Chico Cano, the Last Western Bandit.* Canutillo, TX: Reata Publishing, 1997.

Carrigan, William D. *The Making of a Lynching Culture: Violence and Vigilantism in Central Texas, 1836–1916.* Urbana and Chicago, Illinois: University of Illinois Press, 2004.

Cox, Mike. *Texas Ranger Tales: Stories That Need Telling.* Austin: Republic of Texas Press, 1997.

———. *Texas Ranger Tales II.* Austin: Republic of Texas Press, 1999.

———. *Time of the Rangers: From 1900 to the Present.* New York: a Tom Doherty Associates Book, 2009.

Crouch, Barry A., and Donaly E. Brice. 2011. *The Governor's Hounds: The Texas State Police, 1870-1873.* Denton, Texas: University of North Texas Press.

DuCoin, Candice. *Lawmen on the Texas Frontier: Rangers & Sheriffs.* Round Rock, TX: Riata Books, 2007.

Eckhardt, C.F. *Tales of Bad Men, Bad Women, and Bad Places: Four Centuries of Texas Outlawry.* Lubbock: Texas Tech University Press, 1999.

Franscell, Ron. *The Crime Buff's Guide to Outlaw Texas.* Guilford, CT: Globe Pequot Press, 2011.

Frost, H. Gordon, and John H. Jenkins. *"I'm Frank Hamer": The Life of a Texas Peace Officer.* Austin, TX: Pemberton Press, 1968.

Goodrich, Pat. *Captain Ransom, Texas Ranger: An American Hero, 1874–1918.* Nappanee, IN: Evangel Publishing House, 2007.

Greene, A.C. *The Santa Claus Bank Robbery.* Denton: University of North Texas Press, 1999.

Guinn, Jeff. *Go Down Together: The True, Untold Story of Bonnie and Clyde.* New York: Simon & Schuster, 2009.

Harris, Charles H., III, and Louis R. Saddler. *The Texas Rangers and the Mexican Revolution: The Bloodiest Decade, 1910–1920.* Albuquerque: University of New Mexico Press, 2004.

Harris, Charles H., III, Francis E. Harris and Louis R. Sadler. *Texas Ranger Biographies: 1910–1921.* Albuquerque: University of New Mexico Press, 2009.

Ivey, Darren L. *The Texas Rangers: A Registry and History.* Jefferson, NC: McFarland & Company, Inc., 2010.

Johnson, Benjamin Heber. *Revolution in Texas: How a Forgotten Rebellion and Its Bloody Suppression Turned Mexicans into Americans.* New Haven, CT: Yale University Press, 2003.

Lavash, Donald R. *Wilson & The Kid.* College Station, TX: Creative Publishing Company, 1990.

Malsch, Brownson. *"Lone Wolf" Gonzaullas, Texas Ranger.* Norman: University of Oklahoma Press, 1998.

Martin, Jack. *Border Boss: Captain John R. Hughes—Texas Ranger.* Austin, TX: State House Press, 1990.

McConal, Patrick M. *Over the Wall: The Men Behind the 1934 Death House Escape.* Austin, TX: Eakin Press, 2000.

Paine, Albert Bigelow. *Captain Bill McDonald Texas Ranger: A Story of Frontier Reform.* New York: J.J. Little & Ives Company, 1909.

Paredes, Americo. *"With His Pistol in His Hand": A Border Ballad and Its Hero.* Austin: University of Texas Press, 1958.

Parsons, Chuck. *Captain John R. Hughes: Lone Star Ranger.* Denton: University of North Texas Press, 2011.

Robinson, Charles M., III. *The Men Who Wear the Star: The Story of the Texas Rangers.* New York: Random House, 2000.

Selcer, Richard F., and Kevin S. Foster. *Written in Blood: The History of Fort Worth's Fallen Lawmen*. Vol. 1, *1861–1909*. Denton: University of North Texas Press, 2010.

———. *Written in Blood: The History of Fort Worth's Fallen Lawmen*. Vol. 2, *1910–1928*. Denton: University of North Texas Press, 2010.

Spellman, Paul N. *Captain J.A. Brooks: Texas Ranger*. Denton: University of North Texas Press, 2007.

Sterling, William Warren. *Trails and Trials of a Texas Ranger*. Norman: University of Oklahoma Press, 1968.

Tise, Sammy. *Texas County Sheriffs*. Albuquerque, NM: Oakwood Printing, 1989.

Treherne, John. *The Strange History of Bonnie and Clyde*. New York: Cooper Square Press, 1984.

Umphrey, Don. *The Meanest Man in Texas: A True Story Based on the Life of Clyde Thompson*. Nashville, TN: Thomas Nelson Publishers, 1984.

Underwood, Sid. *Depression Desperado: The Chronicle of Raymond Hamilton*. Austin, TX: Eakin Press, 1995.

Utley, Robert M. *Lone Star Lawmen: The Second Century of the Texas Rangers*. New York: Oxford University Press, 2007.

Webb, Walter Prescott. *The Texas Rangers: A Century of Frontier Defense*. Austin: University of Texas Press, 1935.

Weiss, Harold J., Jr. *Yours to Command: The Life and Legend of Texas Ranger Captain Bill McDonald*. Denton: University of North Texas Press, 2009.

Wilbanks, Dr. William. 1995. *Forgotten Heroes: Police Officers Killed in Bell County, Texas, 1850-1994*. Bell County Museum: Belton, Texas.

Wilkins, Frederick. *The Law Comes to Texas: The Texas Rangers, 1870–1901*. Austin, TX: State House Press, 1999.

Yadon, Laurence J., and Dan Anderson. *200 Texas Outlaws and Lawmen, 1835–1935*. Gretna, LA: Pelican Publishing Company, 2008.

Zoch, Nelson J. *Fallen Heroes of the Bayou City: Houston Police Department, 1860–2006*. Dallas, TX: Taylor Publishing Company, 2007.

NEWSPAPERS

Abilene Morning News
Abilene Morning Reporter News
Abilene Reporter News
Amarillo Daily News
Amarillo Globe

BIBLIOGRAPHY

Avalanche [Lubbock, TX]
Baytown Sun
Big Spring Daily Herald
Big Spring Weekly Herald
Brownsville Herald
Commerce Journal
Commerce Weekly Farm Journal
Corpus Christi Caller-Times
Corpus Christi Times
Daily Express [San Antonio, TX]
Dallas Morning News
Denton Record
El Paso Herald-Post
Evening Light [San Antonio, TX]
Evening News, The Mexia
Galveston Daily News
Laredo Times
Lockhart Post-Register
Mexia Daily News
Mexia Evening Ledger
Mexia Evening News
Mexia Weekly Herald
News [Port Arthur, TX]
Port Arthur Daily News
Port Arthur News
San Antonio Daily Express
San Antonio Evening News
San Antonio Express
San Antonio Gazette
San Antonio Light
Victoria Advocate
Wichita Daily Times
Wichita Weekly Times

Index

About the Authors

Cliff Caldwell has continually cultivated his interest in western history since boyhood. After a stint in the United States Marine Corps during the Vietnam War and a successful thirty-five-year career working for several Fortune 500 corporations, Cliff is now retired and free to pursue his interests as a historian, writer and lecturer on a full-time basis. Cliff holds a bachelor's of science degree in business and is the author of several books and published works, including *Texas Lawmen, 1835–1899: The Good and the Bad; Old West Tales; Good Men, Bad Men; Lawmen: Dead Right; The Lincoln County War; A Day's Ride from Here* (vols. 1 and 2); *John Simpson Chisum: The Cattle King of the Pecos Revisited; Guns of the Lincoln County War: Fort McKavett;* and *Tales of Menard County,* as well as his most recent work, *An Anthology of Old West Tales: The Selected Works of Clifford R. Caldwell.*

Cliff is recognized as an accomplished historian and researcher on the American West, having conducted extensive research on the Texas cattle trails, trail drivers and cattle kings. He is a member of Western Writers of America, Inc., the Texas State Historical Association, the Great Western Cattle Trail Association and the Buffalo Bill Historical Center. When not deeply involved in writing, Cliff volunteers some of his time doing research for the Peace Officers Memorial Foundation of Texas.

Cliff and his wife, Ellen, live in the Hill Country of Texas, near Mountain Home.

Ron DeLord was a patrol officer for the Beaumont, Texas Police Department from 1969 to 1972. He served as a patrol officer and detective for the Mesquite, Texas Police Department from 1972 to 1977. In 1977, DeLord was one of the founders of the Combined Law Enforcement Associations of Texas (CLEAT) and was elected its first president. After thirty years as president, he is currently serving as special counsel. He is a licensed Texas attorney and is a nationally recognized police labor official and author, who is known for his leadership style and visionary ideas.

Ron has a bachelor's of science degree in government from Lamar University (1971), a master's of art degree in police science and administration from Sam Houston State University (1982) and a doctorate of jurisprudence from South Texas College of Law (1986). He has been a licensed Texas attorney since 1987. He graduated from the ten-week Harvard University Trade Union Program (1992).

Ron initiated the legislation to create the Texas Peace Officers Memorial on the grounds of the state capitol in Austin. He was the director of the Peace Officers' Memorial Foundation, Inc., a 501(c)(3) charitable corporation dedicated to honoring the memories of Texas law enforcement and corrections officers who have given their lives in the line of duty. He volunteers his time researching historic cases for the Sheriffs', National, Texas and other state memorials.

Ron is the author and co-author of several books and published works, including *Police Union Power; Politics and Confrontation in the 21st Century: NewChallenges, New Issues* (2nd edition); *Navigating Dangerous Waters: The Real World of Police Labor Management Relations; Working Together: A Police Labor-Management Practitioner's Guide to Implementing Change, Making Reforms and Handling Crisis; Police Association Power, Politics and Confrontation: A Guide for the Successful Police Labor Leader; The Ultimate Sacrifice: The Trials and Triumphs of the Texas Peace Officer;* and *Texas Lawmen, 1835–1899.*

Ron and his wife, Brenda, live in Georgetown, Texas.